CHARTING A PROFESSIONAL COURSE:

ISSUES AND CONTROVERSIES IN EDUCATION

Don Kauchak
University of Utah

Paul Eggen
University of North Florida

Mary D. Burbank
University of Utah

PEARSON

Merrill
Prentice Hall

Upper Saddle River, New Jersey
Columbus, Ohio

Library of Congress Cataloging in Publication Data

Kauchak, Donald P.
   Charting a professional course : issues and controversies in education/
Don Kauchak, Paul Eggen, Mary D. Burbank.
     p. cm.
   Includes bibliographical references and index.
   ISBN 0-13-113371-3
   1. Education—United States. 2. Teaching—United States. I. Eggen, Paul D.
   II. Burbank, Mary D. III. Title.

LA217.2.K38 2005
370′.973—dc22   2004016042

Vice President and Executive Publisher: Jeffery W. Johnston
Executive Editor: Debra A. Stollenwerk
Editorial Assistant: Mary Morrill
Production Editor: Kris Roach
Production Coordination: *The GTS Companies*/York, PA Campus
Design Coordinator: Diane C. Lorenzo
Cover Designer: Ali Mohrman
Cover Image: Corbis
Production Manager: Susan Hannahs
Director of Marketing: Ann Castel Davis
Marketing Manager: Darcy Betts Prybella
Marketing Coordinator: Tyra Poole

This book was set in Berkeley by *The GTS Companies*/York, PA Campus. It was printed and bound by Courier Kendallville, Inc. The cover was printed by Phoenix Color Corp.

Pearson Education Ltd.   Pearson Education Australia Pty. Limited
Pearson Education Singapore Pte. Ltd.   Pearson Education North Asia Ltd.
Pearson Education Canada, Ltd.   Pearson Educación de Mexico, S.A. de C.V.
Pearson Education—Japan   Pearson Education Malaysia Pte. Ltd.

10 9 8 7 6 5 4 3 2 1
ISBN: 0-13-113371-3

PREFACE

At no time in the history of our country has controversy over educational issues been more intense. While discourse and debate are essential in any democracy, the intense differences of opinion about controversial issues has energized the profession and engaged the public. Vouchers, charter schools, accountability, high-stakes testing, bilingual education, and the proper role of technology in teaching are just a few of these controversial topics.

A second trend is also developing. The movement toward professionalism requires that teachers have a deep understanding of all aspects of their profession, including the issues that exist in education today. With this understanding, teachers can make informed decisions that can result in positive change at the local, state, and even national levels. Change is inevitable; the abilities of professional educators to influence that change will depend on their ability to understand the issues and articulate their personal views.

Charting a Professional Course: Issues and Controversies in Education is designed to provide teachers with the knowledge and understanding needed to make informed decisions about major educational issues in today's world. This book is designed to provide teachers with knowledge to shape not only their own personal professional growth but also the future of education. It is intended to accompany any introduction to teaching or foundations of education textbook or to be used as a stand-alone textbook.

Criteria for Selection of Readings

Three criteria were used in selecting the readings for this book. The first was *centrality*. We selected articles that capture and analyze issues that currently have an important influence on today's education. The second was *accessibility*. Teachers must be able to read and understand the articles if they are to apply the information in their professional lives. All the articles are readable, and many are relatively short. The third is *perspective*. To make informed decisions about important educational issues, professionals need to understand all sides, so we selected articles that reflect different perspectives. The book's wide range of writers, including David Berliner, Larry Cuban, Elliot Eisner, Martin Haberman, and Sonia Nieto, helps to ensure these perspectives reflect current thinking on important educational issues.

Organization of the Text

This text is organized into 10 parts. Part One, *Students*, examines the central role that students play in the educational process. Part Two, *Diversity*, analyzes the opportunities and challenges provided by our increasingly diverse student populations. In Part Three, *Schools,* articles describe the different ways that schools are organized to promote student growth and achievement. Part Four, *Curriculum,* examines different perspectives on the selection and organization of learning experiences for students. *Instruction* is analyzed in Part Five, which provides differing views on the most effective ways to involve students in learning. *Technology* is changing the way we live, but the most effective ways to integrate technology into our classrooms remains unclear. Part Six examines different perspectives on technology use in the classroom. *Governance and Finance* are the focal points of Part Seven; many of the deepest controversies in education today focus on financing and governing education in the United States. Part Eight, *Teachers and Teacher Education,* attempts to help teachers better understand the factors influencing the teaching profession today, and how these factors shape who they are as educators. *Foundations,* the topic of Part Nine, reminds us that many contemporary controversies have roots in centuries-old historical and philosophical debates. Finally, Part Ten, *Educational Reform,* examines current efforts to improve education.

Features of the Text

We want this book to make a difference in teachers' professional lives. In addition to selecting articles that are timely and accessible, we have also written the book to maximize learning and encourage personal reflection. To supplement the readings, we have provided the following pedagogical aids:

- *Part openers* introduce each part and provide an overview of the major issues.
- *Article overviews* introduce each article, framing it in terms of its contribution to the field.
- **Think About This** questions direct the reader to key points or issues in the article. The last question in this section is a personal reflection, which asks readers to apply the contents of the article to their own teaching situation.
- *Additional resources* at the end of each part are designed to encourage the reader to explore topics further, either through **Additional Readings** or **Exploring the Internet.**
- The **Correlating Table,** printed on the inside front and back covers, links the articles in this text to topics typically covered in introduction to education and foundations of education textbooks. Arranged alphabetically by topic, the table allows students and instructors to cross-reference articles in this book to topics discussed in others, including our own *Introduction to Teaching: Becoming a Professional,* 2nd Edition.

Acknowledgments

We appreciate the insights provided by the following reviewers, who gave us their honest and knowledgeable opinions about the contents and direction of this text. They are Mary L. Brotherson, Nova Southeastern University, Fort Lauderdale, FL, and Parkland College, Champaign, IL; Carrie Dale, Baker College of Flint, MI; Jeanne Ellsworth, Plattsburgh State University, NY; Lisa A. Kunkleman, Baker College of Flint, MI; and Gayle Mindes, DePaul University, Chicago, IL.

Final Thoughts

For the last two years we have wrestled with the crucial question facing all edited works: what to include and what to leave out. What you have in front of you is our thinking at this time. You may conclude that our selections are lacking in one way or another. This is both expected and desirable. Disagreements indicate that you are thinking about the issues, and encouraging your thoughts about these issues is our primary goal in writing the book.

We are sincerely interested in your comments on the contents of this book and what can be done to improve it in the future. Please share your thoughts by sending us e-mails at kauchak@ed.utah.edu, Peggen@unf.edu, or mary.burbank@ed.utah.edu. We will respond to you promptly.

Good luck with this textbook. We hope it encourages you to reflect on your profession and your work in it, and that it furthers your growth and development as a professional educator.

EDUCATOR LEARNING CENTER: AN INVALUABLE ONLINE RESOURCE

Merrill Education and the Association for Supervision and Curriculum Development (ASCD) invite you to take advantage of a new online resource, one that provides access to the top research and proven strategies associated with ASCD and Merrill—the Educator Learning Center. At **www.EducatorLearning Center.com** you will find

resources that will enhance your students' understanding of course topics and of current educational issues, in addition to being invaluable for further research.

How the Educator Learning Center will Help Your Students Become Better Teachers

With the combined resources of Merrill Education and ASCD, you and your students will find a wealth of tools and materials to better prepare them for the classroom.

Research

- More than 600 articles from the ASCD journal *Educational Leadership* discuss everyday issues faced by practicing teachers.
- A direct link on the site to Research Navigator™ gives students access to many of the leading education journals, as well as extensive content detailing the research process.
- Excerpts from Merrill Education texts give your students insights on important topics of instructional methods, diverse populations, assessment, classroom management, technology, and refining classroom practice.

Classroom Practice

- Hundreds of lesson plans and teaching strategies are categorized by content area and age range.
- Case studies and classroom video footage provide virtual field experience for student reflection.
- Computer simulations and other electronic tools keep your students abreast of today's classrooms and current technologies.

Look into the Value of Educator Learning Center Yourself

A four-month subscription to Educator Learning Center is $25 but is **FREE** when orderd in conjunction with this text. To obtain free passcodes for your students, simply contact your local Merrill/Prentice Hall sales representative, who will give you a special ISBN to give your bookstore when ordering your textbooks. To preview the value of this website to you and your students, please go to **www.EducatorLearningCenter.com** and click on "Demo."

CONTENTS

The Ethics of Teaching 303
Kenneth A. Strike

Reflection Is at the Heart of Practice 306
Simon Hole and Grace Hall McEntee

PART TEN: EDUCATIONAL REFORM 311

April Foolishness: The 20th Anniversary of *A Nation at Risk* 313
Gerald W. Bracey

High Standards for Whom? 319
Donald B. Gratz

Accountability: What's Worth Measuring? 327
Mary Anne Raywid

Accountability Shovedown: Resisting the Standards Movement in Early Childhood Education 332
J. Amos Hatch

Can the Bush School Plan Work? How to Keep "No Child Left Behind" from Dissolving into Fine Print 337
Michael Casserly

No Child Left Behind: Costs and Benefits 340
William Mathis

The Debasement of Student Proficiency: Why We Must Rethink Testing to Encourage Real Learning 349
W. James Popham

REFERENCES 353

PART ONE

Students

Teaching today is more challenging than at any other point in our history. Our students, who have different characteristics than those of generations past, are primary sources of these challenges. Consider the following high school statistics:

- Forty-seven percent of the students consumed alcohol within the last 30 days prior to the Youth Risk Behavior Survey (2001), 13% drove after drinking, and 31% rode in a car in which a driver had been drinking.
- Twenty-four percent of students used marijuana during the previous month, and 10% had tried marijuana before age 13.
- Nine percent attempted suicide during the preceding 12 months, and 19% had thought about it.
- Twenty-nine percent of males and nearly 6% of females reported carrying a weapon on school property during one or more days during the preceding month; 33% were in a physical fight on school property during the same time period (Youth Risk Behavior Survey, 2001).

Fewer of today's students come from "traditional" homes, where the father is the breadwinner and the mother works in the home as the primary caregiver. The traditional American family—a husband who is the primary breadwinner, a mother who does not work outside the home, and two school-age children—now makes up only 6% of the households in the United States (Federal Interagency Forum on Child and Family Poverty, 2001). Families headed by married couples now make up 55% of all households. More of our students come to school hungry, tired, or emotionally drained because of conditions in their homes and communities. They are more sexually active, and they use alcohol and other drugs more often than students have in the past.

As we face the pressures to address standards and increase achievement, we sometimes forget that the welfare of our students is our primary responsibility, and these changing student characteristics make that task even more demanding. The readings from this section focus on questions related to helping our students learn and grow. Some of them include the following: What problems do the students of today face? How good a job are schools and teachers doing to create caring environments that prevent students from becoming simple commodities in an increasingly commercialized world? How does gender influence learning? What can schools and teachers do to maximize learning for all students? And what can individual teachers do to make their classrooms more humane and nurturing? Keep these questions in mind as you study the articles in this section.

"HIS NAME IS MICHAEL":
A LESSON ON THE VOICES WE UNKNOWINGLY SILENCE

Donna M. Marriott

To help our students grow and develop, we must get to know them as human beings. The first step in this process is often getting to know their names. How important is a person's name? Donna Marriott attempts to answer this question with a true story about one of her students who showed up at her classroom door with the school secretary. The student did not speak English, or if he could, was reticent to do so. "His name is Michael," the secretary announced. After several quiet weeks in her classroom, Michael moved away. Only after he was gone did Donna find out his real name was David. As you read this article ask yourself, "How can we make our schools and classrooms more humane places for all students?"

Think About This . . .

1. In what ways did the educational system fail David? What can teachers do to prevent these failures?

2. What role did language play in David's problems? What can monolingual teachers do to address these problems?

3. What were some positive strategies that the teacher used to welcome David? What else could she have done?

4. What strategies will you use to acquaint yourself with the students you will teach?

This is a true story—one that both haunts and inspires me. I wish I could say that the names have been changed to protect the innocent. The names were changed, but, sadly, no one was protected.

I was teaching that year in a full-inclusion, multiage class. My teaching partner and I had 43 children ranging in age from 5 to 9, ranging in ability from average to labeled, ranging in experience from indulged to adequate. I boasted about being a progressive teacher—a teacher bent on changing the system. As I looked around my classroom, I could see evidence of all the latest and greatest in education: child-directed learning, meaning-driven curriculum, responsive teaching, authentic assessment. It took a little boy to show me what I couldn't see: Beneath this veneer of "best practice," there was a layer of fundamental ignorance.

He appeared at my classroom door in the middle of a busy morning gripping the hand of a harried school secretary. He was a tiny child with carefully combed hair, wearing a crisply pressed shirt, tightly clutching his lunch money. The secretary handed this child to me and rattled off the institutional essentials: "**His Name Is Michael.** He is a bus rider. He doesn't speak English." Not much of an introduction, but that's how it happens in schools. New students appear in the office at times that make sense in their lives—not in our lives. These children are unceremoniously placed in whatever classroom has an extra chair. It's not very welcoming—but that's the drill.

We did all the usual new-kid things that day. We played the name game. The kid of the day gave him the grand tour of our room. He got to sit on the couch even though it wasn't really his turn. The children insisted that Michael have a buddy for absolutely everything—learning buddy, recess buddy, bathroom buddy, lunch buddy, cubby buddy, line buddy, water buddy, rug buddy, bus buddy. They thought it would be great if he

From Marriott, D. (2002). "His name is Michael": A lesson on the voices we unknowingly silence. As first appeared in Education Week, *22(6), 35. Reprinted with permission of the author.*

had a sleepover buddy, too, but I was able to convince them otherwise. We were genuinely glad to have this youngster in our learning family. But Michael didn't become part of our family.

Michael existed marginally on the outside of the group. Sometimes he was on the outside looking in; sometimes he was on the outside looking out. I often saw him with his eyes closed—looking somewhere hidden. He was well-mannered, punctual, respectful, cute-as-a-button—but completely detached from me, from the children, and from the learning.

I met with the bilingual resource teacher to chat about concerns and possibilities. She told me she could come do an informal observation "a week from tomorrow." It was a long wait, but that's how it is in schools. She came. She watched. She listened. On her way out she said, "You might have better results, dear, if you call him Miguel."

I could not have been more embarrassed or confused. How could I have been calling this child the wrong name? I was a progressive teacher: How could I have made such a mistake? How could the school secretary have made such a mistake? Why hadn't the parents corrected her? Why hadn't the child corrected me?

Miguel didn't stay with us for long. His family moved on to follow their own calendar of opportunities. We didn't get to say goodbye, but that's how it happens in schools.

Miguel's paperwork arrived about three weeks after he had moved away. I was going through the folder, updating it for his next teacher, when I noticed something that made me catch my breath. His name wasn't Michael. It wasn't Miguel. His name was David.

I wondered how it was that this child could have been part of my classroom for more than a month, and in that entire time he never had enough personal power to tell me that his name was David. What was it about me, about the other children, about the school that made David feel he had to give up his name? No child should have to forfeit his identity to walk through our classroom doors. No child. Ever. It is much too high a price to pay.

I have to do a bit of guessing about what was going on in David's head. I am guessing that he was told to respect *la maestra*—to "be good" in school. I am guessing that he thought if the teacher decided to change his name, well then . . . that was that. I am guessing that he didn't connect school to any known reality. He could be David at home, but at school he was expected to become someone else.

I don't have to do much guessing at my own complicity. It never occurred to me that his name would be anything other than Michael. In the entire breadth of my experience, people had called me by my given name. In those few instances when someone mispronounced my name, I would offer a polite but prompt correction. I was taught to speak up for myself. I was given the power to be me—in my school, in my neighborhood, in my life. I never considered checking in with David about his name. It was beyond the scope of my experience. It was beyond the lens of my culture.

Our power distance was huge. I had all the power. I was white; I was the teacher; I spoke English. David had no power. He was brown; he was a child; he spoke Spanish. Our sense of individualism clashed. I expected him to have a sense of himself—to stand up for himself, to speak up. He denied himself. David expected and accepted that he was "less than" in the culture of school. Our perception of reality was polarized. I trusted in the precision of the system. The name on the registration card just had to be correct. That's how it works in schools. David accepted the imprecision of the system. Having his name changed was just part of the whole befuddling experience.

I have learned many difficult lessons in the years since David sat submissively on the edge of my classroom. I have learned lessons about passive racism—the kind that we cannot see in ourselves, don't want to see in ourselves, and vehemently deny. I have learned lessons about implicit power and explicit powerlessness—about those voices we choose to hear and those voices we unknowingly silence. I have learned that being a good teacher is as much about rapport and relationships as it is about progressive curriculum, pedagogy, and assessment.

If I could go back to that day when the secretary brought in a little boy with carefully combed hair wearing a crisply pressed shirt, I would shake his hand and say, "Hello. My name is Mrs. Marriott. What's your name?" I believe that if I had simply asked him, he would have told me.

OVERBURDENED, OVERWHELMED

Lawrence Hardy

Our primary goal as educators is to promote the growth and development of our students. Our students—and not just the older ones—are facing new pressures that previous generations of students have never encountered. Societal pressures, combined with rising school expectations, are taking a psychological toll on students. These pressures manifest themselves in both physical and psychological symptoms. As you read this article ask yourself, "How can teachers as well as schools help students deal with these pressures?"

Think About This . . .

1. What roles do families and society play in the pressures facing youth? What can schools and teachers do about these external forces?
2. What unique challenges face high school students? How can schools and teachers at this level address these problems?
3. How do parents contribute to the stresses facing students? What can schools and teachers do to minimize these negative effects?
4. What specifically will you do in your classroom to address the kinds of problems identified in this article?

In the elementary and middle schools of Rockingham County, N.C., a rural district north of Greensboro, administrators have to discard as many as 20 test booklets on exam days because children vomit on them.

"Kids [are] throwing up in the middle of the tests," says Dianne Campbell, the district's director of testing and accountability. "They cry. They have to be removed. The stress is so much on the test that they can't handle it."

It's not just tests that are stressing students. Across the country, school nurses, psychologists, counselors, and others concerned about children's mental health say that schools in general have become more stressful places and that many students can't handle the pressure.

What are we doing to our children? Why are we making them sick? What is it about our families, our communities, and particularly our schools that has made their lives so stressful? And what can we do to help?

While there are few studies on stress among K–12 students, two recent surveys show a disturbing trend at the college level. In one of the studies, released in February by the journal *Professional Psychology: Research and Practice,* the counseling center at Kansas State University found that the percentage of students being treated for depression at the center had doubled between 1989 and 2001. The study, one of the most extensive of its kind, followed a 2001 national survey in which more than 80 percent of college counselors said they believed the number of students seeking help for serious psychological problems had increased over the past five years.

And the trend appears to be starting before college. At the K–12 level, school health experts say they are seeing more student stress, much of it coming from outside school. High divorce rates, a sluggish economy, and the rapid pace of society have all put unprecedented pressure on families—and on kids.

Fear of Failure

These societal pressures are difficult enough without schools contributing to the problem, but some observers say that's exactly what's happening. Students

From Hardy, L. (2003). Overburdened, overwhelmed. American School Board Journal, 190(4), 18–23. Reprinted with permission of the American School Board Journal.

are stressed by the climate of schools that have grown too large and impersonal and by the unintended effects of the nationwide effort to raise standards. Parents complain about a glut of homework in the early grades, about elementary school students having to sit through hours of testing, about kindergartens morphing from places where children learned to love school to the start of what could become a grueling 13-year marathon.

"Young children, even first-graders, know where they stand in the achievement hierarchy," says Rhonda S. Weinstein, a psychology professor at the University of California, Berkeley, and author of *Reaching Higher: The Power of Expectations in Schooling*. Rather than creating classrooms that develop talent, Weinstein says, "We magnify minor differences and make them salient."

This relentless sorting is not helping our students. Weinstein says: It undercuts self-esteem and increases the fear of failure. As the late John Holt, the eminent teacher and education writer, wrote in 1964, "Adults destroy the intellectual and creative capacity of children . . . above all by making them afraid, afraid of not doing what other people want, of not pleasing, of making mistakes, of failing, of being *wrong*."

Almost three decades later, that fear has not abated.

Intolerable Levels of Stress

In numerous interviews with professionals in education and mental health—including school nurses, counselors, and psychologists—*ASBJ* found near-unanimous agreement that too many students are suffering from intolerable levels of stress. Of course, much of this stress comes from family and societal factors that are beyond the school's control. But instead of creating schools that are refuges from outside stress, these professionals say, we have too often constructed environments that only add to them.

"It's about as rough as I've seen it in a number of years of talking to schools," says Randy Compton, executive director of the School Mediation Center in Boulder, Colo. "It's hard out there."

Adds Michael Klonsky, director of the Small Schools Workshop at the University of Illinois, Chicago: "The pressures on students are tremendous."

That's certainly the case in Rockingham County. In North Carolina, students are tested in grades three through eight as part of a process that can determine whether they will be promoted. For Rockingham,

that's about 7,500 students. "I probably have, during a three-day period, about 15 or 20 cases where kids get sick during the test," Campbell says, "That's a pretty high rate. As the tests start, they literally fall apart. It would break your heart."

Campbell believes in testing as a diagnostic tool, and she says the teachers in Rockingham try their best not to transfer the pressure they feel to the kids. "Even though you feel the pressure, don't put it on your kids," she says. "There's a fine line between making them feel responsible and making them feel overstressed."

Stress and pressure—both external and self-imposed—affect kids all along the achievement spectrum. For high-achieving students, it's harder than ever to get into a top college or a state's flagship university. In part that's because of the sheer number of students competing for a limited supply of spots. At Berkeley, for example, where admissions officers refer to this generation as "Tidal Wave II," it's almost twice as hard to gain acceptance as it was 10 years ago, the admission rate having dropped from 42.9 percent in 1992 to 23.9 percent last year.

Students respond by loading up on Advanced Placement courses and a dizzying array of extracurricular activities. Sleep becomes "the one part of their schedule that is expendable," says Laura Celestino, a school nurse at Acalanes High School, an academically rigorous public school in Lafayette, Calif. in the valley east of Berkeley.

"I don't know how many kids will sit in my office and say, 'I don't know what I'm going to do when I get out of high school,'" says Lynne Harr, a therapist who leads stress-management groups at Acalanes and other schools. "And this kid will be 15."

Harr describes a meeting with a senior who, by all accounts, has above average credentials for college, including a 3.2 grade point average. "She's absolutely terrified—and probably rightly so—that she won't get into anything," Harr says.

Jeff Maher, 18, a senior at Acalanes, talks about high achievers breaking into tears when they get less than an A in a course. But unlike at many high schools, where grade inflation is rampant, it's not easy to be perfect at Acalanes, and the competition puts incredible pressure on students to stand out. That kind of rigor is why Ivy League admissions offices like the school, Maher said: They know an A from Acalanes means something.

"Harvard takes one or two" students from certain public high schools, Maher estimates. "So what they're doing, early on, is pitting kids against each other."

Maher recently scored a perfect 800 in the SAT-2 writing test; his friend got a 790. "She was pondering studying for it all over again," Maher says. "Why?"

Increased Anxiety

Low-performing students, especially those from poorer areas, face a different challenge—simply staying in school. And being held back a grade raises the stakes. Numerous studies show that grade retention doesn't help students' academic success and may even increase dropout rates, yet between 1980 and 1992 the number of students retained increased from about 20 percent to nearly 32 percent, according to a 1995 study by Melissa Roderick. Anecdotal evidence suggests the rates have increased further since 1992—and will continue to increase—as more states require high-stakes tests for promotion and graduation.

What impact is this retention—and the threat of it—having on students' emotional well-being? Without any national studies to draw on, we can't be sure, but some indications suggest it increases the level of anxiety. Consider a 1987 study in which Kaoru Yamamoto, of the University of Colorado at Denver, and Deborah A. Byrnes, of Utah State University, examined how stressful various events were in the lives of 558 elementary school children. For sixth-graders, fear of grade retention was the third-highest stressor, right behind losing a parent and going blind.

Rose Paolino is a counselor at Bailey Middle School in West Haven, Conn., where a large number of students receive free or reduced-price lunches. Lying just across the river from New Haven, the city shares many the social and economic problems of its larger neighbor. Many of Paolino's students come from single-parent homes and don't have the emotional resiliency of their peers from intact families, Paolino says. She says her caseload has nearly doubled in six years.

"The social-emotional has to come before the academic, and it will always be that way," Paolino says. "Until a child is established socially and emotionally, you can forget about the academics."

And that's true regardless of the student's intellectual ability. Maher, the Acalanes student with the perfect SAT-2 score, had already been accepted at the University of Massachusetts Amherst by February and was waiting to hear from Northwestern University, his first choice. But his high school career was not always so smooth. Coming from an easier middle school, he was unprepared for the work he would have to do at Acalanes.

Counselors say transitions between schools are always tough on students, but for Maher the change was devastating. He was anxious, depressed, distracted—and earning Cs and Ds. Only after being treated for several medical and behavioral problems—including depression, obsessive-compulsive disorder, attention deficit hyperactivity disorder, and Tourette's syndrome—did his health and grades improve. Since then he's had to play catch up and until recently was studying more than six hours a day to make up for his slow start.

Too Much, Too Soon

How much of this stress can be blamed on schools and how much on our fast-paced, fractured society? It's hard to say. With anytime access to cable TV, the Internet, and other kinds of media, kids are no longer shielded from what goes on in the world. They're forced to grow up fast—or, at least, to appear to grow up fast. And a large part of that stepped-up pace of development is facing sexual pressures at an earlier age.

"Some girls will say, 'I'm a lesbian' to keep the boys off them and not be pressured so much," says Brenda Melton, a counselor at Alamo Achievement Center, an alternative school in San Antonio, and president of the American School Counselor Association.

A school may teach values or abstinence or problem-solving skills, but Britney Spears teaches something else. A generation ago, if you skipped school, your neighbor or your relative down the street might report you, and your parents and the teacher would have a talk. Now, your parents are both working, your neighbor doesn't know you, and there is no relative down the street.

In past generations, "there was just a much more consistent and reiterated message" from society, says Dr. Mary Schwab-Stone, a psychiatrist at the Yale Child Study Center who works with the New Haven schools.

Schools also can't control a child's reaction to world events, and the world of late has seemed a strange and treacherous place. Several school nurses and counselors say that Sept. 11, the war in Afghanistan, and the possibility of war in Iraq all cause stress for their students.

Sandra Gadsden, a school nurse in the Worthington Public Schools near Columbus, Ohio, tells of a fourth-grader who came into her office complaining of a stomach ache and saying his eyes were "feeling funny."

"His mother had the television on, and he heard all this rattling about war in Iraq," Gadsden says. "He told me he's afraid our country will go to war. He's 9 years old."

But most of her students' concerns are closer to home. They often involve their parents' expectations and the fear that they cannot meet them. "I've had children tell me, 'My mother says I won't get into a good college if I don't do well on the test,'" Gadsden says.

And these children are in elementary school.

Parent Pressure

Sometimes, parental expectations and school pressure combine to put needless strain on children. More than a year ago, on a state testing day, a third-grader walked into Gadsden's office carrying with her a terrible odor of skunk. It turned out that the girl's dog had been sprayed by a skunk and then jumped on her.

"I had to come up with a plan very quickly to 'de-skunk' her" so she could take the test, Gadsden recalls.

The cafeteria didn't have any tomato juice, a common antidote for skunk musk, so Gadsden doused the girl with catsup, rinsed it off, and put a stocking cap over her wet head. She later recalled the note that had been sent home with the students, telling parents to make sure their children got a good night's sleep and a nourishing breakfast before the test. This test, the note seemed to say, was extremely important.

"This mother didn't have the confidence to say, 'Testing isn't all *that* important,'" Gadsden says.

Obviously, this mother thought the test was more essential than helping her daughter rid herself of an embarrassing and unpleasant odor. But other parents in Worthington are questioning the wisdom of frequent testing and the other academic demands being placed on their children. And they've asked Gadsden to lead a stress-reduction group for interested students.

One of those parents, Pam Nylander, was concerned about her 13-year-old daughter Brittany, a seventh-grader who has juvenile diabetes. A straight-A student, Brittany was staying up too late to finish her homework, and Nylander was worried about her health. She talked to other parents and found their children were also doing homework late into the night, so they approached the school about their concerns.

Of course, it's not all the school's fault. Parents need to limit their children's outside activities, Nylander says, but that, too, can be hard. There was a time a generation ago when students could do well in school, take up a sport, play an instrument, and participate in a youth group—and still have free time.

Not anymore. Noting that her daughter is an accomplished pianist, Nylander says, "If she wanted to, she could be in five music competitions in the next three months." The same is true of the increasingly competitive world of athletics, whether school sponsored or run by a club.

"Everybody has raised the bar on their expectations for these kids for everything," Nylander says, "and it's very difficult to strike a balance."

One school district that is trying to strike a balance is the Adams 12 Five Star Schools in Thornton, Colo. More than two years ago, the district convened the first of 89 focus groups to ask residents what they wanted for the school system and its students. What the district found, says Superintendent Jim Christensen, is "that they have higher expectations and more expectations than just the test scores."

The result is a plan for "Educating the Whole Child" in which students will be assessed according to eight traits. The district says students should be competent, creative, productive, healthy, ethical, successful, thoughtful, and good citizens.

Christensen, who has been working on ways to assess these traits, says the main goals are motivating students and involving their parents. "It really focuses on getting the students, the parents, and the teacher on the same page," Christensen says, "so that [the student's] competence can be enhanced through these traits."

Feeling More Connected

Venice High School is a big school on a big campus—66 acres in an affluent beach town south of Sarasota, Fla. It's got all the advantages of a well-appointed comprehensive high school—and the inevitable drawbacks as well: 2,200 students packed into a sprawling complex that takes up to eight minutes to traverse between classes.

"Personal" wouldn't be the best way to describe it.

"High schools are much too big," says Principal Candace Millington. "They're like mega cities. . . . Venice High School is bigger than the college I attended."

Recognizing that the sheer size of the school and its impersonal atmosphere might be adding to students' stress, the Sarasota Public Schools decided to do something about it. So last fall, armed with a federal Small Learning Communities grant, the district began to break up the campus by grouping the ninth-graders into five "Cornerstone Teams" of about 90 students each. The students will spend four years with their team members, and every new ninth-grade class will be organized into similar teams.

"Day One, we saw an immediate difference on our campus," Millington says. "The campus was calm.

There was a peacefulness and serenity about the campus that we had not experienced."

Breaking up large, impersonal schools as Venice did is a promising way of reducing stress and helping students feel more connected. "Students in these schools are anonymous. Nobody really knows them," says Klonsky, of the Small Schools Workshop. "And they're also heavily tracked and competitive—not just academically, but socially. They're under great pressure to make themselves known or find some kind of identity."

At Venice High, that sense of identity comes more easily now. Each ninth-grade team has become for its students "their neighborhood and their home," Millington says. "And they develop close relationships with their teachers. In fact, during their lunch period, students even go back to the area and have lunch with their teachers and socialize with their friends."

Staff members on each team decide how they will divide the students so that each one has the opportunity to meet regularly with an adult. Students are asked to help develop their own goals for after high school, plus an academic plan to meet those goals. That also helps remove stress, Millington says, "because they know why they're taking the courses they're taking."

The changes have been welcomed by parents, who say they now have a better opportunity to get to know their children's teachers, Millington says. For the parents' benefit (and also the student's), staff members take a picture of each ninth-grader in a cap and gown, a kind of visual reminder of the goals the student has set.

"It's a very powerful, very, very emotional picture," Millington says. "And some of the parents cry when they see these pictures, they're so moved."

MOBILITY

William R. Capps and Mary Ellen Maxwell

Advances in technology, transportation, and opportunities for employment have changed the face of American society and our students. Historically, families remained in the same communities for generations where the work of fathers and mothers became the work of the children. When the nation moved from a relatively agrarian society to one of industry and automation, the mobility of families changed as well.

For many families in the 21st century, movement to new cities is commonplace. Although movement from communities provides access to jobs, life-styles, and differences in culture, there are also limitations. William Capps and Mary Ellen Maxwell discuss the importance of recognizing ways in which schools should respond to the demographic changes within American classrooms. As you read this article ask yourself, "How should schools respond to the number of students who move in and out of their communities? How should I structure my curriculum in ways that recognize the mobility of students?"

Think About This . . .

1. What are some of the challenges faced by students who move from school to school?
2. The school experiences of children often differ from community to community. How will you assess the academic backgrounds of your students?
3. Many schools are developing plans that respond to student mobility. What factors should they consider as they put their plans into action?
4. How will you build a feeling of community in your classroom?

We are a mobile society. Mobility has shaped our history, informed our culture, and helped define what it means to be an American. From 19th-century settlers exhorted to "Go West" to today's immigrants striving to become "upwardly mobile," Americans have accepted movement and change as part of the American Dream.

There is, of course, a downside to all this mobility, and nowhere is it more evident than in the impact on the public schools. Students who change schools can suffer socially and academically. And their schools often suffer as well, as teachers are forced to repeat lessons for a constantly changing student body.

As school board members and administrators, we need to understand the causes and effects of student mobility. While we will never eliminate the problem, we can work to reduce the amount of movement between schools and mitigate the impact of mobility when it does occur. The result will be happier and more productive students and more successful schools.

On the Move

Between March 1998 and March 1999, almost 16 percent of our population moved—that's about one out of every six U.S. residents. The effect on the schools was both predictable and disturbing. According to figures from the National Center for Education Statistics, quoted recently in the *Washington Post,* 32 percent of U.S. fourth-graders in 1998 had switched schools during the course of the two previous years.

Horror stories about student mobility abound in the media and in scholarly reports, but the statistics alone are enough to create an alarming tale. Consider:

- One in 10 students in the United States moved six or more times before the age of 18, according to a 1993 study by researchers Russell W. Rumberger and Katherine Larson.
- In 1996, the *Christian Science Monitor* reported on two students in the Boston area who were attending their 12th and 15th schools in the past three years.
- The same article cited two New Jersey schools—one in Jersey City, the other in Elizabeth—where only 2 percent and 11 percent of the students, respectively, had been in their schools for the full school year.
- In California, nearly 75 percent of students made unscheduled school changes between the first and 12th grades, according to a 1999 report by Stanford professor Russell W. Rumberger and three other authors. This compares to 60 percent

for the nation as a whole. The study found that mobile students suffer psychologically, socially, and academically.

Mobility tends to be a bigger problem in urban schools, but rural and suburban districts are also affected. Some Department of Defense schools report annual transient rates of more than 50 percent, and it is not uncommon for military-dependent children to move 10 times before finishing high school.

Evidence suggests that mobility can hurt children's social, emotional, and academic development. Having to leave friends and known surroundings can create instability in children's lives. According to education researcher Gerald Bracey. "Transient students are not as well adjusted socially as those who are more permanent residents of a school."

It is not difficult to imagine the different expectations these children may encounter from their new teachers, the sense of disconnect from community they experience, and the sense of grief they must feel when forced to break ties with familiar people and places.

"The experience of moving can be similar to death and mourning for a young child," said Jon Newman in his 1988 report "What Should We Do About the Highly Mobile Student?"

Over time, mobility can take an emotional toll on children. Children who move frequently find it difficult to bond with other students, teachers, and a new school culture, which can lead to frustration, loss of self-esteem, lack of interest in school, alienation, and antisocial behavior. And while disadvantaged students are especially vulnerable because of the high transience of their families, middle-class students are not exempt from the consequences of changing schools.

In their 2001 book *Comprehensive Classroom Management: Creating Communities of Support and Solving Problems,* Vernon F. Jones and Louise S. Jones write, "Teachers frequently comment that transfer students often gravitate to a less-than-ideal group of students." The authors stress the importance of teachers modeling appropriate and caring behaviors to negate this tendency.

Mobility and Learning

Mobility also reduces student achievement, numerous studies show. For example, a study by the U.S. General Accounting Office found that 41 percent of highly mobile

From Capps, W., & Maxwell, M. (2002). Mobility. American School Board Journal, *185(5), 26–29. Reprinted with permission of the* American School Board Journal.

third-graders scored below grade level in reading, and 33 percent tested below grade level in math.

Researchers at Minnesota's Family Housing Fund said mobility affects one in five Minneapolis students. The greater the number of moves, the lower the average reading score for students, the researchers said. Average reading scores for those with three or more moves were nearly 20 points lower than for those students who did not move.

Highly mobile students also exhibit developmental delays at a greater rate than their more stable peers, researchers have found. They are more likely to be retained in grade, and they are more apt to drop out of school. In an April 2001 survey, the *Washington Post* noted that "students who have moved four times by eighth grade are four times as likely to drop out, and teenagers who move once during high school are half as likely to graduate." School attendance is also more erratic for mobile children.

The accountability models instituted by states and local school districts assume constancy, stability, and instructional continuity. These models are predicated on the traditional assumption that students will spend the academic year in one school with one teacher or a cadre of teachers. It is not uncommon, however, for teachers in high-mobility schools to witness a 20 percent to 50 percent transient rate in their classrooms between September and June.

Time is a critical element in the accountability equation; there is a set curriculum to be taught and tested within a specified time. Yet teachers in high-mobility schools lose precious hours trying to acclimate new students to their classrooms. They spend valuable time reviewing instructional material and remediating the transient students' academic deficiencies.

High mobility hinders the learning of both transient students and their stable classmates, but teachers are still accountable for academic standards imposed as a result of reform initiatives. Understandably, this causes a good deal of professional angst among teachers, who feel their competency is being judged against unrealistic criteria.

The politics of accountability aside, high mobility raises important ethical issues for administrators and policy makers. Though some accountability models disaggregate mobility as an extenuating factor affecting achievement, is it fair to hold teachers and schools accountable for instruction they were unable to impart through no fault of their own?

When new students come into the classroom, essential questions sometimes go unanswered. New children often come without adequate records, making it hard for teachers and support staff to make classroom and program assignments. Parents often fail to mention that a child has medical or behavioral problems or was receiving special services at the previous school. It is not uncommon for months to go by before records catch up with a highly mobile student. In the interim, there could be gaps in critical services and a loss of instructional continuity.

The U.S. Department of Education and several states have explored the possibility of transferring student records electronically, but privacy concerns are a major issue. Florida has instituted an intra-state system for the electronic transfer of student records between school districts.

Creating Continuity

Student mobility occurs for many reasons, which are often interrelated. Among them are family instability from problems such as divorce, domestic violence, incarceration, or the death of a relative. Other factors are poverty, unemployment, drug abuse, and the lack of affordable housing. New job opportunities, promotions, military transfers, and seasonal employment also contribute to student mobility.

Schools have developed numerous strategies to reduce mobility and mitigate its consequences. Many schools tell parents through letters, handbooks, and conferences of the negative impact that moving during the school year can have on their children's grades, attendance, and standardized test scores.

Some schools have created transition classrooms where students can adapt to a new school culture before moving into a regular classroom. Since affordable housing is a major issue with many transient families, some schools have created partnerships with community service agencies to help families deal with landlords and rent problems.

Teachers in high-mobility schools often present new students with "welcome packets" that include classroom essentials like paper, pencils, and rulers. Some schools have instituted a formal orientation process to quickly determine students' academic needs and help them become better acclimated. This process might include assigning a buddy or peer helper to the new student, providing appropriate tutoring, scheduling parent conferences, and implementing a thorough academic assessment if records are absent.

Vernon and Louise Jones, the authors of *Comprehensive Classroom Management,* propose a greeter program for new students that could be easily incorporated into any orientation process. Students are given coupon books listing the names of adults who assist them at school.

Each student then takes the book to the various adults, who sign it and give the student a small gift. The idea is to have new students interact and become acquainted with key adults in the building as soon as possible. The intent is to foster familiarity and a sense of caring.

The U.S. Army has also begun to deal with some of the bureaucratic problems that affect children of military personnel when their parents are reassigned. This past July, the Army announced an agreement to work with nine school districts that serve large numbers of military dependents. The agreement is intended to address the welfare of these children and the quality-of-life issues that affect their families.

The paradox, of course, is that we live in a society that values mobility. Success in the corporate world is often tied to a willingness to be mobile. When it comes to children, however, we have only recently come to recognize the liabilities associated with mobility.

Parents "need to give children both roots and wings," wrote Marilyn Gardner in an August 2000 article in the *Christian Science Monitor*. "In an age when mobility in all its forms is the mantra of the moment, wings seem an easier gift to offer. Yet roots and a sense of being tethered and grounded still have their place."

Projected increases in enrollment are likely to compound the problem of student mobility in our public schools. Many schools are addressing this issue in creative and imaginative ways, and by doing so, they are helping parents give their children both the roots and the wings they need to be successful learners.

STUDENTS AS COMMODITIES
Anne C. Lewis

One of the dangers of a capitalistic economy is that everything becomes measured in terms of dollars and cents. As educators we have to continually ask, "What are schools for, and what role do educators play in preventing students from becoming commodities?" These are questions Anne Lewis raises as she describes several disturbing trends in our society. Students are increasingly thought of in monetary terms, commodities to be profited from rather than protected. As you read this article ask yourself, "What responsibilities do educators have for protecting our children from becoming commodities?"

Think About This . . .

1. Competition is a pervasive value in U.S. society. What potentially negative effects might it have on our students?

2. One economist compares our educational system to the mail system. How are these two systems similar? How are they different?

3. What arguments does Lewis make against voucher plans and charter schools? How valid are her arguments?

4. What can you as an individual teacher do to prevent your students from becoming commodities?

A story I find useful for all sorts of situations has to do with placing a frog in cold water and gradually warming the water. The frog is lulled into permanent—and fatal—complacency before it winds up on the dinner table. The chance to jump out is gone before the frog realizes it.

Despite belated protests to the contrary, public education seems to be in the midst of a step-by-step movement toward economist Milton Friedman's idea of salvation by competition. The move is very much one of semantics. It can be seen in the words we use to describe our values and our goals, and the words are changing.

I sometimes wonder if it started, innocently enough, with the title of one of the seminal books on education written during the mid-1980s: *The Shopping Mall High School: Winners and Losers in the Educational Marketplace.* The authors, Arthur Powell, David Cohen, and the late Eleanor Farrar, surely did not intend to set off a debate that would incorporate themes about vouchers and the marketplace, but they exposed the realities of the comprehensive high school. It had lost its center, it played to the extremes, and it was breaking up into an array of different accommodations that were made in an effort to keep students in school.

Several recent events serve to remind us of just how thoroughly schools and students are now seen as servants of the marketplace. The Federal Trade Commission, for example, recently settled with companies that have been collecting detailed personal information from students as young as 10 years old, presumably to be used for "educational purposes" but actually sold to other companies that want to market to the children. The companies had amassed information on millions of children.

Or take another example: high school students are spending $2,000 or more to hire sports-recruiting firms to get their applications and video clips to the most promising college athletic programs. This industry matches or bests that of the private consultants who are paid to get students with academic skills into top colleges or to get students who still lack skills into any kind of college.

For a long time, schools, parents, and commercial enterprises have been arguing about the issue of giving businesses access to students—from providing classroom resources, to offering sodas and junk food, to advertising at football stadiums and on school buses. All the objections to these commercial intrusions into schooling faced a tough road until recent studies exposed the problem of obesity in children. At least that might boot the soda and candy machines out of school cafeterias.

However, children often do not have role models to show them how to avoid being commercialized. National education organizations, for example, have always depended on private enterprises, especially those seeking contracts with schools, to fund the "extras" at their meetings. Having just returned from a major education conference, I was struck by how much was now being sponsored or "sold"—major speeches, receptions, awards, and entertainment. The imbibing might not be as intoxicating, but the feeling would be more in keeping with the purpose if Ms. Jones' third-grade class brought lemonade and cookies for these adult parties.

The latest annual study of for-profit education management companies by the Education Policy Studies Laboratory at Arizona State University gives a glimpse of what's happening in the marketplace. Private investors and entrepreneurs who look at the $300-billion K–12 education sector must be rubbing their hands with pleasure and anticipation. They have their own association, advisors, and conferences, unabashedly calling themselves the "education industry." According to the report, charter schools are a growing component of their portfolios, representing 77% of the for-profit schools listed (320 of the 417).

There are 47 management companies operating in 24 states and the District of Columbia that now run schools on a for-profit basis. Like commodities traders, the investors in and leaders of these for-profit companies must be betting on the future. According to Alex Molnar, director of the ASU laboratory, there is insufficient evidence so far that these companies can earn a profit running public schools.

It is ironic that vouchers and choice—pushed as an alternative for parents stuck in low-performing schools—are promoted as purely educational solutions. The major financial backers of vouchers are not education reformers but free-market philosophers and leaders of private enterprise who are often also associated with religious/political extremists. The underbelly of the voucher movement has nothing to do with helping poor families. It is about breaking up the public school system in pursuit of profit or in pursuit of permission to teach the Bible in classrooms.

With last summer's *Zelman* v. *Simmons-Harris* decision by the U.S. Supreme Court, which upheld the Cleveland voucher plan, many governors and state legislators are heeding well-funded campaigns and

From Lewis, A. (2003). Students as commodities. Phi Delta Kappan, *84(8), 563–564. Reprinted with permission of* Phi Delta Kappan.

proposing vouchers. Friedman himself, through his foundation, has provided much of the financing for voucher campaigns in such states as California, Florida, and Michigan. That foundation also subsidizes the Black Alliance for Educational Options, which promotes vouchers among black parents and leaders of the black community.

In an interview in the winter 2003 edition of *Education Next*, Friedman defended his open-market approach to education. Among the public and private choices available through vouchers, the survivors "will be those that satisfied their customers." He anticipates that public schools—the government sector—will "shrink rapidly over time, just as has happened in mail delivery."

It is this attitude that schooling is a commodity and not a value that has changed the vocabulary. That's why a countervailing view expressed in a new report on the civic engagement of youths gives some hope that we can keep schools and children away from the money changers. A joint project of the Center for Information & Research on Civic Learning and Engagement and the Carnegie Corporation, the report calls civic education a necessity.

More than the need to reengage students in civic life, however, the report affirms the role of public schooling as the institution that models and transmits common civic purposes. It is difficult to imagine that free-ranging discussions of contemporary issues, programs of service learning, and the broad experience of diversity—all of which occur regularly in public schools—would continue to exist or have the same impact in a fractured system in which schools reflect individual and exclusive values.

Those who still believe in the worth and possibilities of the common public school need to say so. And they ought first to pledge never to refer to a student as a product.

INSIGHTS INTO MEETING STANDARDS FROM LISTENING TO THE VOICES OF URBAN STUDENTS

Mark G. Storz and Karen R. Nestor

Standards are designed to help all students reach minimal competency in essential content areas, but they can have unintended consequences. One of these is to dehumanize teaching, to focus on the standards rather than the students we serve. Mark Storz and Karen Nestor asked 100 urban middle school students to talk about their teachers and schools and to define a "good education," a caring teacher, effective teaching strategies, and school success. They found that these students wanted their classrooms to be challenging, integrative, and exploratory. As you read this article ask yourself, "How similar are these students to the ones I will teach?"

Think About This . . .

1. How do these students feel about challenge? How can teachers use these feelings to help students meet state-mandated standards?
2. What are the different dimensions of curricular integration? Which of these are easiest for individual teachers to address? Which are most difficult?
3. How might students' desire for opportunities for exploration run counter to standards? What could teachers do to minimize this conflict?
4. How important will challenge, integration, and exploration be in your classroom? How would you implement these ideas in your teaching?

Rigorous, detailed academic standards are driving school improvement efforts across the United States. Local districts and state after state have developed lengthy documents to direct instruction in every discipline. Many of these standards may actually correspond to the charge in *Turning Points 2000* to "teach a curriculum grounded in rigorous, public academic standards for what students should know and be able to do" (Jackson & Davis, 2000, p. 23). However, urban school systems, already reeling from weak performance on high-stakes tests, are facing the challenge of meeting even more demanding expectations for students and teachers. In the rush to implement newly adopted standards, there has been little time to consider standards-based practices that are "relevant to the concerns of adolescents and based on how they learn best" (Jackson & Davis, 2000, p. 23).

As the standards movement has swept the country, the voices of urban middle school students seldom have been heard. Teams of teachers and administrators, district professional developers, education consultants, and university partners have met to design pedagogical approaches based on the new standards, leaving students to observe the process and experience the results from the side-lines. However, when given the opportunity to reflect on their education, urban middle schoolers articulate their own desire for more demanding expectations. At the same time, they also recognize the importance of what middle school professionals call developmentally responsive practice (National Middle School Association [NMSA], 1995).

As consultants, we began our work on standards in a newly configured K–8 school in a large urban district. Being part of a school-based school improvement partnership, we worked with teachers in professional development sessions and in their classrooms to understand the district's new standards and to devise and implement strategies for achieving grade level expectations. As the work progressed, it became clear that students' voices were missing from the planning process. We believed that if teachers heard the students' perspectives, their ability to devise strategies that would help students achieve the increased expectations from the district would be enhanced.

We interviewed 100 seventh and eighth grade students at two urban middle schools. Throughout the interviews, students described in their own words their need for academic experiences that are "challenging, integrative, and exploratory" (NMSA, 1995) in order to achieve the levels of success that they seek and that the new standards demand. The purpose of this paper is to support, through the use of student voices, the notion

that such a curriculum should be the standard for developmentally responsive practice and that it is, in fact, the only way to achieve high academic standards.

Developmentally Responsive Curriculum

First in 1982, and again in 1995, the National Middle School Association (NMSA) published a position paper *This We Believe* that outlined a vision for developmentally appropriate middle level education. Curriculum, viewed as "the primary vehicle for achieving the goals and objectives of a school" (NMSA, 1995, p. 20), was defined by NMSA in its broadest sense to encompass all aspects of a school's educational program. Furthermore, *This We Believe* suggested that what distinguished middle level curriculum from elementary and secondary, was its responsiveness to the various needs and unique characteristics of young adolescents. Thus defined, a curriculum was promoted by NMSA that was "challenging, integrative, and exploratory" (NMSA, 1995, p. 20).

Belair and Freeman (2000) suggested that "young adolescents succeed more and learn best when they are required to become practitioners of knowledge rather than just receivers of knowledge" (p. 5). Similarly, Zemelman, Daniels, and Hyde (1998) asserted that students "learn most powerfully from doing, not just hearing about, any subject" (p. 9). A challenging curriculum actively engages middle school students in their learning, and does so at a level of understanding that affords an appropriate challenge and opportunity for success. Such a curriculum provides students the chance to explore significant issues and address relevant skills in meaningful contexts, and in a way that ultimately leads to the students assuming responsibility for their learning. A challenging curriculum fosters in-depth rather than superficial coverage of topics, provides a balance between following students' interests and concerns and guiding students to new knowledge, and provides opportunities for choice and decision making in the curriculum.

According to *This We Believe*, "curriculum is integrative when it helps students make sense out of their life experiences" (NMSA, 1995, p. 22). Essentially, integrative curriculum attempts to connect what occurs in one classroom or discipline to what occurs in other

From Storz, M., & Nestor, K. (2003). Insights into meeting standards from listening to the voices of urban students. Middle School Journal, *(34)4, 11–19. Reprinted with permission of the National Middle School Association.*

classrooms, other disciplines, and in the lives of the students outside of the classroom and school. Often school curricula are fragmented so that connections between subjects or between subjects and the life experiences of the students are never made. On the other hand, integrative curriculum is both holistic and authentic (see Zemelman, Daniels, & Hyde, 1998). It creates a learning environment that allows students to engage the "big picture" in real, rich, and meaningful contexts.

This We Believe asserted that the total curriculum of a school should be exploratory in nature. The fact that young adolescents are experiencing rapid growth across developmental domains and are beginning to see themselves and their places in the world in new ways suggests that exploration of the many possibilities available to the students is essential to their academic and social growth. Further, given young adolescents' intense curiosity and search to form a conscious sense of identity, an exploratory curriculum provides the opportunity for these students to discover their abilities, talents, interests, values, and preferences, both within the formal curriculum and beyond it. In addition, during adolescence, there is an increased awareness of the social world beyond the students themselves. These developmental characteristics necessitate opportunities for students to examine ways of contributing to the society. Such programs will serve to pique curiosity and broaden the conceptions these students have about themselves and the world around them.

We know that experts in the area of teaching and learning support this position of the National Middle School Association. While many obstacles may impede its implementation (see Thompson, 2000), the literature suggests that developmentally responsive practice remains valid. Currently, however, there is a real concern that the standards movement, along with a reliance on high-stakes testing, will cause middle level educators to abandon developmentally responsive curriculum. This concern has led Vars (2001) to ask the question, "is there any hope for the future of developmentally appropriate curriculum?" (p. 8). The voices of the students we interviewed clearly affirm that such a curriculum is worth fighting for.

Amplifying Student Voices

Through interviews we examined students' views on their educational experiences, particularly on the types of teachers and pedagogical practices that they perceived to be most beneficial to their achievement and success in school. We initially saw the students as a primary source of information in our efforts to work as educational consultants with teams of middle school teachers.

However, as we interviewed the students, their ability to talk about the educational issues that affected their lives led us to believe that a wider audience would benefit from their insights. We were also aware that there is a growing line of research focusing on the voices of the students themselves as a means of examining the impact of educational reform on the lived experiences of students (see Cook-Sather, 2002; Corbett & Wilson, 1995; Erlandson & McVittie, 2001; Nieto, 1994; Oldfather & West, 1999; Powell & Skoog, 1995; Wasley, Hampel, & Clark, 1997; Wilson & Corbett, 2001). Much of this research has involved interviewing and observing students, listening to their reflections on their lived experiences in school, and integrating students' beliefs and expectations into the larger arena. We hoped that our work would amplify students' voices, while providing insight into the impact educational reforms have on the school experiences of these students.

Our study took place in two urban middle schools in a large midwestern metropolitan area. One of the schools had a student population of 480. There were 160 seventh and eighth graders, the majority of whom were African American (99.5%) and low income. The other school had a student population of 600, 420 of whom were seventh and eighth graders. Minority students represented 69% of this school's population, of which the majority were African American. Students came from a wide range of socioeconomic backgrounds.

Together, we conducted 45- to 60-minute, semi-structured group interviews at each of the schools. We randomly selected seventh and eighth grade students at both schools (n=100) and divided them into groups of four or five. Teachers reported that the selected students represented a cross section of personalities and ability levels, providing us with what we think was a balanced perspective of their students' experiences, ideas, and beliefs about education.

An interview protocol was used to ask students to describe what they considered a good education and whether or not they thought they were currently receiving one. We also asked them about the types of teachers and instructional practices that both helped and hindered their learning. Issues surrounding school climate and the environment were also discussed. Going beyond the interview protocol, we probed the students as we sought clarification and elaboration.

We audiotaped and transcribed each of the interviews. Our thematic analysis (Shank, 2002) involved each of us individually reviewing the interview transcripts and reflecting on them, identifying themes that seemed to illuminate the various aspects of our research questions. We then came together, shared our observations, and further discussed the emergent themes.

Students' Perceptions of Their Learning

Our experiences at the middle schools we studied suggest that developmentally responsive curricular practices, as defined in *This We Believe*, are implemented to varying degrees. When such practices are followed, the students are able to articulate the academic and social benefits they receive. Not surprisingly, when such practices are not employed, students are readily able to identify what is lacking and how their learning is impoverished. While the students may not know or understand the educational jargon we use to define developmentally responsive practice, they do understand what constitutes a good education. As the students in our study reflected on and shared their thoughts and beliefs about their school experiences, the characteristics of a developmentally responsive curriculum, namely a curriculum that is challenging, integrative, and exploratory, were illustrated and supported as effective practices.

To illuminate both the effectiveness and lack of developmentally responsive practices in the experiences of the students we interviewed, we have included quotes from the students themselves that we believe are most salient and most representative of the students. In including these excerpts we have chosen not to substantially edit the students' words. We have also been careful not to take the students' words out of context in any way that might change their initial meanings.

Curriculum That Is Challenging

As soon as the interviews began, we were struck by the students' strong desire for challenging academic experiences, in effect, for high academic standards. Throughout the interviews, students emphasized the value they place on rigorous instruction. At both schools, they applauded teachers who "push us to do our work," who "expect a lot of me," who "won't let us give up." One student summarized, "She pushed me to do it and gave me confidence to do it. . . . I thought she was doing it to be mean, but now I see that she wanted me to succeed." On the other hand, students were adamant, and at times even angry, about the low level of work they were experiencing. Take for example this exchange among seventh grade students:

Student 1: We just read a book then do worksheets. Read the next thing, then do a worksheet.

Student 2: It gets played out. It gets boring doing it over and over and over again.

Student 3: We need more work. Harder work.

Student 2: We in seventh grade, and they started giving us multiplication.

Student 3: And they always talking about "you in seventh grade you need to start acting like you all in seventh grade." Well, teach us like we in seventh grade.

An eighth grader said, "We need to challenge our grades a bit . . . if we just sit here and do this easy work like they're giving us now, like most of the teachers are, like the work we did last year, like plusses [addition] and whatever. We don't need that. We need to get a fair break."

While welcoming challenging work, the students also described the importance of developmentally appropriate work that is "achievable, even if difficult" (NMSA, 1995, p. 21). A seventh grader said, "She'd [the teacher] give me stuff like ninth grade work and I was in sixth grade last year. She give me the paper and I didn't know what to do, so I take it home, do research on it, try to learn or whatever. I don't really know it and she knew that." Students accurately described the support they need to perform at high levels. In this excerpt, for example, students discussed the importance of scaffolding their learning:

Student 1: They tell us to do an assignment but they don't tell us how to do it, or why to do it. They just tell us to do it.

Student 2: We were supposed to get up and read our paper and try to persuade her [the teacher], but she didn't teach us how to persuade. She just read out the book and we had to write five paragraphs. But I didn't know how to persuade nobody using that voice.

Students at both schools agreed that challenging work is active, engaging, and explores significant issues and relevant skills. Many students complained that worksheets are boring, like the student who said, "They don't get no action in this school. We sit there and be bored all day. That's why I think some kids don't like coming to school because there don't be no action. We don't do nothing" or the student who added, "right now they give us 15 minutes to do a two minute worksheet, stuff that could have been long done. I need some stuff that is challenging my abilities." Students spoke with great enthusiasm about classroom experiences that focused on significant issues. They particularly emphasized their study of the human body, the

Holocaust, and discussions they had about gangs. Students frequently mentioned their eagerness to learn about their own culture, its history, and its position in society. One asked, "How will I learn without knowing my history?," and others expressed their engagement with class work on racial issues.

In their move toward independence, young adolescents are stimulated by the opportunity to develop their own questions in areas that they find challenging and significant. One boy described a class activity that led him to pose such questions when he said, "When we talked about Black History, I asked him [the teacher], 'What if it was the other way around? What if the Whites were the slaves and the Blacks were rich?'" That same student lamented that there was never a chance to discuss his question. Affirming the value of considering the why as well as the how (NMSA, 1995), he added, "The problem about me is I always think 'What if?' and 'Why not?'" Only a few students mentioned academic choices, like the one who stressed, "She [a teacher] lets you talk about yourself. When you tell her the activities you like to do, she lets you make a project, like who invented this, or like back in the days when all White folks did all the stuff—Black folks did a lot of stuff too." On the other hand, a number of students complained that they have very little independent choice in assignments and none spoke of opportunities for self-evaluation.

This We Believe asserts that a developmentally responsive curriculum provides opportunities for students to guide their own education. The students we interviewed frequently mentioned their own desire to develop personal and academic goals. One defined success in this way:

> To have goals and follow your goals that you have set out for yourself. Like if you want to do something in life . . . you have to be able to, I mean willing to, go to this far extent to get this goal which will lead you to your success. You set your goals out in front of you and for you to be able to walk right into them. If you got something that you want to do, you got to be really, really 100% sure. You have to be really determined to get to these goals.

Some students referred to an ongoing process of goal setting that takes place at the beginning of a marking period. While the students valued goal setting, a number felt that they could gain more from the experience if it were connected more closely with their actual work. One student said, "I don't think they [the teachers] really look at what your goals are. They just kind of have it there to help you and I think they'll just go on regular teaching."

The students we interviewed have a strong desire to reach high standards of achievement and they know how they learn best. Their responses seem to suggest that when the many elements of a challenging curriculum are present, they will be more likely to meet the expectations that state-mandated standards have set.

Curriculum That Is Integrative

Throughout our interviews, the students made it clear that they are looking for the connections between what they are learning in school and their life experiences outside of school. As one student suggested,

> We need to start learning more about the real world instead of things like . . . angles. Give people more science because that's a big thing. You want to know about things. You want to know about yourself. And probably somebody in this school wants to be a doctor. I want to start to learn.

This We Believe suggests a variety of ways that the goals of integrative curriculum can be met. Two of these involve (a) integration across the disciplines and (b) the integration of the core curriculum with other courses and activities within the school. Few of the students we interviewed spoke specifically about these aspects of integrative curriculum. It appeared to us that little curriculum integration of this nature was occurring at the two schools. If such integration was happening, it carried little salience for these students as they responded to our inquiries and interacted with each other. A few students at one of the schools did talk about an exploratory program that integrated technology, research skills, and communication in the creation of a business and a brochure to promote that business. This activity prompted a student to comment, "It [the activity] was real easy because I had watched my mother because she tried to make her own business and she would tell me some of the stuff she did. So it was easy for me and it really helped."

A third way that *This We Believe* suggests for meeting the goals of integrative curriculum is for teachers to explain to the students how the curriculum applies to their daily lives. What seemed most important for the student quoted above was the connection between the business activity and his own personal experiences. This connection made the learning meaningful, or as he put it, "easy." Cast in a somewhat different light, another student remarked,

> We growing up kind of fast and they're [the teachers] trying to slow our growing way slow, like trying to

make us learn things we already know. But I say, "we growing up fast and we need to start learning things more about the real world"!

For the students we interviewed making connections between what they were learning in school and their experiences outside of school was a very important aspect of their learning.

We asked the students to think about the types of activities they believed were most helpful to their learning. One of the more common responses we received was "projects," which were most often described as long term and involved assignments that had some personal meaning for the student. Some of the students were able to recall in detail many of the projects that had been assigned. One of these, the playground project, was a science activity that required students to design and build a playground that was wired for electricity. In reflecting on this experience, one student commented, "We definitely learned a lot about simple machines and how they worked and how to wire for electricity, but I don't know if we're going to use this in real life." While the student suggested that the project did result in learning, he nonetheless wondered about its usefulness outside the classroom. This prompted us to ask the students if their teachers made any attempt to help them see that the information they are learning in the classroom is relevant to real life. The students responded:

> **Student 1:** It seems like a lot of time they're just teaching for the proficiency tests so that we'll pass. I don't think that there's a lot of stuff on these [tests] that's really important to real life.
>
> **Student 2:** And with the playground project, I was thinking that how is this going to help me in real life? I'm going to go in a store and say 'Oh, no, your light bulb is out, let me try to rewire it.' I realized that there are going to be some kids that want to be an electrician. This would help them.
>
> **Student 3:** Like when you're in class, you don't actually get what the thing you are working on is relevant to. Last year, my math teacher had a chart that said careers and then all the subjects in math, and then it had little dots in areas that were relevant, so if you wanted to be a doctor, [it indicated] what kind of math you would need.

A number of other students also articulated the importance of making the school curriculum connected in some way to real life experiences. A student who questioned the value of a particular project stated, "We be having a whole bunch of projects but they don't be necessary. What is a project about paper necessary for?

Paper ain't going to get us no job." This quote reflected a recurring theme that relates the school's curriculum to future occupations. This connection was alluded to in the dialogue presented earlier where the student referred to the math teacher connecting that subject matter directly to occupations. Another student articulated this connection more explicitly when he commented, "Each one of the classes teaches different methods. Like math, that's a clerk in a store. Science class, that's like a scientist or NASA. Spanish class you be an explorer."

The students we interviewed equated good teaching and learning with teachers that connected their subject matter with real life experiences that students perceived as interesting, relevant, meaningful, and useful. According to these students, effective learning that achieves high standards is intimately related to the integration of the school curriculum with the life experiences of the students.

Curriculum That Is Exploratory

Certain aspects of an exploratory curriculum as described in *This We Believe* emerged in our interviews with middle schoolers. Students at both schools, for example, spontaneously mentioned an eagerness to contribute to society, like the student who said: "We don't do no extras so I think that's why kids don't come to school that much. Like people should work in the office and stuff. . . . it would be like helping the principal. Teach people about things. Yeah, jobs, at other schools they have jobs." Another added, "be a role model to the little kids. Like going to their classes, tutor, and teach them." Students referred to times when service learning was part of the academic program: "Mr. S. is into that whole service learning part, and he told us that he just don't want to teach us, but he wants us to actually get out there and use what we've learned and helping people. I like that a lot. . . . I think It's made it easier for me."

In a similar way, students seem to want opportunities in school to develop their personal and interpersonal strengths in addition to their academic strength. Many incorporated such ideas into their definition of a good education, like the student who said, "he encourages us to do good things in the community. He says the most important thing you can learn is not about all the dates and stuff, but he teaches us how to be a good person and that's really cool." At one school students who were elected leaders wanted to exert leadership, but they expressed disappointment that the student council no longer met. Students also articulated a desire to collaborate: "Sometimes we work together on things so it won't be hard for us. . . . We don't do it this year, but last year we were doing it all the time." They add, however, that group work often is ineffective because they have not learned how to manage it.

In addition to defining exploratory curriculum, *This We Believe* highlights teaching strategies that support it. The students we interviewed were particularly insightful in describing the strategies that help them learn. Their ideas are well summarized by the student who said, "You need to be able to learn and have interesting things to *do* [emphasis the student's], because if you're not doing anything, if you're just sitting there listening, then you don't really learn. But when you have things to do, then you learn a lot more." They reiterate that active, exploratory learning promotes understanding: "Instead of having the students write out, do an experiment instead of [just] thinking about it and drawing conclusions. . . . It helps you have a better understanding of what you are learning." In one school, students described their work in a media center that provides opportunities to use technology and other resources to explore their own interests or preferences when they are working on a project. One student also described the value of going outside the school, saying, "She wants us to do research. She says you got to go beyond . . . like go to the library and go to the museum to get more information about what you are going to do. And that's really good. If you want to progress you have to go beyond what you are looking for."

We were surprised that students rarely mentioned extracurricular activities. (It is notable that no student mentioned the arts.) One boy, however, described his approach to running in a way that illuminates the learning connections that could be made with sports or other student interests:

> **Student:** Deshawn had beaten me and I see how he runs so I don't run with my legs. I take little steps.
>
> **Interviewer:** So you studied the way it works?
>
> **Student:** When I start off, I start stretching my legs and I just start taking tiny steps and that's how I beat Deshawn. I ran tiny steps for a minute. Because Michael Johnson, Maurice Green, and Marion Jones.
>
> **Interviewer:** Have you really studied the way they run? Have you looked at it really closely?
>
> **Student:** She runs with her hands down there and bring it up. Maurice Green he just opens up. Michael just starts off and turns his head. That's how they do it, man.

The students we interviewed provided insight into the ways that an exploratory curriculum would help them reach higher levels of achievement. They validate the importance of exploring their own talents, interests, and values within the academic program and beyond the classroom in order to enhance their learning.

Implications for Instruction

Teachers and administrators, who are anxious and frustrated by the demands of mandated academic standards, will find great support for implementing or expanding developmentally responsive practice from listening to the perspectives of middle school students themselves. Since standards have been adopted, schools, and urban schools in particular, have felt pressured to focus on standards rather than on students as they plan instruction. When we listen to the voices of students in these schools, they tell us clearly that they will learn more effectively if we focus first on their unique characteristics as young adolescents and the learning imperatives that will enhance their performance. Their voices affirm, "Standards, yes! Standardization, no!"

As we review the students' discussions, we believe that developmentally responsive practice must be the standard if middle school students are to meet or exceed district and state mandates. The challenge for middle school teachers is to discover ways to teach the formal, standards-based curriculum using strategies that will effectively achieve academic goals and that will continue to help middle school students develop into responsible, fulfilled adults. We believe that the students' insights provide teachers with guidelines for developing their practice:

- Students want their teachers to expect a great deal from them academically and personally. They want difficult work, but just as importantly, they want work that challenges their thinking and understanding. They want teachers to help them set goals and monitor their progress toward their own goals.

- Students know that they are not ready for work that is too far beyond their developmental level. They recognize their need for support when meeting new or more abstract work and for teachers who are eager to identify and meet their individual needs.

- Students are certain that active learning, as evidenced in hands-on activities, projects, experiments, service learning, and the like will help them learn the core curriculum more effectively. In this way, they want to take more responsibility for their learning, with support for gaining the skills necessary to complete their work.

• Students have their own questions that they would like to explore. Many have experienced limited choices in topics, assignments, and assessments. They believe that choice enhances their learning.

• Students benefit from linking their classroom work with their own lives and cultures, and with real-life problems and situations. They know that they need help to make these connections and they want teachers who will make the connections explicit or lead them to their own discoveries.

• Students identify very few connections across the curriculum. If their learning is to be most effective, teachers may need to seek opportunities to integrate learning across disciplines.

• Students are eager to contribute to their school and their community beyond their actual classroom work. They believe that, in the long run, this will help them learn better.

• Students can use their talents, personal interests, or life experiences to improve their knowledge and understanding of academic work. They want teachers who seek to use the students' own strengths to enhance learning. Extracurricular activities may be a way to discover and develop those strengths.

In short, the students we interviewed sent a clear message to middle school professionals: they do want school experiences that are challenging, integrative, and exploratory. They are eager to partner with their teachers to achieve high standards of performance that allow them to develop fully as individuals. After listening to students' voices, teachers can feel confident that they can and should "teach a curriculum grounded in rigorous, public academic standards for what students should know and be able to do, relevant to the concerns of adolescents and based on how they learn best" (Jackson & Davis, 2000, p. 23).

References

Belair, J. R., & Freeman, P. (2000). Providing a responsive and academically rigorous curriculum. *Middle School Journal, 32*(1), 5–6.

Cook-Sather, A. (2002). Authorizing students' perspectives: Toward trust, dialogue, and change in education. *Educational Researcher, 31*(4), 3–14.

Corbett, D., & Wilson, B. (1995). Make a difference with, not for, students: A plea to researchers and reformers. *Educational Researcher, 24*(5), 12–17.

Erlandson, C., & McVittie, J. (2001). Student voices on integrative curriculum. *Middle School Journal, 33*(2), 28–36.

Jackson, A. W., & Davis, G. A. (2000). *Turning points 2000: Educating adolescents in the 21st century.* New York & Westerville, OH: Teachers College Press & National Middle School Association.

National Middle School Association. (1995). *This we believe: Developmentally responsive middle level schools.* Columbus, OH: Author.

Nieto, S. (1994). Lessons from students on creating a chance to dream. *Harvard Educational Review, 64*(4), 392–426.

Oldfather, P., & West, J. (1999). *Learning through children's eyes: Social construction and the desire to learn.* Washington, DC: American Psychological Association.

Powell, R., & Skoog, G. (1995). Students' perspectives on integrative curricula: The case of Brown Barge Middle School. *Research in Middle Level Education Quarterly, 19*(1), 85–114.

Shank, G. D. (2002). *Qualitative research: A personal skills approach.* Upper Saddle River, NJ: Merrill/Prentice Hall.

Thompson, S. C. (2000). Overcoming obstacles to creating responsive curriculum. *Middle School Journal, 32*(1), 47–54.

Vars, G. F. (2001). Can curriculum integration survive in an era of high-stakes testing? *Middle School Journal, 33*(2), 7–17.

Wasley, P., Hampel, R., & Clark, R. (1997). *Kids and school reform.* San Francisco: Jossey-Bass.

Wilson, B. L., & Corbett, H. D. (2001). *Listening to urban kids: School reform and the teachers they want.* Albany, NY: State University of New York Press.

Zemelman, S., Daniels, H., & Hyde, A. (1998). *Best practice: New standards for teaching and learning in America's schools.* Portsmouth, NH: Heinemann.

AN EDUCATOR'S PRIMER ON THE GENDER WAR

David Sadker

How does gender influence our attempts to help students grow and develop? Do schools shortchange girls, or do schools shortchange boys? Surprisingly, the answer to both of these questions is "yes," as asserted by David Sadker, a pioneer in the battle to make schools more gender equitable. In this article, Sadker describes a recent phenomenon in education—the backlash movement—which contends that recent attention to girls' plight in schools has diverted attention from the serious school problems facing boys. Sadker makes a compelling case that schools fail both boys and girls, but in different ways, and the challenge for educators is to address these specific problems strategically. As you read this article ask yourself, "How can schools do a better job of educating both boys and girls?"

Think About This . . .

1. In what areas do schools shortchange girls? Which of these are most and least serious?
2. In what areas do schools shortchange boys? Which of these are most and least serious?
3. What does Sadker mean by the term "backlash movement"? How valid is his response to this movement?
4. What specifically could you do as a classroom teacher to ensure equal opportunities for both males and females in your classroom?

Several recent books, a seemingly endless series of television and radio talk shows, and a number of newspaper columns have painted a disturbing picture of schools mired in a surreptitious war on boys. In such books as *The War Against Boys* and *Ceasefire!*,[1] readers are introduced to education using war metaphors and are informed that boys are daily casualties of zealous efforts to help girls. These "schools-at-war" authors also call for more "boy-friendly" education, including increased testing, frequent classroom competitions, and the inclusion of war poetry in the curriculum—all measures intended to counter feminist influences. They also argue that sections of Title IX, the law that prohibits sex discrimination in education, be rescinded. Teachers are informed that giving extra attention to boys in classrooms and building up school libraries that are dominated by books about male characters are useful strategies to improve boys' academic performance. As one book warns, "It's a bad time to be a boy in America."

After over a quarter century of researching life in schools, I must admit that at first I thought this "gender war" was a satire, a creative way to alert people to the difficulties of creating fair schools that work for all children. Certainly boys (like girls) confront gender stereotypes and challenges, and teachers and parents must work hard every day to make schools work for all children. But these recent books and talk shows were not intended as satire; they purported to present a se-

rious picture of schools in which girls ruled and boys were their victims.

The irony of girls waging a war on boys reminded me of a *Seinfeld* episode that featured "Bizarro World." For those of you not versed in the culture of Bizarro World, it is a Superman comics theme in which everything is opposite: up is down, in is out, and good is bad. When the popular sitcom featured an episode on Bizarro World, Kramer became polite and discovered that doors were to be knocked on, not stormed through. George went from nerdiness to cool, from dysfunctional to popular; he was rewarded with two well-adjusted parents. Elaine's self-absorption was transformed into compassion, a change that would probably lead to a hitch in the Peace Corps and stardom in her own *Seinfeld* spin-off, *Elaine in Africa*. In this topsy-turvy transformation, the entire Seinfeld gang became well adjusted, with their ethical compasses recalibrated to do the right thing. What would schools be like, I thought, if such Bizarro World changes came to pass? What would school look like if "misguided feminists" were actually engaged in a "war against boys"? And then I thought, what if girls really did rule?

From Sadker, D. (2002). *An educator's primer on the gender war*. Phi Delta Kappan, 84(3), 235–240, 244. *Reprinted with permission of the author.*

* * *
(Camera fade-in)

The statue of the great woman dominates the front lawn of suburban Alice Paul High School. (Alice Paul, of course, led the courageous fight for women to be recognized as citizens, and her efforts contributed to passage of the 19th Amendment.) By 2003, Alice Paul, Susan B. Anthony, and Hillary Rodham Clinton have become the most common names for America's schools.

The statue of Alice Paul at the entrance of the school has become a student *talis-woman*. Students rub Alice's big toe before taking the SAT or on the eve of a critical soccer match with their cross-town rivals, the Stanton Suffragettes. Although Alice Paul died in 1977, she remains a real presence on campus.

Once inside Alice Paul High School, images of famous women are everywhere. Pictures of Jeannette Rankin, Mary MacLeod Bethune, Margaret Sanger, Carry Nation, and Mia Hamm gaze down on students as they go to their classes, constant reminders of the power and accomplishments of women. There are few if any pictures of men, as if in confirmation of the old adage "It's a woman's world." Trophy cases overflow with artifacts trumpeting women's role in ending child labor, reforming schools, eliminating domestic violence, confronting alcoholism, and battling for health care reform. It is the same story in the technology and math wing of Alice Paul High, where the influence of such computer pioneers as Ada Loveless and Grace Hopper can be seen everywhere.

Few images of males can be found anywhere in the hallways—or in the textbooks. The typical history text devotes less than 5% of its content to the contributions of men, a percentage that actually shrinks in math and science texts. Other than the one or two "unusual men" who find their way into the curriculum, students learn that their world was constructed almost exclusively by and for women.

Not everyone is happy with female-dominated bulletin boards and textbooks, as school principal Anna Feminie knows all too well. (Most school principals are, of course, female, since they seem better equipped to manage demanding parents and a predominantly male faculty.) From time to time, a few vociferous parents of boys complain about the lack of male images. But Anna has been in her job for five years now, and she knows just how to handle angry parents. She makes a big show of Men's History Month. Almost magically, every March, a new crop of male figures materializes. Anna understands that Men's History Month is nothing more than a nod to political correctness. Luckily, most parents and faculty agree with Anna and feel more comfortable with the well-known female names and images from their own student days. But all that may be changing with the increased emphasis on standardized state tests. New history standards put the traditional female front and center once again, and perhaps the end of Men's History Month is in sight. And if that should come to pass, it would be just fine with principal Anna Feminie.

By 8 a.m., hallway noise is at a peak as students exchange last-minute comments before the late bell sounds. Crowds of girls rule the school's "prime real estate": main stairwells, cafeteria entrance, and the senior locker bay. In groups, the girls can be even more intimidating. Individual boys carefully weave their way around these "girl areas," looking down to avoid unwanted stares and snares. The strategy is less than effective. Sometimes the boys are forced to pretend that they do not hear those louder-than-a-whisper offensive comments. At other times, the boys rapidly sidestep the outstretched arms of some of the more aggressive girls who are trying to impress their friends. Boys at Alice Paul travel in bands for safety, like convoys at sea. They smile a lot and speak a little. Although they do not quite understand it all, they know that they are at some risk, even in their own school, and taking precautions has become second nature.

Girls dominate in classrooms as well. They shout out answers, and teachers accept their behavior as "natural," part of their more aggressive biological makeup. Not true for the boys. When boys call out, they are likely to be reminded to "raise your hand." Even when girls do not shout out, teachers call on them more often than on boys, reward them more, help them more, and criticize them more. With girls as the center of classroom attention, boys seem content to sit quietly on the sidelines: low profiles are safe profiles.

Most boys take to their quiet, second-class role with incredible grace. They enroll in the programs more suitable for their nature: the humanities and social sciences courses, as well as the typical and predictable vocational programs. Few boys are assigned to costly special education programs. While educating boys is relatively inexpensive, there are rewards associated with lower career goals, docility, and conformity. Every quarter, boys are rewarded with higher grades on report cards. Boys are also more likely to be listed on the honor roll and chosen to be the school valedictorian. Teachers appreciate boys who do their work on time, cause few disruptions, demand less in class, rarely complain, and do not need special education.

While these higher report card grades are comforting, low test scores are disturbing. When the SAT and other competitive tests roll around, boys' scores lag behind girls on both math and verbal tests. On virtually every high-stakes test that matters, including the Advanced Placement tests and later the Graduate Record Exam, girls outscore boys. Few adults wonder why boys' high report card grades are not reflected in these very important test scores.

While the athletic field offers a change of venue, it is basically the same story. At Alice Paul, boys' football, baseball, and basketball do not hold a candle to girls' field hockey and soccer. The student newspaper is filled with the exploits of the Alice Paul Amazons, as the female athletes are called. The Gentlemen Amazons draw smaller crowds and less coverage in the school paper. Funding for just one of the girls' teams can equal the entire male athletic budget. Although some parents have tried to bolster male sports, coaches, parents, and the influential state athletic association have thwarted their efforts.

Female domination of athletics is accompanied by the ringing of a cash register. A few female athletes not only have won college scholarships but also have moved into the multimillion-dollar ranks of the professionals. Amazon booster clubs have been generous to Alice Paul, funding the new athletic field, the state-of-the-art girls' training facility, and a number of athletic scholarships. The Alice Paul Amazons ignite school spirit and have won several state championships. No one was surprised five years ago when the former girls' field hockey coach, Anna Feminie, was chosen as the new principal.

If Alice Paul were alive today, she would be proud of her Amazons. Alice Paul women dominate corporate boardrooms and government offices, and many are leaders promoting social reform around the globe. And Alice herself would be no less proud of the men who graduate from her school, true partners with women at work and at home.

(Camera fade-out)

* * *

The description of the fictional Alice Paul High School is a true reflection of hundreds of studies of school life, with one obvious modification (after all, it is Bizarro World): the genders have been reversed. The idea that "girls rule" in school is not only silly, it is intentionally deceptive. So why all the recent commotion about "a war on boys"?

Certainly boys do not always fit comfortably into the school culture, but this has little to do with girls—and a lot to do with how we conduct school. In fact, both girls and boys confront different school challenges, and they respond in different ways. Girls are more likely to react to problems in a quieter and less disruptive fashion, while boys are more likely to act out—or drop out. Males of color in particular drop out of high school more often and enroll in college less frequently than either minority females or white males. Decades of studies, books, and reports have documented the school difficulties of boys generally and of boys of color in particular.

The new twist in the current debate is the scapegoating of the feminist movement. And for those who were never very comfortable with the feminist movement, these new books and their ultraconservative spokespeople have an allure. Many mainstream media fixate on the audience appeal of a "Mars versus Venus" scenario, portraying boys as hapless victims of "male-hating feminists." Even educators and parents who do not blame females for the problems boys experience still buy into the argument that girls are "ahead" in school.

But for people to believe that "girls are responsible for boys' problems," they must repress historical realities: these problems predated the women's movement. Boys' reading difficulties, for example, existed long before modern feminism was even a twinkle in Betty Friedan's eye, and the dropout rate has actually decreased since the publication of *The Feminine Mystique*. Ironically, it was female teachers who fought hard to remove corporal punishment, while promoting new instructional strategies that moved teachers beyond lecture and recitation. Women educators led the movement for more humane classrooms, and the current attack on feminism has the potential of hurting boys as well as girls.

The truth is that *both* boys and girls exhibit different strengths and have different needs, and gender stereotypes shortchange all of us. So where are we in terms of the progress made for both girls and boys in school today? And what challenges still remain? The following "Report Card" takes us beyond the phony gender war and offers a succinct update of salient research findings.

A Report Card on the Costs of Gender Bias
Grades and Tests

Females. Females receive better grades from elementary school through college, but not everyone sees this as good news. Some believe that this may be one of the "rewards" girls receive for more quiet and conforming classroom behavior.[2]

Female test scores in several areas have improved dramatically in recent years. The performance of females on science and math achievement tests has improved, and girls now take more Advanced Placement tests than boys. Yet they lag behind males on a number of important tests, scoring lower on both the verbal and mathematics sections of the SAT, the Advanced Placement exams, and the Graduate Record Exam.[3]

Males. Males (and students from low-income families) not only receive lower grades, but they are also more likely to be grade repeaters. Many believe that school norms and culture conflict with many male behavior patterns.[4] The National Assessment of Educational Progress and many other exams indicate that males perform significantly below females in writing and reading achievement.[5]

Academic Enrollment

Females. Female enrollment in science and mathematics courses has increased dramatically in recent years. Girls are more likely to take biology and chemistry as well as trigonometry and algebra II. However, boys still dominate physics, calculus, and more advanced courses, and boys are more likely to take all three core science courses—biology, chemistry, and physics.[6]

College programs are highly segregated, with women earning between 75% and 90% of the degrees in education, nursing, home economics, library science, psychology, and social work. Women trail men in Ph.D.s (just 40% are awarded to women) and in professional degrees (42% to women). And women are in the minority at seven of eight Ivy League schools.[7]

Computer science and technology reflect increasing gender disparities. Boys not only enroll in more such courses, but they also enroll in the more advanced courses. Girls are more likely to be found in word-processing classes and clerical support programs. Girls are also less likely to use computers outside school, and girls from all ethnic groups rate themselves considerably lower than boys on technological ability. Current software products are more likely to reinforce these gender stereotypes than to reduce them.[8]

Males. Males have a higher high school dropout rate than females (13% to 10%), and they trail females in extracurricular participation, including school government, literary activities, and the performing arts.[9]

Men are the minority (44%) of students enrolled in both undergraduate and graduate institutions, and they lag behind women in degree attainment at the associate (39%), bachelor's (44%), and master's (44%) levels. Although white males and females attend college in fairly equal proportions, African American and Hispanic males are particularly underrepresented at all levels of education.[10]

Gender segregation continues to limit the academic and careers majors of all students. Male college students account for only 12% of elementary education majors, 11% of special education majors, 12% of library science majors, and 14% of those majoring in social work.[11]

Academic Interactions and Special Programs

Females. Females have fewer academic contacts with instructors in class. They are less likely to be called on by name, are asked fewer complex and abstract questions, receive less praise or constructive feedback, and are given less direction on how to do things for themselves. In short, girls are more likely to be invisible members of classrooms.[12]

In elementary school, girls are identified for gifted programs more often than boys; however, by high school fewer girls remain in gifted programs, particularly fewer African American and Hispanic girls. Gender segregation is also evident in the low number of gifted girls found in math and science programs.[13]

Males. Boys receive more teacher attention than females, including more negative attention. They are disciplined more harshly, more publicly, and more frequently than girls, even when they violate the same rules. Parents of male elementary school students (24%) are contacted more frequently about their child's behavior or schoolwork than parents of female students (12%), and boys constitute 71% of school suspensions.[14]

Males account for two thirds of all students served in special education. The disproportionate representation of males in special education is highest in the categories of emotional disturbance (78% male), learning disability (68% male), and mental retardation (58% male).[15]

Health and Athletics

Females. About one million U.S. teenagers get pregnant each year, a higher percentage than in other Western nations. Fifty percent of adolescent girls believe that they are overweight, and 13% are diagnosed with anorexia, bulimia, or binge-eating disorder.[16]

Girls who play sports enjoy a variety of health benefits, including lower rates of pregnancy, drug use, and depression. But despite these benefits, only 50% of girls are enrolled in high school physical education classes. Women today coach only 44% of women's college teams and only 2% of men's teams, while men serve as athletic directors for over 80% of women's programs.[17]

Males. Males are more likely than females to succumb to serious disease and be victims of accidents or violence. The average life expectancy of men is approximately six years shorter than that of women.[18]

Boys are the majority (60%) of high school athletes. Male athletes in NCAA Division I programs graduate at a lower rate than female athletes (52% versus 68%).[19]

Career Preparation, Family, and Parenting

Females. Women dominate lower-paying careers. Over 90% of secretaries, receptionists, bookkeepers, registered nurses, and hairdressers/cosmetologists are female, and, on average, a female college graduate earns $4,000 less annually than a male college graduate. Nearly two out of three working women today do not have a pension plan.[20]

More than 45% of families headed by women live in poverty. For African American women, that figure rises to 55%, and it goes to 60% for Hispanic women. Even when both parents are present, women are still expected to assume the majority of the household responsibilities.[21]

Males. Men make up 99% of corporate chief executive officers in America's 500 largest companies but account for only 16% of all elementary school teachers and 7% of nurses (although this last figure is an increase from 1% of nurses in 1972).[22]

Women and men express different views of fatherhood. Men emphasize the need for the father to earn a good income and to provide solutions to family problems. Women, on the other hand, stress the need for fathers to assist in caring for children and in responding to the emotional needs of the family. These differing perceptions of fatherhood increase family strain and anxiety.[23]

Even this brief overview of gender differences does little more than confirm commonsense observations: neither boys nor girls "rule in school." Sometimes, even progress can mask problems. While a great deal has been written about females attending college in greater numbers than males, this fact has at least as much to do with color as with gender. The disparity between males and females in college enrollment is shaped in large part by the serious dearth of males of color in postsecondary programs. Moreover, attendance figures provide only one indicator; enrollments in specific college majors tell a different story.

As a result of striking gender segregation in college programs, women and men follow very different career paths, with very different economic consequences. Although the majority of students are female, the college culture is still strongly influenced by male leaders. Four out of five full professors are males, more male professors (72%) are awarded tenure than female professors (52%), and, for the last 30 years, full-time male professors have consistently earned more than their female peers.[24] Even at the elementary and secondary levels, schools continue to be managed by male principals and superintendents. If feminists are waging a "war on boys," as some proclaim, they are being led by male generals.

It is not surprising that many educators are confused about gender issues. Both information and misinformation abound. There is little doubt that boys and school are not now—nor have they ever been—a match made in heaven. But this is a far cry from concluding that a gender war is being waged against them or that girls now "rule" in school, as one recent magazine cover proclaimed.

In the midst of the adult controversy, we can easily overlook the obvious, like asking children how they see the issue. Students consistently report that girls get easier treatment in school, are the better students, and are less likely to get into trouble. Yet school lessons are not always life lessons. When researcher Cynthia Mee asked middle school students about boys and girls, both had more positive things to say about being a boy than being a girl. When, in another study, more than a thousand Michigan elementary school students were asked to describe what life would be like if they were born a member of the opposite sex, over 40% of the girls saw advantages to being a boy, ranging from better jobs to more respect. Ninety-five percent of the boys saw no advantage to being female, and a number of boys in this 1991 study indicated they would consider suicide rather than live life as a female. While some adults may choose to argue that females are the advantaged gender, girls and boys often see the world before them quite differently.[25]

The success of the backlash movement has taught us a great many lessons. It has reminded us of the slow pace of social change and of the power of political ideologues to set the agenda for education. How ironic that the gender debate, once thought to be synonymous with females, now hinges on how well boys are doing in school. And in the end, reframing gender equity to include boys may prove to be a very positive development. For now, it is up to America's educators to duck the barrage from the gender-war crowd and to continue their efforts to make schools fairer and more humane environments for all our students.

Notes

1. See Christina Hoff Sommers, *The War Against Boys: How Misguided Feminism Is Harming Our Young Men* (New York: Simon & Schuster, 2000); and Cathy Young, *Ceasefire!: Why Women and Men Must Join Forces to Achieve True Equity* (New York: Free Press, 1999).

2. Myra Sadker and David Sadker, *Failing at Fairness: How American Schools Cheat Girls* (New York: Touchstone Press, 1995).

3. National Center for Education Statistics, *Digest of Education Statistics, 1999* (Washington, D.C.: U.S. Department of Education, 2000), p. 149; Richard T. Coley, *Differences in the Gender Gap: Comparisons Across Racial/Ethnic Groups in Education and Work* (Princeton, N.J.: ETS, 2001); *National Score Report* (Iowa City: ACT, 1999); *Sex, Race, Ethnicity, and Performance on the GRE General Test, 1999–2000* (Princeton, N.J.: ETS, 2000), p. 8; and National Center for Education Statistics, *Condition of Education, 1999* (Washington, D.C.: United States Department of Education, 1999).

4. David Sadker and Myra Sadker, "Gender Bias: From Colonial America to Today's Classrooms," in James Banks and Cherry McGee Banks, eds., *Multicultural Education: Issues and Perspectives* (New York: Wiley, 2001), p. 130.

5. Ibid., pp. 130, 136.

6. *Gender Gaps: Where Schools Still Fail Our Children* (Washington, D.C.: American Association of University Women, 1998).

7. *Digest of Education Statistics, 1999*, p. 290; and 1999 data gathered from university admissions offices of Brown, Columbia, Cornell, Dartmouth, Harvard, Princeton, the University of Pennsylvania, and Yale.

8. *Gender Gaps*, pp. 54–55.

9. *Digest of Education Statistics, 1999*, p. 127.

10. Ibid., p. 290.

11. Ibid.

12. Thomas L. Good and M. J. Findley, "Sex Role Expectations and Achievement," in Jerome B. Dusek, ed., *Teacher Expectancies* (Hillsdale, N.J.: Erlbaum, 1985), pp. 271–94; M. Gail Jones and Jack Wheatley, "Gender Differences in Student-Teacher Interactions," *Journal of Research in Science Teaching*, vol. 27, 1990, pp. 861–74; Linda Morse and Herbert Handley, "Listening to Adolescents: Gender Differences in Science Classroom Interaction," in Louise Wilkinson and Cora Marrett, eds., *Gender Influences in Classroom Interaction* (New York: Academic Press, 1985); Sadker and Sadker, *Failing at Fairness*, pp. 42–46; and Myra Sadker and David Sadker, "Promoting Effectiveness in Classroom Instruction: Year 3 Final Report," ERIC ED 257819, March 1984.

13. Office for Civil Rights, *Elementary and Secondary School Compliance Reports* (Washington, D.C.: U.S. Department of Education, 1999); and *Gender Gaps*, pp. 22–23.

14. "Adolescent Boys: Statistics and Trends," available at www.maec.org/boys.html, 1999; and National Center for Education Statistics, *Trends in Educational Equity for Girls and Women* (Washington, D.C.: U.S. Department of Education, 2000), p. 32.

15. Office for Civil Rights, p. 1.

16. M. H. Zoli, "Centers for Eating Disorders Try to Reprogram Girls' Self-Image," *American News Service*, 25 April 1999, article no. 850; and Centers for Disease Control and Prevention, "National and State-Specific Pregnancy Rates Among Adolescents—United States," *National Vital Statistics Reports*, vol. 49, 2000, p. 607.

17. *Women's Sport Facts*, 15 July 2002, p. 6; and National Collegiate Athletic Association, "Women in Intercollegiate Sport," *NCAA News*, 22 May 2000.

18. Centers for Disease Control and Prevention, "United States Life Tables, 1997," *National Vital Statistics Reports*, vol. 47, 1999, pp. 1–40.

19. *Women's Sport Facts*, p. 2.

20. *Trends in Educational Equity for Girls and Women*, pp. 84–87; "Fact Sheet: Working Women: Equal Pay," American Federation of Labor/Congress of Industrial Organizations, Washington, D.C., 1997; and Bureau of Labor Statistics, *Employed Persons by Detailed Occupation, Sex, Race, and Hispanic Origin* (Washington, D.C.: U.S. Department of Labor, 1999), pp. 1–11.

21. *Poverty in the United States: 1998* (Washington, D.C.: U.S. Bureau of the Census, Current Population Reports, Series P-60-198, 1998); and Haya J. Stier and Noah Lewin-Epstein, "Woman's Part-Time Employment and Gender Inequality in the Family," *Journal of Family Issues*, vol. 21, 2000, pp. 390–410.

22. *Employed Persons by Detailed Occupation, Sex, Race, and Hispanic Origin*, pp. 1–11.

23. Michael Kimmel, "The Gendered Family," in idem, *Gendered Lives* (New York: Oxford University Press, 2000), pp. 111–49; and Eugene August, *Men's Studies* (Littleton, Colo.: Libraries Unlimited, 1986).

24. *Digest of Education Statistics, 1999*, p. 264.

25. Cynthia S. Mee, *Middle School Voices on Gender Identity* (Newton, Mass.: Women's Education Equity Act Publishing Center, March 1995); and *The Influence of Gender-Role Socialization on Student Perceptions: A Report Based on Data Collected from Michigan Public School Students* (Lansing: Michigan State Board of Education, Office for Sex Equity in Education, 1990).

GIVE SAME-SEX SCHOOLING A CHANCE
Christina Hoff Sommers

Can single-gender schools better address the learning needs of developing boys and girls than schools in which they learn together? One experiment in California attempted to answer this question. The interpretation of the results, Christina Hoff Sommers asserts, has been distorted by biased academicians. She claims that the central goal of single-gender schools should be to improve the academic performance of their students. Critics counter that in attempting to improve academic performance, single-gender schools and classrooms are reinforcing societal stereotypes about gender roles and differences. As you read this article ask yourself, "How should schools respond to gender differences in students?"

Think About This . . .

1. How are the educational goals for single-gender classrooms different from those of heterogeneous classrooms? Which of these are most important? Do these goals conflict with other, larger ones for school?
2. Some claim that gender differences are solely constructed socially. How does this perspective differ from other explanations of gender differences?
3. What are the advantages and disadvantages of single-gender classrooms? Do the advantages outweigh the disadvantages?
4. What are the advantages and disadvantages of gender-neutral classrooms? How will you address gender differences in your classroom?

Four years ago, the state of California opened six experimental single-sex academies in its public schools. Then-Gov. Pete Wilson, along with many parents and teachers, believed that same-sex classrooms might improve the prospects of low-achieving, disadvantaged boys and girls. The program has been popular with parents, and there is anecdotal evidence that it is academically successful. But a new study funded by the Ford Foundation has concluded the program is a failure.

California's same-sex education initiative was always fragile. Adequate funding was a problem from the beginning. Groups like the National Organization for Women opposed it on principle. By now, all but one of the academies has been closed. The Ford Foundation report—"Is Single-Gender Schooling Viable in the Public Sector? Lessons from California's Pilot Program"—will probably kill the surviving one. It may also discourage other states from experimenting with single-sex programs.

That would be unfortunate. Even a cursory review of the report shows that its three authors should not have been entrusted with evaluating California's experiment with same-sex education.

The 83-page document claims to be "the most comprehensive study of single-sex public schooling in the United States to date." Yet remarkably, we never find out whether single-sex schools improved grades, test scores, or attendance. The purpose of the California program was to brighten the educational prospects of vulnerable, disadvantaged kids. Did it achieve this goal? The report does not say.

That is because its authors, Amanda Datnow (University of Toronto), Lea Hubbard (University of California, San Diego), and Elisabeth Woody (University of California, Berkeley), had something else in mind. Their goal was to dissect the "sociopolitical context of

From Sommers, C. H. (2001). Give same-sex schooling a chance. As first appeared in Education Week, 21(4), 36. *Reprinted with permission of the author.*

single-gender public schooling." Or, as they explain it: "Drawing upon feminist theory, we provide a critique that illuminates how power which is 'both the medium and the expression of wider structural relations and social forms, positions subjects within ideological matrixes of constraint and possibility.'" True to this murky goal, they devote most of the study to "critiquing" parents, teachers, and students for their "gendered perceptions."

The report classifies as sexist any teacher who believes there may be basic differences between boys and girls that call for different approaches. One unwitting instructor explained why the all-male class voted to read *All Quiet on the Western Front* and why the all-female class chose *Pride and Prejudice*. "The girls tend to choose the romantic spiel . . . and guys tend to go for the action." The study's three authors are electrified by this brazen example of sexism. "Significantly," they say, "teachers did little to change student choices by suggesting alternative book choices or topics that might potentially challenge gendered dispositions."

Another male teacher is censured for having talked to the boys about what it means to become "productive adult males." The teacher stressed the importance of "self-control and being able to control your emotions and making sacrifices for others." Many of the boys in the program don't have fathers; they have never received guidance from an adult male. This teacher was trying to provide some badly needed counsel. The report "critiques" him for promoting gender stereotypes: "Traditional gender-role stereotypes were reinforced, and gender was portrayed in an essentialist manner."

The report repeatedly puts the aim of eliminating gender stereotypes ahead of the academic and moral needs of children. Most of the children entering the program were barely literate and were academically disengaged. Many of the boys had a history of truancy and gang violence. While respected education scholars such as Cornelius Riordan of Providence College

have found that single-sex schooling is especially beneficial to disadvantaged, at-risk children, the Ford report makes a point not to evaluate any of the academic benefits.

Why not? One must first understand something of the intellectual climate of contemporary education. It is, in many quarters, fashionable to deny that there are any significant differences between males and females. Differences in aptitude or preferences are said to be "constructed by the culture." As one feminist theorist explains, all human beings are born "bisexual" and then, through social conditioning, are "transformed into male and female gender personalities, one destined to command, the other to obey." This radical view, once confined to women's studies programs, has become popular in education circles.

The claim that "gender is a social construction" is both ideological and unsupported by science. A growing body of research in neuroscience, endocrinology, psychology, and genetics over the past 40 years suggests there is a biological basis for sex differences in aptitudes, attitudes, and preferences. In general, males have better spatial-reasoning skills, and females, better verbal skills. Young males are drawn to rough-and-tumble play; females are more nurturing. The teachers in the same-sex programs were adapting their teaching styles to the needs and preferences of their students. In doing so, they walked right into a trap set by gender wardens.

Unfortunately, the report's authors are typical of a new generation of gender-obsessed scholars coming out of graduate education programs. Many are scientifically illiterate; most are indifferent to both common sense and the protocols of objective research.

None will succeed in repealing the laws of human nature. But with foundation funds, and credentials from major universities, they have the power to do a great deal of mischief inside and outside the nation's classrooms. The California same-sex experiment will not be the only casualty.

ADDITIONAL READINGS

Barr, R., & Parrett, W. (2001). Hope fulfilled for at-risk youth. Boston: Allyn & Bacon.

Bullough, R. (2001). Uncertain lives; Children of promise, teachers of hope. New York: Teachers College Press.

Hassenpflug, A. (1999). Courts and peer sexual harassment by middle school students. Middle School Journal, 31(2), 49–56.

Hurwitz, N., & Hurwitz, S. (2003). In the shine of the AP Apple. American School Board Journal, 190(3), 14–18.

Navan, J. (2002). Enhancing the achievement of all learners means high ability students too. Middle School Journal, 34(2), 45–49.

Schweinhart, L. (2002). Right from the start. American School Board Journal, 189(6), 26–29.

EXPLORING THE INTERNET

United States Department of Education

http://www.ed.gov/index.jhtml

This home page of the United States Department of Education provides access to a vast array of information, including material about students and what influences their reactions to schools.

U.S. Census Bureau

http://www.census.gov/

At this site you can find demographic information about the changing population of the United States.

Becoming At Risk of Failure in America's Schools

http://www.ed.gov/pubs/EdReformStudies/EdReforms/chap1a.html

This site provides a brief summary of the long-term standing of "learner diversity" as a special characteristic of American schools.

Center for the Study and Prevention of Violence

http://www.colorado.edu/cspv/

This site contains current information on school violence and successful programs to prevent it.

PART TWO

Diversity

American classrooms are changing. For example, during the 1970s and 1980s over 14 million people immigrated to the United States, and between 1980 and 1994 America's classrooms saw the following changes:

- An increase of almost 100% in Asian American students
- An increase in Hispanic students of 46%
- An increase in African American students of 25%
- An increase in Caucasian students of 10% (Kent, Pollard, Haaga, & Mather, 2001).

Experts estimate that by the year 2020 our country will see dramatic increases in the number of Hispanic students (50%) and those who are Asian/Pacific islanders (50%). At the same time, the proportion of the White student population will decrease by 14% (U.S. Bureau of the Census, 1998; U.S. Department of Education, 2000). By the year 2020, almost half of the U.S. school population will consist of members from non-Caucasian cultural groups. Each of these groups brings its own language and a distinct set of values and traditions, all of which influence student learning.

Other forms of diversity also exist. Some students come to school with disadvantaged backgrounds, for example, and learners fall within a broad ability spectrum. Some have unique gifts and talents, and teachers must attempt to provide an enriched array of learning experiences for them. Others have exceptionalities that interfere with their ability to fully benefit from classroom experiences without adaptations. Experts estimate that 1 in 10 students in the United States qualify for special education services (Heward, 2003).

Each of these forms of diversity raises questions, including the following: What can schools and teachers do to best meet the needs of students who have recently immigrated to this country, and how can their language differences best be accommodated? How can schools support children who are homeless or who live in poverty? How effective is inclusion as a mechanism for supporting students with special needs? How effectively do schools serve students at the upper end of the ability spectrum? Keep these questions in mind as you study the articles in this section.

THE NEW IMMIGRANTS AND EDUCATION: CHALLENGES AND ISSUES

Linda Perkins

Education is embedded in culture and students' cultures powerfully affect our efforts in the classroom. In recent years the number of racial and ethnic minorities in the United States has grown dramatically, with a third of all Americans belonging to racial or ethnic groups other than Caucasian Americans of European descent. In states such as California, those once identified as "minorities" now constitute the majority within their communities. These changes in the fabric of our nation require educators to actively evaluate their teaching practices.

Historically, educators and others believed that as immigrants arrived in the United States, they "assimilated" into American communities. Arriving in America was viewed as a chance to "melt" into society, with little attention given to identity preservation and differences among individuals and cultural groups. Linda Perkins encourages educators to recognize "newcomers" by attending to both their home and family needs as well as their needs within classrooms and schools. As you read this article ask yourself, "How can I welcome recent immigrant students into my classroom? How can I organize my classroom to recognize and build upon the cultural and ethnic backgrounds of my students?"

Think About This . . .

1. What are some of the challenges faced by newcomers as they enter American schools? In what ways are these challenges unique to recent immigrants?

2. How can educators learn about the cultural backgrounds of all of their students? How important are these strategies to you as a teacher?

3. Many urban school districts are developing special schools and classrooms for newcomers. What should these schools do to better serve newcomers? What implications does this have for you as a teacher?

4. What strategies will you use to welcome recent immigrants to your classroom?

The dramatic increase in the number of new immigrants entering the nation in the past two decades has generated considerable attention. The 1990 U.S. Census reported nearly 20 million foreign-born residents, the largest number of immigrants in the nation's history. One-third of the population growth of the nation in the last decade is a result of immigration. Although the nation as a whole is impacted by these numbers, three-fourths of all immigrants in the last decade moved to only six states.[1] Because immigrants are younger than members of the native-born population and tend to have more children of school age, these data have profound implications for the nation's public schools. This essay will discuss some of the challenges and issues facing many public school districts impacted by this shifting student clientele. The "newcomers," as they are often termed, differ from previous immigrants from the early part of this century in that they are overwhelmingly non-white and non-European. Like the immigrants of the late nineteenth and early twentieth centuries, these new arrivals come with different languages, religions, customs and worldviews. How the nation's public schools adapt to our newest citizens will be explored.

From Perkins, L. (2000). *The new immigrants and education: Challenges and issues.* Educational Horizons, 78(2), 67–71. *Reprinted with permission of the author.*

Nineteenth Century Immigrants

Except for African Americans and Native Americans, the nation is one of immigrants. However, most people tend to associate American immigration with the massive numbers of non-Anglo-Saxon Protestants who began arriving in great numbers during the last decades of the nineteenth century. Between 1815 and 1860 approximately 5 million people immigrated to the United States. By the eve of the Civil War, 13 percent of the country's population was foreign-born. Two million of these new immigrants came from Ireland and the rest from Germany, the Scandinavian countries and Holland, Switzerland, China, Scotland, and Wales.[2] Until this point, there had been little immigration for the past two generations. Thus, these new immigrants took the nation by surprise.

Between 1860 and 1890, the number of immigrants entering the country doubled that of the earlier period. Between 1890 and 1914, it tripled. During the years 1905-7, 1910, 1913, and 1914, more than a million immigrants arrived annually. By 1920, almost 60 percent of the population of cities of 100,000 or more residents were composed of first- or second-generation immigrants. In large cities like New York City, more than three-quarters of the schoolchildren had foreign-born parents.[3] Immigrants from the British Isles, Germany, and the Scandinavian countries had declined by the end of the nineteenth century. In their place were newcomers from eastern and southern Europe, as well as elsewhere in the Mediterranean basin. By 1896, Italians, Eastern European Jews, Poles, Ukrainians, Slovaks, Bohemians, Hungarians, Greeks, Portuguese, Armenians, Syrians, and Lebanese outnumbered Western Europeans; by 1907 these southern and eastern Europeans were 80 percent of the total number of immigrants. In addition to their varied languages and customs, these new groups reflected varied religious backgrounds. Most were Roman Catholic, along with millions of Jews, Greek and Russian Orthodox, and some Moslems and Buddhists.[4]

With compulsory schooling having become universal in the country by 1918, the public schools were confronted with having to educate students who often could not speak English. In addition, the public schools frequently had overage students with no previous schooling. To address this problem, special classes were often established to accommodate such students.[5] During this period, the notion of Americanization—preparing the students to become Americans—was instituted within the public schools. This process included instructing the students on everything from American customs, foods, and dress to patriotic songs and heroes. Often, this socialization process created tensions between the student and the home. "American" customs, culture, and foods were often viewed as desirable and superior.

Becoming American

The well-known concept of "melting pot" existed in America's desire to "melt" the eastern and southern European immigrants into the existing Anglo-Saxon culture. By the 1920s assimilation had become federal policy and Americanization in the schools was in full force. In addition, in 1924 the Immigration Restriction Act was adopted to restrict the immigration of persons from countries considered difficult to "melt."[6]

Scholars of the immigrant experience note that by the third generation, complete assimilation has usually taken place. The assimilation theory of the sociologist Milton Gordon is that through a series of steps an immigrant can become completely assimilated. This is accomplished through intermarriage, religious conversion, and a variety of other events. By the final stage of this process, the immigrants are "so like the original population that they had reached the point where their actions no longer provoked 'value and power' conflict."[7] Although this process succeeded with earlier European immigrants, how likely is this process with nonwhite immigrants whose physical features will always make it impossible to be indistinguishable from the dominant Anglo image of America? Or will the disproportionate number of nonwhite immigrants so change the complexion of the nation by the next decade that the notions of assimilation and Americanization will be obsolete?

The "New" Immigrants

The 1965 amendment to the Immigration and Nationality Act has resulted in a large-scale immigration to equal that of the late nineteenth and early twentieth centuries. A more equitable distribution of visas worldwide has resulted in more than 85 percent of all immigrants arriving from Asian and Latin America. Some areas of the country have been impacted profoundly by these numbers. For example, by the next census, half the population of California will be Asian or Hispanic. Currently, one person in four in California speaks a primary tongue other than English. More than one million are classified "limited English proficient" and one in five is an immigrant. Similarly, one-third of the population in New York City is foreign-born, as well as one-third of the public schools in the city.[8]

What are school districts doing to adapt to this new population? What challenges are these new students and their teachers facing? Does the assimilation theory of European immigrants of the early part of this century reflect the reality of these new immigrants?

Many issues confront the new students as well as their teachers. For the students, many adjustment problems emerge. First, new immigrant students have to adjust and understand the new racial labeling and categorization of the United States.[9] For example, students who viewed themselves as simply Chinese, Taiwanese, Korean, or Cambodians are now defined as Asian. Similarly, students from varied and culturally distinct Spanish-speaking countries are now considered Hispanics or Latinos. Rarely is the fact that these groups come from different countries with unique histories, cultures, and languages considered. Second, native-born members of these groups are lumped together with the foreign-born. Studies indicate that many American-born members of immigrant groups separate out and make distinctions between themselves and the new arrivals.[10] Further, immigrant children, who were born outside of the United States but educated and socialized here—known as the "1.5 generation"—are often treated the same as recent immigrant students.[11] The adjustment and experiences of this group differ significantly from those who immigrate at an older age. Youths who migrate as teenagers tend to learn English with an "accent." Younger immigrant children will learn to speak the language as a native and usually without an accent.

Many young immigrant students have difficulty with issues of identity and reconciling their home life with their life at school. The lure of America's popular culture and youth culture causes difficulty for many immigrant students from homes that stress standards and expectations of the old country. Teachers should also be aware of the many gender-specific issues that occur in many immigrant families.

In an ethnographic study of a multiracial high school in California, Laurie Olsen found that to "become an American," immigrant students had to undergo the Americanization process. This included academic marginalization and separation; speaking English and the necessity of dropping one's native language to participate in the academic and social life of the school; and taking one's place in the racial hierarchy of the country.[12]

In addition to the above issues, some scholars who are currently analyzing the new immigrants' adjustment to the United States note that because many reside in multicultural urban neighborhoods where employment is scarce and schools are impoverished, poverty may persist from the first to the second generation. This reality debunks the prevailing view of previous immigrant straight-line upward mobility, in which their socioeconomic status improved with each generation.[13] Although many European immigrants experienced class and religious discrimination in the early years of their history in the nation, as noted earlier, most did assimilate, either by choice or coercion. However, because of the persistence of racism in the American society, the sociologist Herbert Gans predicts that dark-skinned non-Caucasian immigrants, particularly the men, can expect to suffer more racial discrimination than other immigrants.[14]

Teachers

The rapid change in the student population obviously causes many issues for teachers. Understanding the background and culture of the children is essential for a more successful experience. As noted above, immigrant children and children of immigrants are usually not distinguished by census data and other data sources. Most teachers are not trained to work with the many various cultures and ethnicities of the new immigrant students. Trueba, Cheng, and Ima suggest that teachers who have immigrant students should learn about their families and previous background. Questions such as the following should be asked:

- What experiences did the newcomer children and their families have prior to their arrival in the United States?
- Might those experiences affect schooling behavior?
- Is the home language of the student the same or similar to English?
- If not, how different is it?[15]

Many immigrant students, particularly those of Asian descent, are bound by such factors as family interdependence, filial piety, "face," respect for teachers, elders and authority, and stoicism.[16] These values are often in conflict with the individualistic, "me"-centered culture prevalent in much of the United States.

Response of School Districts

Many urban school districts throughout the nation have responded to the challenges of educating the new immigrant students by establishing special "newcomer" schools.[17] These are currently for high school students believed to have the most difficulty assimilating into a regular high school. Seven such newcomer high schools exist in New York City. Designed for the limited English-speaking teenage student, these institutions also provide services for the entire family. They function in many ways like the settlement houses of the early part of the century. The newcomer schools helped parents become Americanized and acclimated to the American society. Acculturation programs available to new immigrant families include seminars, speakers, and films.[18]

These special schools for newcomers are not without controversy. Many are concerned that these new students, overwhelmingly nonwhite, are being placed on a separate track that will prevent them from entering a regular school. This controversy may well be one of the key civil rights issues of education in the next decade. Many argue that it is important to mainstream the newcomer students with the regular students as soon as possible.[19] However, the Olson study revealed that even in mainstream classes and regular schools, newcomer immigrants are not always served well. She observed:

> [I]mmigrant students are either placed in inadequately supported classes where they do not have access to English-speaking peers or friends or placed in "mainstream" classes taught by unprepared teachers who do not address their needs and they cannot fully comprehend, hence dooming them to academic failure and loss of access to the academic program. With insufficient English language development and insufficient access to the curriculum in a language they can understand, most immigrant students are (through the force of schooling) denied equal access to an education. Some manage to achieve, but many drop out of school or become stuck in the category of "ESL lifers."[20]

Despite the often poor and inadequate educational institutions available to many newcomers, there is consistent documentation that these students are enthusiastic about school and highly motivated to learn. One study noted:

> Teachers working with Latino immigrant students reported to us, almost unanimously, that the new arrivals are simply the best students they ever had: appreciative, well-behaved, and above all desperate to learn.[21]

Another study stated:

> Immigrants, on the whole, have higher educational and occupational aspiration than indigenous groups, majority as well as minority, and are more determined to use education as a strategy for upward mobility than non-immigrants of comparable class background.[22]

Despite this enthusiasm, immigrant students who have limited English proficiency tend to have much higher dropout rates than those who have English proficiency.[23] Unfortunately, as the younger immigrant students become more Americanized and susceptible to the peer pressure of native-born students, their achievement level and educational aspirations tend to mirror those of the general student population.[24]

Conclusion

Today's immigrant newcomer students are vastly different from those at the beginning of the century. They are largely students of color. These students bring with them a great desire to learn. But, despite their poverty, parents of immigrant children are usually married, self-employed, and not on welfare.[25] However, factors such as inability to speak English, poverty, and inferior schools frequently impede their progress. Educational policy makers are attempting to develop strategies to serve this population. One of the strategies has been to establish "newcomer" schools. These schools are reminiscent of the "special" classes established by urban school districts a century ago to accommodate all the then "new" immigrants. As these schools evolve, it is imperative that educational policy makers and school officials understand the diversity among the various student populations.

Notes

1. U.S. Bureau of the Census, 1993a. Census of Population: The Foreign-Born Population in the United States, 1990, CP-3-1. Washington, D.C.: Government Printing. The six states are California, New York, Florida, Texas, Illinois, and New Jersey. Note: these numbers do not take into account the additional numbers of illegal immigrants in the country.

2. Maxine Schwartz Seller, *To Seek America: A History of Ethnic Life in the United States* (Jerome S. Ozer, 1988), 57.

3. Ibid., 102.

4. Ibid.

5. For more on the establishment of special classes for over-age students, see Joseph L. Tropea, "Bureaucratic Order and Special Children: Urban Schools, 1890s–1940s" in *History of Education Quarterly* 27, no. 1 (Spring 1987): 29–53.

6. David L. Salvaterra, "Becoming American: Assimilation, Pluralism, and Ethnic Identity," in Timothy Walsh, ed., *Immigrant America: European Ethnicity in the United States* (New York: Garland Publishing), 32.

7. Quoted in ibid., 33.

8. U.S. Immigration and Naturalization Service, 1991; Francisco L. Rivera-Batiz, "The Education of Immigrant

Children: The Case of New York City," Institute for Urban and Minority Education, Teachers College, Columbia University, 3.

9. The ethnographer Laurie Olsen terms this "racial mapping"; see Laurie Olsen, *Made in America: Immigrant Students in Our Public Schools* (New York: The New Press, 1997).

10. Ibid.

11. Charles Hirschman, "Studying Immigrants' Adaptation from the 1990 Population Census: From Generational Comparisons to the Process of 'Becoming American,'" in Alejandro Portes, ed., *The New Second Generation* (New York: Russell Sage Foundation, 1996), 70.

12. Olsen, *Made in America*, 240–241.

13. Herbert J. Gans, "Second-generation Decline: Scenarios for the Economic and Ethnic Futures of the Post-1965 American Immigrants," in *Ethnic and Racial Studies* 15, no. 2, April 1992.

14. Ibid.

15. Henry T. Trueba, Lilly Cheng, and Kenji Ima, *Myth or Reality: Adaptive Strategies of Asian Americans in California* (Washington, D.C.: The Falmer Press, 1993), 140–142.

16. Ibid.

17. Olsen discusses one such institution in California in her *Made in America*.

18. Rivera-Batiz, "The Education of Immigrant Children," 43.

19. Ibid.

20. Olsen, *Made in America*, 241.

21. Quoted in Rivera-Batiz, "The Education of Immigrant Children," 33.

22. Ibid., 34.

23. Ibid.

24. Hirschman, "Studying Immigrant Adaptation from the 1990 Population Census": 70–71.

25. Alejandro Portes, editor, *The New Second Generation*

A DIALOGUE AMONG TEACHERS THAT BENEFITS SECOND LANGUAGE LEARNERS

Annela Teemant, Elizabeth Bernhardt, Marisol Rodriguez-Muñoz, and Michael Aiello

Language is an essential component of student diversity because so much of our instruction is verbal. Addressing language diversity contributes to the complexities of teaching, which require educators to juggle multiple demands within their classrooms. For teachers whose classrooms reflect the increasing number of English Language Learners (ELLs), the complexity of teaching is even more profound.

Annela Teemant and her colleagues encourage teachers to work collaboratively on strategies for improving the educational experiences of the ELLs in their classrooms. As you read this article ask yourself, "How can teachers identify the academic needs of the ELLs in their classrooms? How might collaboration among teachers improve their work with ELLs?"

Think About This . . .

1. What suggestions do these authors have for teachers working with ELLs? Which of the seven do you believe are the most useful in addressing the needs of students learning English?

2. Learning through errors can be a valuable part of the educational experience for ELLs. In what ways do you believe errors can improve learning for all students?

3. Collaboration among teachers is one strategy for improving teaching practice. How will you use collaboration with peers in your work as a teacher?

4. In what ways will your classroom provide ELLs with a safe environment where risk taking is encouraged?

It was estimated that by the year 2000 42 percent of public school students will be language minority students (Carrasquillo & Rodriquez, 1995). These youngsters can be overwhelmed learning to adjust to two languages, two cultures, and the demands of American academics. There is a wide gap between what they can understand in English and what they can say in English, between what they can write in English and what they can write in their native languages, between how they conceptualize in English and how they conceptualize in their native languages. Coupled with these facts is a growing tendency to limit English language services (e.g., California's Proposition 227) in favor of mainstreaming for English as a Second Language (ESL) students.

Required to learn English and academic content simultaneously, ESL students depend on both ESL teachers and content-area teachers to help them succeed in school. Teachers with expertise in working with ESL students often remain isolated from colleagues who would benefit from their expertise. In addition, mainstream teachers often have ESL students placed in their classes without the benefits of appropriate professional development opportunities.

Collaboration across academic disciplines and departments within schools on behalf of diverse student populations has emerged as an important tool in the current era of educational reform (Dorsch, 1998; Gelberg, 1997; Hoffman, Reed, & Rosenbluth, 1997; Lipman, 1998; Merritt & Culatta, 1998). Shive (1997) suggested that "collaboration can be one of the significant actions necessary to move all education to more productive levels," (p. 47). Teachers, used to working in isolation with high levels of autonomy, must create opportunities to collaborate with the various specialists, counselors, and administrators who share responsibility for meeting the academic needs of second language learners.

The purpose of this article is to illustrate the value of breaking patterns of isolation in favor of collaborative dialogue among school colleagues. Set in the context of second language and science learning, seven common concerns surrounding ESL students will be presented through a conversation between a science teacher and a language teacher. The eighth grade general science teacher recently attended a regional science conference where he participated in the only presentation on the program about second language issues. In the teachers' lounge, he encounters the ESL teacher, whom he knows only vaguely from in-service meetings, and approaches her with curiosities and frustrations. In theory and practice, their conversation brings together the worlds of science and language for the benefit of the second language students they teach.

1. *Can they learn content and English simultaneously?*
One common question teachers have is why the school system sends students to the mainstream classroom before they can actually speak English. Let's eavesdrop on the conversation between the language teacher (LT) and science teacher (ST). . .

LT: I've had several of your fifth period students come to my language class for help with their lab reports. The one on physics drove me crazy. I know what force means in everyday language, but don't ask me to explain it in terms of science. By the way, how many second language speakers are in that class?

ST: Ten out of the 35 right now. I just got back from our fall science conference. They only had one session on helping second language learners, and that was mainly about little kids. Sometimes, when I see them struggling, I just wonder why they don't learn English first, and then come to science.

LT: In a perfect world, that would be the ideal.

ST: It seems like it would be easier for them if I could understand them better and if they could ask me questions. It's frustrating, especially when I see they have so much potential.

LT: But it takes six to eight years to become fluent. There's a big problem with the idea of waiting until they "know" enough English to compete with their peers.

ST: That's a long time.

LT: If the kids waited until they spoke English before going to science classes, they'd be 12 or 14 before they got any science.

ST: And that's too late from a science perspective! If students haven't had a positive science experience by the time they get to fourth grade, we've lost them.

LT: If we wait, there's no way for the second language speakers to "make up" for the content they'd miss.

ST: Okay, but how much do they get out of class when their language skills are still so limited?

LT: Well, speaking and understanding are two different things.

ST: True! I had that experience myself when I was traveling in Europe.

LT: You always understand much more than you can say. You may understand a concept, like why hot air rises, but not be able to express that concept in English.

ST: So you're saying these students may be able to tell me about why hot air rises in their native language, but can't do it in English.

From Teemant, A., Bernhardt, E., Rodriguez-Muñoz, M., & Aiello, M. (2000). A dialogue among teachers that benefits second language learners. Middle School Journal, 32(2), 30–38. Reprinted with permission of the National Middle School Association.

LT: Exactly. Especially with older kids who have had science in their home countries.

As you've heard from these two teachers, if we wait to send limited English students to the science class, they'll never be ready for or get the science they need. Waiting for mathematics, social studies, or science content is like being on a road to academic failure.

2. *Does a wrong word mean a wrong concept?*

As a second concern, from the outset, it seems the science teacher has to find out if the student has the science, but not the language, or the language and not the science.

ST: So, if you tell me they might understand what I say, but I just can't "hear" it, what am I supposed to do? I know right away if my native English speakers are missing a word, or when they don't know something.

LT: . . . the science concept attached to a specific word.

ST: Right! With words like photosynthesis, I make sure they can read and spell the word, and I make sure that they know it is the process of changing light to energy.

LT: Well, in the bilingual setting, you have to worry about so many more things. Do they know the word in their first language? Do they know the second language word? Do they know the science concept in either language?

ST: Basically, it comes down to figuring out if they understand. And understanding can mean a lot of different things.

LT: Right. Which comes first? The vocabulary or the concept? Many teachers think that because a student doesn't have the right word, they also don't have the right concept. If we take *photosynthesis* as an example, a bilingual student may have the concept "housed" in his native language. He already has it. He just needs to learn the cover term *photosynthesis*. He's just learning to read, pronounce, and spell it in English.

ST: When Abdul was working on a lab assignment classifying rocks, I could see he understood the principle. But when he had to talk about why he classified the rocks the way he did, he froze. He's got the concept, but he's just not in control of the words yet.

LT: What's really messy is when students don't have any of it—not the words, concepts, or understanding.

ST: No matter what, though, I have to figure out if they actually understand the process of changing light to energy, or of force. When I first started teaching, and I didn't have these second language kids, the distinctions were much clearer. I could talk and probe without worrying about a common language. I don't have that luxury anymore.

Distinguishing between content problems and language problems is challenging and exemplifies the difference between teaching in a bilingual versus monolingual setting. Mainstream teachers have to know that the wrong word is not always indicative of a wrong concept. Students can grasp concepts that far exceed their ability to express themselves in English. It's not always fair or accurate to judge these students by what they can say or write.

3. *Are errors a sign of learning?*

Another concern mainstream teachers have relates to understanding the nature of second language learning. Without background in second language acquisition, teachers may struggle to make sense of the language an ESL student produces on assignments or while participating orally in class.

ST: Do you know Carlos Jimenez?

LT: Yes, he comes in for help now and again.

ST: I really want him to go to the science fair; he's put together a great project on saving energy at home comparing incandescent and electronic light bulbs. But when he brought his report in the other day, there were so many errors, we almost had to start from scratch.

LT: Why?

ST: When I watched Carlos do the experiment, he knew exactly what to do. He understood the sequence and was able to follow procedures well. But when I saw this report, the verb tenses didn't match the sequence he'd followed at all.

LT: Tense learning is a really tricky part of second language development.

ST: What do you mean?

LT: It's spooky, but there are rather clear stages in how people learn to use verbs in second languages. Just like little kids learning their first language, second language speakers learn irregular verbs first, like see-saw, or think-thought. Then they start learning the regular verbs.

ST: Like walk-walked.

LT: Talk-talked. Right. But then when they start learning past tense, they get confused. They start saying things like think-thinked. After they sort this stuff out, they start tackling more complex tenses, and then it gets really rough. They start overcompensating. They say "I had previously thinked," or write "I did poured." It's like they want to make absolutely sure they've pointed out the past tense.

ST: I've seen that in their science labs.

LT: They remember something has to be in the past tense, but then they forget that they only have to use the past form once. It's mental overload, and it takes time to get it all under control.

ST: Are you trying to tell me these errors are good?

LT: Sure. The hardest thing to remember is that forms like "I did poured" are really advanced forms. They're good indicators that the kids are learning a lot of English. These kids can't correct one form like "I had thinked" until they've learned "I thought." They have to learn one form—get through one stage—before going on to the next stage.

This third point demonstrates that language learning is a process that's developmental in nature. Bilingual students progress through various stages, sorting through all that they hear and read to master different aspects of language. And through all of this, errors really become signs of learning, and not things to be stamped out. Although most learners traverse the same route in learning, some students go through the stages of language development faster than others do.

4. *Does helping ESL students mean watering down the content?*
Although language learning has its own unique characteristics, teachers often fear that helping their bilingual students means compromising, in some ways, the academic content. This concern over whether helping bilingual students really requires watering down the academic content is the fourth concern discussed between our language and science teachers.

> ST: You've told me that they understand more than they can produce in speaking and writing. I see that's true, but I'm trying to accommodate for the needs of all my students. Sometimes I feel like I have to water down the science, and that doesn't seem fair to the other students.

> LT: Actually, second language kids don't need things simplified. Simplifying doesn't always enhance comprehension.

> ST: I don't get it. Why wouldn't it help?

> LT: Well, it's more a question of the type of modifications we make. For example, if you simplify a reading on sources of energy, you may simplify the grammar or vocabulary. In many ways, you're denying the second language kids access to the very language they need. We do need to modify things, but simplifying the reading can take away the chance for new learning.

> ST: But shouldn't I use special materials—science materials written just for my bilingual students? Wouldn't that help?

> LT: No, it isn't really necessary. You don't need special materials. It's how you exploit the materials you use every day, with all your students, that counts.

> ST: What kind of modifying works then?

> LT: Students seem to do much better with elaborated texts for one thing, rather than simplified texts. If they can make sense of something—if it's comprehensible—they can take the word or the concept and use it later. It's the idea of giving them more than one word or more than one avenue for understanding a concept. In most cases, a second example can be more useful than one example that's been watered down.

> ST: I know all my students, even the second language kids, learn a lot from each other during lab work. A lot of peer teaching is going on.

> LT: Those are the best types of modifications—those that happen during conversation or interaction when we help each other figure out the meaning of something.

Watering down science instruction is not the answer. Second language learners benefit most from academic content that is made linguistically comprehensible to them through appropriate modifications to materials and in instructional practices. For example, if a student cannot write well, let that student illustrate concepts in lab reports and journals. With proper scaffolding of texts (e.g., use of highlighted vocabulary, illustrations, or shortened readings), tasks (e.g., use of multi-stage manageable tasks, routines, and cooperative learning), and participation (e.g., valuing of nonverbal/visual, verbal, and written modes of expression), teachers can maintain high expectations for cognitive engagement while supporting linguistic development. When multiple and varied forms of participation, materials, and instruction are used, the academic content becomes accessible and the academic language more noticeable to ESL students.

5. *What strategies work with ESL students?*
Most content-area teachers do not feel prepared through their undergraduate studies to adequately support ESL students' academic learning. Teachers commonly ask what strategies, techniques, or activities help ESL students. Teachers actually do not lack appropriate strategies for working with ESL students; however, they may lack the explanation for why particular strategies support content learning and language learning. In this lunchroom conversation, several strategies are highlighted that help make content more accessible to language minority students.

> ST: I've noticed my second language students like it when we use concept maps. They only need to use a limited number of words, or even a drawing, to show me what they know.

> LT: That's a good way of helping second language kids without any compromises; it works for all students, even if it's for different reasons.

> ST: Okay, as a language teacher, what other modifications would you use?

> LT: The most effective adjustments you make are those you make when you negotiate with the student.

> ST: Negotiate?

LT: Oh, you know. When you ask questions to see if they have understood what you said, checking for comprehension.

ST: Sometimes I have to clarify what they say to me, too.

LT: You have to make sure you've understood them correctly. Asking yes/no questions or asking questions where you give them a choice between two things makes it much easier for the student to respond.

ST: I find it's easier for them to participate if I ask them a question. It's like I've given them an excuse to speak up.

LT: You can help by breaking down difficult ideas into more manageable pieces. Sometimes, if you pause in the middle of a question, it gives them time to catch up with what you are asking. If you make sure to stress the main word of a sentence, it helps them latch onto what you're looking for. And as we were saying before, elaborating—giving synonyms, or just repeating an idea in different words—helps. Or just repeating to a student what she said in her words helps her hear what she said.

ST: I can see a lot in their faces, and sometimes demonstrating a concept again, with no words, helps more than anything I can say.

LT: You are dealing with both science and language, and the modifications you make have to reflect that. One moment, you're making sure they've used the right word, and a minute later you're making sure they have a very precise understanding of some concept.

ST: The other day I was talking about the way the size and number of holes in balls would affect the bounce of a ball. One student, Marcus, wasn't really able to identify the differences I was looking for. I asked the whole class to create a title for the lesson. Alicia's title, something like "Balls Bounce According to Size and Form," really helped Marcus to see that both the size and the number of holes in the ball affected the bounce.

LT: Those kinds of online adjustments are the modifications that count. Making adjustments in your interaction—negotiating meaning—is more useful than simplifying what they read. Sometimes it's just as simple as allowing them a little more time to think before answering a question.

ST: I see what you mean.

A teacher's sensitivity to language and content is crucial to building up the academic skills and knowledge of second language learners. Through interaction, teachers are creating a scaffold that helps the student identify what is important in both the language and the academic content. Creating scaffolds, however, should not only be limited to listening and speaking adjustments. Teachers can help bilingual students by knowing how to reinforce learning through appropriate adjustments in the way they use reading and writing activities as well.

ST: I use a lot of cooperative activities in my teaching; that seems to support what you are saying about negotiating meaning through interaction.

LT: Different class groupings help, but it isn't really enough. When you only function in a listening–speaking mode, what is said can be elusive.

ST: Elusive—in what way?

LT: The words are hard to hold onto. It helps the bilingual kids if you support what you're saying by writing key words on the blackboard, or by using a handout they can follow along with.

ST: Students need to approach the science from other angles.

LT: They need more opportunities to read and to write about what they're doing in science. If students can read about the structure of matter, for example, in addition to hearing about it in class, they have a better chance of getting the science concept.

ST: Well, one of the best ways for me to see if they understand is by watching them follow a set of procedures in lab.

LT: Yes, if students have a chance to read-and-do or write-and-do, they can show comprehension without the risk or control needed to speak.

ST: Why do you see speech as more of a risk?

LT: With speech, students are carrying a heavier linguistic load, if you know what I mean. They're not only trying to communicate the science to you, but they're also having to use the right words, in the right sequence, with the right tenses. It can be overwhelming—especially if they don't have good control of the science or the language.

ST: Yeah, you're right. We did a unit on crystal formation. Seija needed to write down her hypotheses before she felt comfortable telling me about them.

LT: Sometimes, I think we rely too much on listening and speaking, and don't allow enough time for students to read and write.

ST: I can see how reading and writing would feel more concrete to them.

Good teachers have a repertoire of strategies that will serve them well in working with ESL students. Nevertheless, these strategies can become more powerful tools in the hands of a teacher when connected to an understanding of second language acquisition. For example, redundancy in instruction (e.g., using graphic organizers or transparencies while teaching new content verbally) is good teaching. For ESL students, that redundancy reinforces the vocabulary and grammatical structures the students need to demonstrate content learning. For the learning disabled student, redundancy may serve to improve cognitive processing; however, redundancy may lower the motivation of a gifted/talented student to participate. Similarly, cooperative learning provides a safer linguistic environment for ESL students to demonstrate mastery of academic language and concepts. On the other hand, for a gifted/talented student, cooperative learning may be central to developing successful social relationships with peers. As teachers connect the "what" of good teaching to the reason a strategy serves ESL students, they will refine their ability to select appropriate strategies for engaging ESL students in learning.

6. *What constitutes fair grading for ESL students?* The language problems and insecurities of students with limited English skills manifest themselves in testing, as well as in regular day-to-day classroom interaction. A teacher who is aware of how language learning plays out in science learning, for example, can help bring out these students' best performance in the testing context. Testing can be made fairer for second language learners by using multiple approaches to assessment.

> ST: The whole testing issue is a nightmare. It's frustrating to know these kids are capable and then see them fail a test or get mediocre grades. Kids like Carlos are a good example of what I mean. I know that they know the concepts—I've seen them do the labs, but when I look at the test scores. . . .
>
> LT: It doesn't look like they know anything?
>
> ST: Exactly. But then I look at Mamiko. She hasn't said a word, and she really depends on kids like Carlos to help during labs. She gets fantastic grades on the standardized tests. It makes me crazy to think that we automatically will say that Mamiko "knows" more science than Carlos does, when it isn't really true.
>
> LT: That's why it's important not to be blinded by any one individual assessment. There's nothing worse than asking a student who's really uptight about his oral skills to do a performance assessment. That assessment will naturally reflect more of his anxiety than his knowledge.
>
> ST: But we're interested in the science.
>
> LT: That's the point. We have to make sure that all students have a chance to use the language skill that they're most comfortable with whether it's speaking or writing.
>
> ST: There's no question some students are more comfortable with performance assessment, and others are more comfortable with reading and writing. The lab scares them.
>
> LT: For second language learners, grades are much more accurate if they're based on multiple assessments. Maybe the kids who can't tell you what the lab was about are actually quite knowledgeable; they just need to show you in writing. It makes more sense to

consider reading, writing, and standardized scores along with performance assessments.

7. *Can I invite participation and create a sense of belonging for my ESL students?*
In early adolescence, all students struggle, in one way or another, to connect with peers and to fit into the classroom and school community. For ESL students, their struggle with issues of identity, autonomy, and intimacy play out in a new linguistic and cultural environment.

> ST: It must be difficult to think with subordinate clauses, and then only be able to speak using two-word phrases.
>
> LT: It's much safer for some of these kids to accept the "back of the class," "out of sight, out of mind" position.
>
> ST: That could explain Rita. Her family moved here in early summer, and she still hasn't spoken much. At first, I thought she was just shy. She pays attention, but I can't tell what she's getting.
>
> LT: There can be two explanations for her silence. First, language learning is often marked by what some people call a "silent period," meaning that learners start by listening, taking in what they can from the environment, but don't begin speaking until later.
>
> ST: Rita just may need more time then. What's the other possibility?
>
> LT: Everyone takes on language learning in personal ways. For some, second language learning can be overwhelming, or even threatening.
>
> ST: I've certainly heard my share of these kids being teased for missing some joke, for example.
>
> LT: One of the strategies these students adopt to feel more safe is avoidance. They withdraw psychologically, if not literally, to the back of the class.
>
> ST: It's hard to tell if they just don't like science, which is entirely possible, or maybe they don't like English.
>
> LT: Or peer pressure can keep them quiet too. For a lot of them, they may feel they're betraying their parents' language and culture. Some want to Americanize, and others aren't sure they should. It just takes time to adjust to a new culture and academic competition.
>
> ST: I can see a lot of them are very sensitive. What do you do about correcting their English when they speak up in class?
>
> LT: Fear of correction can keep them silent too. It's about saving face. If they don't say anything, there's nothing to correct. In most cases though, I try to focus on meaning: If I understand what they say, I just go on. But, if I feel like correcting a word would help them, I do. For example, I repeat what they say, or model the right way to say it. That's an indirect, gentle way of correcting.
>
> ST: Yeah, that focuses on what they say rather than how they say it.

For second language learners, patterns of participation in the classroom vary from person to person. These patterns of participation involve both linguistic and psychological components. Unlike the majority of native English speakers, ESL students rely heavily on their teachers to make participation in social and academic conversation possible. For example, a teacher lightens the linguistic burden of participating in class by asking yes/no or either/or questions. A teacher creates a safe learning environment by incrementally involving ESL students in classroom routines and interactions that require more and more language use over time. Assigning buddies, allowing students to write responses before speaking, or assigning roles in cooperative learning activities also support ESL students' participation. Simple measures, such as remembering to greet ESL students both inside and outside of the classroom, can reinforce a sense of belonging in the school and classroom.

Conclusion

Both mainstream and language teachers would benefit from such dialogue. Collaborative dialogue encourages reciprocal relationships and learning. This teachers' lounge conversation illustrates only a first step in making relevant connections across academic boundaries for the benefit of language minority students. The National Center for Science Teaching and Learning has a free audiotape and booklet entitled *Bringing Science and Second Language Together: What Every Teacher Should Know* that can be used to initiate collaboration among ESL specialists and mainstream teachers within your school.

In the education context, the purpose of collaboration is to generate new priorities, alternatives, and solutions in meeting classroom challenges, which intimates concerted, sustained, long-term efforts to collaborate. Collaboration must be built upon the principles of parity, adaptation, interdependence, dialogue, self-study, multiple perspectives, orientations toward change, a concern for student learning, and shared values, power, and control (Clemson, 1990; DiMeo, Merritt, & Culatta, 1998; Ladson-Billings, 1998; Shive, 1997). Clemson (1990, p. 37) noted that "The challenge of collaboration is multifaceted. It includes the sensitive aspects of interpersonal relations, conflicting agendas, incongruent organizational patterns and processes, and the everpresent threat of divorce." Despite these challenges, collaboration, even if it begins in the middle school teachers' lounge, can have substantial academic returns for all teachers working with ESL students, whether in the mainstream classroom or in the ESL program.

References

Carrasquillo, A. L., & Rodriquez, V. (1995). *Language minority students in the mainstream classroom*. Clevedon, Avon, United Kingdom: Multilingual Matters, Ltd.

Clemson, S. (1990). Four models of collaborative teacher education: A comparison of success factors and maturation. *Action in Teacher Education, 12*(2), 31–37.

DiMeo, J. H., Merritt, D. D., & Culatta, B. (1998). Collaborative partnerships and decision making. In D. D. Merritt & B. Culatta, *Language intervention in the classroom* (pp. 37–98). San Diego, CA: Singular Publishing Group, Inc.

Dorsch, N. G. (1998). *Community, collaboration, and collegiality in school reform*. Albany, NY: State University of New York Press.

Gelberg, D. (1997). *The "business" of reforming American schools*. Albany, NY: State University of New York Press.

Hoffman, N. E., Reed, W. M., & Rosenbluth, G. S. (1997). *Lessons from restructuring experiences: Stories of change in professional development schools*. Albany, NY: State University of New York Press.

Ladson-Billings, G. (1998). Forward. In P. Lipman (Ed.), *Race, class, and power in school restructuring* (pp. ix–xv). Albany, NY: State University of New York Press.

Lipman, P. (1998). *Race, class, and power in school restructuring*. Albany, NY: State University of New York Press.

Merritt, D. D., & Culatta, B. (1998). *Language intervention in the classroom*. San Diego, CA: Singular Publishing Group, Inc.

Shive, J. (1997). Collaboration between K–12 schools and universities. In N. E. Hoffman, W. M. Reed, & G. E. Rosenbluth (Eds.), *Lessons from restructuring experiences: Stories of change in professional development schools* (pp. 33–50). Albany, NY: State University of New York Press.

WHERE THE HEART IS
Kathleen Vail

Poverty is a dimension of diversity that affects students in multiple ways. Economic shifts within the United States during the past ten years have had a profound impact on the number of families finding themselves homeless and lacking in financial stability. In response, educators are reconsidering the ways in which they can serve the needs of an increasing number of K–12 students who live in poverty.

Homeless families and their children have unique educational needs that schools need to address in a creative and systematic fashion. As you read this article ask yourself, "How can schools and teachers respond to the unique needs of the poor?"

Think About This . . .

1. In what ways have economic hardships in the United States impacted the housing needs of many families? What are the implications of these trends for educators?

2. What are the unique educational needs of homeless children? Which of these areas should teachers respond to first and in what ways?

3. Who are the major players within school communities who can serve the needs of the homeless? Of these service providers, who will provide you with the most assistance?

4. Describe different ways in which you might integrate community resources to improve the educational opportunities for the students in your classrooms.

Matthew Cardinale never gave up. The vision of graduating from high school and going to college sustained him even when he had no idea where he would sleep at night. When he lived behind a Publix supermarket. When his time ran out at the homeless shelter and he slept in a field. It sustained him during predawn journeys to his Broward County, Fla., high school on three public buses.

"School became my stability," says Cardinale. "I was going to school and making progress toward graduation. It became part of my identity."

Homeless at age 14, Cardinale did more than just survive high school. He was an honor student who earned the rank of Eagle Scout and landed an internship at the *Orlando Sentinel*. Tulane University in New Orleans awarded him a full scholarship.

His odyssey from destitute teen to college graduate is remarkable, but Cardinale does not want his story used as an example of what homeless youth can do if they only try hard enough. He admits he often contemplated dropping out. School sometimes offered more roadblocks than help. "High school was not really designed for people in crisis," he says. "A bus ticket would have helped, and a more supportive principal."

One million children and youth are homeless in any given year, the Urban Institute estimates. Like Cardinale, some are runaways or throwaways—teens abandoned by their parents. Others are children staying with their parents in emergency shelters or doubled up with relatives or family friends. They sleep in weekly rate apartments or motels, campgrounds, or cars. They live on the streets, in alleys, under bridges.

For children in turmoil, school should be a place they can count on for stability. Too often, it is not. Too often, students who are without a home are also missing school. According to U.S. Department of Education statistics, 45 percent of homeless students in kindergarten through 12th grade were not attending school regularly during the time they were homeless, missing 15 or more days of school in a three-month period.

From Vail, K. (2003). *Where the heart is*. American School Board Journal, 190(6), 12–17. *Reprinted with permission of the* American School Board Journal.

A number of school districts make extraordinary efforts to remove barriers for homeless students, while others do not. However, new federal regulations are prodding all districts to do more to identify and help some of their most vulnerable children.

"In a sea of chaos, school can be an anchor for these kids," says Diana Bowman, director of the National Center for Homeless Education in Greensboro, N.C. "When children talk about their experiences, more than anything, school is a bright spot. What happens to children who don't have this bright spot?"

The Homeless Are Always with Us

If you think you don't have homeless families in your district, you are probably mistaken. Homelessness may be more visible in big cities, but is not exclusively an urban problem: 21 percent of the nation's homeless live in the suburbs, and 9 percent live in rural areas or small towns.

"It's common for people not to realize what homelessness is, and if you don't see it in your daily life, easy to think it doesn't exist. It's a problem that is hidden in many communities," says Patricia Julianelle, education staff attorney of the National Law Center on Homelessness and Poverty, in Washington, D.C.

The economic prosperity of the late 1990s did not eradicate homelessness. Jobs were plentiful, but housing prices and rents soared, making it difficult for workers earning minimum wage to afford apartments and houses. And the 1996 welfare reform laws left more women and their children out on the streets. The economic downturn in 2001 has made it even harder for poor families to get by.

As a result, the number of homeless families grew more rapidly in the past decade than the number of homeless individuals, according to Barbara Duffield, the director of education for the National Coalition for the Homeless in Washington, D.C. Duffield worked with Congress on the McKinney-Vento Homelessness Assistance Act. When the No Child Left Behind Act was passed in 2001, the decades-old McKinney-Vento Act was reauthorized with it. The law spells out specific responsibilities for schools, making it clear that the education of homeless students is the responsibility of every school district in the nation. For the first time, the law does not limit the definition of homeless children to those living in emergency shelters, and it requires all districts—not just those that receive McKinney-Vento funds—to designate a staff person as a homeless liaison.

The changes in the law, Duffield says, reflect the growth of homeless families with children. The school liaison will be a catalyst for change, she hopes, and will convince schools that the new requirements are research-based strategies to raise academic achievement among the poorest and most vulnerable students.

The McKinney-Vento requirements may be new to some schools, but districts in large cities have been dealing with the realities of homeless children and their families for years. The New Orleans Public Schools is such a district.

Homeless in New Orleans

It's a week before Mardi Gras, and Carnival season is in full swing. Already, some parades have lurched down Canal Street, krewe members on floats pelting onlookers with purple and gold beads, baubles, cups, and plush toys.

New Orleans is a study in extremes. It's a bountiful city, known for its overabundance of exquisite food and its decadence. But the Crescent City is also a place of crushing poverty, with an overstressed, undersupported public school system. Almost half the children in New Orleans live in poverty, and nearly 75 percent of the New Orleans Public Schools' 77,000 students are eligible for free or reduced-price lunch.

Like other tourist towns, the city attracts poor and unskilled workers with its warm weather and low-paying service jobs. But when those jobs dry up, as they have been doing over the past two years, families who have teetered on the brink of homelessness and poverty stop teetering and fall. The city's homeless population is estimated at 17,000 to 19,000—33 percent are families, mostly women and children.

In a ramshackle neighborhood off St. Charles Street seldom visited by tourists, homeless women and their families come to reclaim their lives. The Baronne Street Transitional Housing, a refurbished school building, is run by Catholic Charities. The mothers get counseling, find jobs, and learn to save money. Their children go to the neighborhood school or the one they attended before they become homeless. The New Orleans Public Schools give bus tokens to the children who want to stay at their home schools.

Most of the women who come to Baronne Street have few job skills, no high school diploma or even a GED. Grief and intergenerational poverty permeate their stories. Delores Stevens is raising her three grandchildren after her daughter stabbed and killed the children's father. Kandre Franklin, at 24, is the mother of six children. She's worried about her 7-year-old son, who brought a knife to school because kids were taunting him.

But the women say their children are content at Baronne Street. Jennifer Evans, who lives at Baronne with her 9-year-old daughter, says the living situation was hard at first. "I remember my daughter saying, 'I'm not getting out of the car—those girls walking down the street will know I live in the shelter.' I let her sit in the car." Now, however, she says, "Some of my daughter's friends call her here, so they know she lives here."

For most of these children, Baronne Street is unlike any place they've lived before. They get regular hot meals. The lights and heat are never shut off. The shelter's comfortable rooms and concerned adults represent stability they haven't experienced much in their young lives.

The homeless label is a stigma, but in the New Orleans Public Schools, where nearly all the children are disadvantaged, it doesn't sting as hard. As Michell Brown, Baronne Street's program director, puts it, "Most kids are in poverty; it's just a different form of poverty."

But children at the shelter have particular needs, she says. They need anger management counseling, which the shelter provides. They are behind in school because they've missed a lot of days. They don't trust people, and their socialization skills are low. "Kids don't come here because of any choices they made," she says.

District Advocates for the Homeless

If the children at Baronne Street have a chance of making it in school, it's no doubt due to the efforts of Sabrina Mays Montana and Laverne Dunn, the district's homeless liaisons.

The women are tireless advocates for homeless children and their parents. They connect families with social services and shelters, organize tutoring sessions at the shelters, and run a summer camp for homeless students and other disadvantaged students. The program serves more than 1500 children and youth.

In addition to working with children and their families, Montana and Dunn educate school employees and the community about the realities of homeless families, trying to dispel the myths that homeless people are dirty, that they deserve to be homeless, that they don't love their children, "People feel [the homeless] are in that position because they want to be," says Dunn. "Children have no choice; they can't help it."

Those perceptions can be barriers to education for homeless children, as well, especially when so much rides on standardized test scores. School secretaries and principals have been known to fight the admission of homeless students by requiring their parents to show documentation that school officials know they don't have, such as utility bills or other proofs of address. "The assumption is that if they are homeless, they will have poor grades and poor attendance," says Montana. "We must educate them, no matter how low or high their test scores are."

In some cases, principals believe families aren't telling the truth about being homeless, because they're trying to get their children into schools outside their attendance area. Montana reminds them that the law says a child must be admitted immediately, even if there is a dispute. "We always tell principals who say, 'They are using us,' that if we find [parents] are using the program to get into a school, we do a home visit, then remove the child if necessary."

The women hope that understanding will foster compassion. Montana uses this example: A homeless boy recently faced expulsion because he brought a toy gun to school. The principal looked in the boy's knapsack and realized he was carrying everything he owned. His family had to be out of the shelter every day by 5 a.m. and take all of their possessions with them. The boy carried the toy gun because he believed he needed to protect his family in the shelter. "Ask why the person does what he's doing," Montana suggests. "Dig a little deeper to see the root."

Classroom teachers must know their children, says Montana. If children aren't doing homework or class projects, it might be because they don't have a quiet place to do their work at night. Some teachers require papers to be typed—an impossibility for a child living in a shelter.

Without advocates or resources, homeless students and their families are at the mercy of school secretaries, registrars, and administrators who may be ignorant of the new requirements of McKinney-Vento. Confusion also ensues when districts interpret the law in various ways—and sometimes the confusion ends in legal actions.

Abiding by the Law

That was the case with the Chicago Public Schools. The city district now runs a program for homeless students that other schools in Illinois emulate, but it wasn't always that way. In fact, Laurene Heybach, head of the Law Project for the Chicago Coalition for the Homeless, says Chicago's treatment of some homeless children in the early 1990s was "appalling." It was not unusual to encounter families who had been forced to switch schools five times, she says.

"Reducing mobility is one primary thing that a school can do to help itself. The course of practice was to keep moving kids out," says Heybach.

When Heybach and others went to shelters, they found children not attending school. Parents said the neighborhood school wouldn't enroll the children, and their old school wouldn't take them back. Other schools wouldn't take the children unless parents physically returned to their old schools to get records: "They were ridiculous situations that could have been resolved," Heybach says.

The lawyers approached the school system in 1992 to report the violations. When the system didn't respond, the coalition went to court with a class action suit and won in 1996. The school system still didn't respond, which forced the lawyers back into court, saying the district was in breach of their agreement. The appellate court agreed, issuing an injunction against the district in 1999.

It cost the Chicago Public Schools more than $1 million to litigate the case—only to be forced to do something it was legally obliged to do in the first place, Heybach says. But that lesson was lost on two districts in Maryland, as Laurie Norris found. A lawyer with Public Interest, a legal advocacy organization in Baltimore, Norris surveyed parents in several shelters in Prince George's County, Md. Three parents said their children weren't attending school because of transportation problems. Norris says she tried to work with the district before filing a class action suit, which the district lost. "Our role is to try to make sure that homeless children are paid attention to, that they aren't the last group on everyone's mind," says Norris.

But Norris wasn't done yet. In neighboring Montgomery County, Stephenie Bullock and her family lost their home and moved in with relatives in Washington, D.C. Montgomery County officials said that because the family was living with relatives in another school district, the children were not considered homeless and could not continue at their schools. Meanwhile, Washington school officials wouldn't let the children enroll because Bullock had no proof of residency in the district. The children were out of school the entire fall semester.

Bullock's oldest son, Brandon, found information about the McKinney-Vento Act on the Internet and sent a letter to Montgomery County school officials saying that it applied to him. Officials did not respond.

The family heard about Norris and contacted her. When Norris approached school officials, they said that because the family had been homeless for 10 months and not living in their district, they no longer had a right to go to school there. "I was flabbergasted," says Norris. "To the extent that they know about McKinney, they are looking at it narrowly. They carved these kids out, for whatever reason."

At the heart of the disagreement was the new McKinney regulation identifying children living with relatives as homeless. Montgomery County officials said that since the Bullock family was in a stable living situation, the regulations did not apply.

A U.S. District Court judge disagreed, however, and decided that Montgomery County had to provide transportation for the children to return to their original schools. Brandon, who had missed nearly a year of classes, finished his senior year at his former high school.

The district's decision to argue its position in court did not mean that it sought to abdicate its responsibility to educate its homeless students, Montgomery County School Board President Patricia O'Neill says. In fact, she says, the system is full of principals and teachers who are always reaching out to homeless and transient children and families. "It's unfortunate that lawsuits like this create this impression that we are a cold-hearted system," she says.

These legal disputes would not surprise Devora Campbell. Campbell was recently appointed to the District 29 Community School Board in New York City, beating out nine other contenders for the seat. The position allows Campbell to advocate for homeless students. She's acutely aware of their needs—Campbell is homeless herself. The 40-year-old woman lives with her husband and two of her three children in a Queens family shelter. "Children in transition are in a lost civilization," she says.

Not all of them are lost, however. Across the country, school districts are serving and helping their homeless children. The ones meeting with the most success are those that reach out to the families as well as the children.

Help the Family, Help the Child

Laura O'Brien was teaching elementary school in California's Fresno Independent School District when school district officials asked her to develop a program for homeless students. That was six years ago, and the temporary assignment has grown into a full-time job. Over those years, Fresno's homeless program has become a national model—90 percent of homeless students graduate from high school, and 80 percent stay at the same school all year.

At first, O'Brien knew nothing about homelessness. "I thought it wasn't in our own backyard," she says. "It was a real eye-opening experience. That's the thing—if you don't know about it, how can you do something about it?"

Fresno's philosophy for helping homeless students is to start by helping their family. "Problems at school stem from issues at home," says O'Brien. "If you don't provide assistance to the whole family, you won't see improvement."

The fourth largest school system in California, Fresno enrolls 82,000 students. Some three-quarters live in poverty, and the area has a 15 percent unemployment rate. The first year of the homeless program, only 125 students were involved. But during the current school year, 3398 students are being served through the program.

Once students and families are identified, a social worker connects them with social services and helps to move them into permanent housing. "A lot of our families can't deal with more than one issue at a time, and school isn't often on the top of the list," says O'Brien. "We try to make it less of an issue by providing help, food, and clothing."

Another successful program that aims to break the cycle of poverty and homelessness is in central Pennsylvania. In the heart of rural Amish country, Lancaster is not a place normally associated with the homeless. But this small city hosts a variety of shelters, including the historic 100-year-old Water Street Rescue Mission, which are of such high quality that they draw homeless from all over the state.

The School District of Lancaster has about 11,400 students. The homeless program served about 900 students last year, a number that shocks people when program director Kenneth Marzinko talks to church groups and civic organizations.

A large network of charitable organizations and churches supports Lancaster's homeless program. These groups provide food and clothing, and they volunteer at an after-school program held twice a week. They shower the children with Christmas presents, and they provide the presents for the monthly parties held to celebrate the birthdays of all the children born that month.

"Our goal is to try and keep today's homeless students in school [so they will] graduate from high school, and go on to higher education so they can support their family," says Marzinko.

The Power of Possibilities

Matthew Cardinale graduated from Tulane University this spring with a degree in sociology. In the fall, he'll go to the University of California—Irvine to earn his master's degree in the same subject. He knows his life could have been very different without his intense belief in the redemptive power of education.

"I see learning as liberating and empowering," Cardinale says. Many of the young people he met at shelters and on the street had experiences in school that made them feel otherwise. "I had a stronger educational background so I had different ideas of what is possible," he says. "Certain homeless teens have lower ideas of what is possible."

But what is possible depends in part on what opportunities are available to young people. And when children and youth are denied access to school for whatever reason, their possibilities are dimmed.

"We are blessed to know what it's like to come home to a warm house, and we assume it's like that for everybody," says Montana, the New Orleans homeless liaison. "We are all part of mankind. We cannot be judgmental of each other. There is not enough time on earth to be like that."

"OUR SCHOOL DOESN'T OFFER INCLUSION" AND OTHER LEGAL BLUNDERS

Paula Kluth, Richard A. Villa, and Jacqueline S. Thousand

What are the legal obligations of teachers toward students with exceptionalities? This article attempts to answer this question by outlining the history of inclusion in the United States. Inclusion is a movement in special education that attempts to integrate students with exceptionalities into the ongoing life of schools and classrooms. Its advocates claim that inclusion benefits students in multiple ways, ranging from an enriched academic curriculum to the learning of social and life skills. There is evidence, however, that many schools still persist in offering separate special programs such as resource rooms, even when these students could benefit from a less restrictive learning environment. As you read this article ask yourself, "What are the major obstacles to inclusion in schools, and what role do teachers play in removing these obstacles?"

Think About This . . .

1. What are the legal arguments for inclusion in schools today? When can students with disabilities be legally removed from a regular education environment?
2. What are the educational arguments against separate, special programs for students with disabilities?
3. What are some different ways that teachers can adapt their instruction to meet the learning needs of students with disabilities?
4. How could you adapt your classroom to meet the special learning needs of students with disabilities?

In 1975, Congress passed the Education for All Handicapped Children Act (Public Law 94-142), guaranteeing for the first time that all students with disabilities would receive a public education. The law, whose name changed in subsequent reauthorizations in 1990 and 1997 to the Individuals with Disabilities Education Act (Public Law 101-476; Public Law 105-17), set the stage for inclusive schooling, ruling that every child is eligible to receive a free and appropriate public education and to learn in the least restrictive environment possible. Specifically, the law ensures

> that to the maximum extent appropriate, children with disabilities, including children in public or private institutions and other care facilities, are educated with children who are not disabled. (Individuals with Disabilities Education Act, 20 U.S.C. § 1412 [a][5])

In 1994, the U.S. Department of Education's Office of Special Education Programs issued policy guidelines stating that school districts cannot use the lack of adequate personnel or resources as an excuse for failing to make a free and appropriate education available, in the least restrictive environment, to students with disabilities.

Schools have taken much time to implement the law. Although many schools and districts have been educating students with disabilities in inclusive settings for years, families often still have to fight to get their children into general education classrooms and inclusive environments.

An analysis of U.S. Department of Education reports found that in the dozen years between 1977 and 1990, placements of students with disabilities changed little. By 1990, for example, only 1.2 percent more students with disabilities were in general education classes and resource room environments: 69.2 percent in 1990 compared with 68 percent in 1977. Placements of students with disabilities in separate classes declined by only 0.5 percent: 24.8 percent in 1990 compared with 25.3 percent in 1977. And, students with disabilities educated in separate public schools or other separate facilities declined by only 1.3 percent: 5.4 percent of students with disabilities in 1990 compared with 6.7 percent of students with disabilities in 1977 (Karagiannis, Stainback, & Stainback, 1996).

More recently, the National Council on Disability (2000) released similar findings. Investigators discovered that every state was out of compliance with the requirements of the Individuals with Disabilities Education Act and that U.S. officials are not enforcing compliance. Even today, schools sometimes place a student in a self-contained classroom as soon as they see that the student is labeled as having a disability. Some students

From Kluth, P., Villa, R., & Thousand, J. (2002). "Our school doesn't offer inclusion" and other legal blunders. Educational Leadership, 83(4), *24–27. Reprinted with permission of the Association for Supervision and Curriculum Development.*

enter self-contained classrooms as soon as they begin kindergarten and never have an opportunity to experience regular education. When families of students with disabilities move to a different district, the new school sometimes moves the student out of general education environments and into segregated classrooms.

In some cases, districts may be moving slowly toward inclusive education, trying to make a smooth transition by gradually introducing teachers and students to change—but moving slowly cannot be an excuse for stalling when a learner with a disability comes to school requiring an inclusive placement.

Clearly, more than 25 years after the law came into effect, many educators and administrators still do not understand the law or how to implement it. Three common misunderstandings still determine decisions about students with disabilities in U.S. schools.

"Our School Doesn't Offer Inclusion"

We often hear teachers and families talking about inclusion as if it were a policy that schools can choose to adopt or reject. For example, we recently met a teacher who told us that her school "did inclusion, but it didn't work," so the school "went back to the old way." Similarly, a parent explained that she wanted her child to have an inclusive education, but her neighborhood school doesn't "have inclusion."

Special education is not a program or a place, and inclusive schooling is not a policy that schools can dismiss outright. Since 1975, federal courts have clarified the intent of the law in favor of the inclusion of students with disabilities in general education (Osborne, 1996; Villa & Thousand, 2000a, 2000b). A student with a disability should be educated in the school he or she would attend if not identified as having a disability. The school must devise an individualized education program that provides the learner with the supports and services that the student needs to receive an education in the least restrictive environment possible.

The standard for denying a student access to inclusion is high. The law clearly states that students with disabilities may be removed from the regular education environment only

> when the nature or severity of the disability is such that education in regular classes with the use of supplementary aids and services cannot be achieved satisfactorily. (Individuals with Disabilities Education Act, 20 U.S.C. § 1412 [a][5])

If schools can successfully educate a student with disabilities in general education settings with peers who do not have disabilities, then the student's school must provide that experience.

"She Is Too Disabled to Be Educated in a Regular Classroom"

A special education teacher recently told us that she was interested in inclusive schooling and that she decided to "try" it with one of her students. Patricia, a young student with Down's syndrome, began 1st grade in September, but the school moved her back to a special education classroom by November. The teacher told us how difficult the decision had been and explained why educators had changed Patricia's placement: "The kids really liked her and she loved 1st grade, but she just wasn't catching on with the reading. She couldn't keep up with the other kids."

Many families and teachers have the common misperception that students with disabilities cannot receive an inclusive education because their skills are not "close" enough to those of students without disabilities. Students with disabilities, however, do not need to keep up with students without disabilities to be educated in inclusive classrooms; they do not need to engage in the curriculum in the same way that students without disabilities do; and they do not need to practice the same skills that students without disabilities practice. Learners need not fulfill any prerequisites to participate in inclusive education.

For instance, a middle-school social studies class is involved in a lesson on the U.S. Constitution. During the unit, the class writes its own constitution and bill of rights and reenacts the Constitutional Convention. Malcolm, a student with significant disabilities, participates in all these activities even though he cannot speak and is just beginning to read. During the lesson, Malcolm works with a peer and a speech and language therapist to contribute one line to the class bill of rights; the pair uses Malcolm's augmentative communication device to write the sentence. Malcolm also participates in the dramatic interpretation of the Constitutional Convention. At the Convention, students acting as different Convention participants drift around the classroom introducing themselves to others. Because he cannot speak, Malcolm—acting as George Mason—shares a little bit about himself by handing out his "business card" to other members of the delegation. Other students are expected to submit three-page reports at the end of the unit, but Malcolm will submit a shorter report, a few sentences, which he will write using his communication device. His teacher will assess Malcolm's grade on the basis of his report and participation in the class activities, his demonstration of new skills related to programming his communication device, and his social interactions with others during the Constitutional Convention exercise.

The Constitutional Convention example illustrates how students with disabilities can participate in general education without engaging in the same ways or having the same skills and abilities that others in the class may have. In addition, this example highlights ways in which students with disabilities can work on individual skills and goals within the context of general education lessons. Most important, his teachers designed and put in place the supports and adaptations that Malcolm needed for success. Malcolm did not have to display all the skills and abilities of other students to participate. Instead, Malcolm's teachers created a context in which Malcolm could demonstrate competence.

For Malcolm to be successful in his classroom, his teachers need to provide him with a range of "supplemental supports, aids, and services," one of the law's requirements (Individuals with Disabilities Education Act, 20 U.S.C. § 1412 [a][5]). Supports, aids, and services might include a piece of assistive technology, use of an education consultant, instruction from a therapist, support from a paraprofessional, peer tutors, different seating or environmental supports, modified assignments, adapted materials (such as large-print books, graphic organizers, or color-coded assignment books), curriculum that is differentiated to meet the needs of the learner, time for teachers' collaborative planning, coteaching, training for school personnel, or any number of other strategies, methods, and approaches. Schools do not need to provide every support available, but they must provide those required by the student with disabilities.

Families do not have to prove to the school that a student with disabilities can function in the general classroom. In *Oberti v. Board of Education of the Borough of Clementon School District* (1993), for example, a U.S. circuit court determined that the neighborhood school of Raphael Oberti, a student with Down's syndrome, had not supplied him with the supports and resources he needed to be successful in an inclusive classroom. The judge also ruled that the school had failed to provide appropriate training for his educators and support staff. The court placed the burden of proof for compliance with the law's inclusion requirements squarely on the school district and the state in-

stead of on the family. In other words, the school had to show why this student *could not* be educated in general education with aids and services, and his family did not have to prove why he *could*. The federal judge who decided the case stated, "Inclusion is a right, not a special privilege for a select few."

"We Offer Special Programs Instead of Inclusion"

A few years ago, one of us went to a neighborhood school to vote. To get to the ballot machines, voters had to walk down a long hallway to a classroom marked *Autistic Center*. Knowing that the district had been providing inclusive education to many students with disabilities, we were surprised to learn that although students with mild disabilities were in general education classrooms, others were still in "special programs." The teacher in the Autistic Center was responsible for educating all the district's students who were diagnosed with autism—eight learners, ages 6 to 14.

Across the United States, many school districts still operate programs for discrete groups of students. Separate programs and classrooms exist for students identified with certain labels—emotional disabilities, for example—and for students with perceived levels of need, such as severe or profound disabilities. In many cases, students enter these self-contained settings without an opportunity to receive an education in a general classroom with the appropriate aids and services.

In 1983, the *Roncker v. Walter* case challenged the assignment of students to disability-specific programs and schools. The ruling favored inclusive, not segregated, placement and established a *principle of portability*. The judge in the case stated,

> It is not enough for a district to simply claim that a segregated program is superior. In a case where the segregated facility is considered superior, the court should determine whether the services which make the placement superior could be feasibly provided in a nonsegregated setting (i.e., regular class). If they can, the placement in the segregated school would be inappropriate under the act (IDEA). (*Roncker v. Walter*, 1983, at 1063)

The *Roncker* court found that placement decisions must be determined on an individual basis. School districts that automatically place students in a predetermined type of school solely on the basis of their disability or perceived level of functioning rather than on the basis of their education needs clearly violate federal laws.

Benefits of Understanding the Law

Implementation of the law is still in its infancy, and educators are still learning about how the law affects students in their classrooms. Reviewing the intent and language of the Individuals with Disabilities Education Act will help administrators shape districtwide or school-based policies and procedures; evaluate the ways in which programs are labeled and implemented; and make more informed decisions about student assessment, placement, and service delivery. Administrators should also consider the following questions:

- Are all students in the least restrictive environment?
- Are we providing students with disabilities with the necessary supplemental supports, aids, and services?
- Do teachers and administrators understand their responsibilities under the Individuals with Disabilities Education Act?
- Do teachers and administrators talk about inclusive education as if it were a choice that can be made by a school or by a teacher?
- Do school personnel require additional training?

School district leaders and school principals who understand the federal law can avoid lawsuits, enhance education experiences for students with and without disabilities, and move toward the development of school communities that are egalitarian, just, and democratic for all.

References

Education for All Handicapped Children Act of 1975, Public Law 94-142 (1975).

Individuals with Disabilities Education Act, 20 U.S.C. § 1400 *et seq.* (1997).

Karagiannis, A., Stainback, S., & Stainback, W. (1996). Historical overview of inclusion. In S. Stainback & W. Stainback (Eds.), *Inclusion: A guide for educators* (pp. 17–20). Baltimore: Brookes.

National Council on Disability. (2000, January 25). *Back to school on civil rights.* (NCD #00-283). Washington, DC: Author.

Oberti v. Board of Education of the Borough of Clementon School District, 995 F.2d 1204 (3rd Cir. 1993).

Osborne, A. G. (1996). *Legal issues in special education.* Needham Heights, MA: Allyn & Bacon.

Roncker v. Walter, 700 F.2d 1058 (6th Cir. 1983), *cert. denied,* 464 U.S. 864 (1983).

Villa, R., & Thousand, J. (Eds.). (2000a). *Restructuring for caring and effective education.* Baltimore: Brookes.

Villa, R., & Thousand, J. (2000b). Setting the context: History of and rationales for inclusive schooling. In R. Villa & J. Thousand (Eds.), *Restructuring for caring and effective education: Piecing the puzzle together* (pp. 7–37). Baltimore: Brookes.

BEAUTIFUL MINDS
Wesley Clarkson

The range of abilities among the learners in our classrooms is considerable. In addition to providing curriculum and instructional strategies that meet the needs of the majority of students, teachers must plan for remediation for slower students and enrichment for faster learners. For students identified as gifted, teachers must create an environment that allows students to grow beyond the standard expectations for given grade levels. As you read this article ask yourself, "What are some of the instructional options teachers can use as they work with gifted students?"

Think About This . . .

1. Wesley Clarkson describes a range of educational services for students identified as gifted. What are the merits and limitations of these different approaches to gifted education?

2. When funding for education is limited, educators must make difficult choices in the distribution of resources. What are the potential ramifications of limited funding for gifted programs?
3. Clarkson identifies specific costs for different gifted programs. In which area do you think educators should invest the most resources?
4. The students in your classroom will possess a wide range of abilities. How will you respond to the academic needs of gifted students in your classroom?

That eminent social philosopher Matt Groening—creator of *The Simpsons*—deftly illustrated our stereotype of gifted education in an early episode of his popular cartoon series. It seems that "Everychild" Bart, through some horrendous error, winds up in the gifted kindergarten class at Springfield Elementary School.

All around him are industrious little geniuses, pursing their passions for art, math, and science with nary a peep from their teacher. Bart, meanwhile, thinks it's neat that he doesn't really have to *do* anything.

Bart's gifted classroom is, in many ways, the one we carry around in our minds. It is a rarified place, populated by children who are somehow different from the rest of us—and great at everything they do.

In reality, gifted education is not a mysterious science reserved for a few geniuses but, rather, a common-sense answer to the special needs of gifted children. And, yes, gifted children do have special needs. At a time when school districts are strapped for dollars, when federal law has mandated that schools focus on their poorest performers, it's easy to see why the budgetary needs of gifted programs are sometimes given low priority.

But gifted programs need not be viewed as a luxury item we cannot afford. They can be both cost-effective and educationally beneficial. Likewise, designing gifted programs isn't rocket science. It just involves common-sense choices for meeting the needs of students who need a more challenging curriculum.

Clearing Up Misconceptions

Most every instructional program seems to attract its share of criticism, and gifted programs are no exception. You might have heard complaints like these:

- Gifted education is elitist. It provides specialized instruction for a small minority of students instead of using scarce funds to enrich the educational experiences of all. Moreover, most gifted students come from wealthier families who can afford to supplement their own children's education.
- It's terribly expensive to provide special programs for the gifted and talented—especially when money is short. We need to concentrate our funding on programs for students who are having problems meeting state and national standards.
- Gifted and talented kids will get along fine without any special help. They don't need special programs or materials.

I'd like to clear up some of these misconceptions and provide some practical advice for school boards. I'll look at three issues: the nature of various gifted programs, the budgets required to support these options, and a cost/benefits analysis of each. If you have a firm grasp of the program options and the quality of instruction you can expect from them, you will have the information you need to make intelligent decisions.

Different Approaches

Since the 1950s, gifted education has been characterized by three main approaches: (1) acceleration of instruction by placing students in higher grade levels so that they graduate sooner, (2) enrichment of instruction within the regular school setting, and (3) grouping of gifted students for special instruction. Current practices have changed little over the past five decades, and all programs provide services based on one of these three models. Today the four most common types of arrangements are within-class programs, pull-out programs, separate classes, and special schools.

From Clarkson, W. (2003). *Beautiful minds.* American School Board Journal, 190(8), 24–28. *Reprinted with permission of the* American School Board Journal.

• *Enrichment programs,* held within the regular classroom, are the most common. Although they are sometimes called schoolwide enrichment programs, the name can be misleading because it doesn't mean that all students are gifted or that all teachers should be gifted teachers. Rather, cluster groups of six to eight gifted students are placed in a teacher's classroom, along with 12 to 20 other students who are not identified as gifted.

The teacher is provided with specialized training, a limited array of books and instructional materials, and perhaps a curriculum guide if the district has developed one. The teacher's job is to carry out all normal teaching duties with the entire class and provide an outlet for the gifted students through in-depth projects that are related to the regular instruction. This is accomplished through independent study units and techniques such as "tiered assignments," in which students work on multiple assignments within the same instructional unit, and "curriculum compacting," a system in which students are provided with alternative activities after they test out of material they have already mastered.

• *Pull-out programs* provide special instruction for gifted students for a short period of time, either daily or weekly. During this time, the gifted education teacher instructs all of the gifted students in a specific grade level, using special activities. Often, these activities are related to leadership and creativity rather than the core curricular areas of language arts, math, social studies, and science, because those subjects are being taught in the regular classroom. Some call this the "you're gifted for an hour a day" model, though that phrase may be a little unfair.

Several researchers and writers have developed excellent plans for this style of gifted instruction, with a clear emphasis on teaching thinking skills, creative problem solving, and a variety of research and presentation methods. In high school this approach might be an independent study class, in which the student works with a teacher or mentor on an advanced-level research paper, science experiment, creative writing assignment, work of art, or other appropriate project.

• *Separate gifted classes,* sometimes confused with pull-out programs; replace core curriculum classes and are made up of gifted students only. These are very common in secondary schools, due to the departmentalization of the teachers and the larger numbers of students on a campus. Common classes include advanced math classes, special science classes, or humanities programs. High school Advanced Placement courses, which are sponsored by the College Board, are similar to this approach, although most districts allow open enrollment for AP classes, rather than limiting them to gifted students.

• *Special schools for the gifted* are much rarer than any of the other models. They can include private and charter schools designed specifically for gifted students or magnet schools whose entrance requirements have a gifted component along with the specialized instructional interest of the school. These schools generally emphasize a rigorous curriculum, a novel approach to instruction, the creative development of the students' talents, or all of the above. Many such schools have stringent entrance requirements and waiting lists due to their popularity with some parents.

Making a Decision

Which program is right for your district? You might decide to go for the cheapest one, but as in life, sometimes the least expensive item on the rack is not the best bargain. Sometimes, it's better to pay more up front to create a program with the desired long-term benefits.

I know from my experience in running and developing these kinds of programs for a large urban school district that program cost is an important issue. There is never enough money to go around for everything we want to do. Still, I think we can develop a framework that you can use to investigate these costs and make decisions based on real information. Let's look at some of the financial information that we can collect.

• *Teacher salaries* are perhaps the biggest consideration, as they are the largest single expense in any district's budget. Enrichment programs and most pull-out programs usually require no additional staff, except in the case of a dedicated gifted teacher who serves all of the school's students and has no other teaching duties. This scenario could result in a one-half or one full-time equivalent (FTE) position per campus, depending on other assignments and/or the number of campuses this teacher serves.

An additional fractional FTE generally is required for all-gifted classes because the classes replace regular content courses for these students, sometimes with classes that are smaller than average for the campus. In a typical middle school with three grade levels and one gifted teacher for each of the four core subject areas, this might result in the need for three additional FTEs overall, depending on the gifted classes' size. However, in some cases, especially in schools that have large numbers of gifted students, there may be no additional FTEs due to the classes' large size.

Special schools have the same teacher loads as gifted classes and could require overall increases in staffing, unless class sizes are comparable to those on other campuses. If class sizes range from 15 to 20 students, as opposed to typical classes of 30 to 35, the net increase in staffing would run between 30 and 50 percent over the number of teachers needed to staff a comparably sized school with a regular curriculum. These issues are sometimes delineated at the time of designing the program to help control overall costs.

• *Training costs* are a factor in all of the programs. Specialized training components may include requirements for teachers to have advanced degrees and state certification as gifted or special education teachers, program training designed to introduce teachers to the specialized curriculum, yearly curriculum development meetings in the summer, and annual training to keep everyone up-to-date on techniques, materials, and regulations.

To calculate a daily training rate, you might need to include the cost of providing a substitute if the training occurs on a school day, the cost of providing a stipend if the training occurs when the teacher is off, the cost of the training materials and books used, a portion of the daily salary of the administrator(s) in charge of the training, and a portion of the consultant's presentation fee and expenses. Taking into account typical consultant fees these days, the expense would range from $100 to $175 per day of training for each teacher in your program.

Training costs would be approximately equal, on a per-teacher basis, in the various programs, but the number of teachers varies by program, thus affecting the total cost. Enrichment programs use the largest number of teachers, with teacher-to-student ratios that range from 1-to-1 (in schools with very few identified gifted students) to 1-to-8.

Pull-out programs require the fewest teachers, especially in schools where one teacher serves all grade levels. In this type of program, the ratio could be as high as one teacher to 75 or more students. Gifted classes and special schools also result in relatively high teacher-to-student ratios, with one teacher serving from 10 to 20 students.

Thus, your total training costs could be calculated by multiplying the total number of teachers providing gifted services by the number of days of training and then by the per-day cost. Additional funds would have to be budgeted to allow some teachers to attend state and national conferences.

• *Classroom materials* are another cost. Choice of program also affects expenditures for books and curricular materials. Enrichment programs typically provide teachers with a simple curriculum guide and a small library of materials to use in class. One such library

currently costs about $2,000 per teacher. Pull-out programs can have a similar cost in materials per teacher, but with fewer teachers the overall cost would be considerably less.

Gifted classes and special schools are always the most expensive because they typically replace the state-purchased textbooks with other materials and seek to build up considerable libraries of classroom materials for each teacher. These programs usually include a technology component that requires hardware and software purchases as well as maintenance for several computers per classroom. A good library of materials for a classroom could run more than $10,000 in startup costs, plus additional yearly purchases per teacher. Computer hardware and software—including a set of five computers and all necessary peripherals, as well as additional funding for yearly upgrades and new software—would add another $10,000 per classroom.

You can save money by consolidating and sharing materials in a well-equipped library, using computer labs for student projects, leasing equipment with a service contract rather than buying it outright, and purchasing software that has a built-in upgrading price structure.

• *Other expenses* include buildings, classrooms, busing, and related items. Enrichment and pull-out programs typically require little, if any, additional expense in this area, although a pull-out program with a dedicated teacher might require one classroom per building. Gifted classes almost always require additional classrooms because the classes are smaller. This cost is akin to the additional staffing needed: If you have additional teachers, then you will need additional classrooms.

Special schools require entire buildings or sections of an existing school that are dedicated solely to this program. Additionally, special schools and some gifted classes may require busing expenses if they are located in magnet schools.

Quality Merchandise or Close-Out Specials?

The biggest question to answer when searching for excellence in an educational program, is, "What are you looking for?" If your goal is to provide a program that meets all of your state's basic educational standards, which are usually set at a minimal level for the average student, then you might decide to choose one kind of gifted program. If, however, your goal is to prepare all students to achieve as much as they possibly can during their years in your school district, then you just might want to choose a different type of program. There are no right or wrong programs in this business, just hard choices that have to be made depending on a host of variables.

The effectiveness of a gifted program is an important variable to consider, even though there is little clear evidence to help you. Gifted classes and special schools, which are the major examples of full-time, gifted-only instruction, have been evaluated as the most effective form of instruction for gifted students. However, these results appear to be most applicable to highly gifted students—the top 1 to 2 percent of all students. So, if your district identifies more than 2 percent of your students as gifted, the benefits of these programs may apply only to a portion of your identified gifted students.

It seems to make sense that a full-time program should challenge gifted students more than a pull-out program, but other factors enter in, such as teacher commitment, parent involvement, curriculum design, quality of materials, and campus leadership.

Enrichment programs provide some benefits that gifted classes and special schools do not, such as heterogeneous grouping for socialization skills, access to gifted instruction in all classes on an as-needed basis, and the stability of having your gifted students remain in their neighborhood schools. These programs have also received positive evaluations, though their quality will vary with the quality of the teacher. Ineffective teachers sometimes provide a gifted program in name only, with little real substance.

Pull-out programs are perhaps the most researched and documented of all these approaches, due to their long history. They are easy to institute, require the least amount of rearranging of facilities and schedules, and are supported by a wide variety of materials from a large number of publishers. The negatives include the need to pull students out of their regular classes, the limited instructional time, and the constant schedule disruptions that can occur because of special events, teacher training, and field trips. All of these factors can diminish the amount of time available for gifted instruction.

Gifted programs can be both cost-effective and educationally beneficial. When deciding on the program that is right for your district, you need to understand the characteristics of these programs, calculate the true costs, and decide on the benefits you want to obtain. It's all a matter of wise, consistent decision making—decision making that you have signed up to do for the benefit of your district's children.

ADDITIONAL READINGS

Borman, G. (2003). How can title I improve achievement? Educational Leadership, 60(4), 49–53.

Callahan, C. (2001). Beyond the gifted stereotype. Educational Leadership, 59(3), 42–46.

Giangreco, M. (1996). What do I do now? A teacher's guide to including students with disabilities. Educational Leadership, 53(5), 56–59.

Halford, J. (1999). A different mirror: A conversation with Ronald Takaki. Educational Leadership, 56(7), 8–13.

Kilgore, K., Griffen, C., Sindelar, P., & Webb, R. (2001). Restructuring for inclusion: A story of middle school renewal. Middle School Journal, 33(2), 44–51.

Meinbach, A. (1999). Seeking the light: Welcoming a visually impaired student. Middle School Journal, 31(2), 10–17.

Miller, J. (1999). More than included. Middle School Journal, 30(4), 44–50.

Nieto, S. (2003). Profoundly multicultural questions. *Educational Leadership, 60*(4), 6–10.

Taylor, D., & Lorimer, M. (2003). Helping boys succeed. *Educational Leadership, 60*(4), 68–70.

Waldron, K., & Allen, L. V., (1999). Successful strategies for inclusion at the middle level. *Middle School Journal, 30*(4), 18.

EXPLORING THE INTERNET

The National Association for Multicultural Education (NAME)
http://www.nameorg.org/
This site contains resources for teachers as well as links to other multicultural sites.

The American Association of University Women
http://www.aauw.org/
As the title suggests, you will find material here about gender equity resources for teachers. This site, maintained by the American Association of University Women (AAUW), includes numerous links to resources for teachers and researchers in gender equity.

The Council for Exceptional Children
http://www.cec.sped.org/
This site contains valuable information on research and resources for teachers.

Urban Education
http://iume.tc.columbia.edu/
You will find valuable information on this site on issues relating to urban education.

PART THREE

Schools

The concept of *school* has different meanings. At a simple level, it is a physical place—a building or set of buildings. At another, it is a place students go to learn. At a deeper level, schools, as with governments, churches, and families, are social institutions with established structures and rules designed to promote certain goals. Promoting both students' growth and development and the well-being of the country and its citizens are the primary goals of our schools.

Conceptions of these goals have changed as the history of our country has unfolded. In colonial times, for example, they were intended to educate the sons of the wealthy. Then, with changes in the perceived needs of our country, came changes in the goals of schools, and their emphasis shifted toward educating all students. Common schools were formed, and the idea of universal public schooling for all children was born. Meeting this goal required the improved preparation of teachers, and many of the universities that now exist in this country were initially designed to be teacher training institutions. Later, as an understanding of adolescent students' special needs and differences were recognized, middle schools and junior highs were created.

Many reforms have occurred in the history of schooling, such as the progressive education movement that featured a child-centered, problem-solving orientation; the back-to-the-basics movement that emphasized reading, writing, and mathematics; and the present emphasis on teacher and student testing and accountability.

Ongoing research gradually began to illuminate some of the questions about the best ways to organize and manage schools and what makes a school effective for promoting optimal learning for all students. However, in spite of a growing body of increasingly high-quality research and an expanding body of knowledge about effective schools and their place in society, a number of questions remain. Some of these include the following: How do the values promoted by effective schools relate to the values of our popular culture? When should quality schooling begin? Are American high schools organized in a way that best meets the needs and interests of all students? How does size influence the effectiveness of a school? What can be done to make schools safe for all students? To what extent do nonacademic policies, such as dress codes, influence student learning? Keep these questions in mind as you read the articles in this section.

WHY GOOD SCHOOLS ARE COUNTERCULTURAL

Patrick F. Bassett

The effectiveness of our schools in helping students grow and develop is influenced by the society in which they exist. Schools are embedded in our culture and reflect many of our cultural values, both good and bad. Counterculture, according to Patrick Bassett, reminds us of the antiestablishment movement of the 1960s and 1970s, with its unkempt look, promotion of uninhibited sex and drug use, and antiwar politics. However, he asserts that our popular culture, as projected in advertising and the media, unfortunately reflects the more sordid aspects of our cultural values. Needed is a countercultural movement of a different kind, one that reflects a healthier set of values. Ironically, Bassett suggests, the most effective schools are actually countercultural, questioning the values of our larger society. As you read this article ask yourself, "How should schools respond to the larger values in our society?"

Think About This . . .

1. According to Bassett, what two characteristics exist in all exceptional schools? What additional characteristics might be added, and why do you think they are important?
2. Summarize Bassett's view of the values of popular culture. Are his assumptions valid? Why or why not?
3. Summarize Bassett's description of the values in effective schools. What values would you add to or delete from the list? Provide a rationale for your suggestions.
4. How will you attempt to promote a positive moral climate in your classroom? Offer a specific example to illustrate your description.

For anyone in the baby boom generation, the term countercultural inspires reminiscences of our '60s and '70s pasts, replete with anti-establishmentarian grooming (basically hirsute), dress (heavy on beads and headbands), behavior (sex, drugs, and rock 'n roll), and politics (anti-war). From the vanilla-flavored culture of the '50s emerged what our elders regarded as a horrific abomination: a generation that seemed to share none of the values of the prevailing adult culture, and in fact snubbed its collective nose at those values.

The irony of youth, of course, is that its possessors eventually become their parents, as the generations replace one another. Witness, for example, the incarnation for this generation with the resurrection of swing music, the resurgence of attendance at church and synagogues, the re-emergence of children's museums, and the revival of sanitized family experiences, such as Disney cruises.

What is unusual about our times is that the American culture projected in the popular media and popular imagination has become so distorted and grotesque—so reflective of only the more sordid aspects of our collective values and aspirations—that counterculture is something we long for. Indeed, when it comes to education, the best schools (both public and private) are now, ironically, countercultural.

What the research shows about schools of all types and in all locations is that the best of the lot share two main characteristics: They have exceptional teachers and appropriate moral climates. (The latter, often a product of small schools with communities sharing common values, tends to attract the former, exceptional teachers wishing to teach in such an environment.) What is equally certain is that the school's internal moral climate runs counter to that of the external culture, at least the prevailing popular culture. Such a paradox is evident in manifest ways:

From Bassett, P. (2002). Why good schools are countercultural. As first appeared in Education Week, 21(21), 35. *Reprinted with permission of the author.*

Values of the Popular Culture	Values in Effective Schools
Rationalizing of dishonesty (*deceits of leaders; meretricious advertising*)	Expecting honorable behavior (*honor codes constraining lying, cheating, stealing*)
Lionizing the individual (*star-worship; limitless greed*)	Proselytizing community (*sacrificing for the team; community service*)
Indulging sexual profligacy (*real scandals and fiery fictions*)	Expecting abstinence (*limits on "PDA": public displays of affection*)
Excusing violence (*"rights" of gun owners and moviegoers*)	Eschewing violence (*conflict-resolution training; media literacy*)
Exhibiting vulgarity (*crude language, coarse behaviors, risqué dress*)	Insisting on civility (*confronting incivility, setting standards for demeanor and appearance*)
Winning at all costs (*hazing of opponents; cheating for advantage*)	Fair play (*sportsmanship credo; no-cut policies*)
Conspicuous consumption (*status markers of clothes and cars*)	Environmental stewardship (*modeling good citizenship*)
Cultural tribalism (*asserting one's differences*)	School as community (*finding the commonalities*)

With all the spotlights on educational reform, we might just pause and shine a light on ourselves: In a democratic society, schools reflect the character of the culture. If we are unhappy with the character of the culture, we may wish to turn to those schools that are countercultural—and allow more such schools to come into existence and flourish. If, in the garden of good and evil, flowers and weeds coexist, perhaps we should allow more flowers to bloom.

INVESTING IN PRESCHOOL

Gerald Bracey

When should quality schooling start and when should it end? Questions like these focus on our country's responsibility to provide a quality education for all of its students. Some critics claim that investing in universal preschool education is an expensive proposition—or is it? Gerald Bracey, a noted educational commentator, presents convincing evidence from a number of studies showing that children who attend quality preschools gain advantages throughout their lives. He argues that preschool programs are a good educational investment because they lay a solid foundation for future educational growth. As you read this article ask yourself, "How do quality preschool programs influence students' successes throughout their lives?"

Think About This . . .

1. What was the Perry Preschool Project, and how did it attempt to help young children? How might instruction in the program help children later in life?

2. Both the Perry Preschool Project and the Chicago Child-Parent Center Program emphasized parental involvement. How might parental involvement contribute to student success?

3. How was Head Start different from the other programs described? How could Head Start be improved using the other programs as a model?
4. What positive aspects of the preschool programs could be incorporated into your teaching? How would they have to be adapted?

"There are problems we do not know how to solve, but this is not one of them," *Washington Post* columnist David Broder wrote in January 2002. "The evidence that high-quality education beginning at age 3 or 4 will pay lifetime dividends is overwhelming. The only question is whether we will make the needed investment."

This statement stands in rather stark contrast to one by educational psychologist Arthur Jensen in 1969: "Compensatory education has been tried, and it apparently has failed." Apparently, the operative word in Jensen's comment was "apparently."

The years between the Jensen and Broder statements have produced a great deal of evidence about the effects of early childhood education, and the evidence is indeed overwhelming. It is also less well known than it ought to be, and it certainly has not had the policy influence it should have. The three major, well-controlled studies of early childhood education differ in some respects but produced highly similar results. In addition, long-term positive outcomes have been found from Head Start. A careful look at these research findings will show why it pays to provide preschool education to all children.

The Perry Preschool Study

The best known and longest term of these studies is referred to as the High/Scope Perry Preschool Project. From 1962 through 1965, 123 African-American children whose parents applied to a preschool program in Ypsilanti, Mich., were randomly assigned to either receive preschool or not (the program did not have room for all applicants).

Random assignment is important in research design. It does not guarantee that the groups will be the same, but it eliminates any systematic bias—only chance differences will occur. Fifty-eight children were assigned to the experimental group, 65 to the control group.

Children who entered the program in 1962 received one year of preschool at age 4. In subsequent years, children received two years of the program at ages 3 and 4. All 123 students received the same sequence of tests and interviews over the years. Testers, interviewers, and subsequent teachers did not know whether the children had been in the experimental group or the control group.

The parents were screened for socioeconomic status, and the children were given the Stanford-Binet IQ test. The children had IQs between 60 and 90 and no evidence of physical handicap. The parents had completed 9.4 years of school, on average, and only 20 percent had completed high school—fewer than the average for all African Americans, which was 33 percent. The half-day program lasted for eight months and included weekly 90-minute home visits by project staff.

The Perry project used a curriculum developed at the High/Scope Educational Research Foundation based on the concepts of Jean Piaget and other theorists who view children as active learners. The teachers rarely assessed specific knowledge, as might happen in a classroom using direct instruction: instead, they asked questions that allowed children to generate conversations with adults.

Instruction focused on what the curriculum developers considered 10 categories of key preschool experiences: creative representation, language and literacy, social relations and personal initiative, movement, music, classification, seriation (creating series and patterns), number, space, and time. The school day included individual, small-group, and large-group activities.

The study so far has looked at the children as they moved through school and at ages 19 and 27. A study of the adults at age 40 is in progress.

What the Perry Study Found

By the time they were 19, the students who attended preschool had higher graduation rates and were less likely to have been in special education. They also scored higher on the Adult Performance Level Survey, a test from the American College Testing Program designed to provide simulations of real-life situations.

From Bracey, G. (2003). Investing in preschool. American School Board Journal, *190(1), 32–35. Reprinted with permission of the* American School Board Journal.

Researchers estimated that—in constant 1981 dollars—a K–12 education cost $34,813 for preschoolers and $41,895 for those who had not attended preschool.

By the time the students turned 27, some 71 percent of the preschool group had attained a high school diploma or GED, compared to 54 percent of the control group. Forty-two percent of the preschool children reported making more than $2,000 a month, compared to only 6 percent of those in the control group. Thirty-six percent of the preschoolers, but only 13 percent of the control group, owned their own homes. The preschool group had longer and more stable marriages.

Preschool did not turn the kids into angels, but it made them more at ease in society. The control group's females had an out-of-wedlock birth rate of 85 percent, compared to 57 percent of the preschool group. Control group members suffered twice as many arrests as preschoolers, and five times as many of the control group (35 percent) had been arrested five or more times. Two females in the control group had been murdered.

At the time, researchers estimated a cost–benefit ratio of $7.16-to-$1—that is, considering the cost of the preschool vs. the cost of special education, retention in grade, and incarceration and considering other benefits of preschool, the public saved more than $7 for every $1 invested in preschool. In contrast, between 1958 and 1981, the Dow Jones Industrial Average had little more than doubled, and from 1962 to 1985 it rose by only 64 percent.

The Chicago Study

A similar cost–benefit ratio emerged from a later study, the Chicago Child-Parent Center Program (CPC). In 2001, when the preschoolers were 21, researchers estimated that, factoring in the participants' reduced crime rates (17 percent vs. 25 percent for those in the control group), higher high school completion rates (61 percent vs. 52 percent), and fewer special education placements (14 percent vs. 25 percent)—plus a significant difference in retentions in grade—the program had returned $47,549 to the public.

The one-year program cost $6,788 per child in constant 1998 dollars, yielding a ratio of almost precisely 7-to-1 ($47,549-to-$6,788). An intervention program initiated after children had begun school returned a much smaller amount.

The CPC study was much larger than the High/Scope Perry Preschool Project, consisting of 989 children who received preschool education, 179 who began kindergarten with no preschool, and 374 who were enrolled in other preschool programs. However, students in the CPC were not randomly assigned.

Because the CPC program was offered in 20 centers, it was more diffuse than the Perry program. Initially, teachers had wide latitude over what materials to incorporate, although later they all incorporated a program developed through the Chicago Board of Education. This program emphasized three general areas of development: body image and gross motor skills, perceptual-motor and arithmetic skills, and language. The language skills taught ranged from the auditory discrimination of sounds to building sentences to story comprehension and verbal problem solving. Arthur Reynolds, the senior researcher in the project, classified seven of the 20 centers as teacher oriented, 10 as child oriented, and three as giving equal emphasis to teacher-initiated and child-initiated activities.

Both the Perry and CPC projects emphasized parent involvement with the children. Project staff made home visits, and parents often accompanied children on field trips.

The Abecedarian Study

Researchers at the University of North Carolina, Chapel Hill, conducted the third study, called the Abecedarian Project. It differed from the first two in that it identified children at birth, and those who participated in the study received full-day day care for 50 weeks a year.

Early interventions consisted of "age-appropriate" adult–child interactions, such as talking to children, showing them toys or pictures, and offering infants a chance to react to sights or sounds in the environment. As children grew older, the content of the interactions became more conceptual and skill oriented and, for older preschoolers, more group oriented. Some students participated in the program only until school began; some until age 8. A school-only intervention was also available to another group of children once they reached kindergarten or first grade. For this group, parents were provided with activities and encouraged to use them with their children.

The children in a separate control group were not completely left to fend for themselves. Researchers supplied them with iron-rich formula, reducing the possibility that differences in nutrition could affect brain growth. Social work and crisis intervention services were also available to control-group families. If assessments indicated developmental lags, the family was referred to a relevant agency for follow-up. A number of families sent their children to other preschool programs available in the area. It seems likely that these various programs provided at least some members of the control group benefits similar to those provided by the Abecedarian program. This means that any differences between the preschool and nonpreschool group are smaller than they would be if the control group had attended no program at all.

Of the 111 children in the original study, 104 took part in a follow-up at age 21 (four children had died, one had been withdrawn from the study, one had developed a severe physical condition that prevented inclusion, and one declined to take part).

Young adults who had received preschool intervention had completed more years of schooling (12.2 vs. 11.6), but this was largely due to the high number of females, who are less likely to drop out of school than males. More were still in school (42 percent vs. 20 percent), and more had enrolled in four-year colleges (35.9 percent vs. 13.7 percent). Forty-seven percent of the preschool group had skilled jobs, such as electrician, compared to 27 percent of the controls. Those in the preschool group were less likely to smoke or use marijuana but no less likely to use alcohol or indulge in binge drinking. Cocaine use was denied by virtually all participants in both groups.

Tests administered at ages 8, 12, 15, and 21 showed that the program paid off in both reading and mathematics. Specifically, for children who participated for eight years, the program had a large impact on reading, ranging from an effect size of 1.04 at age 8 to .79 at age 21. Effect sizes for math ranged from .64 at age 8 to .42 at age 21. (An "effect size" is a metric for analyzing the impact of a program or intervention. The greater the effect size, the greater the impact.)

For those receiving only a preschool intervention, the effect sizes in reading ranged from .75 at age 8 to .28 at age 21. For math, the impact grew over time, being .27 at age 8 and .73 at age 21. Smaller effect sizes were seen for those who had been in a school-only program. In reading the effect size ranged from .28 at age 8 to .11 at age 21. Math effects went from .11 to .26 over the same period.

What About Head Start?

Some have discounted the results from these three studies because they are model programs and perhaps cannot be generalized or because they consider the effects small. In their controversial book *The Bell Curve*, Richard J. Herrnstein and Charles Murray managed to dismiss the studies on both counts—and to dismiss Head Start at the same time. After concluding that Head Start programs neither raise intelligence nor display "sleeper effects" (higher graduation rates, less crime, improved employability), the authors had this to say: "Perry Preschool resembled the average Head Start program as a Ferrari resembles the family sedan. . . . The effects [from Perry Preschool] are small and some of them fall short of statistical significance. They hardly justify investing billions of dollars in run-of-the-mill Head Start programs."

Several rejoinders to the Herrnstein–Murray contentions are available. One can point to longer-term effects now displayed by the three programs (*The Bell Curve* was published in 1994). Or one can point to the effect sizes produced by the Abecedarian and Perry projects (effect sizes have not been published for the CPC program). Not even Herrnstein (were he alive) or Murray would call those effects small.

(Labeling an effect size small, medium, or large is a matter of judgment—there is no formula for such a calculation, no point decisively dividing middle from small or large from middle. Most would call the preschool-only treatment effects in the Perry project "moderate.")

One can also point to studies that show that "run-of-the-mill" Head Start programs, as varied as they might be, do produce long-term results. Researchers looking at such outcomes found that white students who attended Head Start were more likely to finish high school and attend four-year college. The trend for African American students was not significant, although they were less likely to have had run-ins with the law. For both races, there also appeared to be a spillover effect to younger siblings. The young brothers and sisters of students who attended Head Start do slightly better in school and are significantly less likely to have been arrested.

The lack of a significant achievement trend for African-American students themselves could be discouraging. However, the same researchers found in another study that African Americans who attended Head Start also attended schools that had lower test scores than did other African Americans. For whatever reason, this was not true for white students. Thus, the implication is that long-term effects are not seen for African Americans because of the quality of their schooling after Head Start—not because Head Start itself is ineffective. In connection with other findings of preschool effects, this result points to the need to provide for high-quality preschool experiences for minority children while simultaneously improving their schools.

Taken together, the focused research and the Head Start research affirm Broder's conclusion. We know how to provide these services, but we're not doing it. According to *Cellblocks or Classrooms? The Funding of*

Higher Education and Corrections and Its Impact on African-American Men, a study released in August 2002 by the Washington-based Justice Policy Institute, the increase in state spending on corrections between 1985 and 2000 was twice what it was on higher education ($20 billion vs. $10.7 billion). And, the study reported, there are now more African-American men in jail than in colleges and universities.

Something as remote from adulthood as preschool affects the odds of landing in jail in favor of both the individual and society. And that's not all. About the same time as the Justice Policy Institute study was released, *The New York Times* reported a side effect of welfare reform: the "no-parent family." Many more mothers now have jobs, but this leaves their children with no caretakers. The kids are shuttled around to relatives and friends. Obviously these children could benefit from good preschool programs. The question is, as Broder asked, do we have the will to make the investment?

A NEW ORDER OF THINGS
Saul Cooperman

High schools play an essential role in our educational system. For many, they open the doors for success in college, whereas for others they provide the knowledge and skills necessary to succeed not only in jobs but in our society at large. In this article Saul Cooperman argues that the existing organization of American high schools presents a curriculum that is inconsistent with what young people want and need. He offers examples of more effective ways of organizing curriculum and instruction, and he identifies three themes around which the curriculum of a well-organized school should be developed. As you read this article ask yourself, "How can the organization of our high schools be changed to maximize learning for all students?"

Think About This . . .

1. How are high schools currently organized? Having attended high school, how effective is this organization?

2. According to Cooperman, what do young people want in their high school experience? What do you believe teachers can do in their own classrooms to help students meet this need?

3. What are the three themes around which Cooperman would organize his "high school of the future?" Do you believe his suggestion is realistic in today's teaching world? Why or why not?

4. How might Cooperman's suggestions influence your teaching? Provide a concrete example to illustrate your description.

I recently attended my 50th high school reunion, and part of the activities included a visit to my alma mater, West Orange High School, in West Orange, N.J. The building looked the same. So did the classrooms. Having been in hundreds of high schools across the United States during a long career in education, this didn't surprise me. Most educators are all too aware that today's high schools are remarkably like those of the early 1950s. Or, for that matter, the '40s, '30s, or '20s.

From Cooperman, S. (2003). *A new order of things.* As first appeared in Education Week, 22(38), 30, 32. Reprinted with permission of the author.

American high schools have long been organized within a departmental structure patterned after colleges. A typical high school will have an English department, math department, science department, and so on. More often than not, there is little connection, or even communication, between the departments. Each one acts as a sovereign duchy, with positions, course offerings, and budgets to protect.

While the adults organize as separate departmental entities isolated from one another, however, their teenage students seek interconnectedness and relevancy in their school experience. What they get instead is math with no relationship to social studies, science without any connection to literature, and so forth. This relevancy-starved approach continues year in, year out with no alternatives, and any "reforms" seen in public education are invariably found at the elementary or middle school level.

Educators have a phrase they often use—"student centered"—to convey that student needs are the focus of their thinking, planning, and doing. The words are fine, but the reality is often different, because educators know that the high school curriculum and staff organization don't focus on students. "Student centered" is more a statement of what teachers and administrators wish the high school landscape to be than what it truly is. Reality involves an adult-centered curriculum, with both the organization of the faculty and the subject-matter hierarchy molded to suit the convenience of adults, not necessarily the learning needs of students.

For example, let's say the following are some of the educational issues to be taught in a given semester: how the body fights disease (health); identification of geological strata (science); the construction of the Panama Canal (history); writing about a controversial issue (English); math word problems involving cubic yards (mathematics); entrepreneurs (economics). Today, each of these would be taught in its separate discipline. The student would see disconnected issues without coherence, the opposite of how one faces problems in the real world.

Here's how they might be taught: There was controversy about whether the Panama Canal should be built at all, and if so, whether it should be in Nicaragua or what was to become the country of Panama. There were tropical diseases that caused many deaths in the building of the canal, difficult problems dealing with the topography and geology of the land, and an entrepreneur who thought he could make a profit by building the canal in Panama. Good teachers, working together, could weave these various pieces into a curriculum that would be comprehensive in outlook, and yet deal with specific educational issues in a way that made learning seem a joy, rather than the acquisition of a boring hodgepodge of disconnected knowledge.

My goal for secondary education is to see high-performing schools operating within a culture that supports learning as an exciting endeavor, one that reaches inside the student and sets up a desire to learn that will never be stilled. This could be accomplished by making all subjects within a school year "connected."

If the subjects were connected, then the teachers who teach them would be connected to one another as well. Then, for perhaps the first time, entire high school faculties would work *together* as a community of scholars, within an organized, coherent, interdisciplinary approach to the education of young minds. As the enterprise stands now, when a science teacher talks to an English teacher in this country, the venue is usually the lunchroom or the lounge, and the topic is apt to be social, not academic.

What might my high school of the future look like? The curriculum would be organized around three major themes: the universe, the individual, and society.

The Universe

Almost all teenagers look at the sky and wonder: Who made all this? How was it made? When was it made? Explanations usually fall into scientific and religious realms. So our student-centered curriculum, for example, would teach astronomy, a subject not generally taught in high schools today, but absolutely necessary to seeing things from a student's perspective. Since religion has, in almost every society, played a role in explaining the universe, this curriculum might examine the biblical book of Genesis, as well as the basic beliefs about creation from the world's major religions. (Comparative religions can be taught in public schools, as long as a particular point of view is not favored.)

Geometry would be studied in the context of astronomy, a most natural fit. And since we humans inhabit the earth, the study of our planet, within the subject of earth science, would be a necessity.

One of our species' greatest natural advantages was the ability to communicate. As our ancestors needed to understand and be understood by others, so our students would learn a language other than their own. In keeping with the curriculum's theme of connectedness, the foreign-language vocabulary would be taken from the subjects of astronomy, religion, geometry, earth science, and literature. Literature itself (novels, poetry, plays, short stories, and the like), as well as writing, would be studied within the context of the integrated subjects. For example, works of Ray Bradbury and Carl Sagan might be read at appropriate times in the study of astronomy. The necessities of grammar, punctuation, and spelling would be taught within the context of the students' writing.

The Individual

Students wonder how their bodies work. Sure, they know they have digestive, circulatory, and respiratory systems. But how do they work, independently and together? How does the body cope with sickness and pain? Why do we sometimes feel depressed and other times euphoric?

We would begin with the study of biology and chemistry, which would be taught from the perspective of the student's body. We are made of flesh, bone, and chemicals. We have systems beneath our skins, and these systems need to be understood from a biological and chemical perspective. Algebra would be integrated with students' understanding of biology and chemistry.

As teenagers grow they begin to understand their own personalities and those of others. Psychology would be taught, from the point of view of an individual understanding his or her behaviors as well as those of other people. Why do people act that way? What motivates them? Why do some people react differently to similar situations?

The need to communicate is continued, as students develop competency in a foreign language. The foreign-language vocabulary here would be taught within the context of biology, chemistry, algebra, psychology, and literature. Literature and writing would, as before, be inseparable from the subjects under study and would be integrated with biology, chemistry, psychology, and the foreign language. For example, *The Voyage of the Beagle* by Charles Darwin might be read, as would certain selections from Sigmund Freud or B. F. Skinner.

Society

We live on this earth with people, whose journey from hunter to farmer to worker in a postindustrial society represents an amazing story. World history would be taught chronologically, and the history of the United States would be taught within that chronology. Art and music would be a vital part of those offerings.

Because we live in groups, we must understand the complexity of human society, and so would read in the area of sociology. Because economics plays a part in everything we do, and has a profound effect on history, we would need to study that subject as well. Foreign

language might be continued, if desired, and literature and writing would, again, be drawn from the lessons at hand in world history, United States history, economics, and sociology. For example, perhaps *The Federalist Papers*, our Declaration of Independence, *The Communist Manifesto*, John Steinbeck's *Grapes of Wrath*, and other texts could be read at appropriate times to give life and heft to the subject being taught.

One feature of this curriculum would be the Senior Project, a major written paper that would encompass the entire second half of the senior year. This interdisciplinary work would require reading and writing about an important and complex current issue. Students would present an original research paper to a teacher and approximately eight fellow students, who would in turn critique one another's papers using Socratic dialogue.

For example, with the major topic of "The Economy," three choices might be available to students. One might be, "Was competition enhanced or diminished by examining the following situations?" Another, "What healthcare plan would you recommend to the president?" And a third, "After studying your state budget, what changes would you make?" Approximately eight students would work on each of the three options within "The Economy," with one teacher guiding all 24 students.

Such a curriculum would conform to all college requirements. Even though it breaks dramatically with the isolated departmental approach of the past, its innovative course of study would meet all colleges' "credit" requirements. Any state-required proficiencies would be naturally integrated within this curriculum. Whether the goal was mastering the quadratic equation in algebra, gaining the ability to use the proper tense in writing, understanding the contributions of Washington, Jefferson, and Lincoln, or being conversant with simple genetics, the flow of this curriculum would assure compliance with state requirements in a way that went beyond cramming sessions and rote learning.

Nor would any jobs be threatened by this approach. So unions would not be reflexive in their opposition. Certification requirements would remain in place, and no waivers would be necessary. The only changes to the physical plant might be the addition of places where faculty members could talk and work together, if such places could not be adapted from the existing facilities.

Many teachers would look upon the ability to work together as a professional experience heretofore denied them—an opportunity to show that the sum is much more than its isolated parts. But I am not naive enough to think that asking collaborative work of people who have never before worked in a team would be acceptable to all. On the contrary, I know that many faculty members would initially feel threatened. Having worked on their own for so long a time, change would be difficult for some people.

New schools where leadership could choose enthusiastic teachers for such an approach would be an obvious choice for implementing this idea. Districts with more than one high school would be able to give teachers the opportunity to transfer into, or out of, this dramatically different type of high school. Where a district has only one high school, it would be wise to have at least 75 percent of the existing faculty give their support; otherwise, the effort would be scuttled by those comfortable with the status quo.

Nothing that upsets the status quo will ever be met with universal applause. This is a truth that Machiavelli spoke to in 1513, when he advised his Prince that "it ought to be remembered that there is nothing more difficult to take in hand, more perilous to conduct, or more uncertain in its success, than to take the lead in the introduction of a new order of things."

New ideas are not readily accepted. Yet, the great strength of our country—the engine of its dynamism—has always been located in precisely that: new ideas, taking risks, and having leaders with the backbone to see the potential in "a new order of things."

We can do this. All it will take is the leadership to get it done.

CAN THE ODDS BE CHANGED?

Deborah Meier

Some schools are better than others in meeting the needs of their students. What lessons can we learn from the more successful ones? Deborah Meier suggests that specific examples of exemplary schools can be found around the United States. However, she suggests these examples fail to provide a comprehensive basis for widespread reform. She describes existing reform efforts, explains why she believes they generally fail, and offers suggestions for a different approach to reform. Then, she outlines an accountability system that would be needed in order for an alternative approach to school organization to work. As you read this article ask yourself, "What is an exemplary school, and how should it be evaluated?"

Think About This . . .

1. According to Meier, what are at least four examples of ways in which reformers presently attempt to improve schools? How effective do you believe these attempted solutions are likely to be? Why do you think so?

2. What are three common features of exemplary schools, according to Meier? What other characteristics would you add to her list? Why would you add these characteristics?

3. What four steps does Meier recommend to ensure accountability with respect to the work of an effective school? Which of these is easiest to implement? Which is most difficult? Why do you think so?

4. What can you as a teacher do to establish a form of personal accountability in your own classroom? Provide a specific example to illustrate your description.

There are numerous stories of schools that have been successful with students who would otherwise count among society's failures. However, such school successes rarely set the stage for Big Reform agendas. These one-of-a-kind schools flicker brightly. A few manage to survive by avoiding the public's attention or by serving powerful constituents; the rest gradually burn out. Can we change that? Can we make the exceptions the norm?

The Search for Silver Bullets

To the vast majority of serious policy makers, the existing exemplary schools offer no important lessons. Most policy makers define *systemic* so that it applies only to the kinds of solutions that can be more or less simultaneously prescribed for all schools, irrespective of particulars. Solutions, in short, that seek to improve schooling by taking away the already too limited formal powers of those closest to the students. Examples range from more prescriptive curricula to new, more centralized testing systems; fiscal rewards and penalties; or changed school governance bodies.

School-level folks are as skeptical about the capacity of any of these top-down recipes to make a significant impact on the minds of teachers or children as policy-level folks are about the idiosyncratic bottom-up ones. Practitioners—in classrooms and central offices—know at heart that "this too shall pass" or can be gotten around or overcome. They wait out the innovators. Policy makers work overtime to come up with ways to circumvent such resistance. The more things change, the more they stay the same.

This is a climate that encourages impatience: enough's enough! If we can't do a better job of marrying top-down and bottom-up reform, we're probably in for big trouble. Giving up on the new thought that all children can learn to use their minds well is hard, especially for those of us who know firsthand that schools as designed are hardly suited to the job and that vastly more children could be well-educated if we came up with a better design. We've "tasted" it. It seems both so near and so far. Perhaps if we posed the problem differently, the oddball schools might offer us systemic answers. The Annenberg Challenge gave a substantial boost to a wave of projects around the country that were, on the one hand, fueled by the growing interest in vouchers and charters but that sought on the other hand a response more compatible with public education and equity concerns. By seeking a solution to the systemic through looking at the particular, different possibilities became thinkable.

Good schools are filled with particulars—including particular human beings. And it is these human beings that lie at their heart, that explain their surprising successes. In fact, it is these particulars that inspire the passions of those involved and draw upon the best in each. Rather than ignore such schools because their solutions lie in unreplicable individuals or circumstances, it's precisely such unreplicability that should be celebrated. Maybe what these "special" schools demonstrate is that *every school must have the power and the responsibility to select and design its own particulars* and thus to surround all young people with powerful adults who are in a position to act on their behalf in open and publicly responsible ways. That may be the "silver bullet."

Will grown-ups all jump at the chance to be such responsible adults? Of course not. Most have never been asked to have their own wonderful ideas, much less to take responsibility for them. Many will be leery because along with the freedom to design their own particulars must come new responsibilities for defending the outcomes. But the resultant practice, responsible citizenship, is not only a good means for running a good school but also the central aim of public schooling. How convenient.

In designing a way to make it easier to invent powerful and responsible schools, we can stack the deck in favor of good schooling, so that great schools are more likely, good schools become ordinary practice, and poor schools are more quickly exposed and dealt with. This effort will require us to learn how to make judgments about schools with standards in mind, but not with a standardized ruler in hand. For too long we've acted as though, in the name of standards, we have to treat students and teachers as interchangeable parts. Nothing could be worse for standards, and nothing would be more unnecessary.

We already know some of the common features of exemplary schools—public or private—that serve ordinary and extraordinary children well. For example:

• *Smallness.* It helps if schools are of a reasonable size, small enough for faculty members to sit around a table and iron things (such as standards) out, for everyone to be known well by everyone else, and for schools and families to collaborate face-to-face over time. Small enough so that children belong to the same community as the adults in their lives instead of being abandoned in adultless subcultures. Small enough to both feel safe and be safe. Small enough so that phony data can

From Meier, D. (1998). Can the odds be changed? Phi Delta Kappan, 79(5), 358–362. Reprinted with permission of the author.

easily be detected by any interested participant. Small enough so that the people most involved can never say they weren't consulted.

• *Self-Governance.* It helps if those most directly involved have sufficient autonomy over critical decisions. Only then will it be fair to hold people accountable for the impact of their decisions. This will entail creating democratic adult communities that have the power to make decisions about staffing, leadership, and the full use of their budget, as well as about the particulars of scheduling, curriculum, pedagogy, and assessment.

• *Choice.* It helps if there are sufficient choices available for parents, students, and teachers so that schools can afford to be different from one another—to have their own definite characters, special emphases, and styles of operating that appeal to some but not all. Responsibility flows more naturally from willing and informed parties. (If schools are small, they can share big old buildings, and choices can be easily available.)

These three qualities—schools that are small enough in size, sufficiently self-governing, and self-chosen—offer a good beginning. They won't in themselves solve anything, although together they could help solve everything.

Two different historic endeavors in New York City—the 22-year experiment with schools of choice in District 4 and the Alternative High School Division's 12-year effort that created dozens of small alternatives, came together in the 1990s to challenge "business as usual." These ventures caught the public's fancy, stimulating a movement on behalf of small schools of choice for all ages and types of students. The genie was out of the bottle and hard to put back. The idea of small alternative schools attracted the attention of families who did not see themselves as "at risk." Word of mouth suggested that students in these schools matched their counterparts academically and surpassed them on many critical dimensions: college attendance, work preparedness, and ability to perform socially valued tasks. They were also achieving improved scores on typical academic assessments. The research community gradually confirmed such impressions. The studies suggest that such schools provide for the possibility of a community powerful enough to be compelling to young people—a club worth joining.

The skeptics say it still can't work en masse. Whether we create another 100 or 200 small schools of choice—some starting from scratch, others carved out of existing schools—they can't be built to last. Everyone agrees that, under present circumstances, such

schools have a limited future. The reformers argue, however, that "present circumstances" are not engraved in stone.

Why Exceptions Can't Become the Norm

Without deep-seated changes in the system that surrounds these small schools of choice, history suggests that the critics will be right: most will water down their innovations or give up altogether. As their numbers increase, so, oddly enough, does their vulnerability. This is one case in which there may not be more safety in numbers. For one thing, these maverick schools tax the capacities of the existing institutions—both the formal system and the godfatherly individuals and organizations that spring up to provide nurturance and cover. Second, as their numbers increase, they're more noticeable. This visibility, in turn, creates new demands to bring them into compliance. Their mainstream counterparts ask why the mavericks are allowed to "get away" with this or that. Who do they think they are? Third, as new roadblocks appear, which require new Herculean responses, school folks begin to complain of weariness—the original fire in the belly that fueled the pioneering spirit begins to wane. Doing the new and the old at the same time seems more and more unfair, an imposition rather than an opportunity.

The existing system is simply not designed to support such oddball entities. It believes in its mission of control and orderliness. The people who operate the present system do not see themselves in the business of trying to best match teacher to job, child to school. Nor could they do so if they wanted. Instead, whenever they look at a problem, they've been trained to seek, first and foremost, ways to solve it by rule. If it's not good for everyone, it's not good for anyone. To make exceptions smacks of favoritism and inefficiency. Each exception must thus be defended over and over again. How else can we hold everyone accountable?

The results of such rule-boundedness are well-documented—above all by such thoughtful critics of public education as John Chubb and Terry Moe. (We all know that the expression "to work to the rule" describes a form of job sabotage.) Except for small enclaves within the large institution, in which special constituencies carve out their own intimate subschools (the ones designed for the top students or for the most vulnerable), the school as a whole remains remarkably anonymous and unchangeable, the model of a nonlearning institution. But there is an alternative. It means changing the "circumstances" so that those three magic bullets described earlier—small, self-governing schools of choice—can be in the mainstream, not on the sidelines, of the system.

If nearly all good schools in the private sector share these three characteristics, why can't we offer them publicly for all children? Because, it's said, it's not politically feasible when public monies are at stake. If that's the nub of the argument, then we should either roll over and admit defeat or *make* it politically feasible. That means inventing a system of accountability for public funds and aiming for educational results that don't require bad educational practice. It's as simple—and every bit as hard—as that.

Changing the Present Circumstances

Small, self-governing schools of choice could be encouraged to flourish, grow like Topsy, spread like weeds, if we built our system *for them,* not them for our system. To create highly personalized schools, however, we have to be willing to shift both our practices and our mindset cautiously and relentlessly over many years. Present practice isn't inevitable. What we have, after all, is a human invention that's only a hundred years old. But just because it's one of those newfangled ideas that doesn't work doesn't mean it will fade away naturally. In fact, it's got a tenacious hold. But our current practice is not the inevitable product of our human nature. In fact, it's peculiarly in conflict with our humanity and with everything we know about rearing the young.

Until the *relationships* between all the people— parents and teachers—responsible for raising our children are changed, changing the parts (curriculum, pedagogy, or assessment) won't matter very much. But it's precisely because, in the long run, these professional "details" matter a great deal that we need to create a system of schooling that allows us to spend our time and energy honing them, close to home. As Theodore Sizer wisely said when Central Park East Secondary School was started, "Keep it simple, so that you can focus on what will always remain complex—the mind of each individual learner and the subject matter we're trying to help her master." Schools have been doing the reverse for far too long.

We shouldn't declare all schools independent tomorrow. We shouldn't remove all rules and regulations by fiat. We shouldn't even downsize all schools by fiat. Until we have more parents clamoring for change,

more teachers with the skill and confidence to try out new approaches, and more living examples of schools that are both independent and accountable, we need to keep our ambitions in check. We're aiming at a change that sticks, not another fad.

On the immediate agenda, for example, is creating a series of large-scale pilot "laboratories" to see how it might work if we let the existing idiosyncratic schools, with their already eager stalwarts, officially break loose and be different. Add to them all those interested in staffing new schools to replace the worst of our current enterprises. Then we'll need a lean master contract between these schools, the union, the city, and the state—a contract covering the most basic obligations as well as those unwaivable local, state, and federal rules pertaining to health, safety, and equity. If those on the sidelines can sit back and watch, not rush in, as the pioneers develop their own answers—including mistaken ones—then we'll learn something. The present system of schooling and accountability is chock-full of mistakes, after all, not to mention disasters that are perpetuated year after year. Of course we're accustomed to them, so we barely notice. This time, let's notice the mistakes and the disasters—with equal charity. As a way of noticing, let's honor forms of accountability that support rather than sabotage the very qualities such independence is trying to achieve: accountability through the responsible exercise of collective human judgment.

The "magic" three—smallness, self-governance, and choice—provide some of the necessary basic ingredients for more responsible individual schools and thus for more accountability. Smallness creates self-knowledge, self-governance allows for a range of voices now often missing, and choice permits disgruntled parents and teachers to vote with their feet. But while these three elements appear to undercut some of the pressure for more and more external accountability, there's a strong argument for adding several other ingredients that will support the development of a more responsible community of schools. Not just because it's politically smart—but because without a powerful system of public accountability, good individual schools can too easily become stuck in routines, parochial, smug, and secretive. Even tyrannical, Smallness, for example, makes it harder to hide from the impact of bad leadership as well as good leadership.

There are several forms of public accountability that are not only compatible with but actually supportive of school-based initiatives. One way to improve the odds, compatible with the three magic bullets, is to increase constituents' voices about the work not only of their own schools but also of other people's schools in terms of student outcomes, equity, and fiscal integrity. Experience suggests that networks of schools can offer us an opportunity to have the best of both worlds: individuality and close external accountability. We need ways to hold schools up to a mirror and ask, "Is this what you meant to be doing?" We need to tackle professional myopia and defensiveness. We assume that schoolchildren learn by being exposed to criticism, but we have not transferred that to the way teachers and schools learn. For this to happen, we need to create instruments that are consistent with the very quality that led us to propose small schools in the first place: responsiveness to often nonstandard ways of maintaining high standards. What strong democratic schooling needs are new forms of horizontal accountability focused on the collective work of the school.

The first step involves creating stronger internal accountability systems, such as those pioneered at Central Park East Secondary School, Urban Academy, University Heights, and International High School, which use both peers and external critics—college faculty members, parents, community members, and other high school teachers—to examine their students' work. It's the job of the teachers, for example, to grade their own students and to determine when they meet school-wide standards—a task too few schools take seriously today. But the teachers, in turn, need to be publicly accountable for such judgments—both to their internal constituents and to the larger public.

At the next step, schools must answer to one another for the quality of their work. Through the creation of networks of sister schools, not uncommon in private schooling, we can learn how to look at one another's work as critical friends. Such networks can also serve to make up for any problems of scale, if schools choose to use them in that way. Schools that provide feedback on the work of sister schools are creating built-in professional development tools, as well as a powerful form of parent and community education. There is nothing better for one's own learning curve than to formally observe and give support to others.

Third, networks need "cooler," noncollegial audiences to answer to. For this we need formal review panels—public auditors—composed of both critical friends and more distanced and skeptical publics, to attest to the credibility of the networks and the work of their schools. It is such bodies that must demand convincing evidence that the network of schools under review is doing its job, is on the right track, and is acting responsibly. Such review panels must ultimately be responsible to the larger, democratically chosen public authorities.

And finally, everyone—teachers, parents, assessors, legislators, and the public—needs a shared body of credible information (actual student work as well as statistical data) as evidence on which to build reflections and judgments. These are the essentials for creating public credibility, but they are also the essentials for producing good schools. The task of these varied groups of observers—the school's immediate community, the networkers, and the external review panels—is not to find the "one right answer" but to push those closest to the action to act with greater enlightenment.

This is no idle dream. In New York City in 1995, with the support of funds from the Annenberg Challenge, nearly 100 small schools broke themselves down into more than 20 such self-chosen networks and began the work of shared support and accountability. More of these schools were in the works within a year. Simultaneously, a system of review panels to accredit such networks and to maintain audits of their work was being developed, as was a system for collecting credible and accessible data. In return, both the union and the city agreed to negotiate new freedoms and greater flexibility. The largest city in the land was on the brink of the biggest experiment on the potential of smallness. But New York City's inability to keep the same chancellor for more than a few years soon put the more risky and experimental aspects of the project on the back burner.

On a smaller scale, also with support from Annenberg, Boston launched a similar approach—called pilot schools—and throughout the country at other Annenberg sites comparable efforts were begun. Not surprisingly, system folks are always tempted by apparently easier solutions that do not change the locus of power and are simpler to implement—at least on paper.

We periodically imagine that we can avoid the messiness of human judgments and create a foolproof "automatic" system to make everyone good or smart or intelligent. At least, we pretend to believe it is possible. Then we get upset at the bureaucracy it inevitably spawns. But if juries of our peers will do for deciding life-and-death matters of law, why not juries of our peers to decide life-and-death matters of education? As Winston Churchill once said about democracy itself, nothing could be more flawed—except all the alternatives. Of course, juries need guidelines, a body of precedents, rules of procedure, evidence, and the requirement to reach a publicly shared decision. This will not come easily or overnight, and, like democracy itself, such an approach rests on restoring levels of mutual trust we seem inclined to abandon altogether—to our peril.

The criterion we need to keep at the forefront of our minds is clear: How will this or that policy affect the intelligent and responsible behavior of the people closest to the students (as well as the students themselves)? That's the litmus test. Creating forms of governance and accountability that are mindful first and foremost of their impact on effective relationships between teachers, children, and families will not be an easy task. It may not even show up as a blip on next year's test scores. But shortcuts that bypass such relationships are inefficient.

If we do it right, we might in the process help create responsible and caring communities that are more powerful than those adultless subcultures that dominate far too many of our children's lives and that endanger our larger common community. The problem we face is, after all, more than "academic."

IT'S ALL ABOUT SIZE

Tom Vander Ark

How does size influence the effectiveness of a school? Are some schools too large or small, and is there an optimal size for a school? Tom Vander Ark notes that although the war on terrorism is the current focus of our national leaders and policy makers, education remains a high priority for the people of our country. He suggests that creating schools in which all students have the opportunity to achieve at high levels requires the efforts of entire communities, not just school boards and school leaders. The size of a school and its ability to involve all of its clients powerfully influence a school's effectiveness.

Vander Ark continues by offering suggestions on different ways communities can provide schools with a rigorous academic agenda combined with opportunities for positive, personal relationships. As you read this article ask yourself, "How can academic rigor and human relationships be combined in an effective school?"

Think About This . . .

1. How do small and large schools compare with respect to graduation and college attendance rates, discipline and safety issues, and community involvement? Why do you suppose this relationship exists?

2. Vander Ark offers a two-pronged policy for developing learning environments that combine rigor and relationships. What are the two prongs? What do you believe could be done in current learning environments that would approximate what he is suggesting?

3. What three different types of schools can serve as successful models for reaching the goals of combining rigor and relationships? Which of these models do you believe is likely to be most effective? Least effective?

4. You are teaching in a large urban or suburban school. What might you do in your classes or classroom to help meet the goals Vander Ark describes? Offer a specific example to illustrate your description.

Even as the war on terrorism occupies the hearts and minds of our nation's leaders and policy makers, education remains a top priority for people across the country. And ensuring that schools meet the needs of all students is a daunting obligation, one that school boards should not shoulder alone. Communities as a whole need to examine their portfolio of school options and ask themselves: Do all students have an opportunity to achieve at high levels?

Many of our schools, particularly large secondary schools, are based on a one-size-fits-all model. But expanded offerings exist, thanks to growing diversity in our communities and efforts to satisfy a range of needs and interests. Though this desire to add more choice has been appropriate, unfortunately we've gone about it the wrong way.

As communities consider how to provide environments that combine rigor and relationships, school boards can help by developing a new small schools policy for their district. The policy should be two pronged: Create new small schools and redesign large schools. The two complement each other—the former is easier and helps show the possibilities of small schools; the latter is a long, difficult process but one that can make a tremendous difference in the lives of many adolescents.

Why Small Schools?

New small schools can be created quickly, providing valuable incentives for innovative teachers, and changing the communities' sense of what is possible. Overwhelming evidence exists that small schools with unique intellectual missions do a much better job of supporting student success than do large schools. They also offer students and staff the opportunity to experience a more positive school climate.

Small schools have been shown to have significantly higher graduation and college attendance rates, as well as fewer discipline and safety issues than large schools. Small schools also present a tremendous opportunity to involve the community, and examples of this can be seen across the country.

In Oakland, community members, parents, and support groups developed their own ideas for new schools. The project gave the community a voice and sense of ownership. In the Bronx, several community organizations teamed with parents and students to develop plans for 19 new small high schools.

New schools also have the potential to bring new business and community partners to the table. States such as Colorado and Utah are using technology-focused high schools as an integral part of their community development strategy. And a few cities in Washington state, including Seattle and Tacoma, are utilizing small visual and performing arts schools as part of their downtown revitalization strategies.

Finally, cost does not have to be a barrier. Like charters, most small schools operate within the same per-pupil allocation as other public schools and therefore can be created in a cost-effective manner.

Creating Small Schools

In establishing this sort of initiative, districts should examine several small school models. Though there are dozens of models for new schools, only a few, until recently, addressed high schools. Today, however, a number of models for high schools exist, including schools geared toward rigorous applied learning, student-centered structure, and new pathways to college.

Schools such as High Tech High in San Diego and New Tech High in Napa, Calif., offer vocational education in a rigorous applied-learning setting. The schools combine immersion, personalization, and performance-based assessment in a high-tech environment. New Tech High's applied-learning uses a project-based model, digital portfolios, and industry partnerships to prepare students for post-secondary education.

Student-centered schools like the Metropolitan Regional Career and Technical Center (The Met) in South Providence, R.I., or the Minnesota New Country School in Henderson, Minn., tailor learning to a student's interest. The Met uses internships as the primary vehicle for student learning. This model is perfect for engaging students and is great for the 10 percent or so of students who will just not succeed in large, traditional high schools.

A third model allows students an opportunity to earn both a high school diploma and an associate's degree or college credit while in high school. Last fall the National Commission on the High School Senior Year found that the 12th-grade year is often squandered, but in this model, students can be productive as seniors. At Bard High School Early College in Brooklyn, for example, students are immersed in a coherent liberal arts curriculum while also taking college classes.

From Vander Ark, T. (2002). It's all about size. American School Board Journal, *189(7), 34–35. Reprinted with permission of the* American School Board Journal.

They graduate with a high school diploma and an associate's degree in four years.

The three types of schools outlined above could be thought of as applied, alternative, and academic. Any of these models can prepare students for postsecondary success. One is not better than another, and together they represent the sort of options that all students should be able to access. Many schools draw from all three designs and combine the different methods to provide a well-balanced and challenging curriculum.

The Space Challenge

Once a district decides to create a small school, the next challenge is where to put it. Though many districts understand the many advantages of small schools and recognize the need for more quality options, they cannot move beyond the issue of space. There is no easy answer when it comes to creating the space needed for new schools. But small schools can be created without new construction. Small schools can be established in existing space, community space, or leased space.

Some districts use extra space in existing large schools to create smaller campuses. Bard High School Early College, for example, is located on the top floor of a junior high school. Humanities Prep in Manhattan also is located within a larger school. And Chicago's Best Practices High is located with two other schools in a former large high school. The Federal Way Preparatory Academy, near Tacoma, holds classes in six portables in a junior high parking lot.

A number of districts use abandoned buildings or rely on the generosity of the local business and arts community. The Charter School of San Diego uses donated or inexpensive satellite facilities located in office buildings and storefronts. High Tech High is in a former Navy warehouse that was converted with private sector donations. New small arts high schools in Seattle and Tacoma meet in community spaces and museums.

School districts can access various resources to help establish small schools. From community centers to old churches, districts should look in their own backyards to find available space. The point is you have to be creative and use what you can.

Schools of the Future

The coming years will see more than 100 new small schools created, each embracing a different model but all focused on providing the rigor and relationships needed to help all students achieve. Technology-focused high schools like High Tech High will open in more than a dozen communities around the country. Alternative schools that focus on supporting each student's individual interests are gaining favor in Sacramento, Federal Way, Wash., and Minneapolis.

And in the Southeast, the nonprofit group SECME, Inc., will work with historically black colleges and universities, local school districts, and other entities to create eight small early college high schools focused on math, science, and engineering. SECME is a pre-college alliance of school systems, engineering universities, and corporate/government investors who help prepare historically underrepresented students for careers in math, science, and technology.

The Middle College Consortium, which now consists of 23 sites around the country that serve at-risk high school students, will create or redesign 15 small schools in the next decade. Located on community college campuses, these schools will offer five-year programs to help students receive both an associate's degree and a high school diploma.

Districts face daunting challenges today, including improving student achievement on a shoestring budget. But a clear, coherent small schools policy can go a long way toward addressing these and other issues. By creating an array of new small schools, a board can demonstrate its commitment to ensuring that every family has access to a variety of quality educational options that prepare all students for college, work, and citizenship. It is something boards should do for students and for their community.

SCHOOLS SHOULDN'T BE A JUNGLE

Vincent Schrader

Schools are places where students spend the majority of their waking hours. They should be places where students feel comfortable and safe, so that learning can occur. The size of a school can influence the kind of learning environment that occurs. As with Tom Vander Ark in the previous article, Vincent Schrader is a small-school proponent, and he laments the passing of small schools. However, unlike Vander Ark, he focuses on factors other than academic achievement, college attendance, student discipline, and student dropout rates in his discussion. As you read this article, compare Schrader's description of the advantages of small schools to those outlined in the preceding article.

Think About This . . .

1. What do big schools lack that exist in small schools? Why do you suppose this is the case?

2. Schrader describes two higher purposes that have always existed in education. What are they? Do you agree with his assessment of the extent to which our schools are reaching these purposes? Why or why not?

3. What is the ideally sized school? What would be some disadvantages of significantly larger schools? What would be disadvantages of significantly smaller schools? Why do you think so?

4. How will the information in this article influence your decisions when you take your first job? Offer at least two specific factors that you would consider in making your decision.

My first teaching job wasn't in a one-room school, but it was close. Elementary kids were upstairs, 86 high schoolers were downstairs. It was called Ambia School. Once, we got mail addressed to "Amoeba School," a name we thought hilarious, yet a perfect fit. Fresh out of school myself, I was Ambia's entire English department—and frightened by the idea I might be the only English teacher my students ever had.

Yet Ambia glistened as a place of wonder, like Jesse Stuart's school from *The Thread That Runs So True*. Here, small-town and rural kids, rich and poor, smart and otherwise, became family to me. I soon knew each of them so well that I recognized handwriting, even on the restroom walls. We learned, played, laughed, and cried together. I hunted on their parents' farmland, sponsored their student council, scrimmaged with the undermanned basketball team (this was Indiana, so we *did* have a team). Nothing in my career has ever matched this time and place.

But large schools were coming. The drive to close places like Ambia had gathered steam, and we were a target. Sadly, I admit that I supported these efforts to "consolidate." Like many others, I savored the idea of combining nine county schools into a megaschool, complete with planetarium, swimming pool, science labs, and a huge library. The belief that bigger was better was a way of life for me then. It was my first surrender to the notion of reforming education with a "magic bullet"—a mind-set that still permeates education.

An ultramodern school soon bloomed in the middle of the county, and Ambia closed its doors. Kids who once walked or rode short distances to school now rode buses for more than an hour twice a day. At 7:20 a.m., 60 school buses swarmed the new "Benton Central." It was a thrilling sight. But for the kids, it was also terrifying.

From Schrader, V. (2001). School shouldn't be a jungle. As first appeared in Education Week, 21(6), 41, 43. Reprinted with permission of the author.

I joined my Ambia family at the new school. A large-school graduate myself, I thought my students would love the new environment. They did not. After a few months, I knew why. Something here was missing. There was no sense of family. My former students smiled their timid greetings in the hall, and pushed through the milling crowd. Some told me how the big new school oppressed them, how they missed Ambia. I counseled them to be brave, saying they'd get used to their new world. But I missed Ambia, too.

And I noticed other changes. Groups of kids slipped off into subgroups, into cliques, into peripheral cliques outside the mainstream, essentially exiling themselves from their new school society. Suddenly, I didn't know who they all were.

In fact, knowing all the students in this new building was impossible, let alone knowing their brothers and sisters. I didn't know their daily schedules or their teachers. I couldn't simply go next door and discuss a student's progress in other subjects. (All the English teachers were now in our own wing. We had our "club," and didn't talk much to members of other departments.)

At Ambia, the 11 kids in the drama group had all had roles (sometimes even two) in the school play. Now, even talented kids looked on from the sidelines—there weren't enough parts for everyone.

Something else troubled me much more deeply. The new environment had less civility to it, less kindness. The big school wasn't really a bad place, but it was different, and negatively so. It didn't embrace us as had Ambia, where even the neediest child received attention because someone always knew of a problem. Whether the need was for clothes, tutoring, or mothering, a way was found to fill it. We brought used clothes from our own families, taught English after church on Sunday. We were, in a very real sense, a "whole village."

Schools are not like villages anymore. If anything, they are the antithesis. As a society, we dismissed villages years ago as irrelevant. Many disappeared. And every time we took away a neighborhood school, or began busing kids miles down the road to a distant and unfamiliar milieu, we put up walls between children and their metaphorical villages. To be sure, the lucky ones—the bright, the beautiful, the naturally gregarious—survived in these larger settings. But the majority had to settle for a kind of pervasive mediocrity. And what of the truly needy kids? They became invisible.

Most schools today are monuments to impersonality, structured, by their sheer size alone, to allow the disenfranchised to disappear into the brickwork. Rage can fester in such invisibility. Compound the situation with bullying and scapegoating, and you have a recipe for human tragedy. Any teachers or administrators who say that bullying and scapegoating don't go on in their schools are in denial. No school is immune to a determined underground effort to shun or torment the supposed outsider. I've seen it happen every year of my career, even at Ambia. But the difference there was that we adults were able quickly to contain the damage. Kids didn't disappear at Ambia.

Today's world is different, of course, from the one that encompassed Ambia School. We educators need to prepare kids to live in a complex, crowded, and often confusing world. Some policymakers would have us do this by emulating techniques from our most savagely competitive adult social environments. They would have us stress business-honed performance standards, complete with standardized testing for a final Darwinian culling.

But we must ask ourselves: Do we want our kids to believe they have a fair chance to compete in learning and in life if they but apply themselves? Or do we want them to discard aspiration and consent to dreams no larger than their social station? If kids "learn what they live," and their school life is a version of "survival of the fittest," an impersonal jungle, what model of society have we given them? What will they aspire to?

Our schools cannot remain as they are. Education's higher purpose has always been to give kids the knowledge they need, and to present them with a social example they can emulate in order to create the world we all want. It seems to me we've gotten pretty good at delivering knowledge (and testing it). But if our news headlines are any gauge, we are failing in our role of teaching tolerance, celebrating diversity, and protecting personal liberties. At Ambia, I taught two children whose IQs differed by almost 90 points. The smarter one tutored the weaker one. The weaker one worshipped his peer teacher, and the smarter one learned deep and lasting lessons from his tutored friend. Today, both are living full lives.

If we want all our students to succeed, reducing the size of our schools is a place to start. Psychologists have long known of the memory lapses that accompany increases in number. Some argue that the maximum school size for normal minds to deal with effectively (I'm thinking of teachers here) is about 600 students. And even this number can tax the memory. (It always took me until October to remember all the new kids' names.)

There are some efforts under way to restrict various school populations to fewer than 200 students. Research demonstrates that violence and disruption recede in schools of this size. Is such a course costly? Advocates say that if it were done right, achieving such reductions in scale would cost no more than we pay now for schooling. Given that we spend over $40,000 a year to maintain just one young person in a jail, does it not also make sense to consider the human as well as the economic savings that might accrue with reduced school enrollments, especially in high-risk settings?

Is this another silver bullet? I think not. Certainly, small schools can also be terrible places. We still depend on the good hearts and singular talents of dedicated principals and teachers to make schools work. But today, even our very best educators are fighting simple statistical inevitabilities. Massive school size virtually guarantees that at least one student's small fire will go undetected until it rages as an inferno. Smaller schools increase our odds for intervention. They reduce the social space between us, and force us all to see one another as individuals, not as members of an uncaring crowd.

We must put kids back into schools they will love and cherish. We need to return to environments that are able to show children what is best in the society we want them to build and maintain. At the very least, we must foster environments that will allow us to identify those destined to fade into the brickwork—and do so before they begin building walls of their own.

I'm hoping that we start this process by remembering the Ambias that nurtured most of us who now teach. I'm hoping we make things small again, and create worlds where, once again, everyone feels a sense of belonging.

As for me, I look forward to attending this year's Ambia School reunion. All of the graduates from all of the years it existed meet annually to keep Ambia alive in their hearts. I'll be there. After all, I'm part of the family.

PREVENTING SCHOOL VIOLENCE

Karen F. Osterman

Students cannot grow and develop in unsafe learning environments, and school safety is on everyone's minds in light of recent violence in schools. In this article Karen Osterman examines the link between students' emotional health and the problem of school violence. She discusses research that suggests that rejection, by both teachers and peers, can result in serious problems for isolated students. As you read this article ask yourself, "What role can teachers play in creating healthy learning environments for all students?"

Think About This . . .

1. What effect do peer relationships have on learning? What effect do they have on emotional health? Why do you think there is a difference?

2. In terms of peer relationships, how are elementary schools different from secondary schools? What do these differences suggest for teachers?

3. How do teachers and students contribute to the creation of social isolates? What can be done to prevent this problem?

4. What specific actions can you take in your classroom to minimize the possibility of social isolation in your students?

I am both a parent and a professor. A few years ago, after hearing repeated complaints from high school students about how isolated and lonely they felt, I did a small observational study. Two doctoral assistants and I followed six students through an entire day. What we found was that these students—from high-, average-, and low-ability groups—had very little, if any, contact with other students during the school day. There were few opportunities to interact with peers in classes and little interaction in the halls or in the cafeteria.

Many of my professional colleagues didn't seem too concerned about this, so I decided to look into the research more deeply and see what I could learn about peer relationships. Were they important, and what kinds of factors influenced the quality of the relationships among students? What I learned in an analysis of over 150 research studies has, I believe, important implications for preventing student violence.[1]

First, we found that peer relationships were important, but not for the reason that I thought. Originally, I had thought that positive peer relationships would have a direct effect on student learning. But what I found was that the quality of students' relationships with teachers had the most direct and significant effect on students' involvement in learning. Peer relationships, however, had a very significant impact on students' emotional health. Rejection by peers was devastating and particularly so for boys with a high need for affiliation. This gender difference is probably related to the facts that boys have fewer friends and that masculine stereotypes make it difficult for boys to express their need for friends and emotional support. Boys who want to be accepted by other boys can't afford to complain or to seek adult assistance in dealing with their problems.

The other important finding was that many children in elementary and secondary schools have no friends and are not part of any group. Not being a part of a group, however, is not as important as is rejection. It's okay not to be popular. But if you're ostracized from the group, that's when the trouble begins. This is likely to be more problematic in secondary school than in elementary school simply because of the school structure. For the most part students in elementary school remain together with a single group of peers and a single teacher, but even this "family-like" arrangement is no barrier to bullying and victimization. At the secondary level, departmentalization contributes even more to fragmentation, and there are fewer opportunities for students to develop positive relationships with others.

Research also tells us a lot about what happens in schools that contributes to peer rejection and also what can be done to prevent it. The most important fact here is that students who are rejected by their peers are also rejected by their teachers and by other adults in the school. Students who are rejected by the whole school community, in effect, are those who are different in some way: they don't dress well, they're not physically attractive, and they're not socially attractive. They may be bright, but they're not typical learners. They either have behavior problems or are withdrawn. The behavior problems get attention from teachers, but it's negative attention. Those students who are withdrawn are no more able to develop a positive relationship with teachers than with their peers. This lack of support from anyone exacerbates the sense of emotional isolation.

Students who are rejected by teachers and peers become more and more isolated. Teachers avoid them or criticize them, and peers refuse to work with them in class or on projects. Feeling rejected, these students avoid even trying to join in extracurricular activities. It's hard for adults to enter a room where they know no one. It's even harder for a teen to enter a room when he knows that people don't like him and, even worse, might subject him to the type of verbal abuse— including attacks on his sexual identity—that cuts to the quick.

So what can educators do about this? Research also establishes one extremely important point: if you give people a chance to interact, they will get to know one another, and, even if they don't become friends, they'll become more tolerant. What does this mean for schools? I believe that these and other findings suggest a number of strategies.

1. *Establish the ground rules: harassment and abuse in the classroom and in the school are not acceptable.* Young people respond to adult rules, and adults in schools are frequently aware of student harassment. In fact, much of it takes place right in the classroom. Like so many other people in our society, educators assume that this harassment is a natural part of growing up, and they often ignore it or blame the child who is being harassed. Tolerating harassment sends a message that it's okay. The rules need to be clear, and they need to be enforced.

2. *Promote a culture of tolerance and acceptance.* At a minimum, prevent abuse. But go beyond that to develop a culture that encourages not just tolerance for diversity, but caring and respect. This must be done through word and action. Express your values and

From Osterman, K. (2003). *Preventing school violence.* Phi Delta Kappan, 84(8), 622–627. *Reprinted with permission of the author.*

encourage adults and students to extend themselves for others. Do unto others what you would have them do unto one another. Emphasize modeling and recognition, rather than control and punishment.

3. *Reach out to students who are a little different.* Students need adult support, whether they are in sixth grade or ninth grade. Sometimes it's difficult to approach young people, particularly teens, because their body language and even their spoken words convey a message to leave them alone. They don't mean it. Another important research finding is that people—youngsters and adults—need to feel that they belong and that the people they work with care for them. Adults can't tolerate working in a hostile environment; young people are even less prepared to do so.

Sometimes educators get so focused on academic learning that they forget that children have emotional needs. Students need to feel that others care about them, they need to feel that they are competent, and they need to have their autonomy respected. In an action research project designed to remedy the problem of bullying and victimization in elementary classrooms, a group of teachers working with their principal began by examining their own classroom practice.[2] After observing for several weeks, they were surprised to find few occasions when the students were positively involved with the teacher or with peers and few opportunities for students to feel good about themselves.

With this new awareness, they began to interact more with victimized students. They talked to them about classwork and about their lives. They worked with them and figured out how to use their talents in the classroom. As a result, they found that they developed a new appreciation for these children. They liked them more, and they saw sides of their personalities that they had never seen. The children blossomed: they smiled more, they had more self-confidence, they became more engaged in classroom work, and they began to reach out more to the teacher and to their peers. Everyone responded.

Initially, the teachers expressed the opinion that the children—or their parents—were responsible for the way others treated them. This experience led them to change their thinking. They came to realize that they, as teachers, played an important role in shaping these students experience in the classroom. They also realized that the quality of their interaction with these students seemed to affect how the other students treated the "victim." When they began to treat these students differently and demonstrated their affection and concern for them, the other students in the class did so too.

Children who are rejected are children who are neglected. Their behavior is a natural response to this rejection. Adults feel depressed when their colleagues don't like them. It's much worse for children, whose whole world is their school and friends.

4. *Provide opportunities for students to get to know one another.* Most adults, educators included, assume that because teens tend to look alike and act alike, they're all part of one big happy group. That's a myth. Many students are isolated and have no chance in their classes to get to know one another. In the action research project I mentioned above, the teachers observed that cooperative learning groups would refuse to allow certain students to work with them. The teachers established rules that no one could be turned away. And the students who had once shunned some of their peers had experiences similar to those of the teachers: when they had a chance to work with these formerly rejected youngsters, they got to like them better. And students don't bully their friends. We need to help students to become friends.

Educators who work with adults regularly incorporate activities into the classroom that are designed to develop a strong sense of community. They use "ice breakers" to make sure that people in the group get to know one another. They assign people to groups, and they rotate membership in the groups. They use information about learning patterns to develop groups to ensure that they have the resources to be successful. Orientation programs and extracurricular activities are also important, but the largest part of any student's day is spent in the classroom. These strategies can also help younger students get to know and appreciate one another. The students' learning—and their emotional health—depends on it.

Implementing these strategies is not as simple as installing a metal detector, and it requires the effort of everyone in the school community—teachers, librarians, secretaries, administrators, guidance counselors, lunchroom monitors, custodians, and bus drivers. We need to make schools places where students can feel safe emotionally. Making that happen will go a long way toward ensuring their physical safety as well.

Notes

1. Karen F. Osterman, Students' need for belonging in the school community, *Review of Educational Research,* Fall 2001, pp. 323–67.
2. Karen Siris, *Using action research to alleviate bullying and victimization in the classroom,* unpublished Doctoral dissertation, Hofstra University, 2001.

DRESS CODES AND SOCIAL CHAOS

John Northrop

Dress codes have emerged as one attempt to make our schools better places to learn. Advocates claim they minimize social class differences, discourage gangs, and eliminate clothes-related distractions in schools. John Northrop begins his article by describing a television advertisement in which a mother encourages rather than discourages the provocative dress promoted by marketers. He raises the question of whether schools more nearly reflect than define community values and whether educators are more concerned than necessary about issues such as dress codes. Northrop also identifies the mobility of American people and the rise of marketing and entertainment media as forces that are shaping the values of our society. As you read this article ask yourself, "Do dress codes contribute to the learning environment in a school?"

Think About This . . .

1. Describe an important difference in current attitudes compared to those in the past with respect to rules. Why do you suppose this attitude exists?
2. What rationale does Northrop offer for banning forms of dress, such as hip-hugging jeans and bare midriffs? Do you agree that these forms of dress should be banned? Why or why not?
3. According to Northrop, what is the base question for any school? What other questions do you believe schools should be asking in order to best serve students?
4. You are in a school that has a dress code that is strict and unpopular with students. How might you respond to student complaints about the dress code? Provide an example to illustrate your description.

Ok, I admit it: I haven't actually seen the TV ad, but so many people have told me about it that I know it's for real. It's a clothing ad by a mainstream retailer. It depicts a mother tugging her teenage daughter's jeans down to her hips so that the youngster's midriff shows below her blouse. "Now that's the way you do it!" coos the attentive mom. Hmmm. At the risk of sounding a lot like my own mother 20 years ago, that's one media message that rubs me raw.

Secondary schools struggle each day to keep the lid on a tempest of adolescent hormones—for example, by forbidding bare midriffs and other skimpy dress choices. Ads like this make us wonder if there's any use. How can anyone expect to keep children fully clothed in school when national advertisers celebrate parents' peeling back the boundaries during prime time? Talk about holding up an umbrella against a tsunami!

Maybe educators worry too much. After all, schools arguably do less to define community values than to reflect and reinforce the values of the communities they serve. School dress codes are an issue only as community values become fragmented or in flux. Since the 1950s, when communities tended to be more isolated and homogeneous—sometimes in dreadful ways, to be sure—prevailing standards have become harder to define.

These days, at least two powerful forces are at work in the re-valuing of American society. First, Americans are more mobile than they used to be, with more "outsiders" moving into and out of localities, disturbing local conventions and infusing new ideas and expectations. Even more influential than this mobility is the explosive

From Northrop, J. (2002). Dress codes and social chaos. As first appeared in Education Week, 21(8), 36. Reprinted with permission of the author.

rise of new marketing and entertainment media, strategies, and techniques. Modern merchants of thought and sensation jump every geographical boundary and invade every corner of life.

Americans relish fad and fashion. Like dogs chasing their own tails, we race through feverish cycles of consumption, sparked by constant redefinitions of "need." With pressure through all available channels, we find ourselves lured on by successive twists in taste and behavior, drawn toward something faster, more hip, more daring. The frontier of experimentation continues to expand, reaching even into younger age groups.

Maybe it's only human. People love their toys. But I think we cross a dangerous line when we seem to treat our children as toys themselves. No child should become a Barbie or Ken doll to dress or undress according to the style of the month. With children, we really ought to hold on to some conservative old certainties—for example, the notion that how you dress is ultimately far less important than what and how you think. That's one message school systems send when they require student uniforms.

Of course, like birch bark, even superficial concerns can kindle fires—for example, a recent media blaze in Birmingham, Ala., over a boy's desire to wear earrings to his elementary school, despite a school rule to the contrary. Regardless of how you view the fashion or the rule, what really interests me in the earring dispute is how it underscores a huge shift in school–parent relations: Not so long ago, it was rare indeed for a parent to contest a school's authority to set and enforce rules of dress and behavior. These days, every rule seems open to challenge. Why is that?

A retired principal suggests that everything began to come unglued back in the late 1960s, when schools began letting boys into class wearing blue jeans instead of creased slacks. As dress and appearance fell prey to an increasingly permissive attitude in school, a general malaise began to spread. Call it the domino theory of social chaos: By donning denim, we eased down a slippery slope away from enforceable school expectations toward total cultural disintegration.

Even if doomsday for American civilization is just around the bend, it's hard to see jeans alone as responsible—after all, many former "denimistas" like me now wear suits and ties most workdays. I think where we find ourselves today results from a host of cultural influences that began to chip away at certainty and conformity 25 years ago. Remember Watergate and the Pentagon Papers, which convinced a lot of people you can't trust what government says? Remember the burger-ad mantra urging us to "Have it your way"? Remember the bumper sticker, "Question Authority"?

Public schools are reaping some of the consequences of our post-traumatic social rearrangements. Today in schools we often find ourselves answering what may be the single most subversive question it is possible to ask: *Why?* For example, at my school, the state's school of fine arts, there's this: Why will you not let my 15-year-old son or daughter wear a muscle shirt or tank top to class?

Old answers that parents used to give children—answers like "because I said so," or "because that's the way it is"—don't find much traction when grown-ups are posing the questions. More and more, people expect a clear and cogent rationale before they decide to put up with rules and decisions they may not like.

I don't mind giving such answers. For example, it doesn't bother me to say that we ban bare midriffs in our school *not* because we think they are vulgar or offensive; in fact, they have a place on the beach. We ban bare midriffs because we see them as unwelcome and unnecessary distractions that can divert too much student attention from the serious intellectual work we're here to do together.

As tricky as it may be to limit individualism in an art school—art, after all, grows out of individual perception, judgment, experiment, and expression—the basic question here is the same as in any school: How do we strike and hold a workable balance that best serves individual and group needs within a specific community of learners?

From where I stand, that balancing act, like juggling eggs on a high wire, seems to be at least as much art as science.

THE CIVIC PERILS OF HOMESCHOOLING
Rob Reich

In this section we have been reading about different concepts of an ideal school. Perhaps the most radical view of an effective school is one in which students do not go to school at all; instead, they are homeschooled by their parents. Homeschooling is one of the fastest growing trends in education, attracting proponents from both the conservative right and the liberal left. Homeschooling advocates are attracted by the opportunities to customize their children's education, to give them something lacking in the public schools. But this customizing comes at a price, Rob Reich asserts. Children who are homeschooled may not develop the same citizenship skills necessary in a modern, diverse democracy such as ours. As you read this article ask yourself, "How should educators respond to the homeschooling movement?"

Think About This . . .

1. Historically, what two groups have opted for homeschooling? How are their motivations similar and different?
2. What is the "consumption view" of education, and what does Reich feel are limitations of this view?
3. What are the central components of education for citizenship? How do schools address these components?
4. What role will individual needs and requests from parents play in your classroom? How important is it that all of your students receive a common education experience?

Just 10 years ago, educating a child at home was illegal in several states. Today, not only is homeschooling legal everywhere, it's booming. Home-schooling is probably the fastest-growing segment of the education market, expanding at a rate of 15 to 20 percent a year (Lines, 2000a). More children are homeschooled than attend charter schools. More children are homeschooled than attend conservative Christian academies.

And it's not just left-wing unschoolers and right-wing religious fundamentalists who are keeping their children at home. Taking advantage of the Internet and other new technologies, more middle-of-the-road suburbanites are homeschooling, too. *Time* and *Newsweek* have featured homeschooling on their covers. The U.S. Congress passed a resolution in 1999 declaring the week of September 19 to be National Home Education Week. Homeschooling has gone mainstream.

In response to the rise of homeschooling, policymakers and public school administrators and teachers need to consider what makes homeschooling so popular.

Chief among the many reasons to homeschool is the ability to customize a child's education at home.

Customizing Education at Home

The ability to custom-tailor an education for their children is often the motivation for parents to homeschool. No other education arrangement offers the same freedom to arrange an education designed for an individual student; in homeschools, parents are responsible not only for selecting what their children will learn, but when, how, and with whom they will learn. In this sense, homeschooling represents the apex of customization in education.

But is this customization always a good thing? From the standpoint of the parents who choose to homeschool,

From Reich, R. (2002). *The civic perils of homeschooling.* Educational Leadership, 59(7), 56–59. *Reprinted with permission of the Association for Supervision and Curriculum Development.*

it surely is; they wouldn't be doing it otherwise, especially in light of the considerable energy and time it requires of them. But considered from the standpoint of democratic citizenship, the opportunity to customize education through homeschooling isn't an unadulterated good. Customizing education may permit schooling to be tailored for each individual student, but total customization also threatens to insulate students from exposure to diverse ideas and people and thereby to shield them from the vibrancy of a pluralistic democracy. These risks are perhaps greatest for homeschoolers. To understand why, we need first to understand more about the current practice of homeschooling.

Homeschooling Today

Homeschooling is more than an education alternative. It is also a social movement (Stevens, 2001; Talbot, 2001). In 1985, approximately 50,000 children were being educated at home. In 2002, at least 1 million children are being homeschooled, with some estimates pegging the number at 2 million, an increase of 20- or 40-fold. (It's symptomatic of the unregulated environment of homeschooling that precise figures on the number of homeschoolers are impossible to establish.) Depending on the estimate you choose (Bielick, Chandler, & Broughman, 2001; Lines, 2000a), homeschoolers account for 2–4 percent of the school-going population.

Homeschooling parents are politically active. Former Pennsylvania Representative Bill Goodling, the former chair of the House Committee on Education and the Workforce, has called homeschoolers "the most effective education lobby on Capitol Hill" (as cited in Golden, 2000). Homeschoolers have established both local and national networks for lobbying purposes and for offering curricular support to one another. Several national organizations, led by the Home School Legal Defense Association, promote homeschooling. Even the former Secretary of Education, William Bennett, is a fan—he has created a for-profit company called K12, the purpose of which is to supply curricular and testing materials to homeschoolers.

But who homeschools, and why? Two main groups of homeschoolers have emerged, both of which raise difficult questions about customization.

The larger of the groups is the Christian right. Although homeschooling has become a much more diverse enterprise in the past 10 years, its strength as a social movement and the majority of its practitioners are conservative Christians. Precise data are scarce, but researchers tend to agree that whereas homeschools of the 1970s "reflected a liberal, humanistic, pedagogical orientation," the majority of homeschools in the 1980s and 1990s "became grounds of and for ideological, conservative, religious expressions of educational matters" (Carper, 2000, p. 16). Today, most parents choose to educate their children at home because they believe that their children's moral and spiritual needs will not be met in campus-based schools.

Those who educate their children at home for religious reasons often object to the secular bias of public schools. By keeping their children at home, they seek to provide a proper religious education free from the damning influences of secularism and pop culture. These homeschoolers wish to avoid the public school at all costs.

The second group practices a different kind of homeschooling. They seek partnerships with public schools to avail themselves of resources, support, guidance, and extracurricular activities that they could not otherwise obtain or provide at home. For these parents, some participation in public schools is desirable.

Various mechanisms have emerged to allow homeschooled students to connect on a partial basis with the public school system. In California, for example, approximately 10 percent of the charter schools serve students whose primary learning is at home (Lines, 2000b). Other districts have set up "virtual" academies online to aid in the enrollment of homeschoolers. Still other school districts permit students to attend some classes but not others and to participate in extracurricular activities (Rothstein, 2002). Finally, a few public school districts have set up homeschooling resource centers, staffed by public school teachers and professional curriculum developers, that homeschooling parents can use at their convenience.

Democratic Citizenship and Customization

Each kind of homeschooler—the family who teaches the child solely at home and the family who seeks some interaction with the public school system—is practicing customization in education. For the first, parents can tailor the education environment to their own convictions and to their beliefs about what their child's needs and interests are. For the second, parents can select the aspects of the public system they and their child want, creating an overall program designed for their child.

What's to worry about either kind of customization? Let me put the matter quite simply. Customizing a child's education through homeschooling represents the victory of a consumer mentality within education, suggesting that the only purpose that education should serve is to please and satisfy the preferences of the consumer. Education, in my view, is not a consumption item in the same sense as the food we select from the grocery store.

Many homeschoolers would surely protest here that their energetic efforts to overcome numerous obstacles to educate their children at home are motivated by a desire to shield their children from rampant consumerism and to offer their children a moral environment in which they learn deeper and more important values. No doubt this is true.

But my point is not that homeschooling parents are inculcating in their children a consumer mentality. My point is that many homeschooling parents view the education of their children as a matter properly under their control and no one else's. They feel entitled to "purchase" the education environment of their children from the marketplace of learning materials, with no intermediary between them and their child. The first kind of homeschooler actually does purchase learning materials for the home. The second kind of homeschooler treats the public school system as a provider of services and activities from which parents choose what they want, as if it were a restaurant with an extensive menu.

And this attitude is the crucial point. Homeschooling is the apogee of parental control over a child's education, where no other institution has a claim to influence the schooling of the child. Parents serve as the only filter for a child's education, the final arbiters of what gets included and what gets excluded.

This potentially compromises citizenship in the following ways:

• In a diverse, democratic society, part of able citizenship is to come to respect the fact that other people will have beliefs and convictions, religious and otherwise, that conflict with one's own. Yet from the standpoint of citizenship, these other people are equals. And students must learn not only that such people exist, but how to engage and deliberate with them in the public arena. Thus, students should encounter materials, ideas, and people that they or their parents have not chosen or selected in advance.

• Citizenship is the social glue that binds a diverse people together. To be a citizen is to share something in common with one's fellow citizens. As the legal scholar Sunstein (2001) has argued, a heterogeneous society without some shared experiences and common values has a difficult time addressing common problems and risks social fragmentation. Schooling is one of the few remaining social institutions—or civic intermediaries—in which people from all walks of life have a common interest and in which children might come to learn such common values as decency, civility, and respect.

• Part of being a citizen is exercising one's freedom. Indeed, the freedoms that U.S. citizens enjoy are a democratic inheritance that we too often take for granted. But to be free is not simply to be free from coercion or constraint. Democratic freedom requires the free construction and possible revision of beliefs and preferences. To become free, students must be exposed to the vibrant diversity of a democratic society so that they possess the liberty to live a life of their own design.

Because homeschooled students receive highly customized educations, designed usually to accord with the preferences of parents, they are least likely in principle to be exposed to materials, ideas, and people that have not been chosen in advance; they are least likely to share common education experiences with other children; and they are most likely to have a narrow horizon of experiences, which can curtail their freedom. Although highly customized education for students may produce satisfied parents as consumers, and even offer excellent academic training to the student, it is a loss from a civic perspective.

Civic Perils

I do not argue that homeschooling undermines citizenship in all cases. On the contrary, I have elsewhere defended the practice of homeschooling, when properly regulated (Reich, 2002). Many homeschooling parents are deeply committed to providing their children with an education that introduces them to a great diversity of ideas and people. And for those homeschoolers who seek partnerships with public schools, their children do participate in common institutions with other children. I do not intend to condemn homeschooling wholesale, for I have met many homeschooled students who are better prepared for democratic citizenship than the average public school student.

My claim is about the potential civic perils of a homeschooled education, where schooling is customizable down to the tiniest degree. Customization, and, therefore, homeschooling, seem wonderful if we think about education as a consumption item. But schooling, from the time that public schools were founded until today, has served to cultivate democratic citizenship. And though this may be a largely forgotten aim, as many have argued, we should not allow a new consumer mentality to become the driving metaphor for the education of children.

References

Bielick, S., Chandler, K., & Broughman, S. (2001, July 31). *Home schooling in the United States: 1999* (NCES 2001-033). Washington, DC: U.S. Department of Education.

Carper, J. C. (2000, April). Pluralism to establishment to dissent: The religious and educational context of home schooling. *Peabody Journal of Education, 75*(1, 2), 8–19.

Golden, D. (2000, April 24). Homeschoolers learn how to gain clout inside the beltway. *Wall Street Journal,* p. A1.

Lines, P. (2000a, Summer). Home schooling comes of age. *Public Interest, 140,* 74–85.

Lines, P. (2000b, April). When homeschoolers go to school: A partnership between families and schools. *Peabody Journal of Education, 75*(1, 2), 159–186.

Reich, R. (2002). *Bridging liberalism and multiculturalism in American education.* Chicago: University of Chicago Press.

Rothstein, R. (2002, January 2). Augmenting a home-school education. *New York Times,* p. B11.

Stevens, M. (2001). *Kingdom of children: Culture and controversy in the home-schooling movement.* Princeton, NJ: Princeton University Press.

Sunstein, C. (2001). *Republic.com.* Princeton, NJ: Princeton University Press.

Talbot, M. (2001, November). The new counterculture. *Atlantic Monthly, 288*(4), 136–143.

ADDITIONAL READINGS

Black, S. (2003). The creative classroom. *American School Board Journal, 190*(9), 68–71.

Boyer, E. (1995). *The basic school: A community for learning.* Princeton, NJ: The Carnegie Foundation for the Advancement of Teaching.

Darling-Hammond, L. (1997). *The right to learn.* San Francisco: Jossey-Bass.

Hofferth, S., & Jankuniene, Z. (2001). Life after school. *Educational Leadership, 58*(7), 19–23.

Johnson, K. (2002). The downside to small class policies. *Educational Leadership, 59*(5), 27–29.

Marzano, R. (2003). *What works in schools.* Alexandria, VA: Association for Supervision and Curriculum Development.

Oakes, J. (1992). Can tracking research inform practice? *Educational Researcher, 21*(4), 12–21.

Spitalli, S. (2003). Breaking the codes of silence. *American School Board Journal, 190*(9), 56–58.

Wasley, P. (2002). Small classes, small schools: The time is now. *Educational Leadership, 59*(5), 6–10.

EXPLORING THE INTERNET

National School-to-Work Home Page
http://www.lake.k12.fl.us/stw

The Alliance for Parental Involvement in Education
http://www.croton.com/allpie
A nonprofit organization that assists and encourages parental involvement in education, wherever that education takes place—in public schools, in private schools, or at home.

The National Coalition for Parent Involvement in Education (NCPIE)
http://www.ncpie.org
NCPIE is dedicated to developing effective family–school partnerships in schools throughout America.

The National PTA Home Page
http://www.pta.org
Provides information as well as other links for PTA organizations.

PART FOUR

Curriculum

Curriculum can be defined in a variety of ways, including

- the subject matter taught to students
- a course of study . . . a systematic arrangement of courses
- the planned educational experiences offered by a school
- the experiences students have under the guidance of the school
- the processes teachers go through in selecting and organizing learning experiences for their students (Armstrong, 2003; Parkay & Hass, 2000)

Summarizing these definitions, *curriculum* can be described as everything students learn, or do not learn, in school (Kauchak & Eggen, 2005).

The content of the American school curriculum has undergone many changes throughout the history of our country. In colonial times, for example, religion was an integral part of the school curriculum, and educating citizens to thwart Satan's trickery was an important goal. This colonial legacy has left curriculum issues that remain today, such as how religious topics and the development of ethics and morals should be handled. Over time the perceived needs of the colonies changed, and the content of the curriculum quickly expanded to include practical subjects such as navigation, astronomy, bookkeeping, logic, and rhetoric.

With changing conceptions of the needs of our country and its citizenry, further modifications occurred. Religion was downplayed, and content became more practical. Today, for example, only a few private, highly specialized schools include courses in logic or rhetoric. History, geography, science, and—with the westward expansion of our country—agriculture were added to the curriculum. Gradually, the curriculum evolved to what we have today.

World events also have influenced the curriculum throughout history. The Soviet launching of Sputnik in 1957, for example, triggered alarms in this country about the adequacy of our schools, and math and science were given a major boost as a result. Additional concerns precipitated by prominent reports such as *A Nation at Risk,* published in 1983, resulted in a number of reforms and attempts to make the curriculum more rigorous.

As the role and effectiveness of schools continues to be examined and curriculum continues to evolve, historical questions remain and new ones emerge. Some of those questions are as follows: What should the curriculum of the 21st century include and how should it be organized? How has the era of high-stakes testing influenced the curriculum? Should the teaching of values and morals be part of the curriculum, and if so, how should these concepts be taught? To what extent should religious topics be included in the curriculum and how should they be taught? How should controversial issues, such as the teaching of *evolution* versus *creationism* or *intelligent design,* be handled? What role should extracurricular activities play? Keep these questions in mind as you study the articles in this section.

THE CORE KNOWLEDGE CURRICULUM— WHAT'S BEHIND ITS SUCCESS?

E. D. Hirsch, Jr.

What are the benefits of teaching children a core of knowledge as a central component of the school curriculum? E. D. Hirsch, Jr., asks this question and presents arguments for providing all students with a common core of knowledge. These arguments range from the importance of background knowledge in thinking and problem solving to practical ones in which a class of diverse learners has a common knowledge base. As you read this article ask yourself, "How important is a common core of knowledge for successful learning in classrooms?"

Think About This . . .

1. Is a core curriculum the same as a "rich" curriculum? How are they similar and how are they different?
2. From a core curriculum perspective, what is the most important factor influencing individual differences? From this perspective, how can teachers address individual differences?
3. Critics contend that in this age of information overload, students need to know how to access knowledge, not learn more. How valid is Hirsch's reply to these critics?
4. How much will the core curriculum influence your classroom? Provide a specific example.

The Mohegan School, in the South Bronx, is surrounded by the evidence of urban blight: trash, abandoned cars, crack houses. The students, mostly Latino or African-American, all qualify for free lunch. This public elementary school is located in the innermost inner city.

In January 1992, *CBS Evening News* devoted an "Eye on America" segment to the Mohegan School. Why did CBS focus on Mohegan of several schools that had experienced dramatic improvements after adopting the Core Knowledge guidelines? I think it was in part because this school seemed an unlikely place for a low-cost, academically solid program like Core Knowledge to succeed.

Mohegan's talented principal, Jeffrey Litt, wrote to tell me that "the richness of the curriculum is of particular importance" to his students because their educational experience, like that of "most poverty-stricken and educationally underserved students, was limited to remedial activities." Since adopting the Core Knowledge curriculum, however, Mohegan's students are engaged in the integrated and coherent study of topics like: Ancient Egypt, Greece, and Rome; the Industrial

Revolution; limericks, haiku, and poetry; Rembrandt, Monet, and Michelangelo; Beethoven and Mozart; the Underground Railroad; the Trail of Tears; *Brown v. Board of Education;* the Mexican Revolution; photosynthesis; medieval African empires; the Bill of Rights; ecosystems; women's suffrage; the Harlem Renaissance—and many more.

The Philosophy Behind Core Knowledge

In addition to offering compelling subject matter, the Core Knowledge guidelines for elementary schools are far more specific than those issued by most school districts. Instead of vague outcomes such as "First

From Hirsch, E. D. (1993). *The Core Knowledge curriculum—What's behind its success?* Educational Leadership, 50(8), 23–25, 27–30. *Reprinted with permission of the Association for Supervision and Curriculum Development.*

graders will be introduced to map skills," the geography section of the *Core Knowledge Sequence* specifies that 1st graders will learn the meaning of "east," "west," "north," and "south" and locate on a map the equator, the Atlantic and Pacific Oceans, the seven continents, the United States, Mexico, Canada, and Central America.

Our aim in providing specific grade-by-grade guidelines—developed after several years of research, consultation, consensus-building, and field-testing—is *not* to claim that the content we recommend is better than some other well-thought-out core. No specific guidelines could plausibly claim to be the Platonic ideal. But one must make a start. To get beyond the talking stage, we created the best specific guidelines we could.

Nor is it our aim to specify *everything* that American schoolchildren should learn (the Core Knowledge guidelines are meant to constitute about 50 percent of a school's curriculum, thus leaving the other half to be tailored to a district, school, or classroom). Rather, our point is that a core of shared knowledge, grade by grade, is needed to achieve excellence and fairness in elementary education.

International studies have shown that *any* school that puts into practice a similarly challenging and specific program will provide a more effective and fair education than one that lacks such commonality of content in each grade.[1] High-performing systems such as those in France, Sweden, Japan, and West Germany bear out this principle. It was our intent to test whether in rural, urban, and suburban settings of the United States we would find what other nations have already discovered.

Certainly the finding that a schoolwide core sequence greatly enhances achievement *for all* is supported at the Mohegan School. Disciplinary problems there are down; teacher and student attendance are up, as are scores on standardized tests. Some of the teachers have even transferred their own children to the school, and some parents have taken their children out of private schools to send them to Mohegan. Similar results are being reported at some 65 schools across the nation that are taking steps to integrate the Core Knowledge guidelines into their curriculums.

In the broadcast feature about the Mohegan School, I was especially interested to hear 5th grade teacher Evelyn Hernandez say that Core Knowledge "tremendously increased the students' ability to question." In other words, based on that teacher's classroom experience, *a coherent approach to specific content enhances students' critical thinking and higher-order thinking skills.*

I emphasize this point because a standard objection to teaching specific content is that critical thinking suffers when a teacher emphasizes "mere information." Yet Core Knowledge teachers across the nation report that a coherent focus on content leads to higher-order thinking skills more securely than any other approach they know, including attempts to inculcate such skills directly. As an added benefit, children acquire knowledge that they will find useful not just in next year's classroom but for the rest of their lives.

Why Core Knowledge Works

Here are some of the research findings that explain the correlation between a coherent, specific approach to knowledge and the development of higher-order skills.

Learning can be fun, but is nonetheless cumulative and sometimes arduous. The dream of inventing methods to streamline the time-consuming activity of learning is as old as the hills. In antiquity it was already an old story. Proclus records an anecdote about an encounter between Euclid, the inventor of geometry, and King Ptolemy I of Egypt (276–196 B.C.), who was impatiently trying to follow Euclid's *Elements* step by laborious step. Exasperated, the king demanded a faster, easier way to learn geometry—to which Euclid gave the famous, and still true, reply: "There is no royal road to geometry."

Even with computer technology, it's far from easy to find shortcuts to the basic human activity of learning. The human brain sets limits on the potential for educational innovation. We can't, for instance, put a faster chip in the human brain. The frequency of its central processing unit is timed in thousandths rather than millionths of a second.[2] Nor can we change the fundamental, constructivist psychology of the learning process, which dictates that we humans must acquire new knowledge much as a tree acquires new leaves. The old leaves actively help nourish the new. The more "old growth" (prior knowledge) we have, the faster new growth can occur, making learning an organic process in which knowledge builds upon knowledge.

Because modern classrooms cannot effectively deliver completely individualized instruction, effective education requires grade-by-grade shared knowledge. When an individual child "gets" what is being taught in a classroom, it is like someone understanding a joke. A click occurs. If you have the requisite background knowledge, you will get the joke, but if you don't, you will remain puzzled until somebody explains the knowledge that was taken for granted. Similarly, a classroom of 25 to 35 children can move forward as a group only when *all* the children have the knowledge that is necessary to "getting" the next step in learning.

Studies comparing elementary schools in the United States to schools in countries with Core Knowledge systems disclose a striking difference in the structure of classroom activities.[3] In the best-performing classrooms constant back-and-forth interaction among groups of students and between students and the teacher consumes more than 80 percent of classroom time. By contrast, in the United States, over 50 percent of student time is spent in silent isolation.[4]

Behind the undue amount of "alone time" in our schools stands a theory that goes as follows: Every child is a unique individual; hence each child should receive instruction paced and tailored to that child. The theory should inform classroom practice as far as feasible: one hopes for teachers sensitive to the individual child's needs and strengths. The theory also reveals why good classroom teaching is difficult, and why a one-on-one tutorial is the most effective form of instruction. But modern education cannot be conducted as a one-on-one tutorial. Even in a country as affluent as the United States, instruction is carried out in classes of 25 to 35 pupils. In Dade County, Florida, the average class size for the early grades is 35. When a teacher gives individual attention to one child, 34 other pupils are left to fend for themselves. This is hardly a good trade-off, even on the premise that each child deserves individual attention.

Consider the significance of these facts in accounting for the slow progress (by international standards) of American elementary schools. If an entire classroom must constantly pause while its lagging members acquire background knowledge that they should have gained in earlier grades, progress is bound to be slow. For effective, fair classroom instruction to take place, all members of the class need to share enough common reference points to enable everyone to understand and learn—though of course at differing rates and in response to varied approaches. When this commonality of knowledge is lacking, progress in learning will be slow compared with systems that use a core curriculum.

Just as learning is cumulative, so are learning deficits. As they begin 1st grade, American students are not far behind beginners in other developed nations. But as they progress, their achievement falls farther and farther behind. This widening gap is the subject of one of the most important recent books on American education, *The Learning Gap* by Stevenson and Stigler.

This progressively widening gap closely parallels what happens *within* American elementary schools between advantaged and disadvantaged children. As the two groups progress from grades 1–6, the achievement gap grows ever larger and is almost never overcome.[5] The reasons for the parallels between the two kinds of gaps—the learning gap and the fairness gap—are similar.

In both cases, the widening gap represents the cumulative effect of learning deficits. Although a few talented and motivated children may overcome this ever-increasing handicap, most do not. The rift grows ever wider in adult life. The basic causes of this permanent deficit, apart from motivational ones, are cognitive. Learning builds upon learning in a cumulative way, and lack of learning in the early grades usually has, in comparative terms, a negatively cumulative effect.

We know from large-scale longitudinal evidence, particularly from France, that this fateful gap between haves and have-nots *can* be closed.[6] But only one way to close it has been devised: to set forth explicit, year-by-year knowledge standards in early grades, so they are known to all parties—educators, parents, and children. Such standards are requisites for home–school cooperation and for reaching a general level of excellence. But, equally, they are requisites in gaining fairness for the academic have-nots: explicit year-by-year knowledge standards enable schools in nations with strong elementary core curriculums to remedy the knowledge deficits of disadvantaged children.

High academic skill is based upon broad general knowledge. Someone once asked Boris Goldovsky how he could play the piano so brilliantly with such small hands. His memorable reply was: "Where in the world did you get the idea that we play the piano with our hands?"

It's the same with reading: we don't read just with our eyes. By 7th grade, according to the epoch-making research of Thomas Sticht, most children, even those who read badly, have already attained the purely technical proficiency they need. Their reading and their listening show the same rate and level of comprehension; thus the mechanics of reading are not the limiting factor.[7] What is mainly lacking in poor readers is a broad, ready vocabulary. But broad vocabulary means broad knowledge, because to know a lot of words you have to know a lot of things. Thus, broad general knowledge is an *essential* requisite to superior reading skill and indirectly related to the skills that accompany it.

Superior reading skill is known to be highly correlated with most other academic skills, including the ability to write well, learn rapidly, solve problems, and think critically. To concentrate on reading is therefore to focus implicitly on a whole range of educational issues.[8]

It is sometimes claimed (but not backed up with research) that knowledge changes so rapidly in our fast-changing world that we need not get bogged down with "mere information." A corollary to the argument is that because information quickly becomes obsolete, it is more important to learn "accessing" skills (how to look things up or how to use a calculator) than to learn "mere facts."

The evidence in the psychological literature on skill acquisition goes strongly against this widely stated claim.[9] Its fallacy can be summed up in a letter I received from a head reference librarian. A specialist in accessing knowledge, he was distressed because the young people now being trained as *reference specialists* had so little general knowledge that they could not effectively help the public access knowledge. His direct experience (backed up by the research literature) had caused him to reject the theory of education as the gaining of accessing skills.

In fact, the opposite inference should be drawn from our fast-changing world. The fundamentals of science change very slowly; those of elementary math hardly at all. The famous names of geography and history (the "leaves" of that knowledge tree) change faster, but not root and branch from year to year. A wide range of this stable, fundamental knowledge is the key to rapid adaptation and the learning of new skills. It is precisely *because* the needs of a modern economy are so changeable that one needs broad general knowledge in order to flourish. Only high literacy (which implies broad general knowledge) provides the flexibility to learn new things fast. The only known route to broad general knowledge for all is for a nation's schools to provide all students with a substantial, solid core of knowledge.

Common content leads to higher school morale, as well as better teaching and learning. At every Core Knowledge school, a sense of community and common purpose have knit people together. Clear content guidelines have encouraged those who teach at the same grade level to collaborate in creating effective lesson plans and schoolwide activities. Similarly, a clear sense of purpose has encouraged cooperation among grades as well. Because the *Core Knowledge Sequence* makes no requirements about *how* the specified knowledge should be presented, individual schools and teachers have great scope for independence and creativity. Site-based governance is the order of the day at Core Knowledge schools—but with definite aims, and thus a clear sense of communal purpose.

The Myth of the Existing Curriculum

Much of the public currently assumes that each elementary school already follows a schoolwide curriculum. Yet frustrated parents continually write the Core Knowledge Foundation to complain that principals are not able to tell them with any explicitness what their child will be learning during the year. Memorably, a mother of identical twins wrote that because her children had been placed in different classrooms, they were learning completely different things.

Such curricular incoherence, typical of elementary education in the United States today, places enormous burdens on teachers. Because they must cope with such diversity of preparation at each subsequent grade level, teachers find it almost impossible to create learning communities in their classrooms. Stevenson and Stigler rightly conclude that the most significant diversity faced by our schools is *not* cultural diversity but, rather, diversity of academic preparation. To achieve excellence and fairness for all, an elementary school *must* follow a coherent sequence of solid, specific content.

Notes

1. International Association for the Evaluation of Educational Achievement (IEA), (1988), *Science Achievement in Seventeen Countries: A Preliminary Report* (Elmsford, N.Y.: Pergamon Press). The table on page 42 shows a consistent correlation between core knowledge systems and equality of opportunity for all students. The subject is discussed at length in E. D. Hirsch, Jr., "Fairness and Core Knowledge," *Occasional Papers 2,* available from the Core Knowledge Foundation, 2012-B Morton Dr., Charlottesville, VA 22901.
2. An absolute limitation of the mind's speed of operation is 50 milliseconds per minimal item. See A. B. Kristofferson (1967), "Attention and Psychophysical Time," *Acta Psychologica* 27: 93–100.
3. The data in this paragraph come from H. Stevenson and J. Stigler, (1992), *The Learning Gap* (New York: Summit Books).
4. Stevenson and Stigler, pp. 52–71.
5. W. Loban, (March 1964), *Language Ability: Grades Seven, Eight, and Nine,* (Project No. 1131), University of California, Berkeley; as expanded and interpreted by T. G. Sticht, L. B. Beck, R. N. Hauke, G. M. Kleiman, and J. H. James, (1974), *Auding and Reading: A Developmental Model* (Alexandria, Va.: Human Resources Research Organization); J. S. Chall (1982), *Families and Literacy, Final Report to the National Institute of Education;* and especially, J. S. Chall, V. A. Jacobs, and L. E. Baldwin, (1990), *The Reading Crisis: Why Poor Children Fall Behind* (Cambridge, Mass.: Harvard University Press).
6. S. Boulot and D. Boyzon-Fradet, (1988), *Les immigrés et l'école: une course d'obstacles,* Paris, pp. 54–58; Centre for Educational Research and Innovation (CERI), (1987), *Immigrants' Children At School,* Paris, pp. 178–259.
7. T. G. Sticht and H. J. James, (1984), "Listening and Reading," In *Handbook of Reading Research,* edited by P. D. Pearson (New York: Longman).
8. A. L. Brown, (1980), "Metacognitive Development and Reading," in *Theoretical Issues in Reading Comprehension,* edited by R. J. Spiro, B. C. Bruce, and W. F. Brewer (Hillsdale, N.J.: L. Erlbaum Associates).
9. J. R. Anderson, ed., (1981), *Cognitive Skills and Their Acquisition* (Hillsdale, N.J.: L. Erlbaum Associates).

CAN CURRICULUM INTEGRATION SURVIVE IN AN ERA OF HIGH-STAKES TESTING?

Gordon F. Vars

Advocates claim that high-stakes testing can improve the education of all students by holding both students and teachers accountable for learning. But can high-stakes testing have unintended consequences? Gordon Vars is a strong advocate for integration as a way of organizing curriculum content, especially at the middle school level. However, due in part to standards, accountability, and high-stakes testing—which Vars strongly criticizes—interest in curriculum integration has waned. As you read this article ask yourself, "In what ways has the emphasis on high-stakes testing detracted from attempts to provide a high-quality education through curriculum integration? Can high-stakes testing and curriculum integration be made compatible?"

Think About This . . .

1. How does Vars define *curriculum integration*? In what other ways could curriculum be "integrated?"

2. What "sources" or "foundations" should be considered when designing and justifying educational programs. In your view, which of these is most important? Least important? Why do you think so?

3. Vars identifies four steps or factors that should be considered in attempting to design curriculum that is both integrated and standards based. What are they? Are they realistic in today's schools? Explain why you do or do not think so.

4. In your opinion, what are the advantages and disadvantages of attempting to integrate curriculum? In what ways will you attempt to integrate different areas of the curriculum in your teaching?

Public schools are under siege today (Ohanian, 1999), and one of the most likely victims is developmentally-appropriate middle level education as advocated in *This We Believe* (National Middle School Association, 1982/1992, 1995) and detailed in *Turning Points 2000* (Jackson & Davis, 2000). Mandated high-stakes tests, introduced in the mistaken notion that you can improve schools by brow-beating school administrators, teachers, and students to raise test scores, has transformed many schools into dreary test-crammers.

Especially vulnerable is the concept of curriculum integration (Kohn, 2000, p. 31). National Middle School Association called for "integrative" curriculum in its 1995 position paper and the Association has supported this approach in its books, journals, and national conferences. *Turning Points 2000* reiterates the call for integrating subject matter across disciplines that was made in the

original *Turning Points* (Carnegie Council on Adolescent Development, 1989). Yet even educators who have worked most closely with two of today's leading advocates and practitioners of curriculum integration James Beane and Barbara Brodhagen have reduced or abandoned their commitment to the integrative approach, due at least in part to emphasis on mandated standards enforced by high-stakes tests (Weilbacher, 2000).

Is there any hope for the future of developmentally appropriate curriculum? Is curriculum integration worth fighting for? What will it take to save, not only the middle school ideal, but one of its most distinctive features—curriculum integration? Here are some suggestions from

---

From Vars, G. (2001). *Can curriculum integration survive in an era of high-stakes testing?* Middle School Journal, 33(2), 7–17. Reprinted with permission of the National Middle School Association.

one who has taught and advocated curriculum integration for more than 50 years.

What Is Curriculum Integration and Why Is It So Vulnerable?

Curriculum integration is a student-centered approach in which students are invited to join with their teachers to plan learning experiences that address both student concerns and major social issues. The name "core curriculum" was given to this approach by educators who developed it early in the twentieth century (Aikin, 1942; Vars, 1991), and in recent years Beane (1990/1993, 1997) has revived it under the term "curriculum integration." In arguing for integrative curriculum in its recent position paper, National Middle School Association (1995) called for learning experiences that are organized around real-life issues and problems significant both to young people and to adults.

In examining these issues, students draw on pertinent content and skills from many subject areas and acquire many of the "common learnings" or life skills essential for all citizens in a democracy (Vars, 1969, 2000b). Of course these include many, but not all, of the major concepts and skills set forth in the standards proposed by professional associations.

However, in the integrative approach the emphasis is on higher-order thinking processes, cooperative learning, and thoughtful consideration of human values, rather than the minutiae of separate subjects. The intent is to help students "make sense out of their life experiences" (NMSA, 1995) as they and their teachers jointly plan the study of complex issues.

Such a democratic, student-centered approach is clearly anathema to the "military-industrial-infotainment complex" (Ohanian, 1999) that appears to be driving current efforts to impose uniform standards on America's children. Whether this is part of a conspiracy to destroy the public schools may be open to debate, although others besides Ohanian seem to think so (Berliner & Biddle, 1995; Boutwell, 1997; Bracey, 1997).

The problem is not with the standards themselves, because society has a right to define what it expects children to know and be able to do. The problem comes from tying standards to high-stakes tests and expecting all students to reach the same adult-determined level of performance at the same time. This is a blatant violation of everything that is known about individual differences and about the impact of threat on human thinking, not to mention the serious shortcomings of most paper-and-pencil tests. Add the fact that most standards focus on low-level objectives in specific subject areas and the threat to curriculum integration is indeed serious.

Is Curriculum Integration Worth Saving?

Curriculum integration, in various forms and under a number of names, has been advocated for more than a century. Both Beane (1997) and Wraga (1996) have traced the idea back to 1895, but Stack (1960) traced its "philosophical and psychological antecedents . . . in educational theory" back even further. There is a fascinating story here for those interested in the history of ideas!

The Arguments

The literature on curriculum integration is extensive. Since the early 1990s, the National Association for Core Curriculum (1991) has distributed a list of *Selected References* with 65 citations and also *Recent Books on Integrative/Interdisciplinary Curriculum* (published since 1990) with more than 75 titles (NACC, 2001). Succinct summaries may be found in Vars (1987/1993) and Beane (1997).

A number of curriculum theorists have argued that three "sources" or "foundations" should be considered when designing and justifying educational programs: psychological (the learner and learning theory), sociological (social realities and the structure of knowledge), and philosophical (purposes and values) (Vars, 2000b). Moreover, all three must be kept in reasonable balance. A middle school curriculum designed to do this was proposed nearly a quarter century ago by Lounsbury and Vars (1978). Briefly summarized below are some of the major arguments for curriculum integration and a list of a few of its proponents.

I. Psychological

A. Students are more highly motivated and learn better because integrative curriculum relates to their needs, problems, concerns, interests, and aspirations. (Faunce & Bossing, 1951/1958).

B. Students learn better because integrative curriculum is more compatible with the way the brain works, thus enhancing the development of higher-order thinking skills (Caine & Caine, 1991; Hart, 1983).

II. Sociological

A. Students are better prepared for life in contemporary society because integrative curriculum addresses current social problems in all their real-life complexity (Van Til, 1976).

B. Students learn major concepts and processes of the disciplines through studying carefully designed integrated units (Erickson, 1998; Jacobs, 1989).

III. Philosophical

A. Integrative curriculum provides a coherent core of common learnings essential for all citizens in a democracy (Beane, 1997; Vars, 1969).

B. Integrative curriculum provides a meaningful framework for examining values (Apple & Beane, 1995; Zapf, 1959).

The Evidence

It is one thing to list the presumed benefits of curriculum integration, but obtaining evidence to back up these claims is no mean feat, especially since many desired outcomes are difficult to measure. Nevertheless, more than 200 studies have been carried out to assess the effectiveness of the various forms of integrative curriculum and instruction (Vars, 1996, 1997; NACC, 2000a). Unfortunately, most of them used conventional paper-and-pencil tests to measure student achievement. There also are wide variations in the scope and quality of the research. Studies range from highly sophisticated analyses of data on thousands of students to longitudinal qualitative studies of students in one class or taught by one teacher or interdisciplinary team.

The difficulties in summarizing such a range of evidence are formidable. Nevertheless, it is reasonable to assert that:

> Almost without exception, students in innovative interdisciplinary programs do as well as, and often better than, students in so-called conventional programs. In other words, educators who carefully implement any of the various types of interdisciplinary approaches can be reasonably assured that there will be no appreciable loss in student learning, except, perhaps, for the temporary "implementation dip" that occurs whenever people try anything new. (Vars, 1996)

This conclusion may be disappointing to advocates of curriculum integration, but it is essential that we not "oversell" it, especially in these times of single-minded focus on getting kids to do well on high-stakes tests. As Beane often reminds us, curriculum integration (or core, if you prefer the older term) is a complex concept involving both curriculum and instruction and guided by a democratic philosophy. It may result in higher test scores, but even more important are its other benefits such as love of learning, concern for other people, critical thinking, self-confidence, commitment to democratic group processes, and a whole host of other

so-called "intangibles." Educators need to gather data on these objectives, too, if only through surveys of students, teachers, parents, and community members. It is patently absurd to judge all educational outcomes on the basis of tests, state-mandated or otherwise.

What Will It Take to Save Curriculum Integration?

Saving curriculum integration, and the whole idea of developmentally-appropriate education for any age student, involves both political action and wise educational policies.

The politics of curriculum integration have been cogently delineated by Beane (1997). The issue is part of a much larger question of what public schools are for and who will control them. Unfortunately, educators are not noted for being politically savvy and they failed to take a united stand against the high-stakes testing juggernaut when it was just getting under way in the 1980s, signaled by the infamous "Nation at Risk" document. Even today resistance is still spotty and disorganized. Needed are more courageous students, teachers, and parents who will simply refuse to participate in a process that is so grossly unfair and contrary to what we know about teaching and learning. Rare indeed are politicians like the late U.S. Senator Paul D. Wellstone (D-MN) who recognize and fight against the trend toward high-stakes testing. In Wellstone's words: "It is a harsh agenda that holds children responsible for *our own* failure to invest in their future and in their achievement" (emphasis added, Wellstone, 2000).

Everyone concerned about the welfare of children must use all the political processes at their disposal to stop the high-stakes testing craze before it does any more damage (Kohn, 1999, 2000). Until that happy day, educators must hold fast to the ideal of developmentally-appropriate middle level education even if they have to make some accommodations to the realities of their situation. Above all, they must not retreat to long-discredited drill-and-test practices in the mistaken notion that helping students cram in order to raise their test scores is the way to better quality education. Indeed, the opposite is true.

The choice is not between fully implementing *all* the recommendations of NMSA's *This We Believe* versus attempting *none* of them. Large-scale research carried out by Felner and others (1997) demonstrates that the most effective middle schools are those that implement a large proportion of the recommendations found in *Turning Points* (Carnegie Council on Adolescent Development, 1989) and in *This We Believe* (NMSA, 1995).

Here are some ways that educators can retain key elements of curriculum integration and still give reasonable and conscientious attention to mandated standards and proficiencies.

Designing Curriculum That Is Both Integrative and Standards-Based

Standards can be incorporated into the integrative curriculum process during the program design phase and also as teachers and students engage in teacher–student planning for specific units of study. But first it is necessary to face the irrefutable fact that it is impossible to ensure that *all* students will master *all* of the standards that have been proposed. Robert Marzano and associates at the Mid-continent Regional Educational Lab (McREL) have documented the utter futility of trying to teach all of the standards set forth by professional associations and other groups. They concluded:

> A high school diploma would require as much classroom time as has historically resulted in a master's or professional degree. Even the brightest students would need nine additional years of schooling to master the nearly 4,000 benchmarks experts have set in 14 subject areas (Marzano, Kendall, and Gaddy, 1999).

Noddings (2000) asserted that subject matter specialists are bound to recommend too much because "they cannot control their passions." This is not the first time that schools have had to deal with the excess zeal of subject-matter specialists. Remember Jerome Bruner? His 1960 book *The Process of Education* set the tone for an earlier massive effort to organize the school curriculum around the "structure of the disciplines." Ten years later he admitted publicly that that approach was misguided. His words on that occasion are well worth remembering as we endure yet another wave of emphasis on disciplines-based standards:

> If I had my choice now, in terms of a curriculum project for the seventies, it would be to find a means whereby we could bring society back to its sense of values and priorities in life. *I believe I would be quite satisfied to declare, if not a moratorium, then something of a de-emphasis on matters that have to do with the structure of history, the structure of physics, the nature of mathematical consistency, and deal with it rather in the context of the problems that face us.* We might better concern ourselves with how these [social] problems can be solved, not just by practical action, but by putting knowledge, wherever we find it and in whatever form we find it, to work in these massive tasks. *We might put vocation and intention back into the process of education, much more firmly than we had it there before.*
>
> A decade later, we realize that *The Process of Education* was the beginning of a revolution, and one cannot yet know how far it will go. Reform of curriculum is not enough. Reform of the school is probably not enough. The issue is one of man's capacity for creating a culture, society, and technology that not only feed him but keep him caring and belonging (Bruner, 1971, p. 21, emphasis in the original).

Common Learnings

Schools have always had too much to teach, so it is no surprise that it is necessary to be selective. Bruner's comments remind us that there are broad goals of education that are not bounded by academic disciplines or school subjects. These are the "common learnings" or "life skills" that are considered essential for effective functioning as a citizen and human being, regardless of vocation or station in life (Vars, 1969, 2000b).

A few states, such as Maine and Vermont, have identified these "generic" competencies and built them into their state standards. Vermont uses the term "vital results" for standards that "cut across all fields of knowledge." They are arranged in four categories: communication, reasoning and problem solving, personal development, and civic/social responsibility. Similar labels are used in Maine's *Common Core of Learning*: "Communication," "Reasoning and Problem Solving," "Personal and Global Stewardship," and "The Human Record." Although these common learnings or life skills are intended to be developed throughout the entire school program, they should be the primary focus of integrative curriculum.

Three educational "think-tanks" also have compiled lists of "generic" competencies that cut across discipline and subject lines.

1. *Schoolwide Goals for Student Learning.* One carefully-designed set of common learnings has been developed by the Alliance for Curriculum Reform (ACR) and the National Study of School Evaluation (NSSE) (Fitzpatrick, 1997). They examined the proposals of the various academic professional organizations and identified goals that are common across several specific subject standards. Those common learnings, called "Schoolwide Goals for Student Learning," are divided into the following categories: Learning-to-Learn Skills, Expanding and Integrating Knowledge, Communication Skills, Thinking and Reasoning Skills, Interpersonal Skills, and Personal and Social Responsibility.

The rubrics suggested for evaluating student performance in each of these areas are stated in general terms. However, the examples of "Performance Indicators" are "Discipline-Based," as are the *Program Evaluation Guides* to be used for evaluating specific school programs or services. Thus the structure of the handbooks may handicap schools in their efforts to make sure "that their instructional and assessment efforts contribute to a coherent curriculum" (Fitzpatrick, 1997, p. xi).

2. *Core Standards.* An even more comprehensive approach has been used by the Center for Occupational Research and Development (CORD) in Waco, Texas (Edling & Loring, 1996). They identified common learnings embedded in standards proposed by academic organizations and also by groups advocating "workforce education"—businesses, industries, and vocational educators. Tapping the power of computer technology, they created a database of 38 sets of proposed standards. From these they pulled out 53 "Core" standards, similar to the schoolwide goals proposed by the National Study of School Evaluation. These describe a broad array of competencies, everything from "general housekeeping" to statistical analysis and computer literacy to ethics and self-concept.

What CORD calls Integrated Standards also have been generated for various occupational fields like business, engineering, the arts, and service. Field tests of this approach to both common learnings and integrated curriculum are going on in 12 states, and 14 curriculum packages are being developed to help school personnel implement the process (Edling & Loring, 1996).

3. *Life Skills.* Researchers at McREL, an educational research center in Aurora, Colorado, also began their search for "essential knowledge" by building a standards database incorporating 116 national standards documents in 14 content areas (Kendall & Marzano, 1996, 1997). In the process they identified a set of "life skills," which they described as "a category of knowledge that is useful across content areas as well as important for the world of work." These are divided into four areas: thinking and reasoning, working with others, self-regulation, and life work.

An examination of these three formulations reveals a number of similarities. Any set of standards-based common learnings, or, better yet, a composite of all of them, would provide much-needed focus in curriculum planning at all levels and would be especially important in designing integrative curriculum.

Selecting and Prioritizing

After compiling a statement of desired common learnings, it is then necessary to select and prioritize the many standards in the various subjects. It may seem presumptuous for local educators to pick and choose among subject matter standards that have been recommended by experts in prestigious national organizations and sanctioned by state departments of education, but they have no choice. Besides, who is better qualified to design curriculum than those who are closest to the young people being served?

Jackson and Davis in *Turning Points 2000* propose stringent criteria that schools should use to analyze and adapt state and local district standards to provide a basis "for developing a coherent, engaging curriculum." They argue that standards should be "selected and modified or supplemented by consensus" of those who will use the standards, including teachers, administrators, students, parents, and even representatives of higher education, business, and the community (p. 37).

Curriculum specialists have long wrestled with how to solicit meaningful involvement of all these groups and how to coordinate their work. The task is complicated by the fact that the appropriate role in curriculum planning for each category of stakeholder varies widely. For example, it might be inappropriate to expect someone representing local business interests to take part in a team's detailed planning of an interdisciplinary unit. However, that same person's input might be very useful to a curriculum committee outlining the broad features of the district's long-range curriculum design.

Space does not permit examining this issue here, but the "transformative curriculum design and planning" proposed by Henderson and Hawthorne (2000) is notable for its consistent application of principles of democracy. Curriculum planning requires adequate time and support and is best carried out during released time or during the summer months. Viewing state and district standards as guidelines, not absolutes, district and school curriculum committees can design curriculum that addresses the most important standards but that also leaves ample room for input by teachers, parents, and students during teacher–student planning.

Responsibility for developing state- and district-mandated competencies falls heaviest on teachers of language arts, social studies, science, and mathematics, whether organized in interdisciplinary teams, block-time classes, or otherwise. It is the teachers of these "core subjects" who are most likely to have team planning time during the day, while their students are in other classes. This division between so-called "core" and "encore/exploratory" subjects has been a perennial problem in middle level education. Inviting all staff to help define how mandated common learnings will be taught helps to heal this breach, even though certain teachers or teams may bear major responsibility for teaching them.

Designing Integrative Curriculum

After prioritizing the standards to be addressed through integrative curriculum, the next task is to determine its overall design and how staff will be organized to teach it. The options available have been described elsewhere (Vars, 1987/1993).

Teachers accustomed to delivering a curriculum that has required textbooks and prescribed scope and sequence are understandably anxious when asked to do the kind of free-wheeling teacher–student planning recommended by some advocates. They can see that it will be a huge task to design their own curriculum "on-the-spot," incorporating both mandated standards and student concerns, and to do it all without textbooks or other prescribed teaching materials. Is it any wonder that this form of curriculum integration has never been widespread?

Moreover, few teachers have experienced curriculum integration themselves as students, and, with few exceptions, teacher preparation programs give it scant attention. "Lack of qualified teachers" often was cited in early surveys as a major obstacle to implementing "core curriculum" (Vars, 1962), and the situation is not much better today. Organizing a school into interdisciplinary teams is expected to facilitate curriculum integration, but the sheer logistics of team operation often leave little time or energy for planning occasional interdisciplinary units, not to mention full-scale curriculum integration.

Current emphasis on society-imposed standards makes it imperative that teachers and curriculum specialists establish an overall structure for the school's integrative curriculum that addresses both the mandated standards and also the issues, problems, and concerns that are likely to be most meaningful to students. Schools and districts need to reconsider two ideas developed during the core curriculum movement: "problem areas" and "resource units" (Van Til, Vars, & Lounsbury, 1961/1967; Vars, 1999, 2000a).

Problem Areas. "Problem areas" or "centers of experience" are broad centers of human experience around which both student concerns and society's problems tend to cluster. Figure 1 presents Van Til's 1976 formulation, derived from the "interaction of curriculum

Figure 1
Van Til's "Centers of Experience" Compared with Beane's "Themes"*

War, Peace, and International Relations	Interdependence, Conflict Resolution
Overpopulation, Pollution, and Energy	Interdependence, Wellness
Economic Options and Problems	Social Structures, Commercialism
Governmental Processes	Independence, Justice, Institutions
Consumer Problems	Commercialism
Intercultural Relations	Social Structures
World Views	Interdependence, Social Structures
Recreation and Leisure	Wellness
The Arts and Aesthetics	Identities
Self-Understanding and Personal Development	Transitions, Identities
Family, Peer Group, and School	Interdependence, Caring, Institutions
Health	Wellness
Vocations	Social Structures
Communication	Interdependence, Commercialism
Alternative Futures	Transitions
Van Til (1976, p. 197)	Beane (1993, p. 61)

*Beane's ten broad themes have been repeated to illustrate potential parallels.

sources." Note the parallels with the "themes" that Beane identified at the intersections of "personal and social concerns" (Beane, 1990/1993). During the progressive education era, several curriculum scholars generated sets of problem areas that they considered suitable for secondary school core programs. Many of the units taught in junior high core programs appeared to be based on the problem area concept (Van Til, Vars, & Lounsbury, 1961/1967).

Problem areas may be either required or optional. In either case, they should be designed to incorporate both the most critical standards and also the concerns that teachers anticipate will be uppermost in the lives of students. Representative parents and community members also may provide valuable input. Required areas may be assigned to a particular grade level, thus giving the integrative curriculum both scope and sequence. Required or optional, problem areas provide a modest degree of structure to the integrative curriculum.

Resource Units. Within the broad limits of a problem area, teachers and their students are free to develop learning experiences they consider most meaningful. This process is much easier if staff members have prepared "resource units" for each problem area. These are flexible, open-ended curriculum guides that offer a large number of suggested learning activities and instructional materials that might be useful in exploring a particular problem area. They also contain a statement of purpose or rationale, list typical student questions and concerns relating to that area, identify pertinent standards or other mandates, and suggest ways to assess and evaluate student learning. Thus a resource unit serves as a reservoir of ideas to use when planning a specific learning unit with a particular group of students.

The interdisciplinary units currently available from a number of publishers and Internet sources are helpful, but most of them provide for very limited student input (NACC, 2000b). Resource units should be kept deliberately open-ended so teachers and teams can add additional ideas as they encounter them. Loose-leaf notebooks or folders were used in the early days, but modern computers offer even greater flexibility today.

Involving Students

Although teachers are ultimately responsible for what is taught, students have a right to know what is expected of them. Armed with a resource unit, including a pared-down and prioritized set of mandated goals and standards, teachers or teams are now ready to introduce the problem area to their students. It is important to outline the possible ramifications of a problem area,

including the standards that it incorporates. This way, students from the very beginning can join with their teachers to help ensure that mandated competencies are addressed. When students understand the standards that are to be met during any particular year, they can suggest many creative ways to address them. Integrative curriculum, the problem area approach, and teacher–student planning are all likely to be unfamiliar to students' families. It is essential to keep them informed of plans as they evolve and to solicit their support and suggestions.

Should a problem area be presented before, during, or after engaging students in identifying their personal and social concerns? There are pros and cons for each approach.

Before. It is probably best for teachers to delay introducing problem areas until they get to know their students. A reasonable level of trust must be established before students will share their concerns and aspirations with either peers or teachers. Presenting students with a list of required problem areas or mandates too early in the game may suggest that there is little room for negotiation or that teachers are not sincere in inviting student input. And both students and their families will need an introduction to the semi-structured nature of a problem area, as well as the process of teacher–student planning.

Sharing interests is a time-honored way for teachers and students to get acquainted, and this can lead naturally into identifying personal and social concerns. Some students are more outspoken than others, so it is important to solicit written input from everyone before opening up the matter for class discussion. Conducting occasional anonymous surveys and providing a feedback or suggestion box in the classroom can encourage even the most reticent students to express their thoughts and feelings. Once an appropriate level of trust has been established, small group discussions lay the groundwork for classroom or team identification of most-prevalent questions and concerns. Student questions and concerns should be posted in the classroom, along with the major standards to be addressed during that year. These lists should be revisited from time to time during the year, both to check on progress and to tap into changes that take place in the students, the teachers, and the world.

During. Teachers sometimes "back-map" a completed unit to show students and parents where and when they had dealt with content and skills typically taught in separate courses. This sort of "after-the-fact accountability" is especially essential today (see for example, Brodhagen, 1995; Ziegler, 2000a, 2000b, 2000c).

Identifying and labeling the standards and competencies included in a unit not only provides evidence that standards are being addressed, but also may reveal competencies that merit further attention in succeeding units.

It is important for teachers not to panic when they find that certain standards have not been sufficiently addressed. Instead of abandoning the integrative approach and falling back on didactic "drill-and-test" techniques, they should share their concerns with the students and their families, inviting them to join in planning remediation. Teachers who merely "insert" lessons or units to address certain standards without discussing it with their students are bound to lose credibility.

After. Ziegler (2000a, 2000b, 2000c) has described the benefits of keeping a running record of how standards are being addressed through integrative units and learning experiences. Reflecting on these at the end of the year is excellent review and reinforcement for students and provides important evidence to share with parents, administrators, and the community at large.

Balancing student needs, problems, and concerns with societal expectations has always been a challenging task. Inviting students to help in the process gives them excellent opportunities to develop critical thinking. It also demonstrates that their ideas are valued and helps them to see that education is a matter of serious concern for our entire society. Perhaps if more adults had gained this kind of insight while still in school, there would be more societal support for the schools today!

Conclusion

Curriculum integration, in which students are directly involved in planning, conducting, and evaluating their own learning, is a powerful way for middle level schools to demonstrate that they are "developmentally-responsive." Mandated high-stakes testing is a major threat both to curriculum integration and to the middle level school's commitment to meet the needs of young adolescents.

Some reassurance can be drawn from six decades of research which shows that students in interdisciplinary programs usually perform satisfactorily on standardized tests. How students will do in the new state tests remains to be seen. But we have explained how it is possible to retain significant features of curriculum integration, teach the most important state and district standards, and do it all in a way that advances the ultimate purposes of education in a democracy. Whether these efforts will be enough to "save" curriculum integration depends on how committed we all are to the ideals of middle level education. Let us hope that we are up to the task!

References

Aikin, W. M. (1942). *The story of the eight-year study*. New York: Harper.

Apple, M. W., & Beane, J. A. (Eds.). (1995). *Democratic schools*. Alexandria, VA: Association for Supervision and Curriculum Development.

Beane, J. A. (1993). *A middle school curriculum: From rhetoric to reality* (2nd ed.). Columbus, OH: National Middle School Association (1st ed. published in 1990).

Beane, J. A. (1997). *Curriculum integration: Designing the core of democratic education*. New York: Teachers College Press.

Berliner, D., & Biddle, B. (1995). *The manufactured crisis: Myths, fraud, and the attack on America's public schools*. Boston: Addison-Wesley.

Boutwell, C. (1997). *The shell game: Corporate America's agenda for schools*. Bloomington, IN: Phi Delta Kappa.

Bracey, G. (1997). *Setting the record straight: Responses to misconceptions about public education in the United States*. Alexandria, VA: Association for Supervision and Curriculum Development.

Brodhagen, B. L. (1995). The situation made us special. In M. W. Apple & J. A. Beane (Eds.), *Democratic schools*, (pp. 83–100). Alexandria, VA: Association for Supervision and Curriculum Development.

Bruner, J. S. (1960). *The process of education*. Cambridge, MA: Harvard University Press.

Bruner, J. S. (1971). The process of education revisited. *Phi Delta Kappan, 53*(1), 18–21.

Caine, R. N., & Caine, G. (1991). *Making connections: Teaching and the human brain*. Alexandria, VA: Association for Supervision and Curriculum Development.

Carnegie Council on Adolescent Development (1989). *Turning points: Preparing American youth for the 21st century*. New York: Carnegie Corporation.

Edling, W. H., & Loring, R. M. (1996). *Education and work: Designing integrated curricula*, Waco, TX: Center for Occupational Research and Development.

Erickson, H. L. (1998). *Concept-based curriculum and instruction: Teaching beyond the facts*. Thousand Oaks, CA: Corwin Press.

Faunce, R. C., & Bossing, N. L. (1958). *Developing the core curriculum*. Upper Saddle River, NJ: Prentice Hall. (1st ed. published 1951).

Felner, R. D., Jackson, A. W., Kasak, D., Mulhall, P., Brand, S., & Flowers, N. (1997). The impact of school reform for the middle years. *Phi Delta Kappan, 78*(7), 528–532, 541–550.

Fitzpatrick, K. A. (1997). *Indicators of schools of quality, volume 1: Schoolwide indicators of quality*. Schaumburg, IL: National Study of School Evaluation.

Hart, L. (1983). *Human brain, human learning*. New York: Longman.

Henderson, J. G., & Hawthorne, R. D. (2000). *Transformative curriculum leadership* (2nd ed.). Upper Saddle River, NJ: Merrill/Prentice Hall.

Jackson, A. W., & Davis, G. A. (2000). *Turning points 2000: Educating adolescents in the 21st century*. New York: Teachers College Press.

Jacobs, H. H. (1989). *Interdisciplinary curriculum: Design and implementation*. Alexandria, VA: Association for Supervision and Curriculum Development.

Kendall, J. S., & Marzano, R. J. (1996, 1997) *Content knowledge: A compendium of standards & benchmarks for K–12 educators*. Retrieved October 14, 1999 from http://www.mcrel.org.

Kohn, A. (1999). *The schools our children deserve: Moving beyond traditional classrooms and "tougher standards."* Boston: Houghton Mifflin.

Kohn, A. (2000). *The case against standardized testing: Raising the scores, ruining the schools*. Portsmouth, NH: Heinemann. See also: www.alfiekohn.org/teaching/standards.htm.

Lounsbury, J. H., & Vars, G. F. (1978). *A curriculum for the middle school years*. New York: Harper.

Marzano, R. J., Kendall, J. S., & Gaddy, B. B. (1999). Deciding on "essential knowledge." *Education Week, 18*(32), 68, 49.

National Association for Core Curriculum. (1991). *Selected references on block-time, core, and interdisciplinary programs*. Kent, OH: Author.

National Association for Core Curriculum. (2000a). *A bibliography of research on the effectiveness of block-time, core, and interdisciplinary team teaching programs*. Kent, OH: Author.

National Association for Core Curriculum. (2000b). *Sources of interdisciplinary units*. Kent, OH: Author.

National Association for Core Curriculum. (2001). *Recent books on integrative/interdisciplinary curriculum*. Kent, OH: Author.

National Middle School Association. (1992). *This we believe*. Columbus, OH: Author (1st ed. published 1982).

National Middle School Association. (1995). *This we believe: Developmentally responsive middle level schools*. Columbus, OH: Author.

Noddings, N. (2000, March). *Educational standards in a liberal democracy*. Presentation at the 55th Annual Conference. Alexandria, VA: Association for Supervision and Curriculum Development.

Ohanian, S. (1999). *One size fits few: The folly of educational standards*. Portsmouth, NH: Heinemann.

Stack, E. C. (1960). The philosophical and psychological antecedents of the core curriculum in educational theory: 1800–1918. (Doctoral dissertation, University of North Carolina, Chapel Hill, 1960). *Dissertation Abstracts, 20*(07), 1830–1831.

Van Til, W. (1976). What should be taught and learned through secondary education? In W. Van Til (Ed.), *Issues in secondary education*. Seventy-fifth yearbook of the National Society for the Study of Education, Part II (pp. 178–213). Chicago: University of Chicago Press.

Van Til, W., Vars, G. R, & Lounsbury, J. H. (1967). *Modern education for the junior high school years*. Indianapolis: Bobbs-Merrill (1st ed. published 1961).

Vars, G. F. (1962). Leadership in core program development. *Educational Leadership, 19*(8), 517–522.

Vars, G. F. (1969). *Common learnings: Core and interdisciplinary team approaches*. Scranton, PA: Intext. (Digital version available from Questia Media, www.questia.com.)

Vars, G. F. (1991). Integrated curriculum in historical perspective. *Educational Leadership, 49*(2), 14–15.

Vars, G. F. (1993). *Interdisciplinary teaching: Why and how*. Columbus, OH: National Middle School Association (1st ed. published 1987).

Vars, G. F. (1996). The effects of interdisciplinary curriculum and instruction. In P. S. Hlebowitsh & W. G. Wraga (Eds.), *Annual review of research for school leaders* (pp. 147–164). Jefferson City, MO: Scholastic.

Vars, G. F. (1997). Effects of integrative curriculum and instruction. In J. L. Irvin (Ed.), *What current research says to the middle level practitioner* (pp. 179–186). Columbus, OH: National Middle School Association.

Vars, G. F. (1999). Another look back at tomorrow's high schools, part one: Implications for high school curriculum from the Eight-Year Study. *Voices from the Field, 2*(1), 27–34.

Vars, G. F. (2000a). Another look back at tomorrow's high schools, part two: Lessons from the Eight-Year Study for high school methods, guidance, assessment, and the change process. *Voices from the Field, 2*(2), 4–11.

Vars, G. F. (2000b). Common learnings: A 50-year quest. *Journal of Curriculum and Supervision, 16*(1), 70–89.

Vars, G. F., & Beane, J. A. (2000, June). *Integrative curriculum in a standards-based world*. ERIC Digest EDO-PS-00-6.

Weilbacher, G. A. (2000). Why teachers decide to use, then not use, curriculum integration as their curriculum planning philosophy. (Doctoral dissertation, University of Wisconsin, Madison, 2000). *Dissertation Abstracts International, 61*(05), 1735A.

Wellstone, P. D. (2000). High stakes tests: A harsh agenda for America's children. *The Education Revolution, 29*, 31–35.

Wraga, W. G. (1996). A century of interdisciplinary curricula in American schools. In P. S. Hlebowitsh & W. G. Wraga (Eds.), *Annual review of research for school leaders* (pp. 117–145). Jefferson City, MO: Scholastic.

Zapf, R. M. (1959). *Democratic processes in the secondary classroom*. Upper Saddle River, NJ: Prentice Hall.

Ziegler, M. J. (2000a). Standards are our friends. *The Core Teacher, 50*(1), 4–6. (Quarterly newsletter of the National Association for Core Curriculum, 1640 Franklin Avenue, Suite # 104, Kent, OH 44240-4324.)

Ziegler, M. J. (2000b). Standards are our friends. *The Core Teacher, 50*(2), 5–6.

Ziegler, M. J. (2000c). Standards are our friends. *The Core Teacher, 50*(3), 5–7.

MINING THE VALUES IN THE CURRICULUM
Kevin Ryan

> What is the proper place of values in the curriculum? Kevin Ryan answers this question by asking another question, "What is a good person?" Ryan contends that commonalities exist across most cultures in their idea of what constitutes a good person, and this cross-cultural agreement includes common values that our schools should pursue. The values should be pursued in the formal curriculum in the topics we study and the literature we read. These values should also be evident in the hidden curriculum, the implicit messages that students receive as they live and work in our schools. As you read this article ask yourself, "What should be the role of schools in promoting and developing student values?"

Think About This . . .

1. Ryan discusses the role of schools in preparing students for three roles—worker, citizen, and private person. What role do values play in each of these three roles?

2. Are there values in every area of the formal curriculum? If so, what are these? If not, which are some that are discipline specific?

3. How do values influence the hidden curriculum? What values should permeate the hidden curriculum of a school?

4. How do you plan to incorporate values into your classroom? Which values are most important and how would you teach them?

While the development of a child's character is clearly not the sole responsibility of the school, historically and legally schools have been major players in this arena. Young people spend much of their lives within school walls. There they will learn, either by chance or design, moral lessons about how people behave.

In helping students develop good character—the capacity to know the good, love the good, and do the good—schools should above all be contributing to a child's knowing what is good. But what is most worth knowing? And for what purpose? How do educators decide what to teach? Pressing concerns for ancient philosophers, these questions are even more demanding today as we struggle to make order out of our information-saturated lives. New dilemmas brought on by such developments as computers, doomsday weaponry, and lethal viruses challenge us daily.

What Is a Good Person?

Before curriculum builders can answer "What's most worth knowing?" we have to know "For what?" To be well adjusted to the world around us? To become wealthy and self-sufficient? To be an artist? With a little reflection, most of us would come to similar conclusions as our great philosophers and spiritual leaders: education should help us become wise and good people.

What constitutes a "good person" has paralyzed many sincere educators and noneducators. Because the United States is a multiracial, multiethnic nation, many educators despair of coming up with a shared vision of the good person to guide curriculum builders. Our founders and early educational pioneers saw in the very diverse, multicultural American scene of the late 18th and early 19th centuries the clear need for a school system that would teach the civic virtues necessary to maintain our novel political and social experiment. They saw the school's role not only as contributing to a person's understanding of what it is to be good, but also

From Ryan, K. (1993). *Mining the values in the curriculum.* Educational Leadership, 75(3), 16–18. *Reprinted with permission of the Association for Supervision and Curriculum Development.*

as teaching the enduring habits required of a democratic citizen.

Yet the school's curriculum must educate more than just the citizen. Conway Dorsett recently suggested that a good curriculum respects and balances the need "to educate the 'three people' in each individual: the worker, the citizen, and the private person" (1993). Our schools must provide opportunities for students to discover what is most worth knowing, as they prepare, not only to be citizens, but also good workers and good private individuals.

The work of C. S. Lewis may provide us with the multicultural model of a good person that we are seeking. Lewis discovered that certain ideas about how one becomes a good person recur in the writing of the ancient Egyptians, Babylonians, Hebrews, Chinese, Norse, Indians, and Greeks, and in Anglo-Saxon and American writings as well. Common values included kindness; honesty; loyalty to parents, spouses, and family members; an obligation to help the poor, the sick, and the less fortunate; and the right to private property. Some evils, such as treachery, torture, and murder, were considered worse than one's own death (1947).

Lewis called this universal path to becoming a good person by the Chinese name, "the Tao." Combining the wisdom of many cultures, this Tao could be our multicultural answer for how to live our lives, the basis for what is most worth knowing.

Over the years, teachers, curriculum specialists, and school officials have used the Tao, albeit unconsciously, to guide the work of schools. Translated into curriculum, the Tao guides schools to educate children to be concerned about the weak and those in need; to help others; to work hard and complete their tasks well and promptly, even when they do not want to; to control their tempers; to work cooperatively with others and practice good manners; to respect authority and other people's rights; to help resolve conflicts; to understand honesty, responsibility, and friendship; to balance pleasures with responsibilities; and to ask themselves and decide "What is the right thing to do?"

Most educators agree that our schools should teach these attitudes both in the formal and in the hidden curriculum.

The Formal Curriculum

The formal curriculum is usually thought of as the school's planned educational experiences—the selection and organization of knowledge and skills from the universe of possible choices. Of course, not all knowledge

nor every skill contributes directly to knowing the good, but much of the subject matter of English and social studies is intimately connected to the Tao. Stories, historical figures, and events are included in the formal curriculum to illuminate the human condition. From them we can learn how to be a positive force in the lives of others, and we can also see the effects of a poorly lived life.

The men and women, real or fictitious, who we learn about in school are instruments for understanding what it is to be (or not to be) a good person. One of the strengths and attractions of good literature is its complexity. As students read, they learn about themselves and the world. For example, students come face-to-face with raw courage in the exploits of Harriet Tubman and further understand the danger of hate and racism through *The Diary of Anne Frank*. They glimpse in Edward Arlington Robinson's poem "Miniver Cheevy" the folly of storing up earthly treasures. They see in Toni Cade Bambera's "Your Blues Ain't Like Mine" the intrinsic dignity of each human being. They gain insight into the heart of a truly noble man, Atticus Finch, in *To Kill a Mockingbird*. They perceive the thorny relationships between the leader and the led by following the well-intended, but failed efforts of Brutus in Shakespeare's *Julius Caesar*.

Our formal curriculum is a vehicle to teach the Tao, to help young people to come to know the good. But simply selecting the curriculum is not enough; like a vein of precious metal, the teacher and students must mine it together. To engage students in the lessons in human character and ethics contained in our history and literature without resorting to empty preaching and crude didacticism is the great skill of teaching.

The Hidden Curriculum

In addition to the formal curriculum, students learn from a hidden curriculum—all the personal and social instruction that they acquire from their day-to-day schooling. Much of what has been written about the hidden curriculum in recent decades has stressed that these school experiences often lead to students' loss of self-esteem, unswerving obedience to silly rules, and the suppression of their individuality. While true of some students and some schools, the hidden curriculum can lead either to negative or positive education.

Many of education's most profound and positive teachings can be conveyed in the hidden curriculum. If a spirit of fairness penetrates every corner of a school, children will learn to be fair. Through the service of teachers, administrators, and older students, students learn to be of service to others. By creating an atmosphere of high standards, the hidden curriculum can teach habits of accuracy and precision. Many aspects of school life, ranging from homework assignments to sporting events, can teach self-control and self-discipline.

While unseen, the hidden curriculum must be considered with the same seriousness as the written, formal curriculum. The everyday behavior of the faculty, staff, and other students cannot fail to have an impact on a student.

One school concerned with the hidden curriculum is Roxbury Latin, a fine academic high school in Boston. In the spring of 1992, an accrediting team interviewed 27 students, ranging from 7th to 12th grade, asking them the same question, "What do you think is Roxbury Latin's philosophy of education?" Every one of the students came back with the same answer: "This school is most concerned about what kind of people we are becoming." What the review team did not know was that every September, the school's headmaster, Anthony Jarvis, assembles all the new students and delivers a short message:

> We want you to excel in academics and sports and the arts while you are here. But, remember this: we care much more about your characters, what kind of people you are becoming.

End of message. End of assembly. All indications are that the message is getting through.

Policies and Practices

A school that makes a positive impact on the character of young people helps children to know the Tao and make it part of their lives. Such a school has in place the following policies and practices.

- The school has a mission statement widely known by students, teachers, administrators, parents, and the entire school community.
- The school has a comprehensive program of service activities, starting in the early grades and requiring more significant contributions of time and energy in the later years of high school.
- School life is characterized by a high level of school spirit and healthy intergroup competition.

- The school has an external charity or cause (a local home for the elderly or educational fund-raising for a Third World community) to which all members of the community contribute.
- The school has a grading and award system that does more than give lip service to character formation and ethics, but recognizes academic effort, good discipline, contributions to the life of the classroom, service to the school and the community, respect for others, and good sportsmanship.
- The school expects not only teachers but also the older students to be exemplars of high ethical standards.
- The school's classrooms and public areas display mottoes and the pictures of exemplary historical figures.
- The school has regular ceremonies and rituals that bring the community together to celebrate achievements of excellence in all realms: academic, athletic, artistic and ethical.[1]

Our students have a major task in life: to become individuals of character. Character education, then, is the central curriculum issue confronting educators. Rather than the latest fad, it is a school's oldest mission. Nothing is better for the human soul than to discuss excellence every day. The curriculum of our elementary and secondary schools should be the delivery system for this encounter with excellence.

Note

1. Several of these policies and procedures are elaborated in *Reclaiming Our Schools: A Handbook for Teaching Character, Academics and Discipline,* by E. A. Wynne and K. Ryan (Columbus, Ohio: Merrill, 1992).

References

Dorsett, C. (March 1993). "Multicultural Education: Why We Need It and Why We Worry About It." *Network News and Views* 12, 3: 31.

Lewis, C. S. (1947). *The Abolition of Man.* New York: Macmillan.

Author's note: I wish to acknowledge Catherine Kinsella Stutz of Boston University for her contributions to this article.

HOW NOT TO TEACH VALUES: A CRITICAL LOOK AT CHARACTER EDUCATION

Alfie Kohn

Alfie Kohn, a prominent educational lecturer and author, is critical of the use of rewards and punishments in all aspects of education. A proponent of character education, he is also critical of what he sees as the prevailing trends in character development. As you read this article think about the different approaches suggested by character education leaders that you saw in the introduction to the previous article and ask yourself, "How valid are Alfie Kohn's criticisms of alternate forms of character education?"

Think About This . . .

1. How does Kohn describe current approaches to character education? Do you agree or disagree with his assessment? Why or why not?

2. According to the author, what impact does the giving of rewards have on the activity that led to the reward? Do you agree with his analysis? Why or why not?

3. Kohn suggests that five questions should be asked of any character education program. What are these questions? Which do you believe is most important? Least important?

4. How will you attempt to promote moral development in your classroom? Cite a specific example to illustrate your position.

Teachers and schools tend to mistake good behavior for good character. What they prize is docility, suggestibility; the child who will do what he is told; or even better, the child who will do what is wanted without even having to be told. They value most in children what children least value in themselves. Small wonder that their effort to build character is such a failure; they don't know it when they see it.

—John Holt
How Children Fail

Were you to stand somewhere in the continental United States and announce, "I'm going to Hawaii," it would be understood that you were heading for those islands in the Pacific that collectively constitute the 50th state. Were you to stand in Honolulu and make the same statement, however, you would probably be talking about one specific island in the chain—namely, the big one to your southeast. The word *Hawaii* would seem to have two meanings, a broad one and a narrow one; we depend on context to tell them apart.

The phrase *character education* also has two meanings. In the broad sense, it refers to almost anything that schools might try to provide outside of academics, especially when the purpose is to help children grow into good people. In the narrow sense, it denotes a particular style of moral training, one that reflects particular values as well as particular assumptions about the nature of children and how they learn.

Unfortunately, the two meanings of the term have become blurred, with the narrow version of character education dominating the field to the point that it is frequently mistaken for the broader concept. Thus educators who are keen to support children's social and moral development may turn, by default, to a program with a certain set of methods and a specific agenda that, on reflection, they might very well find objectionable.

From Kohn, A. (1997). How not to teach values: A critical look at character education. Phi Delta Kappan, 78(6), 428–439. *Reprinted with permission of the author.*

My purpose in this article is to subject these programs to careful scrutiny and, in so doing, to highlight the possibility that there are other ways to achieve our broader objectives. I address myself not so much to those readers who are avid proponents of character education (in the narrow sense) but to those who simply want to help children become decent human beings and may not have thought carefully about what they are being offered.

Let me get straight to the point. What goes by the name of character education nowadays is, for the most part, a collection of exhortations and extrinsic inducements designed to make children work harder and do what they're told. Even when other values are also promoted—caring or fairness, say—the preferred method of instruction is tantamount to indoctrination. The point is to drill students in specific behaviors rather than to engage them in deep, critical reflection about certain ways of being. This is the impression one gets from reading articles and books by contemporary proponents of character education as well as the curriculum materials sold by the leading national programs. The impression is only strengthened by visiting schools that have been singled out for their commitment to character education. To wit:

> *A huge, multiethnic elementary school in Southern California uses a framework created by the Jefferson Center for Character Education. Classes that the principal declares "well behaved" are awarded Bonus Bucks, which can eventually be redeemed for an ice cream party. On an enormous wall near the cafeteria, professionally painted Peanuts characters instruct children: "Never talk in line." A visitor is led to a fifth-grade classroom to observe an exemplary lesson on the current character education topic. The teacher is telling students to write down the name of the person they regard as the "toughest worker" in school. The teacher then asks them, "How many of you are going to be tough workers?" (Hands go up.) "Can you be a tough worker at home, too?" (Yes.)*

* * *

> *A small, almost entirely African American school in Chicago uses a framework created by the Character Education Institute. Periodic motivational assemblies are used to "give children a good pep talk," as the principal puts it, and to reinforce the values that determine who will be picked as Student of the Month. Rule number one posted on the wall of a kindergarten room is "We will obey the teachers." Today, students in this class are listening to the story of "Lazy Lion," who orders each of the other animals to build him a house, only to find each effort unacceptable. At the end, the teacher drives home the lesson: "Did you ever hear Lion say thank you?" (No.) "Did you ever hear Lion say please?"*

> *(No.) "It's good to always say . . . what?" (Please.) The reason for using these words, she points out, is that by doing so we are more likely to get what we want.*

* * *

> *A charter school near Boston has been established specifically to offer an intensive, homegrown character education curriculum to its overwhelmingly white, middle-class student body. At weekly public ceremonies, certain children receive a leaf that will then be hung in the Forest of Virtue. The virtues themselves are "not open to debate," the headmaster insists, since moral precepts in his view enjoy the same status as mathematical truths. In a first-grade classroom, a teacher is observing that "it's very hard to be obedient when you want something. I want you to ask yourself. 'Can I have it—and why not?'" She proceeds to ask the students, "What kinds of things show obedience?" and, after collecting a few suggestions, announces that she's "not going to call on anyone else now. We could go on forever, but we have to have a moment of silence and then a spelling test."*

Some of the most popular schoolwide strategies for improving students' character seem dubious on their face. When President Clinton mentioned the importance of character education in his 1996 State of the Union address, the only specific practice he recommended was requiring students to wear uniforms. The premises here are first, that children's character can be improved by forcing them to dress alike, and second, that if adults object to students' clothing, the best solution is not to invite them to reflect together about how this problem might be solved, but instead to compel them all to wear the same thing.

A second strategy, also consistent with the dominant philosophy of character education, is an exercise that might be called "If It's Tuesday, This Must Be Honesty." Here, one value after another is targeted, with each assigned its own day, week, or month. This seriatim approach is unlikely to result in a lasting commitment to any of these values, much less a feeling for how they may be related. Nevertheless, such programs are taken very seriously by some of the same people who are quick to dismiss other educational programs, such as those intended to promote self-esteem, as silly and ineffective.

Then there is the strategy of offering students rewards when they are "caught" being good, an approach favored by right-wing religious groups[1] and orthodox behaviorists but also by leaders of—and curriculum suppliers for—the character education movement.[2] Because of its popularity and because a sizable body of psychological evidence germane to the topic is available, it is worth lingering on this particular practice for a moment.

In general terms, what the evidence suggests is this: the more we reward people for doing something, the more likely they are to lose interest in whatever they had to do to get the reward. Extrinsic motivation, in other words, is not only quite different from intrinsic motivation but actually tends to erode it.[3] This effect has been demonstrated under many different circumstances and with respect to many different attitudes and behaviors. Most relevant to character education is a series of studies showing that individuals who have been rewarded for doing something nice become less likely to think of themselves as caring or helpful people and more likely to attribute their behavior to the reward.

"Extrinsic incentives can, by undermining self-perceived altruism, decrease intrinsic motivation to help others," one group of researchers concluded on the basis of several studies. "A person's kindness, it seems, cannot be bought."[4] The same applies to a person's sense of responsibility, fairness, perseverance, and so on. The lesson a child learns from Skinnerian tactics is that the point of being good is to get rewards. No wonder researchers have found that children who are frequently rewarded—or, in another study, children who receive positive reinforcement for caring, sharing, and helping—are less likely than other children to keep doing those things.[5]

In short, it makes no sense to dangle goodies in front of children for being virtuous. But even worse than rewards are *a*wards—certificates, plaques, trophies, and other tokens of recognition whose numbers have been artificially limited so only a few can get them. When some children are singled out as "winners," the central message that every child learns is this: "Other people are potential obstacles to my success."[6] Thus the likely result of making students beat out their peers for the distinction of being the most virtuous is not only less intrinsic commitment to virtue but also a disruption of relationships and, ironically, of the experience of community that is so vital to the development of children's character.

Unhappily, the problems with character education (in the narrow sense, which is how I'll be using the term unless otherwise indicated) are not restricted to such strategies as enforcing sartorial uniformity, scheduling a value of the week, or offering students a "doggie biscuit" for being good. More deeply troubling are the fundamental assumptions, both explicit and implicit, that inform character education programs. Let us consider five basic questions that might be asked of any such program: At what level are problems addressed? What is the underlying theory of human nature? What is the ultimate goal? Which values are promoted? And finally, How is learning thought to take place?

1. *At what level are problems addressed?* One of the major purveyors of materials in this field, the Jefferson Center for Character Education in Pasadena, California, has produced a video that begins with some arresting images—quite literally. Young people are shown being led away in handcuffs, the point being that crime can be explained on the basis of an "erosion of American core values," as the narrator intones ominously. The idea that social problems can be explained by the fact that traditional virtues are no longer taken seriously is offered by many proponents of character education as though it were just plain common sense.

But if people steal or rape or kill solely because they possess bad values—that is, because of their personal characteristics—the implication is that political and economic realities are irrelevant and need not be addressed. Never mind staggering levels of unemployment in the inner cities or a system in which more and more of the nation's wealth is concentrated in fewer and fewer hands; just place the blame on individuals whose characters are deficient. A key tenet of the "Character Counts!" Coalition, which bills itself as a nonpartisan umbrella group devoid of any political agenda, is the highly debatable proposition that "negative social influences can [be] and usually are overcome by the exercise of free will and character."[7] What is presented as common sense is, in fact, conservative ideology.

Let's put politics aside, though. If a program proceeds by trying to "fix the kids"—as do almost all brands of character education—it ignores the accumulated evidence from the field of social psychology demonstrating that much of how we act and who we are reflects the situations in which we find ourselves. Virtually all the landmark studies in this discipline have been variations on this theme. Set up children in an extended team competition at summer camp and you will elicit unprecedented levels of aggression. Assign adults to the roles of prisoners or guards in a mock jail, and they will start to become their roles. Move people to a small town, and they will be more likely to rescue a stranger in need. In fact, so common is the tendency to attribute to an individual's personality or character what is actually a function of the social environment that social psychologists have dubbed this the "fundamental attribution error."

A similar lesson comes to us from the movement concerned with Total Quality Management associated with the ideas of the late W. Edwards Deming. At the heart of Deming's teaching is the notion that the "system" of an organization largely determines the results. The problems experienced in a corporation, therefore, are almost always due to systemic flaws rather than to a lack of effort or ability on the part of individuals in that organization. Thus, if we are troubled by the way students are acting, Deming, along with most social psychologists, would presumably have us transform the structure of the classroom rather than try to remake the students themselves—precisely the opposite of the character education approach.

2. *What is the view of human nature?* Character education's "fix-the-kids" orientation follows logically from the belief that kids need fixing. Indeed, the movement seems to be driven by a stunningly dark view of children— and, for that matter, of people in general. A "comprehensive approach [to character education] is based on a somewhat dim view of human nature," acknowledges William Kilpatrick, whose book *Why Johnny Can't Tell Right from Wrong* contains such assertions as: "Most behavior problems are the result of sheer 'willfulness' on the part of children."[8]

Despite—or more likely because of—statements like that, Kilpatrick has frequently been invited to speak at character education conferences.[9] But that shouldn't be surprising in light of how many prominent proponents of character education share his views. Edward Wynne says his own work is grounded in a tradition of thought that takes a "somewhat pessimistic view of human nature."[10] The idea of character development "sees children as self-centered," in the opinion of Kevin Ryan, who directs the Center for the Advancement of Ethics and Character at Boston University as well as heading up the character education network of the Association for Supervision and Curriculum Development.[11] Yet another writer approvingly traces the whole field back to the bleak world view of Thomas Hobbes: it is "an obvious assumption of character education," writes Louis Goldman, that people lack the instinct to work together. Without laws to compel us to get along, "our natural egoism would lead us into 'a condition of warre one against another.'"[12] This sentiment is echoed by F. Washington Jarvis, headmaster of the Roxbury Latin School in Boston, one of Ryan's favorite examples of what character education should look like in practice. Jarvis sees human nature as "mean, nasty, brutish, selfish, and capable of great cruelty and meanness. We have to hold a mirror up to the students and say, 'This is who you are. Stop it.'"[13]

Even when proponents of character education don't express such sentiments explicitly, they give themselves away by framing their mission as a campaign for self-control. Amitai Etzioni, for example, does not merely include this attribute on a list of good character traits; he *defines* character principally in terms of the capacity "to control impulses and defer gratification."[14] This is note-

worthy because the virtue of self-restraint—or at least the decision to give special emphasis to it—has historically been preached by those, from St. Augustine to the present, who see people as basically sinful.

In fact, at least three assumptions seem to be at work when the need for self-control is stressed: first, that we are all at war not only with others but with ourselves, torn between our desires and our reason (or social norms); second, that these desires are fundamentally selfish, aggressive, or otherwise unpleasant; and third, that these desires are very strong, constantly threatening to overpower us if we don't rein them in. Collectively, these statements describe religious dogma, not scientific fact. Indeed, the evidence from several disciplines converges to cast doubt on this sour view of human beings and, instead, supports the idea that it is as "natural" for children to help as to hurt. I will not rehearse that evidence here, partly because I have done so elsewhere at some length.[15] Suffice it to say that even the most hard-headed empiricist might well conclude that the promotion of prosocial values consists to some extent of supporting (rather than restraining or controlling) many facets of the self. Any educator who adopts this more balanced position might think twice before joining an educational movement that is finally inseparable from the doctrine of original sin.

3. *What is the ultimate goal?* It may seem odd even to inquire about someone's reasons for trying to improve children's character. But it is worth mentioning that the whole enterprise—not merely the particular values that are favored—is often animated by a profoundly conservative, if not reactionary, agenda. Character education based on "acculturating students to conventional norms of 'good' behavior . . . resonates with neoconservative concerns for social stability," observed David Purpel.[16] The movement has been described by another critic as a "yearning for some halcyon days of moral niceties and social tranquillity."[17] But it is not merely a *social* order that some are anxious to preserve (or recover): character education is vital, according to one vocal proponent, because "the development of character is the backbone of the economic system" now in place.[18]

Character education, or any kind of education, would look very different if we began with other objectives—if, for example, we were principally concerned with helping children become active participants in a democratic society (or agents for transforming a society *into* one that is authentically democratic). It would look different if our top priority were to help students develop into principled and caring members of a community or advocates for social justice. To be sure, these objectives are not inconsistent with the desire to preserve certain traditions, but the point would then be to help children decide which traditions are worth preserving and why, based on these other considerations. That is not at all the same as endorsing anything that is traditional or making the preservation of tradition our primary concern. In short, we want to ask character education proponents what goals they emphasize—and ponder whether their broad vision is compatible with our own.

4. *Which values?* Should we allow values to be taught in school? The question is about as sensible as asking whether our bodies should be allowed to contain bacteria. Just as humans are teeming with microorganisms, so schools are teeming with values. We can't see the former because they're too small; we don't notice the latter because they're too similar to the values of the culture at large. Whether or not we deliberately adopt a character or moral education program, we are always teaching values. Even people who insist that they are opposed to values in school usually mean that they are opposed to values other than their own.[19]

And that raises the inevitable question: Which values, or whose, should we teach? It has already become a cliché to reply that this question should not trouble us because, while there may be disagreement on certain issues, such as abortion, all of us can agree on a list of basic values that children ought to have. Therefore, schools can vigorously and unapologetically set about teaching all of those values.

But not so fast. Look at the way character education programs have been designed and you will discover, alongside such unobjectionable items as "fairness" or "honesty," an emphasis on values that are, again, distinctly conservative—and, to that extent, potentially controversial. To begin with, the famous Protestant work ethic is prominent: children should learn to "work hard and complete their tasks well and promptly, even when they do not want to," says Ryan.[20] Here the Latin question *Cui bono?* comes to mind. Who benefits when people are trained not to question the value of what they have been told to do but simply to toil away at it—and to regard this as virtuous?[21] Similarly, when Wynne defines the moral individual as someone who is not only honest but also "diligent, obedient, and patriotic,"[22] readers may find themselves wondering whether these traits really qualify as *moral*—as well as reflecting on the virtues that are missing from this list.

Character education curricula also stress the importance of things like "respect," "responsibility," and "citizenship." But these are slippery terms, frequently used as euphemisms for uncritical deference to author-

ity. Under the headline "The Return of the 'Fourth R'"—referring to "respect, responsibility, or rules"—a news magazine recently described the growing popularity of such practices as requiring uniforms, paddling disobedient students, rewarding those who are compliant, and "throwing disruptive kids out of the classroom."[23] Indeed, William Glasser observed some time ago that many educators "teach thoughtless conformity to school rules and call the conforming child 'responsible.'"[24] I once taught at a high school where the principal frequently exhorted students to "take responsibility." By this he meant specifically that they should turn in their friends who used drugs.

Exhorting students to be "respectful" or rewarding them if they are caught being "good" may likewise mean nothing more than getting them to do whatever the adults demand. Following a lengthy article about character education in the *New York Times Magazine,* a reader mused, "Do you suppose that if Germany had had character education at the time, it would have encouraged children to fight Nazism or to support it?"[25] The more time I spend in schools that are enthusiastically implementing character education programs, the more I am haunted by that question.

In place of the traditional attributes associated with character education, Deborah Meier and Paul Schwarz of the Central Park East Secondary School in New York nominated two core values that a school might try to promote: "empathy and skepticism: the ability to see a situation from the eyes of another and the tendency to wonder about the validity of what we encountered."[26] Anyone who brushes away the question "Which values should be taught?" might speculate on the concrete differences between a school dedicated to turning out students who are empathic and skeptical and a school dedicated to turning out students who are loyal, patriotic, obedient, and so on.

Meanwhile, in place of such personal qualities as punctuality or perseverance, we might emphasize the cultivation of autonomy so that children come to experience themselves as "origins" rather than "pawns," as one researcher put it.[27] We might, in other words, stress self-determination at least as much as self-control. With such an agenda, it would be crucial to give students the chance to participate in making decisions about their learning and about how they want their classroom to be.[28] This stands in sharp contrast to a philosophy of character education like Wynne's, which decrees that "it is specious to talk about student choices" and offers students no real power except for when we give "some students authority over other students (for example, hall guard, class monitor)."[29]

Even with values that are widely shared, a superficial consensus may dissolve when we take a closer look. Educators across the spectrum are concerned about excessive attention to self-interest and are committed to helping students transcend a preoccupation with their own needs. But how does this concern play out in practice? For some of us, it takes the form of an emphasis on *compassion;* for the dominant character education approach, the alternative value to be stressed is *loyalty,* which is, of course, altogether different.[30] Moreover, as John Dewey remarked at the turn of the century, anyone seriously troubled about rampant individualism among children would promptly target for extinction the "drill-and-skill" approach to instruction: "The mere absorbing of facts and truths is so exclusively individual an affair that it tends very naturally to pass into selfishness."[31] Yet conservative champions of character education are often among the most outspoken supporters of a model of teaching that emphasizes rote memorization and the sequential acquisition of decontextualized skills.

Or take another example: all of us may say we endorse the idea of "cooperation," but what do we make of the practice of setting groups against one another in a quest for triumph, such that cooperation becomes the means and victory is the end? On the one hand, we might find this even more objectionable than individual competition. (Indeed, we might regard a "We're Number One!" ethic as a reason for schools to undertake something like character education in the first place.) On the other hand, "school-to-school, class-to-class, or row-to-row academic competitions" actually have been endorsed as part of a character education program,[32] along with contests that lead to awards for things like good citizenship.

The point, once again, is that it is entirely appropriate to ask which values a character education program is attempting to foster, notwithstanding the ostensible lack of controversy about a list of core values. It is equally appropriate to put such a discussion in context—specifically, in the context of which values are *currently* promoted in schools. The fact is that schools are already powerful socializers of traditional values—although, as noted above, we may fail to appreciate the extent to which this is true because we have come to take these values for granted. In most schools, for example, students are taught—indeed, compelled—to follow the rules regardless of whether the rules are reasonable and to respect authority regardless of whether that respect has been earned. (This process isn't always successful, of course, but that is a different matter.) Students are led to accept competi-

tion as natural and desirable, and to see themselves more as discrete individuals than as members of a community. Children in American schools are even expected to begin each day by reciting a loyalty oath to the Fatherland, although we call it by a different name. In short, the question is not whether to adopt the conservative values offered by most character education programs, but whether we want to consolidate the conservative values that are already in place.

5. *What is the theory of learning?* We come now to what may be the most significant, and yet the least remarked on, feature of character education: the way values are taught and the way learning is thought to take place.

> The character education coordinator for the small Chicago elementary school also teaches second grade. In her classroom, where one boy has been forced to sit by himself for the last two weeks ("He's kind of pesty"), she is asking the children to define tolerance. When the teacher gets the specific answers she is fishing for, she exclaims, "Say that again," and writes down only those responses. Later comes the moral: "If somebody doesn't think the way you think, should you turn them off?" (No.)
>
> Down the hall, the first-grade teacher is fishing for answers on a different subject. "When we play games, we try to understand the—what?" (Rules.) A moment later, the children scramble to get into place so she will pick them to tell a visitor their carefully rehearsed stories about conflict resolution. Almost every child's account, narrated with considerable prompting by the teacher, concerns name-calling or some other unpleasant incident that was "correctly" resolved by finding an adult. The teacher never asks the children how they felt about what happened or invites them to reflect on what else might have been done. She wraps up the activity by telling the children, "What we need to do all the time is clarify—make it clear—to the adult what you did."

The schools with character education programs that I have visited are engaged largely in exhortation and directed recitation. At first one might assume this is due to poor implementation of the programs on the part of individual educators. But the programs themselves—and the theorists who promote them—really do seem to regard teaching as a matter of telling and compelling. For example, the broad-based "Character Counts!" Coalition offers a framework of six core character traits and then asserts that "young people should be specifically and repeatedly told what is expected of them." The leading providers of curriculum materials walk teachers through highly structured lessons in which character-related concepts are described and then students are drilled until they can produce the right answers.

Teachers are encouraged to praise children who respond correctly, and some programs actually include multiple-choice tests to ensure that students have learned their values. For example, here are two sample test questions prepared for teachers by the Character Education Institute, based in San Antonio, Texas: "Having to obey rules and regulations (a) gives everyone the same right to be an individual, (b) forces everyone to do the same thing at all times, (c) prevents persons from expressing their individually [sic]"; and "One reason why parents might not allow their children freedom of choice is (a) children are always happier when they are told what to do and when to do it, (b) parents aren't given a freedom of choice; therefore, children should not be given a choice either, (c) children do not always demonstrate that they are responsible enough to be given a choice." The correct answers, according to the answer key, are (a) and (c) respectively.

The Character Education Institute recommends "engaging the students in discussions," but only discussions of a particular sort: "Since the lessons have been designed to logically guide the students to the right answers, the teacher should allow the students to draw their own conclusions. However, if the students draw the wrong conclusion, the teacher is instructed to tell them why their conclusion is *wrong*."[33]

Students are told what to think and do, not only by their teachers but by highly didactic stories, such as those in the Character Education Institute's "Happy Life" series, which end with characters saying things like "I am glad that I did not cheat," or "Next time I will be helpful," or "I will never be selfish again." Most character education programs also deliver homilies by way of posters and banners and murals displayed throughout the school. Children who do as they are told are presented with all manner of rewards, typically in front of their peers.

Does all of this amount to indoctrination? Absolutely, says Wynne, who declares that "school is and should and must be inherently indoctrinative."[34] Even when character education proponents tiptoe around that word, their model of instruction is clear: good character and values are *instilled in* or *transmitted to* students. We are "planting the ideas of virtue, of good traits in the young," says William Bennett.[35] The virtues or values in question are fully formed, and, in the minds of many character education proponents, divinely ordained. The children are—pick your favorite metaphor—so many passive receptacles to be filled,

lumps of clay to be molded, pets to be trained, or computers to be programmed.

Thus, when we see Citizen-of-the-Month certificates and "Be a good sport!" posters, when we find teachers assigning preachy stories and principals telling students what to wear, it is important that we understand what is going on. These techniques may appear merely innocuous or gimmicky; they may strike us as evidence of a scattershot, let's-try-anything approach. But the truth is that these are elements of a systematic pedagogical philosophy. They are manifestations of a model that sees children as objects to be manipulated rather than as learners to be engaged.

Ironically, some people who accept character education without a second thought are quite articulate about the bankruptcy of this model when it comes to teaching academic subjects. Plenty of teachers have abandoned the use of worksheets, textbooks, and lectures that fill children full of disconnected facts and skills. Plenty of administrators are working to create schools where students can actively construct meaning around scientific and historical and literary concepts. Plenty of educators, in short, realize that memorizing right answers and algorithms doesn't help anyone to arrive at a deep understanding of ideas.

And so we are left scratching our heads. Why would all these people, who know that the "transmission" model fails to facilitate intellectual development, uncritically accept the very same model to promote ethical development? How could they understand that mathematical truths cannot be shoved down students' throats but then participate in a program that essentially tries to shove moral truths down the same throats? In the case of individual educators, the simple answer may be that they missed the connection. Perhaps they just failed to recognize that "a classroom cannot foster the development of autonomy in the intellectual realm while suppressing it in the social and moral realms," as Constance Kamii and her colleagues put it not long ago.[36]

In the case of the proponents of character education, I believe the answer to this riddle is quite different. The reason they are promoting techniques that seem strikingly ineffective at fostering autonomy or ethical development is that, as a rule, they are not *trying* to foster autonomy or ethical development. The goal is not to support or facilitate children's social and moral growth, but simply to "demand good behavior from students," in Ryan's words.[37] The idea is to get compliance, to *make* children act the way we want them to.

Indeed, if these are the goals, then the methods make perfect sense—the lectures and pseudo-discussions, the slogans and the stories that conk students on the head with their morals. David Brooks, who heads the Jefferson Center for Character Education, frankly states, "We're in the advertising business." The way you get people to do something, whether it's buying Rice Krispies or becoming trustworthy, is to "encourage conformity through repeated messages."[38] The idea of selling virtues like cereal nearly reaches the point of self-parody in the Jefferson Center's curriculum, which includes the following activity: "There's a new product on the market! It's Considerate Cereal. Eating it can make a person more considerate. Design a label for the box. Tell why someone should buy and eat this cereal. Then list the ingredients."[39]

If "repeated messages" don't work, then you simply force students to conform: "Sometimes compulsion is what is needed to get a habit started," says William Kilpatrick.[40] We may recoil from the word "compulsion," but it is the premise of that sentence that really ought to give us pause. When education is construed as the process of inculcating *habits*—which is to say, unreflective actions—then it scarcely deserves to be called education at all. It is really, as Alan Lockwood saw, an attempt to get "mindless conformity to externally imposed standards of conduct."[41]

Notice how naturally this goal follows from a dark view of human nature. If you begin with the premise that "good conduct is not our natural first choice," then the best you can hope for is "the development of good habits"[42]—that is, a system that gets people to act unthinkingly in the manner that someone else has deemed appropriate. This connection recently became clear to Ann Medlock, whose Giraffe Project was designed to evoke "students' own courage and compassion" in thinking about altruism, but which, in some schools, was being turned into a traditional, authoritarian program in which students were simply told how to act and what to believe. Medlock recalls suddenly realizing what was going on with these educators: "Oh, *I* see where you're coming from. You believe kids are no damn good!"[43]

The character education movement's emphasis on habit, then, is consistent with its view of children. Likewise, its process matches its product. The transmission model, along with the use of rewards and punishments to secure compliance, seems entirely appropriate if the values you are trying to transmit are things like obedience and loyalty and respect for authority. But this approach overlooks an important distinction between product and process. When we argue about which traits to emphasize—compassion or loyalty, cooperation or competition, skepticism or obedience—we are trafficking in value judgments. When we talk about how best to teach these things, however, we are being descriptive rather than just prescriptive. Even if you like the sort of virtues that appear in character education programs, and even if you regard the need to implement those virtues as urgent, the attempt to transmit or instill them dooms the project because that is just not consistent with the best theory and research on how people learn. (Of course, if you have reservations about many of the values that the character educators wish to instill, you may be *relieved* that their favored method is unlikely to be successful.)

I don't wish to be misunderstood. The techniques of character education may succeed in temporarily buying a particular behavior. But they are unlikely to leave children with a *commitment* to that behavior, a reason to continue acting that way in the future. You can turn out automatons who utter the desired words or maybe even "emit" (to use the curious verb favored by behaviorists) the desired actions. But the words and actions are unlikely to continue—much less transfer to new situations—because the child has not been invited to integrate them into his or her value structure. As Dewey observed, "The required beliefs cannot be hammered in; the needed attitudes cannot be plastered on."[44] Yet watch a character education lesson in any part of the country and you will almost surely be observing a strenuous exercise in hammering and plastering.

For traditional moralists, the constructivist approach is a waste of time. If values and traditions and the stories that embody them already exist, then surely "we don't have to reinvent the wheel," remarks Bennett.[45] Likewise an exasperated Wynne: "Must each generation try to completely reinvent society?"[46] The answer is no—and yes. It is not as though everything that now exists must be discarded and entirely new values fashioned from scratch. But the process of learning does indeed require that meaning, ethical or otherwise, be actively invented and reinvented, from the inside out. It requires that children be given the opportunity to make sense of such concepts as fairness or courage, regardless of how long the concepts themselves have been around. Children must be invited to reflect on complex issues, to recast them in light of their own experiences and questions, to figure out for themselves—and with one another—what kind of person one ought to be, which traditions are worth keeping, and how to proceed when two basic values seem to be in conflict.[47]

In this sense, reinvention is necessary if we want to help children become moral people, as opposed to people who merely do what they are told—or reflexively rebel against what they are told. In fact, as Rheta DeVries and Betty Zan add (in a recent book that offers a useful antidote to traditional character education), "If we want children to resist [peer pressure] and not be victims of others' ideas, we have to educate children to think for themselves about all ideas, including those of adults."[48]

Traditionalists are even more likely to offer another objection to the constructivist approach, one that boils down to a single epithet: *relativism!* If we do anything other than insert moral absolutes in students, if we let them construct their own meanings, then we are saying that anything goes, that morality collapses into personal preferences. Without character education, our schools will just offer programs such as Values Clarification, in which adults are allegedly prohibited from taking a stand.

In response, I would offer several observations. First, the Values Clarification model of moral education, popular in some circles a generation ago, survives today mostly in the polemics of conservatives anxious to justify an indoctrinative approach. Naturally, no statistics are ever cited as to the number of school districts still telling students that any value is as good as any other—assuming the program actually said that in the first place.[49] Second, conservative critics tendentiously try to connect constructivism to relativism, lumping together the work of the late Lawrence Kohlberg with programs like Values Clarification.[50] The truth is that Kohlberg, while opposed to what he called the "bag of virtues" approach to moral education, was not much enamored of Values Clarification either, and he spent a fair amount of time arguing against relativism in general.[51]

If Kohlberg can fairly be criticized, it is for emphasizing moral reasoning, a cognitive process, to the extent that he may have slighted the affective components of morality, such as caring. But the traditionalists are not much for the latter either: caring is seen as an easy or soft virtue (Ryan) that isn't sufficiently "binding or absolute" (Kilpatrick). The objection to constructivism is not that empathy is eclipsed by justice, but that children—or even adults—should not have an active role to play in making decisions and reflecting on how to live. They should be led instead to an uncritical acceptance of ready-made truths. The character educator's job, remember, is to elicit the right answer from students and tell those who see things differently "why their conclusion is *wrong.*" Any deviation from this approach is regarded as indistinguishable from full-blown relativism; we must "plant" traditional values in each child or else morality is nothing more than a matter of individual taste. Such either/or thinking, long since discarded by serious moral philosophers,[52]

continues to fuel character education and to perpetuate the confusion of education with indoctrination.

To say that students must construct meaning around moral concepts is not to deny that adults have a crucial role to play. The romantic view that children can basically educate themselves so long as grown-ups don't interfere is not taken seriously by any constructivists I know of—certainly not by Dewey, Piaget, Kohlberg, or their followers. Rather, like Values Clarification, this view seems to exist principally as a straw man in the arguments of conservatives. Let there be no question, then: educators, parents, and other adults are desperately needed to offer guidance, to act as models (we hope), to pose challenges that promote moral growth, and to help children understand the effects of their actions on other people, thereby tapping and nurturing a concern for others that is present in children from a very young age.[53]

Character education rests on three ideological legs: behaviorism, conservatism, and religion. Of these, the third raises the most delicate issues for a critic; it is here that the charge of *ad hominem* argument is most likely to be raised. So let us be clear: it is of no relevance that almost all of the leading proponents of character education are devout Catholics. But it is entirely relevant that, in the shadows of their writings, there lurks the assumption that only religion can serve as the foundation for good character. (William Bennett, for example, has flatly asserted that the difference between right and wrong cannot be taught "without reference to religion."[54]) It is appropriate to consider the personal beliefs of these individuals if those beliefs are ensconced in the movement they have defined and directed. What they do on Sundays is their own business, but if they are trying to turn our public schools into Sunday schools, that becomes everybody's business.

Even putting aside the theological underpinnings of the character education movement, the five questions presented in this article can help us describe the natural constituency of that movement. Logically, its supporters should be those who firmly believe that we should focus our efforts on repairing the characters of children rather than on transforming the environments in which they learn, those who assume the worst about human nature, those who are more committed to preserving than to changing our society, those who favor such values as obedience to authority, and those who define learning as the process of swallowing whole a set of preexisting truths. It stands to reason that readers who recognize themselves in this description would enthusiastically endorse character education in its present form.

The rest of us have a decision to make. Either we define our efforts to promote children's social and moral development as an *alternative* to "character education," thereby ceding that label to the people who have already appropriated it, or we try to *reclaim* the wider meaning of the term by billing what we are doing as a different kind of character education.

The first choice—opting out—seems logical: it strains the language to use a single phrase to describe practices as different as engaging students in reflecting about fairness, on the one hand, and making students dress alike, on the other. It seems foolish to pretend that these are just different versions of the same thing, and thus it may be unreasonable to expect someone with a constructivist or progressive vision to endorse what is now called character education. The problem with abandoning this label, however, is that it holds considerable appeal for politicians and members of the public at large. It will be challenging to explain that "character education" is not synonymous with helping children to grow into good people and, indeed, that the movement associated with the term is a good deal more controversial than it first appears.

The second choice, meanwhile, presents its own set of practical difficulties. Given that the individuals and organizations mentioned in this article have succeeded in putting their own stamp on character education, it will not be easy to redefine the phrase so that it can also signify a very different approach. It will not be easy, that is, to organize conferences, publish books and articles, and develop curricular materials that rescue the broad meaning of "character education."

Whether we relinquish or retain the nomenclature, though, it is vital that we work to decouple most of what takes place under the banner of "character education" from the enterprise of helping students become ethically sophisticated decision makers and caring human beings. Wanting young people to turn out that way doesn't require us to adopt traditional character education programs any more than wanting them to be physically fit requires us to turn schools into Marine boot camps.

What does the alternative look like? Return once more to those five questions: in each case, an answer different from that given by traditional character education will help us to sketch the broad contours of a divergent approach. More specifically, we should probably target certain practices for elimination, add some new ones, and reconfigure still others that already exist. I have already offered a catalogue of examples of what to eliminate, from Skinnerian reinforcers to lesson plans that resemble sermons. As examples of what to add, we

might suggest holding regular class meetings in which students can share, plan, decide, and reflect together.[55] We might also provide children with explicit opportunities to practice "perspective taking"—that is, imagining how the world looks from someone else's point of view. Activities that promote an understanding of how others think and feel, that support the impulse to imaginatively reach beyond the self, can provide the same benefits realized by holding democratic class meetings—namely, helping students become more ethical and compassionate while simultaneously fostering intellectual growth.[56]

A good example of an existing practice that might be reconfigured is the use of literature to teach values. In principle, the idea is splendid: it makes perfect sense to select stories that not only help students develop reading skills (and an appreciation for good writing) but also raise moral issues. The trouble is that many programs use simplistic little morality tales in place of rich, complex literature. Naturally, the texts should be developmentally appropriate, but some character educators fail to give children credit for being able to grapple with ambiguity. (Imagine the sort of stories likely to be assigned by someone who maintains that "it is ridiculous to believe children are capable of objectively assessing most of the beliefs and values they must absorb to be effective adults."[57])

Perhaps the concern is not that students will be unable to make sense of challenging literature, but that they will not derive the "correct" moral. This would account for the fact that even when character education curricula include impressive pieces of writing, the works tend to be used for the purpose of drumming in simple lessons. As Kilpatrick sees it, a story "points to these [characters] and says in effect, 'Act like this; don't act like that.'"[58] This kind of lesson often takes the form of hero worship, with larger-than-life characters—or real historical figures presented with their foibles airbrushed away—held up to students to encourage imitation of their actions.

Rather than employ literature to indoctrinate or induce mere conformity, we can use it to spur reflection. Whether the students are 6-year-olds or 16-year-olds, the discussion of stories should be open-ended rather than relentlessly didactic. Teachers who refrain from tightly controlling such conversations are impressed again and again by the levels of meaning students prove capable of exploring and the moral growth they exhibit in such an environment. Instead of announcing, "This man is a hero; do what he did," such teachers may involve the students in *deciding* who (if anyone) is heroic in a given story—or in contemporary culture[59]—and why. They may even invite students to reflect on the larger issue of whether it is desirable to have heroes. (Consider the quality of discussion that might be generated by asking older students to respond to the declaration of playwright Bertolt Brecht: "Unhappy is the land that needs a hero.")

More than specific practices that might be added, subtracted, or changed, a program to help children grow into good people begins with a commitment to change the way classrooms and schools are structured—and this brings us back to the idea of transcending a fix-the-kid approach. Consider the format of classroom discussions. A proponent of character education, invoking such traditional virtues as patience or self-control, might remind students that they must wait to be recognized by the teacher. But what if we invited students to think about the best way to conduct a discussion? Must we raise our hands? Is there another way to avoid having everyone talk at once? How can we be fair to those who aren't as assertive or as fast on their feet? Should the power to decide who can speak always rest with the teacher? Perhaps the problem is not with students who need to be more self-disciplined, but with the whole instructional design that has students waiting to be recognized to answer someone else's questions. And perhaps the real learning comes only when students have the chance to grapple with such issues.

One more example. A proponent of character education says we must make students understand that it is wrong to lie; we need to teach them about the importance of being honest. But why do people lie? Usually because they don't feel safe enough to tell the truth. The real challenge for us as educators is to examine that precept in terms of what is going on in our classrooms, to ask how we and the students together can make sure that even unpleasant truths can be told and heard. Does pursuing this line of inquiry mean that it's acceptable to fib? No. It means the problem has to be dissected and solved from the inside out. It means behaviors occur in a context that teachers have helped to establish; therefore, teachers have to examine (and consider modifying) that context even at the risk of some discomfort to themselves. In short, if we want to help children grow into compassionate and responsible people, we have to change the way the classroom works and feels, not just the way each separate member of that class acts. Our emphasis should not be on forming individual characters so much as on transforming educational structures.

Happily, programs do exist whose promotion of children's social and moral development is grounded in a commitment to change the culture of schools. The best example of which I am aware is the Child Development Project, an elementary school program designed, implemented, and researched by the Developmental Studies Center in Oakland, California. The CDP's premise is that, by meeting children's needs, we increase the likelihood that they will care about others. Meeting their needs entails, among other things, turning schools into caring communities. The CDP offers the additional advantages of a constructivist vision of learning, a positive view of human nature, a balance of cognitive and affective concerns, and a program that is integrated into all aspects of school life (including the curriculum).[60]

Is the CDP an example of what character education ought to be—or of what ought to replace character education? The answer to that question will depend on tactical, and even semantic, considerations. Far more compelling is the need to reevaluate the practices and premises of contemporary character education. To realize a humane and progressive vision for children's development, we may need to look elsewhere.

Notes

1. See, for example, Linda Page, "A Conservative Christian View on Values," *School Administrator,* September 1995, p. 22.

2. See, for example, Kevin Ryan, "The Ten Commandments of Character Education," *School Administrator,* September 1995, p. 19; and program materials from the Character Education Institute and the Jefferson Center for Character Education.

3. See Alfie Kohn, *Punished by Rewards: The Trouble with Gold Stars. Incentive Plans, A's, Praise, and Other Bribes* (Boston: Houghton Mifflin, 1993); and Edward L. Deci and Richard M. Ryan, *Intrinsic Motivation and Self-Determination in Human Behavior* (New York: Plenum, 1985).

4. See C. Daniel Batson et al., "Buying Kindness: Effect of an Extrinsic Incentive for Helping on Perceived Altruism," *Personality and Social Psychology Bulletin,* vol. 4, 1978, p. 90; Cathleen L. Smith et al., "Children's Causal Attributions Regarding Help Giving," *Child Development,* vol. 50, 1979, pp. 203–10; and William Edward Upton III, "Altruism, Attribution, and Intrinsic Motivation in the Recruitment of Blood Donors," *Dissertation Abstracts International* 34B, vol. 12, 1974, p. 6260.

5. Richard A. Fabes et al., "Effects of Rewards on Children's Prosocial Motivation: A Socialization Study," *Developmental Psychology,* vol. 25, 1989, pp. 509–15; and Joan Grusec, "Socializing Concern for Others in the Home," *Developmental Psychology,* vol. 27, 1991, pp. 338–42.

6. See Alfie Kohn, *No Contest: The Case Against Competition,* rev. ed. (Boston: Houghton Mifflin, 1992).

7. This statement is taken from an eight-page brochure produced by the "Character Counts!" Coalition, a project of the

Josephson Institute of Ethics. Members of the coalition include the American Federation of Teachers, the National Association of Secondary School Principals, the American Red Cross, the YMCA, and many other organizations.

8. William Kilpatrick, *Why Johnny Can't Tell Right from Wrong* (New York: Simon & Schuster, 1992), pp. 96, 249.

9. For example, Kilpatrick was selected in 1995 to keynote the first in a series of summer institutes on character education sponsored by Thomas Lickona.

10. Edward Wynne, "Transmitting Traditional Values in Contemporary Schools," in Larry P. Nucci, ed., *Moral Development and Character Education: A Dialogue* (Berkeley, Calif.: McCutchan, 1989), p. 25.

11. Kevin Ryan, "In Defense of Character Education," in Nucci, p. 16.

12. Louis Goldman, "Mind, Character, and the Deferral of Gratification," *Educational Forum,* vol. 60, 1996, p. 136. As part of "educational reconstruction," he goes on to say, we must "connect the lower social classes to the middle classes who may provide role models for self-discipline" (p. 139).

13. Jarvis is quoted in Wray Herbert, "The Moral Child," *U.S. News & World Report,* 3 June 1996, p. 58.

14. Amitai Etzioni, *The Spirit of Community: The Reinvention of American Society* (New York: Simon & Schuster, 1993), p. 91.

15. See Alfie Kohn, *The Brighter Side of Human Nature: Altruism and Empathy in Everyday Life* (New York: Basic Books, 1990); and "Caring Kids: The Role of the Schools," *Phi Delta Kappan,* March 1991, pp. 496–506.

16. David E. Purpel, "Moral Education: An Idea Whose Time Has Gone," *The Clearing House,* vol. 64, 1991, p. 311.

17. This description of the character education movement is offered by Alan L. Lockwood in "Character Education: The Ten Percent Solution," *Social Education,* April/May 1991, p. 246. It is a particularly apt characterization of a book like *Why Johnny Can't Tell Right from Wrong,* which invokes an age of "chivalry" and sexual abstinence, a time when moral truths were uncomplicated and unchallenged. The author's tone, however, is not so much wistful about the past as angry about the present: he denounces everything from rock music (which occupies an entire chapter in a book about morality) and feminism to the "multiculturalists" who dare to remove "homosexuality from the universe of moral judgment" (p. 126).

18. Kevin Walsh of the University of Alabama is quoted in Eric N. Berg, "Argument Grows That Teaching of Values Should Rank with Lessons," *New York Times,* 1 January 1992, p. 32.

19. I am reminded of a woman in a Houston audience who heatedly informed me that she doesn't send her child to school "to learn to be nice." That, she declared, would be "social engineering." But a moment later this woman added that her child ought to be "taught to respect authority." Since this would seem to be at least as apposite an example of social engineering, one is led to conclude that the woman's real objection was to the teaching of *particular* topics or values.

20. Kevin Ryan, "Mining the Values in the Curriculum," *Educational Leadership,* November 1993, p. 16.

21. Telling students to "try hard" and "do their best" *begs* the important questions. *How,* exactly, do they do their best? Surely it is not just a matter of blind effort. And *why* should they do so, particularly if the task is not engaging or meaningful to them, or if it has simply been imposed on them? Research has found that the attitudes students take toward learning are heavily influenced by whether they have been led to attribute their success (or failure) to innate ability, to effort, or to other factors—and that traditional classroom practices such as grading and competition lead them to explain the results in terms of ability (or its absence) and to minimize effort whenever possible. What looks like "laziness" or insufficient perseverance, in other words, often turns out to be a rational decision to avoid challenge; it is rational because this route proves most expedient for performing well or maintaining an image of oneself as smart. These systemic factors, of course, are complex and often threatening for educators to address; it is much easier just to impress on children the importance of doing their best and then blame them for lacking perseverance if they seem not to do so.

22. Edward A. Wynne, "The Great Tradition in Education: Transmitting Moral Values," *Educational Leadership,* December 1985/January 1986, p. 6.

23. Mary Lord, "The Return of the 'Fourth R,'" *U.S. News & World Report,* 11 September 1995, p. 58.

24. William Glasser, *Schools Without Failure* (New York: Harper & Row, 1969), p. 22.

25. Marc Desmond's letter appeared in the *New York Times Magazine,* 21 May 1995, p. 14. The same point was made by Robert Primack, "No Substitute for Critical Thinking: A Response to Wynne," *Educational Leadership,* December 1985/January 1986, p. 12.

26. Deborah Meier and Paul Schwarz, "Central Park East Secondary School," in Michael W. Apple and James A. Beane, eds., *Democratic Schools* (Alexandria, Va.: Association for Supervision and Curriculum Development, 1995), pp. 29–30.

27. See Richard de Charms. *Personal Causation: The Internal Affective Determinants of Behavior* (Hillsdale, N.J.: Erlbaum, 1983). See also the many publications of Edward Deci and Richard Ryan.

28. See, for example, Alfie Kohn, "Choices for Children: Why and How to Let Students Decide," *Phi Delta Kappan,* September 1993, pp. 8–20; and Child Development Project, *Ways We Want Our Class to Be: Class Meetings That Build Commitment to Kindness and Learning* (Oakland, Calif.: Developmental Studies Center, 1996).

29. The quotations are from Wynne, "The Great Tradition," p. 9; and Edward A. Wynne and Herbert J. Walberg, "The Complementary Goals of Character Development and Academic Excellence," *Educational Leadership,* December 1985/January 1986, p. 17. William Kilpatrick is equally averse to including students in decision making; he speaks longingly of the days when "schools were unapologetically authoritarian," declaring that "schools can learn a lot from the Army," which is a

"hierarchial [sic], authoritarian, and undemocratic institution" (see *Why Johnny Can't,* p. 228).

30. The sort of compassion I have in mind is akin to what the psychologist Ervin Staub described as a "prosocial orientation" (see his *Positive Social Behavior and Morality,* vols. 1 and 2 [New York: Academic Press, 1978 and 1979])—a generalized inclination to care, share, and help across different situations and with different people, including those we don't know, don't like, and don't look like. Loyally lending a hand to a close friend is one thing; going out of one's way for a stranger is something else.

31. John Dewey, *The School and Society* (Chicago: University of Chicago Press, 1900; reprint, 1990), p. 15.

32. Wynne and Walberg, p. 17. For another endorsement of competition among students, see Kevin Ryan. "In Defense," p. 15.

33. This passage is taken from page 21 of an undated 28-page "Character Education Curriculum" produced by the Character Education Institute. Emphasis in original.

34. Wynne, "Great Tradition," p. 9. Wynne and other figures in the character education movement acknowledge their debt to the French social scientist Emile Durkheim, who believed that "all education is a continuous effort to impose on the child ways of seeing, feeling, and acting which he could not have arrived at spontaneously. . . . We exert pressure upon him in order that he may learn proper consideration for others, respect for customs and conventions, the need for work, etc." (See Durkheim, *The Rules of Sociological Method* [New York: Free Press, 1938], p. 6.)

35. This is from Bennett's introduction to *The Book of Virtues* (New York: Simon & Schuster, 1993), pp. 12–13.

36. Constance Kamii, Faye B. Clark, and Ann Dominick, "The Six National Goals: A Road to Disappointment," *Phi Delta Kappan,* May 1994, p. 677.

37. Kevin Ryan, "Character and Coffee Mugs," *Education Week,* 17 May 1995, p. 48.

38. The second quotation is a reporter's paraphrase of Brooks. Both it and the direct quotation preceding it appear in Philip Cohen, "The Content of Their Character: Educators Find New Ways to Tackle Values and Morality," *ASCD Curriculum Update,* Spring 1995, p. 4.

39. See B. David Brooks, *Young People's Lessons in Character: Student Activity Workbook* (San Diego: Young People's Press, 1996), p. 12.

40. Kilpatrick, p. 231.

41. To advocate this sort of enterprise, he adds, is to "caricature the moral life." See Alan L. Lockwood, "Keeping Them in the Courtyard: A Response to Wynne," *Educational Leadership,* December 1985/January 1986, p. 10.

42. Kilpatrick, p. 97.

43. Personal communication with Ann Medlock, May 1996.

44. John Dewey, *Democracy and Education* (New York: Free Press, 1916; reprint, 1966), p. 11.

45. Bennett, p. 11.

46. Wynne. "Character and Academics," p. 142.

47. For a discussion of how traditional character education fails to offer guidance when values come into conflict, see Lockwood, "Character Education."

48. Rheta DeVries and Betty Zan, *Moral Classrooms, Moral Children: Creating a Constructivist Atmosphere in Early Education* (New York: Teachers College Press, 1994), p. 253.

49. For an argument that critics tend to misrepresent what Values Clarification was about, see James A. Beane, *Affect in the Curriculum* (New York: Teachers College Press, 1990), pp. 104–6.

50. Wynne, for example refers to the developers of Values Clarification as "popularizers" of Kohlberg's research (see "Character and Academics," p. 141), while Amitai Etzioni, in the course of criticizing Piaget's and Kohlberg's work, asserts that "a typical course on moral reasoning starts with something called 'values clarification'" (see *The Spirit of Community,* p. 98).

51. Kohlberg's model, which holds that people across cultures progress predictably through six stages of successively more sophisticated styles of moral reasoning, is based on the decidedly nonrelativistic premise that the last stages are superior to the first ones. See his *Essays on Moral Development, Vol. 1: The Philosophy of Moral Development* (San Francisco: Harper & Row, 1981), especially the essays titled "Indoctrination Versus Relativity in Value Education" and "From *Is* to *Ought.*"

52. See, for example, James S. Fishkin, *Beyond Subjective Morality* (New Haven, Conn.: Yale University Press, 1984): and David B. Wong, *Moral Relativity* (Berkeley: University of California Press, 1984).

53. Researchers at the National Institute of Mental Health have summarized the available research as follows: "Even children as young as 2 years old have (a) the cognitive capacity to interpret the physical and psychological states of others, (b) the emotional capacity to effectively experience the other's state, and (c) the behavioral repertoire that permits the possibility of trying to alleviate discomfort in others. These are the capabilities that, we believe, underlie children's caring behavior in the presence of another person's distress. . . . Young children seem to show patterns of moral internalization that are not simply fear based or solely responsive to parental commands. Rather, there are signs that children feel responsible for (as well as connected to and dependent on) others at a very young age." (See Carolyn Zahn-Waxler et al., "Development of Concern for Others," *Developmental Psychology,* vol. 28, 1992, pp. 127, 135. For more on the adult's role in light of these facts, see Kohn, *The Brighter Side.*)

54. "Education Secretary Backs Teaching of Religious Values," *New York Times,* 12 November 1985, p. B-4.

55. For more on class meetings, see Glasser, chaps. 10–12; Thomas Gordon, *T.E.T.: Teacher Effectiveness Training* (New York: David McKay Co., 1974), chaps. 8–9, Jane Nelsen, Lynn Lott, and H. Stephen Glenn, *Positive Discipline in the Classroom* (Rocklin, Calif.: Prima, 1993); and Child Development Project, op. cit.

56. For more on the theory and research of perspective taking, see Kohn, *The Brighter Side,* chaps. 4–5; for practical classroom activities for promoting perspective-taking skills, see Norma Deitch Feshbach et al., *Learning to Care: Classroom Activities for Social and Affective Development* (Glenview, Ill.: Scott, Foresman, 1983). While specialists in the field distinguish between perspective taking (imagining what others see, think, or feel) and empathy (*feeling* what others feel), most educators who talk about the importance of helping children become empathic really seem to be talking about perspective taking.

57. Wynne, "Great Tradition," p. 9.

58. Kilpatrick, p. 141.

59. It is informative to discover whom the proponents of a hero-based approach to character education themselves regard as heroic. For example, William Bennett's nominee for "possibly our greatest living American" is Rush Limbaugh. (See Terry Eastland, "Rush Limbaugh: Talking Back." *American Spectator,* September 1992, p. 23.)

60. See Victor Battistich et al., "The Child Development Project: A Comprehensive Program for the Development of Prosocial Character," in William M. Kurtines and Jacob L. Gewirtz, eds., *Moral Behavior and Development: Advances in Theory, Research, and Applications* (Hillsdale, N.J.: Erlbaum, 1989); and Daniel Solomon et al., "Creating a Caring Community: Educational Practices That Promote Children's Prosocial Development," in Fritz K. Oser, Andreas Dick, and Jean-Luc Patry, eds., *Effective and Responsible Teaching* (San Francisco: Jossey-Bass, 1992). For more information about the CDP program or about the research substantiating its effects, write the Developmental Studies Center at 2000 Embarcadero, Suite 305, Oakland, CA 94606.

TEACHING ABOUT RELIGION
Susan Black

Religion and religious thought have had an enormous impact on history and are therefore an important component of social studies education. However, the author asserts, teaching *about* religion is very different from teaching religion, and schools sometimes go wrong in ignoring the word *about*. The First Amendment to the Constitution, in mandating the principle of separation of church and state, requires that the government and public schools remain neutral with respect to religion. However, maintaining that neutrality is a challenge for schools and teachers, who sometimes cross the line and provide religious instruction, which violates the principle. As you read this article ask yourself, "What is the proper role of religion?"

Think About This . . .

1. According to the "Federal Guidelines for Religious Expression in Public Schools," what is legally permissible with respect to teaching about religion? Do you believe a teacher with strong religious beliefs is capable of adhering to these guidelines? Why or why not?

2. What are some examples of "unconstitutional instruction?" Do you agree with these guidelines? Why or why not?

3. What are several trends revealed by research with respect to teaching about religion in the public schools? Which of these trends is most significant with respect to the curriculum? Why do you think so?

4. If a controversial religious issue came up in one of your classes, how would you handle it? Provide a specific example to illustrate your description.

"One can hardly respect a system of education that would leave the student wholly ignorant of the currents of religious thought that move the world society."

So said Supreme Court Justice Robert Jackson in the 1948 case of *Illinois ex rel. McCollum v. Board of Education.* And 15 years later, Justice Tom Clark echoed that thought in the high court's majority opinion in School District of *Abington v. Schempp* (1963). "One's education is not complete," Justice Clark wrote, "without a study of comparative religion or the history of religion and its relationship to the advancement of civilization."

But teaching about "the currents of religious thought" or about religion's "relationship to the advancement of civilization" is one thing; providing religious instruction is quite another, and that's where some schools have come to grief.

The Supreme Court's interpretation of the First Amendment says the government—and public schools, by extension—must remain neutral toward religion. But maintaining neutrality can be a challenge for teachers. In a November 2002 publication advising teachers how to navigate the subject of religion in their classrooms, the National Education Association says teachers must teach every lesson about religion without bias. At the same time, they must honor their students' personal views on religion and hold and observe their own beliefs privately.

Teachers also need to know which topics are permissible in classroom study of religion, and they need to know which instructional techniques may be used to convey these topics. That means school leaders need to provide guidance and support to teachers who cover curriculum topics related to religion—and they need to be certain that, when it comes to teaching *about* religion, the district abides by the letter of the law.

What's Permissible

According to "Federal Guidelines for Religious Expression in Public Schools," issued in 1995 by then-Secretary of Education Richard Riley, teachers may include the Bible or other scripture in lessons about religion, and they may cover such topics as the history of religion, comparative religions, and the influence of religion on art, music, and literature.

Teachers may also teach about religious holidays, and they may celebrate secular aspects of holidays with their students, but they may not observe holidays as religious events or promote such observances by students. In addition, teachers may teach civic values and virtues—including those held by various reli-

gious groups—but the guidelines specify that such lessons should reinforce "the moral code that holds us together as a community."

In turn—according to the new guidelines and the 1995 document alike—students may express their beliefs about religion in the form of homework, artwork, and other written and oral assignments. When students exercise this right, teachers must treat students without discrimination, and they must judge students' work by academic standards of substance and relevance, as well as other standards set by the school.

Most scholars recognize that religion has a legitimate place in history and civics courses. Indiana University's C. Frederick Risinger, a specialist in social studies curriculum and instruction, says students should understand the religious ideas associated with such topics as nationalism, imperialism, anticolonialism, slavery and antislavery, freedom of conscience, capitalism, and environmentalism.

The study of the conflict in Bosnia, for example, requires understanding the historical enmity among Roman Catholics, Orthodox Christians, and Muslims in the Balkan region. Similarly, studying Northern Ireland's political history requires understanding the roots of the ongoing dissension between Protestants and Catholics.

To uphold constitutionally approved teaching about religion (and refrain from unconstitutional religious indoctrination), Risinger advises schools to: (1) adopt an approach that is academic, not devotional; (2) strive for students' awareness of religions without pressuring students to accept any one favored religion; (3) expose students to a diversity of religious views without imposing viewpoints on students; and (4) educate students about all religions.

The Washington, D.C.-based Americans United for Separation of Church and State (AU) holds a similar position. Interpreting the federal government's guidelines, AU says the history of religion and comparative religion are permissible subjects, providing the instructional approach is objective and serves a legitimate educational purpose.

AU also says that it's permissible for students to study the role of religion in U.S. history, and they may study historic documents (such as the Declaration of Independence) that contain references to God, provided teachers do not use such documents to promote a religious viewpoint.

From Black, S. (2003). Teaching about religion. American School Board Journal, 190(4), 50–53. *Reprinted with permission of the* American School Board Journal.

Getting It Wrong

But reality isn't always in accord with these recommendations. In *Abington v. Schempp,* the Supreme Court held that teaching about the Bible in a public school must be done "objectively as part of a secular program of education." But the People For the American Way Foundation, a Washington, D.C.-based advocacy group, says several schools violate this ruling by teaching the Bible from a sectarian perspective, as historical fact, and to support certain religious faiths.

In a report titled "The Good Book Taught Wrong: Bible History Classes in Florida Public Schools," the foundation describes findings from a yearlong investigation of Bible history courses taught in Florida high schools. Examples of "unconstitutional instruction" include:

- Assuming that all students are Christians.
- Teaching about religion from a Christian perspective without regard for other faiths.
- Treating Biblical events as universally held factual historical events.
- Requiring students to define their personal relationship to God and Jesus.
- Asking students, on a final exam, to use scripture to write essays about "God's Directions for Righteous Living," "God's Plan for the Family," and "Living a Victorious Life in the World Which is So Dark."
- Using Bibles and other resources that represent only one religious translation, usually the Protestant King James translation.
- Assigning students to memorize Bible verses.

In the 1998 case of *Gibson v. Lee County School Board of Florida,* the foundation successfully challenged these unconstitutional practices, and in March 2000, the Florida Department of Education removed two Bible history courses—taught mainly in a Protestant "Sunday School style"—from its approved course list. Beginning with the 2000–01 school year, the department approved two new academic and secular courses that approach the Bible from a literary perspective and allow different interpretations of the text.

A Place in the Curriculum

A 2000 study titled "Teaching About Religion in National and State Social Studies Standards," a joint venture by the Council on Islamic Education and the First Amendment Center, found much to commend and

much to correct in the ways most schools currently teach about religion.

After reviewing state curriculum standards and frameworks and documents from national organizations, Susan Douglass, the study's principal researcher, found widespread support for teaching about religion in the social studies curriculum. Her study reveals a number of significant trends. For example:

- Teaching about religion is included, to some degree, in all national and state standards.
- Teaching about religion is an established curriculum topic in most public schools.
- Teaching about religion mainly occurs in U.S. history and world history, geography, or cultural studies courses.
- Teaching about religion is more deliberate in middle schools and high schools than in elementary schools.
- Teaching about religion is often included in lessons on exploration and colonization, slavery, and 19th century reform movements; religion in American life is seldom mentioned in 20th century studies.
- Teaching about religion is more indepth in elective courses than in required courses.

Douglass concludes, optimistically, that "a place has been made in the curriculum" for teaching about religion in the nation's schools. By the time students have completed 10th grade, she says, most have been exposed to major world religions and ethnic groups and cultures. And, she notes, most high school students have some knowledge of the role of religion in the origin of U.S. democracy and in society.

But she also finds that teaching about religion tends to be uneven and superficial. In elementary grades, for instance, teaching about religion is often a small component included in larger studies of holidays and ethnic customs. In U.S. history courses, in elementary and secondary schools alike, lessons about religions taper off after the colonial period and appear infrequently after the Civil War period. In upper-level courses, students often get mere "thumbnail sketches" of religions and societies.

Lack of teacher training is a major barrier to expert teaching and learning about religion, Douglass concludes. Teachers typically lack the knowledge and training to expand and elaborate on the thumbnail sketches of world religions presented in most national and state standards and curriculum frameworks. Many teachers, she reports, are still "very uncomfortable" with the topic of religion and prefer to gloss over, if not wholly ignore, this component of their curriculum.

Finding Common Ground

How can school districts address the issue? Gary Dei Rossi, superintendent of the San Joaquin County Office of Education in Stockton, Calif., advises school leaders to "get out in front" and be proactive about including the topic of religion in their school's curriculum. Speaking as a representative of the 3Rs Project Steering Committee, which helps school districts and communities find common ground in regard to teaching about religion, Dei Rossi says board members, superintendents, and principals must see to it that schools stand for democratic values and allow all religions and ethnic groups to have a voice in a diverse society.

I'd like to add a few more responsibilities for school officials to the list: First, make sure that curriculum committees and others who develop instruction in your district understand and apply federal laws and guidelines that define and describe what's legal and what's not legal in terms of teaching about religion. Second, don't let special interest groups influence schools to promote their beliefs. Third, make sure that students' beliefs—especially the beliefs of those who are not religious or are otherwise in the minority—are never shortchanged or silenced in studies about religion. And finally, provide top-notch training for teachers before expecting them to teach *about* religion.

References

Douglass, Susan. "Teaching About Religion in National and State Social Studies Standards." Fountain Valley, Calif.: Council on Islamic Education, 2000.

"God and the Public Schools: Religion, Education & Your Rights." Washington, D.C.: Americans United for Separation of Church and State. www.au.org.

Haynes, Charles C., and Oliver Thomas. "Finding Common Ground: A Guide to Religious Liberty in Public Schools." Nashville, Tenn.: First Amendment Center, 2001. www.freedomforum.org/templates/document. asp?documentID=3979.

Holmes, Natalie Carter. "Don't Take Holiday from Educating about Religious Diversity, Experts Urge." *AASA Leadership News*, Nov. 28, 2000. www.aasa.org/publications/1n/11_00/00-11-28religion.htm.

"Navigating Religion in the Classroom." *NEA Today*, November 2002. www.nea.org/neatoday/0211/cover.html.

Riley, Richard. "Secretary's Statement on Religious Expression." Washington, D.C.: U.S. Department of Education, 1995. www.ed.gov/Speeches/08-1995/religion.html.

Risinger, C. Frederick. "Religion in the Social Studies Curriculum." ERIC Clearinghouse for Social Studies/Social Science Education, 1993. ED363553.

"Navigating Religion in the Classroom." *NEA Today*, November 2002. www.nea.org/neatoday/0211/cover.html.

"Religion in the Public Schools: A Joint Statement of Current Law." Washington, D.C.: U.S. Department of Education, April 1995. www.ed.gov/Speeches/04-1995/prayer.html.

"The Good Book Taught Wrong: Bible History Classes in Florida Public Schools." Washington, D.C.: People for the American Way Foundation, January 2000. www.pfaw.org/pfaw.

WHERE DID WE COME FROM?

Lottie L. Joiner

Teaching about explanations for the origin of the species that live and have lived on the earth is one of the most contentious curricular issues in education today. The theory of *evolution* has historically been the most prominent explanation presented in the science curriculum. However, *intelligent design*, which essentially argues that certain features of the universe and living systems can best be explained as the result of intelligent cause, not an undirected process such as natural selection, is being offered in some circles as an alternative to the theory of evolution. In contrast with *creationism*, which grounds explanations for the origin of species in religious scripture and writing, intelligent design attempts to be secular by avoiding references to religion and religious overtones. This position is controversial, however, because critics of intelligent design theory suggest that it is little more than creationism stripped of religious references, and teaching creationism violates the principle of separation of church and state. As you read this article ask yourself, "What role should school play in the evolution–creationism controversy?"

Think About This . . .

1. According to the author, on what does the debate about evolution versus intelligent design center? Do you agree with the author's assessment? Why or why not?

2. How do science educators, such as Eugenie Scott and Gerald Skoog, feel about intelligent design being a viable alternative to evolution? What do you believe the prevailing views of teachers in general would be with respect to the viability of intelligent design? Why do you think so?

3. What four points of guidance do court decisions have with respect to the teaching of evolution? Do you believe these court decisions are consistent with constitutional principles? Why or why not?

4. How do you believe the issue of evolution versus intelligent design should be handled in the public school curriculum? Provide at least one reason for your position.

For a year, Martha Wise listened to presentations, visited constituents' homes, took phone call after long phone call, and spent hours answering e-mail. She was often up until the wee hours of the morning, trying to understand the latest issue dividing her state: the teaching of "intelligent design," one of the alternative theories of the origin of species.

"I'm not a scientist. I don't know much about science," says Wise, a member of the Ohio State Board of Education. "There's nothing the intelligent design people showed me that the science people couldn't say, 'That's not evidence,' or 'That's not a fact.' I can't refute them because I don't know that much about it. I can't believe either side."

The question of which side you believe is central to the controversy surrounding the teaching of evolution, one of public education's longest-running battles. The debate is often less about the science of describing the origins of life and more about a community's moral and ethical belief systems. More often than not, religious values and science collide, leaving a community torn and a school district unprepared to sort out the remains.

Ohio is the latest evolution battleground, following on the heels of state-level debates in Alabama, Louisiana, Oklahoma, and South Carolina and local controversies in Georgia and Pennsylvania over the past several years. Ohio's state board debated for nearly a year before adopting a new set of science standards in December 2002.

The standards require that the state's 1.8 million public school students learn Charles Darwin's theory of evolution as well as be allowed to discuss how "scientists continue to investigate and critically analyze all aspects of evolutionary theory." The statement made Ohio the first state to require districts to let criticisms of evolution be examined in classrooms. However, a disclaimer insists that the board did not support "the teaching or testing of intelligent design," a theory that the complex features of life are the result of intelligent planning and activity.

For many, it was a compromise that satisfied both sides. Some felt that it was not enough. Others believed that the Ohio board had caved to the pressure of Darwin's critics.

"Science education has not convinced a lot of Americans that Darwin was right," says Charles Haynes, senior scholar at the Freedom Forum's First Amendment Center, based at Vanderbilt University in Nashville, Tenn. "Many religious Americans have long felt that evolution or the theory of evolution challenges many of their deeply held beliefs."

Wise falls somewhere in the middle. "I believe in creationism, but I can also believe in the science

From Joiner, L. (2003). Where did we come form? American School Board Journal, 190(4), 30–34. Reprinted with permission of the American School Board Journal.

process," she says. "I do not separate the two. That's where some people have the problem. They separate the two and only believe in one."

The Evolution of a Debate

Central to the long-running controversy, Haynes says, is the fact that people are deeply concerned about the implications of what is taught in science. "What are the implications for understanding humans, for understanding morality, for understanding our place in the universe? Americans see public schools as a place where we define who we are as a people, what we believe as a nation. And it therefore often becomes a battleground where different world views clash."

The first battle was fought in 1925, when famed attorney Clarence Darrow defended biology teacher John T. Scopes in what became known as the Scopes Monkey Trial. Scopes, a high school biology teacher in Dayton, Tenn., was convicted of violating the state's Butler Act, which barred the teaching of "any theory that denies the story of the Divine Creation of man as taught in the Bible." The Butler Act was upheld in the Scopes trial and was not repealed until 1967.

The U.S. Supreme Court has ruled twice on the issue since then. In 1968, the Supreme Court invalidated state laws when it struck down an Arkansas statute that banned the teaching of evolution. And in 1987, the court ruled that a Louisiana law requiring that evolution and creationism be given equal time in the classroom was unconstitutional because it violated the First Amendment's Establishment Clause.

As the intelligent design argument raged in Ohio last summer, the Supreme Court declined to hear the case of Minnesota science teacher Rodney LeVake, who was reassigned by Independent School District No. 656 after he questioned the principles of evolution in his class. LeVake sued the district, claiming that the reassignment violated his constitutional rights to free speech and religion. He lost in the lower courts.

After the Supreme Court refused to hear his case, LeVake told reporters that he did not want to teach creationism or make references to God in his classes, but he wanted to tell students about what he sees as "flaws" in evolutionary theory. According to court documents, LeVake wanted to offer students "an honest look at the difficulties and inconsistencies of the theory without turning my class into a religious one."

The Supreme Court did have precedent for LeVake's lawsuit. In the 1987 Louisiana case, *Edwards v. Aguillard*, the justices ruled that "teaching a variety of scientific theories about the origins of mankind to school-children might be validly done with the clear secular intent of enhancing the effectiveness of science instruction." Haynes says this language provides an open door for evolution critics, including those who want to see the teaching of intelligent design.

"Intelligent design is really a whole new chapter in the debate about what alternative scientific theories may be allowed in the public school classroom," he says. "This is a new effort to open up the science curriculum to alternatives from a different direction."

Bruce Chapman, founder and president of the Discovery Institute, a Seattle-based think tank, believes alternative theories of the origin of species should be taught. He specifically cites intelligent design, which he describes as "a theory that holds that certain features of the universe and living systems can best be explained as the result of intelligent cause, not an undirected process such as natural selection.

"Overwhelmingly, our primary objective is for students to be allowed to learn the scientific evidence against Darwin's theory as well as for it," says Chapman. "Darwin's theory is flawed; that's the issue. It has nothing to do with religion. It has everything to do with science."

The Clash over Theories

The problem with trying to use the Supreme Court language as an argument, evolution advocates say, is that there are no proven scientific alternatives to evolution.

"Teachers are legally allowed to teach scientific—not religious—alternatives to evolution, but there are none," says Eugenie Scott, executive director of the National Center for Science Education in Oakland, Calif.

"If scientific alternatives to evolution are developed and take their place in scientific explanation, then of course it would be appropriate to teach them," Scott says, "but neither creation science nor [intelligent design] has made the grade."

Intelligent design is not a scientific model because it doesn't answer questions about the natural world, Scott says. "Intelligent design presents itself as science education, but it really is a form of progressive creationism—a religious idea. It should not be taught in public schools."

Gerald Skoog, former president of the National Science Teachers Association and dean of the College of Education at Texas Tech University in Lubbock, Texas, agrees.

"Intelligent design simply represents a revolutionary step to neutralize the teaching of evolution," says Skoog. "It's creationism stripped of religious overtones. Instead of saying that God is the creator, it's a designer.

They claim evidence, but the evidence does not stand up to peer review."

Michael Behe, a biochemistry professor at Pennsylvania's Lehigh University and a senior fellow at the Discovery Institute, insists that intelligent design and creationism are different.

"First of all, intelligent design does not refer to any sacred text, any religious writings, any sayings or prophets. It starts simply with the data that biology has presented to us, not religious sources, but from evidence of biology," says Behe. "Intelligent design is a completely scientific hypothesis. Creationism starts from sacred scripture and writing."

Behe, author of *Darwin's Black Box: The Biochemical Challenge to Evolution,* says scientific evidence supports intelligent design, despite what pro-evolution advocates believe.

"The scientific evidence that I point to in my writing appears in many biology textbooks and scientific journals," Behe says. "I haven't gotten my own private pieces of data. I use things in the scientific community. They object to the fact that I don't share the Darwinian interpretation of the data. But the data I use fits more readily with the theory of intelligent design than with Darwinism."

Only one fundamental difference exists between evolution and intelligent design, Behe says. While Darwin's theory says life resulted from natural selection, intelligent design is centered around the belief that a "designer" is behind it all. And even Behe admits that discussing who the "designer" is might not be appropriate in a science class.

"We may need to decide (that) on a basis other than a scientific basis—like historical records such as the Bible or philosophical considerations," says Behe. "You could even base it on a personal encounter with a space alien. But most people will conclude that it's God."

And that's the very problem evolution advocates have with intelligent design.

"Intelligent design is not a scientific theory," says Barry Lynn, director of the Americans United for Separation of Church and State, a Washington, D.C.-based watchdog group. "It's not about science. It's about theology. The religious right is acting as if evolution is one of dozens of ideas that might be true. . . . Their purpose is not to clarify matters of science. It's to confuse religion with science."

Caught in the Middle

It's this very debate that has state and local school boards in a bind. Most board members are responsible for sorting out a scientific discussion of which they have little understanding. The issues are so complex that boards are caught in the middle without "the tools or knowledge to sort out the truth of the matter," Haynes says.

"There are very few people who have enough knowledge of science to make a reasoned judgment as to whether what the intelligent design people are advancing is good science," he says. "When a school board looks at this, often they're listening to really a political debate on both sides where people are trying to convince them that this is good science and that the other is bogus."

Wise says she listened intently to both sides during the Ohio debate but admits that it was difficult at times to understand certain specific elements. In the end, she says she made a faith-based decision. "These are science standards and intelligent design, in my interpretation, is not scientific," she says. "Science standards should identify the science process. Intelligent design is based on a belief system, not a science process, in my estimation."

It took 11 months for Ohio's state board to agree on new science standards, a period in which board members received more than 40,000 e-mails, phone calls, and letters about the evolution issue. More than 20,000 letters were sent to the governor's office. And about 1,500 people attended a $2\frac{1}{2}$-hour debate between evolution and intelligent design experts.

"No other state had dealt with this as openly as we had," says Deborah Owens-Fink, who serves on the state board with Wise. "Initially, there was a huge backlash because people were upset that the education community wanted only one viewpoint. I was totally opposed to censoring scientific evidence that calls into question Darwinian orthodoxy."

The state board's biggest challenge, Owens-Fink says, was integrating the different points of view into the final decision. The key was taking an evenhanded approach.

"A scientist who opposed my decision said he respected the way we dealt with this," says Owens-Fink. "He said, 'No one can dispute the fact that you dealt with this in a very professional, fair manner.'"

"It sounds so fair to teach both sides," says Scott of the National Center for Science Education. "The idea of fairness is just so powerful in American society. The intelligent design people have gotten further on the fairness issue than on science."

Behe, the researcher and author, believes students should be allowed to learn that challenges to evolution exist. "There are many open questions about how life got here and how life developed over the years," he says. "There are many different ideas about how that happened. But students don't even learn that people are skeptical of Darwinian theory or even learn there are alternative theories to it. Too many biology textbooks give the strong impression that all of the big questions are solved and that's simply misleading the students."

But, Scott asks rhetorically, is it fair to teach kids an idea that scientists have rejected "just because the intelligent design proponents have good public relations and are in the op-ed pages and not scientific journals?

"Even if scientists have said that intelligent design is not science, they say teach it anyway because it makes us feel good," says Scott. "That's pretty irresponsible curriculum development."

Teaching the Controversy

Ohio's decision to allow teachers to discuss alternative theories about the origin of species in the classroom raises another prickly question: How will teachers introduce new ideas without getting into religious or philosophical discussions that belong outside a science class?

"The only thing that really matters is what happens in the classroom," says Owens-Fink. "It has to change in the classroom in terms of how evolution is presented to let students know that scientists are still investigating and challenging Darwin's theory. That's indeed the real issue."

But Lawrence Lerner, professor emeritus at California State University–Long Beach, says there's no point in teaching children false history or what he calls "pseudo science."

"Scientists don't think evolution is controversial," says Lerner, author of the Thomas B. Fordham Foundation's report *Good Science. Bad Science: Teaching Evolution in the States,* which gives letter grades to state science standards. "The controversy exists in political and religious groups. It does harm to both science and religion."

Haynes, however, believes that boards wanting to "teach the controversy" must first prepare teachers by providing accurate information and resources to help them understand the science.

"I'm all for exposing students to different viewpoints and students understanding why there's a con-

troversy to the origins, but only if we properly prepare teachers to teach about these issues in ways that aren't prejudiced or subjective," says Haynes. "'Teach the controversy' means nothing without follow-through. It could be a recipe for disaster."

At the Local Level

The evolution controversy can erupt at the local level as well as in state standards. What should you do if the issue is raised in your community?

First, consult your school attorney and your curriculum department to determine what's legal and what's good science. Scott says school boards must think about what's best for their students, and that is to "teach them the scientific consensus."

That's why standards developed at the state level are so important, says Skoog, the Texas Tech dean.

"If evolution is on the standards and the teacher doesn't teach it, the teacher puts the students at risk," Skoog says. "For me it's a breach of the public officials' integrity. It's my job to prepare students."

Lerner, the Cal State professor, notes that local school boards are "constantly assaulted" with issues that have political consequences. Ultimately, though, students are the ones most often put at a disadvantage.

"You have to think whether this is a politically correct thing to do or are you going to do the right, moral thing," says Lerner.

Will there ever come a time when there's a meeting of the minds in the evolution debate?

"The challenge is how can we improve science education in a way that helps people get beyond the cartoon version of both sides and become educated about what science is, what works, and what the prevailing views are and yes, what the criticisms are," Haynes says.

For Ohio board member Martha Wise, the evolution decision ended a painful, tumultuous year. "It's divided a lot of things," says Wise. "It certainly divided the board."

THE WELL-ROUNDED STUDENT

Susan Black

Schools are more than just an accumulation of classes—some of the most powerful learning experiences occur outside the classroom. The *extra curriculum* is commonly described as the learning experiences that extend beyond the core of students' formal studies, such as clubs, sports, school plays, and other activities that do not earn academic credit. The role of extracurricular activities in the school curriculum has historically raised a number of questions, and these questions are becoming ever more significant in an era of tight school budgets and teacher and student academic accountability. Some of these questions include the following: Should extracurricular activities be part of students' overall education? What influence does participation in extracurricular activities have on academic achievement? Is there a relationship between extracurricular participation and student behavior and dropout rates? What impact would the elimination of extracurricular activities have on a school's budget? As you read this article try to answer the following questions.

Think About This . . .

1. What influence does participation in extracurricular activities have on student achievement, social development, school dropout rates, and discipline problems? Why do you think this might be the case?
2. According to research cited in the article, what factor has the greatest effect on both boys' and girls' rates of participation in extracurricular activities? Why do you think this might be the case?
3. What relationship exists between family income and students' participation in extracurricular activities? What implications might this have for teachers?
4. How will the information in the article influence your work as a teacher? Cite a specific example to illustrate your description.

Where do your students go when the last bell rings? At dismissal time, some kids hurry to catch the bus, punch in at a part-time job, or hang out with friends on a street corner.

But others suit up for sports practice, paint props for the drama club, or study their next move in the school chess club. These students are involved in "more than just child's play," according to Steve Duncan at Montana State University.

Students who participate in structured extracurricular activities, Duncan and other researchers say, are likely to have higher academic achievement and higher levels of commitment and attachment to school. And extracurricular programs pay off in other ways as well: Schools that encourage students to participate in after-school programs show significant declines in discipline problems and dropout rates.

School officials who are struggling to balance budgets might consider cutting extracurricular activities. But the savings from such cuts are likely to be meager, according to the National Federation of State High School Associations (NFHS), which encourages cocurricular activities that support the academic mission of schools and teach students "lifelong lessons as important as those taught in the classroom." NFHS estimates that schools typically earmark only 1 to 3 percent of their total budgets for high school extracurricular programs. The funding—which goes to pay teachers' extra-duty salaries, buy equipment, and provide transportation—is "one of the best bargains around," NFHS says.

The Achievement Advantage

Do students involved in extracurricular activities really earn higher grades? Research by Mary Rombokas of Middle Tennessee State University supports that claim. Rombokas interviewed 292 college students, collecting data on social and academic achievement. She found that those who participated in high school extracurricular programs had higher intellectual and social development than those who steered clear of such programs. Extracurricular activities, Rombokas concluded, are

From Black, S. (2002). *The well-rounded student.* American School Board Journal, 189(6), 33–35. *Reprinted with permission of the* American School Board Journal.

often "the only component" that causes some students to stay in school and attend school regularly.

Anecdotal evidence further supports the connection between extracurricular activities and school performance. "It's a little uncanny," a high school counselor told me. "I've charted academic profiles for our seniors that show the students who participated in extracurricular activities have higher grades and better attendance. For instance, students on the traveling tennis team or in the color guard say they have to be super-organized about school work—which means setting aside a specific time to do their homework and study for tests. And they show up for school every day. The students who've joined several activities hardly ever miss a day."

Extracurricular activities provide all students—including those in remedial and advanced classes—with an "academic safety net," according to John Holloway, a consultant with New Jersey's Educational Testing Service. Contrary to the widely held assumption that sports and other activities cut into time for serious school study, Holloway says students tend to do better in school when they participate in after-school activities. A study by Alan Silliker and Jeffrey Quirk is a case in point. Silliker and Quirk examined the effect of extracurricular participation on the academic performance of boys and girls who played interscholastic soccer. They found that grade point averages for girls and boys alike were higher during the soccer season than during the off-season.

Extracurricular participation also is associated with adolescents' prosocial growth, which, Randall Brown has concluded, leads to a stronger connection to school. Examining the "complex developmental process of school connection" in a doctoral dissertation submitted to the University of California, Davis, Brown found that structured after-school activities tend to lessen such problem behaviors as cutting classes and using alcohol and drugs.

Similarly, in a study of seven southeastern public schools, Joseph Mahoney followed 695 children to age 24 and determined that—independent of risk variables such as living in poverty—boys and girls who participated in school extracurricular activities were less likely to drop out or be arrested. In a commentary on the study, Hans Steiner of Stanford University's School of Medicine wrote that Mahoney's findings point to a protective factor in what remains an "incomplete picture" of risk factors that lead to behavior problems and crime. A single intervention won't prevent all students from delinquency and dropping out, Steiner said, but he supports the notion of encouraging all children to participate in extracurricular programs.

The Small-School Advantage

But before they can reap the benefits of extracurricular participation, kids have to join in, and not all choose to do so. In a study of high school extracurricular participation, Ted Coladarci of the University of Maine and Casey Cobb of the University of New Hampshire investigated factors that prompt kids to join school clubs and sports teams. Studying more than 6,000 students—half from small schools and half from large schools—the researchers concluded that school size makes a big difference. Larger schools usually offer more extracurricular activities than small schools, but student participation rates are proportionately higher in small schools, Coladarci and Cobb reported.

This small-school advantage was consistently found in schools with fewer than 800 students and remained constant for all activities, including sports, performing arts, and academic clubs. In fact, the researchers found, small school size was the "greatest determinant" of participation for both boys and girls—a factor more powerful than students' socioeconomic status, academic achievement, or self-esteem.

Small school size also affects the amount of time students spend on extracurricular activities—and time, Coladarci and Cobb discovered, is an important indicator of students' commitment to their activities. In contrast to their counterparts in large schools, where students sometimes show up only to sit on the sidelines, students in small schools are more actively involved and expend more energy on their chosen activities. (Coladarci and Cobb also found "no basis for concern" that time students spend on extracurricular programs detracts from their academic learning.)

In a review of the research, Neil Stevens of the Eureka County (Nev.) High School and Gary Peltier of the University of Nevada identified two factors that influence students to sign up for school activities. In small schools, Stevens and Peltier found, students recognize the need for members to keep teams and clubs functioning—such as filling the ninth spot on a baseball team. And, they found, students respond to personal invitations to join activities—such as a biology teacher seeking out a student and suggesting signing up for the science club. "Every student is needed in the ecological system," Stevens and Peltier wrote, noting that students respond to feeling important and invited.

Seeking to understand the relationship between adolescents' satisfaction with life and their participation in extracurricular activities, Georgia State University's Rich Gilman studied 321 high school students. He found that students who took part in greater numbers of structured extracurricular activities reported significantly higher satisfaction with school than did those with minimal or no participation. Gilman's research confirms findings from several previous studies: Taking part in extracurricular activities increases students' feeling of commitment to school. And that, in turn, translates into higher academic self-concept and other positive outcomes, such as spending more time on homework, taking more advanced courses, and earning higher grades.

But contrary to his expectations, Gilman found that many students who rated themselves high in "prosocial disposition" (that is, being outgoing and getting along with others) weren't involved in many structured school activities. He and other researchers hypothesize that students who see themselves as prosocial might prefer more personal, individual activities rather than extracurricular programs, which often involve group work and teamwork.

Overall, concluded Coladarci and Cobb, the effects of extracurricular participation on students appear to be positive but modest. They reported a "single digit" impact on academic achievement, but they found "more optimistic" and psychologically important effects on students' self-esteem. These effects, they said, should "not be taken lightly by educators or policymakers." Similarly, Gilman advised school leaders to establish strategies and policies that encourage students' participation in extracurricular programs.

The Participation Gap

As it stands, however, extracurricular programs in many schools are not entirely equitable. Eileen O'Brien of Policy Studies Associates and Mary Rollefson of the National Center for Educational Statistics reported "no important differences" in the availability of extracurricular activities between affluent and poor schools. But it's a different story when it comes to student participation. According to O'Brien and Rollefson, participation rates for students from poor families are consistently lower than those for students from wealthy families. (The exception is poor students' higher participation rates in vocational clubs, such as Future Farmers and Future Teachers of America.)

The participation gap O'Brien and Rollefson described also showed up in teacher Jennifer D'Abbracci's case study of 74 junior and senior high special education

students in rural upstate New York. At times, D'Abbracci found, coaches and advisers of extracurricular programs forgot about the students in the school's special education wing. "We seldom get notices or postings of activities," she said, adding that many of her handicapped and disabled students would like to be involved but feel "shut out and shut down" by the rest of the school.

The reasons D'Abbracci's students gave for not joining school activities are telling. Some cited personal weaknesses such as asthma and lack of coordination, while others mentioned such problems as high costs and lack of transportation. Some responses were heartfelt and heartbreaking. During interviews, one junior high school girl said, "I am no good and people would laugh." But most often the students, presented with an activity list that includes ski club, art club, golf, cross country, and other programs, commented, "I didn't know about it"—a finding that prompted D'Abbracci to ask administrators to make sure special education students have an opportunity to sign up for school activities.

Stevens and Peltier agree that building administrators should critically examine their school's extracurricular programs. They recommend monitoring the numbers of students participating in various activities and establishing more options for those interested in participating. A good start is to establish open rather than restrictive participation policies to allow more students to join sports teams, cheerleading, and other traditionally competitive activities.

Schools of all sizes should extend invitations to students—all students—to join extracurricular activities. The students who believe they're "no good" might be the ones who need extracurricular activities most.

References

Brown, Randall. "The Influence of Extracurricular Activity Participation upon Youth Problem Behavior: School Connection as a Mediator." Doctoral dissertation, University of California, Davis, 1999. ED430167.

Coladarci, Theodore, and Casey Cobb. "Extracurricular Participation, School Size, and Achievement and Self-Esteem Among High School Students." *Journal of Research in Rural Education,* Fall 1996, pp. 92–103.

D'Abbracci, Jennifer. "Extracurricular Activities: Participation Rates of High School Special Education Students." Unpublished graduate research project, Elmira College, Elmira N.Y., April 1999.

Duncan, Steve. "Family Matters: What is the Role of 'Extracurricular' Activities?" Montana State University, 2000. *http://www.montana.edu/wwwpb/home/extra.html.*

Gilman, Rich. "The Relationship Between Life Satisfaction, Social Interest, and Frequency of Extracurricular Activities

Among Adolescent Students." *Journal of Youth and Adolescence,* December 2001, pp. 749–767.

Holloway, John. "Extracurricular Activities: The Path to Academic Success?" *Educational Leadership,* December 1999–January 2000. *http://www.ascd.org/readingroom/edlead/9912/holloway.html.*

Mahoney, Joseph. "Children Who Participated in School Extracurricular Activities." *Evidence-Based Mental Health,* February 2001.

National Federation of State High School Associations. "The Case for High School Activities," 2002.

O'Brien, Eileen, and Mary Rollefson. "Extracurricular Participation and Student Engagement." National Center for Education Statistics, June 1995.

Rombokas, Mary, et al. "High School Extracurricular Activities & College Grades." Paper presented at the Southeastern Conference of Counseling Center Personnel, 1995. ED391134.

Silliker, S. Alan, and Jeffrey T. Quirk. "The Effect of Extracurricular Activity Participation on the Academic Performance of Male and Female High Students. *The School Counselor,* vol. 44, March 1997, pp. 288–293.

Stevens, Neil G., and Gary L. Peltier. "A Review of Research on Small-School Student Participation in Extracurricular Activities." *Journal of Research in Rural Education,* Fall 1994, pp. 116–120.

ADDITIONAL READINGS

Doerr, E. (1998). Religion and public education. *Phi Delta Kappan, 80*(3), 223–225.

Fitzhugh, W. (2002). The state of the term paper. *Education Week, 21*(18), 35, 37.

Gibbs, J. (2000). Value-based discipline in a fifth grade classroom. *Middle School Journal, 31*(5), 46–50.

Glasser, W. (1992). The quality school curriculum. *Phi Delta Kappan, 73*(9), 690–694.

Hirsch, E. D. (2001). Seeking breadth and depth in the curriculum. *Educational Leadership, 59*(2), 22–25.

Schaps, E., Schaeffer, E., & McDonnell, S. (2001). What's right and wrong in character education today. *Education Week, 21*(2), 40, 44.

Schuster, E. (2003). The persistence of the "grammar schooling." *Education Week, 22*(33), 43.

EXPLORING THE INTERNET

Content Knowledge: A Compendium of Standards and Benchmarks for K–12 Education
http://www.mcrel.org/standards-benchmarks
A coherent and systematic set of content standards presented in an easy-to-read format for primary, upper elementary, middle school, and high school.

The Character Education Partnership
http://www.character.org/
This site provides several connections to other sites that provide information about character education approaches to moral development.

Integrated Curriculum
http://www.nwrel.org/scpd/sirs/8/c016.html
This site provides an overview of curriculum approaches with emphasis on integrated curriculum. An annotated reference list is also provided.

National Service-Learning Clearinghouse (NSLC)
http://www.servicelearning.org/
This site provides information from different sources that focus on service learning.

PART FIVE

Instruction

Instruction is at the heart of teaching and occupies most of a teacher's day. In addition to providing opportunities to promote student learning and development, it also influences the kinds of interactions teachers have with their students.

As with all other aspects of education, views of effective instruction have changed during the course of history. In colonial times, for example, instruction focused on memorization and recitation; students were expected to sit quietly for long periods of time, and expressing opinions and asking questions were essentially forbidden. As our understanding of the ways students learn and develop increased, improved methods were encouraged. These more effective instructional strategies emphasized student involvement and making students' thoughts about the topics they study open and visible.

In spite of an increased understanding of the ways students learn most effectively, many teachers and lay people continue to believe effective instruction is basically a process of explaining information to students. A large and expanding body of research consistently indicates that this belief is simplistic and naïve (Bransford, Brown, & Cocking, 2000; Eggen & Kauchak, 2004). In fact, instruction is very complex, and effective instruction includes *all* the processes teachers use to help their students learn. Three of the most important processes include the following:

- Establishing and maintaining orderly classrooms. Effective instruction and classroom management are interdependent; learning cannot be maximized in a chaotic environment, and it is virtually impossible to maintain order in the absence of effective instruction.
- Conducting formal learning experiences, such as teacher-led discussions, small group work, and individual projects (Eggen & Kauchak, 2004).
- Using assessment as a tool to promote learning. In productive classroom environments—those that are orderly and focus on learning—teachers use assessment to not only measure but also increase student achievement.

In spite of an expanding literature that discusses learning and effective instruction, many questions remain. Some of them include the following: What role does theory, and particularly constructivist learning theory, play in guiding instruction? How should learners' needs and interests be balanced with the calls for standards and accountability? What teacher characteristics and teaching strategies are most effective with underachieving students? How can rules be most effectively used to help create orderly classrooms? How can we use assessment to increase learning? Keep these questions in mind as you study the articles in this section.

JOINING THEORY AND BEST PRACTICE TO DRIVE CLASSROOM INSTRUCTION

Carol Fuhler

Theories of learning attempt to explain how students learn; research attempts to refine and shape these theories. What role should theory and research play in determining instruction in our classrooms? Although *theory* is not one of the concepts that teachers commonly consider in making their decisions, it can play an important role in guiding practice. In this article Carol Fuhler outlines three of her favorite theories—schema theory, constructivism, and literacy response theory—and offers additional classroom examples of how to improve instruction.

As you read this article ask yourself, "How important is theory to instruction?"

Think About This . . .

1. Which of the three primary theories that Fuhler describes in her article do you believe is most valuable in guiding classroom practice? Why?
2. How does Fuhler link theory to classroom practice? How important do you believe theory is as a guide for teaching? Provide a rationale for your opinion.
3. On what content areas does Fuhler focus in her discussion? Is theory more important in these areas, or is it equally important across the curriculum? Explain why you think so.
4. How will theory influence your instruction in your chosen field of interest? Provide a specific example to illustrate your answer.

"Theory." How did you react when you read that word? In all honesty, it is probably not on every teacher's list of 25 favorite words. What about "best practice"? Is your reaction to that term a little different? Under the right circumstances you have probably engaged in a lively dialogue with a colleague or two about what you considered to be best practice in reading, language arts, or content area classes. Although many of us might not have the time or the inclination to champion our favorite theories on a regular basis, theory as it relates to learning can lead to thought-provoking conversations as well. It is worth noting that there is a strong positive relationship between these terms and that both play a crucial role in our day-to-day teaching. Whether they are on the tip of your tongue during daily conversations or not, there is a good possibility that theory and best practice are alive and well in your classroom. Perhaps, though, they are currently working undercover. If that is the case, they could be much more effective if they were

scrutinized, affirmed, and promoted as you strive to meet the needs of your learners this year.

I would like to share a thumbnail sketch of three of my favorite theories with you. Throughout the article, best classroom teaching practices will be highlighted and tied to the theories that endorse them whenever possible. The particular practices selected are from those advocated by Zemelman, Daniels, and Hyde (1998). Their condensation of best practices across the curriculum is based upon an extensive review of national and state standards and general curricular reform efforts in the United States. Later, I will invite you to reflect upon both theory and these acclaimed practices and how they co-exist in your classroom. While our conversations will revolve around reading, please think

From Fuhler, C. (2003). *Joining theory and best practice to drive classroom instruction.* Middle School Journal, 34(5), 23–30. *Reprinted with permission of the National Middle School Association.*

about how these theories and quality teaching practices move smoothly across the curriculum. Finally, a sample lesson illustrating possible cross-curricular interactions, also considered a "best practice," will conclude our conversation.

A focus question begins our discussion: Do theory and the knowledge of excellent ways to teach reading drive the decisions you make about how you currently instruct your middle school students? Clearly understanding that there is no one best way to teach every child, there is general agreement among a number of authorities in the field about some of the stellar ways to reach our learners (Duffy & Hoffman, 1999; International Reading Association Board of Directors, 2000; Pressley, 2000; Zemelman, et al., 1998). We will examine a collection of them, but let's start with those theories first.

A Few Well-Documented Learning Theories

Schema Theory

Cognitive psychologists have made heroic efforts for the past few decades to examine how the brain works, how people learn in general, and what that might mean for classroom teachers and the learners in their care (Jensen, 1998). One intriguing theory that emerged in the 1970s and 1980s in the field of reading is schema theory. It continues to be relevant today. Rumelhart (1981) and other colleagues have suggested that a schema (the plural is schemata) can be likened to a package of knowledge made up of concepts, events, emotions, and people's roles in life, all of which are interrelated. Theorists go on to explain how people work with that knowledge. An apt analogy is that as knowledge is stored, it is carefully organized into file-like folders of related data. When something new is encountered, an individual searches the mind-filing system for previous knowledge, adding the new to the old in an existing file. If no file currently exists, one is created. However, schemata do not remain entities unto themselves. They are interconnected over the years to yield a vast network of personal knowledge as experiences and learning increase (Rumelhardt, 1984).

How does the knowledge of schema theory affect our classroom practices? One illuminating revelation that applies to reading, in addition to other content area subjects, is that a student's previous knowledge about a topic helps her to acquire new knowledge. Therefore, the ease or difficulty with which she will grasp new information is directly related to what she already knows about the topic. The related theory-based classroom strategy involves accessing that prior knowledge. This means that we should routinely activate our learners' prior knowledge before beginning the next story in reading or a new topic in social studies or science. Such a process can be accomplished in a number of ways like brainstorming together, participating in a bit of drama, watching a snippet of a video, engaging in class discussions, or using an appropriate graphic organizer like a Venn diagram (Merkley & Jeffries, 2001). Supported by theory, we are promoting better learning opportunities for our students.

The Constructivist Approach

A second theory that continues to receive positive support and practitioner interest is the constructivist theory, a theory rooted in several different fields of research. For the purposes of our conversation, we will consider it primarily in its psychological context. In brief, this group of theorists believes that meaning-making is an active, constructive process. For example, when a reader picks up a text, he must actively engage with the words, think about what he is reading, and connect that with what he already knows to make meaning. In addition, constructivists point out that such meaning-making is subjective because each reader is influenced by an accumulation of personal experiences and a particular ability to learn (Fosnot, 1996).

If one believes in a constructivist approach to teaching reading, how might that play out in the classroom? One example is that a teacher would support multiple interpretations of a novel based upon the fact that no two learners come in exactly the same way to the reading situation. Therefore, interpretations of what they read are bound to vary. Under these circumstances, then, there is no such thing as only one right answer. When working with clear cut, informational text, however, the readers will probably construct more similar meanings. There is not as much room for multiple interpretations with this less-subjective text. In another instance, when class work involves completing a project of some kind, students would be actively thinking, talking, and creating their way to its conclusion (Roehler & Duffy, 1996).

An additional theory-related procedure, also lauded as "best practice," is urging students to choose their own reading materials as often as possible. This is especially appropriate for time spent in independent reading. In this case, personal interests and inherent abilities are behind the selection of a student's reading selection. A bonus is that motivation is heightened as these students quickly become involved in a text they can manage on a topic they enjoy (Turner & Paris, 1995). Thus, both best practice and constructivist theory support active involvement in class work and student choice as ways to encourage engagement in learning. The odds are that engaged learners are bound to be more effective learners, a win–win scenario for both teacher and learner (Robb, 2000; Zemelman et al., 1998).

Literary Response Theory

My final favorite is a popular response theory that incorporates the constructivists' thinking. Rosenblatt (1994), recognized literary response theorist, explained how important it is for readers to respond to and connect with the text they read. She remarked that without responding to what is read, the words on the page are merely unintelligible ink spots. Instead, there must be a transaction between the reader and those words. She continued by explaining that readers are typically involved in two stances, either aesthetic or efferent, as the transactions occur. Readers alter their stance depending on the materials being read and the purposes for their reading. Picture a student reading a novel, so engrossed that she is living through the events of the story right along with the main character. Caught up heart and soul in the drama, she is in the aesthetic stance.

If, however, she is carefully reading informational text, researching facts for a self-selected project, she is in the efferent stance. Rosenblatt explained that this is not an either–or situation. Instead, readers slide back and forth along a continuum between the two stances. They may be thoroughly enjoying the reading of their informational text to the point that it also becomes an aesthetic experience (Rosenblatt, 1991). This theorist's work reminds us again that our learners must be involved, cognitively engaged, and active participants in their classroom lives if we are to be the most effective teachers. Quality teaching practices second her beliefs.

A Pause to Focus on Response

There are a myriad of ways to incorporate literary response theory into the classroom. Varying their use piques interest for teacher and student alike, for as Jensen (1998) stated, the brain likes periodic pleasant surprises. One common strategy, also considered an excellent teaching strategy, is to talk about books together (Robb, 2000; Turner & Paris, 1995). Strongly supported are "social, collaborative activities with much discussion and interaction" (Zemelman, Daniels, & Hyde, 1998, p. 54). Middle school learners are social

beings and talk comes quite easily to them. As a result, book talk is natural and motivational. Use it in whole class discussions after students have read materials silently or following literature circles where students are reading the same book together. Build on that willingness to chat by encouraging readers to discuss, listen, and learn from each other as they share their opinions. They are strengthening comprehension in the process (Galda, Ash, & Cullinan, 2000).

In addition, students can respond in numerous ways via writing. Using several different kinds of journals can extend student thinking in connection with both fiction and nonfiction materials. Just look at literature response journals, for example. They give readers an opportunity to react in writing in an informal way to what they are reading. Not graded or corrected, these journals are repositories of students' predictions, connections, and questions regarding what they are reading (Combs, 2003). A variation of this type of journal is the dialogue journal in which you and the student write back and forth to each other about a book. This written dialogue might be changed once again, this time flowing between two students.

Yet another adaptation is to arrange a time when parents and their middle schooler read a book together and exchange written reactions within the journal. Once this particular activity has been completed and you have an opportunity to browse through the journals at a later date, you can count on being amazed at the quality of the written interactions (Fuhler, 1994). For a change of pace when working with content area materials, students might use a double-entry journal, recording facts or important notes in one column on the page and their thoughts and reactions to the information in the second column. Certainly, journals foster a reading, writing, interactive connection between reader and text.

Aside from journals, students might write a poem about their books once they are completed. Working with other students who have read the same book they can write a Readers' Theater script to be performed in front of the class. With communication but a technological keystroke away, students can post a personal book review on the web beginning with popular sites like www.amazon.com or www.barnesandnoble.com.

Moving beyond writing, there is art. Artistic extensions of a book could be the creation of a poster advertising the book, a mural of favorite scenes, or a picture collage involving objects, words, and images related to the novel. The list of response options is only limited by your students' creativity. Remember that as you invite students to react to what they are reading, you are incorporating another aspect of best practice.

Are the preceding theories familiar to you and perhaps favorites of yours, too? Are there others you would ascribe to more readily than these as you teach? At some point, settle back and indulge in a little quiet reflection on what you do from day to day in your classroom world and which theories undergird those actions. In the meantime, let's turn our attention to additional suggestions for affirmed and acclaimed classroom practices in the teaching of reading. As we do so, think about how they, too, can be applied to other subject areas.

A Look at Several More Suggestions for Best Practice

Time for Reading Aloud

Do you read aloud to your students on a regular basis? I honestly think there were too many days when the only time my middle school students were really with me was when I was reading to them. While that may not be the best reason for reading aloud, there are a number of others to underscore its value (Combs, 2003). When you read aloud to your class, you:

- Show readers that reading is worthwhile, reinforcing the fact that it is a pleasurable investment of time.
- Enable students to see themselves within a book as they relate to a particular character or incident.
- Expose listeners to a rich and wide variety of genre and kinds of reading materials, perhaps enticing them to broaden their reading interests in the process.
- Provide a model of good oral reading for students to emulate as you bring print to life.
- Develop a sense of community within your classroom as you and your students share the same book and discuss it. All students, despite their varying reading abilities, are a part of the community.
- Foster literate thinking as students predict, confirm, and question what they are hearing, monitoring their comprehension all the while.

Do not worry about how you will squeeze out the 15 to 20 minutes of reading aloud time on a regular basis. Just do it. Without a doubt, reading aloud to middle grade learners is simply essential to building comprehension skills as you and your students savor a piece of quality literature together (Galda, et al., 2000).

Fostering Independent Reading

Not to be missed is yet another best practice that ties into the preceding theories. This one incorporates the concept of choice and promotes the idea of personal engagement. It dictates devoting classroom time to independent reading (Pressley, 2000; Robb, 2000; Turner & Paris, 1995). Setting aside a specific time for independent reading, preferably between 25 and 30 minutes, on a regular basis is a practice that reaps a number of benefits, all of them reinforcing reading comprehension. First, within the context of one student-chosen book or magazine after another, students have the opportunity to practice recently-taught, newly acquired skills. At the same time, they are polishing previously learned skills and strategies (Fuhler, 2000). Second, word recognition is built through many encounters with words, so reading and plenty of it is in order (Pressley, 2000). Furthermore, extensive reading of a variety of materials is an excellent way to broaden personal knowledge. Charged up by choice, given time to read regularly, and monitored by a wise teacher who can nudge readers on to new and challenging fiction and nonfiction, this practice is invaluable.

The Values of Teacher Modeling

If you think back to your college methods courses, it is highly likely that you learned that "telling" students how to accomplish a task has significantly less value than "showing" them how to do it, and then letting them actually practice the skill or strategy (Fuhler, 2000; Robb, 2000). When you think about it, most human behavior is learned through modeling, so it is not surprising that it is so effective in the classroom (Roehler & Duffy, 1996). Modeling is the final strongly supported teaching strategy to be reviewed here. One method of modeling has already been highlighted, that of reading aloud. However, modeling can occur in various other ways.

In one instance, a teacher might take the students step by step through the strategy being taught, demonstrating its application in the process. After the skill has been taught, its use is modeled again within the context of appropriate materials. Another popular method is thinking aloud as you problem-solve in front of the learners. In doing so they can see the usually invisible thought processes required. For example, you might think aloud as you work through a particularly difficult passage to show students how you try to make sense of the content. Using a different example, the teacher might illustrate how she connects what she is reading to previous personal experiences, talking aloud as she makes those connections.

So much of what we do during the complex process of reading is impossible to see (Worthy, Broaddus, & Ivey, 2001; Pressley, 2000). We cannot assume that our students understand what is going on in an efficient reader's head for they really have no way of knowing. Thus, we turn to modeling in its various guises to demonstrate thought processes along with how to apply a particular skill. Those efforts still are not sufficient, though. The final step is to put the students to work, trying out the skill or strategy right after it is taught and applying it again and again over time until it becomes an effortless part of their repertoire of skills (Fuhler, 2000).

What else would you add to these previously mentioned best practices? Certainly there are others that help us be the most effective teachers we can be for every one of our students. Let us consider a sample lesson that illustrates how theory and best practice could work.

Integrating Theory and Best Practice Across the Curriculum

Weaving the threads from pertinent theory and best practice into the middle school curriculum can bolster teaching and learning. Combining the two offers exciting challenges and invigorating changes to the classrooms where such efforts may not have happened regularly. In the middle grades, students in reading classes are shared with other teachers for various content courses. When reaching across the curriculum, reading teachers will be working with teachers in content areas, effectively dissolving boundaries between subject matter as teaming occurs.

If you are fortunate enough to have a self-contained class, integration could be accomplished more easily perhaps, because you are more in control of blocks of time. Alone or together, integration requires some careful planning with an eye to district curricular requirements, gathering a variety of quality materials, and involving students in parts of the planning (Combs, 2003). One blessing afforded by the interweaving of course materials is that the never-enough-time factor can be eased somewhat. The following lesson demonstrates one way integration might be accomplished as the areas of reading, writing, and social studies are tied together, lightly flavored with technology. It will serve as a practical conclusion to our conversation on theory and best practice as these drive personal curricular decisions.

Figure 1
A Sampling of Poetry Sources

Altman, S. & Lechner, S. (1993). *Followers of the North Star: Rhymes about African American heroes, heroines, and historical times.* Illus. by Byron Wooden. Chicago, IL: Children's Press.

Huges, L. (1994). *The dream keeper and other poems.* Illus. by Jerry Pinkney. New York: Knopf.

Merriam, E. (1996). *The inner city Mother Goose.* Illus. by David Diaz. New York: Simon & Schuster.

Nye, N. S. (1999). *What have you lost?* Photographs by Michael Nye. New York: Greenwillow.

Robb, L. (1997). *Music and drums: Voices of war and peace, hope and dreams.* Illus. by Deb Lil. New York: Philomel.

Volavkova, H. (Ed.). (1993). *"I never saw another butterfly": Children's drawings and poems from Terezin Concentration Camp,* 1942–1944. New York: Schocken Books.

A Lesson Framework
Topic: Oppression Across Cultures

Note the following suggestions for best practice in social studies as they are woven throughout this lesson (Zemelman, Daniels, & Hyde, 1998, p. 155):

- Emphasis on activities that access prior knowledge and engage students in inquiry and problem solving about significant human issues.
- Participation in interactive and cooperative classroom study processes that bring together students of all ability levels.
- Integration of social studies with other areas of the curriculum.

1. *Assessing Prior Knowledge.* Begin the lesson by writing the word "oppression" on the white board or on chart paper. Ask the class to think about its meaning while you read several poems aloud to them (Figure 1). Explain that when you are done reading, they will write a journal response to what they hear, feel, and know about oppression. Afterwards, you will discuss their reactions together as a whole group.

Read several poems from the books in Figure 1 or from others that you have previously collected. Give students time to reflect and journal. Invite student responses, a process that enriches everyone's understanding

Figure 2
A Sampling of Picture Books for Older Readers

Bunting, E. (1998). *So far from the sea.* Illus. by Chris Soentpiet. New York: Clarion.

Coles, R. (1998). *The story of Ruby Bridges.* Illus. by George Ford. New York: Scholastic.

Howard, E. F. (2000). *Virgie goes to school with us boys.* Illus. by E. B. Lewis. New York: Simon & Schuster.

McCully, E. A. (1996). *The bobbin girl.* New York: Dial.

McGill, A. (1999). *Molly Bannaky.* Illus. by Chris Soentpiet. Boston: Houghton Mifflin.

Mochizuki, K. (1995). *Heroes.* Illus. by Dom Lee. New York: Lee & Low.

Nerlove, M. (1996). *Flowers on the wall.* New York: McElderry.

Shrange, N. (1997). *White wash.* Illus. by Michael Sporn. New York: Walker.

Figure 3
A Sampling of Nonfiction Titles

Atkin, S. B. (2001). *Voices from the fields: Children of migrant farm workers tell their stories.* New York: Scholastic.

Alonso, K. (1998). *Korematsu V. United States: Japanese-American internment camps.* Springfield, NJ: Enslow.

Berck, J. (1992). *No place to be: Voices of homeless children.* Boston: Houghton Mifflin.

Cha, D. (1996). *Dia's story cloth: The Hmong people's journey of freedom.* Stitched by Chue and Nhia Thao Cha. Published in cooperation with Denver Museum of Natural History. New York: Lee & Low.

Dash, J. (1996). *We shall not be moved: The women's factory strike of 1909.* New York: Scholastic.

Freedman, R. (1995). *Kids at work: Lewis Hine and the crusade against child labor.* New York: Clarion.

Hansen, J. (1998). *Women of hope: African Americans who made a difference.* New York: Scholastic.

Mochizuki, K. (1997). *Passage to freedom: The Sugihara story.* Illus. by Dom Lee. New York: Lee & Low.

Springer, J. (1998). *Listen to us: The world's working children.* Toronto: Groundwood.

Towle, W. (1993). *The Real McCoy: The life of an African-American inventor.* Illus. by Wil Clay. New York: Scholastic.

of the concept under discussion. As an option, create a web of meaning on the board as students volunteer to share a thought or insight into oppression. Begin the web with the word "oppression" encircled in the center. Each student might add an attached circle containing a phrase or insight to the web as they explain their thoughts. The result will be a visual overview of the word and the growing concept behind it. Conclude this stage of activating prior knowledge when students have shared as much as they wish.

2. *Deepening Understanding: Modeling the Use of Literature to Extend Thinking.* Picture books for older readers often pack a powerful message in just a few pages. Try them as a way to ignite learning from time to time. At this point, explain to the students that you are going to be reading a picture book that depicts some form of oppression. They are to listen, reflect on the instances of oppression within the short story, and be prepared to discuss their thinking in an effort to extend the earlier concept formation. Tell them that this step will prepare them for brainstorming further ways to look at oppression in its various guises in later work.

Select one of the books in Figure 2 or another of your choice. Preview and practice reading it before presenting it to the class. After reading the book, ask students for general reactions. Is there anything else they would like to add to the web or any additional thoughts

they have about oppression based upon the reading and discussion of the book? Next, brainstorm a list of possibilities for engaging in research about the word as it ties to people who have suffered oppression, past and present. Review the list together.

For the next step, students are to select a person, group, or situation that reflects oppression from the list. They are headed toward individual investigations into a particular form of oppression. Personal interest in a specific topic will motivate engagement as students deepen their understanding of this concept. Students might work individually, in pairs, or in triads to complete their work. Begin gathering information. Bring in fiction and nonfiction materials for student use, booktalking them briefly so that students can quickly select materials (Figure 3) that are pertinent for their work.

Figure 4
Sample Web Sites

Global Educator's Guide to the Internet www.bayside.sd63.bc.ca/home/rcoulson/globaled/globalhome.html
An excellent guide for educators wishing to enhance global education themes in the elementary and middle level classroom.

History/Social Studies Web Site for K–12 Teachers
my.execpc.com/~dboals/boals.html
A comprehensive homepage takes educators to a myriad of web links and resources inviting them to learn about and teach social studies better with a technological advantage.

Cultures of the World
www.ala.org/gwstemplate.cfm?section=greatwebsites&template=/cfapps/gws/default.cfm
Heighten multicultural awareness and appreciation for people of varying cultures beginning with a site like this one.

Library of Congress
http://lcweb.loc.gov/homepage/lchp.html
Students might research original documents and endless history resources here.

PBS TeacherSource
www.pbs.org/teachersource/
Makes it easy to locate and use the best television and Web resources available including a variety of lesson plans.

Web-Travelers Toolkit: Essential Kid Lit Web site
www.acs.ucalgary.ca/~dkbrown/general.html
An exciting site designed for readers and writers giving a wealth of information and suggestions evolving from fine literature for readers of varying ages.

Yahoo for Educators
http://dir.yahoo.com/Education
One could get lost in search and discovery investigating one link after another that might yield resources for teacher and student use. Check the link to Web-based education.

Remember that a novel offers a unique perspective that students might miss in a textbook or other non-fiction materials. Invite the learning center director to share possible resources, or use previously previewed sites on the Internet (Figure 4) for additional research. One site to explore is The New York Times' Learning Network (www.nytimes.com/learning/), an excellent resource for both teachers and students. When appropriate, personal interviews with people who are currently enduring, or have endured, oppression might be conducted with interview questions carefully crafted ahead of time.

Reading, writing, and thinking are in high gear as the research comes together. At an appropriate point, students are to select the way they want to present what they have learned from a starter list of options. Students may have their own ideas or select one from the teacher's list. Perhaps it will take the form of a poster display, a written report, a mock interview with a classmate, a scrapbook of a fictional person's memories, a picture book for older readers, or a PowerPoint presentation.

3. *Sharing the Wealth: A Variety of Presentations.* Set aside a couple of class sessions to share the learning and discuss the implications of this cross-curricular project together. In this critical talk time learning is shared and understandings of a pervasive human behavior are digested and stored for future use. Students are still broadening their understanding of oppression as they listen to classmates present what they have learned. When it is their turn to present, they are teaching what they know. If they can do that successfully, it is an indication that they understand the content of their work. Extend the learning

opportunities by inviting another class to attend the presentations.

4. *Assessing What Was Learned.* Assess student learning based upon a previously designed rubric. Involve students in its creation once students understand their responsibilities, perhaps around the time research begins. Include a student self-reflection as a part of this assessment. Reflection on the knowledge gained from work on this project helps students to critique their learning, look for misconceptions, and think about unanswered questions that might prompt further personal investigations. In your own classroom or in collaboration with your cross-curricular colleague, reflect on the strengths and weaknesses of this unit of study and how it can be fine-tuned for future use.

References

Combs, M. (2003). *Developing competent readers and writers in the middle grades* (2nd ed.). Upper Saddle River, NJ: Merrill/Prentice Hall.

Duffy, G. G., & Hoffman, J. V. (1999). In pursuit of a flawed illusion: The search for a perfect method. *The Reading Teacher, 53*(1), 10–16.

Fosnot, C. T. (1996). *Constructivism: Theory, perspectives, and practice.* New York: Teachers College Press.

Fuhler, C. J. (1994). Response journals: Just one more time with feeling. *Journal of Reading, 37,* 400–405.

Fuhler, C. J. (2000). *Teaching reading with multicultural books kids love.* Golden, CO: Fulcrum.

Galda, L., Ash, G. E., & Cullinan, B. E. (2000). Children's literature. In M. L. Kamil, P. B. Mosenthal, P. D. Pearson, & R. Barr (Eds.), *Handbook of reading research, Vol. III* (pp. 361–379). Mahwah, NJ: Lawrence Erlbaum.

International Reading Association Board of Directors. (2000). Excellent reading teachers. *The Reading Teacher, 54*(2), 235–240.

Jensen, E. (1998). *Teaching with the brain in mind.* Alexandria, VA: Association for Supervision and Curriculum Development.

Merkley, D. M., & Jeffries, D. (2001). Guidelines for implementing a graphic organizer. *The Reading Teacher, 54*(4), 350–357.

Pressley, M. (2000). What should comprehension instruction be the instruction of? In M. L. Kamil, P. B. Mosenthal, P. D. Pearson, & R. Barr (Eds.), *Handbook of reading research, Vol. III* (pp. 545–561). Mahwah, NJ: Lawrence Erlbaum.

Robb, L. (2000). *Teaching reading in the middle school: A strategic approach to teaching reading that improves comprehension and thinking.* New York: Scholastic.

Roehler, L. R., & Duffy, G. G. (1996). Teachers' instructional actions. In R. Barr, M. L. Kamil, P. B. Mosenthal, & P. D. Pearson (Eds.), *Handbook of reading research, Vol. II* (pp. 861–883). Mahwah, NJ: Lawrence Erlbaum.

Rosenblatt, L. M. (1991). Literature—SOS! *Language Arts, 68,* 444–448.

Rosenblatt, L. M. (1994). *The reader, the text and the poem: The transactional theory of literary work.* Carbondale, IL: Southern Illinois University Press.

Rumelhart, D. E. (1981). Schemata: The building blocks of cognition. In Guthrie, J. T. (Ed.), *Comprehension and teaching: Research reviews* (pp. 3–26). Newark, DE: International Reading Association.

Rumelhart, D. E. (1984). Understanding understanding. In J. Flood (Ed.), *Understanding reading comprehension* (pp. 1–20). Newark, DE: International Reading Association.

Turner, J., & Paris, S. C. (1995). How literacy tasks influence children's motivation for literacy. *The Reading Teacher, 48*(8), 662–673.

Worthy, J., Broaddus, K., & Ivey, G. (2001). *Pathways to independence: Reading, writing, and learning in grades 3–8.* New York: Guilford Press.

Zemelman, S., Daniels, H., & Hyde, A. (1998). *Best practice: New standards for teaching and learning in America's schools.* (2nd ed.). Portsmouth, NH: Heinemann.

CONSTRUCTIVIST CAUTIONS
Peter W. Airasian and Mary E. Walsh

Theories of learning influence our views of effective instruction, and one of the most prominent theories of learning today is constructivism. Constructivism suggests that learners do not behave like tape recorders, which store information in the form it was presented; rather, learners develop (construct) their own understanding based on their existing background knowledge, so each person's constructed understanding is potentially unique.

> Despite the intuitive appeal of constructivism, translation of these ideas into classroom practice can be problematic, the authors assert. As you read this article ask yourself, "What role should constructivism play in classrooms of the 21st century?"

Think About This . . .

1. Why is constructivism so widely accepted according to Airasian and Walsh? In your opinion, how justified is this popularity?
2. At a conceptual level, what are four questions that constructivists debate? Which of these questions are most important for teachers?
3. What are three cautions about constructivism offered by the authors? Which of these is most important? Explain your answer.
4. How will an understanding of constructivism influence your teaching? Provide a classroom example to illustrate your description.

Recently, the concept of "constructivism" has been receiving a great deal of attention. At the conceptual level, constructivists debate such questions as, What is knowledge? What is teaching? What is learning? And is objectivity possible?[1] At the practical level, these complex issues have, in many cases, been reduced to catch phrases such as "Students construct their own knowledge" or the slightly narrower "Students construct their own knowledge based on their existing schemata and beliefs." Many efforts are under way to translate constructivist epistemology into classroom practices that will enable students to become "constructors of their own knowledge." While readily acknowledging that constructivism has made and will continue to make a significant contribution to educational theory and practice, we wish to sound a cautionary note about the euphoria surrounding constructivism.

What Is Constructivism?

Constructivism is an epistemology, a philosophical explanation about the nature of knowledge. Although constructivism might provide a model of knowing and learning that could be useful for educational purposes, at present the constructivist model is descriptive, not prescriptive. It describes in the broadest of strokes the human activity of knowing and nowhere specifies the detailed craft of teaching. It is important to understand at the outset that constructivism is not an instructional approach; it is a theory about how learners come to know. Although instructional approaches are typically derived from such epistemologies, they are distinct from them. One of the concerns that prompted us to undertake this discussion is the rush to turn the constructivist epistemology into instructional practice with little concern for the pitfalls that are likely to ensue.

Constructivism describes how one attains, develops, and uses cognitive processes. Multiple theories, such as those of Piaget and Vygotsky, have been proposed to explain the cognitive processes that are involved in constructing knowledge. While constructivism provides the epistemological framework for many of these theories, it is not itself an explanation for the psychological factors involved in knowing.

In general, constructivists compare an "old" view of knowledge to a "new," constructivist view. In the old view, knowledge is considered to be fixed and independent of the knower. There are "truths" that reside outside the knower. Knowledge is the accumulation of the "truths" in a subject area. The more "truths" one acquires, the more knowledge one possesses. In sharp contrast, the constructivist view rejects the notion that knowledge is independent of the knower and consists of accumulating "truths." Rather, knowledge is produced by the knower from existing beliefs and experiences. All knowledge is constructed and consists of what individuals create and express. Since individuals make their own meaning from their beliefs and experiences, all knowledge is tentative, subjective, and

From Airasian, P., & Walsh, M. (1997). Constructivist Cautions. Phi Delta Kappan, *78(6), 444–449. Reprinted with permission of the authors.*

personal. Knowledge is viewed not as a set of universal "truths," but as a set of "working hypotheses." Thus constructivists believe that knowledge can never be justified as "true" in an absolute sense.

Constructivism is based on the fundamental assumption that people create knowledge from the interaction between their existing knowledge or beliefs and the new ideas or situations they encounter. In this sense, most constructivists support the need to foster interactions between students' existing knowledge and new experiences. This emphasis is perceived to be different from the more traditional "transmission" model, in which teachers try to convey knowledge to students directly.

These fundamental agreements among constructivists are tempered by some important areas of difference about the process of constructing knowledge. These differences are reflected in two versions of constructivist theories of cognition: developmental and sociocultural. Developmental theories, such as Piaget's, represent a more traditional constructivist framework. Their major emphasis is on describing the universal forms or structures of knowledge (e.g., prelogical, concrete, and abstract operations) that guide the making of meaning. These universal cognitive structures are assumed to be developmentally organized, so that prelogical thinking occurs prior to concrete logical thinking in a developmental sequence. Within this framework, the individual student is considered to be the meaning maker, with the development of the individual's personal knowledge being the main goal of learning.

Critics of developmental theories of cognition point out that this perspective does not take into account "how issues such as the cultural and political nature of schooling and the race, class, and gender backgrounds of teachers and students, as well as their prior learning histories, influence the kinds of meaning that are made in the classroom."[2] Cognitive-developmental theories, it is claimed, divorce meaning making from affect by focusing on isolating universal forms of knowledge and thus limiting consideration of the sociocultural and contextual influences on the construction of knowledge.[3]

A second version of constructivism is reflected in the social constructivist or situated social constructivist perspective. As its name suggests, this type of constructivism puts its major emphasis on the social construction of knowledge and rejects the individualistic orientation of Piagetian theory. Within the sociocultural perspective, knowledge is seen as constructed by an individual's interaction with a social milieu in which he or she is situated, resulting in a change in both the individual and the milieu. Of course, it is possible for an individual to "reside" in many milieus, from a classroom milieu through a much more general cultural milieu. The point, however, is that social constructivists believe that knowledge has a social component and cannot be considered to be generated by an individual acting independently of his or her social context.[4] Consequently, recognition of the social and cultural influences on constructed knowledge is a primary emphasis. Because individual social and cultural contexts differ, the meanings people make may be unique to themselves or their cultures, potentially resulting in as many meanings as there are meaning makers. Universal meanings across individuals are not emphasized.

Critics of this perspective have pointed to the chaos that might be inherent in a multiplicity of potential meanings. While the social constructivists' concern with particular contextual or cultural factors that shape meaning enhances their recognition of differences across meanings, it limits their recognition of the universal forms that bring order to an infinite variety of meanings. Arguably, the critics of each version of constructivism exaggerate the positions espoused by these theories; however, they do set into relief the relative emphasis of each theory on the individual or the context.

This brief overview of constructivism omits many of the nuances and issues that characterize the debate over constructivist theory. However, our purpose is not to provide an in-depth portrait of constructivism, but rather to identify fundamental tenets that most constructivists would endorse and to point out that constructivism is not a unitary viewpoint. This latter fact is often overlooked in practice-oriented activities that derive from the slogan "Students are constructors of their own knowledge." The conflict between the two versions of constructivism is not merely "a matter of theoretical contemplation. Instead, it finds expression in tensions endemic to the act of teaching."[5] The particular version of constructivism one adopts—developmental or social constructivist—has important implications for classroom practices,[6] for the definition of knowledge,[7] for the relative emphasis on individual versus social learning,[8] for the role of the teacher,[9] and for the definition of successful instruction.[10]

Why Is Constructivism So Readily Accepted?

In the broad sense, constructivism represents a shift in the perspective of the social sciences and humanities from a view in which truth is a given to a view in which it is constructed by individuals and groups. There has been an inevitable spillover of this view from the social sciences and the humanities to education.

However, most educational theories and innovations are adopted with high levels of uncertainty. The wisdom of their adoption and the range of their impact are rarely known in advance of their implementation. Thus the justification for adopting a theory or innovation must come from outside the theory or innovation per se.[11] Typically, the justification is supplied by the existence of a pressing need or problem that requires quick amelioration or by the moral symbolism inherent in the theory or innovation. This is as true for constructivism as it has been for all educational theories and innovations that have sought to make their way into practice. However, it is very important to emphasize that there is a crucial difference between evidence that documents the need for change and evidence that documents the efficacy of a particular strategy of change. The specific strategy selected to produce change must seek its own validation, independent of the evidence of the need for change of some kind.

To understand its rapid acceptance, we must examine both present educational needs and the symbolic aspects of constructivism. The pressing educational need that fuels interest in constructivism is the perception that what we have been doing in schools has failed to meet the intellectual and occupational needs of the majority of our students; schools seem not to be promoting a sufficiently broad range of student outcomes. In particular, "thinking" or "higher-order" skills are not receiving sufficient instructional emphasis. A large part of the explanation for the perceived deficiency in pupil learning is thought to be an emphasis on "reductionist" or rote outcomes and forms of instruction. Reorienting instruction to nonrote outcomes makes such skills as generalizing, analyzing, synthesizing, and evaluating very important. From an instructional point of view, it puts much more of the onus on the student to construct personal meanings and interpretations. There is a link, then, between an epistemology that focuses on students' constructing their own knowledge and an education system that seeks to promote higher-level learning outcomes.

Also linking constructivism and educational need is the current emphasis on bottom-up as opposed to top-down approaches to reform. Thus recent reforms have increasingly allocated discretion for reforming the educational process to individual schools, teachers, students, and parents. In particular, teachers are given more discretion to construct their own meanings and interpretations of what will improve classroom teaching and learning. Moreover, because constructivism is an epistemology of how people learn, its focus is

logically on classroom practice. The increased teacher discretion over teaching and learning, combined with the classroom orientation and higher-level focus of constructivism, has sparked teachers' interest in the potential of constructivism for classroom practice.

Of course, it is not just increased teacher discretion and the classroom focus of constructivism that prompt interest. Constructivism is also appealing for other, more symbolic reasons. First, the rhetoric that surrounds constructivism is seductive. It plays off the metaphor of "lighting the flame" of student motivation (constructivism) against that of "filling the bucket" of students' heads with facts (present methods).[12] Constructivists claim that they emphasize autonomy as opposed to obedience, construction as opposed to instruction, and interest as opposed to reinforcement.[13] The implication is that, if one is opposed to constructivism, one is opposed to student autonomy, construction of meaning, and interest. Thus opponents are viewed as being against lighting the flame of student motivation. Such rhetoric plays a potent role in the reception of all innovations, including constructivism.

Second, since knowledge consists of what is constructed by the learner and since attainment of absolute truth is viewed as impossible, constructivism makes the implicit assumption that all students can and will learn—that is, construct knowledge. The vision of the constructivist student is one of activity, involvement, creativity, and the building of personal knowledge and understanding. This is an appealing symbol in an education system that is perceived to be inadequate for meeting the learning needs of many students. However, our consideration of constructivism should extend beyond process to an examination of the nature of the knowledge actually constructed.

Third, in a variety of ways and with a variety of potential consequences, constructivism symbolizes emancipation. From one perspective, constructivism can be interpreted as a symbol of the emancipation of teachers from the primary responsibility for student learning, since constructivism passes the onus of creating or acquiring knowledge from the teacher to the student. This notion is mistaken. The teacher will no longer be a supplier of information, but he or she will remain very much involved in the learning process, coordinating and critiquing student constructions, building his or her own knowledge of constructivism in the classroom, and learning new methods of instruction. Constructivism can also be interpreted as a symbol of the emancipation of teachers from the burden of dealing with the difficult issue of motivation, since many constructivists view the student's sense of ownership of and empowerment over the learning process as providing its own intrinsic motivation.[14]

Constructivism certainly is emancipatory and dovetails well with the agendas of many interest groups through its social constructivist emphasis on context as a critical feature of knowledge construction. When context becomes an important aspect of knowledge construction, it is logical to conclude that involvement in different contexts will lead to the construction of different knowledge, even if the same set of "data" is presented in the different contexts. Given a problem or an issue, a context—which is often designated in social, economic, racial, and gender terms—will influence the interpretations, conclusions, motives, and attitudes of individuals in that context. When confronted with the same problem or issue, individuals in different milieus may construct different interpretations and conclusions. In this case, "truth" becomes what those in a given milieu construct. And since different milieus vary in their constructions and since there is no absolute truth to search for, knowledge becomes relative to the milieu one inhabits.

This view is certainly symbolically emancipatory for many disempowered groups, but with what effect on the classroom? It would be naive to ignore the sociopolitical agendas and potential consequences for education that constructivism can evoke, particularly those emanating from the social constructivist version of constructivism.

Thus there are strong forces that underlie the growing interest in and acceptance of the constructivist epistemology. These forces stem from the perceived need to alter educational practice from an associational approach to one that emphasizes the higher-level knowledge construction needed to cope with the rapid expansion of information. They also stem from symbolic features of constructivism, particularly the symbols associated with the rhetoric of constructivism.

Cautions

Despite the persuasiveness of the above forces, it is important to be aware that the application of constructivism in classrooms is neither widespread nor systemic. This is not to suggest that there are no successful applications of constructivism. In fact, a number of writers have described approaches to constructivist teaching in special education classrooms, in largely African American classrooms, and in afterschool programs.[15] With the exception of Ann Brown's Community of Learning schools, however, most applications of contructivism have tended to be recent, narrowly focused pilot studies.

In discussing her ongoing work, even Brown indicates that, "for the past 10 years or so, my colleagues and I have been gradually evolving learning environments [to foster grade school pupils' interpretive communities]."[16] Accentuating the need for gradual development is important, because in simultaneously mounting constructivist teaching and endeavoring to remain faithful to constructivist tenets, teachers and administrators will be confronted with a number of obstacles and issues.

We turn now to some cautions that need to be kept in mind as teachers attempt to implement constructivism in their classrooms. Some of these cautions are pertinent to any classroom innovation. Others are specific to constructivism.

Do not fail to recognize the difference between an epistemology of learning and a well-thought-out and manageable instructional approach for implementing it. We do not have an "instruction of constructivism" that can be readily applied in classrooms. There are suggestions for methods that are likely to foster student construction of knowledge, primarily those that emphasize nonrote tasks and active student participation in the learning process (e.g., cooperative learning, performance assessments, product-oriented activities, and "hands-on" learning, as well as reciprocal teaching and initiation-reply-evaluation methods). However, it is not clear how such methods relate to learning in different content areas or whether these methods will be equally successful across all subject areas.[17]

It is even more important to recognize that the selection of a particular instructional strategy represents only part of what is necessary in the constructivist approach. Selection of a strategy does not necessarily lead to appropriate implementation or to the provision of individual feedback to students regarding their constructions. Implementing constructivism calls for a "learn as you go" approach for both students and teachers; it involves many decisions and much trial and error. Commenting on the relevance of this theory for contemporary practices and procedures in education, Kenneth Gergen writes:

> There is no means by which practical derivatives can simply be squeezed from a theory of knowledge. As has been seen, theories can specify neither the particulars to which they must be applied nor the contexts in which they may be rendered intelligible. There are no actions that follow necessarily from a given theory. . . . Thus, rather than seeking clear and compelling derivatives of constructionist theory, we should explore the kinds of practices that would be favored by the perspective within current conventions of understanding.[18]

Do not fall into the trap of believing that constructivist instructional techniques provide the sole means by which students construct meanings. This is not the case. Students construct their own knowledge and interpretations no matter what instructional approach is implemented and no matter what name is given to it. What teacher has not taught a didactic, rote-oriented topic or concept only to find that the students constructed a variety of very different meanings from those anticipated by the teacher? Thus no single teaching method ought to be used exclusively. One of the leading advocates of constructivism in education has compellingly argued that, from a constructivist point of view, it is a misunderstanding to consider teaching methods such as memorization and rote learning useless. "There are, indeed, matters that can and perhaps must be learned in a purely mechanical way."[19] One's task is to find the right balance between the activities of constructing and receiving knowledge, given that not all aspects of a subject can or should be taught in the same way or be acquired solely through "hands-on" or student-centered means.

Because students always make their own meaning from instruction, the important curricular and instructional choice is not a choice between making and not making personal meaning from instructional activities, but a choice among the ideas, concepts, and issues that we want our students to construct meaning about. It is in this area that states such as Kentucky, California, and Vermont, among others, are redefining the expectations for student learning and reinforcing those expectations through statewide assessments. Similarly, it is in this area that such organizations as the National Council of Teachers of Mathematics are promulgating and advocating newer, more performance-oriented goals in their subject areas. The issues addressed by states and professional organizations are much more focused on the outcomes than on the means of instruction.

Do not assume that a constructivist orientation will make the same demands on teaching time as a nonconstructivist orientation. Time is an extremely important consideration in implementing constructivist education in two regards.

1. *Time is needed for teachers and pupils to learn and practice how to perform in a constructivist classroom.* If criticisms of "reductionist" education are valid, then substituting another approach, whether in part or in toto, will call for a redefinition of both teachers' and students' roles. In a constructivist approach, teachers will have to learn to guide, not tell; to create environments in which students can make their own meanings,

not be handed them by the teacher; to accept diversity in constructions, not search for the one "right" answer, to modify prior notions of "right" and "wrong," not stick to rigid standards and criteria; to create a safe, free, responsive environment that encourages disclosure of student constructions, not a closed, judgmental system.

Students will also have to learn new ways to perform. They will have to learn to think for themselves, not wait for the teacher to tell them what to think; to proceed with less focus and direction from the teacher, not to wait for explicit teacher directions; to express their own ideas clearly in their own words, not to answer restricted-response questions; to revisit and revise constructions, not to move immediately on to the next concept or idea.

It is easy to *say* that constructivist teachers must create an open, nonjudgmental environment that permits students to construct, disclose, and expose their constructions to scrutiny. But listening and responding to student constructions will be difficult and time-consuming.[20] Teachers will have to become accustomed to working with quite different and more general goals, since the instructional emphasis will be on the viability of varied, idiosyncratic student constructions. Teachers will need to serve as initiators of activities that will evoke students' interest and lead to new constructions and as critics of the constructions that students produce. In a sense, much of the responsibility for learning will be turned over to the students through "hands-on" experiences and activities designed to spur their constructions of meaning. The more teachers become engaged in this process, the more the resulting constructions will be theirs, not the students'.

Finding a balance between teacher involvement or noninvolvement in the process of learning will be a challenge. It is legitimate to ask how well—and how soon—teachers will be able to create such an environment and reorient their practice. In this regard it is noteworthy that, with few exceptions,[21] there is considerably less discussion about the role and activities of the *teacher* in constructivist education than there is about the role and activities of the *students*. But changes in orientation for both teacher and students will not occur immediately, especially for those who have had a long time to become accustomed to the current norms of classroom practice. New ways of thinking, acting, organizing, and judging will always take time to develop.

2. *In the shift to constructivist teaching, considerable time will be required for responding to the individual constructions of students.* Student constructions have

two important properties: 1) they are complex in form, and 2) they differ from student to student. Because constructions represent understandings and connections between prior and new knowledge, they cannot be conveyed in a word or a phrase. To convey one's construction of meaning will require an in-depth presentation about one's knowledge and how one arrived at or justifies that knowledge. If constructions are reduced to multiple-choice items or to some other truncated representational form, the richness and meaning of constructivism will be lost. Hence, to review, understand, and respond to student constructions will require substantial teacher time and perhaps the involvement of parents and community members as well.

Moreover, different students are likely to produce quite different constructions, making it difficult to apply the same frame of reference to the review of their constructions. Each construction and its underlying logic will need to be examined, understood, and reviewed. Hence, the amount of time needed to respond to these constructions will be further increased. Responding to student constructions will be more like reading essays or viewing oral reports than like scoring multiple-choice or short-answer tests.

Implicit in the need for increased time are other important time-related issues, such as the trade off between coverage and depth. It is likely that the quality of students' knowledge constructions will depend in part on the time they are given to construct. More time will mean richer and deeper constructions. Teachers and schools will have to face the question of whether it is better to cover a large amount of content at a rather shallow level or to cover a smaller amount of content in great depth. The constructivist approach fits much better with the latter choice, since it aims for personal meaning and understanding, not rote associations.

Do not believe that the opposite of "one-right-answer" reductionism is "anything-goes" constructivism. Implicit in any form of classroom instruction guided by any theory of learning is the need for standards and criteria of judgment. This matter is both important and challenging in constructivist thought and application. Among the questions that constructivist teachers will have to confront regarding standards and criteria are: On what basis should students have to justify their constructions? Can the teacher who facilitates the constructions also be an objective evaluator of them? What constitutes a "reasonable" or "acceptable" student construction? Should the teacher try to avoid transmitting standards and criteria that end up influencing or controlling the nature of student constructions? If so, how? Are

evaluation standards and criteria independent of context or are they contextually bound?

A teacher who accepts the constructivist tenet that knowledge is constructed by individuals and that knowledge and experience are subjective must inevitably face the relationship between truth and meaning. In practical terms, the teacher must decide how much emphasis will be placed on the relative "truthfulness" of students' constructions or on their "meaningfulness" to the student. Since there is no one best construction and since people must construct their own meanings from personal experiences and understandings, there are many viable constructions.[22] Further, if it is assumed that knowledge is ego- and context-specific, the likelihood of agreeing on common standards of evaluation is diminished greatly. This perspective could create many problems when applied in classrooms.

A rejoinder to this view argues that the lack of one best construction does not mean that some constructions cannot be deemed better than others. Moreover, sole reliance on personal meaning to justify constructions leads to rampant relativism and potentially biased, self-serving, and dishonest constructions.[23] In this view, the role of the teacher is to challenge students to justify and refine their constructions in order to strengthen them.

At the opposite end of the spectrum from meaningfulness is truthfulness. Absolute certainty is alien to the tenets of constructivism. However, there can be intermediate positions between absolute and relative truthfulness. Thus it is possible to evaluate some constructions as being more truthful (i.e., reasonable) than others. If a position of modified or relative truthfulness is adopted, as it inevitably will be in real classrooms, the teacher is directly confronted by the need to establish standards and criteria for evaluating the merits of students' constructions.

However, in facing this need, the teacher also faces an issue that should be approached with awareness and caution. In evaluating some constructions as being better than others, the teacher will find that the more explicit the evaluation standards and criteria, the greater the likelihood that they will be transmitted to and adopted by the students. When standards and criteria are constructed jointly by teachers, students, and parents, transmission and adoption become desirable. However, if the teacher is the sole determiner of standards and criteria, he or she is likely to have the primary influence on the nature of classroom constructions. Students may not construct meaning on their own, for they know that high grades derive from meeting the teacher's standards and criteria. Constructivism is thus compromised. The problem of guiding and evaluating students without undermining their constructivist activities is a thorny one. The development of standards and criteria that are clear but that allow variance in evaluation is paramount, and each teacher will have to find his or her appropriate balance, given that few external guidelines for defining such standards and criteria exist.

In the preceding discussion we have pointed out the difference between the theory of constructivism and its practical application. In particular, we have argued that the consequences of implementing constructivism in the classroom will be considerably more challenging than might be anticipated from the simple slogans that advocates repeat. But our comments and cautions should not be taken as criticisms of the constructivist viewpoint. Indeed, we recognize and appreciate the positive role that this orientation can play in changing educational practice. Rather, our comments are meant to illuminate and anticipate important issues that will inevitably arise in attempts to implement constructivism in practical, classroom settings. These are not reasons to avoid trying to implement constructivism: they are efforts to help readers know something about what they are adopting at a more substantive level. Knowing some of the nuances and problems of a theory or innovation makes one better able to move beyond rhetoric to consider the implications for one's own practice.

Notes

1. Richard S. Prawat, "Teachers' Beliefs About Teaching and Learning: A Constructivist Perspective," *American Journal of Education*, vol. 100, 1992, pp. 354–95; Carl Bereiter, "Constructivism, Socioculturalism, and Popper's World 3," *Educational Researcher*, October 1994, pp. 21–23; Rosalind Driver et al., "Constructing Scientific Knowledge in the Classroom," *Educational Researcher;* October 1994. pp. 5–12; and Neil M. Agnew and John L. Brown, "Foundations for a Model of Knowing: II. Fallible but Functional Knowledge," *Canadian Psychology,* vol. 30, 1989, pp. 168–83.

2. Michael O'Loughlin, "Rethinking Science Education: Beyond Piagetian Constructivism Toward a Sociocultural Model of Teaching and Learning," *Journal of Research in Science Teaching,* vol. 29, 1992, p. 792.

3. Martin L. Hoffman, "Development of Moral Thought, Feeling, and Behavior," *American Psychologist,* vol. 34, 1979, pp. 958–66.

4. Kenneth J. Gergen, "Exploring the Postmodern: Perils or Potentials," *American Psychologist,* vol. 49, 1994, pp. 412–16; and James V. Wertsch and Chikako Toma, "Discourse and Learning in the Classroom: A Sociocultural Approach," in Leslie P. Steffe and Jerry Gale, eds., *Constructivism in Education* (Hillsdale, N.J.: Erlbaum, 1995). pp. 159–74.

5. Paul Cobb, "Where Is the Mind? Constructivist and Sociocultural Perspectives on Mathematical Development," *Educational Researcher,* October 1994, p. 13.

6. Deborah L. Ball, "With an Eye on the Mathematical Horizon: Dilemmas of Teaching Elementary School Mathematics," *Elementary School Journal,* vol. 93, 1993, pp. 373–97.

7. Virginia Richardson, "Constructivist Teaching: Theory and Practice," paper presented at the annual meeting of the American Educational Research Association, New Orleans, 1994; and Bereiter, op. cit.

8. Driver et al., op. cit.

9. Ibid.

10. Ginnette Delandshire and Anthony J. Petrosky, "Capturing Teachers' Knowledge: Performance Assessment," *Educational Researcher,* June/July 1994, pp. 11–18.

11. Peter W. Airasian, "Symbolic Validation: The Case of State-Mandated, High-Stakes Testing," *Educational Evaluation and Policy Analysis,* vol. 4, 1988, pp. 301–13.

12. David Elkind, "Spiritually in Education," *Holistic Education Review,* vol. 5, no. 1, 1992, pp. 12–16.

13. Rhete DeVries and Lawrence Kohlberg, *Constructivist Early Education* (Washington, D.C.: National Association for the Education of Young Children, 1987).

14. Aire W. Kruglanski, *Lay Epistemics and Human Knowledge* (New York: Plenum Press, 1989); Penny Oldfather, "Sharing the Ownership of Knowing: A Constructivist Concept of Motivation for Literacy Learning," paper presented at the annual meeting of the National Reading Conference, San Antonio, 1992; and O'Loughlin, op. cit.

15. Ann Brown, "The Advancement of Learning," *Educational Researcher,* November 1994, pp. 4–12; Richardson, op. cit.; Gloria Ladson-Billing, *The Dreamkeepers: Successful Teaching of African-American Children* (San Francisco: Jossey-Bass, 1994); and Wertsch and Toma, op. cit.

16. Brown, "Advancement of Learning," p. 7.

17. Susan S. Stodolsky, *The Subject Matters* (Chicago: University of Chicago Press, 1988); and Cobb, op. cit.

18. Kenneth Gergen, "Social Construction and the Educational Process," in Steffe and Gale, pp. 17–39.

19. Ernst von Glasersfeld, "A Constructivist Approach to Teaching," in Steffe and Gale, p. 5.

20. Peter W. Airasian, "Critical Pedagogy and the Realities of Teaching," in Henry Perkinson, *Teachers Without Goals, Students Without Purposes* (New York: McGraw-Hill, 1993), pp. 81–93.

21. See, for example, Brown, "The Advancement of Learning"; and Ladson-Billing, op. cit.

22. Geraldine Gilliss, "Schön's Reflective Practitioner: A Model for Teachers?," in Peter Grimmett and Gaalen Erickson, eds., *Reflection in Teacher Education* (New York: Teachers College Press, 1988), pp. 47–54.

23. Bereiter, op. cit.; and Karl Popper, *Objective Knowledge: An Evolutionary Approach* (Oxford: Clarendon, 1972).

WHAT DO WE KNOW ABOUT LEARNERS AND LEARNING?
THE LEARNER-CENTERED FRAMEWORK: BRINGING THE EDUCATIONAL SYSTEM INTO BALANCE

Barbara McCombs

Effective instruction accommodates the learner in multiple ways, ranging from background knowledge to preferred ways of learning. Our educational system is out of balance, Barbara McCombs asserts, focusing too much on standards and accountability, and not enough on students' needs and interests. The Learner-Centered Psychological Principles attempt to address this imbalance by emphasizing student development, motivation, and individual differences. When successfully implemented, these principles encourage educators to refocus their energies away from texts and tests to the learners they serve. As you read this article ask yourself, "How would implementing these principles change instruction in my classroom?"

Think About This . . .

1. In her article, McCombs talks about an imbalance in our current educational system. What is this imbalance, and what can teachers do to address this problem?

2. How is a learner-centered approach different from traditional approaches to teaching? What do teachers need to know to implement a learner-centered approach to teaching?

3. How are the four major categories of the Learner-Centered Psychological Principles similar? How do they differ?

4. How would implementation of the Learner-Centered Psychological Principles change your teaching? Provide a concrete example in your response.

Abstract

This paper introduces "learner-centered" education from a research and theory base that integrates what we know about learners and learning both inside and outside formal school settings and describes the work of the author and colleagues in developing self-assessment and reflection tools for K–20 teachers and their students. Building on the Learner-Centered Psychological Principles (APA, 1993, 1997), data on more than 20,000 students and their teachers in kindergarten through graduate school were collected with the Assessment of Learner-Centered Practices (ALCP) surveys (McCombs, 1997, 1999; McCombs and Lauer, 1997; McCombs and Pierce, 1999; McCombs and Quiat, 1999). The surveys identify teacher beliefs and discrepancies between teacher and student perspectives on practices, and help teachers to reflect on and change practices as well as to identify personalized staff development needs. Data indicated that the best predictor of student motivation and achievement, at all age levels, was a common domain of practice that creates positive relationships between students and teachers and a positive climate for learning. Implications for moving from personal to systems change based on student perspectives will briefly be presented.

From McCombs, B. (2001). What do we know about learners and learning? The learner-centered framework: Bringing the educational system into balance. Educational Horizons, 79(4), 182–193. Reprinted with permission of the author.

Introduction

Our educational system is out of balance. Current reform efforts are focusing primarily on technical issues (e.g., high academic standards, increased student achievement, alignment of curricula and assessment) that emphasize accountability (e.g., "high stakes" testing, teacher responsibility for student achievement) and punitive consequences for teachers, students, and administrators when student achievement standards are not met (e.g., replacing school staff, retaining students in grade). To bring the system into balance and bring some of the joy of learning back into the educational process, the focus must also be on personal issues and the needs of all people in the system, including students and the adults who serve them in the teaching and learning process. First, however, it is important to clarify why this balance is particularly vital at this time.

Imbalance in the Current System

Although focusing school reform efforts on high academic standards does have its merits, this approach puts content, curriculum, and assessment, not students, at the center, contributing to students' feelings of alienation. Even with clearer standards for what learners should know and be able to do, and the shift from what to *teach* to a focus on what content and skills must be *learned* by all learners, the needs of individual learners are often downplayed in the implementation of standards-based programs. Further, with the emphasis on knowledge and skill standards, our current educational paradigm defines the goal of learning as knowledge conservation rather than knowledge production (Carroll, 2000). This contributes to student complaints that school is boring and irrelevant.

From a learner-centered view based on research-validated principles of learning and change in complex human living systems, this focus must be transformed. Why? Because without a corresponding focus on individual learners and their learning needs, we are in danger of continuing to ignore students' and teachers' calls for help when they report that they feel disconnected from each other, think school is irrelevant, or drop out mentally or physically from a punitive and coercive learning environment.

In spite of these negative consequences for students and teachers, current state and federal approaches to increasing student achievement and teacher quality continue to emphasize content knowledge, standards, assessment, and accountability (Chase, 1999; Feistritzer, 1999; Finn, Kanstoroom, and Petulli,

1999; Kanstoroom and Finn, 1999; U.S. Department of Education, 1997). But is this focus the best? It may not be—particularly in light of new crises that have surfaced in our nation's schools. These crises are outside the academic standards, achievement, and accountability area, but they are clearly being magnified as a result of the focus on this area. They include not only rising youth alienation from learning and associated non-academic issues, but also the rising evidence of teacher stress, feelings of being overwhelmed, despair, and departure from the profession.

The Need for Person-Centered Approaches

Schools no longer have the luxury of ignoring the personal needs of students. The rising wave of youth violence, both in the community and in school settings, has generated increased attention to issues facing today's school-age children. Associated rises in youth suicide, alcohol and drug abuse, school disciplinary problems, school dropout rates, and delinquent behaviors are of additional concern. School system and community responses run the gamut from fear-based attempts to expel or suspend all students who even appear to be troublemakers to more positive approaches that build the strengths and assets of even the most troubled youth. At the core of these youth issues, however, many experts as well as the youth themselves say that youth feel alienated, disconnected, and in a spiritual crisis, questioning who they are, their purpose in life, and the meaning of life (Brendtro, 1999; Wheatley, 1999). What is needed are educational models that reconnect youth and adults, models that are person-centered while also providing challenging learning experiences that prepare children and youth to be knowledge producers, knowledge users, and socially responsible citizens. We need models with a balanced focus on learners and learning.

Restoring a Needed Balance

Attention to the knowledge base about learners and learning is essential in focusing on the *personal domain* of educational systems. This domain focuses on the *human processes* and on personal and interpersonal *relationships, beliefs, and perceptions* that are affected or supported by the educational system as a whole. The foundation of research-validated principles is essential to designing person- and learner-centered programs and practices that attend holistically and systemically to the needs of all learners.

Youth alienation, with its relationship to problems such as school dropouts and suicide, is an issue of much current concern. Ryan and Deci (2000) maintain that alienation in any age population is caused by a lack of supports for competence, autonomy, and relatedness. Unfortunately, there are too many examples in the current educational reform agenda of coercive and punitive consequences for students, teachers, and administrators when students fail to achieve educational standards as assessed on state and national tests. Ryan and Deci (2000, p. 76) argue: "Excessive control, nonoptimal challenges, and lack of connectedness . . . disrupt the inherent actualizing and organizational tendencies endowed by nature, and thus such factors result not only in the lack of initiative and responsibility but also in distress and psychopathology."

Open School Movement founder Herb Kohl has thirty-six years of experience as a teacher working in dysfunctional, poverty-ridden urban school districts. In a recent interview (Scherer, 1998), Kohl emphasizes the importance of teachers projecting hope to students—convincing them of their worth and ability to achieve in a difficult world. This means respecting students and honoring their perspectives. Kohl also maintains that quality learning is learning that engages students. He describes learning communities as those that are curious and encourage invention, creativity, and imagination. He believes that the curriculum needs to be shaped by what adults know *and* by student interests and learning preferences. The educational environment has to be changed and communities rebuilt with a focus on caring. Kohl advocates "personalized learning," based on personal relationships between students and teachers and respect for the unique way each student perceives the world and learns.

This article presents a research-validated definition of "learner-centered" that integrates what we know about learners and learning, inside and outside formal school settings. I will describe the work of my colleagues and me in developing self-assessment and reflection tools for K–20 teachers and their students, highlighting the role of student perspectives in defining classroom practices and contexts that best support *both* high academic achievement and high motivation for learning. I will also discuss how self-assessment results are used to promote teacher change and the implications of these results for moving from personal to systems change based on student perspectives. I will

conclude with a summary of what must be done in practice to achieve a balanced focus on technical and personal educational issues.

What Knowledge Base Is Needed to Achieve a Balance Between Learners' Learning and Motivational Needs?

What is the foundational knowledge base needed to define the learning experiences and conditions that create quality learning and meet social, emotional, and cognitive learning needs? Research supports the contention that a focus on personal and motivational outcomes balanced with a focus on high achievement and challenging standards is vital in today's schools. There is growing recognition that schooling must prepare children to behave in moral and ethical ways. For example, many educators are calling for caring, democratic schooling and instructional methods that build on each student's background, experience of reality, and perspective (e.g., Bartolome, 1994; McWhorter et al., 1996; Noddings, 1995; Ruddick, Day, and Wallace, 1997). These models balance attention to the personal domain; the content-focused technical domain; and the organizational domain, which focuses on management structures and process.

For such learner- and person-centered practices to become realities, however, teachers need to become more aware of their relationship with students as knowledge generators and active participants in their own learning. When power is shared by students and teachers, teaching methods become a means to an end rather than an end in themselves. As Schaps and Lewis (1999) report in reflections on the "perils" of building school community, it is essential that schoolwide change have a dual emphasis on (a) a sense of community *and* academic learning and (b) student *and* teacher input in shaping classroom lessons and decisions. Research-validated principles are needed to guide the implementation of such practices. The knowledge base underlying the principles of learners and learning can be a research-validated foundation for comprehensive school reform that focuses on meeting cognitive, social, and emotional human needs and fostering positive teacher–student relationships. These principles lead to understanding students as knowledge generators, active participants in their own learning, and co-creators of learning experiences and curricula.

The Learner-Centered Principles as a Foundational Framework

Education is one of many complex living systems that function to support particular human needs (cf. Wheatley, 1999). Such systems, unpredictable by their nature, can be understood in terms of principles that define human needs, cognitive and motivational processes, development, and individual differences. The research-validated Learner-Centered Psychological Principles (APA, 1993, 1997) provide a knowledge base for understanding learning and motivation as natural processes that occur when the *conditions and context* of learning support individual learner needs, capacities, experiences, and interests. This foundation is essential to designing programs and practices that attend holistically and systemically to the needs of all learners—including students, teachers, administrators, families, and community members.

The Learner-Centered Psychological Principles

In 1990, the American Psychological Association (APA) appointed a special Task Force on Psychology in Education, one of whose purposes was to integrate research and theory from psychology and education in order to surface time-tested general principles that can provide a framework for school redesign and reform. The resulting document originally specified twelve fundamental principles about learners and learning that, taken together, provide an integrated perspective on factors influencing learning for all learners (APA, 1993). This document, revised in 1997 (APA, 1997), now includes fourteen principles, with attention to diversity and standards. (*Note to readers:* Those interested in research support for the principles are referred to the research and theory reviewed in developing the principles, described in McCombs and Whisler [1997]. Further research support is also provided in Alexander and Murphy [1998] and Lambert and McCombs [1998]).

The fourteen learner-centered principles are categorized into four research-validated domains important to learning, as shown in Figure 1: metacognitive and cognitive factors; affective and motivational factors; developmental and social factors; and individual difference factors. An understanding of these domains and the principles within them establishes a framework for designing learner-centered practices at all levels of schooling. It also defines what "learner-centered" means from a research-validated perspective.

Defining "Learner-Centered"

From an integrated look at the principles, the following definition emerges:

> "Learner-centered" is the perspective that couples a focus on individual learners—their heredity, experiences, perspectives, backgrounds, talents, interests, capacities, and needs—with a focus on learning—the best available knowledge about learning and how it occurs and about teaching practices that are most effective in promoting the highest levels of motivation, learning, and achievement for all learners. This dual focus then informs and drives educational decision making. Learner-centered education is a reflection in practice of the Learner-Centered Psychological Principles—the programs, practices, policies, and people that support learning for all. (Summarized from the APA Work Group of the Board of Educational Affairs [1997, November]. *Learner-centered psychological principles: Guidelines for school reform and redesign.* Washington, D.C.: American Psychological Association.)

This definition of "learner-centered" is based on an understanding of the Learner-Centered Psychological Principles as a representation of current knowledge on learners and learning. The principles apply to all learners, in and outside school, young and old. Learner-centered is also related to the beliefs, characteristics, dispositions, and practices of teachers—practices primarily created by the teacher. When teachers derive their practices from an understanding of the principles, they (a) include learners in decisions about how and what they learn and how that learning is assessed; (b) value each learner's unique perspectives; (c) respect and accommodate individual differences in learners' backgrounds, interests, abilities, and experiences; and (d) treat learners as co-creators and partners in the teaching and learning process.

Others who have used the term "learner-centered" (e.g., Darling-Hammond, 1996; Sparks and Hirsh, 1997) refer to learning new beliefs and visions of practice that are responsive to and respectful of the diverse needs of students and teachers as learners. All learning, for students and teachers, must support diverse learners, provide time for reflection, and offer opportunities for teachers and students to co-create practices that enhance learning, motivation, and achievement. This view of "learner-centered" is a research-validated paradigm shift that transforms education—including how best to

Figure 1
The Learner-Centered Psychological Principles

Cognitive and Metacognitive Factors

Principle 1: Nature of the Learning Process
The learning of complex subject matter is most effective when it is an intentional process of constructing meaning from information and experience.

Principle 2: Goals of the Learning Process
The successful learner, over time and with support and instructional guidance, can create meaningful, coherent representations of knowledge.

Principle 3: Construction of Knowledge
The successful learner can link new information with existing knowledge in meaningful ways.

Principle 4: Strategic Thinking
The successful learner can create and use a repertoire of thinking and reasoning strategies to achieve complex learning goals.

Principle 5: Thinking About Thinking
Higher-order strategies for selecting and monitoring mental operations facilitate creative and critical thinking.

Principle 6: Context of Learning
Learning is influenced by environmental factors, including culture, technology, and instructional practices.

Motivational and Affective Factors

Principle 7: Motivational and Emotional Influences on Learning
What and how much is learned is influenced by the learner's motivation. Motivation to learn, in turn, is influenced by the individual's emotional states, beliefs, interests and goals, and habits of thinking.

Principle 8: Intrinsic Motivation to Learn
The learner's creativity, higher-order thinking, and natural curiosity all contribute to motivation to learn.

Intrinsic motivation is stimulated by tasks of optimal novelty and difficulty, relevant to personal interests, and providing for personal choice and control.

Principle 9: Effects of Motivation on Effort
Acquisition of complex knowledge and skills requires extended learner effort and guided practice. Without learners' motivation to learn, the willingness to exert this effort is unlikely without coercion.

Developmental and Social Factors

Principle 10: Developmental Influence on Learning
As individuals develop, they encounter different opportunities and experience different constraints for learning. Learning is most effective when differential development within and across physical, intellectual, emotional, and social domains is taken into account.

Principle 11: Social Influences on Learning
Learning is influenced by social interactions, interpersonal relations, and communication with others.

Individual Differences Factors

Principle 12: Individual Differences in Learning
Learners' different strategies, approaches, and capabilities for learning are a function of prior experience and heredity.

Principle 13: Learning and Diversity
Learning is most effective when differences in learners' linguistic, cultural, and social backgrounds are taken into account.

Principle 14: Standards and Assessment
Setting appropriately high and challenging standards and assessing the learner and learning progress—including diagnostic, process, and outcome assessment—are integral parts of the learning process.

design programs to support the new vision (cf. Sparks and Hirsh, 1997).

"Learner-centeredness" is not solely a function of particular instructional practices or programs (McCombs, 2000; McCombs and Lauer, 1997; McCombs and Whisler, 1997). Rather, it is a complex interaction of qualities of the teacher in combination with characteristics of instructional practices, as perceived by individual learners. That is, "learner-centeredness" is in "the eye of the beholder": it varies as a function of learner perceptions, which in turn are the result of learners' prior experiences, self-beliefs, and attitudes about schools and learning as well as their current interests, values, and goals. The quality of "learner-centeredness" does not reside in programs or practices by themselves, no matter how well-designed the program may be.

When learner-centered is defined from a research perspective that includes the knowledge base on both learning and learners, it also clarifies what is needed to create positive learning contexts and communities. When this approach occurs at the classroom and school levels, it increases the likelihood of success for more students and their teachers. It can also increase clarity about the requisite dispositions and characteristics of those in service to learners and learning—particularly teachers. From this perspective, the learner-centered principles can become a foundational framework for determining how to assess the efficacy of existing programs and practices in enhancing the teaching and learning process. Learner perceptions of how well programs and practices meet individual cognitive, social, and emotional needs are part of the assessment of ongoing learning, change, and improvement.

The Role of Self-Assessment for Learning and Change

Throughout history, all major changes or paradigm shifts have required a transformation in thinking, seeing, or interpreting reality. In this current era of educational reform, many shifts in thinking are being proposed. We are asked to believe that "all students can learn" and to see education as a "shared responsibility" among all constituencies—students, teachers, administrators, parents, and community members. We are also asked to confront old models and beliefs about how we learn and how best to promote the learning process. In any time of significant change, people are forced to confront and revise old assumptions. For this process to be successful, however, people need to know why change is necessary, what it entails, and how to make

the shift. This certainly is the case when educators are asked to consider a learner-centered perspective, to adopt a learner-centered approach.

Even those educators who are open to change may be uncertain what kind of changes will be most effective and how best to go about making the changes. It may seem unlikely that any change can be successful, given the complex and overwhelming set of problems and issues facing educational systems. Feelings of fear, frustration, hopelessness, and despair abound, as well as a sense that "we're already doing so much—how can we possibly do more?" In such an atmosphere, it is easy to hold on to old beliefs and assumptions, to stay within the comfort zone of old ways of thinking about and doing education, and to avoid the issue for as long as possible. Is there a way to break through this resignation and inertia? What might increase willingness to change and hopefulness about the possibilities?

We have taken these questions seriously in our work. We examined our own beliefs and thinking about learning, learners, and teaching; looked to the research literature to learn what needs to change and why; and challenged ourselves to discover a sound foundation of research-based principles that can guide the change process. In our efforts, we have learned to question even the most pervasive assumptions and ideas being proposed. For example, we have learned from research on learning that not only *can* all students learn, but all students *do* learn. Research from cognitive and developmental psychology clearly supports the view that learning is a natural and ongoing process, and that it occurs continuously for all learners, cradle to grave (Alexander and Murphy, 1998; McCombs, 1998). After examining the differences in educational systems based on the "can learn," versus the "do learn," philosophy, we have seen clear evidence of the superiority of those systems that assume all students do learn (McCombs and Whisler, 1997). The "do learn" environments respect and accommodate student diversity by assuming that learning and motivation will be natural and that students can be trusted to guide their own learning process—not selected and sorted into presumed categories of ability. Variable learning methods, content, and performance demonstrations are determined with student input, not selected for students in ways that may limit their potential.

To address motivation, learning, and achievement, as well as variables dealing with health and positive functioning, in addition to focusing on *learning*, our work with the Learner-Centered Psychological Principles has focused on providing tools for addressing the personal domain of educational systems. These tools were developed to foster a process of personal learning and change for teachers.

The Assessment of Learner-Centered Practices (ALCP)

The ALCP contains a set of short teacher and student self-assessment surveys for teachers and students in grades K–20 (McCombs, 1999). The Teacher (or Instructor) Survey measures two primary variables: "Teacher Beliefs" and "Assumptions and Teacher Perceptions of Classroom Practices." Three factors that relate to learner-centered, versus non-learner-centered, beliefs about learners, learning, and teaching are measured in the Teacher Beliefs section of the survey. Depending on the level of schooling, four to five factors that define domains of learner-centered classroom practice are measured in the "Teacher Practices" section of the survey. These domains are based on the principles and cover practices associated with metacognitive-cognitive, affective-motivational, developmental, personal-social, and other individual needs of learners (McCombs, 1997; McCombs and Whisler, 1997).

The student survey measures students' perceptions of their teachers' practices, assessing the same four or five domains of practice from the students' perspective (McCombs, Lauer, and Pierce, 1998; McCombs, 1997; McCombs and Lauer, 1997). This survey provides teachers with feedback about how each of their students experiences classroom practices. (Note: There are other measures in the ALCP for administrators, mentor teachers, and parents, cf. McCombs and Whisler, 1997).

Results of Self-Assessing Personal Beliefs and Perceptions of Practice

Our research (McCombs, 1998; McCombs and Lauer, 1997; McCombs and Quiat, 1999; McCombs and Whisler, 1997) looked at the impact of teachers' beliefs on their perceptions of their classroom practices, as well as how teacher perceptions differ from student perceptions of these practices. In a large-scale study of teachers and students, we confirmed our hypothesis about the importance—for student motivation, learning, and achievement—of those beliefs and practices that are consistent with the research on learners and learning. We also found that teachers who are more learner-centered are more successful in engaging all students in an effective learning process and are themselves more effective learners and happier with their jobs. Furthermore, teachers report that the process of self-assessment and reflection—particularly about discrepancies between their own and their individual students' experiences of classroom practices—helps them identify areas in which they might change their practices to reach more students effectively. This is an important finding that relates to the "how" of transformation. Helping teachers and others engage in a process of self-assessment and reflection—particularly about the impact of their beliefs and practices on individual students and their learning and motivation—creates a respectful and non-judgmental impetus to change. The transformation is completed when this opportunity for self-assessment and reflection is combined with skill training in and dialogue about how to create learner-centered K–20 schools and classrooms.

We found in our research that teachers were not absolutely learner-centered or completely non-learner-centered. At the same time, however, specific *beliefs or teaching practices* could be classified as learner-centered (likely to enhance motivation, learning, and success) or non-learner-centered (likely to hinder motivation, learning, and success). Learner-centered teachers are defined as those with more beliefs and practices classified as learner-centered than as non-learner-centered. For example, *believing that all students learn* is quite different from *believing that some students cannot learn*, the former being learner-centered and the latter being non-learner-centered. Learner-centered teachers see each student as unique and capable of learning, have a perspective that focuses on the learner, understand basic principles defining learners and learning, and honor and accept the student's point of view (McCombs and Lauer, 1997; McCombs and Quiat, 1999). As a result, the student's natural inclinations to learn, master the environment, and grow in positive ways are enhanced.

The results of our research with the ALCP teacher and student surveys at both the secondary and postsecondary levels have confirmed that (a) student perceptions of their teachers' instructional practices are significantly related to their motivation, learning, and achievement; (b) teacher perceptions of instructional practices are not significantly related to student motivation and achievement; and (c) student perceptions of a positive learning environment and interpersonal relationship with the teacher are the most important factors in enhancing student motivation and achievement.

For K–3 students, three domains of classroom practice are best at predicting motivation and achievement:

(1) establishing positive relationships and classroom climate; (2) adapting to individual differences; and (3) facilitating students' learning and thinking skills. For middle and high school students, there were four domains that included the three for K–3 students, but with the addition of (4) honoring student voice and providing individual choice and challenge. Results with undergraduate and graduate students and their instructors revealed five domains of practice important to motivation and achievement: (1) establishing positive interpersonal relationships; (2) facilitating the learning process; (3) adapting to student learning needs; (4) encouraging personal challenge and responsibility for learning; and (5) providing for social learning needs. Thus, at all levels of our educational system, teachers and instructors can improve instructional practices and move toward more learner-centered practices by attending to what students perceive and by creating positive climates and relationships—those critical connections so important to personal and system learning and change.

Moving from Personal Change to System Change

A focus on the learner has also emerged from those who see schools as "living systems"—systems that are in service to learners and serve the basic function of learning for the primary recipient (the learner) as well as for the other humans who support learning (teachers, administrators, parents). Building on the living-systems concept, proponents of this "learner-centered" perspective contend that education must concern itself with how to provide the most supportive learning context for diverse students—a context created primarily when teachers value and understand individual student needs (e.g., Marshall, 1998; Sarason, 1995). From this perspective, curriculum and content are the important but not deciding factors in achieving desired motivation, learning, and achievement. Attention to individual learner needs and assessment of how well these needs are being met are as important and fundamental to learning.

Those working within a living systems framework also contend that systems change is the result of personal change and of critical connections (Wheatley and Kellner-Rogers, 1998). That is, personal change in one's perceptions, values, attitudes, and beliefs results from transformations in thinking. These transformations in thinking most often result from critical connections made in one's own understanding,

knowledge, and ways of thinking, as well as from critical connections—personal relationships—with others of significance in the learning environment. For example, a teacher confronted with the awareness that prior instructional practices aren't working with a new group of students is most likely to change those practices to more learner-centered approaches if (a) he or she learns that this group of students has a higher level of prior knowledge about the topic being covered than prior groups of students (new information component) and (b) a valued colleague has worked with similar students successfully using new instructional practices that give the students more choice and control over the instructional process (personal relationship component).

As people in living systems such as education are given more opportunities to be creatively involved in how their work gets done, Wheatley and Kellner-Rogers (1998) contend that not only will they create conditions that facilitate rapid change (new relationships, new insights, greater levels of commitment), but they will also increase their capacity for learning and growth. When individuals are engaged in designing change, they create more and better connections and relationships that can help the system change from within. Although the availability of new and richer information helps people change personal constructions of meaning and understanding, increasing the number, variety, and strengths of interpersonal connections and relationships is what moves the system toward better functioning and health. Standards of functioning and plans for change should not be imposed or mandated from outside, but need to come from within—through ongoing dialogue and conversations in which people share perceptions, seek out a diversity of interpretations, and agree on what needs to be done. In this process of learning and change, research-validated principles can be guides to what will work well in the current situation or context, helping to create a system designed to take care of self, others, and the place (Wheatley and Kellner-Rogers, 1998).

In most educational institutions and progressively within the K–12 system, teachers and disciplines are isolated from one another. It is difficult to find examples of cross-department collaborations in course design, multi-disciplinary learning opportunities, or organizational structures and physical facilities that allow interactions and dialogue among teachers or instructors. Content and people are isolated and fragmented. Change is often mandated from above or outside the system. Since critical connections are not being made, it is not surprising that change often meets resistance. The fears and insecurities that create resistance disappear when people participate in creating the system through which their work gets done.

In conclusion, by using research that integrates what we know about learners and learning as a framework and foundation for transformed practice at K–20 levels of our educational system, we can achieve a needed balance between meeting personal needs of learners and technical demands for high standards and accountability. Our research shows that learner- or person-centered systems can improve learning and motivation by meeting students' needs for belonging, control, and competence. Transforming our K–20 educational system with a consideration of the needs and perspectives of the people in the system is one of the most powerful ways to enhance learning, motivation, and achievement. Continuing to mandate and coerce higher achievement can at best produce only compliance among those too fearful, disheartened, or tired to contest these practices. We can do better than that, and we have research evidence and research-validated principles to point the way.

References

Alexander, P. A., and Murphy, P. K. (1998). The research base for APA's Learner-Centered Psychological Principles. In N. Lambert and B. L. McCombs (eds.), *How students learn: Reforming schools through learner-centered education.* Washington, D.C.: American Psychological Association.

APA Task Force on Psychology in Education (1993, January). *Learner-centered psychological principles: Guidelines for school redesign and reform.* Washington, D.C.: American Psychological Association and Mid-Continent Regional Educational Laboratory.

APA Work Group of the Board of Educational Affairs (1997, November). *Learner-centered psychological principles: A framework for school reform and redesign.* (Rev. Ed.) Washington, D.C.: American Psychological Association.

Bartolome, L. I. (1994). Beyond the methods fetish: Toward a humanizing pedagogy. *Harvard Educational Review, 64(2),* 173–194.

Brendtro, L. K. (1999, June). *Tools for reclaiming at-risk youth.* Keynote presentation at the 8th Annual Rocky Mountain Regional Conference in Violence Prevention in Schools and Communities, Denver, Colo.

Carroll, T. (2000, July). *New models for education: Using technology to transform learning.* Keynote presentation at the U.S. Department of Education's Regional Conferences on "Evaluating Technology," Atlanta, Ga.

Chase, B. (1999, February). *Education's brave new world: Keeping our schools public by holding them accountable to higher standards.* Washington, D.C.: National Education Association.

Darling-Hammond, L. (1996). The quiet revolution: Rethinking teacher development. *Educational Leadership, 53(6),* 4–10.

Feistritzer, C. E. (1999, November). The making of a teacher: A report on teacher preparation in the U.S.

Finn, C. E., Kanstoroom, M., and Petrilli, M. J. (1999, November). *The quest for better teachers: Grading the states.* Washington, D.C.: Thomas B. Fordham Foundation.

Griffin, G. A. (1999). Changes in teacher education: Looking to the future. In G. A. Griffin (ed.), *The education of teachers.* Chicago, Ill.: University of Chicago Press.

Kanstoroom, M., and Finn, C. F. (1999, July). *Better teachers, better schools.* Washington, D.C.: Thomas B. Fordham Foundation.

Lambert, N., and McCombs, B. L. (Eds.) (1998). *How students learn: Reforming schools through learner-centered education.* Washington, D.C.: APA Books.

Marshall, H. H. (1998). Teaching educational psychology: Learner-centered and constructivist perspectives. In N. Lambert and B. L. McCombs (eds.), *How students learn: Reforming schools through learner-centered education.* Washington, D.C.: APA Books.

McCombs, B. L. (1997). Self-assessment and reflection: Tools for promoting teacher changes toward learner-centered practices. *NASSP Bulletin, 81(587),* 1–14.

McCombs, B. L. (1998). Integrating metacognition, affect, and motivation in improving teacher education. In N. Lambert and B. L. McCombs (eds.), *How students learn: Reforming schools through learner-centered education.* Washington, D.C.: APA Books.

McCombs, B. L. (1999). *The Assessment of Learner-Centered Practices (ALCP): Tools for teacher reflection, learning, and change.* Denver, Colo.: University of Denver Research Institute.

McCombs, B. L. (2000, August). *Addressing the personal domain: The need for a learner-centered framework.* Paper presented in the symposium, "Learner-Centered Principles in Practice: Addressing the Personal Domain," at the annual meeting of the American Psychological Association, Washington, D.C.

McCombs, B. L., and Lauer, P. A. (1997). Development and validation of the learner-centered battery: Self-assessment tools for teacher reflection and professional development. *The Professional Educator, 20(1),* 1–21.

McCombs, B. L., Lauer, P. A., and Pierce. J. (1998, July). *The learner-centered model of seamless professional development: Implications for practice and policy changes in higher education.* Paper presented at the 23rd International Conference on Improving University Teaching, Dublin, Ireland.

McCombs, B. L., and Pierce, J. (1999). *Development and validation of the college level Assessment of Learner-Centered Practices (ALCP) surveys.* Denver, Colo.: University of Denver. Unpublished manuscript.

McCombs, B. L., and Quiat, M. A. (1999) *Development and validation of norms and rubrics for the grades K–5*

Assessment of Learner-Centered Practices (ALCP) surveys. University of Denver Research Institute. Manuscript in preparation.

McCombs, B. L., and Whisler, J. S. (1997). *The learner centered classroom and school: Strategies for increasing student motivation and achievement.* San Francisco: Jossey-Bass.

McWhorter, P., Jarrard, B., Rhoades, B., and Wiltcher, B. (1996, Summer). *Student-generated curriculum: Lessons from our students.* (Instructional Resource No. 30.) University of Georgia and University of Maryland: National Reading Research Center.

Noddings, N. (1995). Teaching themes of care. *Phi Delta Kappan,* 76(9), 675–679.

Perry, K. E., and Weinstein, R. S. (1998). The social context of early schooling and children's school adjustment. *Educational Psychologist,* 33(4), 177–194.

Rogers, C., and Freiberg, H. J. (1994). *Freedom to learn.* (3rd Ed.) New York: Merrill.

Rudduck, J., Day, J., and Wallace, C. (1997). Student perspectives on school improvement (pp. 73–91). In A. Hargreaves (Ed.), *Rethinking educational change with heart and mind: 1997 ASCD yearbook.* Alexandria, Va.: Association for Supervision and Curriculum Development.

Ryan, R. M., and Deci, E. L. (2000). Self-determination theory and the facilitation of intrinsic motivation, social development, and well-being. *American Psychologist,* 55(1), 68–78.

Sarason, S. B. (1995). Some reactions to what we have learned. *Phi Delta Kappan,* 77(1), 84–85.

Schaps. E., and Lewis, C. (1999). Perils on an essential journey: Building school community. *Phi Delta Kappan,* 81(3), 215–218.

Scherer, M. (1998). A conversation with Herb Kohl. *Educational Leadership,* 56(1), 8–13.

Sparks, D., and Hirsh, S. (1997). *A new vision for staff development.* Alexandria, Va.: Association for Supervision and Curriculum Development.

Sylwester, R. (1995). *A celebration of neurons: An educator's guide to the brain.* Alexandria, Va.: Association for Supervision and Curriculum Development.

U. S. Department of Education (1997, August). *Excellence and accountability in teaching: A guide to U.S. Department of Education programs and resources.* Washington, D.C.: Author.

Wheatley, M. J. (1999). *Leadership and the new science: Discovering order in a chaotic world.* (2nd ed.) San Francisco: Berrett-Koehler Publishers.

Wheatley, M. J., and Kellner-Rogers, M. (1998). Bringing life to organizational change. *Journal of Strategic Performance Measurement.* April–May, 5–13.

WHAT ENGAGES UNDERACHIEVING MIDDLE SCHOOL STUDENTS IN LEARNING?

Mike Muir

Student motivation is a concern for teachers at all levels. In this article Mike Muir interviewed six underachieving middle school students about how they thought they learned and how teachers could help in the process. From their responses Muir found that personal relationships with teachers were important. Students also preferred instructional activities that were experiential and involved student autonomy and choice. Content that connected to their own personal lives and experiences were important motivational factors as well. As you read this article ask yourself, "How similar are these students to students in general? Will the students I teach be motivated by the same types of learning experiences?"

Think About This . . .

1. What types of relationships did these students want from their teachers? How would this relationship change for teachers at grade levels different from these students?

2. What kinds of learning activities did these students prefer? What kinds of learning activities did these students not want?

3. How do these students define meaningful learning? What common denominator exists across content areas?

4. How could you improve your instruction by implementing the findings in Muir's study? How would you have to adjust your ideas to meet the unique learning needs of the students you will teach?

Ben, Doris, Eric, Cathy, Mike, and Andy are probably just like some of the students you have. Ben does well when he turns in his work, but often misplaces, loses, and forgets papers and books. Doris' teachers feel that they do not know her well, because she is frequently absent and very quiet when in school. Eric does not do much of his work despite the fact that he is bright, garrulous, and personable. Cathy is the kind of friendly student you would like to have in class, but her mom often keeps her home to care for her six younger siblings. Mike wants to be a pilot or work with computers but does not see how school is preparing him for his future. Andy is an extraordinary artist whose learning style does not seem to match his schoolwork.

These six students are all underachievers. Their teachers identified each of them as such and they readily recognize themselves as being bright but not doing well in school or not liking school much. They happily identify with this characterization, rather than being offended by it. They also each agreed to be interviewed, so that I might gain some insight into what they believe motivates them to learn.

The Challenge

Public education faces a difficult challenge: educating every youth in the country. In the face of this challenge is the fact that there are many children who are undermotivated, disengaged, and underachieving. Even early in the 20th century, there was concern that many students had dropped out physically or mentally (Kaminsky, 1992). In the 1915 book, *All The Children of All The People,* Smith's exploration into the challenge of educating all students, begins:

> However reluctant one may be to acknowledge the fact, it is nonetheless certain that the task of trying to educate everybody, which our public schools are engaged in, has proved to be far more difficult than the originators of the idea of such a possibility thought it would be when they set out upon the undertaking. (Smith, 1915, p. v)

Teachers are challenged daily by students who do not seem interested in learning. Teachers struggle with discipline issues and with meeting the needs of students at widely differing ability and achievement levels. One of the most persistent questions facing individual teachers is, "How do I motivate *all* children to learn?" The real problem facing educators is helping all students achieve optimal learning (conceptual understanding and the ability to apply knowledge to new problems, learning, and creations) with high quality content (from the students' own interests, from state and local curricula, and national standards). If we are serious about educating every child, we must include every child in meaningful, engaged learning. That means using teaching techniques that match what we know about how kids learn.

I decided to ask underachieving students what they thought about how they learn well. There is a lot written about how experts think students learn well. Although these studies and theories can be very helpful to teachers, there is much less written about how *students* think they learn well, especially from the point of view of underachieving students. I asked my underachieving students a series of questions. The first set included open ended questions such as the following:

- Think of a good learning experience. What made that a good learning experience?
- Describe a good class or teacher that you have now or have had in the past. What made them good?
- Imagine that the State Department of Education came to you and asked you how to design courses and units so that you could really learn well. What would you tell them?
- What is the one thing you would change about how your classes are taught or how your teachers teach that would help you to learn better?

From Muir, M. (2001). What engages underachieving middle school students in learning? Middle School Journal, 33(2), 37–43. Reprinted with permission of the National Middle School Association.

These questions did not suggest any factors which might help them learn better, but solicited the students' own ideas. The second set of questions was based on what research advises might help students learn. This set of questions included:

- How do your teachers try to make school interesting to you?
- How do your teachers give you choices and let you help in class decision-making?
- How do your teachers try to help you see how course content is useful or important?
- How is school preparing you for your future?

There are two things that you, the reader, should keep in mind as you read this study. The first is that the sample is small and narrow: There are only six students in the study. This sample includes only middle school students not those in elementary or high school, and it includes students from rural, central New England, rather from other possible demographic regions.

The second is that this is a "theory building" study designed to explore what students think. Because it is a theory building study, and not a theory testing study, I do not have achievement data on these students. While the stories and conclusions are presented to help you build your own theories about what motivates underachieving students to learn, it will not "prove" that any particular motivator will help students. What I have done below, however, is point out where the students' ideas connect with the professional literature on learning.

Keep in mind that with this kind of study, it is up to you to decide if these students' opinions and my conclusions match your own experience base, theories, and beliefs about motivating underachievers.

You do not have to accept my results. This study can be a model for your own action research, and I enthusiastically invite readers to ask your underachieving students questions about how they think they learn well. All six students had clear ideas of how they learn well, what they liked and disliked about how their teachers teach, and what recommendations they would make about changing schools in ways that would help them learn better. This leads me to think that you will find the same when you ask your students.

The six students were seventh graders attending one of two middle schools in rural, western Maine. Both schools are approximately the same size, serving about 500 students in grades seven and eight. Both schools divide students into five academic teams of four teachers (math, science, social studies, and language

Figure 1

Components of Meaningful Engaged Learning

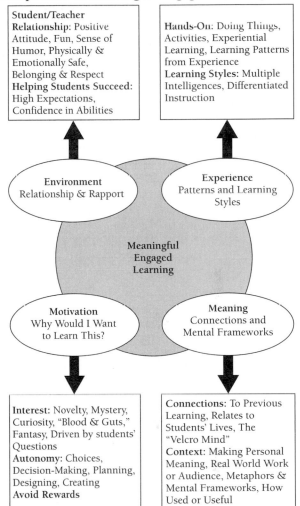

arts) and about 100 students each. Both are consolidated schools located in their respective county seats. They bring in students from a wide surrounding area, creating a diverse student demographic. For example, there are students who live in town and students who live in the woods; there are students of lawyers and doctors and students of farmers, woodsmen, and factory workers.

To add more credibility to the findings from the student interviews, I also interviewed four of their teachers, and conducted classroom observations. Synthesizing these findings with the literature on learning and motivation, a theory for meaningful, engaged learning begins to emerge. There are four key components: the learning environment, experience, motivation, and meaning making.

Environment

I had expected students to focus on intrinsic motivators closely related to content, including hands-on activities, choice, curiosity, pace, and alignment with personal goals. Those were validated by the students, but not as strongly as the importance of relationship, trust, and respect in the classroom. Andy talked about how teachers who nag turn him off to learning and Mike said that he would not learn from a teacher who did not like him. Eric and Ben both feel they learn better from teachers who joke around and create an environment where it is safe to ask questions and make mistakes. Eric says he does not learn well from teachers who are grumpy and Ben equates boring classes with teachers who are too serious and not having much fun. Ben said he would tell the Department of Education that students are not having enough fun in school and that they should have more. Cathy likes caring teachers who give her one-on-one assistance and attention. Doris likes teachers who know her capabilities and push and challenge her, but are not authoritarian. Dowty (1997) and Emerick (1992) also report that the student/teacher relationship is key to improving achievement.

A teacher having clear expectations was especially important to Doris. She wanted teachers to use a lot of repetition so that she would be sure to know what they wanted from her. Interviews and observations revealed numerous strategies that teachers used to help students succeed: giving students personal attention, using a variety of teaching strategies, making sure students start with success before moving on to more challenging work, working from student strengths rather than focusing on their weaknesses, having peers explain a difficult concept, giving students a second chance, creating an environment where mistakes are viewed as a learning opportunity, and using questions to guide students.

Teachers should create a respectful environment within their classrooms. They should get to know their students well, including their interests and aspirations, and personal histories and contexts. This might be facilitated by long term relationships with students, achieved through looping, multiage classrooms, or multiyear classrooms. Teachers should treat students as if they genuinely like and respect them, even when disciplining them.

Experience

Educators should remember that most learning is finding patterns in experiences (Schank & Cleary, 1995). These patterns become schema and help define how a person perceives and understands her world. Experience provides students with rich sensory data, furnishing multiple cues for memory and recall (Rumelhart, 1980; Bruning, Schraw, & Ronning, 1995). It is not surprising, then, that all six students thought they learned best from experiential work such as projects and hands-on activities, especially when they had input into project design or in selecting a topic.

Doris thought that hands-on activities were the best part of school. Eric's favorite classes were the ones that were taught in an active way. Cathy equated "fun" with doing group projects that allowed for individual student input. Ben sees hands-on activities and projects as a way to make school interesting and fun for all students. Eric recommends that more teachers be active and fun, and Cathy recommends less book work in exchange for more activities. Andy talked about how math class was one of his favorites because they did hands-on work. Doris says that fun schoolwork is "doing something," not just reading or studying, and Cathy does not mind reading and writing assignments, as long as the teacher combines it with hands-on activities.

Andy and Doris say that part of what they liked about hands-on activities was that there was often more than one solution, and not everyone had to do the work the same way or at the same pace. They disliked lockstep teaching. Many of the students went on to complain that they did not learn well from too much bookwork. Eric and Cathy said it was because there was too much sitting and they wanted to be more active. The recommendations that several of the students would make to the Department of Education focused on reducing the amount of bookwork and increasing the amount of hands-on work. Nearly all the students liked project-based teaching and thought they learned well from it.

Despite their interest in doing things and hands-on work, none of the students wanted to forego all bookwork. Their descriptions of hands-on activities and project work were full of references to researching, reading, and writing. Cathy was specific about not minding bookwork as long as there were some more active components to the work, as well.

Much of the talk about active hands-on learning revolved around discussions of respecting and providing for students' diverse learning styles. Both Doris and Ben commented on how different students learn differently and that students sometimes might be placed into groups according to how they learn best. Doris saw differentiated assignments as a form of fairness. Ben recommended that teachers help students discover how they best learn. Only Eric thought he learned well with traditional schoolwork, although his math teacher reports that he is doing best in math with the nontraditional activities. Educators should keep in mind that people perceive and process experiences differently (Sternberg, 1997; Gardner, 1983, 1998, 1999; Fairhurst & Fairhurst, 1995; Papert, 1996). Teachers can meet students' diverse needs by using a variety of teaching strategies from learning style or Multiple Intelligence theories. Teachers can also provide assignments, such as projects, that are flexible enough that different students can complete the task in different ways.

Teachers' responsiveness to students' individual learning differences was very important to the six participants. All the students and all the teachers interviewed agreed with Papert (1996) that most failure to learn is a result of instruction not matching the individual's learning style. Further, despite the common motivators (teacher relationship, hands-on work, and choices), there were individual differences between how the students felt they learned well.

Motivation

Motivation is the next key factor. This does not refer to why teachers might want students to learn material, but why students themselves might want to learn it. Subconsciously, students decide every day what they will learn and what they will not. Teachers can increase the likelihood that students will learn when they try to motivate the students intrinsically or extrinsically. Intrinsic motivation is very powerful. Teachers can invoke it by relating learning to student interests and goals, or finding ways to make learning interesting, perhaps by using novelty, mystery, curiosity, "blood and guts," or fantasy.

Each student had typical adolescent interests: playing sports, socializing with friends, toying with computers and video games, and listening to music. So, it may not be surprising that teachers struggle to tie their academics into these fairly non-academic interests and hobbies. Even though much of the work did not tie in with these interests, the students did find some of the work interesting. Much of it was dependent on the individual. Doris liked teachers sharing stories from their past. Cathy liked lessons related to government and books such as *The Outsiders* and *Huck Finn* that related to the South, where she used to live. Ben thought his fourth grade teacher, who dressed up as story characters, was interesting. One of his teachers reports that Ben likes blood and guts and anything that's gory, "books that have gory stuff things in them. He loved Edgar Allan Poe." Of the work that students agreed is interesting, projects and hands-on work giving students choices and limited autonomy headed the list.

Extrinsic motivation can either improve learning or shut it down. A focus on punishments and rewards can be counterproductive to learning (Kohn, 1993, 1994). Autonomous supportive strategies (such as providing students choices and giving them opportunities for decision making, planning, designing, and creating), on the other hand, can make extrinsically required learning as powerful as intrinsically motivated learning (Deci & Ryan, 1985; Deci, Spiegel, Ryan, Koestner, & Kauffman, 1982; Deci, Valler, Pelletier, & Ryan, 1991).

The student participants liked having choices and input into their learning. Choice was one of the key attractions of hands-on and project work. Students also described being given choices among class assignments and required readings, setting schedules, and being flexible in how they meet content requirements. Choice was also one of the teachers' key strategies for meeting students' different learning styles, and several teachers believed that choice is a way to spark student interest or to engage students.

Choices and input were important components of project work for Ben, Doris, and Cathy. Doris said she wanted to do class projects and assignments her own way. Cathy wanted input into the kinds of work she does; she does not mind parameters, but does not want to be told exactly what to do. Ben thinks he learns best when he is doing hands-on activities that students have more control over. Design projects, by definition, involve students in deciding how to solve a problem. In other projects, students were given choices about how to represent their work, and project topics were often student selected.

Meaning

Meaning is the fourth component. People do not compile knowledge in some objective data retrieval system. Memory works primarily to make meaning of experience and functions as a connection machine, making associations between different memories, facts, skills, and attitudes (Anderson, Reynolds, Schallert, & Goetz, 1977; Anderson, Spiro, & Anderson, 1978; Schank & Cleary, 1995; Rumelhart, 1980; Bruning et al., 1995). By providing contexts for learning and mental frameworks for new knowledge, teachers can help students learn material better by helping them develop associations, connections, and contexts for understanding and meaning making.

Seeing connections and believing that content is useful is important to these students. Both Eric's and

Ben's good learning experiences involved learning something they perceived as being useful to them. Eric says he sees how language arts might be useful to him as a businessman and that he can see how math would be useful in everyday life. Cathy says she likes social studies, mostly because of the connections the teacher makes between ancient societies and today's. Ben says his math teacher shows how content and skills are useful through application projects, like building bridges and boats. Eric says that some of his teachers explain how course content might be useful to careers he is interested in.

Teachers say they use a variety of strategies to help students connect to content and understand its usefulness. Eric's and Cathy's math teacher uses problems and projects related to real world problems, and their language arts teacher says she tries to connect her teaching to the student's lives and tries to teach writing skills as the need arises from the students' own writing. Ben's and Doris' science teacher mostly tries to make interdisciplinary connections or connections to lessons the students have had previously. Their social studies teacher shared a variety of ways she tries to connect her teaching to students' lives:

> I guess it's really easy with the geography to connect in their own lives, because you can always compare people and customs. As far as U.S. History connecting to their lives, I guess I would do that more with what is going on now in the world, using topics like gun control, the death penalty, as well as laws and amendments. You can bring it right to their personal life.

Teachers need to find ways to relate learning to student's lives, whether that is showing how new knowledge and skills are useful to them or by connecting it to their own lives. Involving students in work for an audience beyond the teacher and other students, giving them real world work to complete, or using metaphors while presenting new information are strategies that help students make meaning of what they are learning.

Conclusion

It is not surprising that improved instruction, which involves students in meaningful, engaged learning, is viewed as a remedy to the growing concern over the high social and economic cost of large numbers of disengaged and at-risk youth (North Central Regional Educational Laboratory, 1997; Williams, 1996). Identifying practices which help these diverse populations learn well is a step toward creating an educational system serving all students.

Mike, Andy, Ben, Doris, Eric, and Cathy allowed me insights into how they think they learn well, in a hope that I can select teaching strategies that more closely match how students learn. You may wish to follow up with your own action research into how your underachieving students learn well. Finding out what motivates our underachieving students will help inform and equip teachers in the struggle to lead all students to academic achievement.

References

Anderson, R., Reynolds, R., Schallert, D., & Goetz, E. (1977). Frameworks for comprehending discourse. *American Education Research Journal, 14,* 367–381.

Anderson, R., Spiro, R., & Anderson, M. (1978). Schemata as scaffolding for the representation of information in connected discourse. *American Education Research Journal, 15,* 433–440.

Bruning, R. H., Schraw, G. J., & Ronning, R. R. (1995). *Cognitive psychology and instruction.* Upper Saddle River, NJ: Merrill/Prentice Hall.

Deci, E. L., & Ryan, R. M. (1985). *Intrinsic motivation and self-determination in human behavior.* New York: Plenum.

Deci, E. L., Spiegel, N. H., Ryan, R. M., Koestner, R., & Kauffman, M. (1982). The effects of performance standards on teaching styles: The behavior of controlling teachers. *Journal of Educational Psychology, 74,* 852–859.

Deci, E., Valler, R., Pelletier, L., & Ryan, R. (1991). Motivation and education: The self-determination perspective. *Educational Psychologist, 26*(3 & 4), 325–346.

Dowty, G. (1997). *The development of at-risk children's self-efficacy for social functioning and interpersonal relationships: A review of the literature and implications for residential interventions.* Unpublished paper. University of Maine, Orono, Maine.

Emerick, L. J. (1992). Academic underachievement among the gifted: Students' perceptions of factors that reverse the pattern. *Gifted Child Quarterly, 36*(3), 140–146.

Fairhurst, A., & Fairhurst, L. (1995). *Effective teaching effective learning: Making the personality connection in your classroom.* Palo Alto, CA: Davies-Black Publishing.

Gardner, H. (1983). *Frames of mind.* New York: Basic Books.

Gardner, H. (1998). A multiplicity of intelligences. *Scientific American Presents: Exploring Intelligence, 9*(4), 18–23.

Gardner, H. (1999). *The disciplined mind.* New York: Simon & Schuster.

Kaminsky, J. (1992). A pre-history of educational philosophy in the United States. *Harvard Educational Review, 62*(2), 179–198.

Kohn, A. (1993). *Punished by rewards: The trouble with gold stars, incentive plans, A's, praise, and other bribes.* Boston: Houghton Mifflin.

Kohn, A. (1994). *The risks of rewards.* ERIC digest (EDO-PS-94-14). Urbana, IL: ERIC Clearinghouse on Elementary and Early Childhood Education.

North Central Regional Educational Laboratory. (1997). *At risk children and youth.* Retrieved December 11, 1997, from http://www.ncrel.org/sdrs/areas/at0cont.htm

Papert, S. (1996). *The connected family: Bridging the digital generation gap.* Marietta, GA: Longstreet Press.

Rumelhart, D. (1980). Schemata: The building blocks of cognition. In R. Spiro, B. Bruce, & W. Brewer (Eds.), *Theoretical issues in reading comprehension* (pp. 33–58). Hillsdale, NJ: Erlbaum.

Schank, R., & Cleary, C. (1995). *Engines for education.* Hillsdale, NJ: Lawrence Erlbaum.

Smith, W. H. (1915). *All the children of all the people: A study of the attempt to educate everybody.* New York: Macmillan.

Sternberg, R. (1997). What does it mean to be smart? *Educational Leadership, 54*(6), 20–24.

Williams, B. (Ed.). (1996). *Closing the achievement gap: A vision for changing beliefs and practices.* Alexandria, VA: Association for Supervision and Curriculum Development.

USING CLASSROOM RULES TO CONSTRUCT BEHAVIOR
David Bicard

Classroom management concerns teachers at all levels and at every stage of their professional development. Effective teaching cannot occur in the absence of an effective management system. In most schools, David Bicard suggests, teachers attempt to influence students' behaviors by establishing and implementing a series of rules. He further suggests that, in terms of time and effort, establishing and maintaining rules is one of the most "cost-effective" means available to teachers for developing orderly classrooms.

Bicard believes that a number of misconceptions about rules exist, however, and describes differences between positive, negative, and vague rules. As you read this article ask yourself, "What role should rules play in an effective classroom management system?"

Think About This . . .

1. According to Bicard, how much effect do rules alone have on student behavior? Why do you think this is the case?

2. What are the characteristics of positive rules? Which of these characteristics is most important? Why?

3. What are four ways to use rules effectively? What are other ways in which rules can be effectively used?

4. How will you teach and monitor rules in your classroom to incorporate the values described by Muir, in the preceding article? Provide an example to illustrate your description.

I've come to a frightening conclusion that I am the decisive element in the classroom. It's my approach that creates the climate. It's my daily mood that makes the weather. As a teacher, I possess a tremendous power to make a child's life miserable or joyous. I can be a tool of torture or an instrument of inspiration. I can humiliate or humor, hurt or heal. In all situations, it is my response that decides whether a crisis will be escalated or de-escalated and a child humanized or dehumanized.

—Haim Ginott,
The Teacher, January 2000

From Bicard, D. (2000). Using classroom rules to construct behavior. Middle School Journal, 31, 37–45. Reprinted with permission of the National Middle School Association.

In many middle school classrooms, teachers attempt to influence the behavior of students through the use of rules. However, rules alone exert little effect on student behavior. Teachers may sometimes be unaware of the effects their actions have on the behavior of their students. Two classic studies may help to illustrate the effects of teacher-made rules and teacher behavior on the activity of their students. Madsen, Becker, and Thomas (1968) found that when a teacher provided rules alone to her students, the students' appropriate and inappropriate behavior remained at relatively the same level as when she provided no rules. Major decreases in inappropriate conduct and increases in appropriate conduct occurred when the teacher showed approval for appropriate behavior in combination with ignoring some inappropriate behavior. Similarly, Thomas, Becker, and Armstrong (1968) found that teachers could produce or eliminate appropriate and inappropriate behavior by varying approval and disapproval statements. When the teachers delivered positive statements to their students regarding their classroom behavior, the students maintained appropriate conduct; and when the teachers withdrew positive statements and delivered frequent disapproval statements, inappropriate behavior increased.

While rules by themselves may not be effective, they do provide structure, communicate teacher expectations, provide a foundation for learning, and help maintain a well-run and organized classroom. Positive rules, along with consistent action by the teacher, set the stage for praising student achievement that benefits the teacher as much as the students. Good classrooms where students are highly involved do not just happen. They exist because effective teachers have constructed the types of classroom conditions and student interactions necessary for a positive learning environment (Emmer, Evertson, Clements, & Worsham, 1994). In *Middle School Journal,* Mills (1997) described how one effective teacher named Suzan constructed her classroom to ensure successful learning. Suzan "modeled a way of teaching, learning, and behaving that she shared, both explicitly and implicitly, with her students. . . . [Her approach] held expectations for student responsibility, for a caring atmosphere, and for student success" (p. 32). Throughout this article we will return to Suzan's classroom to demonstrate how effective teachers can use words and actions to construct positive rules for their students.

Rules are one of the most cost effective forms of classroom management available to teachers (Catania, 1998). However, not all teachers recognize the benefits of teaching rules. In *Setting Limits in the Classroom,*

Mackenzie (1996) noted 10 common misconceptions held by teachers about the use of rules, among them, "teaching rules is the parents' job," "students should know what I expect," "I can't afford to take precious time away from instruction," and "explaining my rules to students should be enough." The reality is that in the classroom, teaching rules is one of the teacher's jobs, with parents' help. In addition, students need time to learn the rules and expectations of their teachers. Rules need to be taught with words as well as actions; the time invested up front will pay huge dividends in the end.

Ginott (2000) suggested that teachers are the decisive element in the classroom. In that role, they should take the responsibility for constructing and implementing positive rules as a management system to build academic success. This article describes the characteristics of positive rules, offers suggestions for developing and implementing the rules, and provides guidelines for what to do when students break the rules.

Characteristics of Positive Rules

The first part of this section will describe the differences between some common rules that exist in many middle school classrooms. The second part discusses an often overlooked, yet extremely important, component of effective rules. These small differences in the way teachers construct rules may have a big influence on the way students behave in the classroom.

Positive Rules Specify Appropriate Student Behavior in Observable Terms

Rules come in three basic varieties: positive rules that communicate how to behave, negative rules that communicate how not to behave, and vague rules that communicate neither how nor how not to behave (Table 1). A common rule about completing assigned work can be worded positively ("Answer each problem until you are done"), negatively ("Don't stop unless you are done"), or vaguely ("Stay on task"). Small differences in wording make a substantial difference in the way students will respond and how teachers will focus their attention. The positive version of the rule lets the student know how to behave so that teachers can provide approval when students follow the rule. Conversely, in the negative and vague examples, nothing has been said on how to respond; the student is left with only how not to respond. More important, in the negative and vague examples, teachers are more likely to recognize students only when they do not follow the rule. When rules state what the student *can do* in specific

Table 1

Positive	Negative	Vague
Raise your hand when you want to talk.	Don't interrupt others.	Respect others.
Keep your eyes on the teacher.	Don't look around the room.	Listen to the teacher.
Bring a pencil to class every day.	Don't come to class without a pencil.	Come to class prepared.
Before you leave make sure your desk is clean.	You are not ready to leave until your desk is clean.	Keep the classroom neat.
Be in your seat when the bell rings.	Don't be out of your seat when the bell rings.	Be on time for class.

Examples of Positive, Negative, and Vague Rules

and observable terms, both teachers and students can easily recognize whether a rule is being followed. Teachers are more likely to notice appropriate behavior and celebrate student success. Positive rules tell students what to do instead of what not to do and are thus more instructive (Paine, Radicchi, Rosellini, Deutchman, & Darch, 1983).

When rules state only what the student *cannot do* or are *vague,* teacher attention will likely be on punishment for inappropriate behavior (Zirpoli & Melloy, 1993). When teacher attention is focused on punishment, the classroom becomes coercive, authoritarian, and punitive. It becomes a teacher's job to investigate violations, determine guilt, and mete out sentences. Less time is left for teaching. Frequent disapproval may also deter student learning in other ways. Greer (1981) found that the use of disapproval statements by teachers resulted in the students avoiding what was taught during free time. For example, if when teaching reading a teacher delivers frequent disapproval statements to his or her students, the students will be less likely to read books when they have leisure time. As Sulzer-Azaroff and Mayer (1986) noted, "One more critical disadvantage to resorting to punishment too frequently is that the practice inadvertently may teach others to use it as well" (p. 146).

A key component of effective rules is that the rules specify observable student behavior. In this respect *observable* means something a teacher can count, for example raising a hand. When a teacher can count behaviors, students become accountable for those behaviors. Vague rules such as "respect others" or "stay

on task" may be as difficult for students to follow as they are for teachers to enforce because behaviors are extremely difficult to count. A teacher who can observe specific instances of appropriate student conduct is prepared to celebrate students' successes.

When attention is focused on appropriate behavior through the use of positive rules, teachers promote a sense of personal efficacy in students that communicates the trust, competence, responsibility, affiliation, and awareness so important in middle level curriculum (Stevenson, 1998). In short, teachers should be in the business of constructing behaviors, not eliminating them (W. L. Heward, personal communication, February 12, 1998).

Suzan "told her students what she expected and wanted. . . . She reminded the students of proper lab behavior before each lab activity. . . . She gave examples of acceptable comments that focused on their learning and encouraged students" (Mills, 1997, pp. 33–34). Yet simply stating positive rules is only the first step of effective classroom management.

Positive Rules Specify Observable Consequences

Another important, though often overlooked, component of effective rules is a statement of consequences. Consequences are the *quid pro quo* of rules, letting students know what they get in return. Classroom studies conducted by Braam and Malott (1990) and Mistr and Glenn (1992) have shown that rules specifying only response requirements did not reliably guide student behavior; conversely, when rules specified observable behavior *and* consequences, they were effective in maintaining appropriate behavior. Consequences are important because they teach responsibility and accountability to the teacher as well as the student. Providing clear consequences will help to break the cycle of limit-testing so common with middle school students. In the example, "Raise your hand when you want to talk," the students are left to discover what will happen next; they may raise their hands and then begin to talk. If the teacher provides a consequence, for example, "and I will call on you when it's your turn," the students will not have to guess. This is especially significant when we look at negative rules, such as "Don't talk until called upon." When a consequence is provided, "or your name will be written on the board," the focus of attention will necessarily be on elimination of behavior. It is also important that students be aware of the consequences for not following the rules. For example, during science experiments Mills' (1997) expert

Table 2

Keys to Developing and Implementing Positive Rules in Classrooms
Characteristics of Positive Rules
• Positive rules specify appropriate student behavior in observable terms
• Positive rules specify observable consequences
Developing Positive Rules
• Develop a framework before the school year begins
• Include students in the decision-making process
• Get agreement by students, teachers, and parents
Using Positive Rules Effectively
• Teach the rules
• Catch students following the rules
• Monitor your behavior
• Include students as monitors
What to Do When Students Break the Rules
• Use the least intrusive procedures first
• Praise other students for following the rules
• Give verbal redirection
• Remain unemotional yet firm when intervening

teacher "reminded the students of the cost of activities and suggested the principal, 'won't give me money for labs if you're not mature enough to handle them well'" (p. 34).

Developing Positive Rules

Three strategies help develop effective rules. The first strategy helps teachers to conceptualize a basic framework for identifying situations in which rules should be specified. The next two strategies are specific processes teachers can use to develop successful classroom rules.

Develop a Framework Before the School Year

All rules must follow the policies and procedures of the school; however, these are typically general guidelines that can easily be incorporated into a set of classroom rules. Once teachers, or a team of teachers, have information about school policy and procedures, they can begin to plan rules for their classrooms and team areas. Paine and associates (1983) maintained that the best

time to develop rules is *before* the school year begins. Teachers should decide what kinds of situations to cover and what kinds of rules to write for those situations. For example, a science teacher may have one set of rules during experiments and another during whole-class time. This basic framework will help teachers to guide students toward a formalized version of the rules.

Include Students in the Decision-Making Process

Once the guidelines are in place, the next step is involving students in deciding the specific rules. Student participation in rule setting has been demonstrated to be effective for increased compliance (Dickerson & Creedon, 1981), lower numbers of violations (Felixbrod & O'Leary, 1974), and academic success (Lovitt & Curtis, 1969). Emmer, Evertson, Clements, and Worsham (1994) noted that involving students in rule setting helps to promote student ownership and responsibility. Incorporating students in the process communicates respect and concern, lets students know they are important elements in the classroom, and serves to promote student acceptance.

There are a number of techniques teachers can use. For example, the first day of class can begin with a discussion of the role of rules in society and their application to the classroom. A teacher could ask the students to describe model behavior, then use this as a basis for discussing what types of rules are appropriate in the classroom. Specifying student behaviors in observable terms provides the foundation for the rules, and identifying teacher behavior provides the foundation for the consequences. The teacher may need to guide the students in providing positive examples, as middle school students tend to focus on violations (Emmer et al., 1994). Suzan had students "brainstorm appropriate comments and role-play supportive situations" (Mills, 1997, p. 35). It is important to note that student-made rules are sometimes too stringent, so again, it is a good idea to have a basic framework in mind prior to discussing rules with the students.

Try to keep the rules to a minimum: It is recommended that teachers use no more than three or four rules for each situation. To help students remember the rules and help teachers make praise statements within the wording of the rules, keep the wording as simple as possible. When the rules are established consequences must also be established. A simple method for achieving positive rules and consequences is to ask students to list possible consequences for following classroom rules.

These can be favorite classroom activities, free time, or a note to parents. Students should also list consequences for not following the rules—for example, a "three strikes policy," then loss of free time, then a note to parents. An example of a positive rule might be when a student completes assigned work before the end of class, the teacher will give him or her five minutes of free time. Teachers can decide on whole class and individual contingencies based on the list each student completes. This process will allow flexibility in classroom management.

Create a Contract for the Students, Teachers, and Parents

Once the rules are in place have each student write the rules on a piece of paper, sign it, take it home for the parents or guardians to sign, and bring it back to school the next day. Jones and Jones (1990) recommended including a statement about classroom philosophy regarding management and instruction: "This lets you present the issues of rules in a positive manner that indicates their relationship to effective instruction and student learning" (p. 285). The contingency contract provides a number of useful advantages: students cannot say they were unaware of the rules; parents know the expectations of the teachers and have agreed, fostering a home-school partnership; and there is a record on file for future reference. (For more information regarding contingency contracts see Cooper, Heron, & Heward, 1987, pp. 466–485.)

Using Rules Effectively

Now that the rules have been specified and the consequences set forth, teachers are ready to begin using the rules to guide student learning. It is worth mentioning again that, without reliable enforcement by teachers, rules have very little effect on student conduct.

Teach the Rules

A crucial component of positive classroom management is how teachers implement the rules. The first step in teaching the rules is to post them prominently in the classroom. Suzan, "at the beginning of the year displayed a life-size female adolescent labeled 'scientist,' a smaller poster of rules near a frog saying 'hop to it'" (Mills, 1997, p. 33). An effective strategy is to designate a student from each class to make a poster listing the rules and consequences, or, if teachers decide on one set of rules for all their classes, a competition can be held and prizes awarded for the three best posters. For the first two or three days after the rules are in place, devote five minutes of class time to teaching the rules through examples. Doing this at the beginning of each class is an excellent way to keep the students engaged while taking attendance or gathering materials. Teachers can guide this discussion or designate a student to lead the class. It is important to have all the students state the rules, then have students role-play acceptable and unacceptable behavior. This is a perfect time to begin to catch students following the rules and praise them. Teachers can continue teaching the rules in this fashion each Monday for the first month of the school year and again the first Monday after long breaks. Whenever students need a "booster shot" during the school year, teachers can go back to this activity. Although this procedure may seem somewhat elementary, it is useful to teach rule following just as one would teach any other subject.

Catch Students Following the Rules

Teaching positive rules does not end in the first five minutes of class or in the first week of school; it continues throughout the school year. Suzan "provided numerous opportunities for students to experience success. Her students experienced frequent success and received teacher praise for their efforts" (Mills, 1997, p. 35). Praise should be immediate, consistent, and contingent upon "catching the students being good." Consistent means a teacher reliably recognizes student behavior as it occurs. Contingent specifies a relationship between praise and the student's behavior. When students are behaving appropriately, follow the "if, then rule"—*if* students have done something appropriate, *then* praise them (Paine et al., 1983). An example from Mills (1997) illustrates this point. "Suzan once shared the compliments that a substitute teacher had made about the students and thanked them for their good behavior. . . . When I saw the work you had done in groups [while I was gone] I knew you had been wonderful'" (p. 35).

When praising always identify the rule, the behavior, and the student or students by name, "I like the way Jennifer put things away when the bell rang because that shows she is ready to learn. Nice job Jennifer." Public praise can occur in several situations: while teaching, when near a student, or in the presence of other teachers. This may be especially helpful for some students who are having difficulty in other classrooms. Sometimes public praise might be a problem with middle school students, so teachers may want to praise some students only when nearby or in private. Teachers can write a note on a student's paper or praise the student during individual seat work. Sometimes a call home to parents or even to a student is a good technique. For Suzan, "quiet, supportive exchanges with individual students took place literally during every occasion" (Mills, 1997, p. 34).

Monitor Teacher Behavior

An effective way to achieve success using positive rules is for teachers to monitor their own behavior. Initially, teachers can count the number of approval and disapproval statements. It is not as difficult as one would think. Generally, middle level teachers are excellent time managers. Begin counting, and when five minutes have passed, note the number of approval and disapproval statements. This then becomes a measure per unit of time. Teachers may be surprised and somewhat shocked at how little praise has been given. A good rule of thumb is to have a 3:1 ratio of approval to disapproval statements (Englemann & Carnine, 1991).

One technique for helping to pinpoint specific approval statements is a variation of "the timer game" (Lovitt, 1995, p. 322). Identify the behaviors to "catch," for example, students active at work stations making entries in their notebooks. Set a goal such as five praise statements in five minutes. The next and easiest step is for teachers to identify a reward for themselves, maybe a chocolate bar at lunch. Once these are in place, teachers can set a timer for five minutes and begin teaching. During teaching simply make a mark on a spare piece of paper for every praise statement. When the timer goes off, students will probably be very interested in what is going on. This is a good time to let them in on the secret. Take a few minutes to discuss this practice and why it is being used. The students may be willing to assist in counting. It also has the added benefit of notifying students of what behaviors are being monitored and may help to promote appropriate classroom conduct.

Another useful strategy is to place "reminders" in the classroom such as a sign in the back of the room to prompt the teacher. Mills (1997) reported that in Suzan's classroom, "virtually every week, new student work was displayed. . . . Before class started, Suzan would call my attention to the students' work, call students over to show me their efforts or explain the concept, and tell me loudly how proud she was of their efforts" (pp. 35–36). Monitoring teacher behavior helps to promote a positive classroom environment. In the classroom it is the teacher who sets the standards.

By modeling appropriate behavior teachers communicate with words and actions that they value a supportive, responsible, and respectful classroom.

Include Students as Monitors

Students play an active role in controlling peer behavior (Lovitt, 1995). Middle school teachers are well aware of the effects of peer attention on student behavior. Unfortunately, this has usually been correlated with inappropriate behavior. The results of a study by Garden-Smith and Fowler (1984) suggested that peers can serve to increase and maintain appropriate classroom behavior, provided they are given proper instruction and feedback from a teacher. Here is how Suzan involved students as monitors, "One particular day, the students had given oral reports and presented visuals on different animals; following each report the students asked for questions and comments. All students received praise from classmates about some aspect of their reports or drawings" (Mills, 1997, p. 35). Suzan "reminded her students during lab activities to 'check with your buddy' or 'help your partner'" (Mills, 1997, p. 34). Encouraging students to praise their peers has many benefits. In the above example, a mutually reinforcing relationship is established that will increase the probability of more praise statements to follow. Another example shows how involving students frees the teacher to take on other responsibilities:

> During the first observation, a group of students who finished their assignments early were designated by Suzan as "wizards." Suzan explained the next assignment to the wizards, and they were to provide and explain the worksheet to other students as they completed their work. All students were to seek help from the wizards before they asked questions of Suzan. (Mills, 1997, p. 35)

A useful and highly effective strategy for involving students as peer monitors is a variation of "the good behavior game" (Barrish, Saunders, & Wolf, 1969). This strategy is appropriate for whole groups or individual students. The technique requires teachers to model appropriate behaviors and then designate a student or group of students to identify instances of appropriate behavior by other students. In this game all students can win if they simply engage in appropriate behavior. Each team or individual can choose rewards the students and teacher have selected prior to the game. Successfully including peers as monitors may take some time and creativity on the part of a teacher, but the benefits of a cohesive, nurturing classroom are well worth the investment.

What to Do When Students Break the Rules

There will be times when students behave in unacceptable ways. This is as true for the best students as it is for the worst. The decisions teachers make during these times can escalate or de-escalate an already unfavorable situation. Heward has noted that teachers can maintain and increase deviant behavioral patterns even though they are trying to help their students. This process

> begins with a teacher request that the student ignores and follows a predictable and escalating sequence of teacher pleas and threats that the student counters with excuses, arguments, and eventually a full-blown tantrum. The aggression and tantrumming is so aversive to the teacher that she withdraws the request (thereby reinforcing and strengthening the student's disruptive behavior) so the student will stop the tormenting (thereby reinforcing the teacher for withdrawing the request). (Heward, 2000)

This increasing escalation of disruptive behavior is called *coercive pain control* (Rhode, Jensen, & Reavis, 1998) because the student learns to use painful behavior to escape or avoid the teacher's requests. It is best to try to anticipate these times by preparing a plan of action before the situation occurs. The following five proven strategies can be used separately or in combination to assist teachers when students behave unacceptably in the classroom.

Use the Least Intrusive Procedures First

The first technique to use is simply to arrange seating patterns so teachers can reach every part of their classrooms. Second, certain objects may be removed from the classroom if they prove to be distracting. However, keep in mind that having interesting objects in the classroom provides a great teaching opportunity since the student's attention is naturally directed toward the object. Another useful, unobtrusive technique is known as "planned ignoring" (Walker & Shea, 1995). Before attempting to use this technique, first try to determine why the student is engaging in unacceptable behavior. If it is determined he or she is doing this to get attention, then any response (positive or negative) will increase the probability of this behavior re-occurring in the future. With planned ignoring the teacher does not make any contact with the student. This technique works especially well in combination with praising other students. When a teacher uses this technique, at first unacceptable behavior may increase in intensity or

duration. This should not be cause for alarm because it is an indication that the technique is working. It is important to resist the temptation to react. Once the student stops the unacceptable behavior the teacher can catch some appropriate behavior and praise it. If the teacher determines the unacceptable behavior is maintained by other students or is dangerous, then planned ignoring will not work and should not be attempted. At this point a teacher may want to intervene directly.

Praise Other Students for Following the Rules

Praising other students for following the rules serves as a reminder to a student that he or she is not behaving appropriately. This reminder encourages the student to adjust his or her own behavior (Sulzer-Azaroff & Mayer, 1986). For example, if James is staring out the window when most of the other students are working diligently on math problems, the teacher may call a student by name and praise him—"I like the way DeMarco is working; one bonus point for DeMarco." More often than not, James will then begin to work on his math. After a few seconds, praise James to encourage him to keep working. This strategy is effective and has the benefit of notifying the student who is acting inappropriately without having to single him out. At the same time, it recognizes a student who is behaving appropriately.

Use Proximity Control and Signal Interference

Proximity control and signal interference are two less obtrusive techniques that are frequently used in conjunction with one another (Walker & Shea, 1995). When teachers move around the classroom their presence often serves as a cue to students, who stop behaving unacceptably. When a student is misbehaving, casually move in the direction of the student and attempt to make eye contact. Sometimes simply making eye contact is enough, other times nonverbal cues such as facial expressions, toe taps, or body language may be necessary. These nonverbal signals may alert a student that a behavior is disruptive. Walker and Shea noted, "In addition, proximity can have a positive effect on students experiencing anxiety and frustration. The physical presence of a teacher or parent available to assist has a calming effect on troubled children" (p. 228). Often nonverbal signals help the student to "save face" with his peers and promote a sense of respect on the part of the teacher. This technique is also appropriate for reinforcing acceptable behavior. After making eye contact, the teacher can simply smile or give a thumbs-up sign (Walker & Shea, 1995).

Give Verbal Redirection

Occasionally students engage in minor disruptions during daily classroom routines such as attendance, returning homework, or when listening to daily messages over the intercom. This is a good time to channel their energy toward acceptable behavior. For example, Lynn passes a note to Juan through Chuck. Ask Lynn to assist in passing out homework. Ask Juan a question about an upcoming activity and tell Chuck to read today's assignment off the blackboard. Verbal redirection can be an extremely effective technique, but caution should be used if the student is engaging in the behavior to get the teacher's attention.

Remain Unemotional Yet Firm When Intervening

It is best to remain unemotional yet firm when dealing with rule violations. As classroom leaders, teachers set the tone when things do not go as planned. The most effective strategy teachers can use is to handle minor disruptions before they become worse. Jones and Jones (1990) noted, "An inappropriately angry teacher's response creates tension and increases disobedience and disruptive behavior. When a teacher reacts calmly and quickly to a student's disruptive behavior, other students respond by improving their own behavior" (p. 295). The first step when intervening is to make contact with the student. Never assume the student is aware he or she is breaking a classroom rule; let the student know what is unacceptable: "Carlos, the rule is, raise your hand when you want to speak, and I will call on you as soon as possible." As soon as Carlos raises his hand, the teacher should call on him and praise him for behaving responsibly. Teachers can intervene publicly as a message to the entire class; however, it is best to deliver reprimands in private. When teachers show respect for students, they will be more likely to comply with the teacher's instructions, and the teacher has averted turning a minor disruption into a major catastrophe.

Conclusion

Following this four-part framework for constructing behaviors can result in positive approaches to middle level classroom management. Figure 2 provides an outline of this approach for reference. The goal of setting positive rules and procedures is to maintain a healthy and respectful classroom. As the decisive element, teachers can create a supportive, caring community of learners through the words they choose and the actions they take. Mills (1997) captured this approach this way: "Suzan communicated to her students a pervasive caring by helping them feel a sense of belonging; learn acceptable, supportive behaviors; experience frequent success; and assume they have a promising future" (p. 34).

Author's note: Support for this article was provided by a Leadership Training Grant (#H3253980018) from the Office of Special Education and Rehabilitation Services, U.S. Department of Education. I thank David A. and Barbara Bicard for being the decisive elements in my life. I also thank William L. Heward for his constructive comments.

References

Barrish, H. H., Saunders, M., & Wolf, M. M. (1969). Good behavior game: Effects of individual contingencies for group consequences on disruptive behavior in a classroom. *Journal of Applied Behavior Analysis, 2,* 119–124.

Braam, C., & Malott, R. M. (1990). "I'll do it when the snow melts": The effects of deadlines and delayed outcomes on rule-governed behavior in preschool children. *The Analysis of Verbal Behavior, 8,* 67–76.

Carden-Smith, L. K., & Fowler, S. A. (1984). Positive peer pressure: The effects of peer monitoring on children's disruptive behavior. *Journal of Applied Behavior Analysis, 17,* 213–227.

Catania, A. C. (1998). *Learning* (4th ed.). Upper Saddle River. NJ: Prentice Hall.

Cooper, J. O., Heron, T. E., & Heward, W. L. (1987). *Applied behavior analysis.* Upper Saddle River. NJ: Prentice Hall/Merrill.

Dickerson, E. A., & Creedon, C. F. (1981). Self-selection of standards by children: The relative effectiveness of pupil-selected and teacher-selected standards of performance. *Journal of Applied Behavior Analysis, 14,* 425–433.

Englemann, S., & Carnine, D. (1991). *Theory of instruction* (rev. ed.). Eugene, OR: ADI Press.

Emmer, E. T., Evertson, C. M., Clements, B. S., & Worsham, M. E. (1994). *Classroom management for secondary teachers* (3rd ed.). Needham, MA: Allyn and Bacon.

Felixbrod, J., & O'Leary, K. (1974). Self-determination of academic standards by children: Toward freedom from external control. *Journal of Educational Psychology, 66,* 845–850.

Ginott, H. (2000). *The teacher.* Retrieved January 6, 2000 from the World Wide Web.

Greer, R. D. (1981). An operant approach to motivation and affect: Ten years of research in music learning. In Documentary report of the Ann Arbor symposium: *Application of psychology to the teaching and learning of music.* Washington, DC: Music Educators National Conference.

Heward, W. L. (2000). *Exceptional children: An introduction to special education* (6th ed.). Upper Saddle River, NJ: Merrill/Prentice Hall.

Jones, V. F., & Jones, L. S. (1990). *Comprehensive classroom management.* Needham Heights, MA: Allyn and Bacon.

Lovitt, T. C. (1995). *Tactics for teaching* (2nd ed.). Upper Saddle River, NJ: Merrill/Prentice Hall.

Lovitt, T. C., & Curtis, K. (1969). Academic response rate as a function of teacher- and self-imposed contingencies. *Journal of Applied Behavior Analysis, 2,* 49–53.

Madsen, C. H., Becker, W. C., & Thomas, D. R. (1968). Rules, praise, and ignoring: Elements of elementary classroom control. *Journal of Applied Behavior Analysis, 1,* 139–150.

Mackenzie, R. J. (1996). *Setting limits in the classroom.* Rocklin, CA: Prima Publishing.

Mills, R. A. (1997). Expert teaching and successful learning at the middle level: One teacher's story. *Middle School Journal, 29*(1), 30–38.

Mistr, K. N., & Glenn, S. S. (1992). Evocative and function-altering effects of contingency-specifying stimuli. *The Analysis of Verbal Behavior, 10,* 11–21.

Paine, S. C., Radicchi, J., Rosellini, L. C., Deutchman, L., & Darch, C. B. (1983). *Structuring your classroom for academic success.* Champaign, IL: Research Press.

Rhode, G., Jensen, W. R., & Reavis, H. K. (1998). *The tough kid book: Practical classroom management strategies.* Longmont, CO: Sopris West.

Stevenson, C. (1998). Finding our priorities for middle level curriculum. *Middle School Journal, 29*(4), 53–57.

Sulzer-Azaroff, B., & Mayer, G. R. (1986). *Achieving educational excellence using behavioral strategies.* New York: CBS College Publishing.

Thomas, D. R., Becker, W. C., & Armstrong, M. (1968). Production and elimination of disruptive classroom behavior by systematically varying teachers' behavior. *Journal of Applied Behavior Analysis, 1,* 35–45.

Walker, J., & Shea, T. M. (1995). *Behavior management: A practical approach for educators.* Upper Saddle River, NJ: Merrill/Prentice Hall.

Zirpoli, T. J., & Melloy, K. J. (1993). *Behavior management: Applications for teachers and parents.* Don Mills, Ontario: Macmillan Publishing.

ASSESSMENT *FOR* LEARNING: A VISION FOR THE FUTURE

Rick Stiggins

Assessment is an integral part of effective teaching; it informs both teachers and students about learning progress, providing invaluable feedback for future actions. Standards can play a critical role in assessment, highlighting clear learning goals and targets. Rick Stiggins suggests that the process of assessment in the United States has evolved over the past 50 years to the strongly held beliefs that school improvement depends on high and clear standards for student achievement, that assessments should measure the extent to which the standards have been met, and that accountability should hold both students and teachers accountable for meeting the standards.

Assessment can make a broader contribution to the development of effective schools, Stiggins asserts, by becoming a tool for increasing learning, and he differentiates between the concepts of assessment *of* learning and assessment *for* learning. As you read this article ask yourself, "How can assessment *for* learning improve my teaching?"

Think About This . . .

1. How does assessment *for* learning differ from assessment *of* learning? Which of these is more important for the classroom teacher?
2. Which use of assessment does Stiggins argue is largely ignored in attempts to improve schools? Do you agree or disagree with Stiggins' position? Explain your view.

3. According to Stiggins, how effectively do teachers apply principles of assessment *for* learning? Why do you believe this is the case?

4. How will you use assessment *for* learning in your instruction? Provide a specific example to illustrate your description.

———

The evolution of assessment in this country over the past five decades has led to the strongly held view that school improvement requires the articulation of high achievement standards, transformation of those expectations into rigorous assessments, and expectation that educators will be held accountable for student achievement as reflected in student test scores.

To maximize the energy devoted to school improvement, we have "raised the bar" by setting world-class standards for student achievement, as opposed to minimum competencies. To promote greater accountability, policymakers often have attached the promise of rewards for schools that produce high scores and sanctions for schools that do not.

In all of this, we rely on assessments of learning to tell us if schools are delivering. The tests tell us how much students have learned, whether standards are being met, and if educators have done the job they were hired to do. Interested parents, communities, and politicians demand and deserve evidence of student learning.

But there is another way in which assessments can contribute to the development of effective schools, one that has been largely ignored. We also can use assessments *for* learning. Assessments *of* learning provide evidence of achievement for public reporting; assessments *for* learning serve to help students learn more. The crucial distinction is between testing to determine the status of learning and testing to promote greater learning.

Both kinds of assessment are important, but one has been ignored in our attempts to improve schools. Now we need a national, state, and local investment in assessment *for* learning. Compelling evidence gathered here at home and around the world tells us that such an investment will yield unprecedented achievement gains. Simply knowing that schools are to be held accountable for raising test scores is not enough. We must provide teachers with the assessment tools they need to do the job.

Assessments of learning have been the norm throughout the United States for decades. We began with standardized college-admissions testing in the early decades of the previous century, and it continues essentially unchanged today. These tests have not been used merely for college selection, however. For decades, we also have ranked states based on average SAT scores. This is assessment of learning for public accountability.

In response to demands for accountability in public schools in the 1960s, we launched districtwide standardized-testing programs that also remain in place today. In the 1970s, we began the broad implementation of statewide testing programs, and those have spread into every state today. Then we added a national assessment program, which continues today. And during the 1990s, we became deeply involved and invested in international assessment programs.

Across the nation, across the various levels of testing, and over the decades, we have invested probably billions of dollars to ensure the accuracy of the scores on these assessments of learning. Now, in 2002, President Bush has signed into law a school reform measure requiring standardized testing of every pupil in the United States in mathematics and reading every year in grades 3–8, once again revealing our faith in assessment of learning as a school improvement tool.

Assessments of learning are not limited to large-scale testing programs. Teachers also conduct similar "summative" assessments of learning at the end of instruction to determine what students have learned. These feed into the assignment of report card grades. Thus, they serve the same "audit" function as do state assessments.

Clearly, assessments of learning dominate. They are conducted within the classroom and imposed from outside the classroom.

How does assessment *for* learning differ? When it is done properly, teachers use the classroom-assessment process and the continuous flow of information about student achievement it provides to advance, not merely check on, student progress. The basic principles of assessment for learning are these:

From Stiggins, R. (2001). Assessment for learning: A vision for the future. As first appeared in Education Week, *21(26), 30, 32–33. Reprinted with permission of the author.*

- Teachers understand and articulate in advance of teaching the achievement targets that their students are to hit.
- They inform their students about those learning goals in terms that students understand from the very beginning of the teaching and learning process.
- Teachers are assessment-literate and thus are able to transform those expectations into assessment exercises and scoring procedures that accurately reflect student achievement.
- They use classroom assessment to build students' confidence in themselves as learners, helping them take responsibility for their own learning and thus lay a foundation for lifelong learning.
- Classroom-assessment results are consistently translated into informative (not merely judgmental) feedback for students, providing them with specific insights on how to improve.
- Students work closely with their teachers to review assessment results, so that they remain in touch with, and thus feel in charge of, their own improvement over time.
- Teachers continuously adjust instruction based on the results of classroom assessments.
- Students are actively involved in communicating with their teachers and their families about their achievement status and improvement.

In short, the effect of assessment for learning, as it plays out in the classroom, is that students remain confident that they can continue to learn at productive levels if they keep trying to learn. In other words, they don't give up in frustration or hopelessness.

The deeply troubling fact, however, is that few teachers apply these principles of assessment for learning because they have not been given the opportunity to learn to do so. Currently, only a few states explicitly require competence in assessment as a condition for being licensed to teach. No licensing examination now in place at the state or federal level verifies competence in assessment. Since teacher-preparation programs are designed to prepare candidates for certification under these terms, the vast majority of programs fail to provide the assessment literacy required to prepare teachers to face emerging classroom-assessment challenges. It has been so for decades.

Furthermore, lest we believe that teachers can turn to their principals for help, almost no states require competence in assessment for licensure as a principal or school administrator at any level. As a result, assessment training is almost nonexistent in administrator-training programs. This, too, has been the case for decades.

We remain a national K–12 faculty that is unschooled in the principles of sound assessment—whether it is of or for learning. And to date, as a nation, we have invested almost nothing in assessment for learning.

As a result, we miss out on an immensely promising school improvement opportunity. And we face the danger that student progress may be mismeasured, day after day, in classrooms across the nation. The dire consequences for student learning are obvious. School leaders and educational policymakers must come to understand that a hundred layers of differing standardized tests cannot overcome the negative effects of this reality.

The potential impact of the problem has not gone unnoticed. Many have anticipated the consequences and urged action. For example, during the 1990s, virtually every professional association related to teaching, school leadership, and educational assessment adopted standards of professional competence for teachers that include a classroom-assessment component.

In its 2001 report, the Committee on the Foundations of Assessment of the National Research Council advanced recommendations for the development of assessment in American schools, saying that "instruction in how students learn and how learning can be assessed should be a major component of teacher preservice and professional-development programs."

"This training," the committee said, "should be linked to actual experience in classrooms in assessing and interpreting the development of student competence." It further recommended that the balance of resources and mandates be shifted from an emphasis on external examinations to an increased emphasis on the use of formative classroom assessment for learning.

Similarly, the Commission on Instructionally Supportive Assessment, convened in 2001 by the American Association of School Administrators, the National Association of Elementary School Principals, the National Association of Secondary School Principals, the National Education Association, and the National Middle School Association, listed among its requirements the expectation that states ensure that educators receive professional development focused on how to optimize children's learning based on the results of instructionally supportive assessment.

We understand what teachers need to know in order to be able to establish and maintain productive classroom-assessment environments. The challenge we face is that of providing the opportunity for them to master those essential classroom-assessment competencies. The depth of this challenge becomes clear when we realize that we must provide opportunities for new teachers to gain these competencies before entering the classroom, and for experienced teachers who had no chance to master them during their training.

Black and Dylan Wiliam of Kings College, London, examined the literature on assessment worldwide, asking if there was evidence that improving the quality and effectiveness of the use of formative (classroom) assessments raises student achievement, as reflected in periodic summative assessments. They uncovered more than 250 relevant research articles. Upon pooling the information on the estimated effects of improved formative assessment on summative-test scores, they reported unprecedented positive effects on student-achievement positive-effect sizes of between a half and a full standard deviation. That would lead to percentile-score gains of from 15 to 30 points, or three or more years in grade equivalents.

If applied to the most recent Third International Mathematics and Science Study results, effects of this magnitude would have raised the United States from the rank of 21st out of 41 participating nations to the top five. For perspective, the research on reducing class size reveals expected gains of only two-tenths of a standard deviation.

Most importantly, the Kings College researchers report that "improved formative assessment helps low achievers more than other students, and so reduces the range of achievement while raising achievement overall." The implications for those struggling with achievement gaps between subsets of their student populations are obvious. We know of no other school improvement innovation that can make this claim.

There are no good arguments against balancing our assessments of and for learning. Everyone wins and no one loses. Students benefit from greater confidence and achievement. They come to understand what it means to be responsible for one's own learning—the foundation of lifelong learning.

Teachers benefit from greater student motivation, more effective instructional decisions, and greater student success. Parents benefit by seeing greater enthusiasm for learning in their children and greater achievement, and through understanding that their children are learning to manage their own lifelong process of learning. School administrators and instructional leaders benefit from the reality of meeting accountability standards and the public recognition of doing so. Political officials benefit in the same way. Schools work more effectively, and they are recognized as contributing to that outcome.

But the price that we must pay to achieve such benefits is an investment in teachers and their classroom-assessment practices. We need to provide teachers with the professional development needed to assess *for* learning. Moreover, federal, state, and local assessment resources must be allocated in equal proportions to assure the accuracy and the effective use of both assessments of and for learning.

Only then can we assure families that their children are free from the harm that results from the mismeasurement of their achievement in schools. Only then can we maximize students' confidence in themselves as learners. Only then will we raise achievement levels for all students.

TEACHING TO THE TEST?
W. James Popham

In this age of accountability, externally imposed standardized tests take on an increasingly powerful role in classrooms. All teachers want their students to do well on tests, but some instructional efforts, such as teaching to the test, are counterproductive, W. James Popham asserts. He differentiates between item-teaching and curriculum-teaching. Item-teaching focuses on specific test content and formats, whereas curriculum-teaching emphasizes important standards and goals. Item-teaching results in inaccurate inferences about student achievement and provides students, parents, and educators with inaccurate conclusions about student competence and skill. As you read this article ask, "How can teachers align their instruction with test content without succumbing to teaching to the test?"

Think About This . . .

1. How is item-teaching different from curriculum-teaching? Why is this difference becoming increasingly important?
2. Why is item-teaching harmful to students? To parents? To teachers?
3. What suggestions does Popham have for reducing the likelihood of item-teaching? Which of these suggestions are most important?
4. What can you do to ensure that your instruction will focus on the curriculum rather than the test?

American teachers are feeling enormous pressure these days to raise their students' scores on high-stakes tests. As a consequence, some teachers are providing classroom instruction that incorporates, as practice activities, the actual items on the high-stakes tests. Other teachers are giving practice exercises featuring "clone items"—items so similar to the test's actual items that it's tough to tell which is which. In either case, these teachers are teaching to the test.

What Is Teaching to the Test?

Although many use the phrase, educators need to understand exactly what *teaching to the test* means. Educational tests typically represent a particular set of knowledge or skills. For example, a teacher's 20-item spelling quiz might represent a much larger collection of 200 spelling words. Therefore, the teacher can distinguish between test items and the knowledge or skills represented by those items.

If a teacher directs instruction toward the body of knowledge or skills that a test represents, we applaud that teacher's efforts. This kind of instruction teaches to the knowledge or skills represented by a test. But if a teacher uses the actual test items in classroom activities or uses items similar to the test items, the teacher is engaging in a very different kind of teaching. For clarity, I will refer to teaching that is focused directly on test items or on items much like them as *item-teaching*. I will refer to teaching that is directed at the curricular content (knowledge or skills) represented by test items as *curriculum-teaching*.

In *item-teaching,* teachers organize their instruction either around the actual items found on a test or around a set of look-alike items. For instance, imagine that a high-stakes test includes the multiple-choice subtraction item "Gloria has 14 pears but ate 3." The test-taker must choose from four choices the number of pears that Gloria has now. Suppose the teacher revised this item slightly: "Joe has 14 bananas but ate 3." The test-taker chooses from the same four answers, ordered slightly differently. Only the kind of fruit and the gender of the fruit-eater have been altered in this clone item; the cognitive demand is unchanged.

Curriculum-teaching, however, requires teachers to direct their instruction toward a specific body of content knowledge or a specific set of cognitive skills represented by a given test. I am not thinking of the loose manner in which some teachers assert that they are "teaching toward the curriculum" even though that curriculum consists of little more than a set of ill-defined objectives or a collection of vague and numerous content standards. In curriculum-teaching, a teacher targets instruction at *test-represented* content rather than at test items.

Is Teaching to Test Items Wrong?

The purpose of most educational testing is to allow teachers, parents, and others to make accurate inferences about the levels of mastery that students have achieved with respect to a body of knowledge (such as a series of historical facts) or a set of skills (such as the ability to write particular kinds of essays). Because the amount of knowledge and skills that teachers teach is typically too great to test everything, tests sample those bodies of knowledge or skills. For example, on the basis of a student's ability to write one or two persuasive essays on a given topic, we can infer the student's general ability to write persuasive essays. If our interpretation of the student's skill in writing essays is accurate, we have arrived at a valid performance-based inference about the student's mastery of the skill represented by the test.

From Popham, W. J. (2001). *Teaching to the test?* Educational Leadership, 58(6), 16–20. *Reprinted with permission of the Association for Supervision and Curriculum Development.*

Similarly, when a student scores well on a 10-item test consisting of multiplication problems with pairs of triple-digit numerals, we infer that the student can satisfactorily do other problems of that ilk; hence, he or she appears to have mastered multiplying pairs of triple-digit numbers. If a test-based inference is valid and the teacher gets an accurate fix on students' current knowledge or skills, then the teacher can make appropriate instructional decisions about which students need additional help, or, if all the students do well, whether it's time to switch to new instructional targets.

To illustrate, suppose a district-developed reading vocabulary test includes 25 items from a set of 500 words that reflect the target vocabulary words at a particular grade level. If the test yields valid interpretations, a student who answers 60 percent of the items correctly will, in fact, possess mastery of roughly 60 percent of the 500 words that the 25-item vocabulary test represents. If the test yields valid inferences, of course, teachers can make suitable decisions about which students need to be pummeled with more vocabulary instruction. Similarly, district-level administrators can allocate appropriate resources—for example, staff-development focused on enhancing students' reading vocabularies.

Curriculum-teaching, if it is effective, will elevate students' scores on high-stakes tests and, more important, will elevate students' mastery of the knowledge or skills on which the test items are based. If a teacher, however, gets a copy of the district test, photocopies its 25 vocabulary items, and drills next year's students on those 25 items, valid test-based interpretations become impossible. A student's score on the test would no longer indicate, even remotely, how many of the designated 500 vocabulary words the student really knows. Valid inferences disappear as a consequence of item-teaching.

Because teaching either to test items or to clones of those items eviscerates the validity of score-based inferences—whether those inferences are made by teachers, parents, or policymakers—item-teaching is reprehensible. It should be stopped. But can it be?

Detecting Inappropriate Test Preparation

One way of deterring inappropriate conduct is to install detection schemes that expose misbehavior. For example, when professional athletes are informed that they will be subjected to unannounced, random urine testing to determine whether they have been using prohibited substances, there is typically a dramatic reduction in the athletes' use of banned substances. The risk of penalties, at least to many people, clearly exceeds the rewards from engaging in proscribed behavior.

Unfortunately, I have found no practical procedures to detect teachers who are using inappropriate test preparation. Let me illustrate the difficulties by describing a fictitious teacher, Dee C. Ving. A 5th grade instructor in a school mostly serving low-income youngsters, Dee has consulted the descriptive information accompanying the national standardized achievement test that her 5th graders will take in the spring. She finds those descriptions inadequate from an instructional perspective: They are both terse and ambiguous. Dee simply can't aim her instruction at the knowledge or skills represented by the test items because she has no clear idea about what knowledge or skills are represented.

Frustrated by the overwhelming pressure to improve her students' scores. Dee engages in some full-scale item-teaching. One of her friends has access to a copy of the test that Dee's students will take and loans it to Dee for a few days so that Dee can "understand what content your students will really need to know."

Dee, having covertly made a copy of key sections of the test, devotes one or two days each week to what she rationalizes as test-targeted instruction. In her explanations and practice exercises, she uses either actual items taken from the test or slightly modified versions of those items. Not surprisingly, when Dee's 5th graders take the standardized achievement test in the spring, most of them score very well. Her students last year scored on average in the 45th percentile, but her students this year earn a mean score equal to the 83rd percentile.

The scores, of course, provide invalid interpretations about the students' actual mastery of the content. But let's give Dee the benefit of the doubt by assuming that she genuinely believed she was helping her students get high scores and, at the same time, was making her school look good when the district compared schools' test performances. Dee, we assume, is not fundamentally evil. She just hasn't devoted much careful thought to the appropriateness of her test-preparation practices.

Could we have detected what Dee was up to? Let's say that, at some level, she recognizes that she has done something inappropriate. She is reluctant to reveal to colleagues or administrators that she relied on photocopied test items and slightly altered versions of those items. How could we determine that this year's high test scores were attributable to Dee's item-coaching rather than to good instruction?

Detection Procedures Doomed to Fail

What options might we have to apprehend Dee as she dished out item-teaching to her 5th graders?

Teacher self-reports. We might survey a school's teaching staff, and even devise the survey so that teachers' responses will be anonymous, to see whether teachers respond truthfully to questions about item-teaching. But teachers like Dee did not tumble off the turnip truck yesterday and would undoubtedly supply socially desirable, if inaccurate, responses to a self-report. Few teachers gleefully let the world know that they engage in questionable teaching practices.

Teacher-collected materials. We might also require teachers to compile a set of tests and practice exercises that they have used in their classes. Theoretically, we could inspect such materials to see whether they contained any actual items from the high-stakes test or any massaged versions of those items. But Dee will surely be shrewd enough to sanitize the materials that she puts in her required compilation. She'll destroy any incriminating papers and probably rely on chalkboard explanations and practice exercises. Chalkboards can be erased ever so completely.

Oral exercises also are difficult to monitor. Once uttered, they evaporate. Moreover, it is both naive and professionally demeaning to ask teachers to assemble a portfolio of potentially self-incriminating evidence. In most schools, such a requirement would be a genuine morale-breaker.

Pre-announced classroom observations. If Dee's principal lets her know that he or she will visit the classroom on Wednesday of that week, that principal will see no item-teaching. Dee knows how to play the high-stakes score-boosting game. And allowing a principal to walk in on an item-focused teaching activity would violate the rules of the game. The principal will see only good teaching.

Unannounced classroom observations. Whereas pre-announced classroom observations by a school administrator give teachers ample time to disply appropriate lessons, unannounced observations do not. Unannounced visits, therefore, ought to work better than pre-announced ones. But this detection ploy is not promising on three counts.

First, it casts the unannounced visitor in a negative "Gotcha!" role. Few school-site administrators enjoy playing police officer. Second, forcing a school principal or other adminstrator to undertake this surveillance duty will diminish that person's effectiveness as an ally for a teacher's improvement. And reduced effectiveness, in the long run, is certain to harm the quality of instruction for students. Third, visiting teacher's classrooms to ensure that no inappropriate test preparation is underway is enormously time-consuming. The administrator's other responsibilities may suffer.

Student self-reports. There are other eyewitnesses to what goes on in a classroom—the students. Theoretically, students could periodically complete anonymous instructional questionnaires, containing actual or slightly altered versions of high-stakes test items. We could then ask them whether the teacher provided explanations or practice exercises focused on items similar to those on the instructional questionnaire.

Yet most students would have difficulty determining the degree of similarity between a questionnaire's sample items and the practice or explanatory items that they had already seen. Besides, this tattle-on-teacher activity could create an unsavory relationship between teachers and students. Indeed, as soon as they figured out the purpose of the questionnaire, unhappy students could readily get revenge by falsely asserting that they had been given oodles of practice items.

Score jumps. I often advise parents to view with suspicion any substantial year-to-year increases that they see in their children's test scores. There is far too much likelihood that because of pressures to boost students' test scores, teachers have engaged in inappropriate test preparation—or, worse, violations of the prescribed test administration procedures. When student scores jump dramatically from one year to the next, I urge parents to look into what's going on instructionally at the school. Standardized achievement tests are notoriously insensitive to instruction. That is, such tests typically fail to detect the impact of even first-rate instructional improvements.

But, of course, scores can jump because of improved instruction. Suppose, for instance, a school served a large number of students whose first language was not English. Students' poor test performances in the previous year may be directly attributable to their inability to read the actual test items. Recognizing the problem, the school's staff may have directed instructional energy toward students' reading comprehension. And, as a result, students' scores could have improved dramatically.

On the one hand, a score jump may signal the presence of item-teaching or worse. On the other hand, a score jump may arise because of improved instruction. By themselves, score jumps can't detect improper instruction.

Does all this mean that we simply avert our eyes while inappropriate test preparation becomes even more common in U.S. schools? Can this inappropriate practice ever be effectively deterred? Surprisingly, the answer is a decisive *yes*.

Deterrence Strategies

Provide a hefty dose of assessment literacy. I have spoken to many teachers about their test-preparation practices, especially teachers who are seriously pressured to raise their students' test scores. The vast majority of them have never considered the appropriateness of their test-preparation practices. Indeed, after learning that teaching directly toward test items created invalid inferences about their students, most teachers are both surprised and dismayed.

I am not suggesting that once teachers recognize instructional improprieties, such improprieties instantly disappear. Some teachers, unfortunately, already understand quite well the effects of their item-focused teaching. The score-boosting pressures that those teachers experience lead them toward practices that, absent such pressure, they would regard as repugnant.

But I believe that the vast majority of teachers, if they recognize the adverse effects of item-teaching, will abandon such teaching. The first deterrence should be an aggressive attempt to enhance teachers' assessment literacy—especially as it relates to the impact on the validity of test interpretation. Teachers should understand not only the difference between item-teaching and curriculum-teaching, but also the impact that those types of teaching have on their students.

Help policymakers understand what kinds of high-stakes tests they should use. Some teachers succumb to item-teaching because, if they truly believe they are obliged to raise test scores, they think they have no alternative. More often than not, those teachers are correct.

There's no way a pressured teacher can provide students with curriculum-teaching if he or she doesn't have a clear description of the knowledge and skills represented by the test items. Obviously, for a teacher to focus instruction on the curricular content that a test represents, that content must be spelled out sufficiently for the teacher's instructional planning. A teacher, looking over what curricular outcomes a high-stakes test represents, should understand those outcomes well enough to plan and deliver targeted lessons. Anything less descriptive drives teachers down a no-win instructional trail leading to item-teaching.

Thus, the second tactic is to educate policymakers to support only high-stakes tests that are accompanied by accurate, sufficiently detailed descriptions of the knowledge or skills measured. A high-stakes test unac-companied by a clear description of the curricular content is a test destined to make teachers losers. Moreover, because of the item-teaching that's apt to occur, tests with inadequate content descriptors also will render invalid most test-based interpretations about students.

For teachers to direct their instruction toward tangible teaching targets, not only should they have clear descriptions of the curricular content assessed by a test, but they should also have some reasonable assurances that good teaching will pay off in improved student test scores. In an effort to use such an approach, Hawaii education authorities recently overhauled the state's content standards—the knowledge and skills that the Hawaii Board of Education has directed the state's teachers to promote. One element of the process was to reduce the number of content standards to a smaller, more intellectually manageable number of curricular targets. A second element of the revision was to clarify what a content standard actually signified in terms of the knowledge or skill embodied in that standard.

State officials then enlisted an established test-development contractor to develop a test suitable for ascertaining students' mastery of the revised content standards. Each item measured one of the state's content standards. After the contractor developed the test items and identified the designated content standard for each item, committees of Hawaii educators reviewed each item's quality. One of the review questions was "If a teacher has supplied effective instruction directed toward students' mastery of this item's designated content standard, is it likely that most students will answer the item correctly?"

Hawaii education officials attempted to create a test that would allow teachers to engage in curriculum-teaching, rather than item-teaching, by targeting the state's content standards. If Hawaii's teachers can focus their instruction on curricular targets yet feel confident that student test scores will rise with effective instruction, they will have no need to engage in rampant item-teaching.

Deterrence and Detection

The core issue underlying this problem is easy to define. If students' scores jump, is it because those students are really able to leap over higher hurdles, or have the students been surreptitiously given stepladders? We surely do not wish to penalize a teacher who delivers instruction so stellar that students' performances go into orbit. But we don't want that orbit to be illusory.

In 1999, we learned that a United States president can be impeached for high crimes and misdemeanors. I'm not sure whether item-teaching is, technically, a high crime or a misdemeanor. But because it can harm children, I lean toward the high crimes label—and such instructionally criminal conduct is increasing.

No realistic procedure identifies and, hence, dissuades those teachers who choose to engage in item-teaching. Our best approach to deterrence lies first in getting educators to understand the difference between, and the consequences of, item-teaching and curriculum-teaching. Then, we must not use high-stakes, pressure-inducing tests that are not accompanied by content descriptions sufficiently clear for teachers' on-target instructional planning. If we prohibit instructionally opaque tests, teachers will no longer be victims of a score-boosting game that they cannot win. If we use tests with clarified instructional targets, teachers can focus their classroom efforts on getting students to master what they're supposed to learn.

ADDITIONAL READINGS

Amrein, A., & Berliner, D. (2003). The effects of high-stakes testing on student motivation and learning. *Educational Leadership, 60*(5), 32–38.

Brooks, M., & Brooks, G. (1999). The courage to be constructivist. *Educational Leadership, 57*(3), 18–24.

Chappuis, S., & Stiggins, R. (2002). Classroom assessment for learning. *Educational Leadership, 60*(1), 40–43.

Fuhler, C. (2003). Joining theory & best practice to drive classroom instruction. *Middle School Journal 34*(5), 23–30.

Gandal, M., & Vranek, J. (2001). Standards: Here today, here tomorrow. *Educational Leadership, 59*(1), 6–13.

Guskey, T. (1994). Making the grade: What benefits students? *Educational Leadership, 52*(2), 14–20.

Lessinger, L. (2001). Ending chance in classroom teaching. *Education Week, 21*(20), 56, 36.

Ojure, L., & Sherman, T. (2001). Learning styles: Why teachers love a concept research has yet to embrace. *Education Week, 21*(13), 33.

Painter, B. (2001). Using teaching portfolios. *Educational Leadership, 58*(5), 31–34.

Stiggins, R. (2001). Assessment *for* learning: A vision for the future. *Education Week, 21*(26), 30, 32.

EXPLORING THE INTERNET

Forms of Alternative Assessment
http://www.miamisci.org/ph/lpdefine.html
This site includes descriptions of different forms of alternative assessment together with suggestions for using each form.

Teacher Talk
http://education.indiana.edu/cas/tt/tthmpg.html
This site contains basic teaching tips for inexperienced teachers, ideas that can be immediately implemented into the classroom, new ideas in teaching methodologies for all teachers, and a forum for experienced teachers to share their expertise and topics with colleagues around the world.

Teachers Helping Teachers
http://www.pacificnet.net/~mandel//index.html
This site connects you to other teachers for help on lesson plans, professional planning, and similar types of issues.

PART SIX

Technology

We tend to think of technology as a recent innovation in American education, and computers are usually what come to mind when technology is discussed. Technology is much broader in scope, however, and it has been used in instruction as long as schools have existed. For example, teachers in our country's first schools had children use individual slate boards to practice their "letters and numbers." As the multiage one-room school evolved into schools organized by grade levels, the chalkboard became an essential tool for communicating with larger groups of students. These are rudimentary forms of technology.

The invention of electricity revolutionized instruction by allowing teachers to use radio, television, film strips, films, and overhead projectors. Technology further evolved, and teachers now routinely use videotapes, many have access to CD-ROM and DVD, virtually all have at least one computer in their classrooms, and some have sophisticated sound amplification systems and demonstration capability, such as PowerPoint. These are all forms of technology.

Without question the revolution in technology has given most people access to personal computers and information networks, and students should be taught about this technology and how to use it in their daily lives. Some educational reformers suggest that technology has the potential to transform education, and with this goal in mind, the United States has spent billions of dollars to inject technology into the schools. As of 2001, a whopping 99% of public schools had Internet access, and the ratio of students to school computers had steadily dropped over the years, averaging slightly less than 6 to 1 in 2002 (Ansell & Park, 2003; Flanigan, 2003).

However, in spite of this enormous investment, persistent questions remain about educational technology, including the following: Considering the huge amount of money invested, why doesn't technology play a larger role in today's schools? What is necessary to increase its use in schools? What is the future of technology in education? What are the promises and pitfalls of online learning? How can the vast resources of the Internet be used to increase student learning? Keep these questions in mind as you study the articles in this section.

THE TECHNOLOGY PUZZLE

Larry Cuban

Technology has already changed the society we live in, but why doesn't technology play a larger role in today's schools? Some point to teachers as the source of the problem, but Larry Cuban, noted educational historian, says, "No, instead, look to the contradictory and shifting technology goals that teachers have been given. Look also to work conditions and technology equipment that is both in short supply and often unreliable." As you read this article ask yourself, "How will I be able to overcome these obstacles to greater technology use?"

Think About This . . .

1. What criticisms have been leveled at teachers in terms of insufficient technology use? How valid are these criticisms?
2. How have technology goals shifted over time in the schools? Which goals will become important in the future?
3. What work conditions do teachers face that discourage greater use of technology in classrooms?
4. How will you use technology in your teaching? What can beginning teachers do to combat the negative conditions that Cuban describes?

Here's a puzzle for both cheerleaders and skeptics of using new technologies in the classroom. Out of every 10 teachers in this country, fewer than two are serious users of computers and other information technologies in their classrooms (several times a week); three to four are occasional users (about once a month); and the rest—four to five teachers out of every 10—never use the machines at all. When the type of classroom use is examined, we find that these powerful technologies end up being used most often for word processing and low-end applications. And this is after a decade of increases in access to computers, Internet capability, and purchases of software. In other organizations (think hospitals, major corporations, supermarkets), computer use is ubiquitous. Not so in schools.

How can this phenomenon of infrequent, low-end use of technology be occurring in our schools? For experts, there is no puzzle to be solved. The answers are straightforward and all point to teachers: their insufficient preparation in universities, their lack of specific training, too little time to learn, too many older teachers, "technophobia," and so on, ad infinitum. Surely, some of these scattershot explanations have merit in attempting to understand the paradox of increasing access and infrequent use.

What is missing from these neatly packaged reasons, however, is one overlooked fact: Of those same 10 American teachers, about seven have computers at home and use them to prepare lessons, communicate with colleagues and friends, search the Internet, and conduct personal business. In short, most teachers use computers at home more than at school. No technophobes here.

It is this fact that creates the puzzle of limited classroom use of new machines amid a river of technology money. It is this fact, too, that drives me to examine other reasons for the disparity, reasons seldom voiced in the media by either promoters or skeptics. The five areas that follow may offer explanations of the

From Cuban, L. (1999). The technology puzzle. As first appeared in Education Week, 19(43), 47, 68. Reprinted with permission of the author.

puzzle and broaden the debate over teachers' use of new technologies:

• *Contradictory Advice from Experts.* For almost two decades, experts hired by corporate vendors and entrepreneurial academics have exhorted teachers, particularly those in high schools, to use new technologies in their classrooms. Teachers must use the new, information-rich machines, they say, so that students will learn more, faster, and better to be prepared for the 21st century's knowledge-based workplace. But exactly what have these self-appointed experts told teachers about how computers should be used in schools?

When desktop computers began to appear in schools in the early 1980s, corporate leaders urged high school teachers to get their students "computer literate." The phrase then meant learning how to write BASIC programs. Experts said that learning to program would prepare students to think clearly and get jobs. Computer-savvy teachers who had learned BASIC on their own plunged into the task of teaching the language in newly established computer labs.

By the late 1980s, however, BASIC had disappeared. Now, freshly minted experts prodded high school teachers to teach computer applications (for example, word processing, spreadsheets, use of databases) because computers were analytic tools and, in the work world, knowing these applications paid off. Districts invested in more labs, more teachers were trained, and students began taking required courses in keyboarding and learning software applications that were used in the workplace.

By the mid-1990s, the prevailing wisdom among experts had shifted, and computer literacy took on new meanings. Teachers were now asked to integrate the new technologies into their daily classroom routines by placing four to six new machines in each teacher's classroom, rather than sending students to computer labs. Teachers were urged to learn and teach hypertext programming, or HTML, to help their students create multimedia products for an audience. Experts and their allies now said that students who were computer literate knew how to do research on the Internet, communicate via e-mail, and create their own World Wide Web pages. A series of so-called 'Net Days advertised the importance of wiring schools for the Internet, so that students could become part of the real world each and every day.

So, for the last two decades, experts have urged upon teachers an ever-shifting menu of advice: Teach BASIC. Teach HTML. Teach skills of using the Internet, e-mail, and producing multimedia projects. Teach applications relevant to the constantly changing workplace.

Now, let's imagine a couple of average high school teachers in the heart of Silicon Valley who have been around for these years of shifting advice and are eager to help their students learn. They have taken courses on using software applications that their district offers. They bought computers and use them at home extensively to prepare lessons, record grades, and search the Internet for lessons they could use in their classes. They are enthusiastic about using computers with their students. They have listened to the experts; but, since the advice keeps changing, they have largely ignored the wisdom of the moment. What gives them pause is not the experts' contradictions but other factors.

• *Intractable Working Conditions.* Although information technologies have transformed most corporate workplaces, our teachers' schedules and working conditions have changed very little. They teach five classes a day, each 50 to 55 minutes long. Their five classes contain at least three different preparations; that is, for the math teacher among our five, there are two classes of introductory algebra, two of geometry, and one calculus class. In those five classes, she sees 140 students a day. Colleagues in other districts, depending on how affluent the district is and how determined the school board and superintendent are to keep class size down, may see 125 to 175 students a day.

Or take the English teacher in our group, who assigns an essay in three of his 9th grade composition classes and for his two senior classes asks the students to answer five questions on "Hamlet." He will face the prospect of reading and correcting 130 papers for students who expect their homework to be returned earlier rather than later. Like all high school teachers, he has at least one period a day set aside for planning lessons, seeing students, marking papers, making phone calls to parents or vendors, previewing videos, securing a VCR or other equipment, and using the school's copy machines for producing student materials. So he and the math teacher, like most of their colleagues elsewhere, remain people for whom rollerblades would be in order to meet the day's obligations.

• *Demands from Others.* High school teachers are expected to know their subjects inside and out; they are expected to maintain order in their classrooms; they are expected to report instances of abuse and spot signs of behavioral problems; they are expected to be both friendly and demanding of each and every student; and, with district and state mandates for students to meet higher academic standards and take tests that can spell the difference between graduating or staying in school longer, teachers are expected to prod students on homework and other assignments and to be personally accountable for how well the students do on tests.

So teaching high school, in addition to knowing one's subject matter thoroughly and being able to convey it to others, requires the grit of a long-distance runner, the stamina of a boxer going 15 rounds, the temperament of a juggler, and the street smarts of a three-card monte dealer.

• *The Inherent Unreliability of the Technology.* Add serious technology use to the mix, and a teacher needs infinite patience. Ask even the most dedicated teacher-users about the reliability of these machines and their software. Most schools can't afford on-site technical support. When they do have coordinators and eager students who troubleshoot problems and do the repairs, there are still software glitches and servers that crash, torpedoing lessons again and again. Then new software packages and upgraded ones require more memory and speed from machines that are sorely limited in their capacity. More breakdowns; more pulled hair. These caring and techno-enthusiastic teachers ask, "What did I do to deserve this?"

• *Policymakers' Disrespect for Teachers' Opinions.* Teachers seldom are consulted on which technologies make the most sense for them to use with their students, what machines and software are both sensible and reliable for their classrooms. Instead, their classrooms disappear in the equation. Fully stocked labs with donated or purchased equipment appear. Machines pop up on teachers' desks. Administrators exhort teachers to take brand-new courses on technology that the district just made available.

The obvious question that seldom gets asked is this: Why should very busy teachers who are genuinely committed to doing a good job with their students listen to experts' changing advice on technologies when they have to face daily, unyielding working conditions; internal and external demands on their time and stamina; unreliable machines and software; and disrespect for their opinions?

Bashing teachers for not doing more with technology in their classrooms may give us cute media one-liners. What the one-liners miss, however, are the deeper, more consequential reasons for what teachers do every day. What corporate cheerleaders, policymakers, and vendors who have far more access to the media ignore are teachers' voices, the enduring workplace conditions within which teachers teach, inherent flaws in the technologies, and ever-changing advice of their own experts.

Such reasons are ignored because they go to the heart of what happens in schools, are very expensive to remedy, and reflect poorly on corporate know-how in producing machines. Nonetheless, these reasons may have more explanatory power for solving the puzzle of extensive home use of computers and limited, low-end classroom use than do the currently fashionable ones.

OUR TECHNOLOGY FUTURE
Laurence Goldberg

This article also attempts to answer the question, Why doesn't technology play a larger role in today's schools? Laurence Goldberg examines a number of possible reasons, but concludes that a "device dearth" exists and that the quality of machines is to blame. Paradoxically, our current cutting-edge educational technologies are not cutting-edge, and fail to meet the needs of real teachers and students. The technology of the future, Goldberg claims, needs to be mobile, flexible, and widely available. It needs to be reliable, user-friendly, and inexpensive. A tall order? Perhaps, but more user-friendly devices are necessary if technology is ever to have a lasting impact on classrooms and teaching, Goldberg asserts. As you read this article ask yourself, "Are improved machines the key to improved technology use in our schools?"

Think About This . . .

1. What does Goldberg mean by a "device dearth?" How would current technologies need to change to address this problem?
2. What are "disruptive technologies?" Can you think of examples from our everyday lives? Why have they become so "disruptive" and what implications does this have for education?
3. If you had access to the type of "killer devices" that Goldberg describes, how would you use them? How would it change your teaching?

Why does educational technology seem to have such trouble living up to its full potential of transforming the learning process? Conventional wisdom says the solution is simply to find more money for technology, more time and resources for staff development, and more innovative and effective ways to integrate technology into the curriculum. While this may be true, certain substantial roadblocks also have kept educational technology from reaching its potential.

As the state of the information-technology sector and the economy as a whole has changed, along with the mood of the country, many thoughtful educational technology leaders have switched into a reflective mode, looking at schools' substantial investment in technology infrastructure and trying to understand how it is and is not being fully leveraged. They are finding that, while individual educational institutions may do a better or worse job of "infusing technology," all schools face some common limitations.

To have a truly transformational impact on education, technology must become ubiquitous. It must be always available, mobile, and flexible. It must be intuitive, reliable, and user-friendly to the point of being no more difficult to operate than a chalkboard, textbook, or overhead projector. It must be seamless and nearly invisible.

At the moment, educational technology isn't any of these things. How can bulky, wire-tethered computers become invisible? How can students achieve ubiquitous access when there is only one or perhaps half a dozen fixed, shared computers in a classroom, or when they must wait until their next scheduled lab time? How can a quirky, unreliable computer (dependent upon the occasional resuscitative visit of an overstretched support technician) become an intuitive extension of the learner? More to the point, how can technology have a transformational impact on the educational process when it is simply being used to automate the same classroom-management and instructional-delivery tasks that were being done before?

Let's look first at what I'll call the "device dearth." Plenty of computing devices of all sizes and flavors are available for educational uses. Yet, conspicuously absent has been any "killer device" with the potential to transform the educational process by enabling one-to-one, personal, ubiquitous computing, and allowing the computer to take its natural place as a modern-day instructional supply in the bookbag or on the desk of every student and teacher. The ideal educational device should be as common and lacking in mystery as textbooks or spiral-bound notebooks.

Desktop personal computers are inherently awkward and inappropriate for many dynamic uses in an educational setting. While desktops may provide an appropriate medium for administrative uses, classroom-management tasks, and demonstration-style instruction, they are not the best solution for the personalized, portable, and dynamic technology needs for a ubiquitous student or teacher computer. Further, the operating system, hardware, and software of most personal computers sacrifice reliability for wealth of features, many of which are irrelevant to educational settings.

Laptop computers offer an alternative to desktops with some distinct advantages. But their relatively high cost, fragile design, and higher-than-average failure rate have impeded their acceptance as desktop replacements for students or teachers. Moreover, most laptop computers are simply too heavy and bulky to live up to their promise of true mobility. "Slimmed down" models may achieve lower weight and trimmer form by leaving out essential components (and are generally even more susceptible to damage), while "all in one" devices achieve full functionality at the cost of weight and girth.

Handheld computers offer greater mobility, but generally feature cramped keyboards that do not lend

From Goldberg, L. (2002). Our technology future. As first appeared in Education Week, 21(27), 32, 34. *Reprinted with permission of the author.*

themselves to regular use. And palmtop computers, while excelling in mobility and in their original roles as personal organizers, are of very limited use in an educational setting. Unless you are well-schooled in "graffiti," enjoy tiny accordion keyboards, or tapping out sentences on a Lilliputian screen, letter-by-letter, it's fair to say that no viable input method exists on these devices. Nor does the screen of a palmtop computer lend itself to the kinds of rich multimedia content or large chunks of texts that students need to be able to easily create and access in an educational setting.

So what is the killer device that will enable ubiquitous educational computing? It must be portable enough for every student and teacher to carry around in a bookbag, light enough not to further weigh down that bag, and sturdy enough not to get cracked or whacked when tossed in. Significantly, the personal educational computing device must be of a low enough cost to be universally available, whether through outright purchase, loan, or home-school-government-business partnership. The "e-book" devices that have appeared on the market recently (and in some cases, subsequently disappeared) held some promise for education, but are too single-purpose in their design to be useful. The same can be said of digital notepads designed to allow computer input of handwritten notes and diagrams. Why have one device to read digital books, another to take notes, another to keep track of class and activity schedules, another to surf the Internet, and yet another to communicate electronically? Students and teachers need a single, personal educational computing device that seamlessly performs these functions in a reliable, user-friendly way, using an intuitive and flexible input method, such as natural handwriting in a classroom setting or voice recognition at home.

Tablet computing devices currently hold the most promise of meeting these many requirements. Although some tablet devices already exist for specialized markets, expect to wait another year or two for the technology to become mature, reliable, and inexpensive enough to really begin to have an impact on the education market. Microsoft's recent announcement of a new version of the Windows operating system (currently scheduled for release this summer) designed for tablet computers will help spur hardware development and interoperability for this type of device. If hardware and software manufacturers can finally "get it right," they should expect to be rewarded by an explosion of adoptions of some sort of portable, personal computing device in the educational market in the coming years.

But, in the long run, the only viable way to reach ubiquity in educational technology is to free ourselves of wires. All school buildings must sooner or later provide wireless access to all of their students and educators by way of a wireless local-area network, or WLAN. Wired infrastructure can be leveraged by the placement of wireless access points, or be used in selected instances for wired applications with higher needs for security and performance. In classrooms, the killer device will have built-in, high-speed wireless capabilities for handling not just simple data, but also graphics and video content.

Users will be able to move freely within the school building, maintaining always-on connectivity to local network resources, the Internet, printer and file sharing, and e-mail access. Students' group work will be fostered from real-time, controlled connectivity among devices in the classroom. Teacher charts, diagrams, and notes may be integrated into the digital assignments passed to students. Student work will not be limited to written essays or quiz sheets, but may be in graphical or multimedia format where appropriate, and will be submitted electronically from school, home, or somewhere in between.

Outside schools, ideally, the device would automatically switch, to access a wireless wide-area network, or WWAN. For true ubiquity, schools may depend on the development of such networks by commercial providers of cellular telephones or integrated mobile Internet-access devices. Once at home, the student, parent, or teacher should be able to seamlessly access school information on the same device. For the near term, this access may be achieved through some broadband connectivity method, such as a high-speed modem of some sort, but ultimately it also should be wireless.

In the ubiquitous model of educational technology, it is essential for students to be able to continue working, with access to all the same digital educational resources, from anywhere in their community. It's also important for parents to have access to student and school information online, and to have open channels of communication with schools and teachers via the same device, or an online connection on the parents' home computer.

While the convergence and full implementation of these technologies may be rare in the current landscape, none of this is pie-in-the-sky. All these technologies exist today, but are not fully mature or widely available. More important, they are not yet being brought together in a meaningful way for the education community.

Once the right devices are widely available and the proper, ubiquitous infrastructure exists in and out of our schools, the true, transformational capabilities of educational technology can be realized. In industry and science, we sometimes refer to "disruptive technologies" as those that cause paradigm shifts in the way certain processes occur. Nascent "disruptive technologies" for the educational space will bring about this shift. Ubiquitous learning is student-centered and personalized, based on discovery activities. It is both collaborative and self-directed. In a ubiquitous model, students must become adept at information retrieval, management, and synthesis, from a variety of sources. Personal technology puts those resources within their reach, not just in the hands of the teacher, librarian, or lab aide. The ubiquitous model gives students the means of communicating and requires them to develop responsible "netizenship," with guidance from the instructor.

By its very nature, technology lends itself to interactive, bidirectional activities. This is why the insertion of a few computers into the traditional educational model of frontal, unidirectional delivery of facts and instruction has largely not had any substantial effect on learning. Unidirectional use of technology is a great way to foster a "boob tube" mentality of passive consumers. Students should instead be taught and encouraged to be active, creative participants in the learning process. The only way to make this happen is to provide them with the correct technologies, tools, and environments.

Educational technology has made incredible progress in the last decade. The building blocks have been put in place in many schools; we have become accustomed to new digital concepts like the Internet, multimedia presentations, and streamlined classroom management. Yet, in many ways we are in the Digital Dark Ages.

We are on the verge of the dawn of a golden age for educational technology. It may take a few more years for attitudes and technologies to mature to the point that the transformation is possible—but it will happen. Ubiquitous technology will have such an explosive impact on education that its results will become clearly visible to the naked eye, in stark contrast to today's inconclusive empirical studies.

Students will become vastly more involved in both the content and delivery of the learning process, and the walls of the school will crumble, as ubiquitous technology extends that learning process to the home and the community.

THE FUTURE OF COMPUTER TECHNOLOGY IN K–12 EDUCATION

Frederick Bennett

This article presents a third perspective on the question, What would it take to produce greater technology use in the schools? Frederick Bennett says nothing less than a complete rethinking of teachers' instructional roles. Bennett asserts that the best use of educational technology is for schools and teachers to use computers to instruct students directly. Because interaction is at the heart of teaching, teachers need to use computers as responsive tutors in areas like math and reading. As you read this article ask yourself, "Can increased use of computers to directly instruct students improve learning in my classroom?"

Think About This . . .

1. The availability of technology and poor teacher preparation have both been blamed for insufficient technology use. How important are these factors in explaining the current use of technology in today's schools?

2. With computers providing instructional support, what other instructional roles will teachers be free to perform? How important are these roles to you as a teacher?

3. How is Bennett's vision of technology's future in schools different from Goldberg's? Which vision do you think is more accurate?

4. How comfortable would you be in integrating computers in the classroom in a direct instructional role? How would it change your interactions with students? Are these positive changes?

In a piece published in February 2001, syndicated columnist George Will used Hippocrates and Socrates to illustrate the difficulties in contemporary American schooling. "If you were ill and could miraculously be treated by Hippocrates or by a young graduate of Johns Hopkins medical school, with his modern technologies and techniques, you would choose the latter. But if you could choose to have your child taught either by Socrates or by a freshly minted holder of a degree in education, full of the latest pedagogical theories and techniques? Socrates, please."

Teaching has always been more art than science and depends heavily on the talents of the practitioner. Some teachers are outstanding; some are not. In medicine, Hippocrates probably had more innate abilities than many of the new physicians, but his successors have the advantage of modern technology. Teachers, however, rely on basically the same approach that instructors have used throughout history, and, consequently, they must count on their own native skills. This situation presents a difficulty for education because exceptional instructors are in the minority. We see this easily if we think back over the teachers that we ourselves had in our school career. The number we remember as superb is not large.

The Present

Education today, as always, depends on the luck of the draw—who gets the good teachers and who gets the others? Meanwhile, technology has become a powerful force in the world. Theoretically, it might change education, just as it has made the new physician better equipped than Hippocrates and has brought dazzling benefits to innumerable other areas of society. Education authorities apparently hoped for comparable results because they have placed millions of computers in schools. By 1999, there was one computer for every six children.[1] Yet despite this massive infusion of technology, overall improvements in education have been minimal.

Scores on the National Assessment of Educational Progress point up this lack of advancement. Results for 1999 showed no significant change in reading, mathematics, or science for the three age groups tested—9-year-olds, 13-year-olds, and 17-year-olds—from 1994 through 1999.[2] During this five-year period, schools acquired huge numbers of computers and hoped earnestly that this influx of technology would improve education.

Since few people want to despair and conclude that K–12 education seems to be about the only major field that technology cannot benefit, authorities have sought reasons for the current failure. The most frequently suggested explanation is that teachers have not learned how to employ technology in their classrooms. Therefore, if schools could train teachers, the argument goes, technology would finally deliver major benefits to education. President Clinton joined those who wanted additional teacher training when in June 2000 he announced $128 million in grants to instruct teachers in the use of technology.

Lack of teacher training, however, is a myth. In 2000 the U.S. Department of Education issued a study in which half of all teachers reported that college and graduate work had prepared them to use technology. In addition, training continues after formal schooling. The same government document pointed out that, from 1996 to 1999, 77% of teachers participated in "professional development activities in the use of computers or the Internet."[3] Thirty-three percent to 39% of teachers responding to two surveys in 1999 said that they felt well prepared to use computers.[4] Although not the full universe of teachers, this percentage of well-prepared instructors ought to have brought some improvement if technology were going to lift education to a higher plateau.

The failure of test scores to change after schools have added millions of computers, after teachers have received considerable training, and after many years of computer usage leads to a troubling question: Is it possible that technology as currently used can never fundamentally improve today's K–12 education? I believe that

---

From Bennett, F. (2002). The future of computer technology in K–12 education. Phi Delta Kappan, 83(8), 621–625. Reprinted with permission of the author.

such hopelessness is indeed warranted, for one obvious reason: the power of electronic interaction is necessarily diminished because of the way computers must be used in schools today.

Interaction takes place when the instructor and the student react directly to each other's contributions. Interaction between child and teacher has always been found in good instruction. It can make learning enjoyable, can adjust to the varied abilities of different students, and is effective with children of all ages. Very possibly, one of the attributes of the teachers that we remember as being superb was their ability to develop a high degree of interaction with us.

Computer games show the power of electronic interaction. The secret to a large portion of this technology's success in maintaining its iron grip on the attention of game players is the unparalleled ability of the machine to interact continually with the participant. Theoretically, this same interactive power ought to make computers a potent force in education. When computers are used in classrooms today, however, interaction between the computer and the student cannot be strong and ongoing. This is because the teacher, not the computer, must control and direct instruction. Individual teachers must decide how they will use computer instruction in the dissemination of classroom material—how much the machine will teach the student and how much instruction the teacher will provide. These conditions are unalterable in the present system of education, and they drastically curtail interaction between the computer and the student.

Business and Computers

American education, however, is not unique in its poor initial results with computers. Corporate America had a similar experience. For several years, businesses added large numbers of computers, but overall productivity did not improve. Many workers acquired the machines for their desks. They used them for important jobs such as word processing and spreadsheets, but the basic manner in which companies carried on their activities did not change. This kind of computer usage was bound to fail. In time, corporations made the necessary structural changes and thus altered the basic way they carried on their business. When that happened, productivity increased dramatically. In an extensive article about the increase in productivity that technology has brought to business, Erik Brynjolfsson and Lorin Hitt point out, "Investments in computers may make little direct contribution to overall performance of a firm or the economy until they are combined with complementary investments in work practices, human capital, and firm restructuring."[5]

Education is in a position today akin to that of American business in those early days. Despite the millions of computers in schools, teaching has not changed. In the encompassing evaluation of technology in schools mentioned above, the Department of Education notes, "According to the literature, the advent of computers and the Internet has not dramatically changed how teachers teach and how students learn."[6]

An Alternative

There is an alternative to the way we use computers in schools, an alternative that would take advantage of the power of interaction. We could allow computers to tutor children individually and directly, without a teacher in the usual role. This approach seems radical when first considered. Nonetheless, a few schools have tried it for some students or subjects. The usual students in these computerized classes are those who are at risk of dropping out of school. In many cases, these students have been so difficult to teach that authorities have allowed this new approach. The results have been uniformly good.

Several companies have developed fitting teaching software. Among these are Plato Learning, Inc., Scientific Learning, and NovaNet Learning, Inc. All three have Web pages on which the results of their programs are posted.[7]

Lakeland High School in Florida, Lawrence High School in Indianapolis, and Turner High School in Carrollton, Texas, provide three interesting examples of Plato programs. In retests in Lakeland, student FHSCT (Florida High School Competency Test) scores increased dramatically, and the school identified a significant positive relationship between some Plato student performance data and the FHSCT scores. Authorities at Lawrence implemented an extensive remediation program in 1998–99 to increase the passing rate of their students taking the state-mandated competency exam, ISTEP (Indiana Statewide Testing for Educational Progress). At the beginning of the year, 406 students failed either the math or the English component. At the end of the year, only 74 of those pupils continued to fail the exam. At Turner, the pass rate on TAAS (Texas Assessment of Academic Skills) reversed a trend and improved from 69% in 1998 to 83% in 2000.

Scientific Learning has concentrated on reading and comprehension, especially with students who are behind in these vital areas. Pretest and posttest results with standardized, nationally normed tests showed significant gains with various levels of students from kindergarten through grade 12.

Dillard High School in Fort Lauderdale, Florida, provides an example of the results of using NovaNet software. In this program there were 123 students, all of whom were below the 20th percentile on state standards. After three months of using the program, all pupils had made gains. Moreover, half of the students had advanced at least one full grade, and 27 of those pupils had improved by either two or three grade levels.

Although schools have used this form of computerized education primarily with at-risk children, there are other programs that teach average and bright students, and they have recorded equally exciting gains. For example, researchers at Carnegie Mellon University created software to teach algebra through computers. They installed the program in a number of high schools, including some in their hometown of Pittsburgh. The authors made a study of freshmen at three schools, none of whom had taken the subject in middle school. Approximately 470 students enrolled in 21 computer classes. At the end of the year the schools assessed results and compared math achievement for these students with that of a comparable group of 170 ninth-grade students in standard math courses. The results showed the power of the computerized learning. The computer students scored 15% better on standardized tests. Moreover, they scored 100% better on the more difficult questions that "focused on mathematical analysis of real-world situations and the use of computational tools."[8]

In all these successful programs the electronic instruction takes advantage of many of the strengths of computers: children are taught individually and at their own pace, and the software develops interaction between the computer and the student. Moreover, the electronic instructor never retires or gets sick, and programmers can continually improve the software. Teachers continue to be essential, but with a role that differs from our accustomed conception of what teachers do.

Careful consideration of results from these and other studies makes it seem possible that, if this type of computerized education were adopted universally, technology could begin to make real and beneficial changes for students, teachers, and schools. Under this scenario, not only would there be interaction between the computer and the student, but also each pupil would have, in effect, a private tutor throughout his or her educational career. Like a human tutor, the electronic instructor would teach the child at his or her learning level. For example, superior students would constantly have new vistas and challenges opened to them, with continual opportunities for advancement. With sub-par students, the computer would provide appropriate material but would also move at a speed that would fit each pupil's capacity for progress.

Through constant testing and continual interaction, the electronic instructor would be aware of the child's needs and would immediately provide proper material to correct any problems and to encourage and help the student to advance. Students who had more difficulty learning would never be overwhelmed because the class had proceeded beyond their level of scholarship. Moreover, there would be no embarrassment if the computer had to take longer to cover a given lesson for a particular student. The child's classmates would not know. Only the computer and the authorities receiving the computer reports would have this information. At the other end of the learning spectrum, students who were capable of advancing more rapidly would find new excitement and challenges, and much of the boredom that has always engulfed these students would be removed.

Moreover, the electronic instructor could be programmed to emulate the approaches that good teachers have always used with their students. It would point out errors and praise and reinforce all gains. Positive feedback helps the student and makes learning enjoyable, as all teachers recognize. In a classroom of 15 or 20 students, teachers are often unable to give each student individual encouragement. The computer, however, with only one child to attend to, would always be quick to praise his or her accomplishments. Since the computer would interact directly with the child, it could concentrate its power exclusively on the needs of the individual student without affecting the requirements of other children in the class. They would all have their own private tutors.

Teachers

Computerized education would change the role of teachers but would neither eliminate nor downgrade them. On the contrary, human instructors would remain extremely important but with a radically different focus. This possibility often frightens teachers, but computerization would actually enhance their position. Many of the tedious, boring duties that they must endure today, such as preparing daily lesson plans and correcting tests, would vanish. That would leave them more time to function in their true and essential position as educators.

There are two basic roles that I foresee for teachers in computerized education: continuing to conduct group activities and acting as "leader teachers."

Many teachers today conduct a variety of group sessions, such as workshops, seminars, and discussions. In computerized education, these duties would not only continue but would take on more importance than in today's schools. In addition, some aspects of today's group meetings would change. The computer would handle the basic necessities of the assigned curriculum, giving teachers greater freedom to choose topics for a group setting and the prospect of dealing more deeply with those topics than is possible today. Group projects might continue for several class periods or for several days. Despite the length of time used in these activities, the students would not miss any of their computer classes because the computer would begin again exactly where the last lesson ended. Today, teachers usually have all the students from their own classes in their groups and no one else. In computerized education, preset conditions would not determine attendance. Students could choose the workshops that most interested them, and teachers could establish prerequisites for attendance. For a teacher, this type of group would form the ideal teaching environment.

One of the fears sometimes voiced about children learning extensively from computers is that they would lose the valuable human give-and-take that currently happens in classes. In actuality, because of the need for discipline, less interplay among students goes on in today's classrooms than is often imagined. But group sessions in computerized education would provide many legitimate opportunities for student interaction.

Another vitally important activity for humans in the education of children would be to function as leader teachers.[9] Every student at every age level would have a leader teacher whom the pupil and his or her parents would choose and who would be responsible for leading the child as he or she pursued an education. This relationship between student and teacher would last for at least a year at a time and might continue for several years. The student would meet this mentor privately and on a regular basis. These meetings would vary, depending on the age and needs of the child. For example, the leader teacher of a student in the first grade might see and talk with the child several times every day. The leader teacher of a student in high school might meet with the youth only once every couple of weeks if that seemed appropriate.

All children, however, at all age levels would sit down regularly with their teachers, who would have access to their computer records. Time would be available for the instructors to get to know the children well. This system would make directing the education of the children easier and more productive for the teachers and make the children comfortable with this kind of direction. In today's education system, many students go months or even years without meeting privately with a teacher. That could never happen if computers were teaching and leader teachers had both the responsibility of directing children's education and the time to carry out that responsibility.

Parents would have another advantage because a leader teacher directed their child. They would find it easier to arrange parent/teacher conferences. They would need to meet with only one instructor, who would have a thorough knowledge of the student and of all the subjects he or she was studying.

The Future

Can schools ever take advantage of true computerized education? When corporate America learned how it could use computers to improve productivity, the central role of the computer in business was assured. The need for improvement in education is present, as even such staunch defenders of today's schools as the Sandia National Laboratories and Gerald Bracey point out. Moreover, everybody would be delighted if there could be additional gains even among today's best schools.

Emulating the successful employment of computers by business, however, is not simple. There are unique difficulties in education. For example, school boards must alleviate the fears of teachers that they will lose their jobs. In addition, since education is much more involved in the political world, proportionately more people must take part in the process of making changes. The numbers of citizens who must become aware of the potential of computerization in education will be larger than in business, where the decision makers are fewer. In corporate America, when software companies developed programs to enhance productivity, individual businesses bought that software because they wanted to improve and did not fear changes. Education, with some exceptions, has a history of resisting serious change. This tendency lessens the incentive for software companies to develop the necessary programming.

The solution, therefore, must be twofold. First, educators, politicians, parents, and concerned citizens must understand how schools can use computers more effectively to improve education and to benefit students and teachers. Second, commercial companies must create suitable software.

These seem to be monstrous tasks, but both are possible. Many teachers, parents, and administrators want improvements and are engaged in an ongoing search for answers. They will need to examine and debate the value of true computerization as they carry out their quest. If these many searchers for improved education decide that computerization can supply an important portion of the answer, then it will be up to the private corporations to do their part. Some of these are already developing programming, as noted above, and they and other companies could turn more of their resources and ingenuity toward developing outstanding and effective educational software. The potential market is huge, and software corporations will produce the programming as soon as they see that education will accept these changes.

Although there are differences in the paths of education and business in developing the use of computerization, there is one major similarity. American business was not able to take advantage of the power of computer technology until many of its basic practices changed. This is equally true in education. Until schools can permit a major alteration in the way teaching is carried on, they must necessarily continue to miss out on the improvement that computer technology can bring.

Notes

1. Becky Smerdon et al., *Teachers' Tools for the 21st Century: A Report on Teachers' Use of Technology* (Washington, D.C.: National Center for Education Statistics, 2000), p. 5.
2. Jay R. Campbell, Catherine M. Hombo, and John Mazzeo, *NAEP 1999 Trends in Academic Progress: Three Decades of Student Performance* (Washington, D.C.: National Center for Education Statistics, 2000), Figure 1.
3. Smerdon et al., p. iii.
4. Ibid.; and Market Data Retrieval, "New Teachers and Technology: Examining Perceptions, Habits, and Professional Development Experiences," survey conducted in 1999.
5. Erik Brynjolfsson and Lorin M. Hitt, "Computing Productivity: Firm-Level Evidence," p. 2, available at http://grace.wharton.upenn.edu/~lhitt/cpg.pdf.
6. Smerdon et al., chap. 7.
7. Plato Learning, Inc.: http://www.plato.com; Scientific Learning: http://www.scilearn.com; and NovaNetLearning, Inc.
8. Kenneth R. Koedinger et al., "Intelligent Tutoring Goes to School in the Big City," *Journal of Artificial Intelligence in Education,* vol. 8, no. 1, 1997, p. 31.
9. Frederick Bennett, *Computers as Tutors: Solving the Crisis in Education* (Sarasota, Fla.: Faben, 1999), chap. 19.

SCHOOL TECHNOLOGY GROWS UP

Kathleen Vail

What does the future hold for educational technology? Kathleen Vail examines political and societal trends, as well as changes in the machines themselves, to outline educational technology trends for the future. Influenced by No Child Left Behind's emphasis on achievement, accountability, and assessment, school districts are looking for ways to use technology to meet new federal reform efforts. In addition, new technologies such as wireless networking, and smaller, more affordable, and user-friendly personal computers, will change the face of educational technology, Vail claims. As you read this article ask yourself, "Will these new technologies significantly change the shape of instruction in U.S. schools?"

Think About This . . .

1. How have recent economic and political trends influenced technology use in the schools? Are these trends likely to continue or abate in the near future?

2. How have current reform's emphasis on achievement, accountability, and assessment changed technology use in the schools? What new instructional roles and strategies are likely to become more important because of these reforms?

3. In the future, will changes in technology use in the schools be driven more by technological changes, improvements in the machines themselves, or societal changes? Why?

4. How can technology help you meet reform's new instructional demands for teachers?

The second half of the 1990s was a heady time for technology. Education was the eagerly sought-after target market, and money for research and development flowed freely. Nearly every month brought a new piece of equipment or cutting-edge application breathlessly promising to transform education as we know it.

But today, after the dot.com bust and well into a lingering economic downturn, the novelty of educational technology has worn off. Venture capital is scarce. Many of the companies offering must-have services and gadgets no longer exist. States face crippling budget deficits, and school districts are raising real estate taxes, laying off teachers, and cutting programs.

Gone are the days when a well-known and influential software company president could say with a straight face that schools needed to be persuaded to upgrade and replace their hardware and software every two or three years. Schools are lucky these days to find the money to keep their existing network and computer systems up and running.

But despite the current economic realities, education technology is alive and kicking. It did, after all, transform education—just not as quickly as those in the industry had hoped. All school districts have instructional computers, and virtually all school buildings are connected to the Internet. Most states and districts have technology plans, and teachers are being trained to integrate technology into their daily classroom lives.

Some people say the bust was beneficial because, in a Darwinian sense, only the best, most cost-efficient, and most practical education technology survived. "It's gotten rid of silly ideas about technology in education, and people who believed it was magic," says Chris Dede, Timothy E. Wirth Professor in Learning Technologies at the Harvard Graduate School.

Educators and school districts continue to try out cutting-edge technology. Education technology companies are still developing new devices and applications, albeit not at the same prodigious pace. So what does this mean for you?

What new technological advances or trends are headed to your schools and classrooms? What can you expect in the next year or two or even the next decade? *ASBJ* asked practitioners and researchers in the education technology field to give us their vision of the future.

Tech Trends

Educators tend to be traditionalists, so persuading them to latch onto the latest technological advancement has been and probably always will be a challenge. That doesn't mean change won't happen. It means that change will happen slowly, and only after most of a district's teachers and administrators are convinced that the new technology or technique will work.

In marketing terms, educators tend to be at the slow end of the adopter scale, which classifies consumers as innovators, early adopters, early majority, late majority, or laggards. Of course, a few innovators or early adopters can be found in your classrooms. Some teachers buy the first generation of any new device or application and put up with the bugs that accompany it. You'll probably always have a few laggards, too, still attached to their rotary telephones.

But most are in the late majority camp: They want to see if something works—and works well—before embracing it.

Contributing to resistance among educators is that new technology is frequently invented before someone needs it. Instead, Dede points out, teachers should find technology solutions that fit identified needs. "Start with the learning, whom are you teaching and what your strengths are," he says. "If you start with technology, it's a solution looking for a problem."

It's fortunate, then, that folks in the field say education technology is increasingly viewed as a tool, as means to an end, which has been the goal all along. Schools and teachers embrace technology only when they see a need for it. "People don't adopt technology for its own sake," says John Bailey, technology director for the U.S. Department of Education. "They do it to help solve a problem."

Bailey's boss, President Bush, handed schools a big reason to further adopt education technology in the form of the No Child Left Behind Act. Many in the field believe the federal law is driving technological changes in school districts and classrooms. In fact, Bailey says it would be nearly impossible for schools to meet federal requirements without using technology.

From Vail, K. (2003). *School technology grows up.* American School Board Journal, 190(9), 34–37. *Reprinted with permission of the* American School Board Journal.

If this is the case, it's not surprising that a number of new developments focus on the NCLB mantra: achievement, accountability, and assessment. Also, cutting-edge trends are building on or improving existing technology—figuring out different, better, and faster ways to use it, rather than reinventing the school technology wheel.

One-to-One Computing

Get used to the term "one-to-one computing," in which one student works with one computer or one computer-like device. You'll probably hear it frequently in the next few years.

"We won't experience the real potential of technology until we get to one-to-one computing," Bailey says. "Not only are kids sharing computers, but instructional time is being cut. If you want to go to the next generation of learning, you need a one-on-one environment."

Those who say this trend is coming to your district aren't necessarily just talking about students using computers at school. They are also talking about letting students take them home.

Two devices—the laptop and the personal digital assistant (PDA)—are at the top of the one-to-one computing list. Their usefulness and practicality, as well as their cost-effectiveness, are being debated and tested in several states and individual school systems.

Some districts, such as the Henrico County Public Schools near Richmond, Va., are experimenting with providing laptops to large groups of students. Henrico has leased laptops from Apple and loaned them to all middle and high school students. Maine is providing laptops on an even larger scale: one for every middle-schooler in the state.

One-to-one proponents say teaching and learning change in the classroom when students have their own computers. And learning doesn't have to end when the school bell rings. "We are all learning together," says Henrico Superintendent Mark Edwards. "It has really created a dynamic model of lifelong learning. Every day teachers are demonstrating that by learning about a new tool, and they are excited about it."

Handhelds also can help districts achieve one-on-one access, but while they're cheaper than laptops, they don't have as much computing power. Still, they have their champions, such as Elliot Soloway, a professor in the University of Michigan's College of Engineering, School of Education, and School of Information.

Soloway, who founded the Center for Highly Interactive Computing in Education, designs software for handhelds. He predicts the devices will have a profound effect on teaching and learning. Soloway says their relatively low cost—generally $150 to $200 each—will benefit districts and notes that what PDAs lack in power, they make up in portability and ease of use. Kids love them, in part because of their similarities to the ubiquitous Gameboy.

Problems, however, do exist. PDAs were invented for the business market, and their applications haven't quite come around to the classroom, although companies that specifically market to schools are working on that. Soloway and his research partner, Cathie Norris, a professor in the Department of Cognition and Technology at the University of North Texas School of Education, recently posted free software and curriculum for handhelds and got 100,000 downloads.

Norris says most elementary and middle school students don't always need the power of a desktop or laptop computer. "This is overkill to begin with," she says. "The schools are having to buy the technology—bigger, faster, more powerful machines—because we are coming up with newer versions of Windows, when we don't need all the capacity now."

Regardless of the device that gets you there, one-to-one computing and portability open possibilities that previously didn't exist, according to Stephen Arnold, founder and managing general partner of the venture capital firm Polaris Venture Partners and vice chairman of the board of the George Lucas Educational Foundation.

"What it does is collapse the distance between question and answer. In the old days, access to information was a barrier to getting information, because you had to go to the library," says Arnold. "Technology decreases barriers to availability and to browseable, searchable databases."

Portals to the Future

With No Child Left Behind, teachers and schools will live and die by data. This requirement is driving several technology changes in schools and is forcing even the most recalcitrant teacher to learn how to use the computer.

Using electronic tools, teachers are becoming "data miners"—able to drill down through information and pull up the test data they need to make instructional decisions. With data mining, teachers know which students had trouble with certain concepts or skills immediately, rather than waiting for months for test scores to be processed and sent back.

The challenge is helping teachers become comfortable with using computers and data to make instructional decisions.

To address the comfort factor, the Boston Public Schools are developing portals—Web windows or homepages that teachers can use to access student data. No longer will district employees have to have a degree in statistics to find out how their students are doing on standardized tests. Teachers will use customized homepages to get student information from the schools' central database.

"A teacher in fifth grade can look at fourth-grade MCAS results for her students," says Steven Gag, special adviser on technology to Boston Mayor Thomas Menino. "When you go on the [Web] site, you need a little bit of training, not an extensive amount of training."

Although the trend is to make data mining as easy as possible, training is bound to be an issue, especially for teachers who have been particularly resistant to using computers or other technology. Florida's Santa Rosa County School District offers training on how to retrieve data and what to do with it once they get it.

"Data is not any good unless used in the appropriate way," says Vickie Beagle, Santa Rosa's director of in-service and instructional technology. "If teachers have all this data and don't know how to figure it out, how to say, 'Here are my needs and this is what I need to change to help this child's performance,' then they don't need the data. The key is what to do with the information once you get it. It's one part of the big picture."

Santa Rosa uses data teams and data coaches—lead teachers with technology expertise and an interest in student data—to help the other teachers along. Using Santa Rosa's data management system, teachers can get specific and detailed information on each student's skill level. The system also allows teachers to point and click to get strategies and lesson plans to help teach the skills.

Testing, Testing

Before test scores can be available at the click of a mouse, though, a lot of information must be processed and flowed into databases. The need to input test data and compute it swiftly is leading the charge for electronic testing.

To make sure they are making Adequate Yearly Progress, as defined under NCLB, "schools will need information on how kids are doing early in the year and frequently after that," says Randy Bennett, director of strategic planning for Educational Testing Service Research.

"If not, they won't know which kids to target and move forward," he says. "They will need information frequently and [information that] comes back immediately."

According to Bennett, about half the states are either working on an electronic testing program or actually have one in their classrooms. Multiple-choice questions lend themselves to electronic testing, but with the advent of sophisticated essay-reading software, more complex tests also could be given and scored on computers.

The main advantage of electronic testing, Bennett says, is the speed with which districts or classroom teachers get back the results. In the current paper-based system, booklets are mailed or trucked back to an outside agency that scans and processes the test. Tests that require grading of open-ended responses involve more shipping, cataloging, and inputting of scores. It could be six months before results are returned, but in the context of NCLB, a six-month turnaround time is not good enough.

"One attraction to online testing is that the turnaround time can be reduced from months to weeks, days, or maybe hours as processes get put into place to do analysis more quickly," Bennett says.

Access issues arise, of course. Schools might not have enough computers for all students to take the tests at the same time. As electronic testing becomes more prevalent. Bennett predicts, schools will make more use of PDAs for testing. But for electronic testing to move forward, money must be available for teacher training, software, hardware, and maintenance.

"Once you've made that investment, a number of states and districts believe [electronic testing] will be cheaper to operate than the paper-based testing program because you no longer have to ship materials or print materials," says Bennett. "If you can eliminate a good part of human scoring by using reading programs, there's a large cost savings there, too."

Bring on the Broadband

Many schools already have high-speed, or broadband, access to the Internet. So the question isn't whether you have broadband, but what you are doing with it. Unfortunately, even if the connections are robust, the content and the applications are not. The possibilities seem limitless, but good-quality multimedia curricula and applications are in short supply.

Cable in the Classroom, a nonprofit education consortium of cable companies, attempted this spring to get the educational broadband ball rolling by creating a free Shakespeare unit, which uses live-streaming video so students can compare two performances of the "to be or not to be" soliloquy in *Hamlet*.

"This is meant to be a catalyst," says executive director Peggy O'Brien. "Teachers and schools in general would begin to insist on content available like this. It's a big order; it's reinventing a few things."

Milton Chen, executive director of the George Lucas Education Foundation, compares the state of multimedia education with educational television 30 years ago. He believes children's educational television never reached its full potential because it didn't have a consistent source of funding. Without private or public funding, he notes, content won't grow.

"What is needed are breakthroughs in content," says Chen. "We are on the brink of a new, multimedia world, and we need new forms of educational content."

Multimedia content on the Internet has the potential to alter how we think of education and schools. "The argument is when students and teachers have ability to access content from the greatest libraries, museums, that will change the nature of instructional materials and experiences," says Chen.

Going Mobile

Laptops and handhelds are portable, but your Internet connections are in your walls. For the portable revolution to be realized, many people say schools must go wireless, so that students can connect to the Internet anywhere in the school building. Wireless networks, backers say, will encourage more computer and Internet usage among students and teachers.

"If you have the wireless configuration, you can access anywhere in the building. The next step is to find the best ways for technologies to improve learning, so we can capitalize on how best to use technology," says Dean Bergman, technology director for the Nebraska Department of Education.

For example, wireless networks make COWs—computers on wheels—a workable idea. With COW carts, laptops or other portables can move from room to room without the concern of where they would plug in for a connection to the Internet.

Wireless connections also can be useful within a single classroom, says Bergman. A classroom might have only one wired connection to the Internet, but with a wireless tower, that connection can be beamed to a roomful of laptops. Schools then can add computers without making accommodations for additional space and more cable and wiring.

But with wi-fi—as the techies call high-frequency wireless networking—the good news of easy connectivity is bad news for security. You don't have to be a sophisticated hacker to tap into a nearby wireless network, so users suggest limiting wi-fi to the classroom. Keep the school server and other vital systems plugged into the wall.

On the Horizon

No look at the future of education technology would be complete without a peek into what might be coming 10 or 20 years from now.

One vision of the future is a virtual one. Chris Dede has been described as a futurist, but he's also a respected researcher in education technology, particularly on the use of virtual environments in the classroom. Through his work. Dede hopes to reach children who don't perform well in a classroom setting. He's convinced that multimedia technology is key to connecting with these under-performing students.

"We work because we believe it can reach kids whom traditional methods haven't reached," Dede says. "Let's find creative ways, different kinds of pedagogies. That's where learning technologies should focus."

Dede is currently using a National Science Foundation grant to study how multiuser virtual environment experiential simulators, or MUVEES, can be used to teach science. In a unit called River City, for example, students move individually or as a team through a fictional 19th-century town, using clues to figure out why there has been a cholera outbreak among the city's poorest residents.

Another vision involves ever-smaller handhelds. Margaret Riel, a visiting professor at Pepperdine University's Graduate School of Education and Psychology, sees a day when electronic communication devices are as small and portable as sheets of paper. This will change the education culture, she believes, because schools will embrace community among students rather than fight it.

"Schools can take advantage of collective thinking power," says Riel, a researcher in collaboration, communication, and education technology. "With these flat devices, collaboration won't need to be as noisy as it is now."

A changing school culture is also predicted by Terry Rogers, president and CEO of Advanced Network and Services, a nonprofit organization that creates programs to explore the future of education technology. "Each child in our education system should be able to get the learning environment ideally suited to that child," he says. "Technology can deliver this goal, but it will require profound change. Such transformation is difficult for many of us who are invested in business as usual."

But the students of today and tomorrow are not beholden to the status quo, these and other observers note. Whatever the future of technology holds, our children are ready for it. The digital age is their age, and they are looking to us to help them get there.

CLASSROOM OF ONE
Gene Maeroff

The previous articles have assumed a traditional classroom structure of one teacher working face-to-face with a group of 25 to 30 students. Do students really need to attend a classroom to learn? Gene Maeroff's article describes the developing field of online learning, exploring both its potential and possible pitfalls. Maeroff contends that online learning is perfectly suited for today's students, who have grown up with technology and have learned to use it in every facet of their lives. Online learning provides instructional flexibility, but experts suggest that it is not for everyone. It requires students who are tech-savvy, mature, and disciplined. The role of online learning in charter schools and homeschooling is being actively debated, with long-term governance and finance implications. As you read this article ask yourself, "How important will online learning be in education's future?"

Think About This . . .

1. What are the advantages of online learning? The disadvantages? Will online learning expand? Why?

2. What types of students succeed in online learning? How effective do you think online learning would be for the students you will teach?

3. What are some of the larger governance and finance issues involved in online learning? How will these influence the future of online learning in education?

4. How important will online learning be in your future? How important will it be for the students you teach? What factors could change your answer to this question?

A classroom of one—the ultimate in small classes—is now available to any student with a computer and a connection to the Internet. Online learning seems appropriate for youngsters who have grown up with electronic technology.

Computers, cell phones, and fax machines have surrounded this generation since infanthood. Using information technology and computer gadgetry is as natural to them as eating and sleeping. Their earliest toys contained chips to make dogs bark and dolls talk, and playing computer games is a favorite pastime for many young people.

Their music has always traveled with them, and they think it ridiculous to fetter themselves to a telephone by a wire. They are plugged in 24/7. The older ones even attend virtual college fairs, no longer visiting in person all of the campuses that interest them. Instead, they browse through electronic exhibit booths at college Web sites, then submit applications online. They pass from high school to college with their own computers and other accoutrements of the cyber age—cell phones, graphing calculators, DVD players, MP3 files, and perhaps Palm organizers as well. Remember: Most young people getting their bachelor's degrees in 2003 were born in the same year as IBM's first personal computer. The possibility of adapting to an online course would not faze them.

"They come to college with an understanding of the tools of technology," says Bruce Chaloux, director of the Electronic Campus of the Southern Regional Education Board. "They bank this way: they shop this way; they learn this way. When this group floods higher education, you will see signs of change."

It would hardly be a stretch for most of today's high school and college students to take a Web-based course. Online learning requires more than comfort

From Maeroff, G. (2003). *Classroom of one.* American School Board Journal, 190(2), 26–29. *Reprinted with permission of the* American School Board Journal.

with technology, however. Students need some degree of maturity and a measure of self-discipline. Online learning is a kind of independent study that students must be motivated to pursue. Therefore, the first step for youngsters to take before hitting the Web is to determine whether it is an environment in which they are ready to go it alone.

Some institutions try to help students determine if they can exercise the responsibility that distance learning demands before they register for an online course. San Diego State University, for example, provides guidance for students contemplating enrolling in distance or online courses. A self-administered quiz on the university's Web site asks candidates to consider the following questions: Do I like working and learning on a computer or television? Am I comfortable resolving technology problems when they arise? Would I want to learn new software or a set of online procedures just to access the course materials or chat with the faculty and others who are taking the course? Do I work well alone? Am I self-disciplined enough to follow the lessons on my own without peer pressure or pressure from the course instructor? Will I be comfortable if I don't get to see the instructor in person? Will I be comfortable if I have to ask questions via e-mail?

Julie Young, the executive director of Florida Virtual School, a state-sponsored secondary program, readily concedes that online studies are not appropriate for all youngsters. Her simple three-part, self-administered test for potential students asks whether they can manage their time, summon up motivation, and work without a teacher in the room.

Why Online Learning?

The flexibility of online learning is a strong motivator for some students. Katrin Tabellion, for instance, found that the University of Missouri's virtual high school met her needs because her father's job kept the family relocating around the world.

"I wanted to get my high school diploma," she said in an interview by e-mail from Ghana, her residence at the time, "but since I was moving quite often I got the idea of a long-distance course. I just looked up some schools on the Internet, and the University of Missouri was most appealing to me. The biggest advantage is that you can choose the time to study or to take your exams. You don't have to be at one place at a certain time. You can do it from anywhere you like." She conceded that despite these incentives, "it is also hard sometimes to make yourself sit down

and study. It is easy to say, 'Oh, I'll just wait until tomorrow.'"

Online learning has much to offer certain students under the right circumstances. It can potentially present content every bit as good as that conveyed in a classroom. Students taking online classes can interact with teachers who monitor their progress and extend learning through threaded discussions, chat rooms, and exchanges of e-mail when courses operate properly. Students often use books in online courses identical to those found in classrooms.

Many proponents of e-learning envision this approach as primarily an activity at the secondary level for students who might take an extra class or two online. They don't advocate it as a full-time pursuit. Nor do they see it as an appropriate way for elementary children to learn. Online courses can serve youngsters whose own high schools do not offer Advanced Placement and other specialized courses that they want to take. It allows students to add courses when their classroom schedules are full, letting them collaborate online with students and teachers from other schools.

Advanced Placement and specialized courses are available online through a number of sources. Some school districts have turned to for-profit companies that offer these courses, such as Apex Learning, Jones Knowledge, and Pearson Education Technologies.

Scheduling Needs, Special Needs

Students have many other reasons for seeking online education. Adolescents are notorious for their late-to-bed and late-to-rise habits, making it a chore to get up for school in the morning. After-school employment, which causes them to work into the night and do homework (if they do it) afterward, exacerbates the problem. They do not want to harness themselves to society's clock.

Still other secondary students need more time or less time than the regular schedule allows to make their way through a course. At least some online courses may appeal to high school youngsters in these circumstances.

Florida Virtual School schedules courses so that students may tailor them to their time needs. Students indicate when they enroll in each course whether they want to pursue the work on a traditional schedule, an accelerated schedule, or an extended schedule. Those choosing the second option can take less than the usual time to complete a course. Those choosing the third option must obtain the permission of parents or school counselors to pursue the extended schedule, which adds several months to the time allotted for the completion of the course.

Students with disabilities are yet another group for whom online learning holds potential advantages. Students at the Model School for the Deaf in Washington, D.C., as well as hearing impaired children at other schools around the country, participated in the courses of the Virtual High School, an online learning consortium based in Concord, Mass., that was funded by a grant from the U.S. Department of Education. "It put our students on a more level playing field with students at other schools who participated," says Joyce Barrett, who coordinated the use of technology for the Model School, part of Gallaudet University.

The Model School has too small an enrollment to offer the courses in its classrooms, so it turned to the Virtual High School. "Because it involved reading and writing, our students could interact with hearing students in regular classrooms without having to be in those classrooms with interpreters. It gave them exposure to different kinds of kids in different places," Barrett says.

Cyber Charter Questions

Though online learning is proliferating, nagging questions remain about policies regarding these programs and the suitability of the approach for students below the college level, especially for the youngest students.

Pennsylvania and Ohio provide case studies in the problems that can erupt when states allow the creation of cyber charter schools, many of which enroll elementary school students. In both states, cyber schools flew under the radar of legislation authorizing charter schools to reach a safe landing, and some of the results may tarnish what might otherwise be a beneficial enterprise. Advocates of homeschooling, for instance, shrewdly sought to use online learning as a pipeline to public funding. A survey by the Pennsylvania School Boards Association found that almost half the pupils in one of the state's largest cyber charter schools were being schooled at home.

Lawmakers will not easily reconcile this dispute. On the one hand, online learning is supposed to overcome strictures of time and place, facilitating education at settings that students choose, including their homes. Until now, though, home-schooling has not involved taking money away from the public school district in which a youngster resides and awarding it to a cyber charter school.

Officials need to revisit policies to decide if their intent was to allow cyber charter schools to serve as vehicles for home-schooling at public expense. If policy makers see online learning primarily as a service that allows high school students to add a course or two to their schedules, then they must address the cyber homeschooling situation.

Perhaps in this era of wider choice, however, homeschooling might become a more widely accepted option and online learning might be the vehicle to make that more possible. If so, such a development should be the result of carefully considered policy, not an accidental outcome of charter school legislation. Furthermore, officials must also reexamine their regulatory approaches to ensure adequate monitoring of students enrolled in online courses. In Ohio, one cyber school was ordered to return $1.6 million to the state because it could not document its enrollment, and another had to drop hundreds of students from its rolls when it appeared that they weren't going online and doing the work.

Two Clashing Visions

What is the proper role of online learning in public education? Currently, two clashing visions of that role exist. The Virtual High School consortium represents one approach. Its model has students attend regular bricks-and-mortar schools and take online courses in addition to and in place of some regular courses that they pursue in classrooms. The other approach, as embodied in some cyber charter schools, would allow youngsters of elementary as well as secondary age to skip in-person classes altogether and pursue their studies entirely on the Internet at public expense, in some cases supplementing teaching their parents provide around the dining room table.

Most families will almost certainly maintain their allegiance to bricks-and-mortar schools, but online learning could still make serious inroads among the nation's 53 million elementary and secondary students. Cyber charters in particular are growing in popularity, despite the controversy. For example, the Western Pennsylvania Cyber School in Midland, a town near the intersection of Pennsylvania, Ohio, and West Virginia, had 529 students its first year and doubled its enrollment to about 1,100 by its second year. The town of Midland's entire population was 3,300, so the only way the school could grow so large was to enroll students from throughout the state, taking youngsters who resided in 105 school systems in 23 counties. The state school boards association says that only 11 of Western Pennsylvania Cyber School's students lived in the chartering district. Students, ranging from kindergarten to 12th grade, choose courses from nine different curricula.

The instructional methods at Western Pennsylvania Cyber School, depending on the courses, exemplify the four main ways online learning is occurring across the country:

- Real-time online, synchronous instruction, in which students communicate with teachers from their computers as the teachers teach the lessons.

- Asynchronous instruction, in which students work on their own and later receive messages on their computers from the teachers.

- Web-based, packaged programs consisting of a pretest, a tutorial, a practice, and a posttest that the students submit electronically, without contact with teachers.

- Traditional book–based courses, in which students, working online at a pace that they set for themselves, get assignments, turn them in, and receive responses from teachers.

It's clear that state funding regulations will have to be adjusted to address online learning. The mismatch of state regulations and the reality at online schools can be seen at the Daniel Jenkins Academy of Technology, a combination middle school/high school near the center of the Florida peninsula, a rural portion of the state between Tampa and Orlando.

After proceeding through a classroom-based middle school curriculum infused with technology, students continue into a high school at the same site in which the main subjects are offered online through Florida Virtual School. Four days a week they have to show up at the school even though no high-school-level courses are taught there. They might stay home one day a week. State regulations generate per-pupil funding based on their attendance. They can choose to do as much or as little of their course work on computers—at school or at home—as they wish.

"If it were up to me," says Sue Braiman, principal of the combined school, "I would ask them how many days they want to come to school and leave it at that, but Florida has a funding mechanism tied to the time students spend sitting in seats, not to learning objectives. It's absurd." But so long as they had to attend school, even though they did not have to pursue their studies while there, the school promoted the opportunity for socialization for the students who might not get it otherwise.

The future of online courses at the precollegiate level will depend as much on the resolution of policy disputes about the purposes of this kind of learning as on the answers to questions about the quality of the offerings. School boards, teacher unions, advocates for homeschooling, and for-profit education businesses have all jumped into the fray. Online learning could play a constructive role in the education of some children before they reach colleges and universities, but it remains to be seen if it will be allowed to fulfill that potential.

TAPPING THE RESOURCES OF THE WORLD WIDE WEB FOR INQUIRY IN MIDDLE SCHOOL

Mark Windschitl and Janet Irby

Acquiring information is only one educational goal. Students also must learn to think critically and investigate problems on their own. An important question facing teachers today is, How can technology be used to promote student inquiry? Mark Windschitl and Janet Irby describe different ways the World Wide Web can be used to promote student investigations. The World Wide Web is a vast repository of information on the Internet that can serve as a source of information for students. The vastness of this storehouse has both advantages and disadvantages; although the answers to most questions are there, it can often be very difficult to locate specific information.

The wealth of information on the World Wide Web can serve as the basis for authentic inquiry into a variety of subjects ranging from science and math to social studies and language arts. Teachers play a crucial role in helping students learn how to access and use this vast information source. As you read this article ask yourself, "How important will the World Wide Web be for instruction in tomorrow's classrooms?"

Think About This . . .

1. What is inquiry? How appropriate is it as an instructional strategy for the content areas and students you will be teaching?

2. What are the advantages and disadvantages of the World Wide Web as an information source? What can teachers do to minimize the disadvantages?

3. What are the similarities and differences of inquiry in the various disciplines? What can teachers do to help students understand inquiry commonalities across disciplines?

4. What obstacles do you anticipate in attempting to integrate technology-based inquiry into your instruction? What can you do to address these obstacles?

Conducting independent inquiry is a highly valued academic enterprise for middle school learners. Student inquiry cultivates skills such as developing meaningful questions, deciding what information is relevant to problem-solving, critically analyzing sources of data, making inferences from data, and making judgments about claims. As adolescents develop an increasingly comprehensive understanding of subject matter and a growing intellectual independence, they become able candidates for inquiry-based learning.

To accommodate an emphasis on inquiry, powerful computer-based tools are poised to assume a new role in middle school classrooms. The most flexible and multifaceted of these tools is the World Wide Web. The Web opens doors to thousands of information "spaces" filled with text, graphics, and sound—for those who are willing to venture onto it. In addition, the scope of available information on the Web increases daily and many middle school teachers are anxious to learn how to exploit this resource.

In this article we argue for the cautiously expanded use of the Web for inquiry across the middle school curriculum and, along with supporting the *why* of this expanded web use, some examples of *how* the Web can be used for inquiry are included. We begin by examining the call for student inquiry by national curriculum organizations and the attendant call for the use of technology to facilitate inquiry processes. Next, the Web is described, including honest assessments of its distractions and its academic utility. Finally, specific features of the Web are identified that support student inquiry as practiced in science, mathematics, social studies, and language arts.

The Emphasis on Inquiry

Science, social studies, math, and language arts are subjects that typically engage learners in inquiry. The different subject area approaches are distinct in character, but are similar in that they encourage learners to think critically and wrestle with authentic problems as do professional scientists, mathematicians, historians, and writers. National Standards promote inquiry at the middle level: In language arts, students conduct "research on issues and interests by generating ideas and questions, and by posing problems" (Wilhelm, 1996, p. 9); in science, "inquiry is basic to science education and a controlling principle in the ultimate organization and selection of students' activities" (National Research Council, 1996, p. 105); in math, students "understand that there is no one right way to solve mathematical problems, but that different methods have different advantages and disadvantages" (Kendall & Marzano, 1995, p. 91); and, in history, students work "backward from some issue, problem, or event, to explain its

From Windschitl, M., & Irby, J. (1999). *Tapping the resources of the World Wide Web for inquiry in middle school.* Middle School Journal, 30(3), 40–45. *Reprinted with permission of the National Middle School Association.*

causes that arose from some beginning and developed through subsequent transformations over time" (Kendall & Marzano, 1995, p. 122).

These curriculum documents also emphasize the role of technology as a resource for the inquiry process. The National Standards recommend the following uses of technology: In language arts, students use a "variety of technological and informational resources to gather and synthesize information" (Wilhelm, 1996, p. 9); in science, students use "appropriate tools (including computers) and techniques to gather, analyze and interpret scientific data" (National Research Council, 1996, p. 145); and, in math, students understand that "the development of computers has opened many new doors to mathematics" (Kendall & Marzano, 1995, p. 113).

Of the variety of computer-based resources for inquiry, the World Wide Web is unique in that, unlike other computer-based applications like tutorials, simulations, or drill and practice, the Web was not originally designed for educational use. Its domain includes government, private, and commercial interests that all influence what is available on the Web and how this information is "marketed" to the computer-using public. Additionally, Internet service providers have enchanted much of the educational community about visions of global connectedness and access to information, while providing little evidence of its benefit to young readers. The Web has been the subject of so much hyperbole that it is time to take a realistic look at its potential role in the classroom, specifically in supporting the evolving inquiry practices of middle school students. But before we examine this issue, we must first answer the question, "What is the World Wide Web and *how* do students interact with it?"

The World Wide Web

In 1969 the United States Department of Defense linked computers together from several military sites in order to form a research network (Ryder & Hughes, 1997). From this rudimentary beginning, the network grew in size and scope by connecting with networks of other government agencies, educational institutions, and businesses. Today, this mammoth network of networks is known as the Internet. One of the most popular and versatile components of the Internet is the World Wide Web.

The Web is a vast repository of information and misinformation. Thousands of computers all over the world function as Web "sites" with "pages" that can be accessed by anyone connected to the Web. The Web

pages themselves, containing text and graphics (such as photographs, diagrams, or maps), are similar to multimedia; many pages now even include sound and video clips. The text on a Web page contains "hyperlinked" terms that, when clicked on, transport the user to another page that has information related to the linked term. This ability to move, via links, through virtual space has been touted as an intellectual lever for learners, who use this flexibility to construct their own understanding of a body of information.

Another characteristic of the Web is its lack of oversight or regulation; almost anyone can maintain a site. There are hundreds of thousands of pages posted by individuals, businesses, educational institutions, and innumerable special interests. Government entities also have a significant presence on the Web. For example, *Thomas*, a Web site maintained by the United States Congress, contains exhaustive information about voting records of members of the legislature, bills pending before Congress, and timetables for congressional activities. The number of such sites on the Web has grown exponentially in the last two years and will continue to grow at a similar pace in the foreseeable future.

Unfortunately, the characteristic of having large amounts of linked information is a double-edged sword with regard to academic use. Students often lack the skills to search for pertinent information, and the problem is exacerbated when using the Web because of the pervasive presence of useless information. Students can easily get lost in a thicket of pages containing irrelevant or invalid information. The hyperlinks embedded in Web pages pose another problem; they seem to beckon users to jump from site to site without stopping to invest the time to comprehend. Without instructional focus, students often leapfrog from one "cool" site to another. These impulsive and fragmented experiences fuel the notion that Web-supported exercises are like learning from 15-second sound-bytes on TV. This kind of learning, although technically interactive and student-centered, undermines the claims that Web-based activities lead students to construct meaningful ideas or promote higher order thinking.

There are, however, emerging practices with Web-supported activities that show promise for meaningful learning. These practices integrate Web use into a larger framework of inquiry-based instruction and include logistical ways to support productive searches for information.

For example, if one views the Web as a large database of databases, it makes sense that skills in searching for information become a priority for inquiry. There are specially designed search pages into which one can type keywords, and with the click of a mouse, find a list of dozens of Web pages that relate to those keywords. Understanding the nature of keywords, alternative search terms, and Boolean logic (using AND and OR together with keywords) are integral to Web literacy.

Assessing the accuracy and validity of information is another inquiry skill that is important in an environment where there are no restrictions on who can post information. Normal editorial filters do not exist for most Web material, and, as people have become increasingly enamored with the sheer volume of information on the Web, judging the quality of the information and developing the ability to use information productively is often de-emphasized. Students must receive explicit instruction on how valid and convincing arguments are constructed so they can recognize reason when they see it, and so they, in turn, can construct inferences and arguments from the wealth of information available on the Web.

Determining how the Web can be used as a tool for inquiry in the different subject areas is a progressive move toward improving instruction in the core middle school program. Inquiry learning is viewed as a capstone experience for middle school learners because it cultivates students' responsibility for their own learning and introduces students to the authentic intellectual pursuits of scientists, mathematicians, historians, and writers. Inquiry comes in various flavors according to subject area, but in all cases, the students generate questions of interest, investigate the question by accessing and analyzing information, and make reasoned inferences about the subject in question. We will now turn our attention to specific instances of why (and how) the Web should be used in various subject areas.

Inquiry in Science and Mathematics

The term "inquiry" has been closely associated with science learning. Science inquiry is linked with the process skills of observation, question generation, data collection, data analysis, inference, and communication of results. What role can the Web play in middle school science inquiry?

The Web provides access to hundreds of data sets that students can download and analyze. Data collection has been so closely tied to experimentation in science that teachers often do not realize that raw data sets are already available from various surveys, observations, and experiments. Government agencies are particularly rich sources of data (e.g., NASA, National Institutes of Health, Census Bureau). These authentic bodies of information range from human gene data to world wide weather readings. Students can download data sets of gene sequences, global temperatures, or census results and use them to identify relationships and trends.

Sometimes, students simply do not know enough about a topic of interest to generate a meaningful question for inquiry. Using special search pages on the Web, students can find background information on everything from the Amazon Rain Forest to heart disease. Most classrooms do not have exhaustive information resources in print for the variety of topics that an entire class of students, engaged in independent projects, would demand. Students are generally subjected to using limited secondary sources such as textbooks or encyclopediae, but the Web provides a wealth of primary sources with extensive information and links to other pertinent sites.

To add richness to the inquiry process, images are often used as a source of information. Managers of Web sites know that, for visitors to maintain interest in their Web site, images captivate more readily than text. With the technology of just two years ago, it was impractical for Web users to wait the minute or two that it took to download an image for display. But now, with recent improvements in software and hardware, full-screen color images can be called up in seconds. Many inquiry topics require visuals to support student understanding, and middle school learners seem strongly attracted to the pictorial beauty of electron microscopy, astronomical images, and undersea photographs. As an added bonus, some Web sites have sizable archives of images specifically for downloading to the students' computers, enabling students to use the images in class reports or presentations.

Another interesting slant on inquiry for middle school students is the investigation of current events. Currency of information is one of the most intriguing features of the Web. In 1994, students around the world could share in the excitement of viewing the comet Shoemaker-Levy 9 that struck Jupiter. The images of this astronomical collision were made available to students on the Web at the same time that scientists around the world got their first look. The visuals made available were impressive; students and scientists could ponder the emerging questions together, "How might the comet's impact affect the surface of Jupiter?" and, "How many comet fragments were there and why?" In addition to individual science organizations furnishing information, entrepreneurs have started several on-line news services and specialized magazines that post information as it happens, often from sources such as oceanographic expeditions or weather stations that provide minute-by-minute updates on exciting phenomena.

Just as science inquiry explores questions about the natural world, mathematics inquiry is based on the exploration of patterns in the theoretical realm of numbers. Mathematics is often linked with science content to provide learners with real-world problems. Students, however, often need an interesting "hook" to engage them in inquiry problems. Recently, a teaching methods class at the University of Washington tackled the question "How many hamburgers are eaten in Seattle every day?" Some students began by contacting the Web site of the National Beef Council, and others collected data from the U.S. Census Bureau on the populations of the United States and Seattle. After some calculations, groups of students arrived at conclusions which were then discussed by the entire class. More importantly, they developed skills in searching the Web, collecting relevant data, and debating the validity of information gathered from certain sources (i.e., Is the Beef Council the best or only source of information on beef consumption?). The census bureau is one of several government agencies that provide rich data sets from which middle school students can identify questions of interest and perform analyses in search of a solution. It is easy to see how the same features of the Web that stimulate scientific inquiry (availability of data sets, current events, and large volumes of background information) can be useful for inquiry in mathematics.

Social Studies

An exercise designed by Parker and Jarolimek (1997) can be adapted to utilize the Web as an information resource, and it demonstrates how the use of the Web should be part of a larger instructional framework; it explicitly introduces students to the skills of creating hypotheses, collecting information, and reasoning about evidence. This exemplary social studies exercise introduces the whole class to the process of inquiry and involves focusing on a complex problem such as the sinking of the Titanic. Students begin by suggesting hypotheses for the ship's sinking and these are written on the board. Then students are given (or they are asked to find) information relevant to one particular aspect of the Titanic such as entries from the captain's diary, facts about the company that built the ship, details of the hull design, or information about icebergs. One by one, as each one of these perspectives is brought to

bear on the event, students vote to erase implausible hypotheses and new ones are generated. In this way, students come to appreciate multiple sources of information and they learn to resolve new facts with the proposed hypotheses. This diversity of background data is hard to come by with the limited resources in many middle schools; but with an hour or two of searching the Web (by either the students or the teacher) and some sharing of "good" Web sites among social studies colleagues, a teacher can find ample background material for this type of whole-class inquiry.

Social studies inquiry involves not only the process of weighing an accumulation of evidence but also resolving several information sources that contain contradictory information. The unregulated nature of the Web makes it a haven for alternative points of view that would not have an audience without Web technology. These sources of information may provide legitimate, alternative views, but they may also provide information that is erroneous, biased, or compromised by critical omissions. Inquiry into such topics as gun control rights takes on new meaning when students find material describing the Brady Bill only a couple clicks away from the National Rifle Association's Web page. The juxtaposition of discrepant information is unique to the world of the Web, and the young inquirer faces an educative dilemma: identifying which information sources are valid to begin with. Rather than viewing the Web as a flawed medium for locating reliable information, teachers can take advantage of these alternative points of view to illustrate multiple perspectives, rhetoric, or propaganda.

Similar to science classes, students in social studies classes are excited by current events. These can be especially stimulating for middle school learners because the publishers of some of these Web pages are students themselves, seeking to share an experience with the world as well as to provide information. For example, compelling firsthand accounts of the earthquake in Kobe, Japan, and the assassination of Israel's Yitzhak Rabin were available on Web pages minutes after the events took place. Students could suggest hypotheses about how countries like Japan or Israel would react to these events and then gather evidence, day by day, to support or refute their ideas.

Social studies also shares with science its value of the image as a source of data. In the case of social studies, the images can be scans of maps, paintings, historical texts, or other cultural artifacts. Some of these Web-based digital artifacts, such as sculptures from museums or items from an archeological dig, are recreated as three-dimensional objects and can be inspected by rotating the image with the click of a mouse. Additionally, museums all over the world are featuring their respective treasures on Web pages and many provide "tours" in which a student can move freely through the rooms of the virtual museum. These features constitute unique resources for inquiry that would not be possible without technology.

Language Arts

Inquiry in the language arts parallels the ways that language is used within society at large. One of those ways is to pose and answer questions about novels, short stories, and poems in order to make sense out of them and to make sense out of human experience. To understand literature, students are also asked to do research on authors and on the historical and cultural context of the work. If the whole class is doing research on one text, students may search critiques of that work posted by classes elsewhere in the world, or they may attempt to contextualize the work by finding relevant historical or sociocultural resources on the Web.

Beyond the study of literature, research goes on in multiple contexts wherever people are constructing knowledge individually or in communities. Using a method called the "I-Search," students pose a question that intrigues them; brainstorm everything they already know about that question; search the library, the community, and the Web for resources to answer the question; and then organize and share the results (Macrorie, 1988). Approaches such as "I-Search" also focus on inquiry processes as much as on products. In addition to searching for answers to questions, students create a narrative about the inquiry, providing opportunities to monitor their own use of the Web and to build those critical skills needed for sorting out sources and the information they provide.

In the language arts classroom, teachers also want their students to understand how various communities use language differently. Through a feature embedded in most Web browsing software (access to electronic discussion groups), students can study language through their participation in on-line discussions. Participation provides a way to extend questions of language use outside the immediate school and community: what is the specialized vocabulary of certain groups, what topics do they discuss, how do participants communicate bias, what are the unspoken rules for language use? Students can make conscious choices to identify with a particular group on-line and to learn from discussion, but they can also simply monitor the way that that group uses language.

In addition, in the last ten years, inquiry in language arts has been supported by a workshop format which encourages students to explore their own experience as a form of self-understanding as well as develop real contexts for publishing their work (Atwell, 1987). In the workshop setting, students are encouraged to write about personal experience and extend that writing into a variety of genres. The Web provides a connection to other young authors who are doing the same thing. Since the Web is so widely accessible, young authors have the opportunity to read a variety of esoteric or nontraditional literature as they browse. The emerging voice of young writers may not find immediate publication in print form, but their works, as well as background information on them and links to other marginalized artists, are available on the Web. Numerous avenues exist for students to publish their work, from setting up their own home pages to posting their work to discussion groups.

Conclusions and Recommendations

The strongest argument for the use of any tool is that it permits activities or insights that could not be realized without it. Can inquiry take place in the classroom without technology? Absolutely! Technology is merely a tool, not an instructional method. Teachers must provide a meaningful framework for inquiry within which students choose among many informational resources. Students must believe that they can pose meaningful questions and construct knowledge for themselves rather than always accepting predigested views of the world. Teachers must help students cultivate the values and discipline necessary for independent exploration. While all these endeavors are completely independent of technology, there remain many unique reasons to be enthusiastic about the Web and its support of inquiry learning.

1. The Web enables immediate access to a significant volume of content information on a variety of subjects.
2. Multiple perspectives on scientific, social, historical, and literary issues are available for review by students, providing ready resources for practicing critical evaluation of texts and other forms of information.
3. Diverse topics found on the Web can prompt student-generated questions for inquiry.

4. The Web contains a wealth of specialized and unique information that is likely to match students' inquiry interests.
5. Current event information is available, making student inquiry more relevant and exciting.
6. Data sets are available from government agencies and other institutions for inspection or downloading.
7. Information in the form of imagery and sound are available in ever increasing amounts.

This article has examined *why* the Web should be used to facilitate the inquiry process in middle school. There are significant logistical and pedagogical concerns about how Web technology should be used in classrooms. Admittedly, only about 9% of classrooms are currently connected to the Web (West, 1996), and most teachers lack the training opportunities to use technology in teaching (Benton Foundation, 1995). In a report prepared for the Educational Summit, Hawkins (1996) reported that the ratio of students to computers is currently about nine to one and will be about three to one around the turn of the century. Hawkins also stressed to summit leaders the importance of more school connections to the Web and the necessity for extensive preservice and inservice teacher training. Teacher training should begin with the basics of using inquiry in the classroom—*without* technological resources. When teachers are comfortable with the use of inquiry strategies, they are more likely to employ resources such as the Web in a meaningful way.

When teachers have attained this comfort level, they can move on to workshops and inservice that focus on the technical aspects of using Web browsers such as Netscape™ or Internet Explorer™. To support this process, conferences of professional teachers' organizations offer many sessions each year on the use of technology in the classroom. Conferences are also places where teachers can come together and share Web experiences and get a clearer picture of what they can do in *their* classrooms with *their* students.

The Web does not often deserve the hyperbole that surrounds it, but when well-planned instruction includes the Web as a tool for inquiry, learning can take place across broader conceptual territory and at deeper intellectual levels. As middle school students take more responsibility for their learning and initiate investigations of interest to them, they deserve to have the best tools made available to them for the journey.

References

Atwell, N. (1987). *In the middle.* Portsmouth NH: Boynton/Cook.

Benton Foundation. (1995). *The learning connection.*

Hawkins, J. (1996). *Technology in education: Transitions* (Briefing paper prepared for the 1996 Education Summit).

Kendall, J. S., & Marzano, R. J. (1995). *The systematic identification and articulation of content standards and benchmarks.* Aurora, CO: Mid-continent Regional Educational Laboratory.

Macrorie, K. (1988). *The I-Search paper.* Portsmouth, NH: Heinemann.

National Research Council. (1996). *National Science Education Standards.* Washington, DC: National Academy Press.

Ryder, R. J., & Hughes, T. (1997). *Internet for educators.* New Jersey: Merrill/Prentice Hall.

Parker, W., & Jarolimek, J. (1997). *Social studies in elementary education* (10th ed.). Upper Saddle River, NJ: Merrill/Prentice Hall.

West, P. (1996, May 22). Schools, libraries seen bridging technology gap. *Education Week, 9,* 16–17.

Wilhelm, J. D. (1996). *Standards in practice grades 6–8.* Urbana, IL: National Council of Teachers of English.

ADDITIONAL READINGS

Evans, D. (2002). Technological progress: An oxymoron? *Education Week, 10*(6), 37.

Firek, H. (2003). One order of ed. tech. coming up . . . You want fries with that? *Phi Delta Kappan, 84*(8), 596–597.

Joyner, A. (2003). A foothold for handhelds. *American School Board Journal, 190*(9), 42–45.

Snider, J. (2001). Should school choice come via the internet? *Education Week, 21*(16), 41.

Tell, C. (2000). The I-Generation—from toddlers to teenagers: A conversation with Jane M. Healy. *Educational Leadership, 58*(2), 8–13.

Vail, K. (2003). Next generation divide. *American School Board Journal, 190*(7), 23–25.

EXPLORING THE INTERNET

NetLearn: Internet Learning Resources
http://www.rgu.ac.uk/celt/learning/page.cfm?pge=4548
This site contains a compendium of Internet learning resources for teachers.

Reinventing Schools: The Technology is Now!
http://www.nap.edu/readingroom/books/techgap/index.html
You will find valuable information on this site about the status of educational technology across the nation.

Edutech's Online Resource for Education and Technologies
http://tecfa.unige.ch/info-edu-comp.html
This site contains valuable information about different uses of technology in education.

National Center for Technology Planning
http://www.nctp.com
You will find valuable information on this site about how to integrate technology into your school and classroom.

PART SEVEN

Governance and Finance

School governance and school funding may seem remotely related to classroom activities, but veterans know better. How schools are run and how school districts use money make big differences in teachers' quality of life and the quality of students' learning experiences. In addition, reform efforts that address funding inequalities, increase decision making at the school level, and provide more choice to parents are changing teaching today.

The way that the nation's schools are governed and financed grew out of the resolution of issues that were important in the history of our country. For example, the First Amendment to the Constitution, created in 1791 as part of the Bill of Rights, established the principle of separation of church and state. This made federal funding for religious schools illegal. In addition, the Tenth Amendment, also part of the Bill of Rights, said that areas not assigned to the federal government would be handled by each state. This amendment passed the responsibility for managing schools on to the individual states, and in doing so implicitly removed the federal government from a central role in running and operating schools. The way schools are managed today—state offices and boards of education, school districts within states, and the organization and management of individual schools—is an outcome of these historical decisions.

Although education officially is a state responsibility, the federal government has passed a number of mandates that states are required to fulfill. Some notable ones include Title IX, passed in 1972, which forbids discrimination in any school program on the basis of gender; the Individuals with Disabilities Education Act (IDEA), passed in 1975, which requires that learners with exceptionalities be integrated into the regular school environment as much as possible; and more recently, the No Child Left Behind Act, passed in 2001, which requires a high level of school accountability for the achievement of all students regardless of background.

Responsibility for school funding also crosses state and federal lines. For example, in spite of funding being the primary responsibility of the states, Congress passed the *Northwest Ordinance Acts of 1785* and *1787,* which reserved one section of each six-mile square township of 36 sections for the support of public education. So, although not directly involved in governing or operating schools, the federal government provided material support for schools and education, a tradition that persists to this day.

The governance of schools is also a shared responsibility. Although the federal government provides some guidance in terms of funding requirements and guidelines, states are legally responsible for the education of students within their borders. However, the more immediate task of running schools typically falls to school districts and their legal representative in each school, the principal. This complex system of governance and finance raises a number of questions related to school effectiveness. Some of these include the following: Since school principals are arguably the most influential people in the operation of individual schools, what do they do to create positive learning environments for their students? How does a district's central office influence the lives of teachers? What is the proper role of the business world in education? How does school funding influence student learning? How are charter schools and school choice impacting public education? Keep these questions in mind as you study the articles in this section.

A VIEW FROM THE CLASSROOM
Sandra L. Harris and Sandra Lowery

Probably the most visible and influential element of the current school governance structure is the school principal, who can have a powerful effect not only on teachers but on students as well. What do effective principals do to create a positive learning environment in their schools? In this article, the authors asked 123 teachers to describe the different ways their principals created a positive school climate. Responses focused on students and clustered in three areas— respect, communication, and support. As you read this article ask yourself, "What kind of school do I want to work and develop in?"

Think About This . . .

1. The study in this article polled teachers. Do you think the results would have been radically different if the study had asked students the same questions?
2. What was a common theme in terms of principals respecting students? What implications might this have for teachers?
3. Virtually all of the positive principal behaviors focused on students. What are some ways that principals create positive learning environments in schools through their interactions with teachers?
4. How can you use the information in this article to create a positive learning environment in your own classroom?

Our university class in administrative theory for principals-in-training was coming to a close. During the course, we had reviewed literature that supported the importance of creating a positive school climate (National Association of Secondary School Principals, 1996) and had discussed the role of the principal in creating that climate (Blase & Kirby, 2000; Freiberg, 1998). As we wrapped up our discussion, a class member made a suggestion: "I think we need to see what teachers would say about what the principals do at their schools to create and encourage this positive school environment."

We organized a study to survey 123 teachers enrolled in a principal preparation program at a regional university and asked the teachers to respond to this question: Reflecting on principal behaviors that you have observed, describe the most effective thing that the principal does for students at your school to contribute to a positive school climate. The teachers participating in the survey represented all grade levels, K–12, and taught in schools ranging in size from 250 to 1,000 students. Three themes emerged from the responses: respecting students, communicating with students, and supporting students.

Respecting Students

The teachers responding to the survey noted that principals establish a positive climate on their campuses by treating students fairly and equally. For example, one principal tells "students up front what [the] school's expectations are" and then shows respect "by expecting [the students] to live up to" those expectations. Other principals demonstrated respect for students by handling student behavior problems "privately, rather than in front of other students."

Several teachers cited treating students equally as an important aspect of creating a positive school

From Harris, S., & Lowery, S. (2002). A view from the classroom. Educational Leadership, 59(8), 64–65. Reprinted with permission of the Association for Supervision and Curriculum Development.

environment. One principal demonstrated this approach when her own daughter got in trouble at the school. According to the teacher surveyed, "She [the daughter] received the same punishment as all the others involved in the prank." In a similar case, a teacher reported that a principal "would not change a punishment for a student based on who his parents are." The teacher wrote, "Students see this as a sign of respect for all students." Another teacher summed up this behavior by saying that principals treat students equally when they "do not see ethnicity or wealth."

Communicating with Students

Effective principals both talk to and listen to students to learn more about them and "their educational needs, plans, hopes, and dreams" (Beck, 1994, p. 82). The teachers participating in the survey commented on such behaviors as making eye contact and following through on student concerns. Some of the principals eat in the lunchroom with invited student leaders to hear their concerns. One principal sits at different lunch tables throughout the year and listens "carefully not just to what they say, but how they say it."

Others principals interact with students in the hallways between classes or greet students as they enter and leave the building. An elementary school principal has a "Play with the Principal" time. The teachers also listed sending personalized birthday cards and notes recognizing student achievement as valuable ways to increase communication with students. For example, one teacher e-mailed her principal about her at-risk 8th graders at the beginning of the school year. Throughout the year, the principal e-mailed each of these students with encouraging messages. According to the teacher, the students "rush to my room to see if they have mail. I print each response and give it to the student. Most of them punch holes in [the messages] and put them in their notebooks; not one student has thrown the mail away."

Supporting Students

According to Noddings (1992), "schools, like families, are multipurpose institutions" (p. 66). Although academics are the focus of schools, "students need . . . adults to care" about their personal interests (p. 69). To meet this need, the principal can be accessible to students; reward them; be an advocate for them; and provide them with a safe, secure learning environment.

Principals who are accessible to the students—for example, by having an open-door policy—contribute to a positive climate for students. One teacher said that her principal "encourages students to come to him if there are any serious issues." Walking the campus is also important. Teachers commented that when principals want to be "invited to class celebrations, class plays, and other activities, the principals become more visible to the students."

The teachers also pointed out that principals who take extra time to praise students for their achievements over the intercom, in the newspaper, or with personal notes and e-mails create a positive school climate. Principals can also use such rewards as extending lunch time, sponsoring field trips, letting students eat lunch outside, and hosting awards assemblies. One principal created a gift store to reward student achievement. Students accumulate points for academic achievements and then use the points to purchase items from the store. Another principal has a "Wall of Fame" where he places students' photos with descriptions of their achievements.

The surveyed teachers also mentioned that being an advocate for students is a necessary aspect of creating a positive environment. Examples of such advocacy included providing motivational speakers and allowing students flexibility in their schedules to accommodate college visits and other needs. One teacher described how her principal works with students one-on-one to set goals and learning plans. Another teacher noted that her principal provides such physical needs as clothes, glasses, and shoes for low-income students.

In addition to meeting students' emotional needs, supportive principals provide a safe and secure environment in which the students can learn. The surveyed teachers cited such behaviors as enforcing the rules and dealing with conflict immediately. One teacher commented that the principal "checks daily for anything and everything that might lead to conflict among students."

Modeling Caring Behaviors

Principals who treat students with respect, communicate with students, and support students emphasize behaviors that create a positive school climate. After reviewing these survey results, the future principals in our class agreed that although these behaviors are natural for some, others need to learn to act in ways that build a better climate for learning. As Judith Azzara, a mentor principal in Fairfax County (Virginia) Public Schools, wrote, "Learning, after all, is what educators believe in" (2000/2001, p. 64).

References

Azzara, J. (2000/2001). The heart of school leadership. *Educational Leadership, 58*(4), 62–64.

Beck, L. (1994). *Reclaiming educational administration as a caring profession.* New York: Teachers College Press.

Blase, J., & Kirby, P. (2000). *Bringing out the best in teachers: What effective principals do.* Thousand Oaks, CA: Corwin Press.

Freiberg, J. (1998). Measuring school climate: Let me count the ways. *Educational Leadership, 56*(1), 22–27.

National Association of Secondary School Principals. (1996). *Breaking ranks: Changing an American institution.* Reston. VA: Author.

Noddings, N. (1992). *The challenge to care in schools.* New York: Teachers College Press.

THE INVISIBLE ROLE OF THE CENTRAL OFFICE
Kathleen F. Grove

Teachers work in schools that are part of a larger organization called *districts*. Each district has a central office that performs a myriad of tasks. What is a district's central office, and why is it important to teachers? Kathleen Grove attempts to answer these questions by describing the various activities of one central office in a school district in Virginia. The central office plays a crucial role in implementing a district's curricular and instructional goals. Grove uses the metaphor of a skeleton in the human body to emphasize the hidden but essential coordinating functions of the central office. As you read this article ask yourself, "How can the central office in the district I will teach in assist me as a teacher?"

Think About This . . .

1. What roles do a district's central office perform in terms of educational standards? Which of these roles are most useful or important to teachers?

2. How can a district's central office assist new teachers? Which of these forms of assistance will be most useful to you as a beginning teacher?

3. The author uses the metaphor of a skeleton to describe the functions of the central office. What other systems in the body might serve as metaphors for the functions of a district's central office?

4. How will you use the central office in your district as a beginning teacher?

Teachers as leaders. The principal as instructional leader. The superintendent as the first instructional leader. But what about the central office staff?

How many articles and headlines have you read about central office leaders? I suspect you've read very few. You might have noticed some passing acknowledgments. For example, in a recent article on leadership in education, Bolman and Deal noted that "the center mounted a series of studies of superintendents, principals, teachers, and *other school leaders*" (2002, p. 21,

italics added). Are central office staff—the curriculum developers, the best practices guides, the assistant superintendents—no more than "other school leaders"?

As the assistant superintendent for instruction in a 19,000-student school system in Arlington, Virginia, I am proud to serve as a central office instructional leader.

From Grove, K. (2002). The invisible role of the central office. Educational Leadership, 59(8), 45–47. *Reprinted with permission of the Association for Supervision and Curriculum Development.*

Despite the lack of attention to their role, the contributions of central office staff members are crucial to the strength of a school system. In this era of standards, high-stakes testing, and increasing expectations of school staff, the role that the central office plays takes on even more importance. What is the leadership role of the central office staff, and why is it invisible?

Focusing on Priorities

Our state, like so many others, instituted criterion-referenced tests several years ago. These assessments qualify as high-stakes tests, determining the accreditation of each school and the graduation of each student. As anticipated, school staffs reacted to these pressures with a variety of strategies, including more practice worksheets, multiple-choice assessments, direct instruction, and test-taking skills instruction. Still, in their hearts and minds, teachers knew what good teaching and real learning were.

In the central office, we took on the task of articulating the goal of *teaching for understanding*. We used a state grant for addressing Virginia's Standards of Learning (the objectives tested by the criterion-referenced tests) to fund the Lead Teacher Initiative. We joined principals in identifying five lead teachers (one instructional and four core content) in each of our 31 schools. These classroom teachers receive a stipend in return for helping their schools develop the best ways to teach for understanding.

Through an arrangement with George Mason University in Fairfax, Virginia, the instructional lead teachers first took and then taught a graduate course that emphasized designing instruction for students' understanding (Danielson, 1996; Wiggins & McTighe, 1998). For final class projects, teachers designed teaching units following the rigorous standards of Wiggins and McTighe (1998). These lead teachers now help other teachers set clear goals for what they want students to learn, how they will measure that learning, and how students will demonstrate deep understanding. Through this approach, we believe that our district's students will perform well on any standardized assessment because they will understand the content.

Communicating the Message

The lead teacher course generated such a following that principals requested a study group on the course's textbook, and some principals even enrolled in the course. Teachers and administrators heard about teaching for understanding from the lead teachers, from those who took the course, from the central office instructional staff, and from the superintendent. An instructional presentation during a school board meeting expanded the audience. Lead teachers spread the word through school newsletters and staff meetings.

Fortunately, our district enjoys a sophisticated parent community and teaching staff. Both groups appreciate the commitment to teaching for understanding. Still, the pressures of the statewide testing and its impact on accreditation and graduation can lead school staffs away from this commitment. Through the leadership of the central office staff and teacher leaders, the message continues to overcome the countervailing pressures.

Fostering Leadership

The central office fosters leadership among teachers. The Lead Teacher Initiative identifies classroom teachers interested in a leadership role, provides them with enhanced opportunities to learn and grow, recognizes their contributions through stipends and public acknowledgment, and capitalizes on their skills and talents for the benefit of students. Teacher leaders from throughout the district meet to provide input and feedback on the instructional program.

The central office identifies professional conferences and encourages teacher leaders to attend and apply as presenters. It organizes teacher research groups, paying stipends to the teacher leaders and providing them with training so that they, in turn, can work with groups in their schools on action research. Teacher mentors in each school building receive stipends and staff development from the central office, and central office staff members work with teachers seeking National Board certification, outlining the path and sustaining the incredible effort needed to reach this goal.

Orienting New Teachers

Central office staff members lead the orientation of newly hired teachers. The purpose of our four-day program is to help new teachers understand the district's shared values and let them know how we can support them professionally.

Hold high expectations for all students. We start the orientation with a skit to emphasize the importance of this message to our district, where close to 40 percent of students qualify for federal lunch subsidies and more than 30 percent speak a language other than English as their native language and where we are deeply committed to closing all achievement gaps.

Teach the district's curriculum. The newly hired teachers receive their curriculum guides and participate in activities that engage them in reviewing their content. Some teachers come from school systems where the textbook represents the curriculum, but our central office, in collaboration with classroom teachers, has developed a scope and sequence of curriculums based on national, state, and local standards. When teachers honor the curriculums agreed to by their peers, students can progress and teachers can avoid duplicating units of study.

Use best practices. Using Danielson's model (1996) and our own experience, we review instructional practices that will set the standards for teacher observations, teacher evaluations, and self-assessment. The teachers review these best practices and, in groups, present them to one another in different ways to demonstrate an understanding of multiple intelligences.

Use assessment to inform instruction. We discuss using information from all kinds of assessments—from checking homework to examining standardized test results—to improve instruction. We share a sample of test results, discuss their potential for interpretion, and describe the assessments that students will encounter in our schools, stressing the importance of preparing students to succeed on any significant assessment that they will experience.

Recognize and value diversity. An activity on given names and their meanings for different cultures and communities kicks off this discussion. The students in our district speak more than 70 languages, and we have a significant Hispanic and African American student enrollment. Appreciating the diversity of our classrooms and how this diversity contributes to the richness of our school community is an important shared value.

You are not alone! A short video shows a new teacher, whose arms are piled high with curriculum guides and handbooks, entering an empty classroom with blank walls, and then follows her as she learns about the many support resources available to teachers, from in-school technology coordinators to laminating services to teacher mentors. With high expectations for all teachers and students, we want to support their important work as much as possible.

The teachers join their school staffs the following week, aware of the district's values and better prepared for the challenge of their first year in the school system.

Providing Service and Expertise

The demands on school staff members increase every day. The central office provides service and expertise to the schools so that they can fulfill their missions without distraction. For example, central office staff members

- conduct the textbook adoption process,
- order new textbooks,
- evaluate supplementary materials,
- develop programs of studies,
- conduct formal observations of teachers,
- assist teachers having difficulties,
- design and conduct staff development,
- facilitate teacher attendance at professional conferences,
- organize countywide activities, such as art exhibits and science fairs,
- organize informational meetings for parents,
- meet with citizen committees on each instruction area,
- analyze achievement data,
- apply for and manage grant-funded projects, and
- complete required state and federal reports.

These tasks, essential to the instruction program, require much time and effort. School staff members provide input and feedback, but knowing that the central office staff is meeting the many other potential demands on their energies allows them to devote most of their time and effort to the daily challenge of instructing students effectively. In this way, central office and school staff members divide the often overwhelming work of the school system to more efficiently serve the students and their families.

The expertise of central office staff members in specific curriculum areas also enables them to serve as consultants and to develop curriculums and instruction strategies that encompass national standards and research-based practices. For example, each school cannot devote the time to learn about and analyze the latest research on second language acquisition and then design instruction to incorporate these concepts. Instead, the central office works with national authorities in English language learning and develops useful models for teaching speakers of other languages. Central office leaders also share their expertise almost daily in their staff development offerings and small-group work with teachers.

This expertise applies also to teacher hiring, a function of growing importance. Principals continue to interview and personally select their teachers, but they want the content-area experts in the central office to screen the candidates' level of subject proficiency.

Ensuring Consistency

How does a school system set goals and work toward them? How does a school system avoid a balkanization of its neighborhoods and schools? How can families trust that their children will receive a high-quality instruction program at any of the schools in a school district?

Through the central textbook adoption process, the development of curriculums, the publication of programs of studies, the development of services to special populations, classroom observations and feedback, staff development activities, and community forums, we establish ways to achieve the district's goals and consistency of the instruction program. Certainly, school staff members vary the instruction program to better meet the needs of their students and to take advantage of their own strengths and interests. But whenever I attend evening meetings to address families who are considering choices within our school system, I can state confidently that our schools share common goals, curriculums, instructional texts, instructional practices, assessments, teacher training, programs for special populations, resource staff, and much more. The central office leaders maintain this high quality and consistency.

The Invisible Skeleton

Central office staff members do serve behind the scenes. If they perform their jobs well, their efforts often go unnoticed or at least without credit. I am married to a middle school principal. I sometimes overhear him talking at a party with a group marveling at such a demanding and interesting vocation. As he describes his school's in-novative curriculum, the practices of his school's teachers, the materials the teachers use, and the changes his school has made to accommodate the changing population (like the interpreter for the Somali students), I restrain my immediate response. I know that the staff in my department developed the curriculum, identified and taught the best practices, selected the materials, and even found the interpreter. I know how the central office has fostered teacher leadership in the school. I also know that many other principals are speaking possessively of the same components but out of my earshot

And I know that if the school staff members take credit for these elements of the instructional program, then they feel ownership and pride in them. Their enthusiasm indicates that the central office staff members have succeeded in their mission of strengthening the instructional program, encouraging teacher leaders, and supporting student achievement and success.

In these ways, central office leaders are effective, in part, precisely because they are invisible, much as the skeleton in the body is invisible. Vitally important, central office staff members provide the support and consistency necessary for a high-quality instructional program.

References

Bolman, L., & Deal, T. (2002). Leading with soul and spirit. *The School Administrator, 59*(2), 21–26.

Danielson, C. (1996). *Enhancing professional practice: A framework for teaching.* Alexandria, VA: ASCD.

Wiggins, G., & McTighe, J. (1998). *Understanding by design.* Alexandria, VA: ASCD.

THE 500-POUND GORILLA
Alfie Kohn

Education is big business—annually, our country spends billions of dollar to educate our children. Business is necessarily involved in a number of school functions, from supplying textbooks and technology to providing food for cafeterias. The dependence of schools on industry sometimes results in abuses, critics claim. What should be the proper relationship between business and education? In attempting to answer this question, Alfie Kohn describes a number of disturbing recent trends in education that suggest corporations are having an increasingly powerful influence on our schools. Corporations sell texts and tests, they advertise their product within schools, and they are even attempting to run their own for-profit schools. As you read this article ask yourself, "Is corporate America's interest in schools a positive influence?"

Think About This . . .

1. What are the three major ways that corporations profit from education? Which of these are most or least troubling?
2. Kohn criticizes the "economic rationale" for schooling. Should the central mission of schools be to prepare students for the workforce?
3. To what extent does emphasis on standardized testing detract from other important educational goals? What are these other important goals, and how important are they relative to academic achievement?
4. How will you as an individual teacher deal with education's competing goals in your classroom?

The best reason to give a child a good school . . . is so that child will have a happy childhood, and not so that it will help IBM in competing with Sony. . . . There is something ethically embarrassing about resting a national agenda on the basis of sheer greed.

—Jonathan Kozol

These days I give a lot of speeches about the accountability fad that has been turning our schools into glorified test-prep centers. The question-and-answer sessions that follow these lectures can veer off in unexpected directions, but it is increasingly likely that someone will inquire about the darker forces behind this heavy-handed version of school reform. "Aren't giant corporations raking in profits from standardized testing?" a questioner will demand. "Doesn't it stand to reason that these companies engineered the reliance on testing in the first place?"

Indeed, there are enough suspicious connections to keep conspiracy theorists awake through the night. For example, Standard & Poors, the financial rating service, has lately been offering to evaluate and publish the performance, based largely on test scores, of every school district in a given state—a bit of number crunching that Michigan and Pennsylvania purchased for at least $10 million each, and other states may soon follow. The explicit findings of these reports concern whether this district is doing better than that one. But the tacit message—the hidden curriculum, if you will—is that test scores are a useful and appropriate marker of school quality. Who would have an incentive to convince people of that conclusion? Well, it turns out that Standard & Poors is owned by McGraw-Hill, one of the largest manufacturers of standardized tests.

With such pressure to look good by boosting their test results, low-scoring districts may feel compelled to purchase heavily scripted curriculum programs designed to raise scores, programs such as Open Court or Reading Mastery (and others in the Direct Instruction series). Where do those programs come from? By an astonishing coincidence, both are owned by McGraw-Hill. Of course, it doesn't hurt to have some influential policy makers on your side when it's time to make choices about curriculum and assessment. In April 2000, Charlotte Frank joined New York's Board of Regents, the state's top policy-making panel for education. If you need to reach Ms. Frank, try her office at McGraw-Hill, where she is a vice president. And we needn't even explore the chummy relationship between Harold McGraw III (the company's chairman) and George W. Bush.[1] Nor will we investigate the strong statement of support for test-based accountability in a March 2001 *Business Week* cover story about education. Care to hazard a guess as to what company owns *Business Week*?

Stumble across enough suspicious relationships such as these, and your eyebrows may never come down. However, I don't want to oversimplify. The sizable profits made by the CTB division of McGraw-Hill, as well as by Harcourt Educational Measurement, Riverside Publishing, Educational Testing Service (ETS), and NCS Pearson[2]—the five companies that develop and/or score virtually all the standardized tests to which students and prospective teachers are subjected—cannot completely explain why public officials, journalists, and others have come to rely so heavily on these exams. Let's face it: for a variety of reasons, people with no financial stake in the matter have become boosters of standardized testing.[3]

More important, even if one could point to a neat cause-and-effect relationship here, the role that business plays in education is not limited to the realm of testing.

From Kohn, A. (2002). The 500-pound gorilla. Phi Delta Kappan, 84(2), 112–119. Reprinted with permission of the author.

Indeed, its influence is even deeper, more complicated, and ultimately more disturbing than anything that might be revealed in a game of connect the corporate dots. Schools—and, by extension, children—have been turned into sources of profit in several distinct ways. Yes, some corporations sell educational products, including tests, texts, and other curriculum materials. But many more corporations, peddling all sorts of products, have come to see schools as places to reach an enormous captive market. Advertisements are posted in cafeterias, around athletic fields, even on buses. Soft drink companies pay off schools so that their brand—and only their brand—of liquid candy will be sold to kids.[4] Schools are offered free televisions in exchange for compelling students to watch a brief current-events program larded with commercials, a project known as Channel One. And the advertisers seem to be getting their money's worth: researchers have found that Channel One viewers, as contrasted with a comparison group of students, not only thought more highly of products advertised on the program but were more likely to agree with statements such as "money is everything," "a nice car is more important than school," "designer labels make a difference," and "I want what I see advertised."[5]

Even more disturbing than having public schools sanction these advertisements and expose children to them[6] is the fact that corporate propaganda is sometimes passed off as part of the curriculum. Math problems plug a particular brand of sneakers or candy; chemical companies distribute slick curriculum packages to ensure that environmental science will be taught with their slant.[7] A few years ago, someone sent me a large, colorful brochure aimed at educators that touts several free lessons helpfully supplied by Procter & Gamble. One kit helps fifth-graders learn about personal hygiene by way of Old Spice aftershave and Secret deodorant, while another promises a seventh-grade lesson on the "ten steps to self-esteem," complete with teacher's guide, video, and samples of Clearasil.

It's worth thinking about how corporate sponsorship is likely to affect what is included—and not included—in these lessons. How likely is it that the makers of Clearasil would emphasize that how you feel about yourself should not primarily be a function of how you look? Or consider a hypothetical unit on nutrition underwritten by Kraft General Foods (or by McDonald's or Coca-Cola). Would you expect to find any mention of the fact that the food you prepare yourself is likely to be more nutritious than processed products in boxes and jars and cans? Or that the best way to quench your thirst is actually to drink water? Or that a well-balanced diet requires little or no meat? Or that smoking causes cancer? (Kraft General Foods—and Nabisco, for that matter—are owned by a tobacco company.)

A few companies, then, make money by selling books and tests, while many more sell other things to children. The third, and most audacious, way that schooling can be milked for profit is by letting corporations take over the management of the schools themselves or even allowing them to own schools outright as they would a car dealership. Opportunities for such businesses have greatly expanded as a result of a movement simply to privatize education. This effort seems to gather strength as people friendly to its aims find themselves in positions of power, as the Supreme Court votes to allow public funds to pay for tuition at private—including religious—schools, and as proponents become more skilled at public relations (for example, jettisoning the unpopular word *vouchers* and justifying their agenda in terms of the ostensible benefits for low-income people of color).

By way of background, consider that the center of gravity for American education has shifted over the last few years from local schools and districts to state capitals. The commissioner or state superintendent of schools, the state board of education, and the legislature have usurped much of the power that communities have long enjoyed to set education policy. Indeed, even Washington, D.C., has gotten into the act, with new federal legislation requiring that every state test every student every year.

It's understandable, then, that frustrated students, parents, and teachers would be inclined to see government as the problem. Some conservative activists have even begun referring derisively to public schools as "government schools." But there are two problems with this equation. First, the current level of interference in curricular and assessment decisions by politicians is not logically entailed by the idea of public schooling; indeed, it is unprecedented. If your governor began telling your local library which books to order, that would not be an argument against the idea of public libraries. Second, the actions taken by government officials have been offensive precisely to the extent that they have appropriated the slogans and mindset of private enterprise. The problem is that people in the public sector are uncritically adopting the world view of the private sector—and applying it to schools.

Privatizing education is predicated on an almost childlike faith in competition: let self-interested people struggle against one another, and somehow all of them—even their children, presumably—will benefit. This belief, as quickly becomes evident from reading and listening to those who hold it, has the status of religious dogma rather than empirical hypothesis. It is closely related to a second ideological underpinning: a pronounced individualism in which there is no us, just you and her and him and me. To apply a marketplace mentality to education both assumes and exacerbates this perspective, with parents encouraged to focus only on what improves their own children's position. This is the very opposite of an invitation to work together to make schools more effective and inviting places for all our children. Perhaps it was the implications of this threat to the value of community that led the political philosopher Benjamin Barber to observe, "Privatization is not about limiting government; it is about terminating democracy."

Clearly, education is just one arena in which larger ideologies are being played out. These days, as education historian David Labaree has put it, "We find public schools under attack, not just because they are deemed ineffective, but because they are public."[8] Once the struggle over public institutions has been joined in the classroom, though, it isn't hard to understand the consequences of implementing voucher plans and other "school choice" proposals—including, to some extent, charter schools, which many see as a first step toward undermining public schooling altogether.

What happens to schools when they are plunged into the marketplace? To begin with, they must shift much of their time and resources to, well, marketing. (It is those who sell themselves skillfully, not necessarily those who are especially good at what they do, who tend to succeed in a competitive market.) Moreover, the pressure to make themselves look better presents a temptation to screen out less desirable students, those whose education takes more effort or expense. "The problem with public schools," remarked John Chubb, "is that they must take whoever walks in the door."[9] The philosophical core of the privatization movement for which Chubb speaks is neatly revealed in the use of the word *problem* in that sentence.

Deborah Meier writes memorably of the "dictatorship of the marketplace," noting that "privatizing removes schools from democratic control." She observes that private schools "cannot serve as general models; their value and advantages depend on their scarcity. . . . Schools dependent upon private clienteles—schools that can get rid of unwanted kids or troublemaker families . . . and toss aside the losers—not only can avoid the democratic arts of compromise and tolerance but also implicitly foster lessons about the power of money and prestige, a lesson already too well known by every adolescent in America."[10] Meier's indictment extends beyond voucher programs, suggesting the corrosive effect of any sort of interference in public education by business interests. The quest for private profits, in whatever form it takes, can only contaminate efforts to help all students become enthusiastic and expert learners.

* * *

These three basic ways by which corporations can profit from education are all quite straightforward. Vivendi Universal, which owns Houghton Mifflin (at least for the moment), which in turn owns Riverside, makes money selling the Iowa Tests of Basic Skills. Nike makes money by advertising its shoes to young people who are required by law to be in the vicinity of its billboards. Edison, Inc., makes money (or will do so eventually, it assures its investors) by running whole schools.

But there are also more indirect ways to turn learning into a business. When corporations can influence the nature of curriculum and the philosophy of education, then they have succeeded in doing something more profound—and possibly more enduring—than merely improving their results on this quarter's balance sheet. That can happen when businesses succeed in creating "school-to-work" programs, by which children are defined as future workers and shaped to the specifications of their employers. It can happen when the whole notion of education as a public good is systematically undermined—an ideological shift that paves the way for privatizing schools. It can happen when a business ethos takes over education, with an emphasis on quantifiable results, on standardized procedures to improve performance, on order and discipline and obedience to authority. Students expect to be controlled with rewards and punishments, to be set against their peers in competitions, to be rated and evaluated by those who have more power than they do. None of this is particularly effective at preparing children to be critical thinkers, lifelong intellectual explorers, active participants in a democratic society—or even, for that matter, good friends or lovers or parents. But the process is exceedingly effective at preparing them for their life as corporate employees.

Rather ingeniously, some practices simultaneously serve the interests of business in multiple ways. For example, selling products in classrooms may immediately increase a company's market share, but it also contributes to a socialization process whereby children come to see themselves as consumers, as people whose lives will be improved by buying more things.

Standardized testing may be an even better illustration in that it manages to achieve several goals at one stroke:

- it brings in hundreds of millions of dollars a year to the handful of corporations that produce the tests, grade the tests, and supply materials to raise students' scores on the tests;

- it screens and sorts students for the convenience of industry and higher education;

- it helps to foster acceptance of a corporate-style ideology, which comes to be seen as natural and even desirable, in which assessment is used less to support learning than to evaluate and compare people—and in which the education driven by that testing has a uniform, standardized feel to it; and

- when many students perform poorly on these tests (an outcome that can be ensured from the outset and then justified in the name of "raising the bar"), these results can be used to promote discontent with public education. "We are shocked—shocked!—to discover just how bad our schools are!" Again, this can create a more receptive climate for introducing vouchers, for-profit charter schools, and other private alternatives. (Anyone whose goal was to serve up our schools to the marketplace could hardly find a shrewder strategy than to insist on holding schools "accountable" by administering wave after wave of standardized tests.)

To the extent that colleges, too, are increasingly seen as ripe for a corporate makeover, testing younger students would make sense as part of a long-term strategy. In the words of one instructor:

> The whole standards movement, after all, is about restricting learning to what is actually useful: the memorization of information, the streamlining of knowledge to what can be evaluated by a standardized test. By curtailing the excessive autonomy of K–12 teachers and requiring them to teach "to the tests," we are preparing future college students for a brand of higher education designed and administered by the savviest segment of our society: for-profit corporations.[11]

There may be some sort of shadowy business conspiracy at work to turn schools into factories, but this seems unlikely if only because no such conspiracy is necessary to produce the desired results. Most politicians have accepted uncritically the goals and methods outlined by the private sector. And, with the possible exception of attitudes toward vouchers, there are few differences between the two major parties. Marveling that "Democrats and Republicans are saying rather similar things about education," a front-page story in the *New York Times* explained, "One reason there seems to be such a consensus on education is that the economic rationale for schooling has triumphed."[12]

More ominous is the extent to which even educators have internalized a business approach. Many of us defend "partnerships" between schools and businesses,

willingly "align" our teaching to uniform state standards, shrug off objections to advertising in the schools, and refer to learning as "work"[13] or to schooling itself as an "investment." The next time you leaf through one of the leading education periodicals or listen to a speech at a conference, try counting all the telltale signs of corporate ideology.

There's no need for executives in expensive suits to show up in schools if we're already doing their work for them.

* * *

Some readers may dismiss as rhetorical excess any comparison of schools with factories. In fact, though, the analogy was first proposed by people who were quite explicit about wanting to make the former more similar to the latter. Back in 1916, Ellwood Cubberley wrote that "our schools are, in a sense, factories in which the raw products (children) are to be shaped and fashioned into products to meet the various demands of life."[14] In the 1950s, this way of thinking was still in favor. A *Fortune* magazine article titled "The Low Productivity of the Education Industry" informed readers that we should strive "to turn out students with the greatest possible efficiency . . . [and] minimize the input of man hours and capital. In this respect, the schools are no different from General Motors."[15]

The popularity of such parallels may wax and wane over time, but were Cubberley to find himself magically transported to the early 21st century, he would almost certainly feel right at home. He would immediately notice that thousands of American schools, some of them dating back to his own era but still open for, um, business, literally resemble factories. Inside them, he would see, as Linda Darling-Hammond observed in 1997, that

> the short segmented tasks stressing speed and neatness that predominate in most schools, the emphasis on rules from the important to the trivial, and the obsession with bells, schedules, and time clocks are all dug deep into the ethos of late-nineteenth-century America, when students were being prepared to work in factories on predetermined tasks that would not require them to figure out what to do.[16]

Cubberley would no doubt be impressed as well by the remarkable power that business continues to have in shaping education policy. Every few months, he would notice, another report on American schooling is released by a consortium of large corporations. These documents normally receive wide and approving press attention, despite the fact that they all recycle the same set of buzz words. Rather like a party game in which players create sentences by randomly selecting an adjective from one list, then a noun from another, these dispatches from the business world seem to consist mostly of different combinations of terms like "world class," "competitive," and "measurable"; "standards," "results," and "accountability."

A few examples from the past decade might set Cubberley's head to nodding. The Committee for Economic Development, consisting of executives from about 250 large companies, demands that school curricula be linked more closely to employers' skill requirements; it calls for "performance-driven education," incentives, and a traditional "core disciplinary knowledge" version of instruction. Ditto for the Business Roundtable, which describes schooling as "competing in the education Olympics." Besides endorsing narrow and very specific academic standards, punishment for schools that fall behind, and more testing, it approvingly cites the example of taking time in high school to familiarize students with personnel evaluations. The National Association of Manufacturers, meanwhile, insists on more testing as well as "a national system of skills standards designed by industry." And the Business Task Force on Student Standards says that "workplace performance requirements of industry and commerce must be integrated into subject-matter standards and learning environments."[17]

To scan these recommendations is to realize two things. First, most have been adopted as policy. To an extraordinary degree, business' wish becomes education's command. Second, they traffic in the realm not only of methods and metaphors, but of purposes and goals. The question is not just whether we will compare schools to factories or even whether we will prescribe practices that will make schools more like factories. The question is what vision of schooling—and even of children—lies behind such suggestions. While a proper discussion of the purpose of education lies outside the scope of this essay,[18] it is immediately evident that seeing schools as a means for bolstering our economic system (and the interests of the major players in that system) is very different from seeing education as a means for strengthening democracy, for promoting social justice, or simply for fostering the well-being and development of the students themselves.[19]

In the final analysis, the problem with letting business interests shape our country's agenda for education isn't just the executives' lack of knowledge about the nuances of pedagogy. The problem is with their ultimate objectives. Corporations in our economic system exist to provide a financial return to the people who own them: they are in business to make a profit. As individuals, those who work in (or even run) these companies might have other goals, too, when they turn their attention to public policy or education or anything else. But business *qua* business is concerned principally about its own bottom line. Thus, when business thinks about schools, its agenda is driven by what will maximize its profitability, not necessarily by what is in the best interest of students. Any overlap between those two goals would be purely accidental—and, in practice, turns out to be minimal. What maximizes corporate profits often does not benefit children and vice versa. Qualities such as a love of learning for its own sake, a penchant for asking challenging questions, or a commitment to democratic participation in decision making would be seen as nice but irrelevant—or perhaps even as impediments to the efficient realization of corporate goals.

Some people in the business world object to this characterization, of course. They insist that modern corporations have goals similar to those of educators, that business today needs employees who are critical thinkers and problem solvers skilled at teamwork, and so forth. But if this were really true, we would see cutting-edge companies taking the lead in demanding a constructivist approach to instruction, in which students' questions drive the curriculum—as well as a rich, whole-language model for teaching literacy. They would ask why we haven't thrown out the worksheets and the textbooks, the isolated skills and rote memorization. They would demand greater emphasis on cooperative learning and complain loudly about the practices that undermine collaboration (and ultimately quality)—such practices as awards assemblies and spelling bees and honor rolls, or norm-referenced tests. They would insist on heterogeneous, inclusive classrooms in place of programs that segregate and stratify and stigmatize. They would stop talking about "school choice" (meaning programs that treat education as a commodity for sale) and start talking about the importance of giving *students* more choice about what happens in their classrooms. They would publish reports on the importance of turning schools into caring communities in which mutual problem solving replaces an emphasis on following directions.

The sad truth, of course, is that, when business leaders do address these issues, their approach tends to be precisely the opposite: they write off innovative, progressive education reforms as mere fads that distract us from raising test scores. This is evident not only from those reports sampled above (from the Business Roundtable and similar groups) but also from the consistent slant of articles about education that appear in business-oriented periodicals.

Moreover, while there may be more talk in boardrooms these days about teamwork, it is usually situated in the context of competitiveness: that is, working together so we can defeat another group of people working together. Business groups commonly characterize students as competitors—as people who do, or will, or should spend their lives trying to beat other people. Other nations are likewise depicted as rivals, such that to make our schools "world class" means not that we should cooperate with other countries and learn, but that we should compete against them and win.

While "social skills" are often listed as desirable attributes, business publications never seem to mention such qualities as generosity or compassion. While it is common to talk about the need for future employees who can think critically, there is reason to doubt that corporate executives want people with the critical skills to ask why they (the executives) just received multimillion-dollar packages of stock options even as several thousand employees were thrown out of work. Corporations may, as we have seen, encourage high school English teachers to assign students the task of writing a sample personnel evaluation, but they seem less keen on inviting students to critically analyze whether such evaluations make sense or who gets to evaluate whom. In short, what business wants from its workers—and, by extension, from our schools—in the 21st century may not be so different from what it wanted in the 20th and even in the 19th centuries.

Moreover, what business wants, it usually gets. It doesn't take a degree in political science to figure out why politicians (and sometimes even educators) so often capitulate to business. For that matter, it isn't much of a mystery why a 500-pound gorilla is invited to sleep anywhere it wishes. But that doesn't make the practice any less dangerous.

Indeed, we might even go so far as to identify as one of the most crucial tasks in a democratic society the act of limiting the power that corporations have in determining what happens in our schools. Not long ago, as historian Joel Spring pointed out, you would have been branded a radical (or worse) for suggesting that our education system is geared to meeting the needs of business. Today, corporations not only acknowledge that fact but complain loudly when they think schools aren't adequately meeting their needs. They are not shy about trying to make over the schools in their own image. It's up to the rest of us, therefore, to firmly tell them to mind their own businesses.

Notes

1. See Stephen Metcalf, "Reading Between the Lines," *The Nation*, 28 January 2002, pp. 18–22. This article is reprinted in Alfie Kohn and Patrick Shannon, eds., *Education, Inc.: Turning Learning into a Business*, rev. ed. (Portsmouth, N.H.: Heinemann, 2002).

2. Notice that the phenomenon by which a company makes money by testing students, then turns around and sells materials designed to prepare students for those tests, is not limited to McGraw-Hill. Many of the major textbook publishers are represented in this list of test manufacturers.

3. For other explanations of the fascination with standardized testing, see Alfie Kohn, *The Case Against Standardized Testing* (Portsmouth, N.H.: Heinemann, 2000), esp. pp. 2–4; Robert L. Linn, "Assessments and Accountability," *Educational Researcher*, March 2000, esp. p. 4; and Gary Natriello and Aaron M. Pallas, "The Development and Impact of High-Stakes Testing," in Gary Orfield and Mindy L. Kornhaber, eds., *Raising Standards or Raising Barriers?* (New York: Century Foundation Press, 2001), esp. pp. 20–21.

4. See Alex Molnar, "Looking for Funds in All the Wrong Places," *Principal*, November 2000, pp. 18–21. Thanks to Patrick Shannon for calling to my attention this article and the one mentioned in the next note. As of early 2002, between 300 and 400 school districts had signed exclusive beverage contracts—more than double the number in mid-1999—according to the Center for Commercial-Free Public Education.

5. Bradley S. Greenberg and Jeffrey E. Brand, "Channel One: But What About the Advertising?," *Educational Leadership*, December 1993/January 1994, pp. 56–58.

6. For more examples of—and ideas for responding to—this phenomenon, contact the Center for Commercial-Free Public Education (www.commercialfree.org) or Commercial Alert (www.commercialalert.org). See also Alex Molnar, *Giving Kids the Business: The Commercialization of America's Schools* (Boulder, Colo.: Westview, 1996), or contact his Commercialism in Education Research Unit (www.asu.edu/educ/epsl/ceru.htm).

7. "Your child's science teachers may be summering with Weyerhaeuser or the hunting lobby. They may be teaching about our food supply with a lesson plan developed and donated by Monsanto. And the video on how oil is formed? An Exxon production. Andrew Hagelshaw, director of the Center for Commercial-Free Public Education in Oakland, said such programs are an attempt to establish brand loyalty. He said the logging companies and oil industry have figured out what fast-food restaurants have long known: 'If you just start educating people at young ages around these facts, then they accept it as truth, and that means customers for life.'" See Chris Moran, "Education or Indoctrination?," *San Diego Union-Tribune*, 13 May 2002.

8. David F. Labaree, *How to Succeed in School Without Really Learning: The Credentials Race in American Education* (New Haven, Conn.: Yale University Press, 1997), p. 51.

9. Chubb is quoted in Bernie Froese-Germain, "What We Know About School Choice," *Education Canada,* Fall 1998, p. 22.

10. Deborah Meier, *The Power of Their Ideas* (Boston: Beacon, 1995), pp. 79, 8, 104, 7.

11. Nick Bromell, "Summa Cum Avaritia," *Harper's Magazine,* February 2002, p. 76.

12. Ethan Bronner, "Better Schools Is Battle Cry for Fall Elections." *New York Times,* 20 September 1998, p. A-32.

13. On this point, see Alfie Kohn, "Students Don't 'Work'—They Learn," *Education Week,* 3 September 1997, pp. 60, 43; and Hermine H. Marshall, "Beyond the Workplace Metaphor: The Classroom as a Learning Setting," *Theory Into Practice,* vol. 29, 1990, pp. 94–101.

14. Ellwood Cubberley, *Public School Administration* (Boston: Houghton Mifflin, 1916), p. 338.

15. The *Fortune* article is quoted in Daniel Tanner, "Manufacturing Problems and Selling Solutions: How to Succeed in the Education Business Without Really Educating," *Phi Delta Kappan,* November 2000, p. 198.

16. Linda Darling-Hammond, *The Right to Learn* (San Francisco: Jossey-Bass, 1997), p. 40.

17. Jeff Archer, "New School Role Seen Critical to Respond to Modern Economy," *Education Week,* 8 May 1996, pp. 1, 8; Catherine S. Manegold, "Study Says Schools Must Stress Academics," *New York Times,* 23 September 1994, p. A-22; *A Business Leader's Guide to Setting Academic Standards* (Washington, D.C.: Business Roundtable, 1996); Mary Ann Zehr, "Manufacturers Endorse National Tests, Vouchers," *Education Week,* 14 January 1998, p. 14; and Business Task Force on Student Standards, *The Challenge of Change: Standards to Make Education Work for All Our Children* (Washington, D.C.: National Alliance of Business, 1995).

18. Many writers, of course, have grappled with education's ultimate goals. I attempt to sort through some of the underlying issues in *The Schools Our Children Deserve* (Boston: Houghton Mifflin, 1999), pp. 115–20.

19. See, for example, an analysis of the powerful Business Roundtable, whose "main objective is not quality education but the preservation of the competitiveness of corporate America in the global economy," in Bess Altwerger and Steven L. Strauss, "The Business Behind Testing," *Language Arts,* January 2002, pp. 256–62. The quotation appears on page 258.

UNEQUAL SCHOOL FUNDING IN THE UNITED STATES

Bruce J. Biddle and David C. Berliner

Does money affect the quality of experiences students have in schools? Some contend no, but Bruce Biddle and David Berliner make a convincing argument that school funding *does* influence student learning. They document a number of funding inequities in different schools around the country and analyze why these inequities exist. As you read this article ask yourself, "How will funding affect my life as a new teacher?"

Think About This . . .

1. How does the U.S. system of funding education differ from other countries? Which system is better? Why?

2. Research shows that household poverty levels strongly influence student achievement. What are some possible reasons for this relationship? What can schools do about these reasons?

3. In terms of funding level, what kind of district or state would you like to work in? What are the advantages and disadvantages of schools at either end of the funding continuum?

Most people believe that students do better in well-funded schools and that public education should provide a level playing field for all children. Nearly half of the funding for public schools in the United States, however, is provided through local taxes, generating large differences in funding between wealthy and impoverished communities (National Center for Education Statistics, 2000a). Efforts to reduce these disparities have provoked controversy and resistance.

Those who oppose demands for more equitable school funding have embraced the claims of reviewers such as Eric Hanushek (1989), who wrote:

> Detailed research spanning two decades and observing performance in many different educational settings provides strong and consistent evidence that expenditures are not systematically related to student achievement. (p. 49)

But other well-known reviewers disagree. For example, in 1996, Rob Greenwald, Larry Hedges, and Richard Laine wrote:

> [Our analysis shows] that school resources are systematically related to student achievement and that those relations are large [and] educationally important. (p. 384)

Given such disputes, what should we believe about school funding and its impact? And given what we know today, what should we do about inequities in funding for education in the United States?

Differences in School Funding
Funding in the United States

Public school funding in the United States comes from federal, state, and local sources, but because nearly half of those funds come from local property taxes, the system generates large funding differences between wealthy and impoverished communities. Such differences exist among states, among school districts within each state, and even among schools within specific districts.

In 1998, for example, the state with the highest average level of public school funding (adjusted for differences in cost of living) was New Jersey, with an annual funding rate of $8,801 per student, whereas the state with the lowest average level was Utah, with a yearly rate of $3,804 per student (see Figure 1). This means that the typical student attending a public school in New Jersey was provided more than *twice* the fiscal resources allocated to his or her counterpart in Utah.

Disparities in per-student funding levels are actually greater *within* some states than among the states as a group. To illustrate, in 1998, public school districts in Alaska that were ranked at the 95th percentile for per-student funding received an average of $16,546 per student for the year, whereas school districts ranked at the 5th percentile received only $7,379 on average. Other "winners" in the inequality derby included Vermont (where school districts at the 95th and 5th percentiles received an average of $15,186 and $6,442, respectively), Illinois (where the figures were $11,507 and $5,260), New Jersey ($13,709 and $8,401), New York ($13,749 and $8,518), and Montana ($9,839 and $4,774).

In contrast, differences in funding were quite small in such states as Nevada (where better-funded and not-so-well-funded districts received an average of $6,933 and $5,843, respectively, for each student), as well as in Hawaii and Washington, D.C., each of which is served by only one large school district (National Center for Education Statistics, 1998).

Nor is the practice of inequitable public school funding confined to the district level. Schools within a given district or classrooms within a specific school may also experience massive differences in funding (Rothstein, 2000). Such inequities appear because the needs of disadvantaged students are less often heeded in debates about programs, facilities, and funding allocation in local venues.

From the preceding data we learn that a few students from wealthy communities or neighborhoods within generous states attend public schools with funding of $15,000 or more per student per year, whereas some students from poor communities or neighborhoods within stingy or impoverished states attend schools that must make do with less than $4,000 per student per year.

What proportion of students attend well-funded and poorly funded schools? We can get some idea by looking at the school districts that report various levels of per-student funding. Figure 2 provides this information for the 7,206 districts that enrolled 1,000 or more students in 1995. Of these districts, 1,425 (or 20 percent) received less than $5,000 in 1995, and 451 (or 6 percent) provided $10,000 or more per student (National Center for Education Statistics, 1998).

Other data show that communities where student poverty is rare tend to have well-funded schools,

From Biddle, B., & Berliner, D. (2002). Unequal school funding in the United States. Educational Leadership, 59(8), 48–59. Reprinted with permission of the authors.

Figure 1

Average Annual Expenditures (in U.S. Dollars) per Student Within Each State in 1998, Adjusted for Cost of Living

State	Amount	State	Amount
New Jersey	$8,801	New Hampshire	$6,195
New York	7,853	Georgia	5,998
Connecticut	7,635	Washington	5,995
Wisconsin	7,448	Illinois	5,991
Delaware	7,255	Louisiana	5,989
Pennsylvania	7,202	North Dakota	5,979
Rhode Island	6,930	Florida	5,829
West Virginia	6,908	South Carolina	5,827
Michigan	6,873	Missouri	5,817
Iowa	6,823	Texas	5,815
Nebraska	6,799	North Carolina	5,763
Wyoming	6,790	South Dakota	5,667
Minnesota	6,767	Colorado	5,599
Vermont	6,746	Nevada	5,478
Maine	6,739	Hawaii	5,430
Indiana	6,661	Alabama	5,356
Alaska	6,581	New Mexico	5,339
Maryland	6,544	Oklahoma	5,317
Massachusetts	6,518	Arkansas	5,268
Oregon	6,422	Tennessee	5,223
Montana	6,349	Idaho	5,029
Kansas	6,311	California	4,939
Ohio	6,251	Mississippi	4,924
Virginia	6,215	Arizona	4,629
Kentucky	6,196	Utah	3,804

Source: From *Quality Counts 2000*, a supplement published by *Education Week* (2000), p. 82.

whereas schools in communities where student poverty is rampant tend to receive much less funding. Figure 3 shows the relationship between funding and student poverty rates for school districts with enrollments of more than 1,000. Districts reporting higher levels of funding are more likely to be located in communities where student poverty is minimal, whereas those reporting lower levels of funding are more often located in communities where student poverty is sizable (National Center for Education Statistics, 2000b).

Funding in Other Countries

Funding differences in the United States generate huge disparities in the quality of school buildings, facilities, curriculum, equipment for instruction, teacher

Figure 2
Disparities in School District Funding

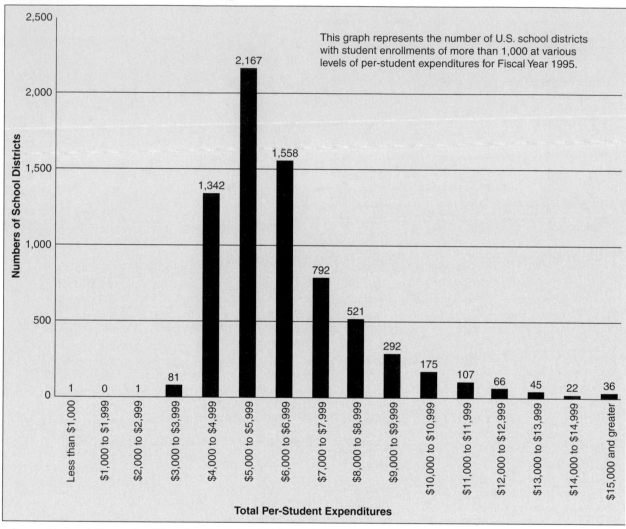

This graph represents the number of U.S. school districts with student enrollments of more than 1,000 at various levels of per-student expenditures for Fiscal Year 1995.

Source: National Center for Education Statistics, 1998, pp. 103–104.

experience and qualifications, class sizes, presence of auxiliary professionals, and other resources. It would surprise most U.S. citizens to learn that disparities such as these are simply not tolerated in other developed countries, where public schools normally receive equal funding in rich and poor communities alike on the basis of the number of students enrolled. Robert Slavin (1999) explains the difference:

> To my knowledge, the U.S. is the only nation to fund elementary and secondary education based on local wealth. Other developed countries either equalize funding or provide extra funding for individuals or groups felt to need it. In the Netherlands, for example, national funding is provided to all schools based on the number of pupils enrolled, but for every guilder allocated to a middle-class Dutch child, 1.25 guilders are allocated for a lower-class child and 1.9 guilders for a minority child, exactly the opposite of the situation in the U.S., where lower-class and minority children typically receive less than middle-class white children. (p. 520)

Poor and minority children always face problems that are not experienced by their peers, and in all advanced nations they tend to have more difficulties with education. But in the United States, those children face additional handicaps because they are often forced to attend poorly funded schools.

Figure 3

Total Per-Student Expenditures Versus Student Poverty Rates for U.S. School Districts with More Than 1,000 Enrollment

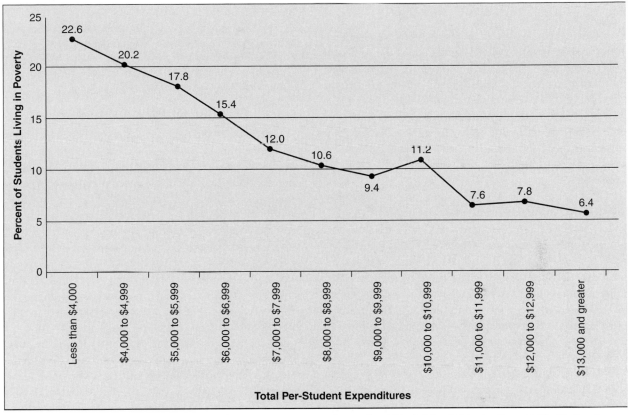

Source: Prepared using information from the "Common Care of Data for 1995." *School District Data Book,* National Center for Education Statistics (2000b).

Excuses for Unequal Funding

As a rule, U.S. citizens say they are committed to the welfare of children, the ideal of equal opportunity, and the notion that public education can and should provide a level playing field for all students. Given these stated values, why are they willing to tolerate unequal funding for public schools?

Perhaps the simplest answer to this question is that some people in the United States are unaware of the problem or think that inequities in school funding are small and don't matter. Many people, however, *are* aware that public schools are not equally supported but are willing to tolerate this form of inequity. Three reasons may lie behind this odd stance.

Historical Experiences

From their beginnings, public schools in the United States have been viewed as institutions that served their local communities. Initially, those schools were often financed by voluntary contributions, but by the end of the 19th century the tradition of funding them through local property taxes was widespread. This tradition had real advantages because many families were living in small, relatively isolated communities with similar standards of living.

But as time passed, fewer people lived in such communities. Instead, more people crowded into major cities, and then—if they achieved "success"—moved to the suburbs that came to surround those urban centers. As the suburbs grew, the inhabitants retained the tradition of funding public schools through local property taxes, but now this system was flawed. Parents who moved to affluent suburbs were generally willing to fund well-equipped, well-staffed public schools for their own children, but—familiar only with the tradition that public schools should be funded locally—they saw little reason to pay additional taxes to fund equivalent schools for the impoverished students left behind in city centers or rural towns.

Beliefs About the Causes of Poverty

Resistance to equitable funding for schools has also been supported by several belief systems about the causes of poverty. One of these, the ideology of *individualism,* holds that success and failure result mainly from individual effort rather than social circumstance. The people of the United States are known around the world for their strong belief in the power of personal effort, but this can lead to associated beliefs that blame impoverished persons for their lack of success in life (see Kluegel & Smith, 1986).

A second belief, *essentialism,* has it that less-privileged groups (such as African Americans, Hispanics, Native Americans, or women) inherit genetic characteristics that account for whatever lack of successes they have experienced. This thesis has appeared repeatedly, in Europe as well as the United States, for more than a century. Advocates such as Arthur Jensen (1972) or Richard Herrnstein and Charles Murray (1994) still promote this theory today. When applied to the poor, essentialism asserts that poverty results from intractable genetic flaws.

Another belief system, the *culture of poverty* thesis, argues that minority persons fail because of inappropriate traditions in the subcultures of their homes, communities, or ethnic groups (see Moynihan, 1969). When applied to the poor, such beliefs suggest that persons in impoverished communities fail because they possess only "limited linguistic codes" or are handicapped by lack of appropriate "cultural or social capital."

Each of these belief systems can lead to the argument that because students from impoverished homes are unlikely to benefit from a "quality" education, funding public schools equally in rich and poor neighborhoods would only waste tax dollars. To voice such arguments openly is not acceptable in the United States today, but the beliefs that would justify them are still embraced privately by many white, affluent people who use them to rationalize resistance to proposals for equal school funding.

Flawed Studies

Reluctance to provide equal funds for U.S. public schools has also been fueled by claims from prominent researchers, reviewers, and others asserting that the level of funding for schools does not affect student achievement. Not surprisingly, such claims often come from sources that are traditionally hostile to public education. For example, the Heritage Foundation (1989) asserted that

> Virtually all studies of school performance, in fact, reveal that spending has little bearing on school achievement. . . . Research demonstrates that [reforms focused on performance assessment] will be far more successful than [those] that concentrate on salary levels and class size. (p. 1)

What could possibly justify such a claim?

Early studies and the Coleman report. To answer this question, we must look at the history of research on school funding and student achievement. In 1966, James Coleman and his colleagues released a major report concerned with student achievement. This document, titled *Equality of Educational Opportunity,* described a massive study that had been commissioned by the National Center for Education Statistics in response to the Civil Rights Act of 1964. Many results discussed in the report concerned other equity issues, but its third section focused on the determinants of achievement and came to a surprising conclusion—that factors related to students' home backgrounds and peer groups in their schools were major generators of achievement, but that school quality and level of school funding had little or no impact after home and peer factors were taken into account.

The Coleman report was lengthy, its procedures and statistics were complex, and its text was murky—and, as a result, almost nobody actually read it. The press, however, widely trumpeted its surprising conclusion about the ineffectiveness of school factors. Thus, the public was led to believe that research had "proven" that schools (and their funding) had little effect, and the fat was in the fire. Conservative forces hostile to the public sector rejoiced because their negative opinions about public schools had been vindicated. Educators, political liberals, and advocates for disadvantaged students became alarmed and began to "explain away" the report's conclusions and to attack its authors.

Somehow, at the time, almost nobody noticed that the report contained major errors likely to have reduced the size of its estimates for school effects on students' achievements. Among other problems, the report's authors had failed to use available scaling techniques to validate their procedures, had made serious mistakes when assigning indicators to major variables, and had failed to measure crucial variables now known to be associated with school effects. In addition, the report had used nonstandard procedures for statistical analyses, which generated falsely deflated estimates of school effects.

To summarize, the Coleman report was badly flawed, although its flaws were not widely understood at the time. Its findings were vigorously promoted, however, and its suspect conclusion that level of school funding has little impact on student achievement passed into the public domain as a confirmed fact.

Efforts by Economists. At about the same time, a sizable group of economists began to publish studies trying to estimate the size of effects (if any) of investing in public education. In doing so, they were responding to ideas expressed by influential leaders in their field. Milton Friedman (1962) had begun to preach a doctrine that favored privatization of most public enterprises (including education), and, about a decade later, Kenneth Boulding (1972) noted that increases in education funding seemed not to have been associated with greater student achievement. These ideas led some of their economist colleagues to pose models for studying the effects of education investments. Many studies based on these models have since appeared, and most have not reported significant net effects of school funding, a fact noted by Eric Hanushek, an influential economist with conservative political ties. Hanushek has declared repeatedly that level of funding is not related to achievement in the real world of public education (see, for example, 1989, 1996a, 1996b)—a conclusion welcomed by those opposed to funding reform proposals.

Hanushek's claims have also attracted opposition. For example, meta-analysts Rob Greenwald, Larry Hedges, and Richard Laine have noted that the bulk of studies by economists have reported positive net effects of funding, and if one combines their findings through statistical aggregation, the resulting pooled estimates suggest *sizable* effects of funding (Greenwald, Hedges, & Laine, 1996; Hedges & Greenwald, 1996; Hedges, Laine, & Greenwald, 1994). Educators and those motivated to redress inequities in funding have welcomed this conclusion, but Hanushek and others have attacked it, and the issue has remained unresolved.

The major trouble with this quarrel is that most of the studies reported by economists have involved serious methodological problems. Most used small samples that did not represent the full range of schools, and most did not examine school funding directly but rather looked at funding-associated school characteristics— such as teacher salaries, student–teacher ratios, or administrative costs—that may or may not be tied to student achievement. Many also employed questionable measures and inappropriate techniques for statistical analysis. Thus, as a group, these studies are poor

tools to use for estimating funding effects in the real world, and it is not clear that much can be learned about the issue by reviewing their findings. Nevertheless, such reviews have certainly appeared and have helped derail efforts to reform school funding practices in the United States.

Strong Studies and Their Findings

Fortunately, other researchers have published a number of strong studies on the topic, and we can gain useful knowledge by reviewing their results.

Features of Strong Studies

As in other fields, the best way to pin down the effects of differential funding would be to conduct experiments in which research subjects are assigned randomly to different process conditions. Needless to say, it would be unethical to design an experiment in which students, classrooms, schools, or perhaps school districts are assigned randomly to conditions of adequate and inadequate funding. Unfortunately, however, such conditions exist in the real world of U.S. education, so our next-best strategy is to examine the outcomes of such conditions using well-designed surveys.

As a rule, all strong surveys collect data from reliable sources, make use of validated measuring and scaling procedures, and employ appropriate statistical tools for analyzing data. In addition, strong surveys on the effects of school funding should meet three specific conditions. First, they should be based on sizable samples that include examples of both well-funded and impoverished schools. (Normally this is done by drawing a large and representative sample, by random means, from schools across the country or a state that exhibits a wide range of funding conditions.) Second, such studies should include statistical controls for level of income, socioeconomic status, or other types of advantage in the home or community that students bring with them to the school. And third, such studies should examine effects associated with only one level of aggregation—for example, if the study examines the effects of funding for classrooms, then all other variables used in the analysis should also apply to classrooms. The reason for this last requirement is that the sizes of statistics change as one goes up the aggregation ladder. If effects from more than one level of aggregation must be examined, then an appropriate multi-level technique must be used for analyzing data.

Surveys that meet the conditions described above have many advantages, but even strong surveys have difficulty pinning down causal relations. Why is this so? Let us assume that a survey examines a sample of schools in which level of funding varies and discovers that schools with greater funding also have higher levels of student achievement (controlling for level of home or community advantage). Does this mean that the funding differences generated the achievement outcomes? Hardly. Perhaps causal relations in the real world go the other way, so that where student achievement is higher, parents are more willing to provide greater funding for schools. Or funding differences might be affected by other conditions in students' homes or communities that no investigator has yet thought to examine.

The point is that no matter how carefully one constructs a survey of funding and its outcomes, critics may point out that it has not ruled out all alternatives that might explain its findings. Thus, to establish the case for a causal relation, one must conduct several surveys, using different techniques, which collectively rule out all reasonably credible, alternative processes that might account for the apparent effect one is studying.

The bottom line: Even if we confine our attention to strong studies of funding effects—well-conducted surveys meeting the criteria set forth above—we must look at findings from various studies before we decide that funding effects have been pinned down convincingly.

Strong Study Findings

Bearing these cautions in mind, can we locate strong studies, and if so, what have those studies found? Indeed, we can find such studies (see, for example, Biddle, 1997; Dolan & Schmidt, 1987; Ellinger, Wright, & Hirlinger, 1995; Elliott, 1998; Ferguson, 1991; Harter, 1999; Payne & Biddle, 1999; Wenglinsky, 1997a, 1997b). Although we do not list all of them here, the examples we cite will indicate typical findings. As a rule, such studies report that level of funding is tied to sizable net effects for student outcome.

To illustrate, a study of 11th grade achievement scores among school districts in Oklahoma found that both student poverty and per-student revenues within schools were associated with achievement. Effects for the former were roughly twice the size of those for the latter (Ellinger et al., 1995). Similar results were found for the determinants of 8th grade achievement scores among school districts from across the United States that participated in the Second International Study of Mathematics Achievement (Payne & Biddle,

1999). And Harold Wenglinsky (1997a), using data drawn from the National Assessment of Educational Progress, found that average student socioeconomic status and per-student expenditures within school districts were both associated with level of mathematics achievement in the 8th grade, but that the effects for socioeconomic status were again larger than those for per-student expenditures.

Collectively, these studies have employed various techniques designed to rule out alternative hypotheses, and all of them have concluded that funding has substantial effects, although level of advantage in the home and community has an even greater impact.

Research on Related Issues

Additional research has also begun to appear on issues related to the effects of unequal funding.

International Studies

How great are the effects generated by differences in school funding and student disadvantage among U.S. schools? One way to answer this question is to compare the sizes of those effects with disparities in achievement among different countries found in international comparisons.

For example, the International Association for the Advancement of Educational Achievement published the *Mathematics Benchmarking Report,* based on data from the Third International Mathematics and Science Study, which compared 8th grade mathematics achievement scores of students in other nations with those of students in specific states, school districts, and school consortia within the United States (Mullis et al., 2001).

The two best-scoring entities in the United States were the Naperville, Illinois, Public School District and the self-proclaimed "First-in-the-World" Consortium (composed of school districts from the Chicago North Shore area). Both of these entities have high levels of funding and serve low numbers of impoverished students, and both earned high achievement scores comparable to those of Hong Kong, Japan, and other top-scoring countries. In contrast, the two worst-scoring U.S. entities were the Miami-Dade County Public Schools in Florida and the Rochester School District in New York. Both of these receive low levels of funding and serve many poor students, and each earned low achievement scores similar to those of the worst-scoring nations in the study— Turkey, Jordan, and Iran.

Thus, differences in student advantage and funding in the United States generate achievement disparities that are comparable to those separating the highest- and lowest-achieving nations in international studies. These sizable disparities suggest that the U.S. public school system includes a *huge* range of education environments.

Funding Differences Over Time

Critics of public schools sometimes claim that funding for schools has increased sharply in recent years, but this increase has not generated achievement gains (Hanushek, 1996b). To illustrate, here is what Benno Schmidt, former President of Yale University, said to justify his decision to head a new, national, for-profit, private school program:

> We have roughly doubled per-pupil spending (after inflation) in public schools since 1965 . . . yet dropout rates remain distressingly high. . . . Overall, high school students today are posting lower SAT scores than a generation ago. The nation's investment in educational improvement has produced very little return. (cited in Rothstein, 1993)

This claim is strongly refuted by a careful study of spending patterns in nine school districts across the United States from 1967 to 1991 (Miles & Rothstein, 1995). Recent legislative mandates and court decisions have assigned to schools a host of new responsibilities designed to meet the needs of disadvantaged students. These mandates have often been underfunded but, taken together, have raised costs for public schools significantly. As a result, about one third of net new dollars during this period went to support special education students; 8 percent went to dropout prevention programs, alternative instruction, and counseling aimed at keeping students in school; another 8 percent went to expand school lunch programs; 28 percent went to fund increased salaries for a teacher population whose average age was increasing; and so forth. Very few additional dollars were provided for needs associated with basic instruction during these years. Small wonder that these types of additional "investments" generated few achievement gains for mainstream students.

How Funding Affects Student Outcomes

If better-funded schools do generate higher levels of achievement, how do they accomplish this task? Various studies have begun to explore this question, with interesting findings. So far, the most impressive findings are associated with teacher qualifications. Better-funded school districts can attract teachers with higher levels of education, more experience, and higher scores on competency tests: these teachers, in turn, seem to generate better achievement scores among students (Darling-Hammond & Post, 2000; Elliott, 1998; Ferguson, 1991; Ferguson & Ladd, 1996).

In addition, better-funded schools are often able to reduce class sizes, and smaller classes seem to help generate better achievement among students. As a rule, the effects so far reported for class size appear to be weaker than those for teacher qualifications, but this conclusion may not be valid. For one thing, some studies of the problem have not examined class size directly but rather the effects of a proxy variable–student–teacher ratio—that is assumed to represent class size but does not. Student–teacher ratio is normally measured at the school or district level and often counts the school's coaches, nurses, social workers, and other service professionals who do not teach.

Moreover, evidence indicates that class size reduction raises achievement *when applied in the early grades*, but evidence has not yet appeared indicating that class size has much effect in the middle school or high school years. Thus, to study the effects of funding-associated differences in class size on achievement properly, one should focus efforts on class size in the early grades. Fortunately, at least one well-crafted study has already done this (Ferguson & Ladd, 1996), and that study reported strong effects for class size. In addition, strong field experiments and trial programs have confirmed that smaller class sizes in the early grades generate both immediate and long-term advantages in student outcomes and that these effects are greater for minority or impoverished students (Biddle & Berliner, 2002a, 2002b).

Differential Impact

Given the evidence reviewed above, it seems obvious that students from disadvantaged families will suffer the most from the U.S. system of unequal school funding because these students are more likely to attend poorly funded public schools. In addition, one assumes that disadvantaged students would suffer particularly when they attend schools with inadequate funding, and research is beginning to support this assumption.

In his recent study, Harold Wenglinsky (1998) found that gaps in achievement between students from high and low socioeconomic-status homes are greater in poorly funded schools than in well-funded schools. And Elizabeth Harter (1999) reported that the achievement effects of funding levels associated with school upkeep are greater in schools serving impoverished students.

Doing Something About the Problem

The funding of public schools through local property taxes has deep historical roots in our country, and suburban hostility to plans for greater equity in public school funding has been intense. Given such facts, what can we do to help solve this problem today?

Because funding inequities exist both within and between states, the ideal way to address them would be through changes in federal policies, but interest in school funding issues has not been great in Washington, D.C., or among the national media. We would need a concerted effort to change this situation as long as most federal politicians depend on support from wealthy donors who often live in the suburbs.

But what about the federal courts? One would think that inequitable school funding creates conditions that violate U.S. citizens' claims for equal opportunities, but in its landmark ruling on *San Antonio Independent School District v. Rodriguez,* issued in 1973, the U.S. Supreme Court denied this contention. By a 5–4 vote, the high court ruled that the U.S. Constitution does not require equal funding among school districts. This decision effectively foreclosed federal court action to remedy inequities in school funding, at least for the near future.

This does not mean that the funding equity issue has been dead in state courts. On the contrary, many state constitutions mandate equal opportunities in education. As a result, suits challenging the legality of unequal funding based on district property taxes have been filed in more than three-fourths of the states, and these suits have been upheld or are still pending in at least 31 states (Morales, 1997; Murray, Evans, & Schwab, 1998; Rothstein, 2000). Details and histories of these efforts have varied sharply from state to state, but we can summarize their results with four statements:

- Particularly when successful, these suits have stimulated both public interest and follow-up actions by state legislatures designed to provide greater funding equity.
- In many cases, such actions have provided additional dollars from state taxes for impoverished school districts while leaving levels of funding for affluent school districts in place.
- These reforms have tended to reduce but not eliminate the within-state inequities that they were designed to address.
- These actions have *not* addressed inequities in school funding among the states.

Meanwhile, the focus of some state litigation has begun to shift away from *equity* to *adequacy* of support for schools, the latter term referring to whether schools have sufficient funds to "provide adequate education so that all students have equal opportunities to play roles as citizens and to compete in the labor market" (Rothstein, 2000, p. 74). This shift opens a can of worms because how one goes about developing valid and agreed-on measures of "adequacy" is by no means clear. Indeed, if people in the United States were to commit themselves to a level playing field in public education, they (like the Dutch) should provide *extra* funding for schools that serve large numbers of impoverished students. Such funds would be needed not only for special educational programs and extra physical facilities but also for additional salaries to recruit and retain qualified teachers who would otherwise migrate to schools serving fewer "problematic" students.

What Do We Now Know?

Taken together, research evidence now available suggests a number of conclusions about unequal funding and its effects:

- Public schools in the United States receive sharply unequal funding. Among the nation's school districts, annual funding per student can range from less than $4,000 to more than $15,000, and although the "typical" school district with 1,000 or more students receives roughly $5,000 per year for each student, affluent districts may receive $10,000 per student or more.
- Large differences in public school funding appear both among the states and within many states.
- Funding differences appear, in part, because much of the financial support for public schools comes from local property taxes, which means that the amount of funding that communities are able to provide for their schools varies according to community affluence.
- Although most people in the United States are not aware of it, other advanced nations do *not* fund public schools with local property taxes. Instead, they provide equal per-student funding from general tax revenues for all schools throughout the country. Some nations also provide extra funding for disadvantaged students.
- Most people in the United States say they support equal funding for public schools, but affluent and

powerful people often oppose efforts to correct funding inequities.

- Opposition to equity in school funding reflects several factors: ignorance about funding differences; unthinking acceptance of traditional methods for funding education; selfish desires to keep personal taxes low; and inappropriate beliefs about the causes of poverty that reflect individualism, essentialism, or the culture of poverty thesis.

- Claims from flawed research and reviews of research have asserted that levels of funding for schools have little or no effect on student outcomes.

- Strong studies indicate that level of student advantage within the home or community matters a great deal to outcomes in education, but sizable (although smaller) net effects are also associated with differences in school funding.

- The joint effects of school funding and student advantage are sizable. Achievement scores from U.S. school districts with substantial funding and low student poverty are similar to those earned by the highest-scoring countries in international comparative studies, whereas scores from districts where funding is inadequate and poverty is high are similar to those of the lowest-scoring countries.

- New demands placed on public schools have driven aggregate increases in school funding during recent years. These increases have not been used for additional resources that would generate increases in average student achievement.

- Two types of resources associated with greater school funding have been tied to higher levels of student achievement: stronger teacher qualifications and smaller class sizes in the early grades.

- The achievements of disadvantaged students are more likely to suffer in response to inequities in school funding for two reasons: Those students are more likely to attend poorly funded schools, and they are more likely to be hurt by lack of academic resources when schools are underfunded.

- Legal and political efforts to reform funding inequities have been weak at the federal level, but considerable activity concerned with unequal funding has taken place in state courts and legislatures. The latter efforts have provoked some increases in state funds for poorly funded districts while leaving funding for rich, suburban districts largely in place.

Policy Implications

Given our traditional beliefs about individual efficacy and the recent flowering of conservative thought in the United States, it is hardly surprising that some argue that access to education is a personal right to be exercised by students and their families solely for their own benefit. And yet, Americans have also long embraced an alternative vision for public education that John Adams, Thomas Jefferson, James Madison, and John Dewey articulated.

This vision has stressed the need for a public school system that generates the informed citizenry needed for democratic government, embraces the welfare of all children in the nation, upholds the ideal of equal opportunity, and stresses the belief that public education can and should provide a level playing field. Dewey's maxim, now a century old, applies here: "What the best and wisest parent wants for his own child, that must be what the community wants for all its children" (1899/1900, p. 3).

References

Biddle, B. J. (1997). Foolishness, dangerous nonsense, and real correlates of state differences in achievement. *Phi Delta Kappan, 79*(1), 8–13.

Biddle, B. J., & Berliner, D. C. (2002a). Small class size and its effects. *Educational Leadership, 59*(5), 12–23.

Biddle, B. J., & Berliner, D. C. (2002b). *What research says about small classes and their effects.* Rockefeller reports on poverty and education. Columbia: Department of Psychological Sciences, University of Missouri; and Phoenix: College of Education, Arizona State University. Available: http://edpolicyreports.org

Boulding, K. (1972). The schooling industry as a possible pathological section of the American economy. *Review of Educational Research, 42*(1), 129–143.

Coleman, J. S., Campbell, E. Q., Hobson, C. J., McPartland, J., Mood, A. M., Weinfeld, F. D., & York, R. L. (1966). *Equality of educational opportunity.* Washington, DC: U.S. Government Printing Office.

Darling-Hammond, L., & Post, L. (2000). Inequality in teaching and schooling: Supporting high-quality teaching and leadership in low-income schools. In R. D. Kahlenberg (Ed.), *A notion at risk: Preserving public education as an engine for social mobility* (pp. 127–167). New York: The Century Foundation Press.

Dewey, J. (1899/1900). *The school and society.* Chicago: University of Chicago Press.

Dolan, R. C., & Schmidt, R. M. (1987). Assessing the impact of expenditure on achievement: Some methodological and policy considerations. *Economics of Education Review, 6*(3), 285–299.

Education Week. (2000, January 13). *Quality counts 2000: Who should teach?, 19*(18) (Supplement). Bethesda, MD: Author.

Ellinger, K., Wright, D. E., III, & Hirlinger, M. W. (1995). Brains for bucks?: School revenue and student achievement in Oklahoma. *The Social Science Journal, 32*(3), 299–308.

Elliott, M. (1998). School finance and opportunity to learn: Does money well spent enhance students' achievement? *Sociology of Education, 71*(3), 223–245.

Ferguson, R. F. (1991). Paying for public education: New evidence on how and why money matters. *Harvard Journal on Legislation, 28*(2), 465–498.

Ferguson, R. F., & Ladd, H. F. (1996). How and why money matters: An analysis of Alabama schools. In H. F. Ladd (Ed.), *Holding schools accountable: Performance-based reform in education* (pp. 265–298). Washington, DC: The Brookings Institution.

Friedman, M. (1962). *Capitalism and freedom.* Chicago: University of Chicago Press.

Greenwald, R., Hedges, L. V., & Laine, R. D. (1996). The effect of school resources on school achievement. *Review of Educational Research, 66*(3), 361–396.

Hanushek, E. A. (1989). The impact of differential expenditures on school performance. *Educational Researcher, 18*(4), 45–65.

Hanushek, E. A. (1996a). A more complete picture of school resource policies. *Review of Educational Research, 66*(3), 397–409.

Hanushek, E. A. (1996b). School resources and student performance. In G. Burtless (Ed.), *Does money matter? The effect of school resources on student achievement and adult success* (pp. 43–73). Washington, DC: The Brookings Institution.

Harter, E. A. (1999). How educational expenditures relate to student achievement: Insights from Texas elementary schools. *Journal of Education Finance, 24*(3), 281–302.

Hedges, L. V., & Greenwald, R. (1996). Have times changed? The relation between school resources and student performance. In G. Burtless (Ed.), *Does money matter? The effect of school resources on student achievement and adult success* (pp. 74–92). Washington, DC: The Brookings Institution.

Hedges, L. V., Laine, R. D., & Greenwald, R. (1994). Does money matter? A metaanalysis of studies of the effects of differential school inputs on student outcomes. *Educational Researcher, 23*(3), 5–14.

Heritage Foundation. (1989). *Education Update, 12*(4).

Herrnstein, R. J., & Murray, C. (1994). *The bell curve: The reshaping of American life by differences in intelligence.* New York: The Free Press.

Jensen, A. R. (1972). *Genetics and education.* New York: Harper & Row.

Kluegel, J. R., & Smith, E. R. (1986). *Beliefs about inequality: Americans' view of what is and what ought to be.* New York: Aldine de Gruyter.

Miles, K. H., & Rothstein, R. (1995). *Where's the money gone?: Changes in the level and composition of education spending.* Washington, DC: Economic Policy Institute.

Morales, J. (1997). The courts and equity: A state-by-state overview. In S. Karp, R. Lowe, B. Miner, & B. Peterson (Eds.), *Funding for justice: Money, equity, and the future of public education* (pp. 61–67). Milwaukee, WI: Rethinking Schools.

Moynihan, D. P. (Ed.). (1969). *On understanding poverty: Perspectives from the social sciences.* New York: BasicBooks.

Mullis, I. V. S., Martin, M. O., Gonzalez, E. J., O'Connor, K. M., Chrostowski, S. J., Gregory, K. D., Garden, R. A., & Smith, T. A. (2001). *Mathematics benchmarking report: TIMSS 1999—Eighth grade achievement for U.S. states and districts in an international context.* Chestnut Hill, MA: Boston College.

Murray, S. E., Evans. W. N., & Schwab, R. M. (1998). Education-finance reform and the distribution of education resources. *The American Economic Review, 88*(4), 789–812.

National Center for Education Statistics. (1998). *Inequalities in public school district revenues.* Washington, DC: Office of Educational Research and Improvement, U.S. Department of Education.

National Center for Education Statistics. (2000a). *The condition of education 2000.* Washington, DC: Office of Educational Research and Improvement, U.S. Department of Education.

National Center for Education Statistics. (2000b). *Common core of data for school years 1993/94 through 1997/98.* [CD-ROM]. Washington, DC: Office of Educational Research and Improvement, U.S. Department of Education.

Payne, K. J., & Biddle, B. J. (1999). Poor school funding, child poverty, and mathematics achievement. *Educational Researcher, 28*(6), 4–13.

Rothstein, R. (1993). The myth of public school failure. *The American Prospect, 4*(13), 20–34.

Rothstein, R. (2000). Equalizing education resources on behalf of disadvantaged children. In R. D. Kahlenberg (Ed.), *A notion at risk: Preserving public education as an engine for social mobility* (pp. 31–92). New York: The Century Foundation Press.

San Antonio Independent School District v. Rodriguez, 411 U.S. 1 (1973).

Slavin, R. E. (1999). How can funding equity ensure enhanced achievement? *Journal of Education Finance, 24*(4), 519–528.

Wenglinsky, H. (1997a). How money matters: The effect of school district spending on academic achievement. *Sociology of Education, 70*(3), 221–237.

Wenglinsky, H. (1997b). *When money matters: How educational expenditures improve student performance and how they don't.* Princeton, NJ: Educational Testing Service.

Wenglinsky, H. (1998). Finance equalization and within-school equity: The relationship between education spending and the social distribution of achievement. *Educational Evaluation & Policy Analysis, 20*(4), 269–283.

BLOWING IN THE WIND

Stephen Smith, John L. Myers, and Julie Underwood

Money is important in education because it can determine the quality of students' educational experiences. It affects the number of students in a class as well as the quality of learning resources available to them, such as technology and textbooks. It also influences teacher salaries, an important factor affecting teacher morale and their decisions to remain in education. States across the nation are currently facing a budget crisis, these authors assert, fueled by declining revenues and increased costs. State incomes have declined because of the nationwide economic downturn. This comes at the same time that states are being asked to pay for costly mandates from federal No Child Left Behind legislation. In addition, choice movements, in the form of charter schools and vouchers, may also prove costly to fund. As you read this article ask yourself, "How do budget issues affect teachers' lives?"

Think About This . . .

1. State governments currently pay for about 50% of school costs. Local governments account for the other large proportion of education funding—44%. Which of these sources is most susceptible to economic downturns? Why?

2. What are the different ways that No Child Left Behind legislation will result in increased state expenditures? Which of these will likely be the most costly?

3. How could the choice movement—charter schools and vouchers—also result in budgetary problems for schools? How could this problem be addressed?

4. In what ways can budget cuts affect beginning teachers? How might this be similar to or different for veteran teachers?

Times are tough all over, but never have they been tougher for the public schools. Gone are the balmy days when many states had enough revenues to cut taxes, bolster rainy day funds, and increase funding for education. Now, as the National Conference of State Legislatures (NCSL) succinctly puts it, "State budgets are under seige." Over the past two years, the drop in state revenues has been at least as severe as the incredible run up during the late 1990s, resulting in a budget crisis the likes of which has not been seen since World War II.

"Nearly every state is in fiscal crisis," according to the November 2002 *Fiscal Survey of States,* published by the National Governors Association (NGA). "Amid a slowing national economy, state revenues have shrunk at the same time that spending pressures are mounting . . . creating massive budget shortfalls," the NGA reported. "As states fight to balance their budgets, the solutions available to them are increasingly dire,

and some of the most difficult fiscal decisions have yet to be made."

With elementary and secondary education making up more than 22 percent of state spending, schools will surely feel the pinch from these budget shortfalls. To compound the budget difficulties, schools are also facing increased responsibility for implementing new federal mandates under the No Child Left Behind Act (NCLB). The federal government initially provided extra funding to states to meet these requirements, but most agree that funding will not cover all costs. Although the Fiscal Year 2003 Omnibus Appropriations Act signed into law this past February increased NCLB funding by 8 percent, the total is still $5 billion less than originally authorized and falls short of fully funding the mandate.

From Smith, S., Myers, J., & Underwood, J. (2003). Blowing in the wind. American School Board Journal, 19(5), 18–21. *Reprinted with permission of the* American School Board Journal.

To top things off, many states are also wrestling with issues related to charter schools and vouchers, both of which have cost implications for the public schools.

How Bad Is It?

Headlines from across the country tell the story: Some school districts in Louisiana and Colorado have moved to a four-day week to save transportation and food service costs. The Portland, Ore., school district considered cutting 24 school days from its school year, and districts in other states have been asked to return a portion of their state funding midway through the school year.

These cutbacks at the local level reflect what's happening with state budgets. Seventeen states cut K–12 education budgets in FY 2002, and so far in FY 2003, 12 states have made cuts in K–12 education. These cuts—often seen as the sacred cow of state budgets—show the severity of the budget crisis. In the past, state funding for K–12 education has often been spared in tough budget times, for two reasons. First, every state has an education clause in its constitution requiring the state to provide a "free and uniform" or "thorough and efficient" education, or words to that effect. Second, opinion polls showing public support for good schools make cutting K–12 education a politically unacceptable choice. Still, when states nationwide began Fiscal Year (FY) 2003 facing a $49 billion budget gap, many governors and legislatures were forced to put everything on the table.

What made a popular and constitutionally required public service like education vulnerable this time around? The answer is that, unlike the federal government, 49 of the 50 states (Vermont being the exception) require a balanced budget every fiscal year. K–12 education consumes a large share of state funding: from 25 percent and 40 percent of general fund expenditures in most states and more than 22 percent of total state expenditures. So, facing shortfalls, many states were left with no choice but to examine possible cuts or at least flat levels of funding for the schools.

States have used a variety of methods to overcome these shortages and deficits. More than half have made cuts in their overall budgets. On the revenue side, 18 states have raised taxes, and others have turned to short-term solutions, such as using tobacco settlement funds (16 states) and dipping into rainy day funds (12 states). Forecasts by NCSL predict difficult budget situations for the foreseeable future, and state budget officers and national organizations say they can't yet see light at the end of the tunnel.

Unfortunately, the available cash and reserves that many states have used to buffer spending cuts over the past two years are shrinking quickly. Nationwide, states had $18.6 billion in cash and $20.3 billion in rainy day funds available in FY 2001. Just two years later, these amounts have been reduced to $5.7 billion in cash and $11.4 billion in rainy day funds.

Of potential concern for education observers is the fact that states are increasingly unwilling to raise taxes as a cure for budget deficits. During the recession of the 1990s, state governments generated $15 billion through tax increases, or 5.4 percent of total budget. But the 18 states that have raised taxes for FY 2003 have generated only $9.1 billion, or only 1.6 percent of total budget, a third of which comes from increases in cigarette taxes. Many worry that the reluctance to raise taxes, coupled with shrinking reserves, will leave states with no other choice than to cut state spending, including K–12 education.

A Costly Mandate

In the face of this budget crisis, states must respond to the 2001 reauthorization of the Elementary and Secondary Education Act, known as No Child Left Behind. NCLB is a logical extension of the standards-based reform movement of the past 20 years, but it is a costly one. Even after increasing funding for NCLB, the federal government still provides only 7 percent of total K–12 funding, and the statute's top-down regulations and requirements will place new funding burdens on states and school districts across the country.

By now, NCLB's requirements are well-known: In addition to requiring states to test students in grades three through eight and then again in high school, the law requires that teachers and paraprofessionals in Title I schools be "highly qualified." States and school districts must also collect student performance information at the individual student level and disaggregate and report the information on the basis of various demographic factors.

Consider NCLB's mandated student assessment programs. Initial estimates for the creation of these tests totaled $1 billion, with the federal government providing roughly half of the funding. The National Association of State Boards of Education estimates the actual cost for designing and implementing these tests to be closer to $7 billion.

Testing is just one of the costs associated with NCLB, of course. The cost of hiring new teachers and paraprofessionals or increasing the skills and qualifications of current personnel has not yet been calculated.

But common sense says this requirement will represent a very real increased cost to local school districts. In addition, states will need to create data collection and warehousing systems, which can cost in the tens of millions of dollars. Again, no federal funding was provided for this requirement.

It is difficult to put a precise price tag on NCLB costs, however. Recent studies undertaken in Vermont and New Hampshire estimate that for every dollar a state receives in federal funding for NCLB, the state will have to spend between $7 and $15 to meet federal requirements. But when calculating state costs, it is important to consider existing expenditures as well. For example, most states had implemented teacher quality initiatives before NCLB. An analysis of what the federal government is requiring *above and beyond* what states were previously engaged in regarding education reform will more accurately reflect the magnitude of this unfunded mandate.

However high the costs of meeting the input and infrastructure requirements of NCLB, the costs of *not* meeting the statute's performance goals could be even greater. Under NCLB, all subgroups of students in a school or district must make annual yearly progress (AYP) toward proficient standards. Failure to meet AYP numbers will result in the following sanctions:

- If a school fails to meet the AYP requirements for two consecutive years, the school is to be identified as needing improvement. At this point, the school will receive technical assistance and, in the next school year, must offer public school choice options unless prohibited by the state. Students may transfer to another school within the local education agency (LEA) or district; if all schools in the LEA or district are labeled as needing improvement, the students may transfer to an outside school. Fulfilling this requirement may be costly for individual schools, but funding for the students who exercise the choice option will remain in the school district. Providing transportation for these students can be an additional cost, however.
- If a school fails to meet AYP for three consecutive years, its students must be provided not only a choice among public schools but also supplementary instructional opportunities from service providers of their choice, from a list of state-approved providers. These services will be paid for by Title I funds in an amount of the cost of the actual services or the national per-pupil allocation under the LEA's Title I Part A grant, which is about $1,000. LEAs may use up to 20 percent of their Title I funds for supplemental services and transportation, though they are not responsible for

providing transportation to and from the site of the services. LEAs may also use resources from the Innovative Education Program Strategies funding pool. States may use funds that are earmarked for program improvement or administration from Title I Part A or Title I Part V. If there is not enough funding to pay for all the services needed, services may be offered for only the lowest-performing students.

- If a school fails to meet AYP for four consecutive years, a series of corrective actions takes place. These include replacing school staff, implementing new curriculum, decreasing administrative authority at the school level, providing an outside expert to advise the school, extending the length of the school day or school year, and/or changing the organizational structure of the school. Each of these actions could result in significant costs to states and school districts.
- If a school fails to make AYP for five consecutive years, it must be restructured. This could take the form of reopening the school as a charter school, replacing all of the staff, or other major actions, such as having the state take over the district's governance structure. Once again, these actions could be costly.

The overall costs of these sanctions are difficult to estimate, but we can safely say they will be high. Approximately one-third of U.S. students currently perform at a proficient level. Getting all students to perform at that level within 12 years will require a 200 percent increase in productivity without significant increases in funding. Given NCLB's lofty goals, we can anticipate that many schools will not meet the adequate yearly progress requirements. The costs associated with sanctions for those schools will be widespread and severe.

Charters, Vouchers, and Overhead Costs

A third and often debated source of costs to the public schools is the movement for charter schools and vouchers. With charter schools, that movement has been swift. What started as a few schools in a couple of states just 10 years ago has expanded to more than 2,600 schools in 36 states today. Although proponents and critics do not agree whether charter schools will take away funding for traditional school systems, a continued increase in charter schools coupled with school vouchers could potentially be costly for the states.

Currently, less than 1 percent of all students attend publicly funded charter schools. Proponents say charter schools can save states money because no school facility funding is required for these students. Opponents counter by citing such additional costs as charter-related administrative units and functions within state departments of education.

More troubling, however, is the question of reducing public school overhead costs if significant numbers of students take advantage of charters and vouchers and leave the traditional public schools. If a school has 500 students, for example, and 20 of those students, or 4 percent, leave the school, the school loses 4 percent of its funding. Some say the school must then reduce expenditures by 4 percent. Others respond that it is not possible to reduce such overhead costs as heating, transportation, and debt service in proportion to the number of students who leave.

With only a small percentage of students attending charter schools or using vouchers, the issue of reducing overhead costs has not been too troublesome—yet. In light of the U.S. Supreme Court's 2002 ruling in *Zelman v. Simmons-Harris* upholding the Cleveland voucher program, and considering the anticipated legislative activity

to promote vouchers, many are worried that reducing overhead expenditures in traditional schools will prove difficult and could further erode K–12 funding.

With state budget difficulties, NCLB requirements, and potential increases in the number of charter and voucher students, funding for traditional K–12 education will be challenging for the foreseeable future. It is difficult to see a silver lining in the dark fiscal cloud that hangs over education, but we can hope that necessity will bring about effective new strategies that can help improve education.

State and local officials must remember that education is a good public investment, in bad economic times as well as in good. Investing in education pays off both monetarily, in terms of increased productivity and tax revenues, and politically. For, as Thomas Jefferson said, "Education is necessary to build an active citizenry and ensure a strong democracy. It is the undergird for our constitutional freedoms of speech, association, and political activity."

PUBLIC-SPIRITED CHOICE: HOW DIVERSE SCHOOLS CAN SERVE THE COMMON GOOD

David Ferrero

School choice in the form of vouchers and charter schools is being heralded as an essential component of education in a democratic society. Parents ought to have a voice in deciding how and where their children will be educated, choice advocates contend. But, how can our schools foster personal individuality and choice while still educating children for productive civic roles in our democracy? This question is at the heart of David Ferrero's concerns about the school choice movement in America. Current market models of choice emphasize individual interests and needs at the expense of a broader, more cohesive view of education in a democracy, Ferrero asserts. Needed is a balanced view of education that emphasizes individual needs with the common good of society. As you read this article ask yourself, "How can the competing goals of meeting individual needs and civic goals be addressed in today's schools?"

Think About This . . .

1. Within the market model, advocates use three rationales for school choice. Which of these do you think is most valid? Least?
2. How does school choice run counter to the Common School movement? Which position best meets the needs of children?

3. Which criteria does Ferrero suggest for judging the adequacy of choice-based schools? Which of these criteria are most important?

4. How will you resolve the dilemma of individual needs versus public good in your classroom? What are specific strategies or actions that you will take to reinforce either position?

Some school choice skeptics worry that choice will erode the civic purposes of schooling. Given the thrust of the most prominent choice advocacy, this concern may be justified. Three approaches prevail: The first, and by far most prevalent, is the market model, wherein families are "customers" and schools are "service providers" competing for market share by catering to diverse tastes and preferences while delivering high test scores. The second is a parents'-rights model, in which parents' interests categorically trump those of the state. The third is a fairness model, where choice is understood as a way to give poor families the same kinds of options that wealthier ones have.

What all three models have in common is a conception of schooling that stresses the individual and private benefits over common, public ones. Schools provide, families consume. And consumers have rights, not obligations. The fairness model breaks somewhat from this pattern by focusing on the public good of equal opportunity, but it too tends to focus on what schools owe poor families, without much regard for what families might owe in return. When proponents refer to poor, minority, or disabled children as "under*served*," they subtly reinforce this tendency.

This privatized conception of schooling is not limited to choice advocates—it increasingly reflects how Americans have come to understand schooling and their relationship to it. From standards-based reform, to multiculturalism, to school choice, school reformers consistently seek changes aimed at extracting greater benefits for specific interest groups, be it business, a minority group, or the family. Some observers, like the political philosopher Michael Sandel, have argued that this tendency further reflects a more general drift away from public commitment to civic virtue and the common good in all areas of American life, as seen in trends ranging from single-issue political organizations to the privatization of public services. If these observers are correct, then market-, rights-, and fairness-based school choice reflects the atrophy of the public sphere more broadly.

This perceived decline in public spiritedness has provoked a bevy of commentary on the importance of a robust public culture to the maintenance of a liberal-democratic society. Liberal values and capacity for democratic self-government, the argument goes, actually require active, sustained cultivation from an early age. Children need to acquire the virtues of tolerance and cooperation, develop some degree of autonomy and taste for public service, and master the essentials of constitutional law and processes. In short, citizens are made, not born. And public schools are regarded as the primary institutional vehicle for making citizens. School choice as it has come to be understood in the United States seems inimical to that strategy. It doesn't have to be.

Over the past century, the favored model of public schooling has been the common school—the zoned, district-based school where students from all walks of life mix and mingle and learn to get along together in what amounts to a little microcosm of our pluralistic society. The enormous gap between the ideal and reality notwithstanding, the common school holds a venerable place in the popular imagination. And while over the past several generations we have made a national ritual of denouncing the common school for failures both real and imagined, school choice cast in the language of providers and consumers, servers and served, seems to awaken in some a dormant allegiance not just to the common school but to the civic purposes it stands for. This reaction should hearten those concerned about the health of our republic, as it suggests that public spiritedness, while atrophied, may not be quite dead yet.

Does this vestigial concern for civic ends constitute grounds for rejecting school choice? Not necessarily. It does provide some resources for rejuvenating our commitment to the public purposes of schooling, whether government-run or not. This would be a most welcome development. In fact, a sizable literature has emerged over the past decade that has attempted to make respectable again talk of civic virtue, robust citizen education, and the common good that also concludes that some form of school choice may actually be a requirement of a fair and robustly public-minded system

From Ferrero, D. (2003). *Public-spirited choice: How diverse schools can serve the common good.* As first appeared in Education Week, 22(28), 28, 30. Reprinted with permission of the author.

of schooling. Many of the philosophers, legal scholars, and sociologists behind this literature—Harry Brighouse, Eamonn Callan, William Galston, John Davison Hunter, Stephen Macedo, Robert Reich, Rosemary Salomone, and others—represent center-right to center-left political and philosophical perspectives that explicitly reject the market model, carefully circumscribe the scope of parents' rights, and vigorously defend the interest of the state in cultivating good citizens. It seems paradoxical that when these thinkers turn to public policy, they endorse school choice.

The conclusion for choice stems from the need to strike a reasonable balance between the liberal-republican state's interest in producing competent, loyal citizens who will uphold liberal values, and its responsibility to accommodate religious, cultural, and value pluralism in a free society. The common school, though invented in the 19th century by people with legitimate concerns for shaping an American character while equalizing opportunity, was designed to stress the common. It has never dealt well with the plural. From Catholic resistance to Protestant indoctrination in the 19th century to charges of secularism, deculturalization, and "linguistic genocide" today, the common school has always had a knack for galvanizing opposition to itself.

The effects of these waves of opposition and their accommodation within the system have proved baleful: ceaseless litigation, increasingly complex regulation, incoherent curricula, timid school and district leaders, and dysfunctional school cultures.

These aren't the only problems schools face, to be sure. But they are deeply significant and under-recognized. It is this condition, along with a liberal respect for some of the claims pressed by religious and cultural minorities, that has led these thinkers to endorse a greater diversity of schools. Which leads them to choice. But it isn't choice based on consumer preferences or unabridgeable parents' rights. It is, rather, choice based on the recognition that schooling is at heart a serious moral undertaking that the state should neither trammel nor trivialize. Call it "public-spirited choice."

This approach to choice resembles the Western European model, where pluralism is regarded as contributing to the good of society, rather than threatening it. It rests on an age-old psychological truism, articulated recently by William Galston: "Genuine civic unity rests on unforced consent. States that permit their citizens to live in ways that express their values are likely to enjoy widespread support, even gratitude. By contrast, state coercion is likely to produce dissent, resistance, and withdrawal."

The theory here is that citizens will give back in loyalty what they gain in liberty. It also assumes that reasonable religious, cultural, and other associative groups will find the resources from within their own traditions to endorse and cultivate the liberal values and republican capacities the polity needs to sustain itself from generation to generation, as the Catholic Church and several immigrant groups did in the 19th and 20th centuries.

This widening of liberty by no means precludes the state from exercising its interests in cultivating a certain kind of citizen. To the contrary, public-spirited choice begins with this interest strongly in mind. But even the most demanding versions of what a citizen should know, value, and be able to do are parsimonious, and reasonable religious or cultural groups already subscribe to them.

These competencies include values of tolerance, cooperation, and service; knowledge of constitutional essentials; a sense of efficacy, a degree of autonomy, and ability to cast informed votes; and literacy, communication, and critical-thinking skills. These sorts of expectations, if included as part of a school accountability system supple enough to include them, should protect the state from schools that teach racial or sectarian hatred, anti-Americanism, or uncritical submission to a particular dogma.

Likewise, the state has the legal and regulatory authority to ensure that schools do not discriminate on the basis of race, religion, gender, or disability; deny parents, students, or teachers civic rights; or neglect their duty to educate students to be virtuous, competent American citizens in the liberal-republican mold. Any school, whether organized on the basis of faith, cultural or vocational emphasis, pedagogical doctrine, or other legitimate basis of association, would have to demonstrate its contribution and commitment to the public good as a condition of its existence.

To date, the case for public-spirited choice has been confined to academic presses and journals that few educators or policymakers read. But it is a powerful case, one that does something far more important than mediating conflicts between choice advocates and critics.

It is also an argument for a renewal of commitment to the civic purposes of schooling and to the public goods it can engender. It provides not only a potentially better institutional arrangement for mediating the sometimes conflicting goods of pluralism and a common culture, but an opportunity to counter consumerism and recover a way of thinking about schooling that honors its moral, formative dimensions.

ADDITIONAL READINGS

Brimley, V., & Garfield, R. (2002). *Financing Education* (8th ed.). Boston: Allyn & Bacon.

David, J. (1996). The who, what, and why of site-based management. *Educational Leadership,* 53(4), 4–9.

Heubert, J. (2003). First, do no harm. *Educational Leadership, 60*(4), 26–30.

Hill, P. (1996). The educational consequences of choice. *Phi Delta Kappan, 77*(10), 671–675.

Johnson, J. (2002). Staying ahead of the game. *Educational Leadership, 59*(8), 26–30.

NEA. (2002). *School vouchers: The emerging record.* A report of the National Education Association.

Smith, K., & Meier, K. (1995). School choice: Panacea or Pandora's box? *Phi Delta Kappan, 77*(4), 312–316.

EXPLORING THE INTERNET

The National School Boards Association
http://www.nsba.org
This site contains valuable information on school board members and issues.

The American Association of School Administrators
http://www.aasa.org
You will find information on different school administrators, including superintendents and principals.

The Council of Chief State School Officers
http://www.ccsso.org
This site contains data on state superintendents as well as the organizational structures found within different states.

About Charter Schools
http://edreform.com/charters.htm
This site, maintained by the Center for Education Reform, contains a large number of links to other sites with information related to topics such as charter school laws, research on charter schools, and books and periodicals of interest to individuals who wish to establish charter schools.

United States Charter Schools
http://www.uscharterschools.org/
This site includes excellent links to information focusing on topics such as (a) starting and running a charter school, (b) state information and contacts regarding charter schools, (c) profiles of individual charter schools, and (d) general resources and information sources regarding charter schools.

PART EIGHT

Teachers and Teacher Education

Views about the extent to which teachers influence students' achievement and how teachers should be prepared, surprisingly enough, have been uneven historically. For example, in the early history of our country teachers had no formal training either in what to teach (the curriculum) or how to teach (instruction). Gradually, emphasis on teacher training increased, but even in the 20th century questions existed about whether or not teachers had a significant influence on achievement. For example, before the 1970s research on teaching and learning, teachers themselves, were given little credit for contributing to student learning. The then-famous Coleman report (Coleman et al., 1966) suggested that students' socioeconomic background was the major significant factor influencing learning; that is, teachers had little to do with it. More sophisticated research began to emerge in the 1970s and 1980s, however. This research left little doubt that teachers are central to the success of our educational efforts, and that the preparation of teachers should be a top priority in the efforts to increase learning for all students in our country. But translating this research into practice was a difficult task, as teachers' work is extremely complex. One observer compared the demands on teachers to those of air traffic controllers, whose decision making is split-second and ongoing. Coupled with the day-to-day logistics of orchestrating lessons, assessing learning, and building relationships with students and their families, teachers face myriad challenges. These challenges are even more complex and demanding with increased calls for accountability and professionalism and the need to serve a student population that is rapidly becoming more diverse.

The complexities of teaching raise a number of questions about teacher preparation and teachers' work. Some of them include the following: What can schools do to retain a higher percentage of quality teachers? What kind of teachers do students in urban schools require? How do professional teachers maintain their zeal for their work? Does a shortage of teachers exist in this country, and if the answer is yes, what can be done to retain more teachers? And perhaps most basic, what makes teachers "highly qualified," and how can we assure that every student in our country has a highly qualified teacher? Keep these questions in mind as you study the articles in this section.

THE SCHOOLS THAT TEACHERS CHOOSE

Susan Moore Johnson and Sarah E. Birkeland

If teachers are essential to school success, then the retention of quality teachers should be a national priority. Each year, the number of new teachers who leave the profession is staggering. Among new teachers, 30% of those working in rural and suburban communities, and 50% of those working in urban districts, leave their positions within the first five years (National Education Association, 2003). Without strong, supportive environments where teachers are mentored and supported, the number of new teachers leaving the profession will remain high.

Although there is a natural level of attrition within any profession, there are a number of factors that can increase stability in the teaching force. As you read this article ask yourself, "What can schools do to ensure that new teachers remain within the profession?"

Think About This . . .

1. Retaining teachers is a challenge for school districts. What is the impact of losing teachers on school districts? What are the implications of these losses for schools?
2. Educators frequently move to schools that provide professional opportunities for growth. Which of the factors identified by Voluntary Movers are most appealing to you? Which are the least appealing?
3. Teaching has been identified as an "isolated profession." What can you do as an educator to minimize the negative effects of professional isolation?
4. What kind of school will you seek in your first years as an educator? How will this type of school promote your personal and professional growth?

If Esther had abandoned teaching after her first year, no one would have been surprised. An experienced engineer and midcareer entrant, she was so demoralized by day-to-day life in her school that she doubted whether she could make it to Christmas. Although confident about the mathematics that she was teaching, Esther was overwhelmed by her near-total isolation from colleagues, inadequate curriculum materials, a phantom mentor, a department head who seemed to resent her presence, an ineffectual principal whom teachers mocked, and a school with few meaningful rules or norms for student behavior and achievement.

By late fall, Esther had deep misgivings about the career change that she had made. Yet she sensed that her doubts were about the conditions of her work rather than the work itself. Instead of returning to engineering, where she could have doubled her salary, Esther moved to a school that offered her more support.

A year later, she was much happier about her career move. Although her engineering friends urged her to "come back," and the prospect of earning twice the pay was "awfully tempting," Esther acknowledged that she wanted to continue teaching: "I have been enjoying this."

The Retention Challenge

At the state and district levels, policymakers are working hard to devise effective retention strategies in the face of alarming statistics about new teacher attrition. Losing teachers to other careers is only part of the problem, however. Ingersoll (2001) found that the

From Johnson, S. M., & Birkeland, S. (2003). The schools that teachers choose. Educational Leadership, 60(8), 20–24. Reprinted with permission of the Association for Supervision and Curriculum Development.

movement of teachers from school to school and district to district, a phenomenon that he calls *migration,* accounts for half of the turnover that schools and districts experience.

For those at the school site, attrition and migration look the same. Losing a good teacher—whether to another profession or to the school across town—means losing that teacher's familiarity with school practices; experience with the school's curriculum; and involvement with students, parents, and colleagues. Losing a teacher means that administrators and teachers must spend precious energy finding a replacement and bringing him or her up to speed. Predictably, schools serving high-poverty communities are particularly vulnerable to this revolving-door effect: the repeated loss of teachers and frantic rush to hire new ones. These schools bear more than their share of the teacher shortage burden (Olson, 2003).

At the Project on the Next Generation of Teachers, we have studied the career paths of 50 new teachers in Massachusetts over the past four years. We began this project in an effort to understand what new teachers seek, what they experience, and what sustains them. By year three of the study, 3 of our original 50 teachers had been involuntarily transferred to other schools; 8 had left teaching for other careers; and 3 had left their public schools to teach in private school settings. Eight others, whom we called *Voluntary Movers,* had chosen to transfer from their original schools to other public schools.

An interesting feature of the Voluntary Movers in our study is that all but one had entered teaching at midcareer, having worked for some years in such fields as law, engineering, accounting, and business. Although these teachers expressed a deep commitment to teaching and a desire to do it well, their experience in other careers had taught them that workplaces differ and that the work environment is crucial in fostering satisfaction and success. When they had taken their first teaching jobs, most had simply expected their new schools to provide basic resources and functioning infrastructures. They had counted on having colleagues to mentor and collaborate with them, and had assumed that principals would be respectful, accessible, and involved in the life of the school. When they found their schools wanting, they looked for different environments.

Unlike those in the study who had left the public school classroom altogether, the Voluntary Movers had not given up on teaching. Instead, they looked for schools that made good teaching possible. The conditions they sought were straightforward and consistent.

In choosing new schools, the Voluntary Movers sought the basic conditions that would allow them to practice their craft day to day: appropriate course assignments; sufficient curriculum guidelines; and efficient systems for discipline, communication with parents, and smooth transitions between classes. They also looked for schools where they could feel like professionals—sharing ideas and resources with colleagues and receiving respect and guidance from the principal. The second time around, they used the hiring process as an opportunity to gather information about prospective schools' cultures, norms, and potential supports, and they weighed their options carefully.

Reasonable Assignments and Basic Support

The first years of teaching are particularly challenging, yet new teachers often get the least desirable courses and classrooms, as well as the most challenging groups of students. For example, in her first year of teaching, Brenda taught Spanish to 10 different classes of 6th, 7th, and 8th graders in an urban middle school. With so many preparations, no classroom of her own, and scant curriculum guidelines, she wryly observed that she had to be "pretty creative" to get through the year. When her principal assigned her an equally "jam-packed" schedule the following September, Brenda decided to look for a different teaching job.

Keisha taught 2nd grade in an inner-city elementary school and, despite some frustrations, had planned to return the next year. When her principal said he was considering moving her to 4th grade, however, she decided to transfer:

> I just felt that that was a really unreasonable thing to ask of me in my second year of teaching. I was just figuring out the 2nd grade curriculum and getting my feet wet, and really getting this together. And now all of a sudden you want me to make what is a huge jump to 4th grade, and a high-pressure [tested] grade. . . . I just didn't think it was really supportive of a first-year teacher.

Theresa, like many new teachers, was assigned to teach a subject for which she was not qualified. Although she was trained to teach science, she accepted a middle school position that required her to teach courses in both math and science. Prepping for two different subjects involved far more work than she had expected, and she felt that she was giving her math students short shrift. Instead of leaving the profession, she decided to look for a different position, saying,

I felt that it was unfair to say that teaching wasn't for me when I had so many things against me.

These Voluntary Movers were far more satisfied after they moved to their new schools. Brenda found a school where she taught 70 students in four classes that met daily, and where she actually had texts and a teacher's book. Keisha found another school where she could continue as a 2nd grade teacher. Theresa chose a job teaching only science, her area of expertise. Given reasonable workloads, these new teachers felt confident that they could succeed.

The Voluntary Movers also left schools with chaotic environments in search of order and predictability. As they strove to create consistent behavior policies and a focus on learning in their first classrooms, they found that the schoolwide norms could either support or undermine their efforts. For example, Mike had hoped "to go into a well-oiled machine" for his first job, to a school with clear and consistent policies in place. Instead, he and his largely inexperienced colleagues were "running around trying to create the infrastructure while we were trying to do our job." The environment wore him out, at a time when he was trying to learn how to teach.

Mary found the atmosphere in her charter school to be similarly chaotic. After a draining first year, she decided that she had to find "a saner environment." She longed for a place in which schoolwide policies were explicit and consistently enforced. "I knew I needed less craziness if I was going to be an effective teacher."

Similarly, Brenda said that the lack of a clear discipline policy in her school caused her to move "from crisis to crisis" and to spend most of her time "babysitting and policing" students. Esther, too, was dismayed by the lack of order in her school and by the kinds of behavior that her colleagues tolerated from students who knew that teachers were "at their mercy."

Mike, Mary, Brenda, and Esther all moved to schools where students and staff shared an understanding about basic expectations, ensuring a positive learning environment.

Opportunities to Learn and Grow

The Voluntary Movers wanted more than workable teaching situations; they also wanted opportunities to interact with other professionals and hone their skills. They left schools in which they felt isolated or philosophically out of sync with colleagues and searched for more sustaining professional cultures.

For example, at Keisha's first school, teachers worked alone and administrators thought stellar teachers were those who "had their kids in rows." Teachers went "from page to page to page to page" in the textbooks rather than use the manipulatives that Keisha tried to incorporate into her own teaching. Although she liked the other teachers in her building personally, their teaching philosophies differed from hers. She wanted a community of teachers who would support her in becoming the teacher she wanted to be.

Doug, too, left an isolating professional culture for a more collegial environment. He gave up eating lunch in the teachers' lounge after a few weeks at his first school because "everybody was complaining all the time. I didn't want to be around it." He wanted to discuss teaching, to share ideas, to learn from other teachers. Instead, his veteran colleagues withheld their lesson plans and guarded their best ideas. He was on his own.

Like other Voluntary Movers, Keisha and Doug sought schools that engaged both veteran and novice teachers in doing better work. Keisha moved to a charter school that "allowed me to do some things that are more innovative and less traditional." At her new school, "we plan curriculum together, we implement curriculum together. . . . No one is working in isolation."

Doug also found more collegial interaction. He described the teachers in his new school as being "extremely proud of the stuff that they are doing, so they are really open about sharing it." He felt encouraged to seek ideas and advice. For example, he said that he would have no trouble saying to a colleague,

> I'm doing this unit in the Interactive Math Project, but I don't have enough time to complete it. Do you have any ideas on how to shorten it?

In searching for a new school, Doug looked for evidence of a facultywide commitment to long-term growth and learning. In explaining why that was important to him, he said,

> I had to start thinking about myself and my own development as a teacher. [At my first school] I was surrounded by mediocrity. I felt I was getting a lot of praise as a teacher. I was a superstar in my first year of teaching. I'm not that good.

Accessible, Respectful Leadership

When explaining their decisions to transfer, the Voluntary Movers in our sample cited dissatisfaction with school administration more often than any other factor.

Some found their principals dictatorial or inept. For example, Brenda was outraged that her principal failed to support her on discipline, even when a student swore at her in class. Mike said that he left his school because of

> the deterioration and incompetence of the administration. Assessment was completely driving instruction.

Some Voluntary Movers said that their principals were aloof or inaccessible. As a team leader, Theresa had several concerns that she wanted to share with her principal, yet she found the principal "so preoccupied" with the needs of a large school and the concerns of veteran teachers that she seldom spoke with him. Mary longed for supervision and instructional guidance from the principal of her first school, but she did not seek help because she knew that her principal was just as exhausted and overwhelmed by day-to-day demands as she was.

When they searched for new schools, the Voluntary Movers paid close attention to what the principal could offer. Doug, who had been dissatisfied with the controlling and distrustful administrative style in his first school, welcomed administrators who expressed confidence in teachers. He found that this respectful attitude influenced the whole school. Mary found a school in which her supervising administrator took time to talk with her about instruction and shared his own mistakes. She commented,

> He will talk about when he first started teaching and some of the really stupid things he did. That's really helpful.

For these new teachers, who were working hard to do a good job, the respect and support of administrators were key to their satisfaction.

Shopping for Schools

Most of these Voluntary Movers had signed on to their first jobs with little information or contact with the school. In choosing their second schools, they were more careful. Some searched extensively; others sought out particular schools that they knew by reputation or recommendation. Always, they examined the hiring process itself for signals about the school's culture.

Mike's second school hired him to replace another teacher in the middle of the year. He was extensively interviewed by a committee that included the vice principal, a department chair, a lead teacher, and a parent. He was surprised and pleased with the parent's involvement:

That struck me immediately as a very good thing, like an empowerment. The parents were taken seriously enough that they had a representative at meetings to hire new staff.

Mary, who applied widely, was looking for "a good match" when she found her new school. She met with the principal, two vice principals, and the department head who would be her immediate supervisor. Right away, she could see that

> it was just the right environment. It was caring, very structured, and I was going to have a lot of supervision.

Months later, Mary reported satisfaction with her new school: "The year has been very much like what my experience at the interview was."

Esther went through a rigorous application process at her new school. Not only did she interview with a team, but she also did a demonstration lesson for observers. Keisha, too, met with a search committee and then visited the school several times "just to see how the school functioned and operated during the academic day." She reflected on the contrast between this and her first hiring experience, where she went through a

> screening interview with someone downtown, who's not connected to any school whatsoever. Then you get on some list. Then some principal calls you and you go in and you interview. And I did interview with a group of people. From there, I was offered a job. They never saw me teach, never saw me interact with children. . . . They really never asked, "Does this particular person and her teaching style and where she wants to go in the future match the culture of our school?"

Teachers' Schools of Choice

The stories of the Voluntary Movers provide important lessons about what matters to new teachers and how schools can support and retain their teachers. When these teachers decided that successful teaching and continuous growth were not possible in their original schools, they left for new sites. The original schools and their students suffered as a result.

One aspect of the stories of the Voluntary Movers is particularly noteworthy. All of them moved to schools that served less impoverished populations of students than their first schools had. In their interviews, most Voluntary Movers described close connections with the students at their first schools. The schools serving these poorer students, however, had working conditions that prompted these teachers to look for new jobs. The fact that the Voluntary Movers found better working conditions in schools serving wealthier students highlights the problem of inequities in public education.

The findings of this study suggest that efforts to stem turnover and attrition must center on the school site and on the factors that support good teaching. The schools that these teachers chose provided them with balanced and appropriate assignments, good curriculums with sufficient resources, colleagues who generously shared their ideas and encouragement, schoolwide practices that kept students focused on learning, and fair-minded principals who were actively engaged in the life of the school. Surely all schools, regardless of the wealth of their communities or the demographic composition of their students, should achieve these conditions.

Although policymakers can mandate and fund recruitment and induction programs, only school leaders can foster the full range of supports that teachers need. New teachers will choose to stay at schools where sustained and consistent supports are in place, where they can do their day-to-day jobs with confidence, and where they can grow in their profession over time.

Authors' note: Susan M. Kardos, David Kauffman, Edward Liu, and Heather Peske participated in data collection and aided in the analysis presented in this article. This research has been made possible by a grant from the Spencer Foundation. The data, findings, and views presented are solely the responsibility of the Project on the Next Generation of Teachers.

References

Ingersoll, R. M. (2001). *A different approach to solving the teacher shortage problem* (Teaching Quality Policy Brief No. 3). Seattle, WA: Center for the Study of Teaching and Policy, University of Washington.

Olson, L. (2003). The great divide. In *Education Week. Quality Counts 2003, 12*(17), 9–18.

SELECTING "STAR" TEACHERS FOR CHILDREN AND YOUTH IN URBAN POVERTY
Martin Haberman

Teaching is a demanding profession, requiring bright, resourceful, and dedicated individuals. All teachers face challenges, but teaching in urban schools brings a special set of challenges. In addition to responding to the increasing diversity in languages and ability levels among students, teachers must address homelessness and poverty.

For many teachers, the demands of working in urban schools lead to attrition rates that far exceed those within rural and suburban schools. Martin Haberman suggests that in order to serve the needs of students in urban schools, educators must be carefully selected and possess critical attributes that allow them to effectively address the special needs of the urban poor. As you read this article ask yourself, "How do my personal teaching strengths address the needs of urban learners?"

Think About This . . .

1. Teachers who are effective with children living in poverty are selected on the basis of their age, life experiences, and demonstrated ability to interact with students. How valid are these criteria?

2. Haberman suggests that teachers who complete their clinical experiences in the most challenging classroom environments will be best prepared to teach. Is it possible for cutting-edge teaching practices to take place in demanding, urban schools?

3. "Star" teachers are capable in 14 distinct areas. Are these criteria unique to the needs of urban students, or do they apply to all students?

4. How can you incorporate the characteristics of a "star" teacher in your classroom? Which areas to do you view as most important for your own personal success?

No school can be better than its teachers. And the surest and best way to improve the schooling of the approximately 12 million children and youth in poverty is to get better teachers for them. The strategy for doing this is not mysterious and has been evolving for more than 35 years.

The premise of the strategy is simple: selection is more important than training. My calculated hunch is that selection is 80% of the matter. The reason is that the functions performed by effective urban teachers of students in poverty are undergirded by a very clear ideology. Such teachers not only perform functions that quitters and burnouts do not perform, but they also know why they do what they do. They have a coherent vision. Moreover, it is a humane, respectful, caring, and nonviolent form of "gentle teaching" that I have described elsewhere.[1] My point here is that teachers' behaviors and the ideology that undergirds their behaviors cannot be unwrapped. They are of a piece.

Nor can this ideology be readily or easily taught in traditional programs of teacher preparation. Writing a term paper on Piaget's concept of conservation or sharing with other student teachers such problems as why Ray won't sit down will not provide neophytes with the ideological vision of "star teachers." This ideology, while it is open to development, must be selected for. What can be taught are the functional teaching behaviors that are built on the foundation of this belief system. And like the ideology, the teaching behaviors are not typically learned in traditional programs of teacher education but on the job, with the benefit of a teacher/coach, a support network, and some specific workshops.

There are four dimensions of excellence that programs claiming to prepare teachers for children of poverty can and should be held accountable for: 1) the individuals trained should be adults; 2) they should have demonstrated ability to establish rapport with low-income children of diverse ethnic backgrounds; 3) they should be admitted as candidates based on valid interviews that reliably predict their success with children in poverty; and 4) practicing urban teachers who are recognized as effective should be involved in selecting candidates.

My colleagues and I have identified three related truths that grow out of the recognition that selection is the heart of the matter where teachers for the urban poor are concerned: 1) the odds of selecting effective urban teachers for children and youth in poverty are approximately 10 times better if the candidates are over 30 rather than under 25 years of age; 2) there is no problem whatsoever in selecting more teachers of color, or more males, or more Hispanics, or more of any other "minority" constituency if training begins at the postbaccalaureate level; and 3) the selection and training of successful urban teachers is best accomplished in the worst schools and under the poorest conditions of practice.

This last truth requires some comment. States routinely give out teaching licenses that are deemed valid for any school in the state. The most reasonable basis for awarding such licenses would be to prepare teachers in the poorest schools and assume they will be able to deal with the "problems" presented by smaller classes, more and better materials and equipment, and safer neighborhoods if they should ever be "forced" to teach in more advantaged schools. Traditional teacher education makes almost the reverse assumption: create professional development centers (the equivalent of teaching hospitals) and then assume that beginners will be able to function in the poverty schools to which city school districts typically assign them. "Best practice" should not be thought of as ideal teaching under ideal conditions but as effective practice under the worst of conditions.

Functions of "Star" Urban Teachers

By comparing the behaviors and undergirding ideologies of "star" urban teachers with those of quitters and failures, my colleagues and I have identified 14 functions of successful teachers of the urban poor that are neither

From Haberman, M. (1995). Selecting "Star" teachers for children and youth in urban poverty. Phi Delta Kappan, 76(10), 777–781. Reprinted with permission of the author.

discrete behaviors nor personality attributes. Instead, these functions are "mid range" in the sense that they represent chunks of teaching behavior that encompass a number of interrelated actions and simultaneously represent beliefs or commitments that predispose these teachers to act.

"Stars" are those teachers who are identified by principals, supervisors, other teachers, parents, and themselves as outstanding. They also have students who learn a great deal as measured by test scores and work samples. Between 5% and 8% of the staff members who now teach in urban poverty schools are such "star" teachers. The quitters and failures with whom their functioning is compared constitute a much larger group: 30% to 50%, depending on the particular district. In a continuing series of interviews with a population of star urban teachers every year since 1959, we have found that the 14 functions have remained stable. What has changed in some cases are the questions needed to elicit interviewees' responses related to these functions.

The structured interview we use has been developed to select beginning teachers who can be prepared successfully on the job. This means that they can function at satisfactory levels while they are learning to teach. The highest success rate for selecting such exceptional neophytes has been achieved by combining both the interview and the opportunity to observe the candidates interacting with and teaching children in the summer prior to their assuming the role of beginning teacher. When the interview is combined with such observation, there is less than a 5% error rate. Use of the interview alone raises the error rate to between 8% and 10%.

Compare these figures with the fact that approximately 50% of newcomers to urban schools who were prepared in traditional programs quit or fail in five years or less. And these "trained" beginners are only the very small, self-selected group who choose to try teaching in an urban school and not a representative sample of those currently being prepared to teach. It boggles the mind to imagine what the failure rate would be if a truly representative sample of those now graduating from traditional programs of teacher education were hired as first-year teachers in the largest urban school districts.

In the rest of this article, I will briefly outline the seven functions that the star teacher interview assesses (and the additional seven for which we have never been able to develop interview questions). In order for a candidate to pass the interview, her or she need not respond at the level of a star teacher. The interview predicts

applicants' potential functioning from "average," through "high," to "star." A zero answer on any of the functions constitutes a failure response to the total interview. The interview is couched in behavioral terms; that is, it attempts to determine what the applicant would do in his or her class and why. (Readers should note that merely reading about these functions does not constitute preparation to conduct an interview.)

The Dimensions of Effective Teaching

1. *Persistence.* Many urban teachers honestly believe that most of their students (all in some cases) should not be in their classrooms because they need special help; are not achieving at grade level; are "abnormal" in their interests, attentiveness, or behavior; are emotionally unsuited to school; or are in need of alternative schools, special classes, or teachers trained to work with exceptional individuals. In some urban districts and in individual urban schools many teachers perceive 90% of their students to be not "normal."[2]

Effective urban teachers, on the other hand, believe it is their responsibility to find ways of engaging all their students in learning activities. The continuous generation and maintenance of student interest and involvement is how star teachers explain their jobs to themselves and to others. They manifest this persistence in several ways. They accept responsibility for making the classroom an interesting, engaging place and for involving the children in all forms of learning. They persist in trying to meet the individual needs of the problem student, the talented, the handicapped, and the frequently neglected student who falls in the gray area. Their persistence is reflected in an endless search for what works best with each student. Indeed, they define their jobs as asking themselves constantly, "How might this activity have been better—for the class or for a particular individual?"

The persistence of star teachers demonstrates several aspects of their ideology: teaching can never be "good enough," since everyone could always have learned more in any activity; teaching inevitably involves dealing with problems and problem students, and such students will be in every class, every day; and better materials and strategies can always be found. The basic stance of these teachers is never to give up trying to find better ways of doing things. The quip attributed to Thomas Edison, "The difference between carbon and diamonds is that diamonds stayed on the job longer," might describe these teachers as well.

2. *Protecting Learners and Learning.* Star teachers are typically involved in some life activity that provides them with a sense of well-being and from which they continually learn. It might be philately, Russian opera, a Save the Wolves Club, composing music with computers, travel, or some other avocation from which they derive meaning as well as pleasure. Inevitably, they bring these activities and interests into their classrooms and use them as ways of involving their students in learning. It is quite common to find teachers' special interests used as foci that generate great enthusiasm for learning among the students. The grandiose explanation for this phenomenon is that people who continually experience learning themselves have the prerequisites to generate the desire to learn in others. A more practical explanation would be that we teach best what we care most about.

In any event, star teachers frequently involve their students in learning that transcends curriculum, textbooks, and achievement tests. Their commitment to turning students on to learning frequently brings them into noncompliance with the extremely thick bureaucracies of urban schools. Stars do not view themselves as change agents, per se, but they do seek ways to give themselves and their students greater latitude within the traditional curriculum.

Consider the following episode. The teacher has succeeded in truly involving the class in a learning activity. It might be an environmental issue (What happens to our garbage?); a biological study (How does a lie detector work?); or the production of a class play dealing with violence in the neighborhood. Imagine further that the intense student interest has generated some noise, the use of unusual equipment, or a need for extra cleaning of the classroom. The principal learns of the activity and requests that it be discontinued. The principal also instructs the teacher to stick with the approved texts and to follow the regular curriculum. At this point the lines are clearly drawn: continuing a genuine learning activity in which the students are thriving versus complying with the directive of a superior and following a school policy.

The way star teachers seek to work through such a problem is in direct opposition to the reaction of quitters and failures. Star teachers see protecting and enhancing students' involvement in learning activities as their highest priority; quitters cannot conceive of the possibility that they would diverge from the standard curriculum or that they would question a school administrator or a school policy.

To the uninitiated, such struggles over red tape may seem atypical. Experienced star teachers, however, find themselves involved in a continuous, day-to-day struggle to redefine and broaden the boundaries within which they work. One reason they so often find themselves at odds with the bureaucracy of urban schools is that they persist in searching for ways to engage their students actively in learning. Indeed, their view that this is their primary function stands in stark contrast to the views of teachers who see their primary function as covering the curriculum.

Star teachers try to resolve their struggles with bureaucracy patiently, courteously, and professionally. They seek to negotiate with authority. Quitters and failures perceive the most professional response to be unquestioning compliance.

3. *Application of Generalizations.* Some teachers have 30 years of experience, while others have one year of experience 30 times over. One basis for professional growth is the ability to generate practical, specific applications of the theories and philosophies. Conversely, successful teachers can also reflect on their many discrete classroom activities and see what they add up to. If you ask stars to give examples of some principle they believe in (e.g., "What would an observer see in your classroom that would lead him/her to believe that you believe all children can learn?"), they are able to cite clear, observable examples. Conversely, if a star is asked to offer a principle or make a generalization that accounts for a series of behaviors in which he or she engages, the star is equally able to move from the specific to the general.

The importance of this dimension is that teachers must be able to improve and develop. In order for this to happen, they must be able to take principles and concepts from a variety of sources (i.e., courses, workshops, books, and research) and translate them into practice. At the same time, stars can explain what their day-to-day work adds up to; they have a grasp not only of the learning principles that undergird their work but also of the long-range knowledge goals that they are helping their students achieve.

At the other extreme are teachers who are "concretized." They do not comprehend the difference between information and knowledge; neither do they see any connection between their daily lessons and the reasons why children and youth are compelled to go to school for 13 years. Indeed, quitters and failures frequently respond to the question, "Would you give an example of a principle in which you believe that guides your teaching?" with, "I don't like to generalize" or "It's wrong to make generalizations."

The ability to derive meaning from one's teaching is also a function of this ability to move between the general and the specific. Without this ability to see the relationship between important ideas and day-to-day practice, teaching degenerates into merely "keeping school."

4. *Approach to "At-Risk" Students.* Of all the factors that separate stars from quitters and failures this one is the most powerful in predicting their future effectiveness with urban children of poverty. When asked to account for the large numbers of at-risk students or to suggest what might be done about cutting down on the number of at-risk students, most teachers are well-versed in the popular litany of causes. The most common causes cited are poverty, violence, handicapping conditions, racism, unemployment, poor housing, lack of health care, gangs, drugs, and dysfunctional families. But while the quitters and failures stop with these, the stars also cite irrelevant school curricula, poor teaching, and overly bureaucratic school systems as additional causes.

Since quitters and failures essentially blame the victims, the families, and the neighborhoods, they do not come up with any measures that schools and teachers can or should take to improve the situation. Indeed, they say such things as "You can't expect schools to be all things to all people" or "Teachers can't be social workers, nurses, and policemen." Stars also see all the societal conditions that contribute to students' problems with school. But they are able to suggest that more relevant curricula and more effective teaching strategies are things that schools and teachers could try and should be held accountable for. Star teachers believe that, regardless of the life conditions their students face, they as teachers bear a primary responsibility for sparking their students' desire to learn.

5. *Professional Versus Personal Orientation to Students.* Stars expect to find some youngsters in their classrooms that they may not necessarily love; they also expect to be able to teach them. Stars expect that some of their students will not necessarily love them, but they expect these students to be able to learn from them. They use such terms as caring, respect, and concern, and they enjoy the love and affection of students when it occurs naturally. But they do not regard it as a prerequisite for learning.

Quitters and failures, on the other hand, cannot and do not discriminate between the love of parents for their children and the love of teachers for their students. They regard such love as a prerequisite for any learning to occur. They also believe that the children should feel a similar sort of love for their teachers. Consequently, it is not uncommon for quitters and failures to become disillusioned about their work in poverty schools. Once they realize that the children do not love them or that they cannot love "these" children, they find themselves unable to function in the role of teacher. For many quitters and failures, this love between students and teachers was a major reason for seeking to become teachers.

Star teachers have extremely strong, positive feelings toward their students, which in many cases might be deemed a form of love. But these feelings are not the primary reasons that stars are teachers, nor are these feelings the basis of their relationships with their students. Indeed, when their students misbehave, star teachers do not take it as a personal attack. Neither do they maintain class order or inspire effort by seeking to instill guilt. Genuine respect is the best way to describe the feelings star teachers have for their students.

6. *Burnout: Its Causes and Cures.* Star teachers in large urban school systems are well aware that they work in mindless bureaucracies. They recognize that even good teachers will eventually burn out if they are subjected to constant stress, so they learn how to protect themselves from an interfering bureaucracy. As they gain experience, they learn the minimum things they must do to function in these systems without having the system punish them. Ultimately, they learn how to gain the widest discretion for themselves and their students without incurring the wrath of the system. Finally, they set up networks of a few like-minded teachers, or they teach in teams, or they simply find kindred spirits. They use these support systems as sources of emotional sustenance.

Without such organizational skills—and lacking the awareness that they even need such skills—failures and quitters are literally beaten down by the system. The paperwork, the conflicting rules and policies, the number of meetings, the interruptions, the inadequate materials, the lack of time, large classes, and an obsessive concern with test scores are just some of the demands that drive the quitters out of the profession. Moreover, quitters and failures are insensitive to many of the conflicting demands that every large, impersonal organization makes. And worst of all, they don't believe a good teacher "should" ever burn out. They believe that a really good person who really wants to be a teacher should *never* be ground down by any bureaucracy. This set of perceptions leads them to experience feelings of inadequacy and guilt when they do burn out. And unlike stars, who use their support networks to offset the expected pressures, quitters and failures respond to the pressures by feeling that they probably should never have become teachers.

7. *Fallibility.* Children and young people cannot learn in a classroom where mistakes are not allowed. One effective way to ensure that we find teachers who can accept the mistakes of students is to select those who can accept their own mistakes. When teachers are asked, "Do you ever make mistakes?" they answer, "Of course, I'm only human!" or "Everyone makes mistakes." The difference between stars and quitters is in the nature of the mistakes that they recognize and own up to. Stars acknowledge serious problems and ones having to do with human relations; quitters and failures confess to spelling and arithmetic errors.

Functions Beyond the Interview

Thus far I have outlined seven teaching functions for which we have been able to create and validate interview questions. While the actual questions we use in the interview cannot be shared, I have described above the goals of the questions. It is noteworthy that there are seven additional functions for which we have never been able to develop interview questions but which are equally powerful in discriminating between stars and quitters. These functions and brief explanations follow.

- *Organizational ability:* the predisposition and ability to engage in planning and gathering of materials.
- *Physical/emotional stamina:* the ability to persist in situations characterized by violence, death, and other crises.
- *Teaching style:* the predisposition to engage in coaching rather than directive teaching.
- *Explanations of success:* the predisposition to emphasize students' effort rather than ability.
- *Basis of rapport:* the approach to student involvement. Whose classroom is it? Whose work is to be protected?
- *Readiness:* the approach to prerequisite knowledge. Who should be in this classroom?

For children in poverty, schooling is a matter of life and death. They have no other realistic options for "making it" in American society. They lack the family resources, networks, and out-of-school experiences that could compensate for what they are not offered in schools. Without school success, they are doomed to lives of continued poverty and consigned to conditions that characterize a desperate existence:

violence, inadequate health care, a lack of life options, and hopelessness. The typical high school graduate has had approximately 54 teachers. When I ask successful graduates from inner-city schools, "How many of your teachers have led you to believe that you were particularly good at anything?" the modal response is none. If graduates report this perception, I wonder what those who have dropped out would say?

I recognize that getting better teachers is not a reconstructive change strategy. Indeed, I may well deserve the criticism that I am offering a Band-Aid solution by finding great people who are merely helping to shore up and preserve bad systems.

As I listened to the great change experts of the 1950s, I bet myself that they would not succeed, and I set myself the modest task of doing whatever I could to save young people in schools as they are currently constituted by getting them a few better teachers. After 35 years the movers and shakers seem further behind than ever. School systems serving poor children have become more rigid, less financially stable, more violent, and further behind their advantaged counterparts.

During the same period the school districts using my selection and training methods have become a national network. We now know how to recruit and select teachers who can succeed with children in poverty. The number of such teachers in every urban school system will continue to grow. So, too, will the impact these star teachers are making on the lives of their students.

Mark Twain once quipped, "To do good things is noble. To advise others to do good things is even nobler—and a lot easier." I fail to understand why *talking* about the reconstruction of urban schools in America is noble work, while what star teachers and their students *actually accomplish* in these schools is merely a palliative. In my own admittedly naive view, it seems that the inadequate nostrums of policy analysts and change agents are being given more attention than the effective behaviors of people who are busy making schools work better. A society that values ineffectual physicists over effective plumbers will find itself hip-deep in insoluble problems.

Notes

1. Martin Haberman, "Gentle Teaching in a Violent Society," *Educational Horizons*, Spring 1994, pp. 131–136.
2. Charles M. Payne, *Getting What We Ask For: The Ambiguity of Success and Failure in Urban Education* (Westport, Conn.: Greenwood, 1984).

WHAT KEEPS TEACHERS GOING?

Sonia M. Nieto

Teachers face many challenges, and these challenges are magnified for urban teachers whose attrition rates are significantly higher than the general population of teachers. In this article Sonia Nieto investigates the problem of urban teacher attrition by collaborating with seven exemplary urban educators who seem to have not only survived but thrived in urban settings. As you read this article ask yourself, "How are the characteristics of successful urban educators similar to successful teachers in general?"

Think About This . . .

1. What is the paradox of teacher quality and urban schools? What are some of the reasons for this paradox?

2. What are the different ways that these urban teachers expressed love and caring for their students? How is this similar to or different from teachers in general?

3. How does intellectual work influence the professional lives of these teachers? What implications does this have for teachers in general?

4. What aspects of these successful urban teachers' lives can you incorporate into your own professional life to enhance its quality?

As a Puerto Rican child from a working-class family, I attended poor schools in Brooklyn, New York, where a small but significant number of teachers helped propel my sister and me—who were the first in our family to graduate from high school—to attend college and become teachers.

As a teacher educator and former classroom teacher, I have become increasingly concerned about the tenuous situation of the most vulnerable students in U.S. public schools—students who attend urban schools with crumbling infrastructures, few resources, and a highly mobile staff. For these students—primarily African American and Latino, but also poor students of all backgrounds—the teachers who believe in and push them, who refuse to accept anything less than the best from them, often make the single greatest difference between a life of hope and one of despair. In many cases, these are veteran teachers who have dedicated their professional careers—and, in many cases, their personal lives—to young people in urban schools.

Unfortunately, many of the most highly qualified and gifted teachers do not teach in the schools where their skills are most sorely needed. Poor students of color are at the bottom of the ladder for receiving services from the most-qualified teachers (Darling-Hammond, 1998).

Moreover, even though most teachers enter the profession for noble reasons and with great enthusiasm, many of those in urban schools know little about their students and find it hard to reach them. Thus, despite their good intentions, many teachers who work with students of racial and cultural backgrounds different from their own have limited experience in teaching them and become frustrated and angry at the conditions in which they must work. Nearly half of all new teachers in urban public schools quit within five years (Haycock, 1998). The teacher dropout rate is certainly not new, but with the predicted looming teacher shortage, recruiting and retaining excellent teachers who are excited about and committed to

From Nieto, S. (2003). *What keeps teachers going?* Educational Leadership, 60(8), 14–18. *Reprinted with permission of the Association for Supervision and Curriculum Development.*

teaching students in urban schools is more urgent than ever.

Why Do They Stay?

What keeps teachers going—in spite of everything? In 1999–2000, I collaborated with a small group of seven urban teachers in the Boston Public Schools to consider this important question.[1] Our inquiry group comprised highly respected high school teachers who had a reputation for success with students of diverse backgrounds. They teach math, English, health, and African American studies in both monolingual English and bilingual settings. Their own backgrounds are quite diverse—African American, Cape Verdean, Haitian, Irish American, and Jewish, among others. Collectively, they have many years of experience; most have been teaching for more than 25 years. They have received numerous awards—five have been named Boston Teacher of the Year—and they are active in professional organizations, writing and reading groups, and other professional activities. They are also known to be movers and shakers, willing to speak up and take a stand.

Besides addressing this question during our meetings, we also read a number of books together and wrote narratives, letters, and e-mails to one another. The teachers spoke movingly about the joys, frustrations, and rewards of teaching. Our conversations were not easy, nor did they come close to solving the problems of urban schools. But the process helped articulate some reasons that these teachers have stayed in teaching, and transcripts of our meetings, writings, and field notes revealed several interrelated themes (Nieto, 2003).

This group of excellent urban teachers might seem to be the exception to the rule. As we have shared our thoughts with educators around the United States, however, we have found that teachers in many different situations—in schools small or large, elementary or secondary, urban or rural—have stayed in teaching for many of the same reasons.

Autobiography

Teachers' identities are deeply implicated in their teaching, and hence in their perseverance. Their identities are defined not only by ethnicity, race, gender, social class, and language background, although these of course are significant. What became clear was that most of these teachers have been involved in movements for social justice. These included movements outside education (civil rights, anti-apartheid) as well as inside education (bilingual education, multicultural education, desegregation).

As a young child in Barbados, English teacher Junia Yearwood learned the value of education early on. She could not divorce her heritage and experiences from the reasons she came to school every day to teach:

> The value of education and the importance of being able to read and write became clear and urgent when I became fully aware of the history of my ancestors. The story of the enslavement of Africans and the horrors they were forced to endure repulsed and angered me, but the aspect of slavery that most intrigued me was the systematic denial of literacy to my ancestors. As a child of 10 or so, I reasoned that if reading and writing were not extremely important, then there would be no need to withhold those skills from the supposed "savage and inferior" African. I concluded that teaching was the most important profession on earth and that the teacher was the Moses of people of African descent. This revelation made my destiny clear. I had to be a teacher.

Love

It seems old-fashioned to speak of teaching as love, yet teachers in the inquiry group often used this word to describe how they feel about their students and the subject matter that they teach. Teacher Stephen Gordon observed that preceding everything else in teaching is "a fundamental belief in the lives and minds of students." Love, then, is not simply a sentimental conferring of emotion. Rather, it is a combination of trust, confidence, and faith in students and a deep admiration for their strengths.

These teachers demonstrate love through high expectations and rigorous demands on students and by keeping up with their subject matter through professional activities. Claudia Bell, a bilingual teacher of Latino students, provides an example. For the first time in her career, she found that most of the students in her health class were failing. With the help of other colleagues in the inquiry group, she developed a questionnaire to try to figure out why. She discovered that the interview process brought the students and her closer together. She explained,

> I always thought I had a really close relationship with them. But somehow, through this process, they opened up to me in ways that I didn't expect.

Within weeks, her students were doing their homework much more consistently, and their schoolwork in general improved. Claudia didn't see this as a miracle cure for low achievement. In fact, it initially bothered her that they were doing these things to please her rather than for themselves. But it also became clear to us that developing a closer relationship with the students had paid off. By the end of the year, many of the students were passing her course.

These teachers also believe in affirming their students' identities. Ambrizeth Lima, who came to the United States from the Cape Verde Islands when she was a child, points out that students should not have to "discard themselves" to be accepted. She encouraged her students, all of whom were from Cape Verde, to hold on to their language and to feel pride in their culture. More than most, she knows that students' identities do not disappear simply because schools refuse to acknowledge them. Teachers' caring promotes an essential sense of belonging for students whose backgrounds differ from the mainstream.

Hope and Possibility

Hope is the essence of teaching, and these teachers demonstrate hope in many ways. They have hope and faith in their students, in their own abilities as teachers, in trusted colleagues and new teachers, in the promise of public education, and in the profession of teaching.

One day, Judith Baker discussed the boys in her classes, mostly African American and Latino, who she knew were capable of doing well in school but were failing. "I'm very, very worried about the boys," she said. But rather than blame the situation on their laziness or lack of intelligence, she said with the greatest confidence, "I'm sure that these guys can do far better than they are, absolutely, positively." And she did everything to see that they would.

Another day, I met with a group of teachers with whom Junia had asked me to speak about what sustained them in teaching. They volunteered that what kept them engaged, in spite of the frustration and heartache that they sometimes experienced, were student teachers who contributed new ideas; colleagues to whom they could turn for support; new teachers who came into the profession with lots of enthusiasm; and students who had graduated and come back to visit. Juan Figueroa, a relatively new teacher, gave an example. He said,

> I was lucky enough to teach a class of seniors. This is the first year when they'll be graduating from college. Knowing that they're going to be graduating this year, and that two of them are going to be teachers, is incredible. They will be entering a profession that I love, and they'll be doing the same thing.

Anger and Desperation

One of the big surprises to emerge from my work with the inquiry group was the level of anger expressed by these excellent teachers. But I came to realize that anger is the other side of hope, and given the conditions in which they work, their hope is constantly tested.

The teachers were angry at the injustices their students have to endure, including racism and poverty. They were impatient with the arbitrariness of society; baffled at school policies made by people far removed from the daily realities of classroom life; and indignant at being treated as if they were children. But no matter how angry they were, they never expressed their frustration in mean-spirited comments about their students. Judith Baker explained, "I would exclude all 'social work' remedies. This is typical talk that teachers always do that leads nowhere." Judith was referring to the vain search for remedies to poverty and other social ills brought on by inequality. Nor did the teachers let their anger interfere with teaching. Junia Yearwood explained that her classroom was her haven. Once she entered the classroom, she said, "What I try to keep focused on is my kids, the students."

Sometimes, however, anger spilled over into desperation. Sonie Felix, the youngest member of the group, came in one day seriously considering leaving the profession. Although she enjoyed teaching and loved her students, she felt that she did not receive support or the opportunity to grow as an individual. She asked plaintively, "But what happens when that job is your life and calling? What do you do then?" The anger and resentment Sonie felt is not uncommon. Nevertheless, I am happy to report that Sonie is still teaching three years later—primarily because of the support of colleagues and her continuing participation in the intellectual life of teaching.

Intellectual Work

Engaging with trusted colleagues in what Stephen Gordon called "adult conversations about unasked questions" is one way in which teachers do intellectual work. When we first started meeting as an inquiry group, I could see the impatience in Sonie's eyes. She wanted us to do something, not just talk. By our last meeting, Sonie had developed not only a desire, but also a need to talk. She said,

> I think that these conversations are important in terms of continuing with teaching. *That's* how and why people tend to leave, because these conversations don't happen.

In addition to participating in the inquiry group, these teachers also took part in individual and collaborative curriculum development, wrote journals, conducted research in their classrooms, attended conferences, were active members in professional organizations, and mentored new colleagues. They also presented workshops for colleagues and visited other schools. In short, these teachers are constantly updating their craft and their knowledge.

Democratic Practice

Students in urban public schools face many problems, but discussions of these problems often place sole responsibility on the children and their families, as if the problems had sprung full-blown from them alone. Rather than the children lacking will or being of unsound moral character, however, it is the schools that often lack the will and the resources to teach these children. Any teacher who works in an urban school system can testify to this fact. A commitment to social justice—the ideals of democracy, fair play, and equality—figures prominently among the reasons why these teachers chose this profession.

I asked the teachers in the inquiry group to write a letter to an imaginary new teacher. What would a new teacher need to know? In his letter, Stephen Gordon expressed the profound desire to engage in democratic practice:

> I am happy that I found a profession that combines my belief in social justice with my zeal for intellectual excellence. My career choice has meant much anxiety, anger, and disappointment. But it has also produced profound joy. I have spent my work life committed to a just cause: the education of Boston high school students. Welcome to our noble teaching profession and our enduring cause.

The Ability to Shape the Future

Teachers' words and actions are of greater consequence than those of almost any other profession. Karen Gelzinis, who had been Sonie Felix's algebra teacher 14 years before, reflected on the power of teaching:

> We change lives forever. Of course, we all know it. But how often do we really think about it? Does it get lost in the piles of paper that we correct? In the scores/grades that we write down? . . . I thought about the teachers I had had, who saw something in "the disadvantaged kids" from the city and gave us the hope that we could do whatever we wanted, and we could do it without giving up who we were. We didn't have to move to the suburbs to be successful.

> We [teachers] need different words to speak about what we do, Standards, Rubrics, Benchmarks, Ninth grader, Important words, yes. But these words do not tell the complete stories of our kids. So, despite everything in our way, why do some of us end up staying? Is it because our lives continue to be changed forever, for the better, by our students? What would my life be without Sonie, without Jeramie? . . . It is an addictive thing, teaching.

The Promise

The promise of public education is a seductive hope. Precisely because of the grim conditions in schools and society, a vigorous commitment to high-quality public education is more necessary than ever. In the past two decades, however, schools have undergone a period of constant reform and restructuring, and the talk surrounding public education has become mean-spirited and antagonistic, giving greater attention to vouchers, "choice," charter schools, and winner-take-all high-stakes tests as the only viable solutions to the crisis in public education. The result is a near wholesale abandonment of the public schools, especially those that serve poor children.

To keep good teachers, we must find ways to achieve the unfulfilled promise of public education. We must rethink teacher education so that it focuses on preparing teachers to work with enthusiasm, competence, and caring among the students in our urban schools. We must prepare teachers—not for missionary work, but for public service. We must rethink professional development—not as a way to fill teachers' heads with new and innovative ideas that may come and go, but rather as an approach that builds on teachers' professionalism and encourages their intellectual activity. Paradoxically, current reforms that focus only on accountability—including standardized testing, teacher testing, and other such policies—may be driving out some of the teachers who are effective with the students who most need committed and caring teachers.

If we are as concerned about education as we say we are, then we need to do more to change the conditions faced by teachers, especially those who work in underfinanced and largely abandoned urban schools. We need to support those teachers who love their students, who find creative ways to teach them, and who do so under difficult circumstances. We need to celebrate teachers who are as excited about their own learning as they are about the learning of their students. And we need to champion those teachers who value their students' families and find respectful ways to work with them. Above all, we need to expect all teachers to do these things. The children in our public schools deserve no less.

Note

1. Ceronne Daly, then head of High School Restructuring for the Boston Public Schools, helped organize the group. Members of the inquiry group who met throughout the year were Judith Baker, Claudia Bell, Sonie Felix, Karen Gelzinis, Stephen Gordon, Ambrizeth Lima, and Junia Yearwood.

References

Darling-Hammond, L. (1998). Teachers and teaching: Testing policy hypotheses from a national commission report. *Educational Researcher, 27*(1), 5–15.

Haycock, K. (1998). No more settling for less. *Thinking 6–16, 4*(1), 3–12.

Nieto, S. (2003). *What keeps teachers going?* New York: Teachers College Press.

THE TEACHER SHORTAGE: MYTH OR REALITY?

Richard Ingersoll

The supply of excellent teachers is a perennial concern, but recently demographic shifts and the "graying" of the work force are major factors impacting the number of teachers in the profession. Each year, states develop a needs assessment profile identifying teaching areas that are in high demand. This *criticality index* assists districts and schools of education in both recruitment and hiring practices.

Experts argue about the reasons for the current teacher shortage. Some blame demographic factors such as increased rates of retirement of an aging teacher force. Others argue that additional factors, ranging from low pay to poor work conditions, impact teacher turnover rates. Richard Ingersoll contends that aggressive recruitment alone will not produce the teachers necessary for contemporary classrooms and schools. As you read this article ask yourself, "How can schools increase the number of qualified teachers who remain in teaching over time?"

Think About This . . .

1. Why is teacher turnover an important issue in education today?
2. What are the differences between movers and leavers in the field of education? What factors impact these teachers' decisions to remain within specific schools?
3. Why do teacher turnover rates differ across different types of schools?
4. What kind of school will you select for your first teaching position and how can the school setting help to support you in your first few years of teaching?

Few educational problems have received more attention in recent times than the failure to ensure that elementary and secondary classrooms are all staffed with qualified teachers. Education researchers and policymakers have told us again and again that severe teacher shortages are confronting our elementary and secondary schools. At the root of these problems, we are told, is a dramatic increase in the demand for new teachers, resulting primarily from two converging demographic

From Ingersoll, R. (2003). The teacher shortage: Myth or reality? Educational Horizons, 81(3), 146–152. Reprinted with permission of the author.

trends: increasing student enrollments and increasing teacher turnover due to a "graying" teaching force. Shortfalls of teachers, the argument continues, are forcing many school systems to fill teaching openings by lowering standards.

The prevailing policy response to these school staffing problems has been attempting to increase the supply of teachers. In recent years a range of initiatives have been implemented to recruit new candidates into teaching. Among these are career-change programs, such as "troops-to-teachers," designed to entice professionals into mid-career switches to teaching and Peace Corps-style programs, such as Teach For America, designed to lure the "best and brightest" into understaffed schools. Many states have instituted alternative certification programs, whereby college graduates can postpone formal education training and begin teaching immediately. Financial incentives, such as signing bonuses, forgiveness of student loans, housing assistance, and tuition reimbursement, have all been instituted to aid recruitment. The "No Child Left Behind Act," passed in winter 2002, provides extensive federal funding for such initiatives.[1]

Over the past decade I have undertaken a series of research projects on teacher supply, demand, quality, and shortages.[2] In this article I will briefly summarize what the data tell us about the realities of school staffing problems and teacher shortages. In my research I adopt an organizational perspective: my view is that looking at these problems from the perspective of the organizations—the schools and districts—where these processes occur is necessary in order to fully understand them. From this perspective, I argue, the data show that such recruitment efforts, however worthwhile, will not solve the teacher-staffing problems schools face. Indeed, I conclude that these efforts are largely a case of the wrong diagnosis and the wrong prescription.

The Project

My primary data source for this research was the nationally representative Schools and Staffing Survey (SASS) and its supplement, the Teacher Followup Survey (TFS), both conducted by the National Center for Education Statistics of the U.S. Department of Education. SASS is the largest and most comprehensive data source available on the staffing, occupational, and organizational aspects of schools. To date, four independent cycles of SASS have been completed: 1987–88; 1990–91; 1993–94; and 1999–2000. Each cycle of SASS administers survey questionnaires to a random sample of some 53,000 teachers and 12,000 principals from all types of schools and from all fifty states. In addition, one year later, the same schools are again contacted, and all those in the original teacher sample who had moved from or left their teaching jobs are given a second questionnaire to elicit information on their departures. This latter group, along with a representative sample of those who stayed in their teaching jobs, comprises the Teacher Followup Survey. The TFS is the largest and most comprehensive data source on teacher turnover, attrition, and migration in the United States.

What do these data tell us about school staffing problems and teacher shortages?

The Importance of Teacher Turnover for School Shortages

The data show that the conventional wisdom on teacher shortages, although partly correct, also errs in important ways. Consistent with shortage predictions, the data show that the demand for teachers has indeed increased. Since 1984, student enrollments have increased, teacher retirements have also increased, most schools have had job openings for teachers, and the size of the elementary and secondary teaching work force has increased. More important, the SASS data tell us that substantial numbers of schools with teaching openings have experienced difficulties filling their positions with qualified candidates.

But the data also show that the demand for new teachers and subsequent staffing difficulties are not primarily due to increases in student enrollment and teacher retirement. Most of the demand and hiring is simply to replace teachers recently departed from their positions; moreover, most of this teacher turnover has little to do with a "graying work force."

Teaching is an occupation with chronic and relatively high annual turnover. One of the best-known sources of national data on rates of employee turnover, the Bureau of National Affairs, has shown that nationwide levels of total employee departures for a range of occupations and industries have averaged a stable 11.9 percent per year for the past decade.[3] In contrast, the TFS data show that teaching has a relatively high annual turnover rate: 14.5 percent in 1988–89; 13.2 percent in 1991–92; 14.3 percent in 1994–95; 15.7 percent in 2000–2001 (see Figure 1).[4]

Two types of teachers are included in these data on total turnover: *movers,* defined as those who move to teaching jobs in other schools, and *leavers,* defined as those who leave the teaching occupation altogether. Total teacher turnover is split fairly evenly between the two

Figure 1

Percentage of Annual Employee Turnover and Percentage of Annual Teacher Turnover

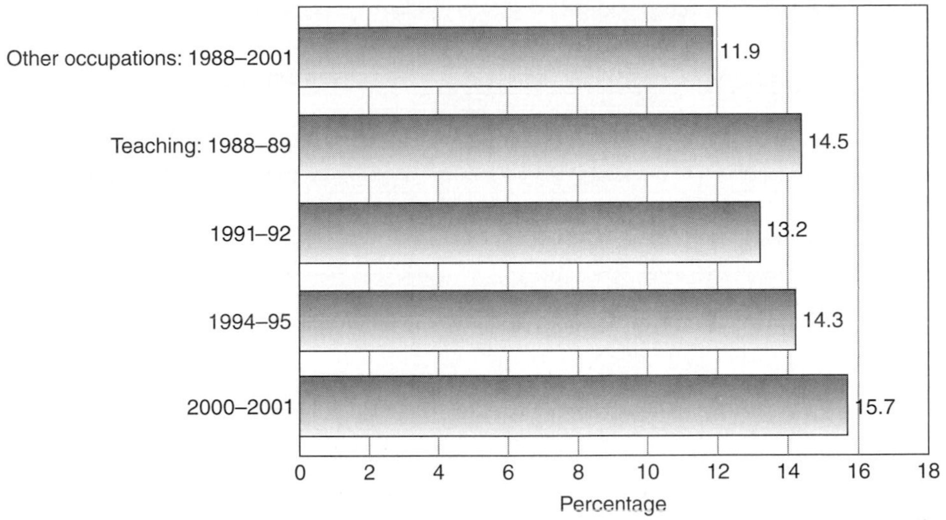

groups. Cross-school migration does not decrease the overall supply of teachers, because departures are simultaneously new hires. As a result, it seems reasonable to conclude that teacher migration does not contribute to the problem of staffing schools and to overall shortages. From a macro and systemic level of analysis, this conclusion is probably correct, and for this reason educational researchers have often de-emphasized or excluded movers. However, from an organizational-level perspective and from the viewpoint of managers, movers and leavers have the same effect—either situation results in a vacancy, which usually must be filled. Hence, research on employee turnover in other occupations and organizations and data such as those from the Bureau of National Affairs almost always include both movers and leavers, and for this reason I include them here.

It is also important to note that teaching is a relatively large occupation: it represents 4 percent of the entire civilian work force. There are, for example, more than twice as many K–12 teachers as registered nurses and five times as many teachers as either lawyers or professors. The sheer size of the teaching force, combined with the relatively high annual turnover of the teaching occupation, means that there are relatively large flows into, through, and from schools each year. The image these data suggest is a revolving door.

Of course, not all teacher or employee turnover is a bad thing. Those who study organizations and occupations in general have compiled an extensive research literature on employee turnover.[5] On the one hand, researchers in this tradition have long held that some employee turnover is normal and efficacious in a well-managed organization. They tie infrequent turnover of employees to stagnancy in organizations; effective organizations usually both promote and benefit from limited turnover by eliminating low-caliber performers and bringing in "new blood" to facilitate innovation. On the other hand, researchers in this tradition have also long held that high employee turnover is both the cause and effect of performance problems in organizations.

From an organizational perspective, employee turnover is especially consequential in work sites like schools, whose "production processes" require extensive interaction among participants. Such organizations are unusually dependent upon commitment, continuity, and cohesion among employees and, hence, especially vulnerable to employee turnover. From this perspective, then, high teacher turnover matters not simply because it may indicate sites of potential staffing problems but because of its relationship to school performance. Moreover, from this perspective high teacher turnover is of concern not only because it may indicate underlying problems in how well schools function but also because it can be disruptive, in and of itself, to the quality of school cohesion and performance.

However, although the data show that teaching has relatively high turnover, the data also show that the revolving door varies greatly among different kinds of teachers and different kinds of schools. As found in previous research, SASS data show that teaching loses many of its newly trained members long before the retirement years.[6] I used these data to calculate a rough estimate of the cumulative occupational attrition of teachers in their first few years of teaching. The data suggest that after

Figure 2

Percentage of Annual Teacher Turnover by Selected School Characteristics (2000–2001)

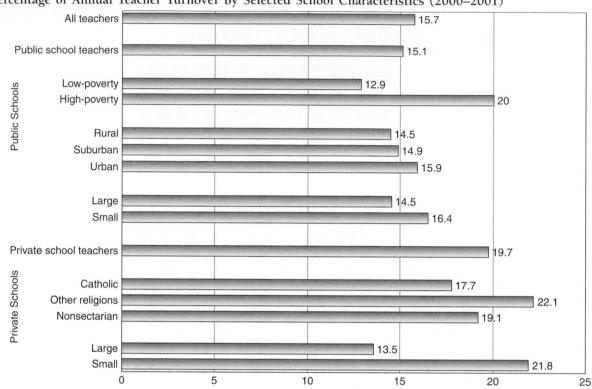

just five years, between 40 and 50 percent of all beginning teachers leave teaching altogether.

Moreover, the data also show that the revolving door varies greatly among different kinds of schools, as illustrated in Figure 2. For example, high-poverty public schools have far higher turnover rates than do more affluent public schools. Urban public schools have slightly more turnover than do suburban and rural public schools.

Private schools have higher turnover rates than public schools, yet there are large differences among private schools. On one end of the continuum lie larger private schools, with among the lowest average turnover rate: about 13.5 percent, close to what is found in other occupations. On the other end of the continuum lie smaller private schools. The turnover rates of smaller private schools have the highest average levels: about 22 percent. The turnover rate in these schools is almost double the national average for many other kinds of employees.

These data raise important questions: Why do teachers depart at relatively high rates, and why do these rates differ so dramatically between schools?

The Sources of Teacher Turnover

To answer these questions I conducted extensive advanced statistical analyses of the data from different SASS/TFS cycles to determine which characteristics of teachers and schools correlate with the likelihood of teacher turnover, and I also closely examined data on the reasons teachers themselves give for their turnover. I found considerable consistency among these different types of data and among different cycles of the survey. In Figure 3, I summarize the principal findings from these different analyses.

Contrary to conventional wisdom, retirement is not an especially prominent factor. The latter actually accounts for only 13 percent of total turnover.

School staffing cutbacks due to layoffs, terminations, school closings, and reorganizations account for more turnover than does retirement. These staffing actions more often result in migration to other teaching jobs than in abandoning teaching altogether. However, the data also show that staffing actions, like retirement, account for little of total teacher turnover.

Figure 3

Percentage of School Teachers Giving Various Reasons for Their Turnover (1994–1995)

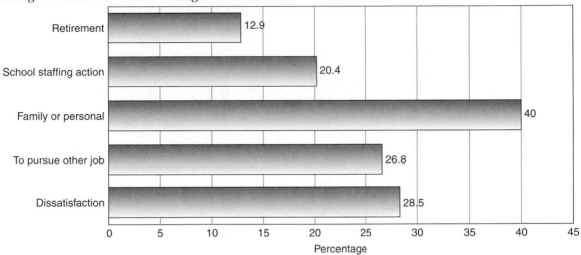

A third category of turnover, personal reasons, includes departures for pregnancy, child rearing, health problems, and family moves. They account for more turnover than either retirement or staffing actions, and the data also show that these motives are common to all schools.

Finally, two reasons directly related to the working and organizational conditions of teaching are, together, the most prominent sources of turnover. Far more turnover results from such factors than from retirements. Almost half of all departures report as a motivation 1) job dissatisfaction or 2) a desire to pursue better jobs, different careers, or improved career opportunities, in or out of education.

Teachers who leave because of job dissatisfaction most often link their departure to low salaries, lack of support from administration, discipline problems, and lack of influence over decision-making. Interestingly, several factors stand out as not serious enough to cause much turnover from schools: large class sizes, intrusions on classroom time, and insufficient planning time (see Figure 4). These latter findings are important because of their implications for policy.

Figure 4

Percentage of School Teachers Giving Various Reasons for Their Dissatisfaction-Related Turnover (1994–1995)

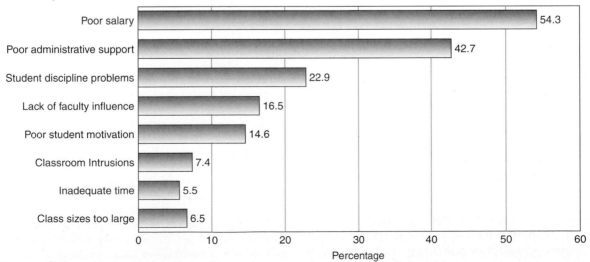

Implications

It is widely believed that two converging demographic trends—increasing student enrollments and increasing teacher retirements—have led to school staffing problems and, in turn, lowered educational performance. In response, school districts, states, and the federal government have developed a variety of recruitment initiatives designed to bring more candidates into teaching.

The data suggest, however, that these efforts, perhaps worthwhile, will not by themselves solve school staffing problems. The data suggest that these problems are not primarily due to shortfalls resulting from increases in student enrollment or in teacher retirement. In contrast, the data suggest that school staffing problems result from a revolving-door syndrome: large numbers of teachers departing from teaching for reasons other than retirement. In short, the problem is not primarily shortages, in the conventional sense of too few teachers being recruited and trained; rather, the problem is turnover: too many teachers departing prior to retirement.

This distinction is important because of its implications for educational policy. Supply-and-demand theory holds that where the quantity of teachers demanded is greater than that supplied, there are two basic policy remedies: increasing the quantity supplied or decreasing the quantity demanded. Teacher recruitment, an example of the former approach, has been and continues to be the dominant approach to addressing school-staffing inadequacies. However, this analysis suggests that recruitment programs alone will not solve schools' staffing problems, if they do not also address the problem of teacher retention. States such as California, where reductions in class size have strained the supply of new teachers, pose exceptions. But for just such reasons, California must, like other states, pay more attention to retention. In short, recruiting more teachers will not solve the teacher crisis if large numbers of such teachers then leave. The image that comes to mind is that of a bucket rapidly losing water because of holes in the bottom. Pouring more water into the bucket will not solve the problem if the holes are not first patched.

One strategy suggested by the data for plugging these holes is increasing teacher salaries, which are, not surprisingly, strongly linked to teacher turnover rates. Increasing salaries is, of course, expensive, given the sheer size of the teaching force.

A second factor suggested by the data is increased support from school administrations, especially for new teachers. Supportive measures could range from ensuring sufficient classroom supplies to providing mentoring for new teachers. The latter is crucial; life for beginning teachers has traditionally been described as a sink-or-swim proposition, and as the data show, turnover is especially high among new teachers.

A third factor suggested by this analysis is enhanced faculty input into school decision-making. Other data from SASS indicate that, on average, teachers have little say in many key decisions concerned with and affecting their work.[7] But these data also indicate large variations among schools, and those where teachers are allowed more input into decisions that affect their jobs have less turnover.

Reduction of discipline problems is a fourth factor tied to teacher turnover. The data tell us that, regardless of the background and poverty levels of the student population, schools vary dramatically in the degree of student misbehavior and again, not surprisingly, that schools with significant student misbehavior problems have significant teacher turnover. One factor tied to both student discipline and teacher turnover is how much decision-making influence teachers themselves have over school policies concerned with student behavioral rules and sanctions: schools where teachers say they are allowed more input into these kinds of issues witness less conflict between staff and students and less teacher turnover.[8]

The data do not suggest that plugging holes through such changes will be easy. But from the perspective of this analysis, schools are not simply victims of inexorable demographic trends, and the management and organization of schools play significant roles in both generating and solving school staffing problems. The data suggest that improvements in such aspects of teaching would contribute to lower turnover rates, in turn diminish school staffing problems, and, hence, ultimately aid school performance.

Notes

1. For a review of these initiatives, see Eric Hirsch, Julie Koppich, and Mike Knapp, *Revisiting What States Are Doing to Improve the Quality of Teaching: An Update on Patterns and Trends* (Center for the Study of Teaching and Policy, University of Washington, 2001).

2. See Richard M. Ingersoll, "The Problem of Underqualified Teachers in American Secondary Schools," *Educational Researcher* 28 (1999): 26–37; Richard M. Ingersoll, "Teacher Turnover and Teacher Shortages: An Organizational Analysis," *American Educational Research Journal* 37, no. 3 (2001): 499–534; and Richard M. Ingersoll, "The Teacher Shortage: A Case of Wrong Diagnosis and Wrong Prescription," *NASSP Bulletin* 86, no. 631 (summer 2002): 16–30.

3. Bureau of National Affairs, "BNA's Quarterly Report on Job Absence and Turnover," *Bulletin to Management* (Washington, D.C.: Bureau of National Affairs, 2002).

4. The 2000–2001 teacher turnover data in figures 1 and 2 are preliminary estimates. As of fall 2002, the 2000–2001 TFS had not yet been entirely released by NCES. However, these figures are consistent with similar data from the earlier cycles of the TFS.

5. See W. A. Mobley, *Employee Turnover: Causes, Consequences and Control* (Reading, Mass: Addison-Wesley, 1982). See also

James Price, *The Study of Turnover* (Ames, Ia.: Iowa State University Press, 1977).

6. See Richard Murnane, Judith Singer, John Willett, J. Kemple, and R. Olsen (eds.), *Who Will Teach? Policies That Matter* (Cambridge, Mass.: Harvard University Press, 1991).

7. Richard M. Ingersoll, *Who Controls Teachers' Work? Power and Accountability in America's Schools* (Cambridge, Mass.: Harvard University Press, 2003).

8. Ibid.

NO CHILD LEFT BEHIND:
THE POLITICS OF TEACHER QUALITY

Leslie Kaplan and William Owings

What constitutes an effective and well-qualified teacher? Knowing *what* to teach and *how* to teach are integral dimensions of teachers' work, but current political debates surrounding teacher preparation challenge the long-held belief that a qualified teacher must be certified.

Proponents of the No Child Left Behind law identify "highly qualified" as those individuals with recognized strengths in their content knowledge, but not necessarily in their ability to teach that knowledge. Others argue that knowledge of content is necessary but not sufficient for teacher competence; teachers are better prepared when they have completed courses on instruction and learner development. As you read this article ask yourself, "What factors should be used to determine whether a teacher is highly qualified? What should schools of education include in their programs to guarantee that teachers are highly qualified?"

Think About This . . .

1. What similarities and differences exist in the opinions of both educators and politicians regarding teacher quality?

2. One criticism of teacher education is the variance in programs from across the country. What type of preparation for teachers do you believe is most important?

3. When evaluating teacher quality, how might evaluators include data from both standardized assessment measures as well as teaching practice?

4. What criteria would you like to be used when you are evaluated as an educator? Why?

A recent bipartisan national poll finds that 42% of respondents felt it was important for teachers to have "skills to design learning experiences that inspire/interest children," while only 19% thought it was important for teachers to have "a thorough understanding of their subject." Similarly, 67% of those who were sampled said that "developing the proper

skills to make information interesting and understandable is a greater difficulty than developing adequate knowledge about subject matter."[1]

From Kaplan, L., & Owings, W. (2003). No Child Left Behind: The politics of teacher quality. Phi Delta Kappan, 84(9), 687–692. Reprinted with permission of the authors.

Overwhelmingly, Americans believe that knowing *how* to teach is at least as important as knowing *what* to teach. High-quality teaching—knowing the material and how to convey it—makes the difference in student achievement. Research supports this view.

Some politicians and education officials, however, seem to be saying just the opposite. U.S. Secretary of Education Rod Paige said in February 2002 that teacher certification does not ensure teacher quality and that "highly qualified teachers may not be required to be certified."[2] He added that the present certification system reflects both low standards and high barriers to professional entry. The No Child Left Behind (NCLB) law's definition of a "highly qualified teacher" reflects this view.

As NCLB brings high-stakes testing and its consequences to all 50 states, everyone wants the best-qualified and most effective teachers. However, the new federal requirements seem to contradict both popular belief and the experiences of educators, which affirm that effective teaching practices—rather than content knowledge alone—increase student achievement. Practitioners worry that, while NCLB widens the potential pool of teaching candidates, many of them will not know how to work effectively with students. Many will not know how to package and deliver their subjects in ways that increase student learning.

Instead of expecting new teachers to be "classroom ready"—that is, equipped with at least the basic teaching skills—NCLB permits content experts who lack teaching knowledge or experience to take over classrooms in the nation's middle and high schools. Once these content experts are on the job, NCLB expects principals and master teachers to educate them using proven, "scientifically based" professional development strategies that will boost student learning. With the federal government saying one thing and the public at large and practitioners believing another, educators are understandably uncertain about how this new definition of "highly qualified teacher" will affect teaching and learning.

Where Educators and Politicians Agree

We use the term "politicians" to refer to knowledgeable thinkers, writers, and political appointees who have an "agenda" about what makes a teacher qualified and who selectively exclude research-referenced views that oppose their agenda. These politicians have had a powerful influence on the current education legislation and on the NCLB guidelines and regulations.

Jeff Archer has noted that there is little actual disagreement about what research on teacher quality says, but the experts from the two camps strongly disagree about how to interpret it and about how policy makers should respond.[3] Consensus does exist about how effective teachers affect student achievement.

The effects on student achievement of working for consecutive years with highly effective or ineffective teachers are known, and we will discuss them only briefly here.[4] The schools students attend and what their teachers know and do are more important influences on student achievement than family characteristics and ethnicity. In addition, the cumulative impact over three years of effective elementary teachers is estimated to produce (on a 100-point scale) more than a 50-point difference in math and a 35-point difference in reading on standardized tests.[5] Consecutive years with highly effective teachers can produce dramatic achievement gains in all groups—low-, middle-, and high-achieving students. Moreover, high school students working with the most effective teachers show reading and math gains that exceed the national median, while their peers with the least effective teachers showed virtually no growth.[6]

Educators and politicians agree that a clear predictive relationship exists between the basic skills of teachers, especially verbal ability, and student achievement.[7] They also agree that teachers' content knowledge affects student achievement. On the 1996 National Assessment of Educational Progress (NAEP), students whose teachers had college majors or minors in the subjects they taught—especially in secondary math and science—outperformed students whose teachers lacked this content knowledge by about 40% of a grade level in each subject.[8] Likewise, evidence suggests that teacher content knowledge in English and social studies may be no less important.[9]

No evidence, however, suggests that possessing content knowledge *alone* is sufficient to be an effective teacher.[10] Some have claimed a mixed connection between teachers' subject-matter knowledge and student achievement that can positively influence student learning. Others have rightly added that college majors vary in rigor and that the college transcript of a prospective teacher may not actually confirm content knowledge.[11]

The bottom line—and the area of disagreement—is that, while teachers' strong content knowledge and verbal skills have demonstrated links to higher student achievement, they may be necessary but not sufficient conditions for high-quality teaching and learning.

Using Research to Advance Political Agendas

Typically, educational research seeks to provide data to support best practices; consumers assume the findings will be objective and informative. The problem with teacher quality research, however, is that it has become a political battleground, and so it is difficult to know what to believe.

A fundamental disagreement exists over whether traditional teacher preparation positively affects student achievement. Experts with opposing political viewpoints differ strongly about the rigor of the methods, about how to interpret the data, and about how policy makers should respond.[12] The tone of such disputes can sometimes turn disagreeable, as when the Progressive Policy Institute refers to a new study of teacher quality as "Putting Lipstick on a Pig."[13]

Traditionalists point to the research affirming that teacher expertise—what teachers know and *can do*—is the most important factor in determining student achievement. Proponents of reduced teacher credentialing, on the other hand, assert that little sound statistical research is available for evaluating which types of training or degrees have the best effect on student achievement or whether teacher preparation even makes a difference.[14] Each camp cites educational research in support of its views.

In this vein, Frederick Hess calls a recent study supporting the benefits of teacher certification on student achievement "Advocacy in the Guise of Research."[15] This statement applies equally to both sides.

Kate Walsh in her report for the Abell Foundation claimed that the research that suggests that teacher knowledge of instructional ideas and practices (i.e., pedagogy) positively affects student achievement is cited selectively, is too old to be reliable, is not subjected to peer review, uses nonstandardized measures, violates sound statistical analysis, doesn't control for key variables such as poverty or prior student achievement, uses too small a sample, or inappropriately aggregates data.[16] Others claim that the research supporting teaching knowledge is biased, arguing that education and pedagogy classes are ideologically rather than research driven.[17]

Citing Walsh's analyses as justification, the *Secretary's Annual Report on Teacher Quality* states that no "scientifically rigorous" research supports the belief that pedagogy or education degrees are linked to higher student achievement.[18] Using this logic, the NCLB legislation removes teacher preparation in educational theory and practice as a requirement for hiring middle and high school teachers.

Directly responding to Walsh's report, Linda Darling-Hammond, although agreeing that legitimate concerns exist about various studies, vigorously argued that Walsh's review ignores evidence, makes unfounded claims, misrepresents research, misunderstands some fundamental issues in research design, uses a double standard in citing studies to support Walsh's own viewpoint, and draws illogical policy conclusions.[19]

Methodological weaknesses can be important when practitioners try to interpret data. True, teacher certification researchers do not account for the fact that teachers are not randomly assigned to classes within schools. The most experienced, credentialed, and respected teachers usually receive assignments to upper-level and advanced courses. School culture and logic dictate that mature teachers with advanced degrees receive these high-status, intellectually rigorous classes, and parents expect it.[20] Comparing certified to uncertified teachers, then, does not present a fair picture of student achievement because students are not starting from the same place. This does not, mean, however, that research limitations undercut all findings.

"As any reader of educational literature knows all too well, one can find experts on both sides of any . . . issues, each armed with his or her supporting data," wrote Howard Gardner in *Education Week*.[21] Ethically, students cannot be randomly assigned from one condition to another "the way that agricultural seeds are planted or transplanted in different soils," he argued. Educators must consume data knowledgeably and consider these limitations and merits along with the reliable data from their own professional experiences to make sense of the issues and determine appropriate responses.

Support for the View That Teaching Knowledge Makes a Difference

Credible research exists showing that teachers' instructional preparation increases student achievement. Darling-Hammond found that teacher preparation is a stronger correlate of student achievement than class size, overall spending, or teacher salaries and accounts for 40% to 60% of the total achievement variance after taking students' demographics into account.[22] In fact, studies show that both subject-matter knowledge and knowledge of teaching and learning strongly correlate with teachers' classroom performance.[23]

It is clear that teachers who learn and practice sound pedagogical techniques can affect students' measured achievement. Harold Wenglinsky's 1996 NAEP study found that students of teachers who conducted hands-on learning activities outperformed their peers by more than 70% of a grade level in math and 40% of a grade level in science. Students whose teachers had strong content knowledge and had learned to work with students from different cultures or special needs tested more than one full grade level above their peers. Students whose math teachers stressed critical thinking skills, such as writing about math, scored 39% of a grade level higher. In addition, "the aspects of teaching quality measured have an impact seven to 10 times as great as that of class size" in affecting student achievement.[24]

Coursework in teacher education is sometimes more influential than extra subject-matter classes in promoting students' math and science achievement.[25] David Monk found a positive correlation between the achievement of students and their teachers' coursework in teaching methods. However, he conceded that variations in the content of the courses made it difficult to draw definitive conclusions.[26]

Education classes do appear to have a point of diminishing returns. Several studies have found that teachers with advanced subject-matter degrees, rather than advanced education degrees, have students who perform better in math and reading, especially beyond elementary school as students need a deeper and more complex understanding of content.[27]

In addition, systematically studying learning processes results in more effective teaching behaviors and increased student achievement. And when teachers examined contemporary learning approaches and developed their own explicit learning theories, researchers found that the number of their effective classroom teaching behaviors increased significantly. Similarly, they found that 73% of these teachers' students—especially the lowest-achieving students—showed statistically significant learning gains.[28]

Moreover, research also suggests that teachers without teacher education preparation can be less effective at helping students learn. Teachers who lack effective classroom management skills, regardless of how much content they know, cannot create a classroom environment that supports student learning. A study of alternatively certified teachers with only subject-matter knowledge demonstrated that they had strongly held misconceptions about appropriate ways to teach the content and were unable to integrate their subject knowledge with teaching practices to allow effective instruction.[29] Likewise, a study of the impact of different disciplinary practices on student achievement found that student disorder results in lower achievement.[30]

To a degree, both sides make valid points. Supporters of traditional teacher preparation admit certain shortcomings. Schools of education vary in standards for candidates, programs, teacher education curricula, and quality of faculty members. Most U.S. teachers have had a "relatively thin" preservice teacher education experience, usually involving tradeoffs between content and pedagogical preparation. Typically, prospective teachers learned subject matter and pedagogical techniques in unrelated courses; the two were not always integrated into real-world teaching experiences. In addition, most teaching candidates have had only short supervised student teaching experiences. It is small wonder that beginning teachers often report that their professional preparation was of little use to them.[31]

In sum, data supporting the impact of pedagogical training on student achievement are available, credible, and substantial, but the research remains open to challenge on logical and methodological grounds. However, the ambiguity of the data invites political use. Both evidence and experience show that effective teaching requires a set of professional practices different from but connected to the content taught. While content knowledge is unarguably essential, knowing *how* to teach content—whether learned in preservice training or on the job—makes a measurable impact on student achievement.

Connecting Certification and Teacher Quality

The research connecting teacher certification and teacher quality is also mixed. Teacher certification lacks consistent standards to classify the effectiveness of candidates. As a profession, teaching has "no consensus on how to train good teachers or ensure that they have mastered essential skills and knowledge," Hess has argued.[32] And this makes certification based on common, mutually agreed upon, and nationally accepted standards difficult.

Complicating matters further, teacher preparation programs vary dramatically in quality. States have broad flexibility to set their own criteria for teacher education and to define which institutions are "low performing." When states recently reported information on teacher preparation, much of it was "inconsistent, incomplete, and utterly incomprehensible."[33] Only one teacher preparation institution among more than 1,300 in the U.S. was classified as "low performing." Thirteen others were considered "at risk" of being low performing.

Moreover, licensing varies in rigor, and exceptions differ from state to state. The Education Trust reviewed the licensure exams of the states and noted that "most of the content on licensing exams is typically found in high school curricula. . . . [The content was] never at the level of a bachelor's degree."[34] In spite of the strong evidence relating student achievement to teachers' knowledge of subject matter, 23 states do not require subject-area knowledge for secondary English or math.[35]

In addition, some states make no effort to screen out even the weakest applicants. Six states reported 100% passing rates, and only 24 states had teacher standards tied to their respective academic content standards.[36] Even the highly regarded National Board for Professional Teaching Standards has been criticized for its vague and broad standards and can show no evidence that certified teachers are more effective than others at raising student achievement.[37]

What is more, teacher certification places "fiscal barriers to teacher preparation and entry [that] produce both chronic shortages of qualified teachers in some fields and dramatically uneven levels of preparation across the teaching force."[38] Traditional teacher preparation requires many professional courses that cost students time and money. Requirements vary by state for entry into a profession with a salary scale that is lower than that offered to college graduates in other fields and is tied to seniority and advanced degrees rather than to productivity. These factors discourage many promising candidates from pursuing a teaching career.

Stating the facts objectively—warts and all—is one thing. Inadvertently or knowingly misrepresenting them to advance an agenda is another. For instance, *The Secretary's Annual Report on Teacher Quality* for 2002 states that "fewer than 36% of new teachers feel 'very well prepared' to implement curriculum and performance standards . . . and less than 20% feel prepared to meet the needs of diverse students or those with limited English proficiency" (p. 15), citing the National Center for Education Statistics as the source. The terms "fewer than" and "new," however, do not appear in the original report from which the statistics were taken.[39] In fact, the statistics reported were actually from a survey of practicing classroom teachers in 1998, most of whom were not new. From these and similar data, the *Secretary's Annual Report* concludes that a majority of teacher education graduates believe that traditional teacher preparation programs left them poorly prepared for real classroom challenges. Conclusions from such misleadingly presented data can be confusing.

What are practitioners to make of these conflicting views? Considering all the evidence, teacher certification standards are too varied and in most cases too low to ensure teacher quality. For candidates from strong education schools where students have content knowledge linked to teaching practices and many real-world opportunities to integrate and use what they learn with students in well-supervised settings, certification can be a strong predictor of teacher quality. For those with weaker backgrounds, certification cannot.

The practical question is whether "content experts" with academic majors—who lack formal coursework in education—are *equal* in potential effectiveness to traditional teacher candidates. Although wide variations exist, research nevertheless suggests that teacher candidates from accredited, respected teacher preparation programs probably have an edge—although by no means a guarantee—in terms of potential teaching effectiveness.

There can be no doubt that students need high-quality teachers. The academic and political arguments surrounding teacher quality also affect how educators do their jobs. Research can offer useful guidance about which teacher candidates are most likely to increase student achievement, but the findings must be used critically and cautiously.

Notes

1. Peter D. Hart and Robert M. Teeter, *A National Priority: Americans Speak on Teacher Quality* (Princeton, N.J.: Educational Testing Service, 2002), p. 9, available at www.ets.org; search on the title.

2. Julie Blair, "Teacher-Trainers Fear a Backfire from New ESEA," *Education Week on the Web,* 6 March 2002, p. 4.

3. Jeff Archer, "Research: Focusing in on Teachers," *Education Week,* 3 April 2002, pp. 36–39.

4. Kati Haycock, "Good Teaching Matters . . . A Lot," *Thinking K-16,* Summer 1998, pp. 3–14; Linda Darling-Hammond, "Teacher Quality and Student Achievement: A Review of State Policy Evidence," *Education Policy Analysis Archives,* 1 January 2000, available at http://epaa.asu.edu/epaa/v8n1; Leslie S. Kaplan and William A. Owings, *Teacher Quality, Teaching Quality, and School Improvement* (Bloomington, Ind.: Phi Delta Kappa Educational Foundation, 2002); idem, "The Politics of Teacher Quality: Implications for Principals," *NASSP Bulletin,* December 2002, pp. 22–41; idem, "Teacher Quality and Student Achievement: Recommendations for Principals," *NASSP Bulletin,* November 2001, pp. 64–73; and Grover J. Whitehurst, "Scientifically Based Research on Teacher Quality: Research on Teacher Preparation and Professional Development," paper presented at White House Conference on Preparing Tomorrow's Teachers, 5 March 2002.

5. William Sanders and June Rivers, *Cumulative and Residual Effects of Teachers on Future Student Academic Achievement*

(Knoxville: Value-Added Research and Assessment Center, University of Tennessee, November 1996).

6. Haycock, op. cit.

7. Kate Walsh, *Teacher Certification Reconsidered: Stumbling for Quality* (Baltimore: Abell Foundation, 2001), available at www.abell.org; Darling-Hammond, op. cit.; Haycock, op. cit.; and Whitehurst, op. cit.

8. Julie Blair, "ETS Study Links Effective Teaching Methods to Test-Score Gains," *Education Week,* 25 October 2000, pp. 24–25; Daniel D. Goldhaber and Dominic J. Brewer, "Does Teacher Certification Matter? High School Teacher Certification Status and Student Achievement," *Educational Evaluation and Policy Analysis,* Summer 2000, pp. 129–45; and Harold Wenglinsky, *How Teaching Matters: Bringing the Classroom Back into Discussions of Teacher Quality* (Princeton, N.J.: Milken Family Foundation and Educational Testing Service, October 2000).

9. Haycock, op. cit.

10. Barnett Berry, "No Shortcuts to Preparing Good Teachers," *Educational Leadership,* May 2001, pp. 32–36; Suzanne M. Wilson et al., "Teacher Preparation Research: An Insider's View from the Outside," *Journal of Teacher Education,* vol. 53, 2002, pp. 190–204.

11. Marci Kanstoroom and Chester E. Finn, Jr., eds., *Better Teachers, Better Schools* (Washington, D.C.: Thomas B. Fordham Foundation, July 1999).

12. Archer, op. cit.; Goldhaber and Brewer, op. cit.; idem, "Evaluating the Evidence on Teacher Certification: A Rejoinder," *Educational Evaluation and Policy Analysis,* Spring 2001, pp. 70–86; and Walsh, op. cit.

13. "New Teacher Quality Studies: Putting Lipstick on a Pig," *Bi-Monthly Bulletin: Progressive Policy Institute 21st-Century Schools Project,* 3 September 2002, pp. 1–2.

14. Kirk A. Johnson, "The Effects of Advanced Teacher Training in Education on Student Achievement," *Report of the Heritage Center for Data Analysis, No. 00-09,* 14 September 2000, pp. 1–17; and Walsh, op. cit.

15. Frederick M. Hess, "Advocacy in the Guise of Research: The Laczko-Kerr-Berliner Study of Teacher Certification," *Bi-Monthly Bulletin: Progressive Policy Institute 21st-Century Schools Project,* 3 September 2002, p.2.

16. Walsh, p. iv.

17. Johnson, op. cit.; and Dale Ballou and Michael Podgursky, "Teacher Training and Licensure: A Layman's Guide," in Kanstoroom and Finn, pp. 31–82.

18. Rod Paige, *The Secretary's Annual Report on Teacher Quality: Meeting the Qualified Teacher Challenge* (Washington, D.C.: U.S. Department of Education, 2002), p. 8.

19. Linda Darling-Hammond, "The Research and Rhetoric on Teacher Certification: A Response to 'Teacher Certification Reconsidered,'" National Commission on Teaching and America's Future, 15 October 2001, available at www.nctaf.org.

20. Hess, p. 3.

21. Howard Gardner, "The Quality and Qualities of Educational Research," *Education Week,* 4 September 2002, p. 72.

22. Darling-Hammond, "Teacher Quality and Student Achievement," p. 27.

23. Edith Guyton and Elizabeth Farokhi, "Relationships Among Academic Performance, Basic Skills, and Subject-Matter Knowledge and Teaching Skills of Teacher Education Graduates," *Journal of Teacher Education,* September/October 1987, pp. 37–42.

24. Wenglinsky, p. 31.

25. David H. Monk and Jennifer A. King, "Multi-level Teacher Resource Effects in Pupil Performance in Secondary Mathematics and Science: The Case of Teacher Subject-Matter Preparation," in Ronald G. Ehrenberg, ed., *Choices and Consequences: Contemporary Policy Issues in Education* (Ithaca, N.Y.: ILR Press, 1994), pp. 29–58.

26. David H. Monk, "Subject-Matter Preparation of Secondary Mathematics and Science Teachers and Student Achievement," *Economics of Education Review,* vol. 13, 1994, pp. 125–45.

27. Johnson, op. cit.; and Rob Greenwald, Larry V. Hedges, and Richard D. Laine, "The Effect of School Resources on Student Achievement," *Review of Educational Research,* vol. 66, 1996, pp. 361–96.

28. John Munro, "Learning More About Learning Improves Teacher Effectiveness," *School Effectiveness and School Improvement,* June 1999, pp. 151–71.

29. G. Williamson McDiarmid and Suzanne Wilson, "An Exploration of the Subject-Matter Knowledge of Alternative Route Teachers: Can We Assume They Know Their Subject?," *Journal of Teacher Education,* vol. 42, no. 3, 1991, pp. 32–35.

30. Paul E. Barton, Richard Coley, and Harold Wenglinsky, *Order in the Classroom: Violence, Discipline, and Student Achievement* (Princeton, N.J.: Educational Testing Service, 1998).

31. Linda Darling-Hammond and Deborah L. Ball, "Teaching for High Standards: What Policymakers Need to Know and Be Able to Do," paper prepared for the National Education Goals Panel, June 1997, p. 18.

32. Hess, p. 2.

33. Sandra Huang, Yi Yun, and Kati Haycock, *Interpret with Caution: The First State Title II Reports on the Quality of Teacher Preparation* (Washington, D.C.: Education Trust, June 2002), p. 1.

34. Ruth Mitchell and Patte Barth, "How Teacher Licensing Tests Fall Short," *Thinking K–l6,* Spring 1999, p. 15, available at www.edtrust.org. (under Reports and Publications, go to *Not Good Enough*).

35. Huang, Yun, and Haycock, p. 8.

36. Paige, p. 25.

37. Frederick M. Hess, "Tear Down This Wall: The Case for a Radical Overhaul of Teacher Certification," Progressive Policy Institute Policy Report, 27 November 2001, p. 8, available at www.ppionline.org.

38. Darling-Hammond and Ball, p. 11.

39. Laurie Lewis et al., *Teacher Quality: A Report on the Preparation and Qualifications of Public School Teachers* (Washington, D.C.: National Center for Education Statistics, January 1999), p. l–xxxviii.

ADDITIONAL READINGS

Cross, C., & Rigden, D. (2002). Improving teacher quality. *American School Board Journal,* *189*(4), 26–29.

Darling-Hammond, L. (2001). The challenge of staffing our schools. *Educational Leadership,* *58*(8), 12–17.

Ference, R., & Rhodes, W. (2002). Preservice teachers are making a difference by mentoring middle school students. *Middle School Journal, 33*(5), 41–46.

Laczko-Kerr, I., & Berliner, D. (2003). In harm's way: How undercertified teachers hurt their students. *Educational Leadership, 60*(8), 34–39.

Temes, P. (2001). Can teaching become an elite profession? *Education Week, 21*(14), 40, 43.

Williams, J. (2003). Why great teachers stay. *Educational Leadership, 60*(8), 71–75.

Wise, A. (2003). What's wrong with teacher certification? Making the case for a professional beginning-teacher licensing process. *Education Week, 22*(30), 56, 42.

EXPLORING THE INTERNET

Teaching as a Career
http://www.aft.org/career/index.html
This site provides information about the need for new teachers, some of the requirements for becoming a teacher, and sources of financial aid for people who want to major in education.

American Society for Ethics in Education
http://www.edethics.org/
This site provides a variety of additional Web sites that examine ethical issues relevant to education today.

Gallup Organization
http://www.gallup.com/
You will find valuable information about teachers' attitudes as well as the public's attitudes toward education.

The Association for Supervision and Curriculum Development
http://www.ascd.org
This site contains a number of valuable resources for beginning as well as experienced teachers.

Job Satisfaction Among America's Teachers
http://nces.ed.gov/pubsearch
This report by the National Center for Educational Statistics investigates factors that influence teachers' job satisfaction.

Teaching in Elementary/Secondary Schools
http://www.eric.ed.gov/
This site contains current information on teacher salaries, motives for entering teaching, and how teachers spend their time.

PART NINE

Foundations

275

The area of *foundations* raises fundamental questions about the nature of schools, teachers, and the processes involved in education. Two of the most fundamental are, What is the purpose of schooling, and what are the characteristics of an educated person? These questions also raise ethical issues—decisions about right and wrong, duties and obligations, and rights and responsibilities. Answers to these questions lead to decisions about what should be taught, how it should be taught, and how our schools and classrooms should be operated. For example, in colonial times, the purpose of schooling was thought to be the development of a scripture-literate citizenry capable of overcoming the negative influence of Satan. An educated person was knowledgeable about the Bible and lived a moral life according to religious principles. As a result, reading, writing, and religion were important parts of the curriculum. And because adherence to authority was highly valued, instruction focused on recitation of factual information and asking questions was discouraged. Teachers were men, they were commonly preparing for the clergy, and they had no formal training as educators.

As the history of our country unfolded, views changed. The purpose of schooling took on a more practical orientation, and educated citizens were viewed as those capable of adapting to their environments as the country expanded westward. As a result, practice-oriented content areas such as geography, science, and agriculture were added to the curriculum. Many women were teachers, but they were forbidden to marry, and society frowned on them having a social life.

Views of the purpose of education continued to change as the country experienced a huge influx of immigrants during the 19th century. Most did not speak English, so developing an English-literate population became a primary purpose of schooling, and people able to contribute to the economy and participate in decisions that made our country stronger were viewed as educated. And thus the two fundamental questions mentioned above continue to be asked today. Answering them has become more difficult in an era where contentious disagreements about the purposes of schooling exist, such as the view that all learners should acquire a common core of knowledge compared to the position arguing that education should be grounded in learners' needs and interests. Attempts to grapple with these issues raise additional questions. Some of them include the following: What are the basic assumptions on which our present system of schooling is based? How can ideological differences about the purposes of education be resolved? What role does philosophy play in helping answer fundamental questions? What are the characteristics of a "good" teacher? How can teachers accommodate the many ethical issues that exist in teaching? And, how can reflection help teachers analyze and improve their practice? Think about these questions as you study the articles in this section.

QUESTIONABLE ASSUMPTIONS ABOUT SCHOOLING
Elliot W. Eisner

Schools can have a profound impact on how young people think and what they believe about themselves. Schools influence students' thinking about what it means to be successful and intelligent, how they think about knowledge and understanding, and what they see as their place in society and the world at large. The organization and goals of schools and the content typically taught are so much a part of our culture that much of what we do as educators is taken for granted. Elliot Eisner, a noted expert on curriculum and schools, suggests that as a result, the assumptions on which they are based are rarely examined. Many of the assumptions on which our schools are based are faulty, he further asserts, and he lists and discusses 12 of these assumptions in this article. As you read this article ask yourself, "How valid are these assumptions and Eisner's response to them?"

Think About This . . .

1. As opposed to getting all the students to the same place at the same time, what does Eisner suggest the aim of schooling should be? In the real world, how do you believe this might be accomplished?

2. According to Eisner, what is assumed to be the primary indicator of an effective school? Do you agree or disagree with his argument? Why or why not?

3. According to Eisner, why is it faulty to tacitly assume that students learn what their teachers intend for them to learn? What do you believe teachers can do to accommodate differences in students' background knowledge?

4. Describe at least two ways in which Eisner's position on the assumptions will influence your teaching. Offer two specific examples to illustrate your description.

The aims, content, and organization of schools are so embedded in our culture that the assumptions on which they rest are seldom examined. Schools are a part of the furniture of our communities, historically rooted institutions that we take as much for granted as the streets upon which we walk, the stores from which we purchase goods, and the houses in which we grow up and raise our families. Yet the fundamental features of schooling—its dominant practices, its mode of organization, its reward system, its aims, its *culture*—have an extraordinary impact on how the young come to think about knowledge, how they regard success, what they consider intelligent, and how they see their place in the world. In short, the institution we know as "school" teaches by its very nature.

And the nature of schools is rooted in the historical traditions, values, and assumptions into which we have been socialized. Although we act on these values and assumptions, we seldom examine them, even as we try to influence schools.

Schools have a special difficulty in changing their nature. Part of this difficulty stems from the fact that all of us have served an apprenticeship in them—and from an early age. Indeed, teaching is the only profession I know in which professional socialization begins at age 5 or 6. Students, even those of so tender an age, learn early what it takes to "do school."[1] They learn early what a teacher does in a classroom. They learn early how they must behave in order to get on. In fact, aside from their sleeping hours, most children spend more time in the presence of their teachers than they spend

From Eisner, E. (2003). Questionable assumptions about schooling. Phi Delta Kappan, 84(9), 648–657. *Reprinted with permission of the author.*

in the presence of their parents. In short, students and parents, like the rest of us, know what to expect of schools. Those expectations, rooted as they are in our past, also shape our present.

Given the impact that schools have on the young, it seems useful to examine some of the assumptions, indeed some of the questionable assumptions, that give direction to our schools. I want to look at 12 questionable assumptions about the aims, content, and structure of schooling. I hope to problematize what seems to be taken for granted, especially by those who shape education policy.

1. *The aim of schooling is to get all students to the same place at about the same time.* Schools are sometimes likened to railroads. Students are to get aboard as 5- or 6-year-olds and, when teaching and learning go well, to arrive at a relatively common destination by the time they're 18. The basic assumption is that the goals of schools should be common; the differentiation of destinations is problematic since it is believed that to differentiate aims is to condemn the less able to positions in society that are neither as lucrative nor as personally rewarding as those destinations available to the more able. Thus a common set of goals is, some believe, a mark of educational equity.

As we all know, the destinations that so well suit the children of the educationally savvy often have the very effects that those who worry about the differentiation of goals want to avoid. Those talented in ways the school does not reward—or even recognize—continue to fall short when they compete in a race that they must struggle to win. Rather than conceive of educational progress as a race whose garlands go to the swiftest, running on a track for which their life experiences have advantaged them, we would do well to recognize both the array of talents that all youngsters possess and our need to honor and foster competence in a considerably wider range of abilities than we now acknowledge.

Given this perspective, the good school, in my view, does not expect all students to arrive at the same destination at the same time. Indeed, it provides conditions in which variability among students can be increased. What we ought to be doing in schools is increasing the variance in student performance while escalating the mean. In an ideal approach to curriculum and instruction—an approach in which every aspect of teaching is ideally suited to each student, and each aspect of curriculum is appropriate for the abilities students possess—variability among students will increase, not decrease.

The virtue of such an outcome for society is that it promotes self-actualization by enabling students to play to their strengths and so to give to one another and to society precisely those gifts that others cannot give. What we have in the model of education that I am talking about is a model of complementarity, a synergistic model, a model that pursues the development of what is productive, yet idiosyncratic.

2. *A teacher should work with 30 youngsters for an academic year, and then students should move on to another teacher.* The way we have organized schools in the United States, with few exceptions, is to have youngsters at the elementary level work with a particular teacher for nine or 10 months and then move on. What is especially ironic about this arrangement is that, at about the time the teacher gets to know the child, the child leaves the teacher and heads elsewhere. What is doubly ironic is that the test data that are usually secured from tests given near the end of the academic year are unavailable to the teacher in whose class the students were tested, since by the time the teacher receives the scores, the students have moved to another teacher.

It is not unusual for teachers to resist working with the same group of students for a two- or three-year period. Elementary school teachers, like professors, develop a repertoire of skills and acquire a body of content knowledge that they bank upon using in their teaching. Their closets are filled with materials that are quite familiar to them, and the prospect of assuming responsibility for students at a grade level higher or lower than the one they know requires them to become competent in new material. For many teachers this is daunting. In describing this state of affairs, I am not defending it, only explaining that since efficiency and effort are issues for teachers, as they are for all of us, it is understandable that some teachers balk at the prospect of staying with the same class for more than a year.

Not all schools organize themselves along these lines or build their programs on the assumption of a nine-month contact. Many Waldorf schools, for example, have students remain with the same teacher for six to eight years. They also operate in many locales without a principal. Both can be done. What would our schools look like if we problematized the assumption of annual mobility? What would it mean for students? What would it mean for teachers?

3. *The best form of school organization is age-grading.* In many ways, this assumption is related to the previous two. The graded school system was invented in America in Quincy, Massachusetts, in 1847.[2] The idea is very simple. Children of the same age should be grouped together, and that grouping should be enumerated by grade level. Thus 6-year-olds should be in the first grade,

QUESTIONABLE ASSUMPTIONS ABOUT SCHOOLING **279**

7-year-olds in the second grade, 8-year-olds in the third grade, and so on.

The age-graded school system is an administrative and organizational convenience, but it has very little to do with what we know about child development. For example, consider the range of reading ability in an average elementary school classroom. It turns out that the range of reading ability approximates the grade level.[3] This means that in the second grade, when children are approximately 7 years old, the range of reading ability is about two years. In the third grade, the range is about three years; in the fourth grade, about four years. Thus in a typical fourth grade, some students will be reading at the sixth-grade level, and some will be reading at the second-grade level. By the time students reach the sixth grade, some will be reading at the third-grade level, and some will be reading at the ninth-grade level.

As children mature, their personalities become increasingly distinctive. Their aptitudes develop, their proclivities emerge, they develop distinctive interests, traits, and ways of working. The idea that all children who are 10 are or should be at the same level is a bogus expectation. In fact, a teacher who taught only a body of content defined by a single grade level would be providing a level of teaching inappropriate for most of the class.

4. *The real outcomes of schooling can be measured by tests employed within the school.* In the United States, we have developed a sophisticated technology of testing. This technology was given a major push during the *First World War* when tests were first used to select men suitable as candidates for officers' training. American schools give more tests to students each year than schools in any other country in the world. The testing industry in the U.S. is large and highly profitable. One argument for using tests is that teacher judgment cannot be trusted, while tests, which are standardized and therefore yield comparable data, have a degree of precision that teachers cannot match. Moreover, tests are statistically reliable instruments, and equivalent forms yield scores that are highly correlated. Thus tests possess a scientific aura and are used extensively as the primary data source for making judgments about the quality of education students are receiving.

One important educational purpose of testing is to provide information that has some relationship to tasks that go beyond the particular items to which students are asked to respond. However, getting a high score on a test that has little predictive or concurrent validity is no educational virtue. Yet this is precisely the problem that pervades testing practice. What test scores predict best are other test scores. Their status as proxies for other forms of performance is dubious.

In any case, the function of schools is surely not primarily to enable students to do well on tests—or even to do well in school itself. What one wants, it seems to me, is to provide a curriculum and a school environment that enable students to develop the dispositions, the appetites, the skills, and the ideas that will allow them to live personally satisfying and socially productive lives. In other words, the really important dependent variables in education are not test scores or even skills performed in the context of schools; they are the tasks students are able to complete successfully in the lives they lead outside of schools. There is a huge difference between knowing how to read and having an interest in doing so. And interest shows up in out-of-school contexts.

I must confess that this conception of what matters educationally has not yet been used to define ways in which out-of-school data could be secured and interpreted. The challenge is enormous, and confounding information is treacherous. The longer one is out of school, the more difficult it is to explain what one is able to do as a function of school. Yet it is precisely such lasting outcomes that we ought to be most interested in producing.[4]

Despite these practical and empirical difficulties, we ought not to forget that what we are after is far more than high scores on standardized tests. We need to remind ourselves that the function of schools is broader and deeper and that what really counts is what people do with their lives when they can choose to do what they want to do. In fact, I would argue that the major aim of schooling is to enable students to become the architects of their own education so that they can invent themselves during the course of their lives.

5. *Knowledge consists of true assertions about empirical states of affairs. Therefore, what students cannot say, they do not know.* This belief is rooted in classical Greek epistemology and silently permeates modern schools and, even more broadly, modern culture. *Logos* was the term the Greeks used not only for words, but also for knowledge—more specifically, for reason. Reason, the Greeks believed, required the use of language, since it depended upon logic, and logic deals with relationships between the meanings of words that are used to form propositions. Indeed, to have scientific knowledge one must provide warrants for one's assertions. What is not assertable is not testable. And what is not testable cannot be warranted.

In schools, we place a premium on the use of words and on the use of number. Literacy and numeracy, as they are referred to, are regarded as not only the primary processes we wish to promote, but also the most sophisticated manifestations of human intelligence. As a result, this view—often unarticulated, but expressed in the choices we make about what to teach and about how much time to devote to doing so—has substantial implications for the breadth of our curriculum and for the equity of our treatment of students whose aptitudes are irrelevant to the school's priorities.

During the past century such philosophers as John Dewey, Nelson Goodman, Susanne Langer, Richard Rorty, and Michael Polanyi have explored in-depth the nonlinguistic—indeed the ineffable—characteristics of particular modes of knowing. The limits of our cognitive life are not defined by the limits of our language. As Polanyi points out, "We know more than we can tell."[5]

To take such an acknowledgment into serious consideration we would need to provide opportunities for students to work in areas in which reasoning is employed, but such reasoning would have to pertain to forms of problem solving that depend not on the uses of logic but on the organization of qualities, including, but not limited to, linguistic qualities. This kind of work is best exemplified by artists who make sophisticated judgments about the ways qualities are composed. Such qualities emerge in the visual arts in the context of visual imagery, in music in the context of sound, in movement in the context of dance, in poetry and fiction in the context of language chosen for its expressive and evocative potential. I speak also of those who work in the universe of practical activity, where the application of algorithm, rule, and even logic is often irrelevant or inappropriate to the successful execution of a task.

Clearly, considerable thought must be devoted to the place of such matters in our curriculum, the amount of time to be devoted to them, the manner in which they are to be employed in classrooms, and the like. But as long as the nonlinguistic expression of human intelligence is marginalized in school programs, our programs will fail to develop the rich varieties of human potential that our students possess. We will also continue to emphasize curricular content and aims that create educational inequities for students whose areas of greatest potential are either marginalized or absent from school programs.

6. *Teaching at its best is the application of scientific knowledge to practical states of affairs emerging in the classroom.* One of the dominant assumptions in universities is that the scientific work that researchers do will yield the theories and generalizations that will provide the procedures that can then be disseminated to those who function in particular contexts. For example, research in agronomy is designed to produce knowledge that will enable farmers to increase yield per acre. The dissemination process is from the university researcher, to the field extension officer, to the farmer, and ultimately to the society. It is a top-down, scientifically based approach to improvement. The same model has dominated our assumptions about the dissemination of research in the field of education.

What is discounted, however, are the limitations of generalizations and theories when practitioners need to apply them to the particular situations in which they work. First, most theories and generalizations in the social sciences are inadequate for addressing the problems within their own discipline, let alone the particular circumstances in which individual teachers and students work. As Joseph Schwab has pointed out, theory addresses ideal states of affairs.[6] Teachers, however, deal with what is particular or idiosyncratic. Second, theories used to understand phenomena reveal only one side of the issue, the side theory addresses. All problems in education are multifaceted, and no single theory can encompass the variety of factors that must be considered. Third, while the aim of the researcher is to know, the aim of the practitioner is to act and to make good decisions in the process. Practitioners are not primarily concerned with the production of scientific knowledge; they are concerned with the conduct of efficient, effective, and, at its best, satisfying and morally right action.

What the dominant assumption about the connection between research and practice neglects is the kind of practical knowledge that Aristotle alluded to when he contrasted productive and theoretical knowledge. Practical knowledge aimed at the achievement of moral ends is what the Greeks referred to as *phronesis*.[7] Practical knowledge is concerned with moral decision making. But even more than Aristotle's characterization of practical knowledge, teachers are not only engaged in practical activity, they are also engaged in artistic activity. They are engaged in the act of creating something—an explanation, a relationship between themselves and their students, an activity that will effectively introduce students to an issue, problem, or dilemma. In short, teachers are makers of things, and to the extent that things well made constitute an art, a theory of teaching predicated on the assumption that teachers simply or mainly implement what researchers discover is naive and ill-founded.

The conception of teaching that I have discussed implies that we need to address the conditions through which artistry in teaching and in other forms of practical action can be promoted, improved, and developed. It also implies that there should be a much greater parity between those who work in the university and those who teach in our schools. Practitioners have a kind of knowledge that might be referred to as "insider knowledge," a kind of knowledge that can be secured only in the context of practice itself.[8] This is a context to which teachers have access, and it is one that can inform the views of theoreticians. And even beyond this characterization of the conditions of improved teaching, we need to recognize that teachers can also inform one another if they have opportunities in the course of their day to discuss with their peers common problems and individual achievements. We need to think about the ways in which such arrangements can be created, for in the end such arrangements will have much to do with the improvement of teaching.

7. *The best way to organize the curriculum is to identify its constituent disciplines and then to create a series of small steps within each so that the discipline can be learned.* A disciplinary orientation to curriculum is especially attractive to professors and other academics who themselves work within a disciplinary structure. The tacit view is that a solid education prepares students to think like those in the academic disciplines. This view of curriculum was salient in the United States in the 1960s.[9] It was the view that Jerome Bruner advanced at a time when America was concerned with its position in the race for space. People who were anxious about the quality of education and who believed that curricula had softened under the onslaught of progressive education saw in a return to the disciplines a return to intellectual rigor.[10]

What we learned was that, although a disciplinary orientation to curriculum was conceptually appealing, it also tended to lack relevance for many students.[11] Each discipline addressed problems that often had little bearing on the students' lives. Academic hurdles were set up that resulted in a reduction of high school enrollments in physics, chemistry, and other fields believed to be intellectually rigorous. Thus the push toward a curriculum that was discipline-oriented had just the opposite effect from the one we wanted to achieve.

The kinds of problems that the average citizen addresses are, as I suggested above, transdisciplinary or multidisciplinary. They are seldom adequately addressed through a single discipline. In fact, they often require modes of thought that are not defined within a specific discipline. Trying to understand the social conditions of young people requires much more than the application of economic theory or sociology or history; it requires something that might be called firsthand contact with the

young themselves. Furthermore, designing an educational program that is almost exclusively mediated through disciplinary language denies youngsters the opportunity to think with and within forms of representation that are nonlinguistic.

The development of mind is related to the modes of thought that schools enable and encourage students to use. The curriculum that is provided in schools is essentially a mind-altering device, and our choices about what students will attend to and the forms in which that material is presented and responded to are of critical importance. In *Cognition and Curriculum Reconsidered,* I describe these issues and offer examples of the ways in which the sensibilities can come into play in learning in the classroom.[12] I argue that the use of a wide variety of sensibilities provides students with opportunities to secure forms of experience, including forms of understanding that otherwise would be absent. In short, I urge readers to think outside of the box about how we select content and organize curricula for school programs. The assumption that the disciplines ought to define what and how we teach is limiting. We need to explore alternatives.

8. *School reform is most effective when competition among schools is promoted and when supervisors can mandate goals, manage teachers, monitor students, and measure outcomes.* Public anxiety over the quality of schools typically leads to pressures that, in turn, lead to higher levels of prescription for schools. These include the articulation of standards and milestones to be met and the use of an assessment program to measure student performance. In the U.S., test data on student performance are arrayed for schools within school districts and from state to state. Test scores are then produced and published in local newspapers in what are the equivalent of league tables that identify the position or rank of each school or district. School reform is being driven by a competitive model in which student scores constitute the data to be rank-ordered. That competition should be seen as motivating is, of course, entirely consistent with the values of a capitalist economy. The tacit belief is that, if competition is good for business, it's good for schools because schools, when you get down to it, are businesses, and the business of schools is producing measurable student performance.

This argument seems impeccable, but it has a number of troubling consequences. First, knowing someone's position in a distribution tells you *nothing* about what needs to be done to improve it. As a woman once told me after I gave a lecture on educational evaluation to a group of teachers in Nebraska, everyone in that cattle-raising state knew that you can't fatten cattle by putting them on a scale. Of course, she was correct. You can't fatten cattle by putting them on a scale; you need to pay attention to their diet. Locating your position in a distribution tells you nothing about how to change the diet and what to substitute.

Second, the belief that education reform is likely to endure if a top-down approach to school improvement is employed is another dubious assumption. Top-down approaches often begin and end with changed education policies, while schools continue on their merry way, largely oblivious to policy changes. Or when schools are not wholly oblivious to policy changes, they engage in forms of adaptation that give the illusion of change but do not constitute its reality. Indeed, unless teachers and school administrators buy into reform efforts, unless they are a part of the group that participates in designing the reforms, little is likely to happen. After all, the only place where education reform makes an educational difference is where the rubber meets the road: in classrooms. And in classrooms, teachers are kings and queens. Thus the idea that policy can be prescribed from on high, issued ex cathedra, is a comforting one for policy makers, but it is a problematic one as far as school improvement is concerned.

9. *Artistry in teaching, when it occurs, is basically the result of the absence of scientifically grounded knowledge of teaching practices.* This questionable assumption is, again, rooted in the belief that science is the only dependable source of knowledge and that artistry is neither a realistic aspiration nor a dependable resource for the conduct of practice. I would argue that any practice at its best is an artistically crafted affair. In the practice of surgery, when decisions about a course of action must be made, artistry is present, since scientific knowledge is never entirely adequate for the treatment of a particular patient with any particular disease. Indeed, one of the important criticisms of modern-day medicine is that individuals are reduced to generalized cases—he's a tonsillectomy, she's an appendectomy, he's a fractured femur, and the like. Somehow, the individuality and personal particulars of the patient get lost. The loss of individuality is not simply a psychological liability; it has consequences for the success of medical practice, since to miss the distinctive features of the individual case is to hamper diagnosis and treatment.

Artistry in teaching represents high levels of pedagogical performance. Artistry depends on sensibility, it uses imagination, it employs technique, it takes pride in its craft. Teachers as artists are sensitive to the tempo of the classroom, to matters of timing, and to the qual-

ity of their own performance and the ways in which it can be shaped to be appropriate for the occasion. Such considerations are in no way prescribable from scientific research.[13]

I wish to make it clear that, as I speak about the limits of scientific theory in education, I have no intention of dismissing research by consigning it to the junk heap. Science gives us one very useful approach to the comprehension of action and its improvement, but it is only one approach. The arts and artistic forms of thinking have generally been neglected as ways of knowing and as qualities of performing. My aim here is not to dismiss science, but to call attention to additional ways of thinking about thinking in the context of practice.

10. *The best way to identify schools that work well is to examine their students' test scores.* As I indicated above, there is probably no nation that makes greater use of tests than does the United States. Tests are contrived tasks that are intended to sample behavior that will make it possible to determine what a student knows and can do. Test scores are believed to be proxies for the quality of education that students have received and for what it is that they have learned. Yet what test scores predict best are other test scores. Ironically, we encounter tests in just a few places outside of the context of schools. Thus we have designed a system that employs culturally rare events to make significant judgments about the quality of education students receive.

This system has several important consequences for schools. First, the curriculum typically gets narrowed so that it reflects a relatively narrow array of what tests are capable of measuring. Second, the tests themselves have very little predictive validity on most of the tasks and forms of action that students engage in outside the context of schools. Third, the use of tests leads students to focus their attention on grades or scores and thereby diverts attention away from engagement in the task itself. Extrinsic rewards gradually displace intrinsic satisfaction.

The quality of education students receive is determined by much more complex and subtle forms of attention. To know about the quality of education students receive, one must be in a position to appraise the significance of the ideas, skills, and attitudes that a school is developing. This typically requires attention to the culture of schooling and not only to the behavior of students. One needs to know something about the kinds of questions that are being raised by both students and teachers; about the sorts of opportunities students have to formulate their own purposes and to design ways of achieving them; about the degree to which multiple forms of representation are promoted, not only through the literal use of language and correct computation, but also through such poetic means as the visual arts, music, and dance. The forms of consciousness and understanding of which humans are capable are not exhausted by what is measurable or by what can be articulated in the literal use of language.[14]

To call for this wider agenda for education and to identify its features as criteria for appraising the quality of educational practice is not to reject the need to promote literacy and numeracy in their conventional forms. It is a plea to recognize a wider educational mission and to use a vision of that mission as a basis for judging and improving schools. Raising test scores on narrow measures of educational achievement is no significant educational victory.

11. *The primary content that students learn in school is what their teachers intend to teach them.* John Dewey once remarked that the greatest fallacy in education is the assumption that students learn only what they are being taught at the time.[15] In fact, what students learn is both more and less than what teachers intend to teach. They learn less because students seldom achieve the lofty aims that teachers hold for them; our ambitions, educationally speaking, virtually always exceed our capacity. Indeed, if all students achieved what we hoped they would, we would probably regard our aims as being too low.

At the same time, students learn more than we intend to teach. They learn more because what they learn is not simply a function of what teachers intend to teach, but of what students themselves bring to the table. The concept of interaction is key here. The meanings that are made by students are a function of their intentions and the conceptual material they bring to the situation that teachers create. And since for each student that background is in some degree different, meanings always differ. These meanings are related to the interaction between the individual and the situation that is created. Teachers may think they are teaching one thing, but what students learn may be quite another. A teacher might intend to help students understand quadratic equations, while the student may intend to get a passing grade in the course or to use the math class to do homework for a history class.

These observations imply that schools need to create situations that engender aims for the student that are congruent with those of the teacher. To say that they ought to be congruent is not to say that they must overlap completely. Indeed, they cannot. Yet, when the student's aims are educationally marginal—or worse, miseducational—teaching cannot have educational value. Students learn quickly to make the kind of moves that enable them to get by without being touched by the material they study.

12. *Some subjects are primarily affective while others are primarily cognitive.* It is unfortunate that our general conception of cognition is that it requires linguistic forms of mediation. As I indicated above, we associate knowing with linguistically mediated thought. But cognition as a term is not limited to what can be linguistically mediated.[16] Cognition refers to the process of becoming aware.[17] Cognition depends on human sensibility, and the more differentiated the sensibilities, the greater the degree of awareness. Indeed, it is the content of such sensibility that serves as the material to which language refers. The best way to ensure that students will engage in meaningless verbal learning is to make sure they have no experience of that to which their language refers.

Concept formation, therefore, is embodied in experience with qualities, and qualities are pervaded by human affect. Thus the mathematician and the logician, two individuals whose work seems to be unrelated to qualitative matters, are in fact dealing with relationships that, at their best, are themselves qualitative and from which feeling is evoked. When it comes to the arts, we have a paradigmatic case of affect-laden qualities being composed to serve human experience. Education in the arts is the education of feelingful thought at its most acute level.[18]

But even those arenas of activity that seemingly are without affect are, in fact, freighted with affect. To be kissed without feeling is to know that one has been kissed without feeling because of the feeling that unfeeling kisses reveal. Experience always has an affective aspect, and the so-called absence of affect is itself an affect. To think in terms of qualities, said John Dewey, is to think about relationships that are often more subtle, more delicate, and more complex than much of the thinking that goes on among those who pride themselves on being intellectuals.[19] The development of intelligence in all areas of human action is never complete without attention to the affective part of the materials with which we compose, regardless of the domain in which we function. The practice of a science at its best is an art that depends upon the affective experience of the scientist in the context of doing his or her research. The absence of attention to such matters in our own teaching is a form of fundamental neglect, for it robs our students of the opportunity to secure the satisfactions of genuine work.

Dimensions of School Reform

What are we to make of this formidable list of questionable assumptions upon which our schools operate? Is it to be merely a taxonomy of erroneous beliefs, or is there some way to think about these assumptions in relation to dimensions of school reform? I believe there is a way to connect this analysis to school reform. Consider the following five dimensions.

First, I believe it would be well for us to think about school reform in relation to the aims of our schools. What really matters? Do we harbor contradictory aspirations? What are our priorities? Why do we have them? Such questions provide a beginning for deep examination.

Second, we can examine our assumptions about the conduct of schools in relation to the structure of schooling. By structure I mean the ways in which time and space are parsed, how roles are defined within the school, how, for example, we organize classes and what it does to the way we treat time. Such questions can be grouped under structural features that need attention.

A third dimension under which questionable assumptions can be examined pertains to the curriculum itself. We make assumptions about the centrality of the disciplines, about the autonomy of subjects, and about the emphasis on language as the virtually exclusive carrier of meaning. These assumptions may interfere with more creative views of how curricula can be selected and organized and, most important, how they are encountered by students.

A fourth dimension pertains to pedagogy. We appear to work with the assumptions that teachers should work alone, that 30 or more children should be assigned to a teacher, and that students should remain with a teacher for a year and then move on to another teacher. Assumptions about pedagogy need to be examined critically, for it is their practical translation in the classroom that determines significantly what students will or will not have an opportunity to learn. At the same time, though, the context in which the teacher functions—both in the classroom and as a part of the school organization—also influences pedagogical practice. We need to think about the environment as a whole.

Fifth, we need to examine our assumptions about evaluation practices. All too often we tend to equate evaluation with testing. But tests are only a mechanism, a procedure, a way through which information about how students are doing can be secured. But it is not necessary either to test or to measure in order to evaluate. Evaluation is a process of making value judgments about phenomena, and most of the value judgments that we make in the course of ordinary life have nothing at all to do with tests and very little to do with measurement. They are judgments made about the quality of this or that, and we make such judgments in order to make decisions that affect our lives. Assumptions about evaluation need to be examined because evaluation practices influence the priorities of schools and affect the kinds of incentives that both teachers and students come to believe are important in "doing school."

Thus we have a scheme in which aims, structure, curriculum, pedagogy, and evaluation become five major dimensions for thinking about school reform. The dozen questionable assumptions that I have addressed here are all candidates for attention within one or more of these dimensions.

Given the questionable assumptions I have identified and the conceptual structure I have described, how shall we think about the practice of reform? There are two salient models of reform, one systemic and the other incremental. Systemic approaches to reform emphasize the need to pay attention to virtually everything, since everything affects everything else. Incremental approaches recognize that we can't pay attention to everything and that, even if we could, it is unlikely that everything could be addressed at the same time. To the extent that factors that one cannot change influence what is to be changed, the problem of reform is enormous.

Schools have demonstrated themselves to be robust institutions, something like giant gyroscopes that, when pushed to the side, accommodate the push and then come back to their upright position. Although "tinkering toward utopia," as my colleagues have put it, may not be ideal, it may be the most realistic approach.[20] What can we actually do? I believe it is possible to think big but start small. I believe that a comprehensive plan can be drafted and that undertaking incremental efforts toward the realization of such a plan is the most realistic option.

With a plan that addresses the problematic assumptions that I have described and with procedures developed for dealing with them, progress toward creating schools that genuinely educate is a real possibility. In so many efforts at school reform, superficial factors are addressed. As a result, the "reforms" are short-lived and lead to no real reform at all. This is not the picture I have tried to paint. I am trying to penetrate the surface and identify our deep-seated assumptions. By problematizing questionable assumptions, we may put ourselves in a position to create a better vision of what schools might become.

Notes

1. Denise Clark Pope, *Doing School: How We Are Creating a Generation of Stressed Out, Materialistic, and Miseducated Students* (New Haven, Conn.: Yale University Press, 1999).

2. David Tyack, *The One Best System* (Cambridge, Mass.: Harvard University Press, 1974).

3. John I. Goodlad and Robert H. Anderson, *The Nongraded Elementary School* (New York: Teachers College Press, 1987).

4. Tom Barone, *Touching Eternity: The Enduring Outcomes of Schooling* (New York: Teachers College Press, 2001).

5. Michael Polanyi, *The Tacit Dimension* (Garden City, N.Y.: Doubleday, 1966).

6. Joseph J. Schwab, "The Practical: A Language for Curriculum," in Ian Westbury and Neil Wilkof, eds., *Joseph J. Schwab: Science, Curriculum, and Liberal Education* (Chicago: University of Chicago Press, 1978).

7. Elliot Eisner, *The Arts and the Creation of Mind* (New Haven, Conn.: Yale University Press, 2002).

8. Myron Atkin, "Teaching as Research: An Essay," *Teaching and Teacher Education*, vol. 8, 1992, pp. 381–90.

9. Jerome Bruner, *The Process of Education* (Cambridge, Mass.: Harvard University Press, 1960).

10. Diane Ravitch, *Left Back: A Century of Failed School Reform* (New York: Simon and Schuster, 2000).

11. Bruner, op. cit.

12. Elliot Eisner, *Cognition and Curriculum Reconsidered,* 2nd ed. (New York: Teachers College Press. 1994).

13. Elliot Eisner, "From Episteme, to Phronesis, to Artistry in the Practice of Teaching," *Teaching and Teacher Education*, vol. 18, 2002, pp. 375–85; and idem, "What Education Can Learn from the Arts About the Practice of Education," *Journal of Curriculum and Supervision*, Fall 2002, pp. 4–16.

14. Eisner, *Cognition and Curriculum Reconsidered.*

15. John Dewey, *Experience and Education* (New York: Macmillan, 1938).

16. Susanne Langer, *Mind: An Essay on Human Feeling* (Baltimore: Johns Hopkins University Press, 1967).

17. Rudolf Arnheim, *Visual Thinking* (Berkeley: University of California Press, 1969).

18. Eisner, "From Episteme, to Phronesis."

19. John Dewey, *Art as Experience* (New York: Minton, Balch, 1934).

20. David Tyack and Larry Cuban. *Tinkering Toward Utopia* (Cambridge, Mass.: Harvard University Press, 1995).

DICHOTOMIZING EDUCATION: WHY NO ONE WINS AND AMERICA LOSES

Carl D. Glickman

Which is superior—standards and high-stakes testing or no described standards and no high-stakes testing, direct instruction or instruction based on constructivist views of learning, phonics or whole language? These either/or debates are symptomatic of ideologies that attempt to crush each other, leaving only one dominant, Carl Glickman asserts. Those who take one position believe they possess the truth, and those who oppose them are demonized as ignorant and extremist, he further argues.

These debates are unproductive and ultimately destructive, the author further notes, emphasizing that no one best approach to education exists, just as no one best way to teach exists. "Any single truth or concept of an educated American will be fraught with contradictions," he concludes. As you read this article ask yourself, "If no one best way to educate exists, what will guide teachers' decision making about what approaches to use in their instruction?"

Think About This . . .

1. What are three ideological "single truth" wars that Glickman identifies in the article? Which position do you favor in each case? Explain why you feel that way.

2. How does Glickman feel about a single governmental (local, state, or national) conception of education? Why do you suppose he feels that way?

3. What does Glickman suggest that educators in our country do in response to disagreements about what constitutes a high-quality education? What is the probability that his suggestions will be put into practice as educational reform continues to unfold?

4. What will you do in your classroom to accommodate different views regarding the ways learners should be educated? Offer a specific example to illustrate your description.

I did not lightly take pen in hand (yes, I still use a pen) in writing this article. I have devoted my entire professional life to working with colleagues to create, establish, and sustain public schools that are driven by collaboration, personalization, and active and participatory student learning.[1] And I will continue to do so, as I personally believe such is the best way to prepare all students for the intellectual, social, and aesthetic life of a democracy.

Yet, even in the fervor of my beliefs, I still see other concepts of education that generate degrees of uncertainty in me. My memories of my own best teachers are revealing. Most taught in highly interactive ways, but one grand elder taught from behind a podium in a huge auditorium and engaged in little interaction with students. He was perhaps my greatest teacher. Such discrepancies don't change the strength of my own beliefs; they simply remind me that the viable possibilities of educating students well are broad indeed.

Ultimately, an American education must stand on a foundation that is wider than the beliefs of any one individual or any one group. It should encourage, respect, and support any conceptions—no matter how diametrically opposed to one's own—that are willing to be tested openly and freely. Furthermore, it should involve the willing and nondiscriminatory participation of *all* students, parents, and educators. That is what should be at the core of an American education. But with the "winner take all" wars being fought today, I am seriously concerned about the future of our students and of our public schools and about the vitality of a better democracy.

Ideological Absolutes

The either/or debates about standards versus no standards, intrinsic versus extrinsic motivation, core versus multicultural knowledge, direct instruction versus constructivist learning, and phonics versus whole language are symptomatic of ideologies that attempt to crush one another and leave only one solution standing. Whether the ideology is education anchored in traditional, behaviorist authority or progressive, inquiry-based learning,

the stance toward the final outcome is the same. One group possesses the truth, and the other side is demonized as a pack of extremists: scary, evil persons. Articles and books present educators and the public with a forced choice that unfortunately disregards reality and endangers the very concept of an American education.[2]

Let me illustrate the incompleteness of ideological absolutes with one of today's most emotional issues, the relationship of race to socioeconomic achievement. One side of this debate argues that America is the land of opportunity, where freedom rings, where anyone—regardless of race, religion, gender, or class—can work hard and rise to a position of authority, success, and accomplishment. The other side argues that America is a hegemonic system, protecting the ruling class and extant privilege while keeping the poor, the dispossessed, and people of color stifled, oppressed, and marginalized. Well, which side of this debate is correct? The answer to that question has important implications for what our society needs to change in terms of practices, programs, and the targeting of resources. But the truth is that both contradictory realities have compelling evidence and must be used together to figure out what needs to be done next.

Consider the economic component of this debate. Seymour Martin Lipset compares the United States with other Western industrialized nations.[3] Since the post-Civil War era, America has been the wealthiest country, with a steady rise in living standards and unparalleled social and economic advances for the poor and working class. Yet the income of the poorest fifth of this nation continues to *decline* relative to that of other Americans.

The African American scholar Henry Louis Gates, Jr., takes on this same dichotomy in reference to race. He observes that, since 1967, the number of middle-class African American families has quadrupled. Since 1973 the top 100 African American businesses have moved from sales of $473 million to $11.7 billion. In 1970 "only one in ten blacks had attended college; today one

From Glickman, C. (2001). *Dichotomizing education: Why no one wins and America loses.* Phi Delta Kappan, 83(2), 147–152. *Reprinted with permission of* Phi Delta Kappan.

in three has." He then goes on to discuss the continuous wrenching poverty of a third of African Americans today and concludes: "We need something we don't have: a way of speaking about black poverty that doesn't falsify the reality of black advancement, a way of speaking about black advancement that doesn't distort the enduring realities of black poverty. I'd venture that a lot depends on whether we get it."[4]

In truth, America has been one of the leading countries of opportunity for disenfranchised persons and, at the same time, a country of the greatest economic stratification between the luxury of the wealthiest and the wretched conditions of the poorest.[5] In essence, the beliefs of Ayn Rand and Pete Seeger are both correct. To speak only of one side and ignore the other is to create disbelief in most ordinary citizens, who know firsthand of counterexamples to any single view. And this is what I believe to be the danger of ideological truth in education. Many educators in classrooms and schools feel that they have become pawns in the reformers' and policy makers' propaganda game that insists there is a single best way to change the system of American schools.

Ideology in Education

The attacks by E. D. Hirsch, Jr., against progressive education and the equally strident attacks by others such as Alfie Kohn against traditional education are wonderful examples of this either/or ideological stance. Hirsch argues that a common core of knowledge is essential for all students, if they are to succeed in mainstream society. Without a common framework of spoken and written English, historical and cultural references, and direct instruction, marginalized and poor children are deprived of the education that wealthier children pick up automatically from their parents and peers. Thus there is the need to rid our schools of the overwhelming "permissive" practices of activity-based education and to use tests of common knowledge to ensure that all children are acquiring the "cultural capital" needed for success in later life. Kohn in turn speaks against standards, core knowledge, and tests and says that children, regardless of their circumstances, are innately curious and that teachers should explore the topics that intrigue them to open up new freedoms and possibilities. Each proponent has his version of "truth." Each sees little validity in any research supporting the methods that oppose his ideology. Again, the reality is that education is composed of many complexities that defeat any singular truth of how the world can and should work.

For example, might it be that both Hirsch and Kohn have valid perspectives? Focusing on core knowledge that students themselves might not choose but that gives them access to a society in which they might possibly change the current balance of power, wealth, and control seems quite reasonable. Using the curiosity of students to learn multiple histories and cultures and to explore a variety of intelligences in an intensely involving way also seems quite reasonable. It is important that schools be joyful and engaging places. Yet is all learning intrinsically or extrinsically motivated? Most would say it's both—we learn for the joy of it, but some of the most useful learning has taken place because others, not we ourselves, demanded that we do it, do it well, and do it until we got it right.

The polemics surrounding standards versus no standards do not account for complex realities. Are external standards bad or good? Might they be both? Might we have state standards and assessments for most (but not all) public schools in the same state? Some states have standards and assessments that have been well received by educators and the public—not seen as heavy-handed, intrusive, or unfair. Many states have standards and assessments that are volatile in makeup, format, pressure, and consequences.

The standards polarization—again, only one side can win—has come about because people have applied the term "standards" to all systems as if they were identical. However, Maine's standards are quite different from Virginia's. Elements of standards systems can be quite good, such as using disaggregated data to focus on the progress of all students, equalizing funding for poor students and communities, and targeting additional resources. Some states grant variances allowing schools and districts to develop their own assessments. And yes, there are cases in which it is good that standards can be used to close and reorganize schools that have done a disservice to students and parents. Standards systems can be demeaning and harmful—when they equate education with narrowly derived assessments and tests. They can also be tremendously positive in challenging schools and communities to leave no student behind.[6] We need to acknowledge simultaneous realities if we are to educate all students better than before.

Pedagogical Pain

The "single-truth" wars have created much pain among teachers and school leaders who are swept into the battles. When whole language gained currency as "the" way to teach reading, teachers using phonics were lambasted, swept aside, and made to feel that they were evil, archaic, fascist practitioners of an indefensible method. Recently, the opposing force has "won" in states led by California and Texas. They have blamed whole language and invented spelling for declining literacy in America. Now teachers of whole language are made to feel abandoned and rejected as "feel-good," self-esteem-promoting contributors to the demise of basic skills.

These periodic surges and countersurges occur because one set of believers ignores any possible merits of the other side. Isn't it possible that many highly literate and culturally diverse people—people that you and I both know—were taught how to read mainly by decoding, phonics, and grammatical rules? Isn't it equally obvious that many highly literate and culturally diverse people have learned to read through literacy immersion, writing workshops, and experiential learning? Why is it so difficult to accept that an open mind about possibilities in education should be seen as a virtue rather than a liability?

Cooperative versus competitive learning is another such brawl. Cooperation is a key aspect of how one learns with and from others, and it undergirds much of community, civic, and business life. Research exists that demonstrates the power of structured team activities for academic and social development. Yet humans, as part of the animal kingdom, are also moved to learn by traits that have helped them to survive: dominance, power, and the need to test oneself against others. Cooperation and competition are not different versions of humanity; they are different dimensions of the same humanity. And thus there is evidence that both cooperation and competition bring out high performance in individuals.

The overarching debate about progressive, learner-centered schools versus teacher-centered, direct-instruction schools will be my last venture into the foolishness of single truths. This debate simplifies and silences the cultural and family values that Lisa Delpit so eloquently writes about in *Other People's Children*.[7] Asking students to conform to certain manners, expecting them to learn what adults determine is important for them, being didactic in instruction, and using "call and response" methods have resulted in great success for teachers and leaders such as Marva Collins, Jaime Escalante, and Lorraine Monroe and for a number of school programs.[8] Regardless of what one personally believes about the atmosphere of such classrooms and schools, students and parents in these settings see such didactic methods as expressions of teachers' love,

care, and cultural solidarity.[9] The teachers are proud to demand that their students learn, and they go to almost any length to see that their students can compete with other students.

Yet progressive classrooms and schools that are activity- or project-centered and that cultivate imagination, problem solving, responsibility, and a variety of intellectual pursuits have, in the hands of the most dedicated teachers, also attained incredible success for students. Educators such as Eliot Wigginton, Deborah Meier, George Wood, Gloria Ladson-Billings, Sonia Nieto, and Jabari Mahiri have shown the power of inquiry-centered, progressive learning.

My point is *not* that all methods, techniques, curricula, and structures are of equal worth or that the attitude "anything goes" is acceptable. My point is that, when a group of students and parents choose to be with a group of educators dedicated to a particular philosophy and way of learning, the results for students can be awesome. No one group should have the presumption or power to tell another group that only its way is the right way. Instead, in accordance with publicly determined purposes and criteria, we should be seeking, testing, and developing research-based alternative conceptions and practices of successful education. Kenneth Wilson, a Nobel laureate in physics, remarked about the need to test a multitude of educational approaches through longitudinal research and self-correction to find out what works well, what can be adapted, and what should be discarded.[10] The idea is not to prove that one way is the only way but instead to allow for different conceptions of education to flourish in the marketplace of public education.

Religion in America and an Educated American

Of all Western nations, America is the country with the highest percentage of citizens actively involved in religious and spiritual practices.[11] Why? Because it has no official state religion and no divine story behind its creation. Those countries that do have histories of such official state religion—a one way to believe for all—tend to have lower percentages of citizen involvement in religious practice. This example suggests why we must avoid a single governmental (local, state, or national) conception of education. The analogy with religion ends at a certain point, as the U.S. government needs to remain neutral and not use public funds to promote any particular set of religious beliefs. But government must use public funds to support a public education consistent with democratic ideals.[12] And the best way for doing so is to create a system of state schools that promote various publicly determined conceptions of an educated American.

Public education can be defined in several overlapping ways. Public education is funded by taxpayers, it is an education for the public, it is open and without cost to students and parents, it is compulsory, it is governed by public authority, it is nonprofit, and it always *should be* nondiscriminatory and nonrepressive of students and parents.[13] It is public because it serves a common good: the education of students to have choices of "life, liberty, and the pursuit of happiness" and to acknowledge those choices for others.

Within these definitions of public, American education is always an experiment—one hopes a thoughtful one—that must constantly test ways to further realize the hopes and aspirations of all the nation's people. Whenever one truth stamps out all others—whether it be through one system of tests, one approach to curriculum, one conception of knowledge, a single method of instruction, or a uniform structure for all public schools—democracy itself and education for a democracy are subverted.

In first proposing the need for common schools, Horace Mann wrote in the 1840s that public schools would be the great equalizers of human conditions, the balance wheel of the social machinery. Poverty would disappear and with it the discord between the haves and the have-nots; life for all men would be longer, better, and happier. The common school would be free, for poor and rich alike, as good as any private school, and nonsectarian. (The common school was not to be a school for common people but rather a school common to all people.) And the pedagogy of the common or free school would stress the "self-discipline of individuals, self-control, and self-governance." The issue for Mann was that the educated person was to have a free, deliberate choice between obedience and anarchy.[14]

Another view of the educated person in a democracy was shaped by the Lockean sympathies of early American thought. The educated person would be the one who renounced self-indulgence, practiced restraint, and saw the virtue of frugality and labor. In this view, one would work not for what one could accumulate but in order to focus the human mind and body.

Jefferson's concept of the educated person was the farmer—a person who lived apart from others; pursued his own curiosity about science, philosophy, and art after a long day of self-sustaining chores; and then determined those times that he should partici-

pate in neighborhood and community affairs. The farmer's life was a combination of aloneness, individuality, and self-learning with minimal but significant civic responsibility.

W. E. B. Du Bois, referring to the need for African American children to learn, saw public education as giving "our children the fairness of a start which will equip them with such an array of facts and such an attitude toward truth that they can have a real chance to judge what the world is and what its greater minds have thought it might be."[15]

Education might also be defined as making a good neighbor—one who cares for and respects others, who takes care of his or her own family needs, and who contributes to the welfare of others.[16] Such a person would possess a respect for other people and an understanding of life conditions locally, nationally, and internationally; the ability to communicate with diverse others; analytic and problem-solving skills; and the competence to choose what to do with one's own life in economic, social, recreational, and aesthetic pursuits. Does one need three years of high school or college-level preparatory mathematics to develop these attributes? Does one need to learn French? How about Chinese? What level of mastery does one need in the various disciplines? Is it better to study discrete subjects or an integrated curriculum with applications to the world outside of school? The question here is, What knowledge, skills, and understandings are needed to be a good neighbor and citizen?

In a high school curriculum controlled by college admission requirements, there are expected core courses, and good scores on the SAT or ACT have become essential measures of an educated American. Whether going to college or not, most students will not use most of what they are required to learn, whether mathematics or history or language or science. Is it still essential? Again, says who? Dare I ask the unspeakable: Can one be a good neighbor and a wise and productive citizen without going to college?

Is the purpose of public education to train a highly skilled work force to support American corporations? If so, the definition of a well-educated American as a good worker will place a great deal of emphasis on technology. But again, who should determine what is a well-educated person? For example, the Waldorf schools in America have children work with natural materials for the first three to five years of schooling.[17] Children work only with wood, clay, water, and paint, in long, painstaking projects for several years before the manmade world becomes a source of their learning—no televisions, no phones, no computers in early childhood and primary classrooms. The prime emphasis is on imagination and work in an all-natural environment. Are these students educated less well than others? According to what criteria?

To be blunt, any single truth or concept of an educated American will be fraught with contradictions. The real danger of any one reform effort, such as a standards movement that relies on a single test, is the promotion of a single definition of the well-educated citizen as a college graduate who is technologically prepared to lead a successful economic life. The idea that an educated citizen might not want to make vast sums of money or work in a corporation but instead might seek success in quietness, resistance, or even detachment from corporate/college-controlled work, has eroded in America. Even to mention the idea that education is not mostly about jobs or money but about choosing how to live one's life among others is to be seen as a romantic, a throwback to another time.

My point is not to convince others of any one definition of a well-educated person but to share the need for varied conceptions of education, conceptions that must be in conformance with "public" criteria and equally based on data about student accomplishments and successes.

What Do We Do?

As a reformer who advocates the progressive tradition and assists schools in keeping it alive, I do not seek a common ground for public education—an eclectic "all things of equal merit" ground—but instead wish to move beyond that to a higher ground that incorporates complexity and competing conceptions. A higher ground where contradictory truths must be part and parcel of American democracy. We need an education system that supports multiple conceptions of an educated American, that subjects all such conceptions to the scrutiny of research and public accountability, and that fixes all actions of classrooms and schools within the boundaries of equity. American students and schools lose each time one "truth" gains currency and suppresses competing notions of public education.

So let me end by stating that, in my experience with schools, education reformers, policy makers, legislators, corporate persons, community activists, and citizens at large, I have found people of astonishingly good will and passionate intent who labor in the light of controversy about what our schools need or deserve. They are accused by their opponents of being self-indulgent conspirators with sinister motives, but most of them, or at least those that I know, are not. However, many of those who are most influential or powerful are singularly convinced that theirs is the true way to improve education and that all other ways are false, bad, and corrupt.

We need to realize that, most often, life does not contain single truths but instead is about predicaments, competing views, and apparent conflicts. The public school system must value and allow multiple conceptions of education that students, parents, and faculty members can choose from—some purebreds, some hybrids, and some yet to be known, but all devoted to students and their pursuit of the American Dream.

We must fight against any single model, structure, method, or system of education. We must expand the freedom of schools to test new concepts of standards, assessments, and accountability. Ultimately, we must hold every school and district responsible for whether it has provided an education for all children that can be documented to increase choices of "life, liberty, and the pursuit of happiness." *That* is an American education.

Notes

1. Carl D. Glickman, *Revolutionizing America's Schools* (San Francisco: Jossey-Bass, 1998).

2. See E. D. Hirsch, Jr., *The Schools We Need and Why We Don't Have Them* (New York: Doubleday, 1996); Alfie Kohn, *The Schools Our Children Deserve* (Boston: Houghton Mifflin, 1999); Susan Ohanian, *One Size Fits Few: The Folly of Educational Standards* (Portsmouth, N.H.: Heinemann, 1999); and I. de Pommereau, "Tougher High School Standards Signal Greater Demands on Students," *Christian Science Monitor,* 16 June 1996, p. 12, 1-C.

3. Seymour Martin Lipset, *American Exceptionalism: A Double-Edged Sword* (New York: Norton, 1996).

4. Henry Louis Gates, Jr., and Cornel West, *The Future of the Race* (New York: Vintage Books, 1996), pp. 19, 38.

5. Jim Myers, "Notes on the Murder of Thirty of My Neighbors," *Atlantic,* March 2000, pp. 72–88.

6. Chris Gallagher, "A Seat at the Table: Teachers Reclaiming Assessment Through Rethinking Accountability," *Phi Delta Kappan,* March 2000, pp. 502–7.

7. Lisa Delpit, *Other People's Children: Cultural Conflict in the Classroom* (New York: New Press, 1995).

8. See, for example, such schools as P.S. 161 in New York, KIPP Academies in Texas and New York, and the Frederick Douglass Middle School in New York.

9. Samuel Casey Carter, *No Excuses: Seven Principals of Low-Income Schools Who Set the Standards for High Achievement* (Washington, D.C.: Heritage Foundation, 1999); and Jacqueline

Jordan Irvine, "Seeing with the Cultural Eye: Different Perspectives of African American Teachers and Researchers," DeWitt Wallace-Reader's Digest Distinguished Lecture presented at the annual meeting of the American Educational Research Association, New Orleans, April 2000.

10. Kenneth Wilson and Bennett Daviss, *Redesigning Education* (New York: Teachers College Press, 1994).

11. Lipset, op. cit.; and Warren A. Nord, *Religion and American Education: Rethinking a National Dilemma* (Chapel Hill: University of North Carolina Press, 1995).

12. John Dayton and Carl D. Glickman, "Curriculum Change and Implementation: Democratic Imperatives," *Peabody Journal of Education*, vol. 9, no. 4, 1994, pp. 62–86; Benjamin R. Barber, *An Aristocracy of Everyone: The Politics of Education and the Future of America* (New York: Ballantine, 1992); and Amy Gutmann, *Democratic Education* (Princeton, N.J.: Princeton University Press, 1987).

13. Gutmann, op. cit.

14. Lawrence A. Cremin, *The Transformation of the School: Progressivism in American Education 1876–1957* (New York: Vintage Books, 1964), pp. 3–11.

15. W. E. B. Du Bois, "The Freedom to Learn," in Philip S. Foner, ed., *W. E. B. Du Bois Speaks* (New York: Pathfinder, 1970), pp. 230–31.

16. George H. Wood, *A Time to Learn* (New York: Dutton, 1998).

17. Todd Oppenheimer, "Schooling the Imagination," *Atlantic*, September 1999, pp. 71–83.

GOOD TEACHERS, PLURAL
Donald R. Cruickshank and Donald Haefele

In the previous article Carl Glickman argues that no one best way to educate America's children exists. The authors of this article have similar views in suggesting that there are several variations of "good" teachers, and no one variation by itself has proven to be superior to the others. Further, they assert, no single variation will satisfy all of the stakeholders in education.

Suggesting that there are several variations of "good" teachers raises a number of questions. Some of them include the following: Are there additional variations of good teachers? To what extent do the variations overlap? Are some variations more valuable than others? Who decides which variations are most valuable? If a variety of "good" teachers exists, how are highly educated professionals prepared? Keep these questions in mind as you study this article.

Think About This . . .

1. What are the different types of "good" teachers that Cruickshank and Haefele identify in the article. In your opinion, are some of them "better" than others?

2. The term *effective teacher* is commonly used in education. How do the authors define effective teachers? How appropriate is this description?

3. The term *expert* has also been commonly used in reference to skilled professionals. According to the authors, what is the difference between an *effective teacher* and an *expert teacher*? How important is this distinction?

4. Which type or types of teachers described in the article best represents the teacher you want to be as you develop your professional abilities? Why do you believe this type or these types are most important?

There are as many kinds of good teachers in our schools as there are varieties of good apples in supermarkets. Unfortunately, we tend to recognize and honor only one kind of teacher at a time. We currently glorify teachers whose students pass standardized tests (Bradley, 2000). In the 1990s, we admired those who had proven they could bring about greater student achievement. In the 1980s, good teachers were those who followed Madeline Hunter's prescriptions for teaching success (Garman & Hazi, 1998). And the list goes on.

Let us identify some of these visions of good teachers. Only then can we begin to explore how we can value them all and how school districts can support the development of many kinds of teachers and create ways to evaluate them.

Visions of Good Teachers

Ideal Teachers

For the first half of the 20th century, school principals, supervisors, and education professors determined the attributes of good teachers. Schools, school districts, and colleges cranked out checklists and rating scales that scored such traits as professional attitude, understanding of students, creativity, control of class, planning, individualization, and pupil participation. During this period, scholar Dwight Beecher (1953) developed the popular Teaching Evaluation Record, and Arvil Barr and his associates (1961) drew up a comprehensive list of ideal attributes that included buoyancy, emotional stability, ethical behavior, expressiveness, forcefulness, and personal magnetism.

Thus, an ideal teacher met subjective standards of excellence determined by selected, significant others. Because the standards were subjective, many disagreements developed over what the standards meant and which teachers met them (Mitzel, 1960; Morsh & Wilder, 1954).

Analytic Teachers

By the early 1960s, administrators encountered problems associated with measuring the attributes of ideal teachers (Cruickshank, 1990). In a search for some other way to judge teacher quality, experts soon began describing good teachers as analytic.

Analytic teachers methodically inspected what they did in the classroom. They recorded and examined their classroom practice using a variety of observation techniques (Simon & Boyer, 1968). Many teachers and observers used the Flanders System of Interactional Analysis (Flanders, 1960) to make a detailed record of the teacher–student interactions occurring during a lesson: how much and about what the teacher talked, how much and about what students talked, and the extent and nature of student silence or confusion. Teachers modified their practice on the basis of these analyses. Becoming an analytic teacher required being investigative and self-correctional. Over time, the work involved in being analytical seemed to overwhelm even proponents of this vision of good teachers.

Effective Teachers

In 1966, the influential Coleman Report asserted that students' socioeconomic backgrounds influenced their learning more than their teachers did (U.S. Department of Health, Education, and Welfare). Immediately, dozens of educational researchers set out to show that teachers made a crucial difference in student achievement. First, researchers identified teachers whose students scored higher on tests than did comparable students taught by others. Next, they examined these overachieving teachers, referred to as *outliers* or *effective teachers,* to determine exactly what they were like and what they did so that other teachers might benefit from such knowledge.

The findings of many studies (Rosenshine, 1971; Rosenshine & Furst, 1971) consistently found that effective teachers carefully monitor learning activities and are clear, accepting and supportive, equitable with students, and persistent in challenging and engaging them. Nonetheless, researchers disagreed about the methods used in the studies and about whether student gain is the most important outcome of teaching (Cruickshank, 1990).

Paralleling the development of the concept of the effective teacher has been a significant increase in the amount of student-achievement testing. As a result, we have become more focused on the product—better student scores on standardized tests—and on rewarding teachers who succeed in teaching to the test. In many states, teachers and principals are deemed effective and are rewarded monetarily when students demonstrate satisfactory gains on standardized tests. Opposition to this narrow definition of teacher effectiveness is mounting (Hoff, 1999; Kohn, 1999).

From Cruickshank, D., & Haefele, D. (2001). Good teachers, plural. Educational Leadership, 58(5), 26–30. *Reprinted with permission of the Association for Supervision and Curriculum Development.*

Dutiful Teachers

Those less than satisfied with the attributes originally assigned to effective teachers argued that teachers who do not display the typical attributes of effective teachers, such as enthusiasm, may yet bring about student learning. They asserted that studying the attributes of effective teachers can be useful, especially for guiding preservice and inservice development, but these attributes should not be used as standards for judging teacher quality. Rather, we should evaluate teachers according to how well they understand and perform their duties: knowledge of the subject matter, school, and community; demonstrated classroom skills, including testing and grading; personal characteristics that encourage learning; and service to the profession (Scriven, 1990).

Competent Teachers

The U.S. accountability movement in the 1970s spurred an effort in education to identify competencies that teachers should possess. Specifically, the public wanted to know what teachers needed to know and be able to do.

To identify teacher competencies, scholars studied the early research on teacher effectiveness, analyzed what teachers do, and obtained the opinions of expert teacher practitioners and other educators. The most thorough compilation (Dodl et al., 1972) organized competencies in the areas of planning instruction, implementing instruction, assessing and evaluating students, communicating, and performing administrative duties.

The public also wanted to make certain that teachers used their knowledge and performed well in the classroom. Consequently, the teacher-testing movement was born, soon to be given a boost by the 1983 publication of *A Nation At Risk* (National Commission on Excellence in Education). Thereafter, teachers or teachers-to-be had to pass tests developed by state education departments or by such national organizations as the Educational Testing Service and the National Board for Professional Teaching Standards.

The Educational Testing Service developed the Praxis teacher competency series of tests for use in teacher preparation programs and entry into the teaching profession. Praxis assesses three areas: reading, writing, and math skills near the beginning of a preservice teaching program; professional academic and pedagogical knowledge near the end of a teaching program; and on-the-job classroom performance. Thirty-eight states currently require some Praxis testing.

The National Board for Professional Teaching Standards provides national certification for experienced teachers who meet competencies set forth by discerning teachers (King, 1994). Teachers seeking National Board certification submit portfolios that include lesson plans, videotapes of lessons taught, and samples of student work. They also come to regional sites for further inspection and testing. States now offer incentives for teachers to obtain Board certification. For example, in Massachusetts, the Veteran Teachers Board offers up to $50,000 over 10 years to any public school teacher who receives National Board certification (Bradley, 1998).

Even the National Council for Accreditation of Teacher Education is moving toward assessing the competence—the knowledge and skills—of preservice teachers and away from merely reviewing their programs of study (Bradley, 1999).

Expert Teachers

In the 1980s and into the 1990s, many scholars decided that what makes a teacher good is expertise. Expert teachers are different from nonexperts in three ways: they have extensive and accessible knowledge that is organized for use in teaching; they are efficient and can do more in less time; and they are able to arrive at novel and appropriate solutions to problems (Sternberg & Horvath, 1995). Thus, expertise is more than experience. Teachers could be experienced and have less expertise than some novices.

Reflective Teachers

The definition of the reflective teacher was developed at Ohio State University in the late 1970s. Reflective teachers are students of teaching, with a strong, sustained interest in learning about the art and science of teaching and about themselves as teachers (Cruickshank, 1987, 1991). Reflective teachers are introspective, examining their own practice of teaching and seeking a greater understanding of teaching by reading scholarly and professional journals and books, including teachers' autobiographies. Because they want to be thoughtful practitioners, they constantly monitor their teaching—for example, by using videotape or audiotape.

Satisfying Teachers

Satisfying teachers please students, parents or caregivers, teaching colleagues, administrators, and supervisors by responding to their needs. In Rochester, New York, for example, parents rate their children's teachers on the basis of 20 questions that inquire about such qualities as the teacher's accessibility, clarity, responsiveness, and optimism (Janey, 1997).

School or parent organizations recognize satisfying teachers by presenting them with awards for good teaching. More often, however, admiration shows up in daily responses to the teacher: students advise one another to take this teacher's courses, fellow teachers look to this teacher for guidance and inspiration, most parents want their children in this teacher's class, and administrators trust this teacher to respond positively to difficult students.

Of course, knowing and meeting the expectations of others is a daunting task, and considerable disagreement can develop about what expectations are appropriate. We can all think of instructors who did or did not satisfy us or others but who were nonetheless effective teachers.

Diversity-Responsive Teachers

Diversity-responsive teachers take special interest in and are particularly sensitive to students who are different culturally, socially, economically, intellectually, physically, or emotionally. For example, Jacqueline Irvine and James Fraser (1998) believe that African American students are best served by "warm demanders" (p. 56). Warm demanders use a culturally specific pedagogical style that is substantively different from the approaches described in effective teaching research. Such teachers perceive themselves as parental surrogates and advocates, employ a teaching style filled with rhythmic language and rapid intonation, link students' everyday cultural experiences to new concepts, develop personal relationships with the learners, and teach with authority.

Diversity-responsive teachers are also dedicated to bettering the lives of students both inside and outside the classroom. Often working with children who have special needs, this kind of teacher demonstrates great tenderness, patience, and tact. A well-known exemplar is Annie Sullivan, Helen Keller's teacher (Peterson, 1946).

Respected Teachers

Respected teachers, real and fictional, sometimes are idolized in books and films. Some of the real ones include LouAnne Johnson in *Dangerous Minds,* Jaime Escalante in *Stand and Deliver,* and Marva Collins in *The Marva Collins Story.* Fictional, virtuous teachers have been crafted in *Mr. Holland's Opus; The Prime of*

Miss Jean Brodie; Up the Down Staircase; To Sir, with Love; and *Goodbye, Mr. Chips.*

Historian Richard Traina (1999) explored the autobiographies of some 125 prominent Americans to determine what qualities in teachers they valued. He notes that three attributes stand out: subject-matter competence, caring about students and their success, and distinctive character. Respected teachers possess and demonstrate virtuous qualities, including honesty, decency, fairness, devotion, empathy, and selflessness. Most such teachers also have determination, overcoming great odds to ensure student success.

Moving Forward

None of these categories is mutually exclusive. And no variation, by itself, has proven or is proving to be just right: None satisfies all education stakeholders. In a utopian world, teachers would demonstrate all aspects of teacher "goodness" and possess the attributes of all 10 visions. In the real world, we must learn how to recognize and appreciate the many models that teachers can follow to be good teachers.

Further, we need to answer some questions. Have we identified all of the possible exemplars of good teaching? To what extent do the exemplars overlap? Are some models more valuable than others? Who decides which exemplar is more valuable? Should all teachers be good teachers according to at least one of the 10 or so models? What should be the standard for good teachers within each vision of a good teacher? How can we prepare teachers and help them become good by some criteria? How can teachers document what kind of good teachers they are? How can we reward good teachers?

In addition, we need to conduct research. To what extent do various education stakeholders agree on what makes teachers good? How do perceptions of good teachers differ by age, gender, socioeconomic background, educational level, geographic area, and political persuasion? Which exemplars of good teachers are related to which educational outcomes? To what extent can good teachers be readily distinguished from bad teachers?

Evaluating Different Kinds of Teachers

School districts that appreciate multiple kinds of good teachers need to create teacher evaluation systems corresponding to the full range of teaching exemplars. To meet legal requirements, an evaluation system must be both formal (guided by public, written policies and procedures) and standardized (applied evenly and fairly). For example, all teachers must meet the criteria of one of the exemplars. Evaluations of *effective teachers* should require that teachers demonstrate such attributes as clarity and enthusiasm—qualities associated with student achievement. *Dutiful teachers* should be judged on such criteria as knowledge of subject matter and classroom skills.

Clearly, to judge each vision of a good teacher, we must use valid criteria that are related to the particular exemplar that the teacher strives to emulate. A good teacher evaluation system should also have predictive validity and make the desired impact on students; an evaluation of a *satisfying teacher,* for example, should include surveys of students and parents. Of course, any teacher evaluation system should require that evaluators—administrators, supervisors, teaching peers, or others—receive training so that each evaluation is objective and would result in approximately the same outcome if done by another evaluator.

Accepting Many Exemplars

Substantiating that there are all kinds of good teachers serves several useful ends. First, it dispels the traditional notion that there is only one kind of good teacher. Second, it permits teachers to describe which kind of good teacher they are and, when necessary, submit evidence to that effect. Third, it provides positive direction for teachers and persons responsible for teachers' continuing development. Finally, such knowledge enables the teaching profession to identify and remove teachers who are unable to meet any definition of what makes teachers good.

Meanwhile, Wyoming Governor Jim Geringer, chairman of the Education Commission of the States, whose membership consists of governors and top state education officials, reports that he hopes to work with the states to define what it means to be a good teacher (Sandham, 1999). Is the time right for educators, educational researchers, and elected officials to join hands in broadening the scope of this ambitious and important task?

References

Barr, A., Worcester, D., Abell, A., Beecher, C., Jenson, L., Peronto, A., Ringness, T., & Schmidt, J. (1961). Wisconsin studies of the measurement and predictability of teacher effectiveness. *Journal of Experimental Education, 30,* 1–156.

Beecher, D. (1953). *The teaching evaluation record.* Buffalo, NY: Educators Publishing Company.

Bradley, A. (1998, February 25). A better way to pay. *Education Week, 17*(24), 29–31.

Bradley, A. (1999, January 13). NCATE unveils a plan for aspiring elementary teachers. *Education Week, 18*(18), 5.

Bradley, A. (2000, March 22). L.A. proposes linking teacher pay to tests. *Education Week, 19*(28), 3.

Cruickshank, D. (1987). *Reflective teaching: The preparation of students of teaching.* Reston, VA: Association of Teacher Educators.

Cruickshank, D. (1990). *Research that informs teachers and teacher educators.* Bloomington, IN: Phi Delta Kappa Educational Foundation.

Cruickshank, D. (1991). *Reflective teaching.* Bloomington, IN: Phi Delta Kappa Educational Foundation.

Dodl, N., Elfner, E., Becker, J., Halstead, J., Jung, H., Nelson, P., Puriton, S., & Wegele, P. (1972). *Florida catalog of teacher competencies.* Tallahassee: Florida State University.

Flanders, N. (1960). *Teacher influence, pupil attitudes, and achievement: Final report.* Minneapolis: University of Minnesota.

Garman, N., & Hazi, H. (1998, May). Teachers ask: Is there life after Madeline Hunter? *Phi Delta Kappan, 69*(9), 669–672.

Hoff, D. (1999, September 22). Standards at crossroads after debate. *Education Week, 19*(3), 1, 9.

Irvine, J., & Fraser, J. (1998, May 13). Warm demanders. *Education Week, 17*(35), 56, 42.

Janey, C. (1997, October 1). Seeking customer satisfaction. *Education Week, 17*(5), 39.

King, M. (1994). Locking themselves in: National standards for the teaching profession. *Teaching and Teacher Education, 10*(1), 95–108.

Kohn, A. (1999, September 15). Confusing harder with better. *Education Week, 19*(2), 68, 52.

Mitzel, H. (1960). Teacher effectiveness. In C. Harris (Ed.), *Encyclopedia of educational research* (3rd ed.) (p. 1481). New York: MacMillan.

Morsh, J., & Wilder, E. (1954). *Identifying the effective instructor: A review of quantitative studies.* Lackland Air Force Base, TX: Air Force Personnel and Training Center.

National Commission on Excellence in Education. (1983). *A nation at risk.* Washington, DC: U.S. Department of Education.

Peterson, H. (1946). *Great teachers.* New York: Random House.

Rosenshine, B. (1971). *Teaching behaviors and student achievement.* London: National Foundation for Educational Research.

Rosenshine, B., & Furst, N. (1971). Research on teacher performance criteria. In B. O. Smith (Ed.), *Research in Teacher Education* (pp. 37–72). Upper Saddle River, NJ: Prentice Hall.

Sandham, J. (1999, August 4). ECS members take closer look at the teaching profession. *Education Week, 18*(43), 23.

Scriven, M. (1990, September). Can research-based teacher evaluation be saved? *Journal of Personnel Evaluation in Education, 4*(1), 19–32.

Simon, A., & Boyer, E. (1968). *Mirrors for behavior: An anthology of classroom observation instruments.* Philadelphia: Research for Better Schools.

Sternberg, R., & Horvath, J. (1995, August/September). A prototype view of expert teaching. *Educational Researcher, 24*(6), 9–17.

Traina, R. (1999, January 20). What makes a teacher good? *Education Week, 18*(19), 34.

U.S. Department of Health, Education, and Welfare. (1966). *Equality of educational opportunity: Summary report* (The Coleman report). Washington, DC: U.S. Government Printing Office.

FROM DEWEY TO BEANE: INNOVATION, DEMOCRACY, AND UNITY CHARACTERIZE MIDDLE LEVEL EDUCATION

Kevin B. Kienholz

John Dewey is one of the most influential philosophers of the early 20th century, and his work continues to be studied to this day. He did a great deal of writing in a variety of areas including art, science, democracy, and in particular, education. He is arguably the most influential philosopher in the history of American schooling.

Dewey's views are consistently credited with fostering the progressive era in education, a movement that featured a learner-centered curriculum and emphasized individual problem solving. Kevin Kienholz suggests that the rise of America's middle schools, schools that also feature a learner-centered curriculum, are closely related to Dewey's work. With an emphasis on real-world problem solving, active learning, and attention to learners' emotional development, middle schools attempt to apply Dewey's ideal of school as relevant to students' present lives rather than something to be endured in preparation for a later life. "The connections that exist between the critical theory of John Dewey and the agenda of the middle school movement are numerous and undeniable," the author asserts. As you read this article ask yourself, "What are these connections between Dewey's philosophy and the middle school movement?"

Think About This . . .

1. What is the goal of the middle school movement? How effectively has it met this goal?

2. What is the organizing framework for most students' experiences in schools? How effective is this framework?

3. According to the author, what is the role of conflict in education? Do you agree with this assertion?

4. How will the philosophy of John Dewey, as described in the article, influence your values and beliefs about teaching as you attempt to grow as a professional? Offer a specific example to illustrate your description.

John Dewey's Drive for Reconciliation

Like so many of the giants of philosophy who came before him, John Dewey worked to bring a certain degree of unity to his world. As one might reasonably expect from a man so committed to the pursuit of harmony among diverse arenas of study, he wrote prolifically in many fields, including art, philosophy, science, democracy, and—most notably—education. Dewey quietly sought a Hegelian synthesis meant to unite two schools of thought, writing articles and teaching from his laboratory school in Chicago, all in a concerted effort to bring closer together the long-time antagonists of theory and practice.

Dewey lived in an era characterized by both terrific upheaval and tremendous potential. He was born in Vermont in 1859—one year after Abraham Lincoln met Stephen Douglas in their famous debates, the same year in which Charles Darwin rocked the stability of the natural and religious world with the publication of his *On the Origin of Species,* and just one year before South Carolina seceded from the union. As an adult, he worked and thought and wrote in the first half of a century shaped dramatically by the brutal realities of two world wars fought within the span of just three decades. Out of this unprecedented era of conflict, discord, and potential for change rose the philosophy and practice of John Dewey, an educator committed to the idea of education as a powerful, workable tool for the improvement of one's self and one's community.

The Middle School Movement

America's middle school movement had its genesis some ten years after the 1952 death of John Dewey, although the seeds for its inception had been planted many years before the first middle school opened its doors. Like Dewey himself, the middle schools were borne out of an era of conflict and upheaval. They emerged from a cloud of controversy centered around the complex relationship among the realities of high schools, the demands of universities, and the unique needs and characteristics of adolescents trying to find their way in a confusing, complicated world. Educators in the 1960s began to attend seriously to the question of how to deal with the experiences and present realities of youth in a school system perhaps overly concerned with preparation for the future and paying homage to the past.

The middle school movement attempted to close the gap between what we know about young adolescents and what we do with them in schools, to narrow the chasm between theory and practice in our public schools. Dewey, too, wanted desperately to push theory and practice closer and closer together. He pursued synthesis and unity in much the same spirit as did the pioneers of the middle school reform movement. Thus, John Dewey's words and actions, which echo clearly out of the first half of this century, inform our understanding of today's middle school movement. In many ways, Dewey and the middle schools exist as part and parcel of the same whole—they both represent attempts to create more humane and practical places for young people to learn and experience an ever-changing and complex world.

In contrast to Dewey's ideas and tracing their roots back to the classical humanists, many educators have created schools that, more often than not, exist as places where the future meets the past so that students find themselves passive recipients of a body of knowledge apparently unrelated to and disconnected from their present realities. That is to say, schools have long thrived on the assumption that the past and the future take precedence over the present. This approach created schools in which the students found themselves to be strangers within their own curriculum. Middle school educators have sought to reposition the students and the curriculum at the center of the educational process and to make the present relevant to students' lives in schools.

The idea of using the experiences of students by paying attention to their world rests at the very heart of the middle school reform movement. Lounsbury (1993) suggested that "Schooling has been seen primarily as a preparation for future life, rather than as life itself. . . . The middle school does not exist to prepare students for high school" (p. 59). Sadly, junior high schools quite often have become preparation for high school; high schools existing as preparation for college; and college claiming its significance only as a stepping stone for some life which looms off in the distant future.

John Dewey (1938) also recognized the danger inherent in treating school as something to be endured simply until the real business of living happens along. He wrote: "When preparation is made the controlling end, then the potentialities of the present are sacrificed

From Kienholz, K. (2001). From Dewey to Beane: Innovation, democracy, and unity characterize middle level education. Middle School Journal, 32(3), 20–24. Reprinted with permission of the National Middle School Association.

to a suppositious future" (p. 49). In fact, Dewey placed the present moment in the forefront of his pragmatic pedagogy, recommending that school be used as the place where students develop personal values and character ethics. Caspary (1990) noted that "Dewey's goal was not to subdue desire under the rule of reason but to develop more reasonable desires" (p. 155). Dewey hoped, along with the middle school movement reformers, that the students would find the curriculum presently helpful and relevant, that schools would have an immediacy about them which prevents them from becoming anachronistic preservers of the past or irrelevant factories built for a preparation based on an unknowable future. In the writings of both Dewey and many middle school educators, one recognizes the condemnation of this impoverished approach to schooling which overvalues the past and the future. Schools cannot simply be holding places where students tread water until something bigger and better comes along; the past will never repeat itself exactly as before, and tomorrow—in the strictest sense of the concept—never actually arrives.

Connecting the Past, Present, and Future

It would be a mistake, however, to suggest that either Dewey or middle school educators have abandoned the idea of studying the past or giving attention to future considerations. In fact, the present moment provides the perfect starting point for an examination of both the past and the future. Beane (1993) proposed that the current concerns and interests of young students should serve as the foundation from which to view larger social issues. "If we look carefully at the personal concerns of early adolescents and the larger issues that face our world," wrote Beane, "it is readily apparent that there is a good deal of a particular kind of overlap between them" (p. 59). Anticipating such a claim, Dewey (1916) argued that "The present, in short, generates the problems which lead us to search the past for suggestion, and which supplies meaning to what we find when we search" (p. 76). Both of these educators recommended tapping into the power of the present in an effort to deal effectively and genuinely with that which has come before and that which is yet to happen. Either way one looks at it, the present becomes—quite logically—the starting line for student inquiry. The past and the future become particularly relevant through their relationships to the current moment.

Perhaps the past and the present have held such a prominent position in our schools' curriculum because placing the focus there takes us, at least temporarily, away from our own problems and concerns. Simply looking forward or looking back might provide a convenient excuse for neglecting our present difficulties. Middle school reformers such as Beane (1993), however, have reminded us that problems should actually rest at the center of our curriculum, and that conflict should be embraced rather than ignored. "Important information and skills may often be found within subject matter areas," noted Beane, "but in real life the problem itself is at the center and the information and the skills are defined around the problem" (p. 45). This suggestion runs counter to the typical situation found in schools, where the facts and skills presented to students are most likely sanitized and free of conflict due to their distance from any potentially meaningful or complicating context. John Dewey, too, recognized the power to encourage learning which rests latent within problems; he noted that conflicts push students to make judgments, decide on courses of action, and—in the quest to move out of cognitive dissonance—to think. "Unless a given experience leads out into a field previously unfamiliar no problems arise, while problems are the stimulus to thinking," submitted Dewey (1938). "Nonetheless, growth depends upon the presence of difficulty to be overcome by the exercise of intelligence" (p. 79). Rather than push conflicts off to the side in an effort to maintain control and peace in the classroom, Beane and Dewey both argue for the carefully considered articulation of those problems which should lead naturally and inevitably to growth. For both of these educators, placing the problem at the heart of the curriculum makes the most sense for the teacher concerned with creating a genuine, authentic learning environment.

Moving real-life problems and concerns to the center of the curricular debate suggests that the customary, perennial organizing structure of schools would necessarily be supplanted. In most cases, of course, this organizing framework which is entrenched in the experience of most students is that of the subject-centered curriculum. As one might reasonably expect, then, both the middle school reformers and Dewey point out the weaknesses inherent in such an approach to organizing the educational experiences of students. The Carnegie Council on Adolescent Development (1989) warned that students have a difficult time seeing the natural connections among ideas from various disciplines because middle grades curricula are so often delivered strictly through a subject-centered approach. Beane (1993) furthered this position when he claimed that "The subject approach presents numerous problems to schools in general and the middle level in particular . . . it is alien to life itself" (p. 45). And John Dewey (1938) noted that students have trouble learning—which he differentiates from memorizing—because schools often present material in subject-centered, "water-tight" compartments (p. 48). Perhaps one should remember that Dewey lived and wrote in an era marked by a distinct sense of alienation; he witnessed the rise of America's lost generation and the disconnected fragmentation associated with that group of young people. Like the middle school reformers of the latter twentieth century, Dewey recognized a significant danger in living in a fractional world where knowledge and people fail to connect in any meaningful way. The schools emerge, then, full of possibility as the places where those essential connections might most effectively be created.

Democratic Connections Among Students

The connections which might be forged in schools need not be limited to those which exist between people and facts, however. Classrooms contain the kinetic potential for authentic, meaningful relationships to be created between and among people. Kochan (1992) reminded us that the changing nature of society necessitates the emergence of a new place where individuals can fashion consequential and meaningful connections:

> The lack of community in our society and the changing nature of the family structure make it vital that our schools provide numerous opportunities for students to think and operate as family and community units. This necessitates developing or strengthening support systems for students, teachers, and staff within the environment. (p. 67)

As has often been the case, school emerges as the place where society's ills might be rectified; education serves a corrective function for the world at large. This added responsibility is not, of course, a recent trend or development. Even in the first half of this century, Dewey viewed schools as the starting point for societal change, and called for education to nurture both the individual as such and the individual as a part of the larger society. Ozmon and Craver (1995) pointed out that, due to the confusion and chaos of the modern world, Dewey

himself argued that "the school should be an institution where both the individual and the social capabilities of children can be nurtured. The way to achieve this is through democratic living" (p. 135). Understood in this light, schools clearly fulfill a role well beyond the typical conception of that as a place one spends twelve years while waiting for the "real world" to arrive; schools function as microcosms of that real world where people must act not only as independent individuals, but as autonomous citizens working within the framework of a larger society.

The phrase "autonomous citizens working within the framework of a larger society" might rightly appear as a part of a larger discussion of democracy. Significantly, the concept of democracy appears again and again, and in many different ways, in the writings of middle school educators and of John Dewey. Beane (1993) called strongly for the overt presence of democratic ideals in the schools: "The idea of democracy ought to permeate the middle school, including its curriculum" (p. 65). And Goodman (1989) argued that Dewey's vision of education embraces the belief that schools should be seen as "forums for cultural politics that reflect, mediate, and potentially transform the societal order within which they exist" (p. 88). Dewey called for a critical democracy. Remembering that John Dewey was born in the year just before South Carolina seceded from the union, we might correctly assume that he remained well aware of a democratic society's need for a degree of cultural unity, for a common set of experiences. Naturally, Dewey (1916) viewed the schools as the place where this synthesis of experience might best originate:

> But with the development of commerce, transportation, intercommunication, and emigration, countries like the United States are composed of a combination of different groups with different traditional customs. It is this situation which has, perhaps more than any other one cause, forced the demand for an educational institution which shall provide something like a homogenous and balanced experience for the young. Only in this way can the centrifugal forces set up by juxtaposition of different groups within one and the same political unit be counteracted. (p. 21)

Like Dewey, many within the middle school movement have issued a call for a certain degree of unification within the nation's school curriculum. Lounsbury (1993) suggested that we need a common curriculum within the schools such that "all Americans can be together and work together, where distinctions based on ability, economic status, national origin, race, religion, or anything else do not predetermine who will experience success" (p. 54). The call for a core curriculum, in the traditional sense of that term, has long been offered up as a viable option for America's schools. And perhaps the request for common experiences and unity made by Dewey near the turn of the century rings even more significantly today as the face of our nation becomes more diverse and varied and interesting by the day.

The connections which exist between the critical theory of John Dewey and the agenda of the middle school movement are numerous and undeniable. Both seek to take an American institution marked by tradition, authority, and fragmentation and infuse it with innovation, democracy, and unity. The crossroads at which Dewey meets the middle schools may be significant to recognize for a number of reasons. First, the middle school movement may simply be riding on the crest of a wave first made by John Dewey, and recognizing that fact might shed illumination on the lack of real progress made over the past eighty years. Also, John Dewey may be the best thinker—educational or otherwise—produced by the United States this century, and we may be well advised to give attention to what this seminal figure had to say. And finally, Dewey himself suggested that our future emerges inevitably out of the synthesis which we construct out of our past and our present; perhaps even today he invites and encourages us to seek connections between our past and our present in an effort to create new possibilities and realities for the future of our schools, for our students, and for ourselves.

References

Beane, J. (1993). *A middle school curriculum: From rhetoric to reality* (2nd ed.). Columbus, OH: National Middle School Association.

Carnegie Council on Adolescent Education. (1989). *Turning points: Preparing American youth for the 21st century*. New York: The Carnegie Corporation.

Caspary, W. (1990). Judgments of value in John Dewey's theory of ethics. *Educational Theory, 40,* 155–169.

Dewey, J. (1916). *Democracy and education*. New York: The Free Press.

Dewey, J. (1938). *Experience & education*. New York: Macmillan.

Goodman, J. (1989). Education for critical democracy. *Journal of Education, 171*(2), 88–113.

Kochan, F. (1992). A new paradigm of schooling: Connecting school, home, and community. In J. Irvin (Ed.), *Transforming middle level education: Perspectives and possibilities* (pp. 63–72). Boston: Allyn and Bacon.

Lounsbury, J. (1993). A fresh start for the middle school curriculum. In T. Dickinson (Ed.), *Readings in middle school curriculum* (pp. 53–62). Columbus, OH: National Middle School Association.

Ozmon, H., & Craver, S. (1995). *Philosophical foundations of education*. Upper Saddle River, NJ: Prentice Hall Merrill/ Prentice Hall.

TEACHING FOR WISDOM IN OUR SCHOOLS

Robert J. Sternberg

Something is fundamentally wrong with education in this country Robert Sternberg asserts. He uses managers of failed companies such as Enron and Global Crossing as examples of people who are highly intelligent and educated. He also notes that, in contrast with popular perception, many terrorists are highly educated, and some of them acquired this education in the United States.

Sternberg asserts that the fundamental problem with education in this country is that our students are taught to be smart and knowledgeable, but they are not being taught *how* to use their intelligence and knowledge. Schools need to go beyond teaching for factual recall and superficial levels of analysis; they need to teach for wisdom, and this can be accomplished in every content area. Only through conscious and explicit teaching for wisdom can some of the fundamental problems in our education system be solved. With these assertions in mind, as you study this article ask yourself, "How can schools teach for wisdom?"

Think About This . . .

1. What are four fallacies that exist in the thinking of people who lack wisdom? Are there other fallacies that also exist?
2. How does the author define *wisdom*? How could this definition be modified to be more applicable in classrooms?
3. The author lists four reasons why schools should include wisdom-related skills in the curriculum. What are they? Which is the most important? Why do you think so?
4. How will you attempt to teach wisdom in your classroom? Offer a specific example to illustrate your description.

The top-level managers who brought down companies such as Enron, Global Crossing, and World-Com were, for the most part, nothing if they were not smart and well-educated. Yet one cannot help feeling that something fundamental was missing in the way they were educated. Similarly, today's consummate terrorist defies the stereotype of the poorly educated ignorant peasant who, having nothing better to do, joins up with a movement and blindly follows orders while showing no personal initiative at all. On the contrary, many of the terrorists who are covertly walking our streets are smart and well-educated—in the United States, in some cases. When their plans go awry, they use their wits to figure out how to get those plans back on track. Once again, it appears that something was fundamentally wrong in their education.

What is that something? I believe it is that, for the most part, we are teaching students to be intelligent and knowledgeable, but not how to use their intelligence and their knowledge. Schools need to teach for wisdom, not just for factual recall and superficial levels of analysis.

When schools teach for wisdom, they teach students that it is important not just what you know, but how you use what you know—whether you use it for good ends or bad. They are teaching for what the Bush administration referred to recently, in a White House conference, as the "fourth R": responsibility. Smart but foolish and irresponsible people, including, apparently, some who run or have run major businesses in our country, exhibit four characteristic fallacies in their thinking.

The *fallacy of egocentrism* occurs when people think the world centers around them. Other people come to be seen merely as tools in the attainment of their goals, to be used and then discarded as the egomaniacs' needs change. Why would smart people think egocentrically? Conventionally smart people often have been so highly rewarded for being smart that they lose sight of the needs and desires of others.

Wisdom requires one to know what one knows and does not know, as well as what can be known and cannot be known at a given time and place. Smart people often lose sight of what they do not know, leading to the second fallacy.

The *fallacy of omniscience* results from people's starting to feel that not only are they expert in whatever they trained for, but that they are all-knowledgeable about pretty much everything. They then can make disastrous decisions based on knowledge that is incomplete but that they do not recognize as such.

The *fallacy of omnipotence* results from the feeling that if knowledge is power, then omniscience is total power. People who are in positions of power may start to imagine themselves to be all-powerful. Worse, they forget the old saw that power corrupts, but absolute power corrupts absolutely. At the same time, they fail to reckon with the potential consequences of their actions because of the fourth fallacy.

The *fallacy of invulnerability* comes from people's view that if they are all-knowing and all-powerful, they can do what they want. And because they are all-knowing, they can get away with anything. Most likely, they convince themselves, they won't get caught. Even if they do, they figure they can weasel their way out of being punished because they are smarter than those who have caught up with them.

If foolish (but smart and often highly accomplished) people commit these fallacies, what do wise people do?

From Sternberg, R. (2002). Teaching for wisdom in our schools. As first appeared in Education Week, 22(11), 56, 42. *Reprinted with permission of the author.*

I define wisdom as the application of intelligence and experience toward the attainment of a common good. This attainment involves a balance among (a) intrapersonal (one's own), (b) interpersonal (other people's), and (c) extrapersonal (more than personal, such as institutional) interests, over the short and long terms. Thus, wise people look out not just for themselves, but for all toward whom they have any responsibility.

An implication of this view is that simply being smart is not enough. It is important to be wise, too. There are several reasons why schools should seriously consider including instruction in wisdom-related skills in the school curriculum.

First, knowledge is insufficient for wisdom and certainly does not guarantee satisfaction, happiness, or behavior that looks beyond self-interest. Wisdom seems a better vehicle to the attainment of these goals.

Second, wisdom provides a way to enter considered and deliberative values into important judgments. One cannot be wise and at the same time impulsive, mindless, or immoral in one's judgments.

Third, wisdom represents an avenue to creating a better, more harmonious world. Dictators such as Adolf Hitler and Joseph Stalin may have been knowledgeable. They may even have been good critical thinkers, at least with regard to the maintenance of their own power. They were not wise.

Fourth and finally, students, who later will become parents and leaders, are always part of a greater community. Hence, they will benefit from learning to judge rightly, soundly, and justly on behalf of their community.

If the future is plagued with conflict and turmoil, this instability does not simply reside *out there somewhere*. It resides and has its origin *in ourselves*. For all these reasons, students need not only to recall facts and to think critically (and even creatively) about the content of the subjects they learn, but also to think wisely about it.

Wisdom can be taught in the context of any subject matter. Our own current research, funded by the W. T. Grant Foundation, involves infusing teaching for wisdom into American history. Students learn to think wisely, and especially to understand things from diverse points of view across time and space. For example, what one group might call a "settler," another might call an "invader." What one group might call "Manifest Destiny," another group might call "land theft." Students also learn that in the current world, peace, or at least absence of conflict, depends in large part upon being able to understand how other nations and cultures see problems and their solutions differently from the way we do. The goal is not necessarily to accept these other points of view, or even necessarily to achieve some kind of accommodation, but rather to understand that resolution of difficult life problems requires people to want to understand each other and to reach a resolution, whenever possible, that all of those people can somehow live with. In our own research, students being taught to think wisely are being compared with a control group that learns the historical material in a standard way.

The road to teaching for wisdom is bound to be a rocky one. First, entrenched educational structures, whatever they may be, are difficult to change. Wisdom is not taught in schools. In general, it is not even discussed.

Second, many people will not see the value of teaching something that does not have as its primary focus the raising of conventional test scores. Teaching for wisdom is not inconsistent with raising test scores, but teaching to tests is not its primary goal. Teaching for wisdom relates to President Bush's "fourth R"—responsibility—more closely than it relates to the conventional "three R's" that tend to be tested.

Third, wisdom is much more difficult to develop than is the kind of achievement that can be developed and then readily tested via multiple-choice tests, such as "What is the capital of France?"

Finally, people who have gained influence and power in a society via one means—through money, high test scores, parental influence, or whatever—are unlikely to want either to give up that power or to see a new criterion be established on which they do not rank as favorably. Thus, there is no easy path to wisdom or teaching for wisdom. There never was, and probably never will be.

Wisdom might bring us a world that would seek to better itself and the conditions of all the people in it. At some level, we as a society have a choice. What do we wish to maximize through our schooling? Is it just knowledge? Is it just intelligence? Or is it also wisdom? If it is wisdom, then we need to put our students on a much different course. We need to value not only how they use their outstanding individual abilities to maximize their attainments, but how they use their individual abilities to maximize the attainments of others as well.

We need, in short, to value wisdom. And then we need to remember that wisdom is not just about what we think, but more importantly, how we act.

THE ETHICS OF TEACHING

Kenneth A. Strike

Three factors make an issue ethical, Kenneth Strike asserts. First, ethical issues concern questions of right and wrong, and they include concepts such as responsibility, duty, and individual rights. Discussions of ethics often include terms such as *fair* or *unfair,* and *ought* or *should,* such as, "In order to be *fair* in grading, a teacher *should* attempt to score all students' work according to the same criteria."

Second, facts alone do not resolve ethical issues. For example, if one student works very hard, but falls one point below a B according to the teacher's grading criteria, would it be fair or unfair to raise the students' grade to the B? And third, ethical questions should be distinguished from values. Values are a matter of choice or preference, and often they are neither right nor wrong. Ethical decisions must be made independent of values, and they may even run counter to what we value. We may value jewelry and find a nice watch in the locker room of a gym as we are getting dressed. This does not mean that it is ethical to keep the watch.

Teaching is filled with ethical dilemmas, which are situations that have both positive and negative consequences regardless of the action taken. For example, you have two students who have worked hard but still earn a failing grade in your class. Failing them may destroy their motivation. On the other hand, passing them when they did not achieve at the required level is unfair to those who meet the criteria. A dilemma such as this requires moral reasoning. As you read this article ask yourself, "What influences the ability to reason effectively about ethical dilemmas?"

Think About This . . .

1. As described by the author, what are two stages involved in ethical reasoning? What else is necessary in order to reason ethically?

2. What two ethical principles does the author suggest can guide people's thinking as they confront ethical dilemmas? Are there other guidelines that you would suggest as an aid in resolving these dilemmas?

3. What three features exist about the ethical principles identified in the article? In your opinion, which is most important?

4. How will you attempt to deal with ethical issues when they appear in your teaching? Cite a specific example to illustrate your description.

Mrs. Porter and Mr. Kennedy have divided their third-grade classes into reading groups. In her class, Mrs. Porter tends to spend the most time with the students in the slowest reading group because they need the most help. Mr. Kennedy claims that such behavior is unethical. He maintains that each reading group should receive equal time.

Miss Andrews has had several thefts of lunch money in her class. She has been unable to catch the thief, although she is certain that some students in the class know who the culprit is. She decides to keep the entire class inside for recess, until someone tells her who stole the money. Is it unethical to punish the entire class for the acts of a few?

From Strike, K. (1988). The ethics of teaching. Phi Delta Kappan, 70(2), 156–158. Reprinted with permission of the author.

Ms. Phillips grades her fifth-grade students largely on the basis of effort. As a result, less-able students who try hard often get better grades than students who are abler but less industrious. Several parents have accused Ms. Phillips of unethical behavior, claiming that their children are not getting what they deserve. These parents also fear that teachers in the middle school won't understand Ms. Phillips' grading practices and will place their children in inappropriate tracks.

The Nature of Ethical Issues

The cases described above are typical of the ethical issues that teachers face. What makes these issues ethical?

First, ethical issues concern questions of right and wrong—our duties and obligations, our rights and responsibilities. Ethical discourse is characterized by a unique vocabulary that commonly includes such words as *ought* and *should, fair* and *unfair.*

Second, ethical questions cannot be settled by an appeal to facts alone. In each of the preceding cases, knowing the consequences of our actions is not sufficient for determining the right thing to do. Perhaps, because Mrs. Porter spends more time with the slow reading group, the reading scores in her class will be more evenly distributed than the scores in Mr. Kennedy's class. But even knowing this does not tell us if it is fair to spend a disproportionate amount of time with the slow readers. Likewise, if Miss Andrews punishes her entire class, she may catch the thief, but this does not tell us whether punishing the entire group was the right thing to do. In ethical reasoning, facts are relevant in deciding what to do. But by themselves they are not enough. We also require ethical principles by which to judge the facts.

Third, ethical questions should be distinguished from values. Our values concern what we like or what we believe to be good. If one enjoys Bach or likes skiing, that says something about one's values. Often there is nothing right or wrong about values, and our values are a matter of our free choice. For example, it would be difficult to argue that someone who preferred canoeing to skiing had done something wrong or had made a mistake. Even if we believe that Bach is better than rock, that is not a reason to make people who prefer rock listen to Bach. Generally, questions of values turn on our choices: what we like, what we deem to be worth liking. But there is nothing obligatory about values.

On the other hand, because ethics concern what we ought to do, our ethical obligations are often independent of what we want or choose. The fact that we want something that belongs to someone else does not entitle us to take it. Nor does a choice to steal make stealing right or even "right for us." Our ethical obligations continue to be obligations, regardless of what we want or choose.

Ethical Reasoning

The cases sketched above involve ethical dilemmas: situations in which it seems possible to give a reasonable argument for more than one course of action. We must think about our choices, and we must engage in moral reasoning. Teaching is full of such dilemmas. Thus teachers need to know something about ethical reasoning.

Ethical reasoning involves two stages: applying principles to cases and judging the adequacy or applicability of the principles. In the first stage, we are usually called upon to determine the relevant ethical principle or principles that apply to a case, to ascertain the relevant facts of the case, and to judge the facts by the principles.

Consider, for example, the case of Miss Andrews and the stolen lunch money. Some ethical principles concerning punishment seem to apply directly to the case. Generally, we believe that we should punish the guilty, not the innocent; that people should be presumed innocent until proven guilty; and that the punishment should fit the crime. If Miss Andrews punishes her entire class for the behavior of an unknown few, she will violate these common ethical principles about punishment.

Ethical principles are also involved in the other two cases. The first case involves principles of equity and fairness. We need to know what counts as fair or equal treatment for students of different abilities. The third case requires some principles of due process. We need to know what are fair procedures for assigning grades to students.

However, merely identifying applicable principles isn't enough. Since the cases described above involve ethical dilemmas, it should be possible to argue plausibly for more than one course of action.

For example, suppose Miss Andrews decides to punish the entire class. It could be argued that she has behaved unethically because she has punished innocent people. She might defend herself, however, by holding that she had reasons for violating ethical principles that we normally apply to punishment. She might argue that it was important to catch the thief or that it was even more important to impress on her entire class that stealing is wrong. She could not make these points by ignoring the matter. By keeping the entire class inside for recess. Miss Andrews could maintain, she was able to catch the thief and to teach her class a lesson about the importance of honesty. Even if she had to punish some innocent people, everyone was better off as a result. Can't she justify her action by the fact that everyone benefits?

Two General Principles

When we confront genuine ethical dilemmas such as this, we need some general ethical concepts in order to think our way through them. I suggest two, the principle of benefit maximization and the principle of equal respect for persons.

The principle of benefit maximization holds that we should take that course of action which will maximize the benefit sought. More generally, it requires us to do that which will make everyone, on the average, as well off as possible. One of the traditional formulations of this principle is the social philosophy known as utilitarianism, which holds that our most general moral obligation is to act in a manner that produces the greatest happiness for the greatest number.

We might use the principle of benefit maximization to think about each of these cases. The principle requires that in each case we ask which of the possible courses of action makes people generally better off. Miss Andrews has appealed to the principle of benefit maximization in justifying her punishment of the entire class. Ms. Phillips might likewise appeal to it in justifying her grading system. Perhaps by using grades to reward effort rather than successful performance, the overall achievement of the class will be enhanced. Is that not what is important?

It is particularly interesting to see how the principle of benefit maximization might be applied to the question of apportioning teacher time between groups with different levels of ability. Assuming for the moment that we wish to maximize the overall achievement of the class, the principle of benefit maximization dictates that we allocate time in a manner that will produce the greatest overall learning.

Suppose, however, we discover that the way to produce the greatest overall learning in a given class is for a teacher to spend the most time with the *brightest* children. These are the children who provide the greatest return on our investment of time. Even though the least-able children learn less than they would with an equal division of time, the overall learning that takes place in the class is maximized when we concentrate on the ablest.

Here the principle of benefit maximization seems to lead to an undesirable result. Perhaps, we should consider other principles as well.

The principle of equal respect requires that our actions respect the equal worth of moral agents. We must regard human beings as intrinsically worthwhile and treat them accordingly. The essence of this idea is perhaps best expressed in the Golden Rule. We have a duty to accord others the same kind of treatment that we expect them to accord us.

The principle of equal respect can be seen as involving three subsidiary ideas. First, it requires us to treat people as ends in themselves, rather than as means to further our own goals. We must respect their goals as well.

Second, when we are considering what it means to treat people as ends rather than as means, we must regard as central the fact that people are free and rational moral agents. This means that, above all, we must respect their freedom of choice. And we must respect the choices that people make even when we do not agree.

Third, no matter how people differ, they are of equal value as moral agents. This does not mean that we must see people as equal in abilities or capacities. Nor does it mean that we cannot take relevant differences between people into account when deciding how to treat them. It is not, for example, a violation of equal respect to give one student a higher grade than another because that student works harder and does better.

That people are of equal value as moral agents does mean, however, that they are entitled to the same basic rights and that their interests are of equal value. Everyone, regardless of native ability, is entitled to equal opportunity. No one is entitled to act as though his or her happiness counted for more than the happiness of others. As persons, everyone has equal worth.

Notice three things about these two moral principles. First, both principles (in some form) are part of the moral concepts of almost everyone who is reading this article. These are the sorts of moral principles that everyone cites in making moral arguments. Even if my formulation is new, the ideas themselves should be familiar. They are part of our common ethical understandings.

Second, both principles seem necessary for moral reflection. Neither is sufficient by itself. For example, the principle of equal respect requires us to value the well-being of others as we value our own well-being. But to value the welfare of ourselves *and* others is to be concerned with maximizing benefits; we want all people to be as well-off as possible.

Conversely, the principle of benefit maximization seems to presuppose the principle of equal respect. Why, after all, must we value the welfare of others? Why not insist that only our own happiness counts or that our happiness is more important than the happiness of others? Answering these questions will quickly lead us to affirm that people are of equal worth and that, as a consequence, everyone's happiness is to be valued equally. Thus our two principles are intertwined.

Third, the principles may nevertheless conflict with one another. One difference between the principle of benefit maximization and the principle of equal respect is their regard for consequences. For the principle of benefit maximization, only consequences matter. The sole relevant factor in choosing between courses of action is which action has the best overall results. But consequences are not decisive for the principle of equal respect; our actions must respect the dignity and worth of the individuals involved, even if we choose a course of action that produces less benefit than some other possible action.

The crucial question that characterizes a conflict between the principle of benefit maximization and the principle of equal respect is this:

When is it permissible to violate a person's rights in order to produce a better outcome? For example, this seems the best way to describe the issue that arises when a teacher decides to punish an entire class for the acts of a few. Students' rights are violated when they are punished for something they haven't done, but the overall consequences of the teacher's action may be desirable. Is it morally permissible, then, to punish everyone?

We can think about the issue of fair allocation of teacher time in the same way. Spending more time with the brightest students may enhance the average learning of the class. But we have, in effect, traded the welfare of the least-able students for the welfare of the ablest. Is that not failing to respect the equal worth of the least-able students? Is that not treating them as though they were means, not ends?

The principle of equal respect suggests that we should give the least-able students at least an equal share of time, even if the average achievement of the class declines. Indeed, we might use the principle of equal respect to argue that we should allocate our time in a manner that produces more equal results—or a more equal share of the benefits of education.

I cannot take the discussion of these issues any further in this short space. But I do want to suggest some conclusions about ethics and teaching.

First, teaching is full of ethical issues. It is the responsibility of teachers, individually and collectively, to consider these issues and to have informed and intelligent opinions about them.

Second, despite the fact that ethical issues are sometimes thorny, they can be thought about. Ethical reflection can help us to understand what is at stake in our choices, to make more responsible choices, and sometimes to make the right choices.

Finally, to a surprising extent, many ethical dilemmas, including those that are common to teaching, can be illuminated by the principles of benefit maximization and equal respect for persons. Understanding these general ethical principles and their implications is crucial for thinking about ethical issues.

REFLECTION IS AT THE HEART OF PRACTICE

Simon Hole and Grace Hall McEntee

Teaching involves making an enormous number of decisions, most of which cannot be reduced to simple rules. How do teachers know if their decisions are valid and wise? This is a tough question, because they receive little feedback about the effectiveness of their work. They are observed by administrators a few times a year at most and receive only vague, sketchy, and uncertain feedback from students and parents. In addition, they get virtually no feedback from their colleagues, unless the school has a peer coaching or mentoring program. To improve, teachers must be able to assess their own classroom performance.

The ability to conduct this self-assessment can be developed, but it requires that teachers develop a disposition for examining what they are doing. This is the essence of a simple yet powerful notion called *reflective teaching,* which is the process of conducting an analytical self-examination of an individual's work. Reflective teachers are observant, thoughtful, and self-critical about their work.

The authors of this article offer some suggestions to help make the process of reflection more systematic. As you read this article ask yourself, "How can I use reflection to help myself grow as a professional?"

Think About This . . .

1. According to the authors, what is the essential beginning step in the process of reflection? Do you think this step is essential? Why or why not?
2. What are the steps in the guided reflection protocol? Which of these steps most nearly exemplifies the essence of reflection? Why do you think so?
3. What are the steps in the critical incidents protocol? Which—the guided reflection protocol or the critical incidents protocol—do you believe is more realistic in today's classrooms? Why do you think so?
4. How will you attempt to use reflection in your own teaching? Offer a specific example to illustrate your description.

The life force of teaching practice is thinking and wondering. We carry home those moments of the day that touch us, and we question decisions made. During these times of reflection, we realize when something needs to change.

A protocol, or guide, enables teachers to refine the process of reflection, alone or with colleagues. The Guided Reflection Protocol is useful for teachers who choose to reflect alone. The Critical Incidents Protocol, which we developed through our work with the Annenberg Institute for School Reform at Brown University, is used for shared reflection. The steps for each protocol are similar; both include writing.

Guided Reflection Protocol

The first step in guided reflection is to collect possible episodes for reflection. In his book *Critical Incidents in Teaching: Developing Professional Judgement* (1993), David Tripp encourages us to think about ordinary events, which often have much to tell us about the underlying trends, motives, and structures of our practice. Simon's story, "The Geese and the Blinds," exemplifies this use of an ordinary event.

Step One: What Happened?

Wednesday, September 24, 9:30 a.m. I stand to one side of the classroom, taking the morning attendance. One student glances out the window and

sees a dozen Canada geese grazing on the playground. Hopping from his seat, he calls out as he heads to the window for a better view. Within moments, six students cluster around the window. Others start from their seats to join them. I call for attention and ask them to return to their desks. When none of the students respond, I walk to the window and lower the blinds.

Answering the question "What happened?" is more difficult than it sounds. We all have a tendency to jump into an interpretive or a judgmental mode, but it is important to begin by simply telling the story. Writing down what happened—without analysis or judgment—aids in creating a brief narrative. Only then are we ready to move to the second step.

Step Two: Why Did It Happen?

Attempting to understand why an event happened the way it did is the beginning of reflection. We must search the context within which the event occurred for explanations. Simon reflects:

It's not hard to imagine why the students reacted to the geese as they did. As 9-year-olds, they are incredibly curious about their world. Explaining my reaction is more difficult. Even as I was lowering

From Hole, S., and McEntee, G. H. (1999). Reflection is at the heart of practice. Educational Leadership, 56(8), 34–37. *Reprinted with permission of the Association for Supervision and Curriculum Development.*

the blinds, I was kicking myself. Here was a natural opportunity to explore the students' interests. Had I stood at the window with them for five minutes, asking questions to see what they knew about geese, or even just listening to them, I'd be telling a story about seizing the moment or taking advantage of a learning opportunity. I knew that even as I lowered the blinds. So, why?

Searching deeper, we may find that a specific event serves as an example of a more general category of events. We need to consider the underlying structures within the school that may be a part of the event and examine deeply held values. As we search, we often find more questions than answers.

> Two key things stand out concerning that morning. First, the schedule. On Wednesdays, students leave the room at 10:00 a.m. and do not return until 15 minutes before lunch. I would be out of the classroom all afternoon attending a meeting, and so this half hour was all the time I would have with my students.
>
> Second, this is the most challenging class I've had in 22 years of teaching. The first three weeks of school had been a constant struggle as I tried strategy after strategy to hold their attention long enough to have a discussion, give directions, or conduct a lesson. The hectic schedule and the need to prepare the class for a substitute added to the difficulty I've had "controlling" the class, so I closed the blinds.

There's something satisfying about answering the question Why did it happen? Reflection often stops here. If the goal is to become a reflective practitioner, however, we need to look more deeply. The search for meaning is step three.

Step Three: What Might It Mean?

Assigning meaning to the ordinary episodes that make up our days can feel like overkill. Is there really meaning behind all those events? Wouldn't it be more productive to wait for something extraordinary to happen, an event marked with a sign: "Pay attention! Something important is happening." Guided reflection is a way to find the meaning within the mundane. Splitsecond decision making is a crucial aspect of teaching. Given the daily madness of life in a classroom, considering all the options and consequences is difficult. Often, it is only through reflection that we even recognize that we had a choice, that we could have done something differently.

> Like a football quarterback, I often make bad decisions because of pressure. Unlike a quarterback, I don't have an offensive line to blame for letting the

pressure get to me. While it would be nice to believe that I could somehow make the pressure go away, the fact is that it will always be with me. Being a teacher means learning to live within that pressure, learning from the decisions I make and learning to make better decisions.

Our growing awareness of how all events carry some meaning is not a new concept. In *Experience and Education* (1938), John Dewey wrote about experience and its relationship to learning and teaching: "Every experience affects for better or worse the attitudes which help decide the quality of further experiences" (p. 37). He believed that teachers must be aware of the "possibilities inherent in ordinary experience" (p. 89), that the "business of the educator [is] to see in what direction an experience is heading" (p. 38). Rediscovering this concept through the examination of ordinary events creates a fresh awareness of its meaning.

The search for meaning is an integral part of being human. But understanding by itself doesn't create changes in classroom practice. The last phase of guided reflection is more action oriented and involves holding our practice to the light of those new understandings.

Step Four: What Are the Implications for My Practice?

Simon continues:

> My reaction to the pressure this year has been to resort to methods of control. I seem to be forever pulling down the blinds. I'm thinking about how I might better deal with the pressure.
>
> But there is something else that needs attention. Where is the pressure coming from? I'm sensing from administration and parents that they feel I should be doing things differently. I've gotten subtle and overt messages that I need to pay more attention to "covering" the curriculum, that I should be finding a more equal balance between process and product.
>
> Maybe they're right. What I've been doing hasn't exactly been a spectacular success. But I think that what is causing the lowering of the blinds stems from my not trusting enough in the process. Controlling the class in a fairly traditional sense isn't going to work in the long run. Establishing a process that allows the class to control itself will help keep the blinds up.

Cultivating deep reflection through the use of a guiding protocol is an entry into rethinking and changing practice. Alone, each of us can proceed step-by-step through the examination of a particular event. Through the process, we gain new insights into the implications of ordinary events, as Simon did when he analyzed "The Geese and the Blinds."

Whereas Guided Reflection is for use by individuals, the Critical Incidents Protocol is used with colleagues. The goal is the same: to get to the heart of our practice, the place that pumps the lifeblood into our teaching, where we reflect, gain insight, and change what we do with our students. In addition, the Critical Incidents Protocol encourages the establishment of collegial relationships.

Critical Incidents Protocol

Schools are social places. Although too often educators think and act alone, in most schools colleagues do share daily events. Stories told in teachers' lounges are a potential source of rich insight into issues of teaching and learning and can open doors to professional dialogue.

Telling stories has the potential for changing individual practice and the culture of our schools. The Critical Incidents Protocol allows practitioners to share stories in a way that is useful to their own thinking and to that of the group.

Three to five colleagues meet for the purpose of exploring a "critical incident." For 10 minutes, all write a brief account of an incident. Participants should know that the sharing of their writing will be for the purpose of getting feedback on what happened rather than on the quality of the writing itself.

Next, the group decides which story to use with the protocol. The presenter for the session then reads the story while the group listens carefully to understand the incident and the context. Colleagues ask clarifying questions about what happened or why the incident occurred, then they discuss what the incident might mean in terms of the presenter's practice. During this time, the presenter listens and takes notes. The presenter then responds, and the participants discuss the implications for their own practice. To conclude, one member leads a conversation about what happened during the session, how well the process worked, and how the group might change the process.

The sharing of individual stories raises issues in the fresh air of collegial support. If open dialogue is not already part of a school's culture, however, colleagues may feel insecure about beginning. To gain confidence, they may choose to run through the protocol first with a story that is not theirs. For this purpose, Grace offers a story about an incident in the writing lab from her practice as a high school English teacher.

Step One: What Happened?

We went into the computer lab to work on essay drafts. TJ, Neptune, Ronny, and Mick sat as a foursome. Their sitting together had not worked last time. On their single printer an obscene message had appeared. All four had denied writing it.

The next day Ronny, Neptune, and Mick had already sat together. Just as TJ was about to take his seat, I asked him if he would mind sitting over at the next bay of computers. He exploded, "You think I'm the cause of the problem, don't you?"

Actually I did think he might be, but I wasn't at all certain. "No," I said, "but I do want you to sit over here for today." He got red in the face, plunked down in the chair near the three other boys, and refused to move.

I motioned for him to come with me. Out in the hall, I said to him quietly, "The bottom line is that all of you need to get your work done." Out of control, body shaking, TJ angrily spewed out, "You always pick on me. Those guys. . . . You. . . ." I could hardly hear his words, so fascinated was I with his intense emotion and his whole-body animation.

Contrary to my ordinary response to students who yell, I felt perfectly calm. I knew I needed to wait. Out of the corner of my eye, I saw two male teachers rise out of their chairs in the hallway about 25 feet away. They obviously thought that I, a woman of small stature, needed protection. But I did not look at them. I looked at TJ and waited.

When he had expended his wrathful energy, I said softly, "You know, TJ, you are a natural-born leader." I waited. Breathed in and out. "You did not choose to be a leader; it was thrust upon you. But there you are. People follow you. So you have a tremendous responsibility, to lead in a positive and productive way. Do you understand what I am saying?"

Like an exhalation after a long inbreath, his body visibly relaxed. He looked down at me and nodded his head. Then he held out his hand to me and said, "I'm sorry."

Back in the room, he picked up his stuff and, without a word, moved to the next bay of computers.

Step Two: Using the Critical Incidents Protocol

At first you'll think that you need more information than this, but we think that you have enough here. One member of the group will take the role of Grace. Your "Grace" can answer clarifying questions about what happened or why it happened in whatever way he or she sees fit.

Work through the protocol to figure out what the incident might mean in terms of "Grace's" practice. Finally, discuss what implications the incident in the writing lab might have for her practice and for your own as reflective educators. Then, try an event of your own.

We think that you will find that whether the group uses your story or someone else's, building reflective practice together is a sure way to get to the heart of teaching and learning.

References

Dewey, J. (1938). *Experience and education*. New York: Macmillan.

Tripp, D. (1993). *Critical incidents in teaching: Developing professional judgement*. New York: Routledge.

ADDITIONAL READINGS

Adler, M. (1998). *Paideia proposal: An educational manifesto*. New York: Simon & Schuster.

Boyer, E. (1995). The educated person. In J. Beane (Ed.), *Toward a coherent curriculum*. Alexandria, VA: Association for Curriculum Development.

Dewey, J. (1897). *My pedagogic creed*. New York: Kellog Co.

Good, H. (2002). Off to see the wizard: What does it mean to be educated? *Education Week, 22*(15), 29, 31.

Jacobsen, D. (2003). *Philosophy in classroom teaching* (2nd ed.). Upper Saddle River, NJ: Merrill/Prentice Hall.

Pulliam, J., & Van Patten, J. (1999). *History of education in America* (7th ed.). Upper Saddle River, NJ: Merrill/Prentice Hall.

Ravitch, D. (2000). *Left back: A century of failed school reforms*. New York: Simon & Schuster.

Schlessinger, A. (1992). *The disuniting of America*. New York: Norton.

EXPLORING THE INTERNET

Overview of Educational Philosophies
http://jan.ucc.nau.edu/~jde7/ese502/assessment/lesson.html
This site provides overviews of essentialism, perennialism, progressivism, existentialism, and behaviorism, which it suggests is as much a philosophy as it is a theory.

Educational Theory
http://www.ed.uiuc.edu/EPS/Educational-Theory/default.asp
This journal publishes articles related to philosophies of education.

Biographies of Philosophers
http://www.blupete.com/Literature/Biographies/Philosophy/BiosPhil.htm
An ever-growing database of biographies developed by Peter Landry, Dartmouth, Nova Scotia, Canada.

History of Education on the Internet
http://library.gcsu.edu/~sc/magepages/magelink.html
This site contains a number of links to Web sites that feature information about American educational history.

History of American Education Web Project
http://www.nd.edu/~rbarger/www7/index.html
This site contains numerous links to topics associated with the development of American education. Most links are to particular time periods, such as the Colonist Period or the Progressive Era.

History of Education in the United States
http://reading.indiana.edu/
This site contains both citations to and brief abstracts of materials from the ERIC database that focus on the history of education.

PART TEN

Educational Reform

The history of educational reform in the United States is as old as education itself. The first reform began with the Bill of Rights shortly after our country became a nation. The First Amendment to the Constitution established the principle of separation of church and state, which fundamentally changed the role of religion in the curriculum, and the Tenth Amendment clearly established states' central roles in educating America's citizens. Many other reforms followed, such as the rise of state support for public education, improved teacher training, compulsory school attendance in the early to middle 19th century, and establishing standards, programs, and methods for high schools in the late 19th and early 20th century.

The rate of reform has increased in recent years, however, as education is increasingly viewed as essential to our country's economic success. During the past 30 years, educators, parents, and government officials have made repeated calls for attempts to improve education. Legislation at state and national levels has prompted educators to reconsider how teachers and public school students are taught and how their learning is evaluated. Reform movements have been initiated to improve the performance of both K–12 students and their teachers.

The challenges of improved learning for students in the 21st century raise a number of questions. Some of them include the following: What standards should be formed and how should we hold students and teachers accountable for these standards? How should we evaluate the learning progress of students in K–12 classrooms? How do current reform movements impact student learning, school climate, and the decision making of educators? And perhaps most important, will current reform efforts result in beneficial and lasting change? Keep these questions in mind as you study the articles in this section.

APRIL FOOLISHNESS:
THE 20TH ANNIVERSARY OF *A NATION AT RISK*

Gerald W. Bracey

During the past 30 years, repeated calls for educational reform in education have led to the publication of federal reports and mandates for change. A seminal document published in 1983, *A Nation at Risk: The Imperative for Educational Reform,* found our educational system and our economic system at risk because of these deficiencies. It suggested the need for education programs emphasizing rigor in math, science, and language arts as well as increases in the efficiencies and productivity of school communities. Increased attention to professional development and teacher induction programs were deemed essential for quality educators in every classroom.

Nationwide, in response to *A Nation at Risk,* committees were formed to define and establish standards for outstanding teaching, with the ultimate goal of improving student learning. Reformers proposed assessment standards and criteria designed to advance the performance of both students and teachers.

Gerald Bracey, a noted defender of education, argues that *A Nation at Risk* painted an overly dire picture of the state of education when, in fact, students in American schools were succeeding nationally and internationally. Limited data as well as unrealistic comparisons and selective reporting are among the weaknesses cited. As you read this article, try to answer the following question, which is at the core of Bracey's article: "How valid were the shortcomings of American education identified by *A Nation at Risk?*"

Think About This . . .

1. *A Nation at Risk* linked economic survival to educational excellence. How valid is that link? What other factors influence the health of the country's economy?

2. Bracey discusses some of the limitations of international comparisons of student performance between Japan and the United States. What are some of the factors educators and policy makers must consider when making comparisons between different groups of students?

3. International competition has been suggested as one way of improving the quality of U.S. schools. In what ways might competition improve school systems? In what ways might competition negatively impact schools?

4. As a teacher, what indicators, or forms of evidence, will you use to determine students' success in your classroom?

Twenty years ago this month (April, 2003), James Baker, Ronald Reagan's chief of staff, and Mike Deaver, Reagan's close advisor, defeated Attorney General Ed Meese in a battle of White House insiders. Over Meese's strong objections, they persuaded President Reagan to accept *A Nation at Risk: The Imperative for Educational Reform,* the report of the National Commission on

Excellence in Education. Secretary of Education Terrel Bell had convened the commission. In his memoir, *The Thirteenth Man,* Bell recalled that he had sought a

From Bracey, G. (2003). April foolishness: The 20th anniversary of A Nation at Risk. Phi Delta Kappan, 84(8), 616–621. *Reprinted with permission of the author.*

"Sputnik-type occurrence" that would dramatize all the "constant complaints about education and its effectiveness" that he kept hearing. Unable to produce such an event, Bell settled for a booklet with 36 pages of text and 29 pages of appendices about who had testified before the commission or who had presented it with a paper.

Meese and his fellow conservatives hated *A Nation at Risk* because it did not address any of the items on President Reagan's education agenda: vouchers, tuition tax credits, restoring school prayer, and abolishing the U.S. Department of Education. Baker called those issues "extraneous and irrelevant." He and the moderates on the White House staff thought the report contained a lot of good stuff to campaign on.[1]

The President accepted the report, but his speech acknowledging it largely ignored the report's content and simply reiterated his own agenda. According to Bell, the speech was virtually identical to the draft of a Reagan speech that he had read and rejected the previous day. *The Washington Post* called it a "homily." Bell tells of looking around as Reagan spoke and noticing that "Ed Meese was standing there with a big smile on his face."[2]

Despite Meese's sabotage, *A Nation at Risk* played big in the media. In the month following its publication, the *Washington Post* carried 28 stories about it. Few were critical. Joseph Kraft did excoriate conservatives for using the report to beat up on liberals without offering anything constructive. William Buckley chided it for recommendations that "you and I would come up with over the phone." The *New York Times* humor columnist Russell Baker contended that a sentence containing a phrase like "a rising tide of mediocrity" wouldn't be worth "more than a C in tenthgrade English." About the authors' writing overall, Baker said, "I'm giving them an A+ in mediocrity."[3]

Any students who were in first grade when *A Nation at Risk* appeared and who went directly from high school graduation into the work force have now been there almost nine years. Those who went on to bachelor's degrees have been on the job for nearly five years. Despite the dire predictions of national economic collapse without immediate education reform, our national productivity has soared since those predictions were made. What, then, are we to make of *A Nation at Risk* 20 years on?

The report's stentorian Cold War rhetoric commanded and still commands attention: "If an unfriendly foreign power had attempted to impose on America the mediocre educational performance that exists today, we might well have viewed it as an act of war" (p. 5).

By contrast, the report's recommendations were, as Buckley and others observed, banal. They called for nothing new, only for more of the same: more science, more mathematics, more computer science, more foreign language, more homework, more rigorous courses, more time-on-task, more hours in the school day, more days in the school year, more training for teachers, more money for teachers. Hardly the stuff of revolution. And even those mundane recommendations were based on a set of allegations of national risk that Peter Applebome of the *New York Times* later called "brilliant propaganda."[4] Indeed, the report was a veritable treasury of slanted, spun, and distorted statistics.

Before actually listing the indicators of risk, *A Nation at Risk* told America why those indicators meant that we were in such danger. Stop worrying so much about the Red Menace, the booklet said. The threat was not that our enemies would bomb us off the planet, but that our friends—especially Germany, Japan, and South Korea—would outsmart us and wrest control of the world economy: "If only to keep and improve on the slim competitive edge we still retain in world markets, we must dedicate ourselves to the reform of our educational system" (p. 7).

In penning this sentence, the members of the National Commission tightly yoked the nation's global competitiveness to how well our 13-year-olds bubbled in test answer sheets. The theory was, to be kind, without merit. A few, such as the historian Lawrence Cremin, saw these claims for the nonsense that they were. In *Popular Education and Its Discontents*, Cremin wrote:

> American economic competitiveness with Japan and other nations is to a considerable degree a function of monetary, trade, and industrial policy, and of decisions made by the President and Congress, the Federal Reserve Board, and the Federal Departments of the Treasury, Commerce, and Labor. Therefore, to conclude that problems of international competitiveness can be solved by educational reform, especially educational reform defined solely as school reform, is not merely utopian and millennialist, it is at best a foolish and at worst a crass effort to direct attention away from those truly responsible for doing something about competitiveness and to lay the burden instead on the schools. It is a device that has been used repeatedly in the history of American education.[5]

Alas, Cremin's wisdom was read only by educators—and not by very many of them, either. It certainly did not reach the policy makers who needed to absorb its message.

In fact, the theory propounded by *A Nation at Risk* became very popular in the late 1980s, when the nation slid into the recession that would cost George H. W. Bush a second term. One then heard many variations of "lousy schools are producing a lousy work force and that's killing us in the global marketplace." The economy, however, was not listening to the litany and came roaring back. By late 1993 and early 1994, headlines over stories about the economy expressed energy and confidence: "The American Economy: Back On Top" (*New York Times*), "America Cranks It Up" (*U.S. News & World Report*), and "Rising Sun Meets Rising Sam" (*Washington Post*).

Of course, it was *possible* that the comeback of the U.S. economy had actually been spurred by true and large improvements in the schools. It was at least as possible as that school improvements after Sputnik in 1957 had put a man on the moon in 1969. If it was true, though, it was a national secret. In fact, the school critics denied that there had been any gains. Three months after the *New York Times* declared the American economy to be number one in the world again, Lou Gerstner, CEO of IBM, took to that paper's op-ed page to declare "Our Schools Are Failing."[6] One reads Gerstner's essay in vain for any hint that schools are on the way up.

Indeed, evidence abounds that Gerstner and other school critics, especially those in the first Bush Administration, strove mightily to keep the dire warning issued by *A Nation at Risk* alive, and they continue to strive today. In 2001 Gerstner was back in both the *Washington Post* and the *New York Times*. The CEOs of Intel, Texas Instruments, and State Farm Insurance all penned op-ed essays for national newspapers about the poor quality of schools, as did Secretary of Health and Human Services Tommy Thompson, former Sen. John Glenn, former Gov. Pete DuPont of Delaware, and former Secretary of Education William Bennett.

During the years after the publication of *A Nation at Risk*, critics of the schools not only hyped the alleged bad news but also deliberately suppressed good news—or ignored it when they couldn't actually suppress it. The most egregious example of suppression—that we know about—was the suppression of the Sandia Report. Assembled in 1990 by engineers at Sandia National Laboratories in Albuquerque, the report presented 78 pages of graphs and tables and 78 pages of text to explain them. It concluded that, while there were many problems in public education, there was no systemwide crisis. Secretary of Energy James Watkins, who had asked for the report, called it "dead wrong" in the *Albuquerque Journal*. Briefed by the Sandia engineers who compiled it, Deputy Secretary of Education and former Xerox CEO David Kearns told them, "You

bury this or I'll bury you." The engineers were forbidden to leave New Mexico to discuss the report. Officially, according to Diane Ravitch, then assistant secretary of education, the report was undergoing "peer review" by other agencies (an unprecedented occurrence) and was not ready for publication.[7]

Lee Bray, the vice president of Sandia, supervised the engineers who produced the report. I asked Bray, now retired, about the fate of the report. He affirmed that it was definitely and deliberately suppressed.[8]

There were other instances of accentuating the negative in the wake of *A Nation at Risk*. In February 1992, a small international comparison in mathematics and science appeared.[9] America's ranks were largely, but not entirely, low, although actual scores were near the international averages. Secretary of Education Lamar Alexander and Assistant Secretary Ravitch held a press conference that garnered wide coverage in both print and electronic media. "An 'F' in World Competition," was *Newsweek's* headline. *Newsweek* had fallen for the hokum that high test scores mean international competitiveness. The *Washington Post* quoted Alexander as saying that the study's outcome was a "clear warning that even good schools are not properly preparing students for world competition."[10]

Critics would hammer the schools with this international study for years. In January 1996, for instance, a full-page ad in the *New York Times* showed the rankings of 14-year-olds in math. Out of 15 countries, the U.S. ranked 14th. "If this were a ranking in Olympic Hockey, we would be outraged," said the large-type ad. The immediate source of the ad was the Ad Council, but the sponsors were, in the order in which they were listed in the ad, the Business Roundtable, the U.S. Department of Education, the National Governors' Association, the American Federation of Teachers, and the National Alliance of Business.[11] Clearly, with friends like these, public schools needed no enemies.

Five months after the math/science study, another international comparison appeared, this one in reading. No one knew. *Education Week* discovered the study first, but only two months after the results were published and then only by accident. Robert Rothman, an *EW* reporter at the time, received a copy from a friend in Europe. American 9-year-olds were second in the world in reading among the 27 nations tested. American 14-year-olds were eighth out of 31 countries, but only Finland had a significantly higher score.

Education Week ran the story on its front page. *USA Today* played off the *EW* account with its own front-page piece. *USA Today's* article included a quote from Deputy

Assistant Secretary of Education Francie Alexander that reflected the Bush Administration's handling of such good news. She dismissed the study as irrelevant. (I was told by someone in the Office of Educational Research and Improvement that Ravitch handed the results to a group of researchers in the office and told the group to make the study disappear. The study was conducted by an educational organization based in The Hague, so, unlike the federally funded Sandia Report, it couldn't be suppressed. The group of researchers produced about six inches' worth of reports but couldn't make the results go away.)

While *A Nation at Risk* offered a litany of spun statistics about the risks the nation faced, its authors and fellow believers presented no actual *data* to support the contention that high test scores implied competitiveness —only the most circumstantial of evidence. The arguments heard around the country typically went like this: "Asian nations have high test scores. Asian nations ['Asian Tigers' we called them then], especially Japan, have experienced economic miracles. Therefore, the high test scores produced the economic good times." Thus the National Commission on Excellence in Education—and many school critics as well—made a mistake that no educated person should: they confused correlation with causation.

The "data" on education and competitiveness consisted largely of testimonials from Americans who had visited Japanese schools. On returning from Japan, educational researcher Herbert Walberg said that many features of the Japanese system should be adopted here. "I think it's portable. Gumption and willpower, that's the key."[12] The believers overlooked cautionary tales such as Ken Schooland's *Shogun's Ghosts: The Dark Side of Japanese Education* or the unpretty picture of Japanese schools presented in the education chapters of Karel van Wolferen's *The Enigma of Japanese Power*.

How representative were the Japanese schools that these American visitors saw? No one knows for sure, but doubtless they saw only the good side. I once asked Paul George of the University of Florida about the difficulty of gaining entrance to any less-than-stellar Japanese schools. George has spent years in Japanese schools of various kinds. His reply was succinct: "Look, there are 27 high schools in Osaka, ranked 1 to 27. You can easily get into the top few. You would have a much harder time getting into number 12 or number 13. Not even Japanese researchers can get into number 27."

The proponents of the test-score theory of economic health grew quiet after the Japanese discovered that the emperor's palace and grounds were actually *not* worth more than the entire state of California, a bit of misinformation widely disseminated as fact in Japan in the Eighties. Japan has foundered economically now for 12 years. The government admits that bad loans from banks to corporations amount to more than 10% of its Gross Domestic Product. Some estimate the size of the bad loans as high as 75% of GDP. We now see headlines such as "The Sinking Sun?" (*New York Times*) and "A Second Decade of Economic Woes?" (*Washington Post*).

The case of Japan presents a counterexample to the idea that high test scores ensure a thriving economy. But there is a more general method available to test the hypothesis put forth in *A Nation at Risk* that high scores equal competitiveness. For this test, I located 35 nations that were ranked in the Third International Mathematics and Science Study (TIMSS) eighth-grade tests and were also ranked for global competitiveness by the World Economic Forum (WEF), the Geneva think tank. Among these 35, the U.S. was number one in 2001. Among all 75 countries that the WEF ranked in its *Global Competitiveness Report 2001–2002*, the U.S. was number 2, trailing Finland. But Finland did not take part in the first round of TIMSS in 1995. The rank order correlation coefficient between test scores and competitiveness was $+.19$, virtually zero. If five countries that scored low on both variables were removed from the list, the coefficient actually became negative.

A Nation at Risk fabricated its case for the connection between education and competitiveness out of whole cloth, but to make its case for the dire state of American education, it did provide a lot of statistics. It was the spin on these numbers that led Peter Applebome to characterize the report as propaganda. Consider these.

• "Over half the population of gifted students do not match their tested ability with comparable achievement in school" (p. 8). I have asked both commissioners and members of the commission staff to tell me where this statistic came from. No one knows. And, of course, it makes no sense because 20 years ago, the principal instruments for identifying gifted students were achievement tests.

• "Average tested achievement of students graduating from college is also lower" (p. 9). Another nonexistent statistic.

• "There was a steady decline in science achievement scores of U.S. 17-year-olds as measured by national assessments of science in 1969, 1973, and 1977" (p. 9). Maybe, maybe not. The National Assessment of Educational Progress (NAEP) was not originally designed to produce trends, and the scores for 1969 and 1973 are backward extrapolations from the 1977 assessment. In any case, the declines were smaller for 9- and 13-year-olds and had already been wiped out by gains on the 1982 assessment. Scores for reading and math for all three ages assessed by NAEP were stable or inching upward. The commissioners thus had nine trendlines (three ages times three subjects), only one of which could be used to support crisis rhetoric. That was the only one they reported.

• "The College Board's Scholastic Aptitude Tests demonstrate a virtually unbroken decline from 1963 to 1980" (pp. 8–9). This was true. But the College Board's own investigative panel described a complex trend to which many variables contributed. It ascribed most of the decline to changes in who was taking the test—more minorities, more women, more students with mediocre high school records, more students from low-income families.

When the standards for the SAT were set, the students who received 500 as an average score were members of an elite: 10,654 high-schoolers, mostly living in New England. Ninety-eight percent were white, 61% were male, and 41% had attended private, college-preparatory high schools. In 1982, the year *A Nation at Risk's* commissioners labored, 988,270 seniors took the SAT. Eighty-four percent were white, 52% were female, 44% had mothers with a high school diploma or less, 27% came from families with incomes under $18,000 annually, and 81% attended public schools. All of those demographic changes are associated with lower scores on any test. It would have been very suspicious if the scores had *not* declined.

• "Average achievement of high school students on most standardized tests is now lower than 26 years ago when Sputnik was launched" (p. 8). The commissioners could not have known if this were true for "most standardized tests." At the time, most companies that produced standardized tests did not equate them from form to form over time. Instead, they used a "floating norm." Whenever they renormed their tests, whatever raw score corresponded to the 50th percentile became the new norm. Only the Iowa Tests of Basic Skills (ITBS, grades 3–8) and the Iowa Tests of Educational Development (ITED, grades 9–12) were referenced to a fixed standard and equated from form to form, beginning in 1955. In order to examine trends in test scores over time, one needs a test that is referenced to a fixed standard where each new form is equated to the earlier form. Among achievement tests, only the ITBS-ITED battery met this requirement.

It *was* true that on the ITED, scores were lower than when Sputnik was launched. Barely. The commissioners could have noted that the scores had risen for five consecutive years and that their statement about test scores and Sputnik didn't apply to most middle or elementary grades. The five-year rise had been preceded by a decade-long decline, which itself was preceded by a 10-year rise. Scores rose from 1955, a baseline year when the test was renormed and qualitatively changed as well, to about 1965. Scores then fell until about 1975, reversed, and climbed to *record high* levels by 1985 (something unnoticed or at least unmentioned by critics or the media).

It is instructive to examine what the nation was experiencing during the 10 years of falling test scores from 1965 to 1975. Just one year before the decline began, the Civil Rights Act of 1964 was passed, and 1965 opened with the Watts riots in Los Angeles. Urban violence then spread across the nation. The decade also brought us the Black Panthers, the Symbionese Liberation Army, Students for a Democratic Society, the Free Speech Movement, the Summer of Love, Woodstock, Altamont, Ken Kesey and his LSD-laced band of Merry Pranksters, the Kent State atrocities, and the 1968 Chicago Police Riot. Martin Luther King, Jr., Robert Kennedy, and Malcolm X were all assassinated. The nation became obsessed with and depressed by first the war in Vietnam and then Watergate. "Recreational drugs"—pot, acid, speed, Quaaludes, amyl nitrate—had become popular. If you remember the Sixties, the saying goes, you weren't there.

Popular books included such anti-Establishment tracts as *The Making of a Counter Culture, The Greening of America,* and *The Pursuit of Loneliness.* Books critical of schools included *Death at an Early Age, The Way It Spozed to Be, 36 Children, Free Schools, Deschooling Society, The Death of School, How Children Fail, The Student as Nigger, Teaching As a Subversive Activity,* and, most influential, Charles Silberman's 1970 tome, *Crisis in the Classroom.*

Under these conditions of social upheaval, centered in the schools and universities, it would have been a miracle if test scores had *not* fallen.

When *A Nation at Risk* appeared, universities and education associations fell over themselves lauding it. The education associations said that they welcomed the attention after a decade of neglect. "We are pleased education is back on the American agenda," wrote Paul Salmon, executive director of the American Association of School Administrators. They also said, later, that they didn't want to appear defensive by challenging the report. They also said, much later and in private, that they were certain that, with all these problems in education, money would surely follow. They were wrong.

As for the universities, well, a crisis in our schools always presents a great opportunity for educational researchers seeking to liberate money from foundations and governments. *A Nation at Risk* was to the research universities as September 11 was to the arms and security industries.

The National Commission on Excellence in Education commissioned more than 40 papers that laid out the crisis. Virtually all of them were written by academics. The report acknowledged only one that was written by someone actually working in a school, and it was not a commissioned work. Harvey Prokop, a teacher in San Diego, wrote a critique of a National Commission seminar in his town. He called it "Intelligence, Motivation, and the Quantity and Quality of Academic Work and Their Impacts on the Learning of Students."[13]

Alas, nothing else is new and, indeed, we must recognize that good news about public schools serves no one's reform agenda—even if it does make teachers, students, parents, and administrators feel a little better. Conservatives want vouchers and tuition tax credits; liberals want more resources for schools; free marketers want to privatize the schools and make money; fundamentalists want to teach religion and not worry about the First Amendment; Catholic schools want to stanch their student hemorrhage; home schooling advocates want just that; and various groups no doubt just want to be with "their own kind." All groups believe that they will improve their chances of getting what they want if they pummel the publics.

It has been 20 years, though, since *A Nation at Risk* appeared. It is clear that it was false then and is false now. Today, the laments are old and tired—and still false. "Test Scores Lag as School Spending Soars" trumpeted the headline of a 2002 press release from the American Legislative Exchange Council. Ho hum. The various special interest groups in education need another treatise to rally round. And now they have one. It's called No Child Left Behind. It's a weapon of mass destruction, and the target is the public school system. Today, our public schools are truly at risk.

Notes

1. Quoted in Terrel H. Bell, *The Thirteenth Man: A Reagan Cabinet Memoir* (New York: Free Press, 1988) p. 29.

2. Ibid., p. 131.

3. Joseph Kraft, "A Note to Conservatives: Come Off It," *Washington Post,* 3 May 1983, p. A-19; William F. Buckley, Jr., "The Obvious Solution: Tuition Tax Credits," *Washington Post,* 3 May 1983, p. A-19; and Russell Baker, "Beset by Mediocrity," *New York Times,* 30 April 1983, p. A-23.

4. Peter Applebome, "Dire Predictions Deflated: Johnny Can Add After All," *New York Times,* 11 June 1983, p. A-31.

5. Lawrence J. Cremin, *Popular Education and Its Discontents* (New York: Harper & Row, 1989), pp. 102–3.

6. Louis V. Gerstner, "Our Schools Are Failing: Do We Care?," *New York Times,* 27 May 1994, p. A-27.

7. Quoted in Julie Miller, "Report Questioning 'Crisis' in Education Triggers an Uproar," *Education Week,* 9 October 1991; and Diane Ravitch, letter to the editor, *Education Week,* 30 October 1991. The David Kearns quote comes from a personal communication from Sandia engineers, and the *Education Week* article stated that "Administration officials, particularly Mr. Kearns, reacted angrily at the meeting."

8. The report finally appeared in full in 1993 in the May/June issue of the *Journal of Educational Research* under the title "Perspectives on Education in America." Its authors were Sandia engineers C. C. Carson, R. M. Huelskamp, and T. D. Woodall.

9. Archie Lapointe, Nancy Mead, and Janice Askew, *Learning Mathematics* (Princeton, N.J.: Educational Testing Service, 1992); and Archie Lapointe, Janice Askew, and Nancy Mead, *Learning Science* (Princeton, N.J.: Educational Testing Service, 1992).

10. Mary Jordan, "Students Test Below Average in World, U.S. Fares Poorly in Math, Science," *Washington Post,* 6 February 1992, p. A-1.

11. *New York Times,* 31 January 1996.

12. Quoted in Keith B. Richburg, "Japanese Education: Admired but Not Easily Imported," *Washington Post,* 19 October 1985, p. A-1.

13. Harvey Prokop, "Intelligence, Motivation, and the Quantity and Quality of Academic Work and Their Impacts on the Learning of Students," a critique of the National Commission on Excellence in Education seminar, "The Student's Role in Learning," submitted to the National Commission on Excellence in Education, 1982.

HIGH STANDARDS FOR WHOM?

Donald B. Gratz

Reform can affect many different aspects of education. One of these aspects is that of standards. Initiating changes in education through the development of standards is not a new phenomenon. Historically, reform movements have followed a pattern where problems are often identified in considerable detail. However, solutions often lack specificity and are portrayed as global panaceas, and reform goals do not always match the realities and demands of classrooms and schools.

Donald Gratz argues that for standards to result in lasting change, several factors must be considered. First, the purposes of standards must be clearly defined. Educators must determine whether standards are designed to bolster competition or to promote the success of low achievers. Second, educators must be realistic in their expectations for change.

As you read this article ask yourself, "What problems should educators avoid as they attempt to use standards to improve education?"

Think About This . . .

1. According to Gratz, there are multiple purposes for professional standards (e.g., standards for testing, as the basis for high-stakes testing, and punishment for lack of improvement). Which of these purposes for professional standards seem the most valuable or useful? Why?
2. What are the "unintended consequences" of standards and high-stakes testing described by Gratz? How could these be minimized?
3. In what ways can the use of standards improve the educational system? What are some of the potential limitations?
4. Describe the assessment practices you will use in your classroom. In what ways will your assessment plans reduce the likelihood of the "unintended consequences" described by Gratz?

Reforms in education tend to follow a pattern. First, the statements of the problems are more compelling, complete, and accurate than the proposed solutions. Second, the reforms overpromise, but underdeliver. Third, even the most promising initiatives usually fail when tried on a broader scale. Some are "adopted" in name but not truly implemented; others are implemented too quickly, too rigidly, with too little attention to differences between schools, or with too little regard for unintended consequences. Finally, too many education reforms are driven by political ideology rather than by what actually works in schools. Given this pattern, it is hardly surprising that most reforms have little lasting impact on schools.

If success were easier to measure, of course, the most successful practices could be identified. But educational accountability is still in its infancy, consisting primarily of average scores for an entire school on national or state tests. Testing is often handled poorly, and the tests are changed regularly, so reliable long-term data are rarely available. In fact, while we know much about how children learn, few districts can demonstrate what works for which students in which settings. In the absence of proof, opinion reigns, and reform

From Gratz, D. (2000). *High standards for whom?* Phi Delta Kappan, *81(9), 681–687. Reprinted with permission of the author.*

ideas proliferate. How are we to know whether the remedy is a new wonder drug or more snake oil?

The biggest current reform initiative is "world-class" standards and accountability. But as with past reforms, the compelling ideas underlying the standards movement are being distorted by poor implementation and political opportunism. Indeed, because many states are implementing standards and accountability for political rather than educational purposes, this reform will likely follow the familiar pattern. Standards will be adopted in word but not in deed by politicians and educational opportunists. They will be misused and abused for political gain. Voices of moderation will be drowned out, and negative outcomes will be obscured. When they fail to produce the promised results, teachers and students will be blamed.

An emerging rebellion—driven by negative consequences for children, parents, and teachers—will cause political support to wane. Stories of overstressed children and teachers will replace the success stories now so popular in the press. Politicians will find new villains to excoriate. The original ideas will be lost or judged failures, the good discarded along with the bad. Finally, the movement itself will be abandoned in favor of the next hot idea. Some effects will certainly linger, but the promised results will not be achieved.

If standards and accountability are to avoid this fate, they must be more than just a world-class sound bite for political leaders. If standards and accountability are to *improve* schools and help children learn rather than *punish* teachers, schools, and children for political advantage, advocates must ensure that the standards are appropriate, the tests are fair, and the implementation is reasonable. They must wrest control from the politicians and opportunists who are currently calling the shots and reshape the movement to serve educational rather than political ends.

Purposes and Professional Standards

Standards grow out of the century-old debate over tracking, the 50-year-old discovery of the impact of teacher expectations, the 40-year struggle for educational equity, and the timeless desire for highly skilled (but compliant) workers to drive the nation's economic engine. These trends have converged to create support—temporarily and for various reasons—from politicians, educators, and business leaders.

Standards have two primary purposes. The first is economic: to address the concern that America is losing its competitiveness and the belief that both the country's and the students' best interests require demanding more from each child and each school. Fed by fear that we are falling behind other countries and fueled by international studies of achievement, the need to push students to learn more and faster has become a national obsession. Our students can't compete because of poor preparation, the argument goes. America is falling ever further behind, and our economy will suffer.

The second purpose of standards is to address the disparity between high- and low-achieving students. Proponents argue that raising standards for all students, teachers, and schools—especially in urban schools where students fall way below current standards—will improve education for poor and minority children. America's growing income gap is made worse, they say, by a growing education gap. Expecting little of students places them at great disadvantage. All children can live up to much higher expectations, and most will.

Standards proponents Marc Tucker and Judy Codding put it this way:

> One of the most striking features of countries that are more successful than we in educating their students to high standards is the assumption made by parents, teachers, and the students themselves that the students can do it. By contrast, the most important obstacle to high student achievement in the United States is our low expectations for students—not just students who are poor and come from minority backgrounds, but . . . most of our students.[1]

Failure is built into our system, they argue. What we have is "a vast sorting system based largely on social class and racial background, with the outcome determined for many children before the game began."[2]

In years past, the same kind of analysis led to more *child-centered,* rather than *test-centered,* approaches to learning. But today's standards proponents point to students' weak motivation to take tough courses and to work hard in school as the source of failure. The answer, they conclude, is competition. Students in Germany and Japan are motivated to compete for the best jobs. Poor grades or lack of a diploma may mean no job or no access to college. American students and schools need an incentive to strive for higher levels of performance. Standards and accountability have emerged as the means to combat these problems. After a brief fling with national standards, proponents have shifted their efforts to the states, and it is state action that seems likely to derail the legitimate purposes of standards. Before taking up these state actions, let us review the professional standards for the standards themselves, drawn from sources across the political spectrum.

Standards for Standards

There is significant agreement on the standards for standards. Proponents agree that standards should be grounded in core academic disciplines and should cover what students should know (content) and be able to do (performance). Moreover, they should address only the essentials. "A laundry list that satisfies everyone will leave teachers right where they are now—facing the impossible task of trying to rush through overstuffed textbooks and ridiculously long sets of curriculum objectives."[3] Standards should *not* "prescribe teaching methods, devise classroom strategies, or substitute for lesson plans. Standards are about ends, not means."[4] The choice of means should be left to local discretion. Finally, standards should be crystal clear to everyone: students, parents, and teachers.

Most proponents agree that standards should be "rigorous" and "world class." Some refer to standards in Germany, France, Japan, or England and say that ours should be "at least as high."[5] Furthermore, and most critically, students should be compared with the agreed-upon standard, not with one another.

All the major proponents agree that standards must have broad support among teachers and the general public. Ownership of the standards is crucial. Even where states have created standards, districts should "engage in the process of examining, refining, and supplementing the state standards. There is simply no other way to have people 'own' the importance and the power of standards or the standards themselves."[6] Finally, standards imply assessment. That is, they must have "teeth." Accountability should be tied to standards for students, teachers, and schools in such a way that everyone knows what is expected and that no allowances will be made for substandard performance.

Standards for Testing

Given this focus on accountability, standards for testing are also critical. And such standards already exist in the *Standards for Educational and Psychological Testing*[7] and many other sources. To begin with, each test should be evaluated for *construct* and *content validity,* ensuring that it measures what it purports to measure (content) and that the constructs it measures are relevant and fair. For job-related tests, such as teacher certification, constructs must be relevant to the actual job to be performed, and the content of the test must fairly measure those constructs. For tests measuring student achievement, the constructs are academic standards. They need to be relevant, age-appropriate, and fair. A separate bias review, sometimes called a sensitivity review, attempts to make certain that material that is irrelevant to the construct does not favor or derogate any particular group.

In addition to the test itself, the *passing score* must be valid as well. A test that fairly measures content can still fail too many students who should pass or pass too many who should fail. The passing score on a test used for important decisions must be carefully considered and independently validated. Finally, each aspect of test creation and validation should be documented in a *technical manual* or *review*. This is time-consuming, but fairness demands that tests, particularly high-stakes tests, be demonstrably valid and reliable.

High-Stakes Testing

Many states have decided that their assessments must be "high-stakes" ones—tests that significantly determine opportunities and outcomes for the test-takers. Today, radically more difficult tests (sometimes poorly designed) are being used to determine who will graduate, who will be licensed to teach, and which schools will get rewards or sanctions. In a recent study of high-stakes testing, the National Research Council concluded that educational decisions "that will have a major impact on a test taker should not be made solely or automatically on the basis of a single test score." Even if the test is a *good* one. Furthermore, the NRC strongly urged that decisions about children below age 8 or grade 3 should not be made on the basis of such a test.[8] A 1998 study of the Chicago schools reached a similar conclusion: that the district's much-vaunted improvement should not be judged solely by standardized test scores.[9]

Punishment or Improvement

Mandatory tests are the main mechanism for implementing state standards. But it is important to note that accountability can be exercised for more than one purpose. Methodologies differ depending on the intent. As now implemented in most states, standards and accountability appear to be designed primarily to identify and punish "poor-performing" schools and students. If that were not so, leaders pushing accountability would focus on how much students within a given school have improved rather than on total scores at one school compared with scores at others.

Accountability systems designed to *help schools improve* and *help students learn* will downplay cross-school comparisons in favor of improvement for individual children. They will give students time to reach the goals. They will break down or disaggregate data to make sure that all students in a school are improving, and they will use those data to identify and learn from the "pockets of success." A suburban school may do well for its college-bound students but serve its non-college-bound, low-income, or minority students poorly. Aggregate test scores are excellent tools for identifying targets for punishment, but they mask these discrepancies. Accountability for the purpose of improvement highlights them.

Standards for All

Surprisingly, many states appear to have excused themselves from applying high professional standards to their own actions. Most focus on punishing poor-performing schools, creating great political opportunity but little improvement. In many states, standards and tests drive most of the curriculum: almost all states measure students against one another at a specific time rather than providing time to meet goals. High-stakes tests are being used as the sole determiners for important decisions, even for young children. Some of these tests bear little relation to the adopted standards; others are poorly constructed, not validated, too hard, politically driven, and shrouded in secrecy. Many districts have their own high-quality standards and assessment rubrics, but statedriven tests are currently setting the agenda. These implementation policies, already breeding skepticism and resistance, seem likely to widen the gap between the educational haves and have-nots, a sad irony for a movement intended to increase equity for all children.

Politics and the Problem of Implementation

Public institutions are often accused of having entrenched bureaucracies with scant ability to accomplish even the simplest improvements. They are highly resistant to change. As Charles Lindblom observed many years ago, bureaucratic action and slow change can be understood as adaptive measures that help public institutions survive in a hostile and rapidly changing environment.[10] Imagine the chaos if schools transformed themselves with each new educational idea. This organizational attribute helps suggest how to proceed in order to create lasting change. In both education and business, a constituency for change must be developed over time, with maximum local latitude and slow, careful implementation. The notion that a school district can fully implement substantive change in a year or two is absurd.

Value of Failure

Politics, by contrast, requires decisive action. Politicians thrive on tough talk. Instead of proposing complex solutions to complex problems, many politicians seek villains to fight. Government has been an enemy of choice for years. Attacking the bureaucracy wins elections; tilting at perceived governmental windmills has advanced many careers. Candidates promise to root out corruption, fire lazy bureaucrats, and get government off our backs. If one believes the current political rhetoric, lazy, incompetent teachers, administrators, and students are destroying the fabric of society and endangering the economy. Naturally, we need tough politicians to take on these demons.

In this context, consider the critical value of tough new standards and massive failure, whether by students, schools, or aspiring teachers. High standards are set. State tests, which provide apparent objectivity, are developed or chosen. Suddenly we have *proof* of massive incompetence, sloth, and ineffectiveness. What politician can resist the temptation to take a tough stance, even if it means using invalid or unfair assessments, accelerating the speed of improvement demanded, ignoring complaints about fairness, or castigating innocent people caught in the middle? The answer, it appears, is not many. Forcing tough standards on "failing schools" has helped elect many sitting governors and legislators. But will these same politicians (or their successors) provide the long-term support those tough standards require?

Linking state-driven assessments to state-developed standards has created political salience for education reform and given politicians a marvelous opportunity to show their mettle. But in the rush to implement tough tests and standards, professional standards have not been maintained. The failure of children, teachers, and schools to meet standards—no matter how unclear, inadequate, or unfair—has created a crisis of great value to some politicians. Massachusetts made headlines last year for the nation's dumbest crop of aspiring teachers, while most of Virginia's students are apparently headed for failure. California has developed and mandated its own state standards, but it is measuring them with a nationally normed test that does not match those standards. It is now "augmenting" that test with new tests aligned to its standards, but it may reconstitute hundreds of schools and flunk thousands of students before it can validate and use the augmentation. How likely is it that these crises will remain politically valuable in the coming years, particularly if the "solutions" don't work or produce negative consequences?

Despite evidence to the contrary, state officials argue that their tests are reasonable, have been "validated" by "panels of experts," will not result in teaching to the test, and will not cause students or teachers to give up, cheat, or drop out. They say that tough tests are needed to promote world-class standards. These tests and standards often fail to meet professional standards, but they do meet the standards for political expedience. They make headlines, provide the veneer of objectivity, and offer up plenty of villains to be denounced. They provide a political platform, as Gerald Bracey has noted regarding Virginia, but "the results mean a great loss of credibility for the standard-setting procedure. There's no evidence that setting these standards results in higher performance."[11] There is evidence, however, that they are causing resistance.

Redefining the Problem

This massive educational experiment has been based primarily on the first purpose stated above: fear that American students can't compete in the world marketplace and are endangering America's future. But, as columnist Robert Samuelson has asked, "If our students are so bad, why is the economy so good?"[12] The Japanese schools to which we still compare ours unfavorably have not kept Japan from deep economic problems. Furthermore, as Henry Levin has noted, "There is no doubt that education, more generally, is an important determinant of earnings. But there is an enormous chasm between this fact and the assertion that new educational performance standards for students will lead to greater economic productivity."[13]

And many of the strongest supporters of standards have begun to shift the grounds for their support. Even the Hudson Institute, which in 1987 equated higher standards in schools with international competitiveness, now emphasizes "equitable distribution of income" as the reason for standards.[14] While the significant disparity between and within American schools is a serious problem, the political need to focus on competition with the Germans and Japanese still drives the movement for "world-class" standards and punitive accountability in most states. Unfortunately, a system of standards designed to level the playing field between urban and suburban schools—which might help

students who are struggling—would not look the same as one designed to be the world's toughest.

Most suburban schools today teach such topics as algebra, biology, and Shakespeare years earlier than they did a generation ago. Today's students also have more homework. Those who do the work get into the best colleges in the world. These students don't need higher standards. By contrast, some schools are inferior, and students in them learn little. While *equivalent* standards and accountability based on how much each child *improves* might address the equity questions, the relentless drive toward ever higher standards serves to *widen* the performance gap between and within schools. In Texas, for example, higher standards and high-stakes tests have resulted in much higher dropout and failure rates for poor and minority students.[15]

By all means let us have standards. But let us also design them appropriately, implement them fairly, provide help rather than punishment, and recognize improvement for students from their various starting places. Finally, let us apply high standards to everyone, including those political and educational leaders who have enforced standards on others. That would be real reform.

Unintended Consequences

Beyond this political and bureaucratic hypocrisy, the biggest reason for the growing disenchantment with standards and high-stakes tests is that the unintended consequences of ill-considered implementation in many states are already being felt. In service of the contradictory goals described above, we are creating higher levels of competition and stiffer sanctions for "low" performance, substantially increasing the pressure on students and schools.

In response, schools are resorting to a range of improvement strategies. Some of them are promising. Schools in many states are upgrading and realigning curricula, training parents to help their children, creating faculty task forces to draw up plans for improvement, and providing extra help to struggling students. Chicago's summer schools are a frequently cited example.

At the same time, many schools and teachers are resorting to such strategies as piling on homework, abolishing recess for young children, cheating on tests, transferring pressure to students, flunking more students, teaching to the test, and seeking ways to rid themselves of low performers. It is easy to fault schools for taking such actions, but these tactics are the direct result of "rigorous" standards, unfair tests, harsh sanctions, unrealistically stringent expectations for change, implementation strategies designed to punish rather than improve, and a system built to satisfy political rather than educational needs. Below I list some of the unintended consequences already emerging for children and families. And remember, most of the high stakes—retaining students, preventing them from graduating, and reconstituting schools—have not yet been applied.

Stress

In his 1981 book, *The Hurried Child,* David Elkind wrote that "today's child has become the unwilling, unintended victim of overwhelming stress—stress borne of rapid, bewildering social change and constantly rising expectations. . . . Tests are now determining school curriculum, and the conduct of teaching is beginning to look more and more like that of a factory foreman than that of a true teacher."[16] That was 1981. What about today? As of the beginning of the 1999–2000 school year, 19 states had "exit exams" that students must pass in order to graduate. Seven more were planning similar tests. Six states planned to tie promotion to tests. Louisiana has tests for fourth and eighth grades, for example, and Ohio will soon have a fourth-grade test.[17]

If anyone doubts that increasing stress is a consequence of such testing, there is plenty of evidence. Homework has increased, free play has been curtailed, recess has been eliminated, and pressured teachers are pressuring children. The comments of a South Carolina kindergarten teacher, feeling the pressure of that state's third-grade test, are telling. "I used to teach letters of the week," notes the teacher. But times have changed. They can "play and nap" at home, she says. "They are here to learn."[18]

We used to believe that play was the work of young children, that play was how they learned. The headmaster of an elite private school draws the following conclusion from statistics about the dramatic drop in free play among preschoolers. "For those of us in education who know that childhood's 'free play' is as critically effective in building SAT scores as time spent on 'academics,' these data explain, in part, why today's children arrive at our privileged school doors with social skills and vocabularies *far* less developed than those of prior generations" (emphasis in original).[19]

Homework

Despite the apparently widespread belief that kids are lazy and homework a thing of the past, *Time* last year highlighted too much homework as a serious and growing problem. In a cover article, Romesh Ratnesar wrote, "The sheer quantity of nightly homework and the difficulty of assignments can turn ordinary weeknights into four-hour library-research excursions, leave kids in tears and parents with migraines, and generally transform the placid refuge of home life into a tense war zone."[20] Part of the problem, he argues, is parents who push their children hard and demand that teachers deliver enough "academic rigor" to get students into top secondary schools and colleges. But the greater part comes from increased pressure from schools. In 1981, the year *The Hurried Child* was published, the average time that grade school students spent on homework was 85 minutes a week; by 1997, it had grown to 134 minutes, an increase of nearly 60%.

The *Time* story also noted that some urban schools assign little or no homework because the students don't do it, while many suburban schools are piling on more than ever. Mandatory standards are supposed to make lazy students and teachers change their ways. But if motivated students who have internalized the high expectations of their parents and teachers have trouble completing their homework, students who struggle with academic work, who don't care, who work long hours, whose parents are working when the students are at home, or whose households provide little support or room for homework will have even more difficulty. Pressure from homework that is too hard or too long is a symptom of problems in some schools, just as the absence of homework is a symptom of problems in others. Until parents put a stop to homework overload, which they eventually will, the most likely effect of this trend will be more pressure on students and an increasing disparity between the achievement of students in suburban and urban schools—just the opposite of the intent of standards.

Recess

Recess for elementary children has become another casualty of high standards in many schools. "Across the country," according to *Education USA,* "educators are doing away with the once standard breaks, citing increasing academic pressure as the primary reason." Child advocates estimate that as many as 40% of the nation's 16,000 school districts—including large districts such as Atlanta and Orlando—have either curtailed or eliminated recess.

Educators engaged in this practice say that "time, safety, and academic pressure" are all factors that contribute to the decline of recess. Eliminating the breaks allows students to spend more time in the classroom. "We are intent on improving academic performance," explains Benjamin Canada, who served as Atlanta's school superintendent before taking over the system in Portland, Oregon. "You don't do that by having kids hanging from monkey bars."[21] Some schools have not only eliminated recess but significantly scaled back the lunch period. Others have combined physical education and recess, providing some physical activity a few times a week, but no "free time" for children.

Child development experts are concerned about this trend, for reasons of physical and mental fitness and social development. Most adults get coffee breaks, but children need breaks much more than adults. Children who get breaks are more alert and pay better attention. They also need unstructured social time to learn to interact with their peers. Eliminating free play and physical activity for children runs counter to both research on child development and common sense. And it will not improve achievement. Parents in some cities have prevented the elimination of recess, and child advocates are fighting back. But if this is the result of world-class standards and high-stakes tests, how long will they last? How long *should* they last?

Social Promotion

Critics complain about students who are passed on year after year without learning, a problem that affects many students in some cities. "Social promotion" is another dream issue for politicians, another chance to get tough. However, flunking or retaining students is a "solution" with an unbroken record of failure. In many cases, researchers say, retaining students actually pushes them to drop out of school. "If you look at the evidence about kids retained, they don't get better over the long term. They fall further behind," according to Arthur Reynolds.[22] "Students who have been held back," says Robert Hauser, chair of the National Research Council's panel on testing, "are much more likely to drop out before completing high school." He cites a Chicago study that found that retaining students in grades 1–8 increased the dropout rate by 12%, corrected for student background. This is a huge negative effect. Unless massive extra help is provided, large-scale retention may dramatically increase the dropout rate. As Hauser observes, "We should know that a new policy works before we try it out on a large scale."[23]

If more students drop out, of course, test scores will go up. But does the goal of increasing test scores justify the probable impact on struggling students? The problem may be real, but the solution has been shown to make things worse.

Motivation

Promoters of world-class standards argue that competition pushes students to excel, but human motivation is more complex than this one-size-fits-all approach. There is no single problem of student motivation, nor is there a single solution. Moreover, stiff competition already exists for entry into the best colleges and access to the best jobs, and students motivated by this kind of competition already work very hard. State tests mean little to these students, but they instill the fear of failure in others. Studies have repeatedly shown that such methods *reduce* learning for many students.

Students who have slacked off may work harder, but others simply stop working in order to justify the expected failure. "Motivation experts say many elements of the current push to hold schools and students to higher academic standards work against the very classroom conditions that research has shown can spark a desire to learn," according to *Education Week*.[24]

Labeling students failures because they do not reach a particular standard or national norm at a particular point in time counters one of the central standards for standards. Yet most states do just that. With standards rising at every level, the only chance students have to "catch up" is in high school, where most states allow a retake. By that point, however, students think they know how smart or dumb they are. Turning up the pressure will not help these youngsters care more or achieve more. Mandated after-school and summer programs may help some students, but not those who already believe they are failures. Thoughtfully implemented standards, along with the funding to create instructional alternatives, might help. Sanctions against schools are supposed to lead to such innovation. The current sledgehammer approach seems more likely to drive students away from learning.

Increasing Inequity

One of the fundamental reasons cited for developing high standards has always been that students who graduate from a low-standards school will be unable to compete in the marketplace, thus increasing the pronounced economic division that already exists in our country. But high-stakes tests don't solve this problem; they make it worse. In Texas, for example, low-income and minority students have been denied graduation in much greater numbers than other students. Will this help their economic prospects? Will high-stakes tests force more students to drop out? Will states be willing to fund the summer and after-school programs, tutoring, additional professional development, and the other strategies these students need to succeed? There has been no great funding bonanza so far. As of January 1999, only 11 states offered extra funding to help schools pay for improvements, and, while the tests affect every school, the funding does not.[25]

Summary

Negative Consequences

In a high-stress world, greater pressure on schools is creating greater pressure on children and families. Policies governing homework, recess, retention, and testing are ignoring research on student learning and motivation in favor of conventional wisdom and political expediency. Inconsistent, hurried, thoughtless, mean-spirited, and politically motivated implementation of standards and accountability is leading to negative consequences for children.

In response, schools are devising some policies that may help, but they are also cheating on tests, teaching to the test, and transferring pressure to the students who need the most help. The results of this pressure are still unclear, but the possibilities are troubling. Forcing schools to adopt increasingly rigid curricula, with more knowledge of more subjects expected at earlier ages, seems unlikely to produce the desired results. Retaining low-performing students because it is politically expedient to do so is likely to increase the number of dropouts—the opposite of the stated goal of increasing the achievement of "failing" students. Certainly, passing students from grade to grade without regard to what they have learned is a serious problem in some districts, but flunking struggling students is demonstrably not the solution.

By downplaying children's need to play, to be active, to experiment, and to develop socially and physically, we may be producing children who are physically unfit, mentally uncreative, and socially inept. "When young people's developmental needs for protection and nurture are ignored," Elkind warns, "when their human differences in growth rates and behavior are deemed deviant, and when they are given little or no space to live and to grow, they are stressed."[26] He continues:

On every measure that we have, children and youth today are doing less well than they did hardly a quarter century ago. On tests of strength, endurance, and general muscle tone, young people today perform less well than did young people of comparable age even ten years ago. There has been a 50% increase in obesity in children and youth. . . . Many of our curriculum-focused schools, in an effort to cut costs or to increase time spent on academic work, have eliminated recess . . . there is not time during the school day for young people to get up, run about, and play. . . . The postmodern perception of children as competent and teenagers as sophisticated has resulted in pushing advanced curricula down even further into the lower grades.[27]

Elkind links these pressures to the increase in escapist and destructive behaviors. Higher standards and harsh categorizations may lead more youths to decide that they can't win in the race. It seems likely, therefore, that greater pressure on "low-performing" schools and students will result in greater numbers of dropouts—both because they can't do the work and because they don't see the point. These are not intended consequences of high standards, but they are the predictable results of greater stress and the breakdown of supportive environments.

Rebellion

The signs of rebellion grow daily. Evidence includes regular reports of increased pressure, competition between suburban communities for the highest test scores, cheating on tests, cheating on test reporting, outrage over the elimination of recess, and lawsuits over and boycotts of high-stakes tests.

The ideas underlying the standards and accountability movement have merit, and the inequities among schools must be addressed. But if standards and accountability are to survive and support student learning, significant changes in implementation must occur. Educators, parents, and other taxpayers must demand that state leaders strictly follow professional standards. They must make sure that the impact of new policies is evaluated. They must publicize what is known about how children learn and are motivated, and they must ensure that children are treated in accordance with their developmental needs.

It is not too late to slow down the runaway train that is the standards movement. But that effort must be made soon. If standards were implemented as they have been so often described, and if multiple accountability measures were used to improve schools rather than to punish them, real school improvement might follow. If the creators and proponents of standards held themselves to high professional and ethical standards, everyone would benefit. Unfortunately, continuing the tradition of education reform, political expediency is once again trumping educational need. The vision for standards is far from the reality, the list of unintended consequences is growing longer, and new signs of the coming rebellion are appearing every day.

Notes

1. Mare S. Tucker and Judy B. Codding, *Standards for Our Schools* (San Francisco: Jossey-Bass, 1998), p. 33.

2. Ibid., pp. 33–34.

3. Matthew Gandal, "Not All Standards Are Created Equal," *Educational Leadership*, March 1995, p. 19.

4. Chester E. Finn, Jr., Michael J. Petrilli, and Gregg Vanourek, "The State of State Standards: Four Reasons Why Most 'Don't Cut the Mustard,'" *Education Week*, 11 November 1998, p. 39.

5. Tucker and Codding, p. 45; and Gandal, p. 19.

6. Christopher T. Cross, "The Standards Wars: Some Lessons Learned," *Education Week*, 21 October 1998, pp. 32–35.

7. American Psychological Association, American Educational Research Association, and the National Council of Measurement in Education, *Standards for Educational and Psychological Testing* (Washington, D.C.: American Psychological Association, 1999).

8. National Research Council, *High Stakes* (Washington, D.C.: National Academy Press, 1999); "Tests Alone Shouldn't Decide a Student's Fate, NRC Warns," *Education Today*, 9 September 1998, pp. 4–5; and "NRC Criticizes High-Stakes Testing," *FairTest Examiner*, Fall 1998, p. 1.

9. Lynn Olson, "Study Warns Against Reliance on Testing Data," *Education Week*, 25 March 1998.

10. Charles E. Lindblom, "The Science of Muddling Through," *Public Administration Review*, vol. 19, 1959, pp. 79–88.

11. Gerald W. Bracey, "Mass Failure on Va Test Shakes Up Standards Drive," *Education USA*, 25 January 1999, p. 6.

12. Quoted in Mary Ann Zehr, "Weak Scores, Strong Economy: How Can This Be?," *Education Week*, 1 April 1998.

13. Quoted in Gerald W. Bracey, "The Eighth Bracey Report on the Condition of Public Education," *Phi Delta Kappan*, October 1998, p. 123.

14. Zehr, op. cit.

15. Peter Schmidt, "Judge Sees No Bias in Tex. Test for High-School Graduation," *Chronicle of Higher Education*, 21 January 2000, p. A-27.

16. David Elkind, *The Hurried Child* (Reading, Mass.: Addison-Wesley, 1981), pp. 3, 53.

17. Robert C. Johnston, "Turning Up the Heat," *Quality Counts* (Bethesda, Md.: Editorial Projects in Education, 11 January 1999), p. 57.

18. Kathleen Kennedy Manzo, "Trickling Down," *Education Week*, 18 November 1998, p. 27.

19. Nicholas S. Thacher, "Truth, Statistics, and Entertainment," *Education Week*, 24 February 1999, p. 51.

20. Romesh Ratnesar, "The Homework Ate My Family," *Time*, 25. January 1999, p. 56.

21. "More Schools Are Giving Kids a Break from Recess," *Education USA*, 11 January 1999, p. 11.

22. Quoted in Johnston, p. 55.

23. Robert M. Hauser, "What If We Ended Social Promotion?," *Education Week*, 7 April 1999, p. 64.

24. Debra Viadero, "Lighting the Flame." *Education Week*, 10 February 1999, p. 24.

25. "Improving Low-Performing Schools," *Quality Counts* (Bethesda, Md.: Editorial Projects in Education, 11 January 1999), p. 95.

26. David Elkind, *Ties That Stress: The New Family Imbalance* (Cambridge, Mass.: Harvard University Press, 1994), p. 188.

27. Ibid., p. 202.

ACCOUNTABILITY: WHAT'S WORTH MEASURING?

Mary Anne Raywid

Accountability, like standards, is at the core of most current reform efforts, but Mary Anne Raywid asks, accountability for what? In answering this question, Raywid identifies important student outcomes that go beyond the types of learning that can be easily measured by paper-and-pencil tests. She also identifies important expectations for schools, criteria that can be used to gauge their effectiveness. As you read this article ask yourself, "How well do standardized tests measure all of the important goals of schooling?"

Think About This . . .

1. How is accountability different from standards-based education? Why is one more desirable than the other?
2. What important learning goals for schools does Raywid identify? Which of these are most important? Why?
3. What important expectations for schools does Raywid identify? Which of these are most important? Why?
4. What type of "unobtrusive" measures could you use in your classroom to assess the effectiveness of your instruction? What would they tell you?

I wish the accountability movement that is now so strong had been launched for different reasons. It emerged, of course, from a growing mistrust of public schools and just how well they are serving us. Because that sentiment continues strong and is likely to be with us for some time to come, the press for accountability is likely to remain with us as well.

We can't beat the accountability movement, so we had better join it and try to shape it. Actually, there are things we can do that could turn it into a very positive force. After all, at root, accountability demands an openness on the part of the education system that we've not always seen and are all entitled to expect: information on just how well or how poorly each public school is doing. And what accountability then demands is that something be done about those schools that are failing.

I am very sympathetic to both these demands. Regarding the first, surely the public is entitled to know how the schools it pays for are faring. If they are *public* schools, surely information about them should be accessible to all. And regarding the second, there are schools in some places that have been failing for years, with little or nothing being done about it. In what was a new and very different kind of move in 1983, the chancellor of New York City's schools simply closed down a high school that was failing. Its numbers had been steadily worsening each year until finally it was failing, expelling, or otherwise pushing out 93% of its students. Only 7% of those enrolled were graduating. It is unforgivable to let things deteriorate to such a point.

Thus I am receptive to the idea of holding schools accountable and of forcing the failing ones to change. To my mind, accountability is a good thing. But the word is often used interchangeably with standards-based education, and they are not quite the same thing. For reasons that I hope will become clear, I think we ought to talk in terms of—and insist on—*accountability* rather than *standards-based education*. Doing so is by no means an abandonment of standards, but rather a broadening of concern.

The hard questions begin with "Accountable for what?" It seems reasonable to expect schools to do what they set out to do and thus to hold them accountable for fulfilling their own goals. This means that some school-to-school differences in accountability make sense, given the differences among us as to the goals to be sought in our schools. But there is also a great deal of commonality as to what we want schools to accomplish with our children. It is this that concerns me here: the goals and expectations for schools that I believe we share.

I've put the matter in the form of the question "What's worth measuring?" Of course, what's worth measuring depends on what's worth learning and acquiring and, hence, what's worth teaching and cultivating. What's worth measuring also depends on our expectations about the conditions and circumstances under which this teaching and cultivating ought to occur.

Our Goals for Children

There are really an awful lot of things we want our children to learn and our schools to teach them. We also have a number of different *kinds* of goals that we want to see fulfilled with and for our children, and we have some surrounding expectations that we want to see met. I'm going to present six rather different kinds of things that are worth learning—and thus worth measuring. I don't agree with the psychologist who launched the measurement movement in education by declaring

From Raywid, M. A. (2002). Accountability: What's worth measuring? Phi Delta Kappan, 83(6), 433–436. Reprinted with permission of the author.

that "whatever exists, exists in some amount and can be measured." He thought everything could be quantified, and I don't. But we can assess without quantifying, and, for me, if we have goals for children and expectations for schools, it's reasonable to try to find out whether they are being met. The short answer to my own question, then, is that whatever we're committed to accomplishing is worth measuring.

First, of course, are the things we call "basic skills"—the ability to read and report accurately on what one has read, to write, and to do elementary calculations. So important are these fundamental skills that they fill a lot of the time for the first three grades of a child's schooling. Much of the teaching that takes place in schools after the first three years calls for the application of these skills, so they really are essential groundwork. Thus it is important that we measure how well a child has learned them.

Second, there are all those pieces of information we want students to pick up: number facts, spelling facts, grammar facts, history facts, biology facts, geography facts, cultural facts, etc. There are lists and lists of these facts, without which you can't be an educated person. You can't even function very well in our society without many of them—like the number facts necessary to determine whether you are being given the right change. Teaching these facts is a perfectly reasonable expectation for schools, it seems to me, even though in some respects facts are really the lowest level of what we want youngsters to learn. They are necessary. But they are only a beginning.

Third, we want learners to be able to do something with all the facts they've learned. There's not much point in having learned the rules of grammar if you can't put together a grammatical sentence. Other applications are even more involved. We want learners to be able to select and retrieve from the information stored in their heads those facts relevant to a given situation, to be able to assemble them, and then to apply them so as to appropriately respond to a challenge or solve a problem.

Fourth, something else that's well worth measuring because it's so very much worth learning is the set of skills involved in using one's mind. We're not born knowing how to do that. And ironically, schools tend to give the most exercise—and hence developmental assistance—along these lines to the ablest students. The youngsters who need the most help in developing such intellectual skills and inclinations as weighing evidence, judging sources, making legitimate inferences, and distinguishing observations from assumptions are the very ones we tend not to bother with such

matters. Instead, we focus on getting them to concentrate on those things that can be acquired by rote and drill—the fact-type learnings. But unless all youngsters are helped to acquire the habits of mind involved in sound judgment and good decision-making, they can never be aware of themselves as creatures of intellect, as beings with the ability to take control of their lives and to alter their circumstances if need be. They can thus never be the citizens we want them to be, with the power to realize their own goals while helping to shape society.

Then there's a whole different kind of learning, the fifth type I find to be important, that we want very much for children to acquire. One principal summed it up recently: "Schools are about all those things that make individuals good and bad." We want our children to grow up as caring, empathetic, compassionate human beings with a sense of stewardship for the land and for one another. We also want them to grow up with integrity, initiative, a sense of responsibility, and a sense of humor. Schools really are in the person-shaping business: they can operate in ways that encourage and reinforce the traits and dispositions just mentioned, or they can operate so as to discourage and squelch them. Since these are the attitudes and inclinations that distinguish a good citizen and a good neighbor from a parasite or an assassin, we certainly want schools to instill them and children to acquire them. So this is yet another sort of goal, and we ought to measure progress toward it.

The sixth goal covers a lot of territory: we expect a school to contribute to a child's individual development. It means, for instance, that we want to see school make a difference in a child's cognitive development. Learning those facts and learning what to do with them are important, but we want school to do more than that. We want school to stimulate young minds to grow and expand their capacity. A school that doesn't lead to such growth isn't fulfilling reasonable expectations, and we need a way to find out whether this is the case. In other words, a school loaded with high achievers has got to make them still better learners. If not, there's been no value added, and that's what individual development is about. It's also about helping youngsters to develop whatever may be their particular talents. Whether it's music or writing or leading others or gymnastics, school ought to be a place that helps young people develop their talents.

These, then, are six different goals for learners that I think most of us can agree are important for schools to work toward: learning basic skills, learning facts, learning how to use information, acquiring desirable habits of mind, developing character and other desirable traits, and developing individual talents. But this isn't all. In addition to these goals and expectations for learners, we have certain expectations that apply specifically to schools.

Reasonable Expectations of Schools

First, given that children are required to attend them, it seems reasonable to expect schools to be *effective* in teaching our children. This means we expect them to be successful with their students. We wouldn't accept a doctor's diagnosis of "incurable" without going elsewhere for another opinion, and we shouldn't settle for the diagnosis "uneducable" from a school. In other words, we don't expect schools to say, "Well, if you've got success in mind, you really should be sending us a different batch of kids."

On the contrary, we expect schools to be welcoming, user-friendly places, where all six of those different kinds of goals I named are pursued with all youngsters, where all are treated with respect and compassion, and where all can meet with some degree of success. This is a tall order.

But, as if this weren't enough, we also expect schools to carry out their functions in particular ways. For instance, we don't want any of those goals of ours to be pursued lackadaisically or perfunctorily. It's not enough merely to take a class to a concert; the teacher must demonstrate genuine engagement with the music. If instead, the teachers are grading papers or chatting together while the music plays, that's not modeling much by way of music appreciation.

Similarly in a classroom, if the teacher isn't fully engaged in listening and attending when children speak but is demonstrating what it is to half listen to another person, then it's anybody's guess whether children can take from these experiences the lessons we want them to learn. So just going through the motions in classrooms isn't enough. Activities must be conducted with a quality—an emotional tone—that can be as important as the content. Just how serious are teachers about what they are doing? We don't want them to appear to be in dead earnest all the time—in fact, that would be awful—but we do want them to be focused and trying all the time. This is certainly a central enough dimension of what we want school to be that it is worth measuring.

Another thing we expect from schools is that they teach in such a way that youngsters acquire positive attitudes toward what they are learning. If a teacher manages to convey the essentials of reading but strips all pleasure and delight from doing so, it's a questionable success. If a youngster manages to stumble his way through geometry but acquires a hatred for math in the process, that is also a questionable success. As a famous educational thinker put it many years ago, "It's not that children should do what they want, but it's important that they want what they do." And being able to generate this kind of positive receptivity with respect to learning is a legitimate expectation of schools and teachers. If learning new things is drudgery to be undergone only under duress, we haven't done much toward creating a lifelong learner. And since this is so widely voiced a concern, we surely ought to be making regular checks on how well teachers and schools are dealing with it.

These last several lessons are a part of the school's culture and hence of its "hidden curriculum." This curriculum consists of the messages typically delivered otherwise than directly in words and usually only as an accompaniment to announced purposes and content. Sometimes it is conveyed in the arrangements. For instance, one famous principal insists that sending children to schools that are too large for teachers and administrators to learn their names teaches students that who they are as individuals, what they are experiencing, and how they feel about it are things that don't matter. Sending them to schools where the toilets are broken or the doors to the stalls have been removed also conveys a message about what doesn't matter. In this case, their need for privacy has no importance. It seems reasonable to expect schools to treat both the children required to attend them and the teachers who teach in them with respect. And since this expectation is as reasonable as it is important, it's worth measuring.

So to our six goals we've added five expectations of schools: that they be successful, that they be welcoming and user-friendly places, that teachers be fully engaged in their teaching, that schools cultivate a receptivity to learning, and that the school's unspoken messages—its hidden curriculum—be positive and desirable ones.

Some Notes About Measuring

Just how do we measure success with these goals and expectations? That is a matter that must be left to another time. But I can underscore some things to be kept in mind in seeking an answer to the question. Several things need to be said about the six goals for learners and five expectations of schools stated here. First, all appear reasonable, widely shared, and well worth seeking. This means that all are worth measuring in order to determine whether students and schools are living up to what we want from them.

It is also worth noting that holding schools accountable for meeting our list of school expectations directly implicates a number of people beyond teachers: principals, in particular, and their office staffs, but also librarians and counselors and coaches and cafeteria workers and security guards and custodians. Moreover, another thing our two lists make clear is that the answer to how well students and schools are faring is not going to be accessible simply through a single observation of a school; it takes a lot more than that. This is why ongoing evaluation is absolutely necessary to school accountability. The public can't determine whether its goals and expectations are being met without real evaluation—which must rely not only on what is directly observable but also on a great deal of indirect observation.

Another thing that merits emphasis is that, of our 11 goals and expectations, the standards-based education that many states have embarked on addresses only the first two goals for learners that we identified as widely shared (basic skills and information). The best tests perhaps address a bit of the third goal (ability to use information). That's why I think we ought to talk about "accountability" in preference to "standards-based education." Many people talk as if the standards we've set are sufficient to render the schools accountable, but they certainly won't render them accountable for all our goals and expectations. It's going to take a lot more than a series of tests to do that.

It seems clear that paper-and-pencil tests aren't going to suffice. For half of our goals for students (the fourth through the sixth), we'll need some other measure, just as we will for all five of the expectations for schools. I have several suggestions in this regard. At the outset, we must recognize that there's not going to be any single test for any one of them. We can't afford the bad judgments that reductionist measures are sure to support. Many of us find it absurd to think you can determine how much a youngster knows from a single test score, and the same is true for each of these other goals and expectations. We'll need to have a lot of other data to consider, and we'll have to construct an answer to how well students and schools are faring from weighing a variety of evidence that must first be gathered and then assembled. So don't look for a single measure that will reveal all, and don't settle for any measure that purports to do so. There aren't any. But here are several things you might put together.

First, you might look to what are called "unobtrusive measures" for evidence that can be revealing about both goals and expectations. Such measures don't involve any special test or assignment or activity, but rather the devising of telling questions that can be answered from observations. Actually, a lot of the data we need to gather with respect to our school expectations will provide unobtrusive measures for everybody but the data collector. These measures make no demands on class time. They include such data as the attendance rates in schools and classrooms, the school dropout rate, the number of suspensions and expulsions, retention rates, the extent of teacher turnover. Each of these offers powerful testimony on whether schools are meeting our expectations.

But these are not what school evaluators usually have in mind when they speak of "unobtrusive measures." Here are a couple of the sorts of things they might be more likely to cite. John Goodlad used to say that one measure of how user-friendly first-grade classrooms are is the number of children who vomit before leaving home on school days. Another measure might be how quickly, and with what sorts of facial expressions, children *and* teachers leave school at the end of the day. Or we might look at the incidence of graffiti in and around the building. You can put together a set of such observations that should yield partial answers on some of the school expectations.

Student performance and behavior are other unobtrusive evaluation measures. Our fifth goal for learners, for instance—the development of character and other personal traits—could be measured by how youngsters carry out service-learning activities: how responsible they are, how sincere their efforts are, the degree of integrity and commitment and stewardship they display. The sixth goal for learners—individual development—may best be displayed through exhibitions in which the community is invited at intervals to observe students' artwork, dancing, singing, storytelling, or debating. In judging such performances, we need a set of carefully devised criteria for judging that are to be applied by a review panel consisting of parents and community members, some relevant experts, some teachers, and some fellow students.

Figuring out the measurements and doing the measuring will not be a simple task. But it is one that real accountability requires. If you agree that the goals and expectations I've stated here are both important and desirable, then we must try, despite the difficulty, to arrive at reliable and credible ways to check how well schools are succeeding at them. In this era of extreme accountability, it just might be our only way to keep test scores from deciding everything.

ACCOUNTABILITY SHOVEDOWN: RESISTING THE STANDARDS MOVEMENT IN EARLY CHILDHOOD EDUCATION

J. Amos Hatch

Supporters of standards-based reform efforts argue that our current approaches to curriculum and instruction must move beyond current practice. Evaluating the effectiveness of educational programs must include outcomes-based performance. While most educators believe improving the quality of experiences for children in K–12 classrooms is essential, we must also attend to the individual needs of learners and those within school communities.

J. Amos Hatch argues that it is imperative for educators to consider multiple factors in our attempts to improve educational quality. He suggests that the developmental needs of learners, breadth of school experiences, the value of learning versus performance, and the professionalization of educators are also important factors to consider in any reform efforts.

As you read this article ask yourself, "Do standards-based movements reflect the developmental needs of students?"

Think About This . . .

1. What factors related to the needs of learners must educators consider when establishing standards for student performance? Are there learner needs that are universal?

2. How is the work of teachers impacted by the standards movements? What can be done to minimize the negative aspects of this influence?

3. Hatch argues that the "corporate mentality" of many standards-based movements may negatively impact school communities. What are some of the strengths and limitations of a "corporate mentality" for educators?

4. What are some of the ways in which teachers can learn more about the abilities and interests of their students? How will you identify the developmental needs of the students in your classroom?

During the 1980s, early childhood educators waged a battle to resist attempts to require more and more of young children at younger and younger ages. This movement to push expectations from the primary grades down into kindergarten and preschool programs was characterized as "curriculum shove-down" by the mainstream early childhood educators, who argued that young children were not developmentally ready for the academic emphasis of such an approach. David Elkind, an articulate spokesperson for the early childhood community, argued that young children were being "miseducated" in settings where they were experiencing stress from academic pressure for no apparent benefit. In *The Hurried Child* and *Miseducation: Preschoolers at Risk*, Elkind provided powerful indictments of curriculum shovedown and related attempts to make children grow up faster.[1]

My view is that the standards movement—so pervasive across educational settings today—is threatening children in early childhood in the same ways as the curriculum shovedown movement did in the 1980s. The point of attack has changed from curriculum to outcomes, but the consequences for young children may be the same. Standards for such federal programs as Head

From Hatch, J. A. (2002). *Accountability shovedown: Resisting the standards movement in early childhood education.* Phi Delta Kappan, 83(6), 457–462. Reprinted with permission of the author.

Start are already in place, and the discourse in many states and across the early childhood field assumes the inevitability of standards.[2] After all, who could be against standards? Who would have the nerve to say that standards are not important? Who would try to build an argument toward the conclusion that standards are somehow bad? Not I, certainly. I am all for standards in early childhood education, unless they fail to pass muster in the 10 areas discussed below.

1. *Pressure on Children.* I support standards for early childhood programs—except when the implementation of those standards puts children as young as 3 and 4 at risk of feeling pressured in the classroom environment. Elkind noted that young children experience significant and sometimes debilitating stress when they are expected to perform at academic levels for which they are not ready. Further, he argued that waiting until they are ready puts children at no real academic disadvantage in the long run.[3]

It is axiomatic in early childhood that children develop at different rates. Some young children will be ready to meet the challenges of the new expectations associated with the standards movement; many will not. Holding all children to the same standard guarantees that some will face failure. And just setting up a situation in which failure is possible creates stress for even the most capable child, who might be wondering if he or she is achieving "high enough or fast enough."[4] Getting children to do more sooner sounds like a logical way to cure the ills of education. But ask someone who has comforted a child who cries because she cannot distinguish between a 3 and a 5 or who has coaxed a child to keep trying when he refuses to demonstrate (once again) his inability to match the letters with the sounds. Those who know young children understand that putting them under stress is an unacceptable by-product of accountability efforts designed to achieve dubious educational advantages.

2. *Pressure on Teachers.* I see standards as vitally important in early childhood education—unless they are used in ways that put pressure on teachers to abandon their mission of teaching young children in favor of teaching a core set of competencies. The pressure to accelerate achievement gets translated to teachers as "Do a better job of getting your kids up to the standards—or else." If meeting the standards is what is valued in the school where they teach and if student performance provides the basis for how they are evaluated, teachers will feel pressured to meet the standards and to raise student performance. On its face, that kind of pressure may not seem so bad. Indeed, standards are set up to demand

more of schools and teachers based on the belief that "demands will result in behavior that conforms to them."[5]

But pressuring early childhood professionals with demands and threats may work against the best interests of teachers and the children they serve. By training and disposition, teachers of young children are concerned with understanding and teaching the whole child. Teachers are motivated to know children's individual capacities and needs and to do whatever is necessary to develop those capacities and meet those needs, whether they are emotional, social, physical, or cognitive. It causes genuine anxiety when other domains of children's development are ignored or put at risk because of an overemphasis on something as narrowly defined as academic standards. In addition, early childhood teachers feel some anxiety when they see themselves as the agents of stress in their students' lives. When they are forced to implement standards-driven programs that focus on academic outcomes and put pressure on young children, teachers experience conflicts between what they believe to be best for their students and the accomplishment of what is required by their programs.[6]

Pressuring teachers to abandon practices that recognize the complexity of children's development is wrong. Demanding that they undertake practices that may ultimately harm children's chances for success in school and life is foolish.

3. *Narrowing of Experiences.* I think standards are fine—except in cases where moving to a standards-based curriculum reduces a rich set of experiences to a narrow sequence of lessons. The consequences of implementing standards with older students are clear enough—when standards are in place, the curriculum is reduced to an emphasis on the content on which children, teachers, and schools will be assessed.[7] This narrow emphasis on easily measured objectives seriously limits what is being learned in elementary, middle, and high schools, and critics are not even convinced that the content on which the narrowed curriculum focuses is necessarily the right stuff.[8] Narrowing the preschool curriculum to accommodate standards such as those being promulgated by Head Start and promoted by the Bush Administration[9] not only limits the scope of what is learned but will also take the life out of young children's initial experiences in classrooms.

The best early childhood programs are those that give children opportunities to explore meaningful content in meaningful ways. Skills and concepts—the same ones found in the standards-based approaches—are learned, but they are learned in the context of meaningful activity. Such programs are characterized by a sense of joyful discovery. Substituting a narrow, skills-based approach for a dynamic, child-responsive curriculum will rob young children of the joy of discovering how much they can learn and just how fulfilling school experiences can be.

4. *Accountability as Punishment.* I believe standards are the centerpiece of reform in early childhood education—unless children, teachers, and programs are systematically identified as deficient in an effort to make them accountable. The logic of the accountability movement is based on the premise that students and teachers will not work hard unless they are afraid of the consequences of being found to be below the standard. What happens to 3- and 4-year-old children who are found to be below the standard? Kohn describes what happens in the primary grades:

> Skills develop rapidly and differentially in young children, which means that expecting everyone of the same age to have acquired a given set of capabilities creates unrealistic expectations, leads to one-size-fits-all (which is to say, bad) teaching, and guarantees that some children will be defined as failures at the very beginning of their time in school.[10]

It's wrong to label a 7-year-old second-grader a failure; it's criminal to do it to a 4-year-old preschooler. Using the threat of failure as a tool to motivate young children and their teachers is an absurd notion that characterizes a system designed to "punish rather than improve."[11] That some children will fail to meet a standard is inevitable.[12] That many who fail will come from groups that have historically been shortchanged by the system is highly likely.[13] While it may be politically expedient to join the call for tougher standards, systematically labeling large populations of our youngest students as failures is a price we should never agree to pay.

5. *Teacher Deprofessionalization.* I am a proponent of early childhood standards—as long as teachers are not stripped of their roles as professional decision makers. Across the education landscape, the movement toward standards is a movement away from teacher responsibility and agency. As curricula, teaching strategies, outcomes, and evaluation techniques are standardized, teachers' opportunities to make decisions based on their professional judgment are systematically reduced. The implementation of standards-based programs signals students, parents, and society at large that teachers are not to be trusted or respected and that technical/managerial control is what is needed to fix problems that teachers helped create.[14]

For the past five years, I have been working with colleagues in Australia studying how early childhood teachers use child observation in their teaching. One of the striking findings from our work is that teachers in the United States and Australia have reduced their use of child observation as a strategy for shaping curriculum and increased their use of observation as a device for monitoring student progress. Instead of studying children in an effort to better meet their needs and improve their learning opportunities, teachers are now filling out checklists so that they can chart the achievement of a narrow set of competencies. We (and the teachers we have interviewed) see this as evidence of teacher deprofessionalization in the areas of assessment and curriculum development.[15] Early childhood assessment appears to be becoming a form of "product control, closely tied to industrialization and the creation of an end product."[16] Early childhood teachers appear to be becoming what Jonathan Kozol calls "technicians of proficiency" whose task it is to monitor children's progress through a hierarchy of prescribed outcomes.[17] Something important is lost when the work of teachers is downgraded from professional to technical status.

6. *Performance over Learning.* I support the standards movement—unless it teaches young children to value the attainment of certain objectives over their ability to learn. Why do children think they are in school? What do we teach them about why they are there? Systems set up on the premise that there are certain standards that everyone must attain teach students that meeting those standards is the reason they are in school. Children learn that doing the work that's put in front of them at a level that will get them by is the stuff of schooling.

In such a system, performance goals dominate learning goals. School tasks have no intrinsic value; they are only means to achieve the extrinsic rewards or avoid the punishments built into the system. Carol Dweck has contrasted performance goals and learning goals.[18] When learning goals are what's important, children are taught that learning itself has inherent value and that the reason they are in school is to learn. It's clear enough that performance-goal structures drive education from elementary through graduate school,[19] but preschoolers are just beginning to form their conceptions of what school is for and where they fit in. The goal in high-quality early childhood programs is to help students see themselves as able learners and see learning as an exciting adventure that has meaning and importance in their immediate experience. On the effects of standards, Eisner summarizes, "In our desire to improve our schools, education has become a casualty."[20] If we continue down the road to standards-based reform in early childhood education, *learning* will be a casualty.

7. *Individual Devaluation.* I like the idea of standards in early childhood education—except when their use encourages us to ignore the individual strengths and needs of young children. Susan Ohanian describes those who advocate standards as the cure-all for the ills of school and society as *standardistos,* who try to force their will on others in the form of one-size-fits-all curriculum plans. She argues that such an approach assumes that knowledge is pure and unrelated to the knowledge-seeker, so education can be prepackaged and delivered without regard for the individual needs and interests of the learners.[21] I agree with Ohanian and others who see standards-based approaches as systems that operate as if individual differences do not exist.[22] What is even more troubling for children is that accountability systems operate as if individual differences *should not* exist; that is, if you don't fit the mold, there's something wrong with you.[23]

Such thinking turns contemporary best practices for teaching young children upside down. Knowing what individual children are like and providing the educational experiences they need are the cornerstones of sound early childhood programming. Anyone who has spent 30 minutes in a classroom full of 4- and 5-year-olds can tell you that children bring striking differences to their school experience. Imposing common standards on all students ignores individual differences, limiting the development of the most talented and jeopardizing the learning opportunities of those who need the most help and support.[24] In early childhood education, we should continue to have high standards for ourselves and for our students. But we should avoid implementing one-size-fits-all standards that devalue the uniqueness of the children we serve.

8. *Sameness Versus Diversity.* Standards seem like a good way to improve early childhood education—except in those instances where family and cultural differences are out of place because programs emphasize sameness. I am not surprised—but I am disappointed—that a tone of cultural elitism runs throughout the standards-for-accountability argument. It's clear that those who are making decisions about what should be taught are those who represent the dominant elite in our society. It's easy for those with cultural power to reach consensus about which knowledge is of the most worth: it's the knowledge they already have.[25] So small groups of privileged individuals are deciding what goes into children's heads based on an artificial consensus that may "underrepresent, misrepresent, or exclude groups of voices from the community."[26]

Children who are already excluded from access to the resources and supports of the mainstream will be further marginalized with the imposition of standards-based reform. They will be expected to perform at prescribed levels on prescribed tasks based on the false assumption that equal opportunities to learn exist.[27] In a model driven by an obsession with sameness, diversity becomes a problem, and children from diverse groups are likely to become casualties simply because of their differences. As a field, early childhood education has not been perfect in its attempts to recognize and celebrate the strengths that diversity brings to educational settings, but early childhood educators are well ahead of most segments of society. Moving to standards-based models that promote sameness and punish diversity is the wrong way to go if we are to continue to improve the life chances of every child in our society.

9. *Who Benefits?* I will speak up for standards in my field—unless it is difficult to make a compelling case that young children actually benefit from this movement. There is little empirical evidence of a causal link between standard setting and enhanced student learning.[28] But even if we buy into the idea that young children's performance on academic tasks could be improved, it is reasonable to ask if those gains are worth the cost of the unintended consequences I have enumerated here. A number of respected researchers, educators, and social critics say the costs are too high.[29] So if students don't actually learn more or must pay dearly for improved performance on a narrowly defined set of arbitrary standards, who benefits from the mania to implement standards?

Michael Apple calls the standards movement "reform on the cheap."[30] He and others point out that politicians and other individuals who use their power to influence educational change seek out simple and inexpensive strategies that give the appearance of providing solutions.[31] Politicians make political hay by offering quick fixes that put responsibility on others for their success. When the poorly thought out and inadequately funded reform strategies are unsuccessful, those in power are quick to blame educators, families, and children.

The standards movement is just such a strategy. It provides an opportunity for those in power to "get tough" with students and educators, spending small amounts of money developing outcomes without investing the large sums it would take to achieve significant change. If the standards are not met, you can be sure the victims, not the politicians, will be blamed. It's hard to see how our youngest and least powerful citizens will benefit from standards in early childhood education.

10. *Corporate Mentality.* I am aboard the standards bandwagon—unless it means that the forces driving

corporate America are being applied in early childhood classrooms. It amazes me that business executives and their political cronies are deciding how children ought to be educated. It makes my head spin to think that the "bottom line" mentality of giant corporations like IBM is having a profound influence on the lives of untold numbers of 3-, 4-, and 5-year-old children. Young children are not PCs to be efficiently assembled according to a set of profit-driven standards. Teachers are not "blue suits" who either meet corporate quotas or are fired. Education is not a commodity to be produced, marketed, and sold. Classrooms are not marketplaces where beating the competition at any cost is all that counts.[32]

It says something profound about what matters in our nation that folks who have committed their lives to caring for and educating young children are being told what to do by individuals whose expertise lies in running large companies or winning political elections. In spite of the rhetoric of those who have the media's attention, early childhood education has a long history of standard setting and accountability.[33] What's different is that our standards presume that young children are complex human beings who learn best when they are guided, nurtured, and cared for, not lifeless commodities that must meet standards of production. Our accountability comes from an ethical commitment to do what is right for every child, not from measuring productivity according to an arbitrary set of narrowly defined outcomes.

Accountability Shovedown

In sum, I see the proliferation of standards for early childhood settings as "accountability shovedown" that threatens the integrity of early childhood professionals and the quality of educational experiences for young children. In spite of the seemingly unassailable logic of the standards movement, I believe educators and others interested in the well-being of our youngest citizens ought to mount a resistance movement to accountability shovedown that parallels the curriculum battles of 20 years ago. Elkind is publishing a new edition of *The Hurried Child.* The field needs to challenge aggressively the appropriateness of standards-based approaches to reforming early childhood education.

I don't see such resistance as a mindless defense of the status quo. Knowledge about how young children develop and learn is expanding rapidly, and the field is opening up to new thinking and expanding its perspective on what is appropriate in early childhood

classrooms. I count this as forward movement, designed to improve the experiences of young children and maximize their chances for a rich, full life in school and beyond. Standards-based approaches represent backward movement, designed to force early childhood programs into molds that don't work with older students and are downright harmful for young children.

Kohn characterizes the dominant philosophy for fixing schools as a return to the methods of the past, only using them "harder, longer, stronger, louder, meaner."[34] This article constitutes a plea to resist adding "earlier" to the list. Let's continue to improve the quality of early childhood programs, but let's not do it by forcing children and teachers to suffer the consequences of implementing standards-based reform.

Notes

1. David Elkind, *The Hurried Child* (Reading, Mass.: Addison-Wesley, 1981); and *Miseducation: Preschoolers at Risk* (New York: Knopf, 1987).

2. Lawrence J. Schweinhart, "Assessing the Outcomes of Head Start: Where Is the Early Childhood Field Going?," *High/Scope Resource,* vol. 20, 2001, pp. 1, 9–11.

3. David Elkind, "Educating the Very Young," *NEA Today,* January 1988, p. 23.

4. Elkind, *The Hurried Child,* p. xii.

5. John Kordalewski, *Standards in the Classroom: How Teachers and Students Negotiate Learning* (New York: Teachers College Press, 2000), p. 5.

6. J. Amos Hatch and Evelyn B. Freeman, "Kindergarten Philosophies and Practices: Perspectives of Teachers, Principals, and Supervisors," *Early Childhood Research Quarterly,* vol. 3, 1988, pp. 158–59.

7. Elliot W. Eisner, "What Does It Mean to Say a School Is Doing Well?," *Phi Delta Kappan,* January 2001, pp. 368–69; and Robert L. Linn, "Assessments and Accountability," *Educational Researcher,* March 2000, p. 8.

8. John Goodlad, quoted in John Merrow, "Undermining Standards," *Phi Delta Kappan,* May 2001, p. 656; Alfie Kohn, "Fighting the Tests: Turning Frustration into Action," *Young Children,* vol. 56, 2001, p. 19; and Donald B. Gratz, "High Standards for Whom?," *Phi Delta Kappan,* May 2000, p. 687.

9. See Jacques Steinberg, "Bush's Plan to Push Reading in Head Start Stirs Debate," *New York Times,* 10 February 2001.

10. Kohn, p. 19.

11. Gratz, p. 685.

12. Linn, p. 11.

13. Anita Perna Bohn and Christine E. Sleeter, "Multicultural Education and the Standards Movement," *Phi Delta Kappan,* October 2000, p. 156; and Gratz, p. 682.

14. Gunilla Dahlberg, Peter Moss, and Alan Pence, *Beyond Quality in Early Childhood Education and Care: Postmodern*

Perspectives (London: Falmer Press, 1999), p. 2; Bohn and Sleeter, p. 158; and Merrow, p. 655.

15. Susan Grieshaber, Gail Halliwell, J. Amos Hatch, and Kerryann Walsh, "Child Observation as Teachers' Work in Contemporary Australian Early Childhood Programs," *International Journal of Early Years Education,* vol. 8, 2000, pp. 50–53; and J. Amos Hatch, Susan Grieshaber, Gail Halliwell, and Kerryann Walsh, "Child Observation in Australia and the U.S.: A Cross-National Analysis," *Early Child Development and Care,* vol. 169, 2001, pp. 39–56.

16. Gaile S. Cannella, *Deconstructing Early Childhood Education: Social Justice and Revolution* (New York: Peter Lang, 1997), p. 103.

17. Jonathan Kozol, Foreword to Deborah Meier, ed., *Will Standards Save Public Education?* (Boston: Beacon Press, 2000), p. xii.

18. Carol S. Dweck, "Motivational Processes Affecting Learning," *American Psychologist,* vol. 41, 1986, pp. 1040–48.

19. Alfie Kohn, *The Schools Our Children Deserve: Moving Beyond Traditional Classrooms and "Tougher Standards"* (Boston: Houghton Mifflin, 1999), p. 26; and Eisner, p. 369.

20. Eisner, p. 370.

21. Susan Ohanian, *One Size Fits Few: The Folly of Educational Standards* (Portsmouth, N.H.: Heinemann, 1999), pp. 3, 14.

22. Ohanian, pp. 17–29; Kohn, "Fighting the Tests," p. 19; and Marion Brady, "The Standards Juggernaut," *Phi Delta Kappan,* May 2000, p. 650.

23. Rex Knowles and Trudy Knowles, "Accountability for What?," *Phi Delta Kappan,* January 2001, p. 392.

24. William E. Coffman, "A King over Egypt, Which Knew Not Joseph," *Educational Measurement: Issues and Practices,* Summer 1993, p. 8.

25. Brady, p. 649; Alan C. Jones, "Welcome to Standardsville," *Phi Delta Kappan,* February 2001, p. 463; and Lisa Delpit, *Other People's Children* (New York: New Press, 1995), p. 24.

26. Pamela A. Moss and Aaron Schutz, "Educational Standards, Assessment, and the Search for Consensus," *American Educational Research Journal,* vol. 38, 2001, p. 65.

27. Bohn and Sleeter, p. 157; and Kohn, *The Schools Our Children Deserve,* p. 55.

28. Bill Nave, Edward Miech, and Frederick Mosteller, "A Lapse in Standards: Linking Standards-Based Reform with Student Achievement," *Phi Delta Kappan,* October 2000, p. 128; and Gratz, pp. 683–84.

29. See, for example, Linn, p. 14; Ohanian, p. 23; and Michael W. Apple, *Cultural Politics and Education* (New York: Teachers College Press, 1996).

30. Apple, p. 157.

31. Gratz, pp. 683–84; Ohanian, p. 32; and Merrow, p. 657.

32. Brady, p. 651; Eisner, p. 370; and Kohn, *The Schools Our Children Deserve,* pp. 15–16.

33. Marilou Hyson, "Reclaiming Our Words," *Young Children,* vol. 56, 2001, pp. 53–54.

34. Kohn, *The Schools Our Children Deserve,* p. 16.

CAN THE BUSH SCHOOL PLAN WORK? HOW TO KEEP "NO CHILD LEFT BEHIND" FROM DISSOLVING INTO FINE PRINT

Michael Casserly

Currently the most powerful and pervasive force in educational reform is the federal initiative No Child Left Behind. The impact of No Child Left Behind (NCLB) is far-reaching; the law challenges educators to provide multiple forms of data as indicators of student and teacher performance. Specifically, school districts must formulate plans for establishing strategically defined, measurable goals for student performance. They must also implement a coherent, systematic curriculum as well as professional development plans for educators. Finally, states must implement a regular testing program using detailed data to measure progress, including plans for diagnoses and intervention. In a nutshell, NCLB legislation calls for results, accountability, regular assessment, coherent professional development, supplemental services, and improved teacher quality.

Michael Casserly asks the question, "Will the legislation work?" If states are given freedom in how the act is implemented, with little flexibility when it comes to outcomes, is there a danger in limiting the ability of states to respond to local conditions and needs? Casserly highlights four cities' success in putting the NCLB proposals into action.

As you read this article ask yourself, "How can school communities respond to the legislative demands of No Child Left Behind legislation in ways that meet both the spirit and the letter of the law?"

Think About This . . .

1. Describe three strategies used by districts whose plans resulted in gains in student performance. Which strategies appear the most promising in terms of a lasting impact on student learning?

2. Casserly raises questions about long-term reform even if school districts can successfully implement the mandates from NCLB. How significant are those limitations?

3. Which aspects of the NCLB legislation are teachers most likely to embrace, and which elements might spawn skepticism?

4. As an educator, how can you integrate research on the practices of effective school districts into your own attempts to meet the requirements of NCLB?

The federal "No Child Left Behind" Act of 2001, signed into law with great bipartisan fanfare last January, is in danger of giving way to a national catfight over whether the letter of the law is more important than its grand intent.

States are struggling over whether they should jettison their current tests. Local school districts are gasping at the requirements they have to meet. Special interests continue to press their narrow concerns. And the press is reveling in the thought of having an endless stream of stories about how everyone is out of compliance with one provision or another.

Yet, this new law could work if schools view it, as most major city school systems now do, as an opportunity to focus anew on student performance.

The law calls for all children to be proficient in reading, math, and science within 12 years; requires tests of progress in grades 3–8; and holds educators accountable for the results. Schools lose varying degrees of authority and control if achievement does not improve.

Schools traditionally have not worked under these kinds of pressures. Results often take a back seat to the schooling process. Credentials trump expertise. And teachers and staffs often think accountability is a threat rather than an opportunity.

Congress wanted to end this mind-set and the poor results it achieved by borrowing liberally from the lessons learned in Texas. There, schools gave tests frequently, supported teachers, and measured results for each racial and economic group. The state's progress on the National Assessment of Educational Progress bolstered the claim that Texas was on the right track. Little other empirical data existed, however, about whether the Texas approach would work elsewhere, allowing one set of partisans to argue that the state's gains were sensational and the other to claim that the "Texas miracle" was overstated.

A new report—one out of the cities, not the states—suggests that the framers of the No Child Left Behind Act may have actually been on to something. More importantly, the research on which the "Foundations for Success" report is based suggests a path along which cities might meet the act's goals, and bolsters the law in places where it is silent—for example, school district improvement.

The Council of the Great City Schools and the independent research firm Manpower Demonstration Research Corp. completed a two-year analysis of city school systems that had improved reading and mathematics performance at rates faster than their states', and had simultaneously narrowed their racially identifiable achievement gaps. The study asked the question: How did they do it?

Researchers also contrasted these city school systems—Charlotte, N.C.; Houston; Sacramento, Calif.; and New York City's Chancellor's District, a unit composed

From Casserly, M. (2002). Can the Bush school plan work? How to keep "No Child Left Behind" from dissolving into fine print. As first appeared in Education Week, 22(14), 48, 38. Reprinted with permission of the author.

of the city's lowest-performing schools—with other districts getting less traction under their reforms.

The reforms pursued by these faster-improving city school systems were strikingly similar to one another and were often in concert with the strategies outlined in the No Child Left Behind Act.

Overall, each district took a comprehensive, systemwide approach to reform, rather than rely on each school to figure it out for itself. This approach helped spur improvements across the district, rather than in pockets of schools. In each city district, reform was initiated and led by a superintendent and a school board that pursued a common agenda over an extended period about how to boost student performance, did so in a steady but relentless fashion, and minimized the political game-playing and zero-sum decision making found in other districts.

The analysis also found that the districts shared three common strategies that a contrasting group of districts without student gains had not implemented.

First, each district set hard-nosed and measurable goals for itself and its individual schools, with an accountability system based on a number of measures. These districts' accountability systems went beyond what their states had established and held district leaders and school staffs personally responsible for results. Eric Smith, who headed North Carolina's Charlotte–Mecklenburg County schools before moving to the Anne Arundel County, Md., school district, had a contract that tied his evaluation to the attainment of the detailed goals set by his board. Similarly, members of the school board in Sacramento signed a public pledge to resign if they could not raise achievement.

Second, the districts implemented a coherent, somewhat prescriptive, districtwide curriculum and professional-development program. This meant that the central office took direct responsibility for raising student achievement, rather than remaining passive and leaving individual schools to devise their own curriculum and training. The Sacramento schools had 17 different reading programs at one time; Houston had seven; and the Chancellor's District in New York had too many to count. The sheer number and variation of these programs stretched the districts' capacity to implement them effectively.

A districtwide instructional approach, however, allowed these districts to mitigate the effects of high student mobility and large numbers of inexperienced teachers.

Third, the districts instituted regular testing and used detailed data to measure progress, diagnose weaknesses, and intervene as problems arose. They provided teachers and principals with early and ongoing assessments and training on how to use the data throughout the school year. Most districts wait until the end of the school year, when it is too late to make adjustments and improve results.

Charlotte administers short assessments in many schools every 10 days or so. Houston and Sacramento give quarterly tests and use the results to target supplementary services for students and professional development for teachers.

The experience of these districts suggests that doing all of these things together can have a much greater impact on a district's success than doing any one of them alone. Indeed, unless a district tried to reform its system as a whole, trying any one of these approaches or pursuing a school-by-school strategy was probably a waste of time and effort.

The findings are not particularly surprising. Nevertheless, they take the discussion about systemic reform out of the realm of speculation and into the empirical.

The research could not answer all questions, of course. It was not clear, for instance, whether the improvements were due to the uniformity or to the prescriptiveness of the curriculum. The analysis could not determine the relative importance of each reform. Neither could it tell where the effects of systemic reform ended and the effects of individual school reforms began. And it could not calculate whether any of the districts met the federal legislation's literal definition of "adequate yearly progress."

Still, the results—and the uncertainties they raise—suggest that No Child Left Behind is actually a solid framework within which to think about reforming America's public schools. The legislation's emphasis on results, accountability, regular assessments, coherent professional development, supplemental services, and teacher quality are clearly on the mark.

What remains unclear is whether the internal gears of the legislation are calibrated to spur higher achievement. The law, if some provisions are followed literally, could have the unintended effect of restricting instructional time in order to accommodate various procedural reviews.

The law's minutiae probably say more about Congress' skepticism that educators will do what works than about its certainty that the law's levers are the right ones. Many of the nation's educators, for their part, feed the skepticism by whining about the details rather than embracing the law's overarching intent.

Likewise, the Bush administration and Congress may have unwittingly confused people by suggesting that there was broad flexibility in the act in places where there shouldn't be. There should be lots of flexibility in how the act is implemented programmatically—its inputs. But there should be little flexibility when it comes to what the legislation strives to achieve—the outcomes.

In other words, there ought to be maximum flexibility in areas such as the selection of instructional interventions, and limited latitude in areas where the bill specifies performance targets and accountability. It is in the latter area where attempts at the state level to game the system can do the most damage to the act's underlying purpose.

Congress and the U.S. Department of Education should not be so worried about compliance with the inputs that the process of achieving it chokes off the outcomes. But they should stick to their guns in insisting on results.

How ironic it would be if No Child Left Behind—in some ways, the capstone of a reform movement to emphasize results rather than process—devolved into a squabble over how tightly to comply with the law's technical provisions, rather than how to spur student performance.

The point here is to make sure that we are flexible about the right things and hard-nosed about the bottom line—and don't confuse one with the other.

President Bush's school plan can and should work if the administration adheres to the academic framework of its legislation, funds it adequately, focuses compliance on schools making little or no progress, and uses the new research to provide better technical assistance to schools and districts that need it most.

The job for educators is to stop fretting about being ticketed over every flashing light in the legislation and get on with the business of boosting student achievement.

NO CHILD LEFT BEHIND: COSTS AND BENEFITS

William Mathis

A hallmark of the No Child Left Behind legislation is providing children with a quality education through schools that promote success for all children, particularly those who have struggled historically. To guarantee quality teaching, educators are evaluated and provided with professional development opportunities that foster the success envisioned under the law.

Although the goals of NCLB are worthy of considerable attention, William Mathis challenges us to examine the costs and resources necessary for adequately meeting the requirements of the law. In addition to performance and cost comparisons between the United States and other nations, we must also make comparisons across states *within* the United States. As you read this article ask yourself, "Will the benefits outweigh the costs of implementing No Child Left Behind?"

Think About This . . .

1. Mathis argues that the costs to reach the goals stipulated in NCLB are considerably more than what is currently spent per pupil. Of the costs that states will incur under the new requirements of NCLB, which are likely to be the greatest?

2. Creators of tests attend carefully to the validity and reliability of those tests. What are some of the concerns raised by Mathis regarding the validity and reliability of tests under NCLB? Which of these concerns are most troublesome?

3. Mathis warns of "unintended consequences" of NCLB legislation such as high dropout rates. How might NCLB impact students' classroom performance? Who is most likely to drop out and what could teachers do to minimize these negative effects?
4. How will NCLB influence your instruction? What could you do as a teacher to minimize the potentially negative effects of NCLB?

It is the cruelest illusion to promise far more than we will ever deliver. Yet throughout time reformers of all persuasions have offered Utopian visions in exchange for permission to shape the world to their view. With great fanfare about historic turning points and fervent promises to America's children, in January 2002 President Bush signed into law the No Child Left Behind (NCLB) Act, the latest reauthorization of the Elementary and Secondary Education Act (ESEA).

The rhetoric was certainly noble, and the law was sold with the guarantee that, at last, we would leave no student behind. The poor would have the same as the rich, and the strong arm of a resolute government would make it so. Public support for equality, periodic testing, highly qualified teachers, and other provisions of the law was strong.[1] As shown by the 87–10 Senate vote, the law passed with substantial bipartisan support.

President Bush and Secretary of Education Rod Paige have said much about the great investments the federal government has made in education. And in strident tones, the material accompanying the passage of the law says that the public has a right to demand great returns on this investment.[2]

Alas, the promises are far greater than the reality. When the "historic" federal investments in education are scrutinized, the first-year increases to Title I compensatory funds amount to a mere 0.4% of total education spending. When the much-touted "flexibility" procedures that NCLB gives to local districts are examined, they allow, at best, a local district to shift around about 4.3% of its already-committed money.[3] When the so-called adequate yearly progress provisions of the law are examined, independent reviewers, almost without exception, say the plans are unrealistic.[4] Submerged beneath emotional appeals and rhetorical demands, hard questions about costs, the adequacy of resources, and the strength of commitments lie hidden.

The Nation's Financial Commitment

Throughout the last century, critics loudly proclaimed the nation's peril owing to the alleged poor condition of the schools. Yet results from the National Assessment of Educational Progress show that at the end of the century scores in reading and mathematics had leveled off at a 30-year high, dropouts were near all-time lows, and our nation's economic supremacy was unquestioned.[5] This is hardly a picture of a "failed" system. But these facts hide the nation's true educational problems.

Much has been made of the "merely average" test scores of U.S. students in comparison with those from other countries. To be sure, U.S. scores on international examinations—such as the Third International Mathematics and Science Study (TIMSS) and the Program of International Student Assessment (PISA)—are at international averages in reading, math, and science.[6] However, it is just as clear that the U.S. investment in K–12 education is also less than stellar. We spend the same average amount of our gross domestic product on elementary schools as other developed countries, but we fall to the bottom half in our commitment to high schools.[7]

The greater and more insidious danger, however, is the disparity in achievement *within* the United States. International test data tell us that we have the greatest inequities between our highest- and lowest-scoring students of any nation.[8] In a UNICEF follow-up study, the gap between our average scorers and our low scorers gives the U.S. an abysmal ranking of 21st out of 24 industrialized nations in educational equality.[9] While we are getting more productivity than we pay for, the troubling disparities in achievement reflect our disparities in funding.

NCLB Costs: What We Spend Versus What We Need

In 1989 the Kentucky Supreme Court ruled that the state constitution requires the state to provide schools and students with the resources necessary to meet high state standards. Since that time, state courts in

From Mathis, W. (2003). *No Child Left Behind: Costs and benefits.* Phi Delta Kappan, 84(9), 679–686. *Reprinted with permission of the author.*

New Hampshire, Tennessee, Arkansas, Ohio, North Carolina, and New Jersey have issued similar rulings on behalf of children. In addition to court actions, the vast majority of states have enacted standards-based reforms. NCLB adopts these state standards and imposes progressively harsher penalties on schools if students do not get passing scores.

Thus figuring out how much NCLB will cost requires knowing how much it will take to ensure that all students meet the standards and pass the tests. But how do we know how much money is enough? Different methods have been used to estimate what is an *adequate* amount of money.

The "professional judgment" method uses panels of experts to carefully define the resources needed for each child to meet the standards. These resources are then added up to arrive at a state figure. The "successful school" technique identifies a set of high-achieving schools, examines their resource allocations and spending levels, and generalizes to other schools. The "statistical analysis" approach calculates what it takes to predict a passing score. These models are particularly useful in determining regional costs, such as what it would take to attract qualified teachers to a remote location.

Within the last four years, a new generation of finance studies has estimated the costs of raising all children's test scores up to a particular state's standard. While some of these studies expressly include NCLB costs, most have been based on achieving the state's own standards—which have since been folded into each state's NCLB system. Since each state determines its own standards, has its own social and political culture, and has its own level of student needs, a great variety of outcomes exists.

Nevertheless, recent studies in different states, by different researchers, using different methods, reveal a picture of the massive costs of making sure all children pass the mandated NCLB tests.

Indiana

To enable a school to meet the "commendable" level on state tests, Indiana would have to increase its base spending from $5,468 to $7,142 per pupil—a 31% increase—according to an analysis by Augenblick and Myers, Inc. These estimates do *not* include any added costs for special education students, which range between $7,500 and $8,300 per pupil. They also do not include the cost of "hard-to-serve students," who average an additional $4,200 to $5,300 per student.[10]

Maryland

Calculating the costs for Maryland students to meet state standards, Augenblick and Myers, Inc., arrived at a total education cost of $12,060 per pupil for elementary schools, $9,000 for middle schools, and $9,599 for high schools. The firm further calculated that having a low-income student meet standards would require an average excess cost of $7,748 per student, or 1.7 times the base cost. The analysts used both a market-basket model and a high-achieving-school model to arrive at costs for their standards-based models. The results from both methods were similar.[11]

The total cost for the system for fiscal-year 2000 would have been between $7.9 and $8.8 billion. Since the expenditures for that year were $5.9 billion, the required percentage increase was between 34% and 49%. To Maryland's credit, its lawmakers boosted education spending by $1.3 billion in spring 2002.[12]

Montana

Montana's 2002 study was sponsored by five education organizations and assisted by the National Council of State Legislators. The analysts used a professional-judgment approach to cost out meeting NCLB requirements based on the current level of performance. They found that a base cost between $6,004 and $8,041 per pupil (depending on district type) was required, while the current base was only $4,471. Additional special-needs and remedial costs were $8,000 and $2,000 per pupil respectively. Thus base costs in Montana would increase between 34% and 80%, depending on location and level of need.[13]

Nebraska

The state department of education, in cooperation with various education organizations, commissioned a study of what it would take to meet current Nebraska standards under NCLB in 2002–03. Estimated costs range from $5,845 per pupil in a large K–12 district to $11,257 in a small, isolated K–12 district.

On top of this figure, at-risk and special-needs students would require an *additional* $1,500 to $12,000 each, depending on the level of need. "Total costs would vary, on average, from $8,103 per student in large K–12 districts to $13,525 per student in very small K–12 districts," says the report.[14] Nebraska currently spends about $5,600 per pupil. Thus the state is looking at a 45% cost increase. NCLB testing and labeling have brought cries of outrage from Nebraska state and local officials. The state senate called for full federal funding of the mandate.[15]

New Hampshire

Mark Joyce, executive director of the New Hampshire School Administrators Association, sent his members and the citizens of the state his analysis of NCLB costs. He found that the state will receive an average of $77 of new federal money for each of the Granite State's 220,000 students, while the obligations imposed by the law will cost $575 per student. In other words, New Hampshire will receive about $17 million in new money for new obligations of $126.5 million.[16]

To arrive at this number, Joyce estimated a state cost for each of the elements of the law and added them together. He contends that his estimates are conservative, and he is probably right. The reason is that his analysis was confined to increased costs for local and state staff and administration. He assumed that the number of special education students would increase by 2%, but he did not include the costs of remedial programs for underachieving children. As compared to other states, this procedure results in a significant underestimate.

New York

Using a statistical technique primarily focused on regional differences in the costs of meeting standards, Professors William Duncombe of Syracuse University and Anna Lukemeyer of the University of Nevada, Las Vegas, arrived at a median statewide figure of $7,927 for *extra* remedial costs, on top of the regular per-pupil expenditure of $9,781. They provide several regional cost variations at different proficiency standards. Their overall regional cost adjustments add 16% to total education spending. New York's Campaign for Fiscal Equity launched a major costing study using both the successful-schools and professional-judgment models. A report of the results is expected in early 2004.[17]

South Carolina

To estimate the costs of getting 85% of South Carolina students to the "basic" level of the state's Palmetto tests and all students to pass the graduation tests in 2011, the 1999 base cost of $4,990 would have to be increased to $6,189 by 2005–06. This figure represents a 24% increase. However, it does not include the costs of at-risk and special education students. When figures for these populations are added in, the cost rises to $9,182 per pupil (an 84% increase), according to Augenblick

and Myers, Inc., whose analysts used a professional-judgment model.[18] Spending in South Carolina must nearly double— going from $3.1 billion in 1999 to a projected $6 billion in 2006.

Texas

While Texas saw large increases in the percentage of students passing the state test, these tests were at an eighth-grade, basic-skills level.[19] Even with the low standards, statistical modeling of NCLB costs on earlier data would require an increase in state aid of 101% or 6.9 billion new state dollars. Assuming the local contribution remained the same, this is about a 35% increase in spending. For comparison purposes, the Bush Administration has proposed a $1-billion increase for the nation as a whole for fiscal year 2004.[20] In Texas, the largest increases are needed in the districts with very low-wealth populations and in the very large-city districts. A new test is being implemented in Texas. Obviously, if the standards are raised, the remedial costs will go up proportionately.

Vermont

In my own study of Vermont's situation, I counted the number of students below state standards. Depending on the test and grade level, Vermont scores between 22 and 32 percentile points above national norms, and this advantage over the nation is increasing. Nevertheless, because Vermont has extremely high standards, 46.5% of the students "fail" one of the tests. I assumed that one-fourth of these students would be able to reach the standards within existing resources. Using estimates from adequacy-cost studies and looking at the number of students affected by poverty and those with moderate needs, I arrived at additional remediation costs for the state of $149.5 million. Testing costs and lost instructional time added $8.7 million to that figure, for a total of $158.2 million in new costs. However, the state receives only $51.6 million in all titles of ESEA combined.[21] Vermont would add 15.5% to its total school costs for remediation and testing alone.

Wisconsin

Using parameters supplied by the Institute for Wisconsin's Future, Whitney Allgood and Richard Rothstein found that adequate funding in Wisconsin would be $11,231 per pupil, averaged across all pupils in the state. For high-risk pupils, the cost would be $27,879 per pupil— more than 2.5 times the cost of previous estimates. In arriving at this figure, the authors demonstrated that overcoming the effects of poverty requires interventions beyond the traditional school. Thus they included community clinics, before- and after-school programs, early childhood intervention, and summer school programs.[22]

Simply teaching children will have little effect if they return to bad neighborhoods, single-parent homes, foster care, inadequate health care, and a general lack of support. The authors marshaled convincing evidence that expecting students to reach high standards without essential support systems in place overestimates the ability of schools to cure social ills.[23]

A follow-up study in 2002 by the Institute for Wisconsin's Future determined that $11,121 per pupil in school spending was needed, but the current level was only $8,241. The difference represents a 35% increase for Wisconsin spending.[24]

Estimating the National Costs of NCLB

These cost studies from 10 states are all based on bringing the state's children up to an academic standard. As we have seen, they vary considerably in methods, assumptions, and procedures, and they use a variety of analytic techniques. All are recent. Yet, for all their diversity, a number of unambiguous findings emerge.

- Providing a "standards-based" NCLB education for all children will require massive new investments in education spending. Seven of the 10 studies show increases in base cost that are greater than 24%, and of these, six were between 30% and 46%; two were in the 15% range; one did not directly address the base cost.
- Traditional estimates of the costs of remedial instruction, such as Title I or state-funded programs, are clearly underestimates at both the state and federal levels.[25] Eight of the 10 studies found the real additional costs to be approximately 100% higher—that is, double the cost of regular instruction. The other two studies did not address or break out these costs.
- The federal government boasts that it is fully paying Title I NCLB costs with the additional $1 billion planned for fiscal year 2004. As indicated by the New Hampshire study, it is not likely that such a small appropriation will pay for the added bureaucracy, testing requirements, qualified-teacher costs, paraprofessional tests, and other mandates in the law.
- Perversely, states with high standards, such as New York, Michigan, and Vermont, will have the highest remedial needs and costs while those with low standards will have the lowest costs.[26]

Public spending on K–12 education was $422.7 billion in 2001–02.[27] If we use a broad—yet easily justified and extremely conservative—estimate of 20% added costs for the nation as a whole, that translates into a national increase of about $84.5 billion. An estimate of 35% additional costs yields a national increase of $148 billion.

For comparison purposes, the current federal Title I appropriation is $11.3 billion, and the Administration's budget request of $12.3 billion is below the authorized amount of $18 billion in NCLB.[28] President Bush said in his weekly radio address of 4 January 2003 that the additional $1 billion was "more than enough money" and that "we are insisting that schools use that money wisely."[29]

Who Has to Pay the NCLB Bill?

Legal scholars have opined that the federal government cannot be sued to force adequate funding of the law. In fact, Secretary of Education Richard Riley in a letter dated 19 January 2001 said that states have the responsibility of providing educational resources to meet new standards: "Indeed, raising standards without closing resource gaps may have the perverse effect of exacerbating achievement gaps and of setting up many children for failure."[30]

The alternative for states is to reject the federal money and, along with it, the mandates. However, if states take the money and require local districts to meet state standards, then these same local districts can legally demand that the state provide adequate money to meet these standards. Local districts can cite a growing number of financial adequacy studies to support their case in the courts.

With the National Governors' Association estimating that states face a total fiscal-year 2003 deficit of $58 billion, state governments will be hard pressed to fund an additional $84.5 billion—to say nothing of $148 billion. In many states, budgets are being balanced in part by cutting education dollars. Tax cuts, a sluggish economy, and the cost of war in Iraq all suggest that significant fiscal help will not be forthcoming from the federal government.

Few reasonable people argue against the idea that all children must be well educated or that extra services must be made available for our most needy. In fact, it has been the dream of many educators throughout our nation's history. However, if funding remains inadequate, then at best the law will represent the attenuated efforts of an overpromising government, which will leave behind our poorest and most needy children.

Promised Benefits: Accountability

The primary promised benefit of NCLB is that 95% of all student groups will reach their state test standards by 2014. Obviously, we don't know if that goal can or will be reached. But if the system is not adequately funded, then reaping that benefit is a remote and forlorn hope.

Assessing the possible benefits of NCLB requires answering two questions—one technical, the other about values. The technical question is whether the system can ever work. At the heart of the plan is the requirement that each subgroup of students in each school improve test scores in equal yearly increments. That is, they are required to make "adequate yearly progress" (AYP). The values question is whether the goals of the system, narrowly conceived as improved test scores, are the right goals for public education in a democratic society.

Promised Benefits: "Adequate Yearly Progress"

There is simply no body of accepted scientific knowledge that says that all students and all subgroups of students can reach meaningful high standards, at the required AYP pace, given the levels of funding and the lack of social, economic, and family assets of many of our children. It is also doubtful that the "machinery" will work. Indeed, there is scant evidence that the AYP train can even get out of the station.

Test Score Reliability

The centerpiece of NCLB is the requirement that test scores must improve annually. Before NCLB became law, Thomas Kane and Douglas Staiger demonstrated that 70% of the year-to-year change in test scores for grade levels or schools is simply random variation.[31] Differences in the student body from one year to the next, combined with the statistical error in the tests themselves, make it impossible to know whether the tests are measuring real gains (or losses) or whether the changes are merely random noise.

Similarly, Walt Haney examined the scores of all Massachusetts schools. He found that those that received a medallion for large gains in one year saw those gains disappear the following year.[32] In Florida, the same pattern emerged, with 69% of the schools that posted gains in the first cycle of testing falling back in the next cycle.[33] In Maine, Jaekyung Lee found the same phenomenon and noted that the random fluctuation,

not surprisingly, increased as the size of the school decreased.[34]

The problems become far more difficult as the number of subgroups increases. A school with a diverse population (and many subgroups) has many more opportunities to fail. Thus the diverse school, which faces greater challenges, is penalized.

Likewise, many rural and small schools do not have enough students in a grade level or a population subgroup to draw valid conclusions. While some states call for a minimum of 30 or 50 students in a subgroup, new analyses are finding that these cell sizes are still too small to validly measure AYP gains. For example, modeling in Vermont shows that 170 students per grade level are needed for the scores to be stable.[35]

Validity

Most states claim that their testing systems are "aligned" with their state curriculum standards. Generally, this means that they are not grossly incompatible. It does not mean that they are a faithful, accurate, and balanced representation of the state's standards for instruction. Since most tests are geared toward reading and mathematics, social studies and science get short shrift. Even within math and reading, the ability of any test to sample validly an ever-expanding knowledge base is suspect. The reading and math wars demonstrate that even these basic areas are subject to great controversy. Moreover, different tests give different results for the same students—even when they are supposedly measuring knowledge of the same subject matter.[36]

Testing companies, state agencies, and local districts all have their own incentives to keep the time, amount, and expense of testing to a minimum. The result, unfortunately, is a tradeoff. Thus it is doubtful that any state accountability test can be considered a valid and representative sampling of the state's curriculum expectations for an educated youth.

Improvement of Learning Through Tests

Each year, the NCLB system progressively increases sanctions against schools that do not meet annual growth targets. Ultimately, the state could take over the school, change its management, or disband it altogether. The assumption is that the fear of these penalties will drive schools to even higher levels of performance.

Leaving aside whether schools have the resources and whether students have the social capital to reach the high levels sought by NCLB, it is questionable whether punitive incentive systems work. (B. F. Skinner disproved negative reinforcement systems 45 years ago.) In looking at 18 states with high-stakes testing systems, Audrey Amrein and David Berliner considered the scores on the high-stakes tests along with the scores on other tests. If all scores went up, they concluded that learning was taking place. If only the high-stakes scores went up, they concluded that test preparation and curriculum narrowing were taking place. They found that scores on the other tests were not related to scores on high-stakes tests. Thus the basic assumption that high-stakes systems lead to improved learning must be suspect at least.[37]

Texas is cited as a state in which the increase in the percentage of students meeting the standards was paralleled by increases in the state's scores on the National Assessment of Educational Progress. However, the low level of the state's tests and the very different trend lines of the state and NAEP tests call this conclusion into question. More troubling still is that the increase in test scores was *not* accompanied by increases in outcomes of high value, such as increased high school completion or college attendance.[38]

Unintended Consequences

The assumption of the NCLB system is that the test results represent what an educated person should know and be able to do. Few would say that an educated person only has high test scores. Most would say good scores are desirable but not sufficient to define an educated person. Most would say that schools must also produce good citizens, strong family members, contributors to society, and people engaged in democratic governance. None of these characteristics are measured by or deemed of importance in the federal accountability system. Along the way, a number of unintended consequences also appear likely.

Curriculum Narrowing

As noted above, statewide achievement tests do not measure the vast expanse of curriculum set forth by states and school districts. Tests tend to measure those things that are easy to measure, in an efficient and economical way. This means that the focus is on lower-order thinking skills, with a light smattering of higher-order skills, such as writing a short essay.[39] Schools and teachers, faced with ever-increasing demands to avoid the "failing school" label, will logically focus on the curriculum content that is most likely to improve test scores. Leaving aside the fact that these tests provide little useful instructional feedback, the inevitable results will be that the nation's curriculum will be narrowed and the level of expectations will be lowered.[40]

Failing Schools

While the federal government has recently announced that the "failing" label for schools should be replaced with the more politically acceptable term "in need of improvement," the negative moniker sticks in the minds of the people and of the media. Regardless of the solid record of achievement test scores and the good graduation rates of the nation's schools, public school critics have been successful in painting schools as "failing," and they have made the most of the cooperation of the media, which have natural incentives to report negative news.

A plethora of estimates have been put forth regarding the number of schools across the U.S. that will turn out to be failing under NCLB. The Center for Assessment says 75%, North Carolina estimates 60%, Vermont calculated 80% over three years, and Louisiana reports 85%—even though two-thirds of their schools show improved scores.[41]

Furthermore, as Lowell Rose has pointed out with regard to Indiana, "A failing label will be assigned frequently, based on the crushing impact of poverty." Students with large and diverse populations will find it most difficult to show progress while schools with a breakout group in special education will find it impossible.[42] Black students showed a 94% failure rate, while Hispanics registered a 68% failure rate. Students who received free and reduced-price lunches showed a 56% failure rate.

Schools labeled as "failing" will not receive their label because they have failed. Rather, schools will be branded because they are in poor or diverse neighborhoods, because they are small and rural, because they are underfunded, and because the AYP system cannot tell the difference between a learning gain and random noise.

Dropouts

While it is still too early to determine whether students will drop out of school as a result of the NCLB requirements, an examination of the national longitudinal database shows that students subjected to eighth-grade promotion examinations are more likely to drop out by 10th grade.[43] Anecdotal evidence suggests that some students are encouraged (or provided subtle incentives) to drop out. This is consistent with the "uncertainty principle" mechanisms set forth by Amrein and Berliner. Simply put, the more intense the negative consequences held over a system in an effort to get high results, the more likely the system is to game the rules to show better results.

Conclusion: Sure Costs, Uncertain Benefits

The No Child Left Behind law claims noble aims and sets unyielding expectations for schools. Yet there is a troubling difference between the language of the federal government and its actions. While asking for the highest educational achievement scores in the world, we ignore that we are, at best, mediocre in the commitment of our substantial wealth to our schools. When it comes to equality for all our children, the U.S. is among the least equitable nations in the world.

It is in this context that NCLB has promised equality for all. Yet in the 10 states profiled in this analysis, the costs for making these promises a reality are far from being met. Seven of the 10 states require new base investments in education of at least 24%. The federal Administration has asked for an increase of $1 billion in Title I, but we need at least $84.5 billion if we are to make a realistic effort to leave no child behind. The states, currently wallowing in deficits totaling $58 billion, will be legally forced to take on these added burdens, but they lack the capability. With war pushed to the front burner and another tax cut planned, there is little reason to believe that federal commitment in the form of federal dollars will follow federal rhetoric.

If we were willing to fund our educational obligations to the poor and the needy, the social benefits would be enormous. But funding alone will do little to stop an unworkable AYP system from randomly assigning punitive sanctions to our schools. The system does not recognize that a hungry child with a poor, single parent and a violent home may not be focused on phonics each morning. The system does not ensure adequate money for an underfunded school. It gives no promise that children will not have to go to a dilapidated school. The system makes no distinction between a school with well-educated parents and generous resources and an impoverished school. Both schools are held to the same standard.

The program is likely to increase the number of dropouts, narrow the curriculum, and label a great many schools as failing—even as NAEP reading and mathematics scores are at very high levels. The effect will not simply be to punish schools and children for failing when they never had a chance. The effect will be that our society accepts a meaner vision of what it means to be educated in America. The effect will be to take money from those schools and those communities that need it most and transfer it to "successful" schools. Ultimately, the effect will be to shift the purpose of schools away from education for a democracy and away from the provision of equal opportunities for all children.

If we are to work seriously to attain the goal of educating all children, there are a number of requirements that must be met.

• Funding for education, prevention, and remediation must be adequate. This will require major new investments—particularly in poor, rural, and inner-city environments. We must undertake this effort not because it is the law but because it is what we should do.

• Ultimately, adequate funding is not a matter of fiscal capacity as much as it is a matter of political will. Obtaining adequate funding will require a level of political involvement not traditionally seen from educators.

• States and districts must conduct their own cost/benefit analyses. Even though schools desperately need the small Title I sums they receive, districts and states should reject Faustian bargains that fail to compensate them adequately for the obligations they take on. The inevitable result is that the district agrees to being publicly branded a failure when it never had a reasonable chance for success.

• States and districts must work with federal officials—elected and appointed—for the repeal or massive revision of the NCLB law so that it provides a workable accountability system. This system must include comprehensive and democratic conceptions of educational goals rather than a narrow reliance on tests. It must also measure gains according to where students are coming from as much as where they are going.

• Finally, educators must embrace accountability. We must work to ensure that no school provides substandard, inadequate, or inequitable educational programs. We must do so not because it is politically expedient but because it is what we owe the children, our society, and ourselves.

Notes

1. Lowell C. Rose and Alec M. Gallup. "The 34th Annual Phi Delta Kappa/Gallup Poll of the Public's Attitudes Toward the Public Schools," *Phi Delta Kappan*, September 2002, pp. 41–56.
2. "Fact Sheet: No Child Left Behind Act," White House, Washington, D.C., available on the Web at www.whitehouse.gov/news/releases/2002/01/20020108.html.

3. "Federal Education Department Budget Request," *Education Week,* 4 September 2002, pp. 37, 43. Total education spending in fiscal-year 2001 was $422 billion, and the Title I increase was $1.5 billion.

4. Richard F. Elmore, "Unwarranted Intrusion," *Education Next,* Fall 2002, available on the Web at www.educationnext. org/20021/30.html; Walt Haney, "Lake Woebeguaranteed: Misuse of Test Scores in Massachusetts, Part I," *Education Policy Analysis Archives,* vol. 10, 6 May 2002, available at http://epaa.asu.edu/epaa/v10n24/; Thomas J. Kane and Douglas O. Staiger, "Volatility in School Test Scores: Implications for School-Based Accountability Systems," unpublished paper, Hoover Institution, Stanford University, Stanford, Calif., April 2001; and Jaekyung Lee, "Evaluating Rural Progress in Mathematics Achievement: Is 'Adequate Yearly Progress' (AYP) Feasible, Valid, Reliable, and Fair?," paper prepared for the ACCLAIM conference, SUNY-Buffalo, 3–6 November 2002.

5. Jay R. Campbell, Catherine M. Hombo, and John Mazzeo, *Trends in Academic Progress: Three Decades of Student Performance* (Washington, D.C.: National Center for Education Statistics, NCES 2000-469, 2000); and *Dropout Rates in the United States: 2000* (Washington, D.C.: National Center for Education Statistics, NCES 2002-114, 2001).

6. *Knowledge and Skills for Life: First Results from PISA 2000, Fifteen-Year-Old Students* (Paris: Organisation for Economic Co-operation and Development, 2001).

7. *Education at a Glance: OECD Indicators 2000* (Paris: Organisation for Economic Co-operation and Development, 2000).

8. *Knowledge and Skills for Life.*

9. *A League Table of Educational Disadvantage in Rich Nations* (Florence: UNICEF Innocenti Research Center, Innocenti Report Cards, no. 4, November 2002).

10. "Calculation of the Cost of an Adequate Education in Indiana in 2001–2002 Using the Professional Judgment Approach," Augenblick and Myers, Inc., Denver, 2002, p. 22.

11. Justin Silverstein and Anne Barkis, "A Look at Two Different Adequacy Studies: The Maryland Report," American Education Finance Association, Albuquerque, 8 March 2002; and "Calculation of the Cost of an Adequate Education in Maryland in 1999–2000 Using Two Different Analytic Approaches," Augenblick and Myers, Inc., Denver, 2001.

12. Lori Montgomery, "Maryland Seeks 'Adequacy,' Recasting School Debate," *Washington Post,* 22 April 2002, page A-1.

13. "Calculation of the Cost of an Adequate Education in Montana in 2001–2002 Using the Professional Judgment Approach," Augenblick and Myers, Inc., Denver, 2002.

14. "Calculation of the Cost of an Adequate Education in Nebraska in 2002–03 Using the Professional Judgment Approach," Augenblick and Myers, Denver, 2003.

15. David L. Greene, "Bush Education Policy Gets States' Rights Jolt," *Baltimore Sun,* 30 December 2002.

16. Mark V. Joyce, "Analysis of Cost Impact of ESEA—No Child Left Behind Act—on New Hampshire," NHSAA Memorandum of 26 November 2002, Penacook, N.H., available at www.nhsaa.org.

17. "More States 'Cost-Out' Education," *Access: Newsletter for the Campaign for Fiscal Equity,* Winter 2002.

18. "A Survey of Finance Adequacy Studies," *ECS StateNotes,* Education Commission of the States, September 2001.

19. Robert L. Linn, Eva L. Baker, and Damian W. Betebenner, "Accountability Systems: Implications of the Requirements of the No Child Left Behind Act of 2001," *Educational Researcher,* August/September 2002, pp. 3–16. See also Martin Carnoy, Susanna Loeb, and Tiffany L. Smith, *Do Higher State Test Scores in Texas Make for Better High School Outcomes?* (Philadelphia: Consortium for Policy Research in Education, Graduate School of Education, University of Pennsylvania, CPRE Research Report Series, RR-047, November 2001).

20. Andrew Reschovsky and Jennifer Imazeki, *Let No Child Be Left Behind; Determining the Cost of Improving School Performance* (Madison: Consortium for Policy Research in Education, University of Wisconsin, May 2002).

21. William J. Mathis, "The Federal 'No Child Left Behind' Law: Should Vermont Take the Money?," discussion paper produced for the Vermont Society for the Study of Education Policy, Brandon, 22 October 2002.

22. Whitney Allgood and Richard Rothstein, "Adequate Education for At-Risk Youths," memorandum to Karen Royster, Institute for Wisconsin's Future, Madison, 18 October 2000.

23. See Richard Rothstein, "Out of Balance: Our Understanding of How Schools Affect Society and How Society Affects Schools," paper presented at the 30th Anniversary Conference of the Spencer Foundation, Chicago, 24–25 January 2002.

24. Jack Norman, "Funding Our Future: An Adequacy Model for Wisconsin School Finance," Institute for Wisconsin's Future, Madison, June 2002.

25. Kevin Carey, "State Poverty-Based Education Funding: A Survey of Current Programs and Options for Improvement," Center on Budget and Policy Priorities, Washington, D.C., 7 November 2002.

26. William Duncombe and Anna Lukemeyer, "Estimating the Cost of Educational Adequacy: A Comparison of Approaches," paper presented at the annual meeting of the American Education Finance Association, Albuquerque, March 2002; Linn, Baker, and Betebenner, op. cit.; and Richard Rothstein, "How U.S. Punishes States with Higher Standards," *New York Times,* 18 September 2002.

27. "Total Expenditures of Educational Institutions, by Level and Control of Institution: 1899–1900 to 2000–01," *Digest of Education Statistics, 2001* (Washington, D.C.: National Center for Education Statistics, 2002), Table 30.

28. Diana Jean Schemo, "Critics Say Money for Schools Falls Short of Promises," *New York Times,* 4 February 2003.

29. "Bush Proposes $1 Billion School Aid," MSNBC News, 4 January 2003.

30. "Dear Colleague" letter, Richard W. Riley, 19 January 2001.

31. Kane and Staiger, op. cit.

32. Haney, op. cit.

33. David Figlio, "Aggregation and Accountability: Will No Child Truly Be Left Behind?," Fordham Foundation, Washington, D.C., 13 February 2002.

34. Lee, op. cit.

35. Richard Hill, unpublished analysis of Vermont New Standards Reference Examinations scores, Vermont Department of Education, Montpelier, 2002.

36. Audrey L. Amrein and David C. Berliner, "High-Stakes Testing, Uncertainty, and Student Learning," *Education Policy Analysis Archives,* 28 March 2002, available at epaa.asu.edu/epaa/v10n18; see also Linn, Baker, and Betebenner, op. cit.

37. Amrein and Berliner, op. cit.

38. Carnoy, Loeb, and Smith, op. cit.

39. W. James Popham, "The Debasement of Student Proficiency," *Education Week,* 8 January 2003, available at www.edweek.org/cw/ewstory.cfm?slug=16popham.h22.

40. Amrein and Berliner, op. cit.

41. Michael A. Fletcher, "States Worry New School Law Sets Schools Up to Fail," *Washington Post,* 3 January 2003, p. A-1.

42. Lowell C. Rose, "Hard Facts Regarding Adequate Yearly Progress (AYP) Under the No Child Left Behind Act," special analysis for the Indiana Urban Superintendents Association, 2002.

43. Sean F. Reardon and Claudia Galindo, "Do High-Stakes Tests Affect Students' Decisions to Drop Out of School? Evidence from NELS," paper presented at the annual meeting of the American Educational Research Association, New Orleans, April 2002.

THE DEBASEMENT OF STUDENT PROFICIENCY: WHY WE MUST RETHINK TESTING TO ENCOURAGE REAL LEARNING

W. James Popham

The legislative mandates of the No Child Left Behind Act of 2001 require that schools must demonstrate "adequate yearly progress," as evidenced by schoolwide testing data. Teachers and school districts are challenged to demonstrate the degree to which students meet identified proficiency standards.

Popham argues that the real challenge for educators and policy makers will be to identify the degree to which current assessment measures accurately evaluate students' mastery of content. At present, traditional measures of assessment fail to address the impact of curriculum and instruction on students' performance.

As you read this article ask yourself, "What do tests actually measure and what alternative formats should educators and policy makers consider in implementing current reform efforts?"

Think About This . . .

1. In what ways are traditional assessments of students' proficiencies limited? Are these limitations inherent in paper-and-pencil tests?

2. What type of changes in traditional tests are needed to better evaluate students' proficiencies?

3. Standardized achievement tests are often used as tools for evaluating student performance. What are some of the possible limitations of standardized tests? Describe some alternative measures, identifying their strengths and weaknesses.

4. As a future classroom teacher, describe your plans for assessing student learning. What types of tests will you use and how will these address the concerns raised by Popham?

The "No Child Left Behind" Act of 2001, an enormously important federal law intended to improve America's public schools, may actually produce the opposite effect. Such an unforeseen consequence stems from the law's requirement that substantially larger numbers of students must be judged proficient each year according to their performances on statewide achievement tests. If a school's teachers don't get sufficient numbers of students to meet each year's "adequate yearly progress" toward test-determined proficiency, the school is considered to be low-performing. And if a school remains low-performing for more than a year, a series of heavy-duty penalties are dished out, such penalties leading to serious staff shake-ups or, ultimately, to outright closure of the school.

Most states, based on existing test data, anticipate that the bulk of their schools will fail to meet the new federally decreed proficiency targets. Accordingly, some states have simply lowered their definitions of proficiency in an effort to avoid the prospect that most of their educators will soon be seen as ineffectual. ("States Revise the Meaning of 'Proficient,' " Oct. 9, 2002.) But the lowering of educational expectations for our nation's students was surely not what the architects of the No Child Left Behind Act intended.

On first reading, this federal legislation appears to leave many key decisions to the states. For example, although the law requires that statewide achievement tests must assess students' mastery of a state's "challenging" curricular aims, each state can decide which achievement tests it will use. And states are even allowed to set up their own year-by-year schedule of schools' adequate-yearly-progress targets. However, the law also stipulates that, by 2014, all of a state's students must be proficient or better.

Moreover, whatever schedule of annual proficiency targets a state's officials establish, that schedule's annual increases toward the 12-year, total-proficiency goal must, by federal law, be equal. Thus, given the current performance levels of students in many states, and the size of the annual progress increases to be required, the number of test-determined low-performing schools will surely be staggering.

Unfortunately, the statewide achievement tests currently used in the United States do not accurately measure students' mastery of most states' frequently sprawling curricular aims. Even worse, most of today's state-adopted achievement tests are instructionally insensitive; that is, they really can't detect even first-rate instruction on the part of teachers. Statewide tests are constructed according to a traditional measurement model aimed chiefly at providing comparisons among students, rather than at producing evidence regarding school quality. Such traditionally constructed tests, because they are highly related to students' socioeconomic status, dominantly measure what students brought to school, not what they were taught there.

As long as traditionally constructed achievement tests are the major measure of educators' instructional success, state policymakers will be faced with an unsavory choice between (a) seeing the bulk of their state's educators labeled as incompetent, and (b) lowering state curricular expectations so that most schools appear to be making adequate yearly progress. Neither of these options will benefit children.

There is, however, a test-focused solution strategy that can allow the federal law to attain its intended educational improvements. A state can base its proficiency targets on students' assessed mastery of a modest number of the state's most important curricular aims. Achievement tests can be built to measure students' mastery of such truly pivotal skills as a child's ability to: (1) read varied kinds of written materials and comprehend their meaning, (2) solve diverse kinds of age-appropriate mathematical problems, or (3) compose a compelling persuasive essay.

We now know how to build statewide achievement tests so they provide accurate and credible evidence of how many students at a school are actually proficient with respect to their mastery of such powerful curricular aims. But those very same achievement tests, if constructed with their instructional implications clearly in mind, can also be catalysts for improving classroom instruction. If the appropriate kinds of statewide achievement tests are installed, there can be genuine progress toward worthwhile curricular goals, rather than public-relations progress toward trivialized levels of student accomplishment.

If states install instructionally supportive tests to satisfy the accountability requirements of the No Child Left Behind Act, there will be no need to lower a state's definition of proficiency. However, if state officials rely on the "same-old, same-old" sorts of traditionally constructed achievement tests—tests that give teachers and students no real chance to succeed—we should prepare ourselves for an avalanche of test results reflecting debased student "proficiency."

From Popham, W. J. (2003). The debasement of student proficiency: Why we must rethink testing to encourage real learning. As first appeared in Education Week, 22(16), 30. Reprinted with permission of the author.

ADDITIONAL READINGS

Falk, B. (2002). Standards-based reforms: Problems and possibilities. *Phi Delta Kappan, 83*(8), 612–620.

Gandal, M., & McGiffert, L. (2003). The power of testing. *Educational Leadership, 60*(5), 39–42.

Haycock, K. (2001). Closing the achievement gap. *Educational Leadership, 58*(6), 6–11.

Jennings, J. (2002). Knocking on your door. *American School Board Journal, 189*(9), 25–27.

Levinson, C. (2000). Student assessment in eight countries. *Educational Leadership, 57*(5), 58–61.

Meier, D. (2002). Standardization versus standards. *Phi Delta Kappan, 84*(3), 190–198.

Neill, M. (2003). The dangers of testing. *Educational Leadership, 60*(5), 43–47.

O'Neil, J. (1999). Core knowledge and standards: A conversation with E. D. Hirsch, Jr. *Educational Leadership, 56*(6), 28–31.

Popham, W. J. (2003). The debasement of student proficiency: Why must we rethink testing to encourage real learning. *Education Week, 22*(16), 30.

Popham, W. J. (2003). The seductive lure of data. *Educational Leadership, 60*(5), 48–51.

Schmoker, M. (2000). The results we want. *Educational Leadership, 57*(5), 62–65.

Sizer, T. (2003). 20 years later: A nation at wait, two reports. *Education Week, 22*(32), 36, 24.

Starnes, B. (2003). Saffy's big idea. *Phi Delta Kappan, 84*(8), 631–632.

EXPLORING THE INTERNET

Center for Education Reform
http://edreform.com/
A national, nonprofit organization, the CER supports fundamental reforms in the schools and serves as "a clearinghouse for information on innovative reforms in education." The site includes information pertaining to charter schools including demographics, statistics, and other relevant information.

The Fall and Rise of Standards-Based Education
http://www.mcrel.org/topics/topics.asp?topicsid=4.
This site provides an overview and predictions for the future of standards-based education.

Assessment Reform: Are We Making Progress?
http://www.education-world.com/a_issues/issues029.shtml
Education World offers a brief summary of findings from a recently released study of assessment reform. Is assessment reform working? How are teachers handling new approaches to assessment? Are students and curriculum benefiting from new assessment methods approaches?

REFERENCES

Airasian, P., & Walsh, M. (1997). Constructivist cautions. *Phi Delta Kappan, 78*(6), 444–449.

Ansell, S., & Park, J. (2003). Tracking tech trends. *Education Week, 22*(35), 43–49.

Armstrong, D. (2003). *Curriculum Today*. Upper Saddle River, NJ: Merrill/Prentice Hall.

Bassett, P. (2002). Why good schools are countercultural. *Education Week, 21*(21), 35.

Bennett, F. (2002). The future of computer technology in K–12 education. *Phi Delta Kappan, 83*(8), 621–625.

Bicard, D. (2000). Using classroom rules to construct behavior. *Middle School Journal, 31*, 37–45.

Biddle, B., & Berliner, D. (2002). Unequal school funding in the United States. *Educational Leadership, 59*(8), 48–59.

Black, S. (2002). The well-rounded student. *American School Board Journal, 189*(6), 33–35.

Black, S. (2003). Teaching about religion. *American School Board Journal, 190*(4), 50–53.

Bracey, G. (2003). Investing in preschool. *American School Board Journal, 190*(1), 32–35.

Bracey, G. (2003). April foolishness: The 20th anniversary of *A Nation at Risk. Phi Delta Kappan, 84*(8), 616–621.

Bransford, J., Brown, A., & Cocking, R. (Eds.). (2000). *How people learn: Brain, mind, experience, and school*. Washington, DC: National Academy Press.

Capps, W., & Maxwell, M. (2002). Mobility. *American School Board Journal, 185*(5), 26–29.

Casserly, M. (2002). Can the Bush school plan work? How to keep "No Child Left Behind" from dissolving into fine print. *Education Week, 22*(14), 48, 38.

Clarkson, W. (2003). Beautiful minds. *American School Board Journal, 190*(8), 24–28.

Coleman, J., Campbell, E., Hobson, D., McPortland, J., Mood, A., Weinfield, F., & York, R. (1966). *Equality of educational opportunity*. Washington, DC: U.S. Department of Health, Education and Welfare.

Cooperman, S. (2003). A new order of things. *Education Week, 22*(38), 30, 32.

Cruickshank, D., & Haefele, D. (2001). Good teachers, plural. *Educational Leadership, 58*(5), 26–30.

Cuban, L. (1999). The technology puzzle. *Education Week, 19*(43), 47, 68.

Eggen, P., & Kauchak, D. (2004). *Educational psychology: Windows on classrooms* (6th ed.). Upper Saddle River, NJ: Merrill/Prentice Hall.

Eisner, E. (2003). Questionable assumptions about schooling. *Phi Delta Kappan, 84*(9), 648–657.

Federal Interagency Forum on Child and Family Statistics (2001). *America's children: Key national indicators of well-being*. Washington, DC: U.S. Government Printing Office.

Ferrero, D. (2003). Public-spirited choice: How diverse schools can serve the common good. *Education Week, 22*(28), 28, 30.

Flanigan, R. (2003). Common measures: A challenging year for schools. *Education Vital Signs, American School Board Journal, 190*(2), 21–25.

Fuhler, C. (2003). Joining theory and best practice to drive classroom instruction. *Middle School Journal, 34*(5), 23–30.

Glickman, C. (2001). Dichotomizing education: Why no one wins and America loses. *Phi Delta Kappan, 83*(2), 147–152.

Goldberg, L. (2002). Our technology future. *Education Week, 21*(27), 32, 34.

Gratz, D. (2000). High standards for whom? *Phi Delta Kappan, 81*(9), 681–687.

Grove, K. (2002). The invisible role of the central office. *Educational Leadership, 59*(8), 45–47.

Haberman, M. (1995). Selecting "star" teachers for children and youth in urban poverty. *Phi Delta Kappan, 76*(10), 777–781.

Hardy, L. (2003). Overburdened, overwhelmed. *American School Board Journal, 190*(4), 18–23.

Harris, S., & Lowery, S. (2002). A view from the classroom. *Educational Leadership, 59*(8), 64–65.

Hatch, J. (2002). Accountability shovedown: Resisting the standards movement in early childhood education. *Phi Delta Kappan, 83*(6), 457–462.

Heward, W. (2003). *Exceptional children* (6th ed.). Upper Saddle River, NJ: Merrill/Prentice Hall.

Hirsch, E. D. (1993). The core knowledge curriculum—What's behind its success? *Educational Leadership, 50*(8), 23–25, 27–30.

Hole, S., & McEntee, G. H. (1999). Reflection is at the heart of practice. *Educational Leadership, 56*(8), 34–37.

Ingersoll, R. (2003). The teacher shortage: Myth or reality? *Educational Horizons, 81*(3), 146–152.

Johnson, S. M., & Birkeland, S. (2003). The schools that teachers choose. *Educational Leadership, 60*(8), 20–24.

Joiner, L. (2003). Where did we come from? *American School Board Journal, 190*(4), 30–34.

Kaplan, L., & Owings, W. (2003). No Child Left Behind: The politics of teacher quality. *Phi Delta Kappan, 84*(9), 687–692.

Kauchak, D., & Eggen, P. (2005). *Introduction to teaching: Becoming a professional* (2nd ed.). Upper Saddle River, NJ: Merrill/Prentice Hall.

Kent, M., Pollard, K., Haaga, J., & Mather, M. (2001). *First glimpse from the 2000 U.S. Census.* Available at http://www.prb.org/AmeriStatTemplate.cfm

Kienholz, K. (2001). From Dewey to Beane: Innovation, democracy, and unity characterize middle level education. *Middle School Journal, 32*(3), 20–24.

Kluth, P., Villa, R., & Thousand, J. (2002). "Our school doesn't offer inclusion" and other legal blunders. *Educational Leadership, 83*(4), 24–27.

Kohn, A. (1997). How not to teach values: A critical look at character education. *Phi Delta Kappan, 78*(6), 428–439.

Kohn, A. (2002). The 500-pound gorilla. *Phi Delta Kappan, 84*(2), 112–119.

Lewis, A. (2003). Students as commodities. *Phi Delta Kappan, 84*(8), 563–564.

Maeroff, G. (2003). Classroom of one. *American School Board Journal, 190*(2), 26–29.

Marriott, D. (2002). "His name is Michael": A lesson on the voices we unknowingly silence. *Education Week, 22*(6), 35.

Mathis, W. (2003). No Child Left Behind: Costs and benefits. *Phi Delta Kappan, 84*(9), 679–686.

McCombs, B. (2001). What do we know about learners and learning? The learner-centered framework: Bringing the educational system into balance. *Educational Horizons, 79*(4), 182–193.

Meier, D. (1998). Can the odds be changed? *Phi Delta Kappan, 79*(5), 358–362.

Muir, M. (2001). What engages underachieving middle school students in learning? *Middle School Journal, 33*(2), 37–43.

National Education Association. (2003). *Status of the American school teacher, 2000–2001.* Available at http://www.nea.org

Nieto, S. (2003). What keeps teachers going? *Educational Leadership, 60*(8), 14–18.

Northrop, J. (2002). Dress codes and social chaos. *Education Week, 21*(8), 36.

Osterman, K. (2003). *Preventing school violence. Phi Delta Kappan, 84*(8), 622–627.

Parkay, F., & Hass, G. (2000). *Curriculum planning: A contemporary approach* (7th ed.). Boston: Allyn & Bacon.

Perkins, L. (2000). The new immigrants and education: Challenges and issues. *Educational Horizons, 78*(2), 67–71.

Popham, W. J. (2001). Teaching to the test? *Educational Leadership, 58*(6), 16–20.

Popham, W. J. (2003). The debasement of student proficiency: Why we must rethink testing to encourage real learning. *Education Week, 22*(16), 30.

Raywid, M. A. (2002). Accountability: What's worth measuring? *Phi Delta Kappan, 83*(6), 433–436.

Reich, R. (2002). The civic perils of homeschooling. *Educational Leadership, 59*(7), 56–59.

Ryan, K. (1993). Mining the values in the curriculum. *Educational Leadership, 75*(3), 16–18.

Sadker, D. (2002). An educator's primer on the gender wars. *Phi Delta Kappan, 84*(3), 235–240, 244.

Schrader, V. (2001). School shouldn't be a jungle. *Education Week, 21*(6), 41, 43.

Smith, S., Myers, J., & Underwood, J. (2003). Blowing in the wind. *American School Board Journal, 19*(5), 18–21.

Sommers, C. H. (2001). Give same-sex schooling a chance. *Education Week, 21*(4), 36.

Sternberg, R. (2002). Teaching for wisdom in our schools. *Education Week, 22*(11), 56, 42.

Stiggins, R. (2001). Assessment *for* learning: A vision for the future. *Education Week, 21*(26), 30, 32–33.

Storz, M., & Nestor, K. (2003). Insights into meeting standards from listening to the voices of urban students. *Middle School Journal, 34*(4), 11–19.

Strike, K. (1988). The ethics of teaching. *Phi Delta Kappan, 70*(2), 156–158.

Teemant, A., Bernhardt, E., Rodriguez-Munoz, M., & Aiello, M. (2000). A dialogue among teachers that benefits second language learners. *Middle School Journal, 32*(2), 30–38.

U.S. Bureau of Census. (1998). *Statistical abstract of the state.* Washington, DC: U.S. Department of Commerce.

U.S. Department of Education. (2000). *Condition of Education, 2000.* Washington, DC: U.S. Government Printing Office.

Vail, K. (2003). School technology grows up. *American School Board Journal, 190*(9), 34–37.

Vail, K. (2003). Where the heart is. *American School Board Journal, 190*(6), 12–17.

Vander Ark, T. (2002). It's all about size. *American School Board Journal, 189*(7), 34–35.

Vars, G. (2001). Can curriculum integration survive in an era of high-stakes testing? *Middle School Journal, 33*(2), 7–17.

Windschitl, M., & Irby, J. (1999). Tapping the resources of the World Wide Web for inquiry in middle school. *Middle School Journal, 30*(3), 40–45.

Youth Risk Behavior Survey. (2001).